MW01251032

Proceedings

Eighth International Symposium on
High-Performance Computer Architecture

HPCA-8

Proceedings

Eighth International Symposium on
High-Performance Computer Architecture

2–6 February 2002 • Cambridge, Massachusetts

Sponsored by

IEEE Computer Society Technical Committee on Computer Architecture

virtutech

COMPAQ

intel

IEEE
COMPUTER
SOCIETY

IEEE

Los Alamitos, California

Washington • Brussels • Tokyo

IEEE Computer Society Order Number PR01525
ISBN 0-7695-1525-8
ISSN 1530-0897

Additional copies may be ordered from:

IEEE Computer Society
Customer Service Center
10662 Los Vaqueros Circle
P.O. Box 3014
Los Alamitos, CA 90720-1314
Tel: + 1 714 821 8380
Fax: + 1 714 821 4641
http://computer.org/
csbooks@computer.org

IEEE Service Center
445 Hoes Lane
P.O. Box 1331
Piscataway, NJ 08855-1331
Tel: + 1 732 981 0060
Fax: + 1 732 981 9667
http://shop.ieee.org/store/
customer-service@ieee.org

IEEE Computer Society
Asia/Pacific Office
Watanabe Bldg., 1-4-2
Minami-Aoyama
Minato-ku, Tokyo 107-0062
JAPAN
Tel: + 81 3 3408 3118
Fax: + 81 3 3408 3553
tokyo.ofc@computer.org

Editorial production by A. Denise Williams

Cover art production by Alex Torres

Printed in the United States of America by The Printing House

Table of Contents

Eighth International Symposium on
High-Performance Computer Architecture

Keynote Speaker

Energy and Thermal Management I

Speculative Multithreading

Panel

Work-in-Progress

Organizers: Bruce Childers, University of Pittsburgh, USA
Koji Inoue, Fukuoka University, Japan
Sally A. McKee, University of Utah, USA
Martin Schultz, Technische Universität München, Germany

Keynote Speaker

Multiprocessor Systems

Pipelining and Microarchitecture

General Co-Chairs' Message

We welcome you to Cambridge, Massachusetts, and the New England region of the United States. We are pleased to host HPCA-8, and hope that you enjoy the conference. New England played a critical role in the early history of America, and we hope that you get a chance to visit some of the various historical landmarks around Cambridge, Boston, and the New England area during your visit.

History also plays a critical role in our field, and we believe that the field of Computer Architecture research continues to make significant contributions year after year. HPCA-8 will provide a diverse technical program, covering both advances in existing and emerging research areas. HPCA has always felt that workshops and tutorials play a critical role in our meetings, and this year is no exception.

David Lilja and Pen Yew have put together an excellent technical program. Antonio González played a large role in attracting six quality workshops and Gus Uht carefully selected a top-rate tutorial program. We want to thank the organizers of these programs for their time and effort.

Much of the administrative work of a conference is handled by a few people that typically do not get the recognition that they deserve. Shubu Mukherjee managed the finances for HPCA-8, Bobbie Manne handled registration, Kevin Skadron ran publications, John Kalamatianos handled local arrangements, and Andreas Moshovos both maintained the HPCA website and handled publicity for the conference. These people deserve a large round of thanks from the HPCA community for their service.

Finally we would like to thank IEEE Computer Society TCCA and our industrial sponsors for supporting HPCA-8. Mary-Kate Rada at IEEE helped us through the TMRF process, and we can not forget to acknowledge the advice provided by Yale Patt, Mark Franklin, and the Steering Committee.

We invite you to sample the local winter activities available. Enjoy the conference, Boston and winter in New England.

Joel Emer and David Kaeli

HPCA-8 General Co-Chairs

Program Co-Chairs' Message

Welcome to the Eighth International Symposium on High-Performance Computer Architecture. Since the first HPCA in 1995, this symposium has grown to become one of the premier forums for presenting new and innovative research in all aspects of computer architecture. We are pleased to present you with this compilation of the papers that comprise the main body of this year's symposium.

A total of 130 manuscripts were submitted from throughout the world for consideration by the program committee. Each paper was assigned to three different members of the program committee who carefully reviewed the papers and provided detailed and thoughtful comments. In addition to providing their own reviews, the thirty members of the program committee solicited additional reviews from more than 240 external reviewers. As a result, each paper received an average of almost six reviews with no paper receiving fewer than three.

In spite of travel and security restrictions imposed as a result of the tragic events in the U.S. on September 11, twenty-one of the program committee members were able to travel to Minneapolis on September 29 to discuss each paper. The remaining committee members were able to participate by telephone, or supplied written summaries of each paper before the meeting. After assessing and debating each paper's originality, technical content, relevance to the conference, and overall presentation, the committee selected a total of twenty-six papers for presentation at the conference and publication in the proceedings you are now reading. These papers represent some of the best research being done today in the field of high-performance computer architecture. We are confident that you will find the program stimulating, insightful, and filled with new ideas.

Tremendous efforts are required by a large number of people to pull together this type of symposium. We first would like to thank all of the authors for their time and effort in submitting their work for review. We also would like to thank all of the reviewers for their efforts in carefully reading and commenting on each individual paper. The program committee did an excellent job in not only providing their own reviews, but in guiding the overall review process and ultimately in selecting a very strong set of papers to include in the program. We gratefully acknowledge all of their contributions and extend our heartfelt thanks.

In addition to the authors, reviewers, and program committee, numerous individuals made important and substantial contributions to ensure the success of this symposium. We appreciate the opportunity to shepherd the overall program provided to us by Dave Kaeli and Joel Emer. We also deeply appreciate their ability to have gently kept all of us on schedule and within budget. We also wish to thank all of the other members of the organizing committee who worked to publicize the symposium, to pay the bills on time, to produce this proceedings, to arrange the hotel accommodations, and to control the myriad other details that are necessary to mounting a successful conference. The names of these talented individuals are listed elsewhere in this proceedings.

Finally, Joshua Yi and AJ KleinOsowski went far beyond the call of duty in keeping our web site up and running to collect the papers from the authors, to distribute the papers to the reviewers, to collect all of the reviews, and to print out reams of reviews for use at the program committee meeting. They maintained a calm sense of urgency as they went about these tasks while simultaneously communicating efficiently and courteously with a wide range of authors, reviewers, program committee members, and short-tempered advisors. Their help is tremendously appreciated.

We hope that you find this symposium enjoyable and informative, and that you leave with a renewed sense of excitement for this dynamically changing field.

David J. Lilja and Pen-Chung Yew
Program Co-Chairs

Organizing Committee

General Co-Chairs
Joel Emer, *Intel*
David Kaeli, *Northeastern Univ.*

Program Co-Chairs
Pen-Chung Yew, *Univ. of Minnesota*
David Lilja, *Univ. of Minnesota*

Steering Committee
Dharma P. Agrawal, *Univ. of Cincinnati*
Laxmi Bhuyan, *Texas A&M Univ.*
Yale Patt, *The Univ. of Texas at Austin*
Mark A. Franklin, *Washington Univ.*
Wen-Mei Hwu, *Univ. of Illinois at Urbana-Champaign*
Ashwini Nanda, *IBM*
Gabriel M. Silberman, *IBM*

Local Arrangements
John Kalamatianos, *Sun Microsystems*

Finance Chair
Shubu Mukherjee, *Intel*

Registration Chair
Srilatha Manne, *Intel*

Tutorial Chair
Gus Uht, *Univ. of Rhode Island*

Workshop Chair
Antonio González, *Universitat Politècnica de Catalunya, Barcelona*

Publications Chair
Kevin Skadron, *Univ. of Virginia*

Publicity Chair
Andreas Moshovos, *Univ. of Toronto*

Program Committee

Dharma P. Agrawal	*Univ. of Cincinnati*
John Carter	*Univ. of Utah*
Frederic T. Chong	*Univ. of California-Davis*
Alok Choudhary	*Northwestern Univ.*
Tom Conte	*North Carolina State Univ.*
Kemal Ebcioğlu	*IBM*
Joel Emer	*Intel*
Babak Falsafi	*Carnegie Mellon Univ.*
Manoj Franklin	*Univ. of Maryland College-Park*
Jesse Fang	*Intel*
Wei-Cheung Hsu	*Univ. of Minnesota*
Lizy John	*The Univ. of Texas at Austin*
David Kaeli	*Northeastern Univ.*
Kim Keeton	*Hewlett-Packard*
Steven Kunkel	*IBM*
Mikko Lipasti	*Univ. of Wisconsin-Madison*
Gyungho Lee	*Iowa State Univ.*
Steven S. Lumetta	*Univ. of Illinois at Urbana-Champaign*
Margaret Martonosi	*Princeton Univ.*
Trevor Mudge	*Univ. of Michigan*
Shubu Mukherjee	*Intel*
Lawrence Rauchwerger	*Texas A&M Univ.*
Mike Schlansker	*Hewlett-Packard*
Kevin Skadron	*Univ. of Virginia*
James E. Smith	*Univ. of Wisconsin-Madison*
Per Stenström	*Chalmers Univ. of Technology*
Josep Torrellas	*Univ. of Illinois at Urbana-Champaign*
Dean Tullsen	*Univ. of California San Diego*
Gary Tyson	*Univ. of Michigan*

Reviewers

Santosh Abraham	George Chrysos	Derek Gottlieb
Shail Aditya	Michal Cierniak	Michael Gschwind
Ali Adl-Tabatabai	Marcelo Cintra	Manish Gupta
Michael Adler	Douglas Clark	Erik Hagersten
Sarita Adve	Jamison Collins	Timothy Heil
Aneesh Aggarwal	Jeffrey Cook	Tom Heller
Anastassia Ailamaki	Jesus Corbal	Michael Hobbs
Marcosde Alba	Toni Cortes	Mark Horowitz
David Albonesi	Darren Cronquist	Zhigang Hu
Guillermo Alvarez	David Crowe	Michael Huang
Eric Anderson	Jose-Lorenzo Cruz	Christopher Hughes
Boon_Seong Ang	Chita Das	Hillery Hunter
Krste Asanovic	Al Davis	Mike Ignatowski
Todd Austin	Andre DeHon	Bruce Jacobs
Jean-Loup Baer	Alex Dean	Jaehon Jeong
Nader Bagherzadeh	Ashutosh Dhodapkar	Ross Johnson
Iris Bahar	Jose Duato	Russ Joseph
Serene Banerjee	Michel Dubois	Roy Ju
Ronald Barnes	Sandhya Dwarkadas	Toni Juan
Luiz Barroso	Susan Eggers	Philo Juang
Kia Bazargan	Todd Ehrhart	John Kalamatianos
Todd Bezenek	Rick Eickemeyer	Mahesh Kallahalla
Ravi Bhargava	Rudolf Eigenman	M. Kandemir
Jeff Bradford	Kevin Elphinstone	Gokul Kandiraju
David Brooks	Roger Espasa	Tejas Karkhanis
Mats Brorsson	Brian Evans	Magnus Karlsson
Doug Burger	Brian Fahs	Vinod Kathail
Greg Byrd	Ayose Falcon	Stefanos Kaxiras
Brendon Cahoon	Keith Farkas	Steve Keckler
Harold Cain	Matthew Farrens	Diana Keen
Brad Calder	Stephen Felix	Rick Kessler
Ramon Canal	Enrique Fernandez	Ho-Seop Kim
Jason Cantin	Michael Fertig	Tom Kistler
Nicholas Carter	Dick Flower	Artur Klauser
Calin Cascaval	Tryggve Fossum	John Knight
Robert Chappell	Maria Garzaran	Peter Kogge
Howard Chen	Chris Gniady	Christoforos Kozyrakis
S. Chiu	Seth Goldstein	Rakesh Krishnaiyer
Sangyeun Cho	Antonio Gonzalez	Jih Kwon Peir
Yuan Chou	Eddie Gornish	Josep-Maria LLaberia

Josep-Lluis Larriba
Alvin Lebeck
Jaejin Lee
Charles Lefurgy
Kevin Lepak
Wei Li
Zhiyuan Li
W. Liao
Ran Libeskind-Hadas
Foo Lim
Ken Lueh
C.K. Luk
Steven Lumetta
Ken MacKenzie
Tara Madhyastha
Wojciech Magda
Scott Mahlke
Bill Mangione-Smith
Srilatha Manne
Pedro Marcuello
Morris Marden
Peter Markstein
Ivan Martel
Jose Martinez
Xavier Martorell
Matthew Mattina
John McCanne
James McCormick
Sally McKee
G. Memik
Arif Merchant
Brian Mestan
Jaime Moreno
Andreas Moshovos
Todd Mowry
Robert Muth
Gregory Muthler
D. Nagle
Walid Najjar
Vijaykrishnan Narayanan
Wayne Nation

Shashank Nemawarker
C.J. Newburn
Tin-Fook Ngai
Anthony Nguyen
Brian O'Krafka
Mark Oskin
Vijay Pai
Joan-Manel Parcerisa
Enric Pastor
Sanjay Patel
Milos Prvulovic
Thomas Puzak
Ram Raghavan
Umakishore Ramachandran
Alex Ramirez
Parthasarathy Ranganathan
Ravishankar Rao
B. Ramakrishna Rau
Steve Reinhardt
Glenn Reinman
Jose Renau
Erik Riedel
Scott Rixner
Jim Rose
Eric Rotenberg
Amir Roth
Kaushik Roy
Juan Rubio
Kevin Rudd
Julio Sahuquillo
Jesus Sanchez
Oliver Santana
Vivek Sarin
Subramanya Sastry
Sumedh Sathaye
Aaron Sawdey
Michael Scott
Resit Sendag
John Seng
Mauricio Serrona
Tatiana Shpeisman

Gabby Silberman
Balaram Sinharoy
Mukund Sivaraman
Anand Sivasubramaniam
Brian Slechta
Allan Snavely
Yan Solihin
Arun Somani
Francesco Spadini
Susan Spence
Simon Steely
John Strasser
Sree Subramoney
Neeraj Suri
Ram Swaminathan
Deepu Talla
Renju Thomas
Mithuna Thottethodi
Eric Tune
Augustus Uht
Mustafa Uysal
Neil Vacharajani
Amin Vahdat
Steve VanderWiel
Stephen van Doren
Alistair Veitch
Miroslav Velev
Mary Vernon
N. Vijaykrishnan
T.N. Vijaykumar
Hangzheng Wang
David Webb
Charles Weems
Shlomo Weiss
Chris Wilkerson
Youfang Wu
Tse-Yu Yeh
Donald Yeung
Mohamed Zahran

Keynote Speaker

The Software Industry: Ten Lessons for Long Life

Timothy Chou

President, Oracle.com

Abstract

The software industry is headed into a major transition, fueled by the increasing availability of high quality, pervasive networking. This change is as fundamental as the transformation of the hardware industry over the past 25 years that was driven by advances in microprocessor technology. Whether one thinks of this software as service, ASPs, web services, or network computing, the face of the software industry will never be the same. This talk will focus on some of the key issues that challenge the industry, academia, and the research community and help determine who will succeed and who will fail.

Energy and Thermal Management I

Microarchitectural Simulation and Control of di/dt-induced

Power Supply Voltage Variation

Ed Grochowski
Intel Labs
Intel Corporation
2200 Mission College Blvd
Santa Clara, CA 95052
Mailstop SC12-303
edward.grochowski@intel.com

Dave Ayers
Enterprise Processor Division
Intel Corporation
2200 Mission College Blvd
Santa Clara, CA 95052
Mailstop SC12-502
david.ayers@intel.com

Vivek Tiwari
Intel Architecture Group
Intel Corporation
2200 Mission College Blvd
Santa Clara, CA 95052
Mailstop SC12-603
vivek.tiwari@intel.com

Abstract

As the power consumption of modern high-performance microprocessors increases beyond 100W, power becomes an increasingly important design consideration. This paper presents a novel technique to simulate power supply voltage variation as a result of varying activity levels within the microprocessor when executing typical software. The voltage simulation capability may be added to existing microarchitecture simulators that determine the activities of each functional block on a clock-by-clock basis. We then discuss how the same technique can be implemented in logic on the microprocessor die to enable real-time computation of current consumption and power supply voltage. When used in a feedback loop, this logic makes it possible to control the microprocessor's activities to reduce demands on the power delivery system. With on-die voltage computation and di/dt control, we show that a significant reduction in power supply voltage variation may be achieved with little performance loss or average power increase.

1. Introduction

Over the past 25 years, microprocessor power consumption has grown from under one watt to over 100 watts. The dramatic increase in power is a result of transistor scaling, which has produced many more transistors on a chip running at much higher frequencies [1]. Traditionally, voltage scaling has been used to reduce power to manageable levels; however, with supply voltages approaching one volt, further large reductions in voltage are unlikely.

Today power has emerged at the forefront of challenges facing the microprocessor designer. There are two distinct sets of problems - those associated with absolute power level and those associated with changes in power level. On absolute power level, it is clear that a microprocessor consuming 100W requires a power supply, voltage regulator, and power distribution network capable of supplying 100W, as well as a thermal solution (package, heat sinks, and fans) capable of dissipating the resulting heat. Such components are costly and cannot be expected to scale to higher power levels as transistor dimensions shrink. Changes in power level are also problematic - a hypothetical 100W microprocessor running at 1.0V draws 100A. The voltage regulator and power distribution network must maintain the supply voltage to within +/-5%, meaning that no more than 100mV peak-to-peak ripple can be tolerated regardless of what the microprocessor and the software its running do. The power distribution network must have sufficient capacitance, and small enough inductance and resistance, to maintain the supply voltage to within 100mV even though the microprocessor's supply current may change dramatically within a few nanoseconds. This latter problem is referred to as the *di/dt problem* after the definition of inductance $V=L*di/dt$. V is the voltage across an inductor of value L when subject to a change in current di/dt.

2. Microarchitecture Simulators

There are many existing microarchitectural simulators: SimpleScalar [2], SMTSIM [3], etc. These simulators work by simulating the flow of instructions through the microprocessor's pipeline. The simulator contains an implementation of the microprocessor's pipeline and control logic as well as an architectural simulator needed

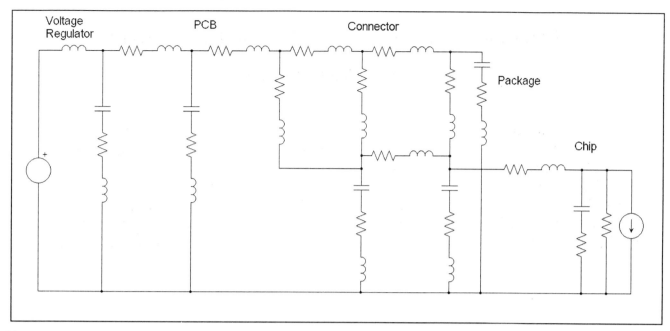

Figure 1: Electrical Model of Power Distribution Network

to execute the program. The simulator determines how many clocks are required to execute a given benchmark, and produces statistics such as pipeline stalls, cache misses, mispredicted branches, etc.

Recent work has shown how to augment a microarchitectural simulator with power computation [4]. The power simulator makes use of a feature of modern microprocessors – extensive clock gating. Each functional unit is equipped with a circuit that turns on the clock when the unit is active and shuts off the clock when the unit is inactive. This technique minimizes power consumption in inactive units but results in large variations in overall power levels that depend on the software being run. In a very power-conscious design, the clock gating may be done with extremely fine granularity - unit by unit and pipestage by pipestage - resulting in a large number of clock gating signals. For every clock the simulator knows which units and pipestages are active, and can compute the total power consumption during that clock by simply adding up the active power and idle power of blocks that are *on* and *off* respectively. Although usually thought of as a power simulator, the simulator can readily compute the total supply current and multiply current by a constant voltage to produce power. *Current* is the interesting quantity, as we'll see in the following section.

Several such simulators have been built for internal use at Intel. The active and idle currents for each block are based on low-level circuit simulations or estimates. The accuracy of these simulators has been determined to be sufficient for pre-silicon comparisons between different

microarchitectural design points across a range of software applications.

3. From Current Simulator to Voltage Simulator

Once a current simulator has been constructed, the power supply voltage may be computed based on an understanding of how the power distribution network responds to new demands for current. Figure 1 shows an electrical model of the power distribution network for a high performance microprocessor. The model includes decoupling capacitors on the die, in the package, and in the voltage regulator, as well as the parasitic inductance and resistance associated with the package, socket, printed circuit board, and devices within the voltage regulator. The microprocessor is modeled as a variable current sink, and the remainder of the voltage regulator is modeled as an ideal voltage source. Component values are chosen to be representative of those in this application. A discussion of how to construct such a model is beyond the scope of this paper. Refer to [5] for a description of the relevant techniques.

The result of applying a 25A current step to the power distribution network is shown in figure 2. The supply voltage as seen by the microprocessor dips and *rings* due to the inductance and capacitance of the power distribution network. The voltage reaches a minimum value 25 clocks after the current step began (each clock is 0.3ns).

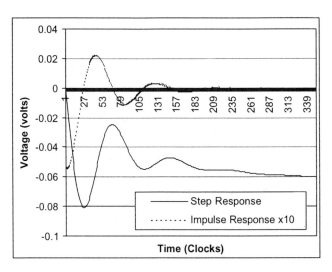

Figure 2: Step and Impulse Response of Power Distribution Network

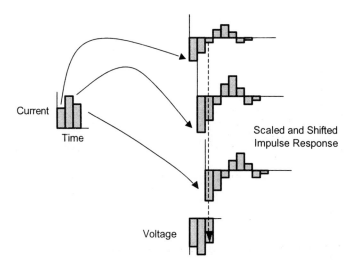

Figure 3: Voltage Computation using Convolution

The step response was determined by running a Spice-like circuit simulation on the network in figure 1. Also shown is the impulse response, which is the response of the power distribution network to a single 25A pulse of 0.3ns duration. The impulse response was computed from the step response by taking the difference between adjacent samples. For simplicity, we've considered only the high-frequency (50-100 MHz) components caused by the circuit board, connector, package, and chip. We've neglected a low-frequency (~1 MHz) resonance caused by the voltage regulator's LC filter. We'll discuss the implications of including this in a later section.

Now that we've determined the response of the power distribution network to a fixed current step, how can we determine its response to an arbitrary current waveform such as the processor's variable activity over time? At first glance, this might appear to require solving systems of differential equations. However, a much simpler method is possible based on the observation that the power distribution network is, to rough approximation, a linear network. Linear systems satisfy two properties:

1. Scaling the input by a certain amount causes the output to scale in proportion. Mathematically, $f(c*x)=c*f(x)$ where c is a constant. Thus, if we were to double the amplitude of the input current step in figure 2, we would expect the output voltage drop to double.

2. The result of applying the linear function to the sum of two inputs is the same as if the function were applied individually to each input and the results summed. Mathematically, $f(x+y)=f(x)+f(y)$. Thus, we can compute the response to a sum of two input waveforms by applying the linear function to each input individually and summing the results. This property is known as *superposition*.

The two properties of linear systems make possible simulation of power supply voltage for arbitrary currents using simple mathematics. This is done by decomposing the current waveform into a series of pulses (one pulse per clock), scaling and shifting the impulse response by the height and time offset of each current pulse, and adding together the results. The algorithm is illustrated in figure 3. Since the current simulator computes average current per clock, it is natural to use the clock as the unit of time for a pulse in the voltage simulator. Readers familiar with digital signal processing will recognize that our supply voltage simulator is computing a convolution of the processor's simulated power supply current and the impulse response of the power distribution network [6].

The results of the combined current and voltage simulator are shown in figures 4 and 5. This is a 2000 clock excerpt of a simulation of a future Itanium™ processor running the Apache web server and gzip file compression program. As one would expect, the current graph reflects phases of program execution, each phase having its own unique IPC and current levels. The voltage graph roughly follows the current graph, with phases of high IPC and high current having low supply voltage. Over the entire 20 million clock simulation the processor's supply current varies from 52A to 73A. The peak-to-peak voltage variation is 40mV with a 1.2V supply. Note that the voltage variation is well within the allowable tolerance since the Apache/gzip workload is not a worst-case di/dt pattern.

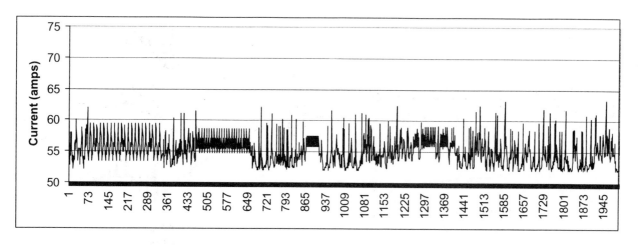

Figure 4: Microprocessor Supply Current versus Time

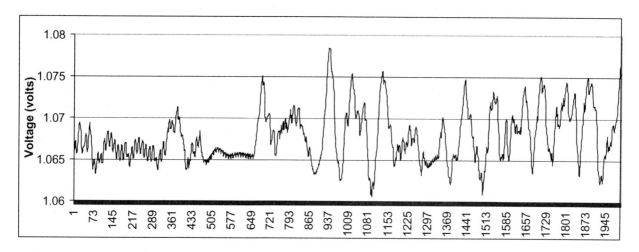

Figure 5: Microprocessor Supply Voltage versus Time

4. From Simulation to Control

So far, we've focused on simulating the microprocessor's power supply current and voltage as a function of the microarchitecture and software being run. Such simulations are invaluable to the microprocessor designer to perform design-time optimizations [7]. We now examine the possibility of controlling the microprocessor's activities in real-time to limit both absolute power and variations in supply voltage.

To understand why control of power related parameters is beneficial, consider how microprocessor power delivery systems are designed today. A microprocessor's power delivery system must be designed for the *worst-case* software that can ever be run. This is usually a program with extremely high IPC (for maximum power consumption), or a program that rapidly alternates between extremely high IPC and extremely low IPC (for maximum di/dt). We call such programs *power viruses* because they stress the power delivery system much

more than normal application software. Consider now the possibility of adding on-die power computation and regulation hardware. This hardware can detect when abnormally high power demands are made by software and slow down execution of that software to reduce power, or artificially inject activity to raise power in order to keep supply voltage within preset limits. With such controls, the microprocessor and its power delivery system need only be designed to meet the needs of *typical* software, with the control hardware ensuring that the typical values are never exceeded. The cost savings in designing for typical rather than worst-case software behavior can be substantial. The Intel® Pentium® 4 processor implements a thermal monitor to limit die temperature so that the processor and system thermal solutions may be designed according to the power envelopes of real applications rather than worst-case power viruses [8].

We began our research by examining shift-register approaches to di/dt control. Shift registers have been

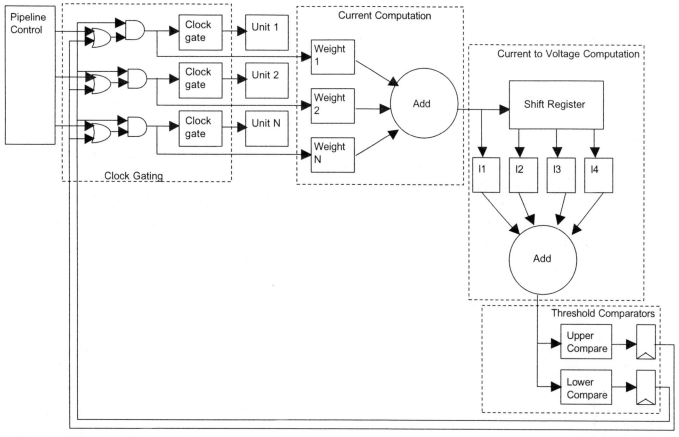

Figure 6: di/dt Controller Block Diagram

proposed as a means to reduce di/dt induced power supply voltage swings [9]. The idea is to spread out the clock gating transitions of functional units over multiple clock cycles by dividing the unit into a number of blocks and turning each block *on* and *off* at different times. This scheme is successful in spreading out large current changes over several clock cycles; however, it cannot effectively address changes in current over a time period longer than the hardware pipeline. With ever increasing clock frequencies, a different approach was needed.

We initially considered using a shift register to maintain a history of the processor's activity over time, the length being set according to the duration of the response of the power distribution network (approximately 25 clock cycles in figure 2). When a large transition is detected, such as going from a period of low activity to a period of high activity, logic connected to the shift register determines that the processor has exceeded its budget for current change, and limits the processor's future activities. This technique evolved into the shift register containing small integers (rather than single bits), the values being proportional to the supply current in that clock. The transition detection logic evolved into a weighted sum computation with both positive and negative weights. Several methods for determining the weights were experimentally tried and the best results were obtained by using weights that were proportional to

the first derivative of the step response of the power distribution network. The final step was achieved when it was noted that this method was the same as setting the weights according to the impulse response of the power distribution network so that the algorithm used by the simulator to compute power supply voltage and the algorithm used by the shift register/weighted sum logic to minimize voltage variation were identical! Thus was born a systematic method to design logic that maintains the processor's supply voltage to within preset limits by computing what the supply voltage should be and controlling the microprocessor's activities to maintain those limits.

A block diagram of the complete di/dt controller is shown in figure 6. It consists of the current computation hardware that monitors the clock gating signals of each block and adds up the active current and idle current to compute the total chip current. The result is fed to a shift register that computes a weighted sum of current over time, the weights being proportional to the impulse response of the power delivery network. This is the convolution engine. The result is then fed to two digital comparators. When a lower voltage threshold is crossed, current is reduced either by shutting off the clock directly or by shutting off instruction fetch or issue causing the clock-gating circuits to shut off the

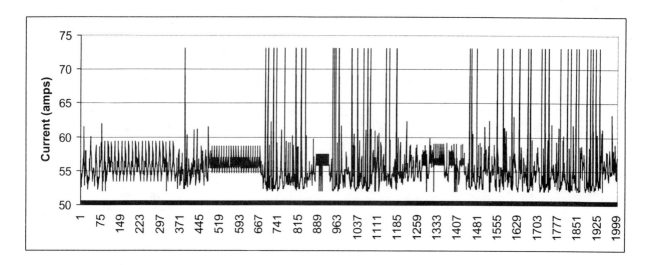

Figure 7: Current versus Time with di/dt Controller

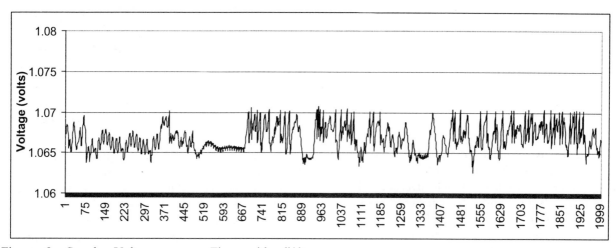

Figure 8: Supply Voltage versus Time with di/dt Controller

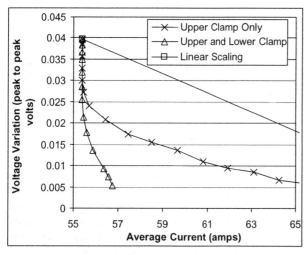

Figure 9: Supply Voltage Variation versus Current

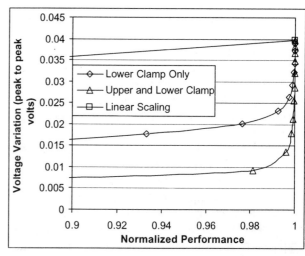

Figure 10: Supply Voltage Variation versus Performance

downstream clocks. When an upper voltage threshold is exceeded, current is increased by forcing on functional units that would otherwise be clock gated off (of course, one needs to ensure that essential state information doesn't get clobbered – the details of how to do this are beyond the scope of the paper). In between the upper and lower thresholds, the processor is allowed to run normally. The voltage computation, threshold comparison, and clock manipulation are performed every clock. As shown in figure 6, the di/dt controller is a feedback loop since the action of forcing on or off the functional units affects the computed supply current and voltage, which in turn affects the controller's subsequent actions.

The result of using a di/dt controller on power supply current and voltage is shown in figures 7 and 8. In these figures the di/dt controller's upper and lower thresholds have been set close together to illustrate their operation. Compared to figures 4 and 5, one can see that the di/dt controller has introduced sharp one clock spikes to both the maximum and minimum current levels. The spikes are a result of the di/dt controller forcing the clock on or off in response to the computed voltage falling outside predetermined limits. Inspite of the spikes, the peak-to-peak variation in supply voltage is less than the uncontrolled case because the di/dt controller has regulated the current in such a way as to avoid exciting RLC resonances in the power distribution network. Due to the contributions of DC resistance to the impulse response, the average power consumed by the microprocessor is also held to within fixed upper and lower bounds.

5. Voltage, Current, and Performance Tradeoffs

The effects of di/dt controls as described in the previous section are slower program execution and/or increased average power. This section examines the tradeoff between the amount of power supply voltage variation and slower program execution/increased average power.

Figures 9 and 10 show the current and performance effects of using a di/dt controller to reduce power supply voltage variation. Because it is possible to independently set the upper and lower thresholds, the effects of each are shown separately, and then the combination is shown. *Upper clamp only* means that only action taken by the di/dt controller is to force on functional units that would otherwise be idle when the computed supply voltage is too high. This results in a net current increase but no loss in performance. *Lower clamp only* means that the only action taken by the di/dt controller is to shut off the clock to units that would otherwise be active when supply voltage is too low, resulting in a net performance loss

and also a reduction in current. *Upper and lower clamp* combines two control mechanisms. In these figures, the input is a 20M clock trace from the Apache web server and gzip file compression program. The simulator is an Intel internal tool that simulates a future Itanium™ microprocessor. The results of using the di/dt controller are compared against simple linear scaling of voltage variation against current and performance. Linear scaling assumes that supply voltage variation can be linearly reduced to zero either by reducing the delta between minimum and maximum current by artificially raising the minimum towards the maximum, or by reducing the processor's performance towards zero. The goal of the di/dt controller is to perform much better than linear scaling.

From figures 9 and 10 one can see that di/dt induced power supply voltage variation can easily be cut in half with less than 2% performance loss and less than 2% current increase on the Apache/gzip workload (neglecting the current consumed by the di/dt controller itself). The performance loss and current increase are proportionally much smaller than the reduction in supply voltage variation because the supply voltage follows a statistical distribution, and the di/dt controller can cut off the peaks without affecting the majority of clocks in between. The sharp knee in the curves is very desirable - it indicates that the di/dt controller can do its job without noticeably affecting program execution time or average current.

6. Implementation

The previous section assumed that the di/dt controller implements the current computation, a convolution with the 300 clock impulse response, and threshold comparisons, with a total latency of one clock. This is a very accurate but enormous amount of computation for one cycle latency. This section examines how relaxing the amount of computation and increasing latency affects the effectiveness of the di/dt controller.

Figures 11 and 12 show the performance and current effects of reducing the number of elements in the impulse response by truncating all elements after a given element. Satisfactory operation may be achieved using as few as the first 25 elements of the impulse response. In the next section, we'll discuss an alternative method to further reduce the amount of computation.

Latency presents a more difficult problem. The main sources of latency are the current computation logic and the convolution engine. The current computation logic adds up the current consumed by all blocks in the microprocessor and produces a result in the same clock that the microprocessor is drawing that amount of current. This might seem to be an impossible task, but

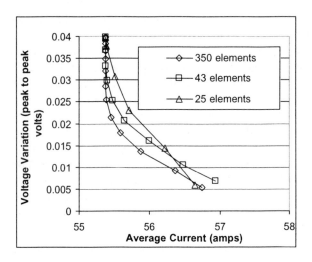

Figure 11: Supply Voltage Variation versus Current with Truncation

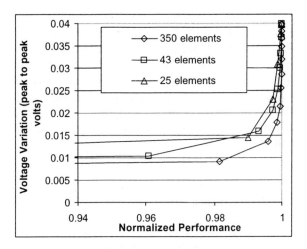

Figure 12: Supply Voltage Variation versus Performance with Truncation

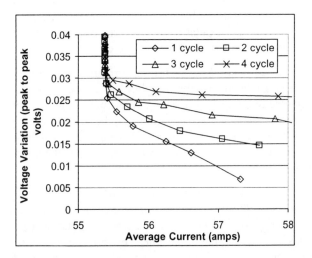

Figure 13: Supply Voltage Variation versus Current with Latency

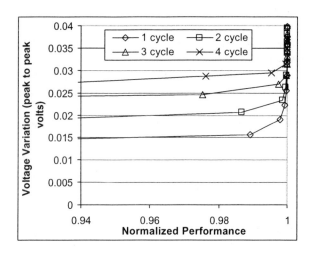

Figure 14: Supply Voltage Variation versus Performance with Latency

the current computation logic can take advantage of the microprocessor's pipeline. The supply current of blocks later in the pipeline can be precomputed at an earlier stage in the pipeline. If necessary, two computations can be performed at an early stage with a late-select choosing the correct sum according to whether the block was active or inactive. These techniques can reduce amount of logic that must operate with short latency (as viewed by the di/dt controller's feedback loop).

Latency in the convolution engine can also be addressed through pipelining. Since the convolution engine maintains a history of supply current over time, it is naturally pipelined. Only the first element of the impulse response need be computed with one cycle latency. The second element can take two clocks; the third can take three; and so on.

Figure 13 and 14 show the effects of adding latency to the di/dt controller's feedback loop. Latency is simulated by zeroing out the initial elements of the impulse response. Because the di/dt controller regulates something that is fairly fast (the "ring" in the step response), its effectiveness decreases rapidly with increasing latency, becoming ineffective with latencies greater than about 3 clocks. While the di/dt controller shares many characteristics with hardwired digital signal processors, one important difference is that achieving short latency is much more important to the di/dt controller.

Because of the need for short latency, it is expected that a realistic implementation of the di/dt controller will not likely rely on one centralized controller, but rather multiple distributed di/dt controllers, each regulating a portion of the microprocessor die. Each di/dt controller can be built alongside a microprocessor pipeline to regulate activities within its corresponding pipeline. This approach relies on loose coupling between the pipelines (through queues, for example) so that if one pipeline is momentarily stopped, incoming bits from neighboring pipelines don't fall on the floor. With a distributed implementation, we believe that a di/dt controller can be built that obtains most of the performance of the centralized controller. Clearly the performance of the distributed di/dt controller cannot be as good because each portion of the controller must operate within a fixed budget that assumes all other portions are experiencing worst-case conditions.

The di/dt controller is subject to other implementation considerations as follows:

1. The weights need to be programmable to allow for changes in operating frequency.

2. The general implementation in figure 6 is overkill – since the end result is a comparison against two thresholds, a practical implementation of the di/dt controller will use small integers with specialized logic rather than multiplier-accumulators.

3. The microarchitectural di/dt controller relies on the processor clocking much faster than the period of the "ring" in the power distribution network - it cannot control di/dt events shorter in duration than a few clocks. Adequate on-die decoupling capacitance and the pipelining technique described in [9] are required to control supply voltage swings shorter in duration than a few clock cycles.

7. Future Work

While our initial work on microarchitectural di/dt controls shows promising results, several questions remain. This section discusses possible areas for future work.

Perhaps the biggest question is "what accuracy can be achieved by the on-die supply current computation?" The current computation needs to be reasonably accurate for the di/dt controller to do its job, and furthermore it must achieve good accuracy within a limited hardware budget. If that is not possible with conventional circuit designs, we must ask the converse question: "how can a microprocessor be designed so that on-die supply current computation logic can achieve good accuracy?" Data-dependent current variations will likely set a lower bound on accuracy. The microprocessor designer may need to take steps to minimize data-dependent current variations through the use of dual-rail and differential circuit topologies, for example. The microprocessor designer may also need to formulate an error budget so that large current consuming blocks are accurately accounted for while small current consuming blocks are

not considered in the current computation, but rather treated as part of the error budget.

Another question concerns the convolution engine at the heart of the di/dt controller. The convolution engine computes supply voltage from current. It is an example of a finite impulse response (FIR) filter. FIR filters are straightforward to design but not well suited to a lengthy impulse response. A recursive filter, or infinite impulse response (IIR) filter, offers the ability to handle a long impulse response with less hardware and shorter latency. A IIR filter would enable the di/dt controller to compensate for low-frequency (~1 MHz) LC ringing in the voltage regulator in addition to the high-frequency (50-100 MHz) ringing associated with circuit board, package, and high-speed decoupling capacitors. We believe the design of the filter is a good topic for future research and one that can offer significant implementation benefits.

Another area for future work is in determining the stability of the di/dt controller's feedback loop. Feedback loops are normally never used around networks with a complex phase response due to the impossibility of making the loop stable. We've worked around this problem by creating a non-linear system with two thresholds – an upper and a lower threshold – that deprive the feedback loop of the gain necessary for oscillation when the voltage is in between the two thresholds. Future work should examine the relationship between the thresholds and the response of the power distribution network on the feedback loop's stability.

A final question is to examine the tradeoff between analog and digital techniques. One may ask why build logic that computes power supply voltage when this physical quantity can be measured using analog circuits? There are advantages to each approach: the digital method can be built using the same logic gates as the rest of the microprocessor and operates completely deterministically (when fed the same input, two microprocessors will compute exactly the same result). The analog method is potentially more accurate and requires less hardware.

8. Conclusion

In this paper, we've presented a novel algorithm for simulating power supply voltage as a function of a microprocessor's activity. We've shown how the same algorithm can be implemented on the microprocessor die to reduce di/dt-induced power supply voltage variation with minimal effects on program execution speed or average power. We believe that in the future the use of such techniques will become widespread. Microprocessors containing hundreds of millions of transistors can be expected to devote a small percentage of those transistors to power computation and control.

9. Acknowledgements

The authors would like to acknowledge the contributions of David Sager and Ian Young to the development of microarchitectural di/dt controls, to Jeff Chamberlain and others for the development of the Dante simulator, and also to John Shen, George Cai, and Steve Gunther for their valuable feedback.

10. References

[1] S. Borkar, "Design challenges of technology scaling", IEEE Micro, Volume 19 Issue 4, July-August 1999, Pages 23-29.

[2] D. Burger and T.M. Austin, "The SimpleScalar toolset, version 2.0," Computer Architecture News, Vol. 25, No. 3, Jun. 1997, Pages 13-25.

[3] D.M. Tullsen, "Simulation and modeling of a simultaneous multithreading processor", 22nd Annual Computer Measurement Group Conference, December 1996.

[4] D. Brooks, V. Tiwari, M. Martonosi, "Wattch: a framework for architectural-level power analysis and optimizations", Proceedings of the 27th International Symposium on Computer Architecture, 2000. Pages 83-94.

[5] D.J. Herrell, B. Beker, "Modeling of power distribution systems for high-performance microprocessors", IEEE Transactions on Advanced Packaging, Volume 22, Issue 3, August 1999, Pages 240-248.

[6] S.W. Smith, "The Scientist and Engineer's Guide to Digital Signal Processing", California Technical Publishing, 1997. Pages 107-122, http://www.dspguide.com

[7] D.M. Brooks, P. Bose, S.E. Schuster, H. Jacobson, P..N. Kudva, A. Buyuktosunoglu, J. Wellman, V. Zyuban, M. Gupta, P.W. Cook, "Power-aware microarchitecture: design and modeling challenges for next-generation microprocessors", IEEE Micro, Volume 20, Issue 6, Nov-Dec 2000, Pages 26-44.

[8] Intel® Pentium® 4 Processor in the 423-pin Package at 1.30 GHz, 1.40 GHz, 1.50 GHz, 1.60 GHz, 1.70 GHz and 1.80 GHz Datasheet, 2001. Pages 78-79.

[9] M.D. Pant, P. Pant, D.S. Wills, V. Tiwari, "Inductive noise reduction at the architectural level", Thirteenth International Conference on VLSI Design, 2000. Pages 162-167.

Control-Theoretic Techniques and Thermal-RC Modeling for Accurate and Localized Dynamic Thermal Management

Kevin Skadron[†], Tarek Abdelzaher[†], Mircea R. Stan[‡]
[†]Dept. of Computer Science, [‡]Dept. of Electrical and Computer Engineering
University of Virginia
Charlottesville, VA 22904
skadron@cs.virginia.edu, zaher@cs.virginia.edu, mircea@virginia.edu

Abstract

This paper proposes the use of formal feedback control theory as a way to implement adaptive techniques in the processor architecture. Dynamic thermal management (DTM) is used as a test vehicle, and variations of a PID controller (Proportional-Integral-Differential) are developed and tested for adaptive control of fetch "toggling." To accurately test the DTM mechanism being proposed, this paper also develops a thermal model based on lumped thermal resistances and thermal capacitances. This model is computationally efficient and tracks temperature at the granularity of individual functional blocks within the processor. Because localized heating occurs much faster than chip-wide heating, some parts of the processor are more likely to be "hot spots" than others.

Experiments using Wattch and the SPEC2000 benchmarks show that the thermal trigger threshold can be set within 0.2° of the maximum temperature and yet never enter thermal emergency. This cuts the performance loss of DTM by 65% compared to the previously described fetch toggling technique that uses a response of fixed magnitude.

1. Introduction

Recent research in the computer architecture field has explored techniques for making the processor's response *adapt* to the current workload. Unfortunately, almost all this work has used engineering solutions whose effectiveness is only verified experimentally for a limited set of applications. This paper introduces the notion of using *formal feedback control theory* to precisely control the adaptivity and minimize performance losses. The use of control theory provides an established design methodology that yields several benefits: runtime adaptivity, very tight control over the value of interest, the ability to avoid large parameter-space searches, and adaptive controllers that are easy to design.

In particular, we demonstrate its effectiveness for adaptive control of chip temperature—*dynamic thermal management* or DTM [2].

Researchers have recently expressed interest in managing heat dissipation in order to reduce the growing cost of the CPU's thermal package. Borkar [1] estimates that above 35–40 Watts (W), additional power dissipation increases the total cost per chip by more than \$1/W. Without some sort of dynamic technique for managing temperature, thermal packages must typically be designed for peak power in order to ensure safe operation—even though peak power may rarely be observed. Unfortunately, peak power dissipation may soon be as high as 130 W [18], making thermal packages expensive. As the sophistication of high-performance processors grows, much of the added complexity and transistors are dedicated to extracting further ILP. Yet in some cases, these features are only intermittently active during the program. This only widens the gap between peak and average power dissipation.

The gap between peak and average power dissipation suggests that, instead of designing the thermal package for sustained peak power dissipation, designers should instead be able to target the thermal package for some lower temperature and hence lower cost. In those cases when power dissipation does approach peak levels and temperature approaches the limits of the thermal package, various techniques for DTM can be engaged to force a reduction in power dissipation and hence avoid thermal emergency. Because these techniques typically entail slowing down the processor in some way, there may be performance penalties whenever DTM is triggered. The decision to deploy DTM therefore requires a tradeoff between savings in thermal packaging costs and consequent losses in performance. Yet speed remains critically important for high-performance computing, and many embedded-systems applications as well. The challenge of DTM is to adapt the thermal management to the application's needs in order to minimize the slowdown and extract the optimum combination of temperature and performance. For any chosen thermal package, better performance can be accomplished either by developing new mechanisms for implementing DTM, or by more precisely engaging and disengaging the DTM mechanisms to minimize the performance loss. Precision is what feedback control provides.

To better evaluate our techniques, this work also develops a more detailed model of thermal effects. Prior work by Brooks and Martonosi [2] on architecture-level DTM used a moving average of chip-wide power dissipation as a proxy for temperature. We instead apply a model from the thermal-packaging literature that uses thermal resistances (R) and thermal capacitances (C) to directly model temperature. This model is also used in the TEMPEST work by Dhodapkar *et al.* [6], but only for average, chip-wide temperatures to capture packaging effects. Our work uses the RC model to derive a computationally efficient thermal model for temperature effects in individual structures, and hence lets us model "hot spots" and appropriate DTM responses. This is important, because localized heating occurs much faster than does chip-wide heating, and so thermal emergencies may occur at individual hot spots well before the chip as a whole shows any signs of entering thermal emergency. DTM mechanisms must take this fact into account. Other work—the most recent by Yuan and Hong [25]—has also modeled non-uniform heating effects, but not in conjunction with architecture-level modeling. We are unaware of any other work that combines localized thermal modeling with a microarchitecture-level model.

Overall, this paper introduces the use of thermal-RC modeling for architecture-level thermal effects, and introduces the use of control theory to guide architecture-level thermal management. We find that the control-theoretic DTM techniques (CT-DTM) that are based on the commonly used PID industrial controller (Proportional-Integral-Differential) substantially outperform the non-control-theoretic (non-CT) techniques. Indeed, the PI and PID controllers are able to respond so quickly that thermal response can be delayed until the chip temperature comes within $0.2°$ of the desired maximum temperature. This responsiveness provides savings of 65% in performance loss compared to the best DTM technique described by Brooks and Martonosi while never causing thermal emergencies. The results presented here suggest that feedback control would be beneficial in a range of other adaptive architecture techniques as well.

The rest of this paper is organized as follows. The next three sections provide some necessary background on DTM, controller design, and thermal modeling. Then Section 5 describes our specific simulation and thermal-modeling techniques, Section 6 evaluates the effectiveness of our control-theoretic DTM techniques, and Section 7 concludes the paper.

2. Dynamic Thermal Management

2.1. Non-Control-Theoretic DTM Techniques

The DTM work by Brooks and Martonosi [2] proposed three microarchitectural and two scaling techniques for controlling temperature. All are engaged at some trigger level close enough to the emergency threshold that a trigger indicates emergency is imminent, and far enough from the threshold to give the DTM mechanism enough time to successfully reduce temperature before an emergency occurs. For their work, Brooks and Martonosi used power dissipation as a proxy for temperature. They chose an emergency threshold of 25 W and a trigger threshold of 24 W, both based on the boxcar average of per-cycle power dissipation over the last 10 K cycles. Unfortunately, chip-wide power is a poor proxy for measuring temperature. Chip-wide measurements do not account for the fact that localized heating occurs much faster—typically orders of magnitude faster—than chip-wide heating. And while power and temperature are clearly related, heating is an exponential effect (like an electrical RC circuit) that a boxcar average cannot capture. Instead, Section 4 of this paper describes a way to model temperature directly and permit the modeling of hot spots at various granularities.

For the DTM mechanisms studied here, we set the goal that the techniques we study should *never* allow the chip to enter thermal emergency. The most effective microarchitectural mechanism that Brooks and Martonosi explored consists of *toggling*: every N cycles, instruction fetch is disabled. This reduces the average number of instructions in the pipeline and reduces the rate of accesses to the major structures on the chip. They explore values for N of 1 (instruction fetch stops completely until the DTM mechanism is disengaged) and 2 (instruction fetch occurs every other cycle until disengaged). "Toggle1" is able to eliminate emergencies, because it stops fetching entirely; "toggle2" is not. For the control-theoretic DTM mechanisms, we consider more fine-grained variations of the toggling rate. Compared to these responses of fixed strength, the control-theoretic approach lets us use mild reductions in fetch toggling when the thermal stress is mild, but more aggressive toggling as the thermal stress becomes more severe.

Brooks and Martonosi also explored two other microarchitectural techniques, *throttling* [17] and *speculation control* [14]. In throttling, instruction fetch is performed every cycle, but the number of instructions fetched is reduced from the normal operating bandwidth. This has the problem that the number of accesses to many structures, especially the branch predictor and I-cache, are not reduced, and this technique often cannot prevent certain hot spots. These problems point out the importance of monitoring temperature on a per-structure basis; the chip-wide average of power dissipation will not capture these effects. With speculation control, whenever more than M unresolved branches are present in the pipeline, no further instructions are fetched until the number of unresolved branches falls below M. Unfortunately, this technique is ineffective for programs with excellent branch prediction or periods of excellent branch prediction.

The scaling techniques consist of either scaling just the clock frequency or scaling both the frequency and the operating voltage. The advantages of the microarchitectural techniques are that they can be engaged and disengaged quickly, and that in some cases, the program's ILP characteristics permit the DTM mechanism to work well without penalizing performance. The scaling mechanisms, on the other hand, necessarily entail some loss in performance because the entire processor operates more slowly. In addition, the processor must stall for as much as 10–20 millisec. while the clock re-synchronizes. The overhead of invoking a scaling policy also means that it must be left in place for a significant *policy delay* in order to ensure that the temperature has been sufficiently reduced so that scaling will not be re-initiated in the near future. But as mentioned, during this period of time the slower clock rate entails a loss in performance, even after temperature decreases. For these reasons, Brooks and Martonosi found that the microarchitectural techniques had less impact on performance. Of course, if a microarchitectural technique fails to stem rising temperatures, scaling can also be performed as a backup policy.

Based on the inferior performance of fetch throttling, speculation control, and the scaling techniques, we do not consider them further, even though a realistic implementation might employ a hierarchy of DTM techniques. More detail can be found in an extended version of this paper [19].

The prior DTM work also explored two ways in which DTM may be triggered. In the first case, a thermal trigger engages an interrupt, which invokes a handler that then sets the DTM policy. After a specified time, another interrupt checks the thermal condition and if there is no longer a triggering condition, the DTM policy is turned off. The use of interrupts, however, introduces some delay (*e.g.*, 250 cycles) for each event. This incurs some small but unavoidable loss in performance even for an ideal DTM policy. Brooks and Martonosi also postulate the existence of a microarchitectural mechanism by which a thermal trigger immediately engages the DTM policy, with no delay. The only performance loss is then from the interaction of the DTM policy and the program's natural instruction throughput. This can be implemented by having each temperature sensor assert a signal indicating that it has been triggered, a feature we assume in our model.

As mentioned, a policy delay is also necessary, even for microarchitectural mechanisms. Once a DTM policy is invoked, it must stay active for a long enough period of time to sufficiently reduce the temperature. The delay must be set empirically: too short a policy, and the system will stay at or near trigger; too long a policy, and the system will incur an unnecessary loss in performance. The trigger level is also set empirically. Too close to the emergency threshold, and DTM will not be engaged soon enough to prevent emergency. Too far, and DTM is engaged unnecessarily.

The use of better thermal modeling and the application of control theory to the design of DTM mechanisms solves these problems. Simulating temperature directly provides more realistic indicators of how fast temperature changes, how different structures move in and out of thermal stress, and a more faithful replica of what actual temperature sensors in a real chip would observe. Section 4 discusses issues related to thermal modeling.

2.2. Control-Theoretic DTM Techniques

Clearly, any one DTM policy with fixed response (*e.g.* toggle1) will be sub-optimal. To guarantee elimination of thermal emergencies, a policy must aggressively reduce activity whenever triggered. But in many cases, such aggressive response is not needed. For example, mild thermal stress need not employ the very aggressive toggle1 policy, but of the mechanisms described so far, only toggle1 can completely avoid emergencies. An adaptive policy, on the other hand, can adjust the degree of response to the severity of the thermal situation. Yet designing adaptive mechanisms by hand is difficult, because it typically requires large parameter-space searches.

In this paper, we propose to use formal feedback control theory to manage the DTM and avoid the difficulties associated with ad-hoc techniques. A control-theoretic approach provides a number of advantages. It permits the DTM policy to adapt its response in proportion to the thermal emergency and also permits it to take account of prior history and the rate of change in temperature. The degree of response to each of these factors is controlled by a formal methodology, avoiding the need for ad-hoc methods. The toggling mechanisms provide an excellent basis for using a controller. Instead of a fixed toggling policy, the rate at which fetching is permitted is set by the controller and adjusted every n cycles, where n is the sampling rate—every 1000 cycles in our experiments. As the control output ranges from 0% to 100%, the fetch toggling ranges proportionally from all the way off to all the way on (toggle1). An output of 50%, for example, corresponds to toggle2.

The use of control theory also provides other benefits. Although beyond the scope of this work, controllers can be designed with guaranteed settling times (*i.e.*, how quickly the temperature settles back to a desired, safe level), and an analysis of the maximum overshoot can be used to choose a setpoint that, in conjunction with the appropriate controller, is as high as possible without risking an actual emergency.

For this paper, we focus on integrating DTM with more

accurate thermal modeling and explore only variations of the PID controller, commonly used in industry. This simple controller is sufficient to demonstrate our techniques and to provide substantial gains in performance. The next section presents some basic precepts of controller design and uses them to derive the adaptive controllers we test in Section 6.

3. Basic Control-Theoretic Techniques

Feedback control theory has been very successful at developing analytic frameworks and algorithms for robust performance control in physical systems. Using a mathematical model of the controlled process (such as the thermal dynamics relating power dissipation to temperature output of various microprocessor structures), it produces controllers which help achieve the desired output. Control-theoretic approaches have been applied to a variety of aspects of computer systems design to achieve adaptive response, *e.g.*, CPU scheduling [13, 22] and Internet congestion control [9]. Closer to the topic of this proposal, Dragone *et al.* have described a feedback technique for voltage scaling [8], and Wong *et al.* [24] have described a feedback circuit for canceling leakage currents.

Temperature control of a physical device such as a microprocessor is a natural application of control theory. A commonly used industrial controller is the PID (Proportional-Integral-Differential) controller. It has been proven very successful and robust even in controlling highly non-linear and poorly modeled systems. This subsection explains our derivation of a PID controller for DTM; those familiar with such derivations may wish to skip to the next section.

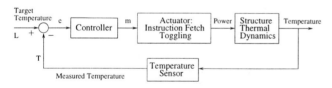

Figure 1. Control Loop

3.1. The Feedback Control Loop

Figure 1 presents the control loop being modeled. Let E be the thermal emergency level, such that heating of some chip structure beyond E poses a threat to that structure. We set a target temperature $L < E$ for the structure, that is very close to, but does not exceed, the emergency limit. A feedback control loop works by sampling the actual temperature, T, at discrete time instances (*e.g.*, once every 1000 cycles) and comparing it to the target L. The difference, $e = L - T$ is the current error in achieving the performance target. If the error is negative, the system is overheated, hence power dissipation should be reduced during the next

sampling interval. If the error is positive, the system can relax any power-reduction techniques that are currently engaged.

3.2. Controller Derivation

The basic PID controller responds to error by a correction that is an algebraic superposition of three actions (or forces). The first is the proportional action. It changes power in proportion to the value of the error and in the direction that reduces the error. The second is the integral action. It adjusts power incrementally, in proportion to the time integral of previous errors. This action tends to accumulate a slowly-changing bias that becomes constant when the error becomes zero, hence maintaining the system at the zero-error state. The last component is the derivative action. It adjusts power in proportion to the rate of change of error in the direction that reduces the rate of change, damping the response to avoid overshoot. At any time t, controller output, $m(t)$, is the weighted sum of the above three terms:

$$m(t) = K_C \left(e(t) + K_I \int e(t)dt + K_D \frac{de(t)}{dt} \right) \quad (1)$$

where K_C, K_I, and K_D are constants that need to be tuned according to stability analysis to ensure that the system will not oscillate. The selection of weights in the above equation gives a rich design space for controller functions. Finding the best weights requires a model of the controlled system. This model depends on whether the system is continuous or discrete. While in principle the system is discrete by virtue of sampling, our sampling period is much smaller than the time-scale of the thermal dynamics for the controlled chip structures. Hence, for all practical purposes, the system behaves in a continuous manner. Continuous controller design is typically performed in the Laplace transform domain. The Laplace transform of the controller transfer function is:

$$m(s) = K_C \left(1 + \frac{K_I}{s} + K_D s \right) e(s) \quad (2)$$

where s is the Laplace transform operator. The thermal dynamics of the controlled structure are represented by its thermal time-constant, τ, and a steady state gain, K_p, representing the steady state ratio of the change in output temperature to the change in input power that produces it—the thermal R in this application. In addition, sampling introduces an effective delay, T_d, in the loop, equal to half the sampling period. Hence, in the Laplace domain, the controlled system model of temperature is:

$$G(s) = \frac{K_p e^{-T_d s}}{1 + \tau s} \quad (3)$$

where $K_p = R_{block}$. Note from Figure 1 that any deviation, e, traveling through the feed-forward path of the loop will be transformed by the combined function $G(s)m(s)$,

Thermal quantity	unit	Electrical quantity	unit
P, Heat flow, power	W	I, Current flow	A
T, Temperature difference	K	V, Voltage	V
R_{th}, Thermal resistance	K/W	R, Electrical resistance	Ω
C_{th}, Thermal mass, capacitance	J/K	C, Electrical capacitance	F
$\tau_{th} = R_{th} \cdot C_{th}$, Thermal RC constant	s	$\tau = R \cdot C$, Electrical RC constant	s

Table 1. Equivalence between thermal and electrical quantities

which is the product of all components on that path. If the actuator and the temperature sensor introduce some gain into the system, K_a and K_s, then the total transformation is $G(s)K_s m(s)K_a$.

In the interests of space, we omit the rest of the derivation and stability analysis, and merely observe that this yields two equations in four unknowns: w, K_C, K_I, and K_D. To solve this set, the simplest approach is to set $K_I = K_D = 0$. This solution yields a proportional controller which has the benefit of computational efficiency. Alternatively, it is possible to set only one of K_I and K_D to zero, producing a PI or PD controller respectively. This makes it possible to introduce an additional design constraint via a phase constant, ω. For the PI controller, we set ω to $\pi/6$; for PID, 0; and for PD, $-\pi/6$. Finally, in more complex systems, two additional design constraints may be accommodated which uniquely determine both K_I and K_D. In our PID controller for fetch toggling, we set $K_I = 1/4K_D$. All the preceding values are common values that are known to work well in practice. They were successful with no tuning, making the derivation of effective controllers extremely easy. We did test other values for these parameters, but found that they were no better than the conventional values. This also illustrates the robustness of control-theoretic techniques: the performance of feedback-control systems remains largely unaffected even when the controlled system has not been accurately modeled in the analysis, or when external factors that have not been accounted for at design time interfere with its operation.

The final values for the PID controller were were $K_s = 1$ (idealized temperature sensor), $K_a = 3$ (actuator gain), $K_C = 4.42$, $K_I = 2.36 \times 10^6$ and $K_D = 1.06 \times 10^{-7}$ for a sampling frequency of 1000 clock cycles or 667 nanosec. The time constant of the system is the RC time constant from the thermal model; we used the longest time constant of the various blocks under study.

3.3. Actuator Saturation Effects

In designing the controller, it is important to consider saturation effects. In general, actuator saturation may have a negative effect in the presence of integral action, which is commonly known as *integral windup* and is a common problem in the design of industrial controllers. In our example, if the application produces only a small power dissipation, it may be impossible to reach the target chip temperature even when the processor operates at full speed. In this case, a positive error persists causing an arbitrarily high increase in the output of the integral action. This increase is meaningless to the actuator, which in this case becomes saturated. Eventually, if power dissipation does increase and temperature overshoots the set point, it will take the integral output a long time to "unwind", *i.e.*, return to a reading that is within the actuator's input range. During that time the actuator continues to be saturated, and the processor continues to operate at full speed, possibly entering a thermal emergency. Integral windup can be easily avoided by freezing the integrator when controller output saturates the actuator. Hence, once the error changes sign due to an overshoot, this permits controller output to immediately decrease below saturation (*i.e.*, *within* the actuator range), causing it to slow down pipeline execution and reduce power dissipation immediately, as needed. As mentioned above, we implemented this mechanism in our PI and PID controllers by preventing the integral from taking on a negative value.

4. Thermal Modeling

4.1. Using an Equivalent RC Circuit to Model Temperature.

For an integrated circuit at the die level, heat *conduction* is the dominant mechanism that determines the temperature. There exists a well-known duality [11] between heat transfer and electrical phenomena as summarized in Table 1. Any heat flow can be described as a "current", and the passing of this heat flow through a thermal "resistance" leads to a temperature difference equivalent to a "voltage". This is really Ohm's law for thermal phenomena. Thermal resistances are enough for describing steady-state behavior, but dynamic behavior is important for DTM, and this requires thermal "capacitances" as well. Thermal capacitances imply that even if the power flow changes instantaneously, there is a delay before the temperature changes and reaches steady state. The thermal resistances and capacitances together lead to exponential rise and fall times characterized by thermal RC time constants similar to the electrical RC constants.

Figure 2A shows a typical IC package with a heatsink and an equivalent simplified thermal model. The IC die consumes power when active and this power needs to be dissipated as heat. In order to simplify the analysis it is general

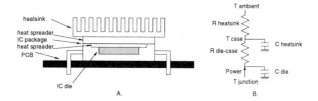

Figure 2. IC package with heatsink.
A. physical structure, B. simple lumped thermal model.

practice to ignore all large thermal resistances and only consider a simplified model as in Figure 2B with very little loss of accuracy. Large thermal resistors in parallel with smaller ones can safely be ignored because they cannot transfer enough heat to further reduce the temperature determined by the smaller values. Thermal capacitances are necessary for dynamic behavior and these have been also represented. To see the usefulness of the model, assume an IC that dissipates 25 W, die-to-case thermal resistance of 1 K/W, and heatsink resistance (conduction plus convection to ambient) of another 1 K/W. For an ambient temperature of 27 degrees Celsius, we can predict that the steady state average die temperature will be $25W \cdot 2K/W + 300K = 350K$ or $77°$ Celsius. Furthermore, if dynamic behavior is desired, the thermal capacitances can be used to derive such information. For example, assuming a heatsink thermal capacitance of 60 J/K and a much smaller die thermal capacitance, we can determine that the time constants involved in how fast the circuit heats up when powered on, or cools down when powered off, are on the order of $60J/K \cdot 1K/W = 60s = 1$ minute.

4.2. Modeling Localized Heating

Large ICs have a heterogeneous structure with many different areas on the die working at different rates, which implies that power is not dissipated uniformly on the chip. This *spatial non-uniformity* is complemented by a *temporal non-uniformity* in power density as many structures on the die go from idle mode to full active mode and vice-versa at different times. Recent emphasis on low-power design techniques such as power modes, clock gating, etc. are exacerbating the spatial and temporal non-uniformity for on-chip power density. As a result of this non-uniformity, the chip will exhibit so-called "hot spots". These hot spots have a spatial distribution as a result of the non-zero thermal resistivity of silicon and also a temporal distribution due to changing program behavior and the time constants implied by the thermal mass (capacitance).

A model for localized heating allows simulation of the actual physical temperature at different locations on the chip. In order to derive a lumped circuit model we first need to decide on the level of granularity for the lumped

elements. We decided to use a natural partitioning where functional blocks on the chip are the nodes in the lumped circuit model. This has the advantage that there is a one-to-one correspondence between the model in the architectural simulator and the thermal circuit, which leads to a good coupling between the two. We also currently make the simplifying assumption that it is feasible to have thermal sensors associated with each functional block. This is unrealistic, since the number of sensors is likely to be limited, and they may not be co-located with the most likely hot spots. Developing a model for temperature sensor behavior (as distinct from true physical temperature) is an important area for future work.

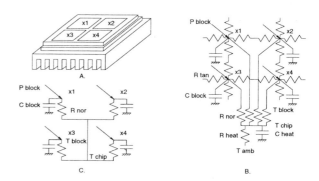

Figure 3. IC die with 4 functional blocks.
A. physical structure with die, heat spreader and heatsink, B. detailed lumped thermal model with tangential and normal block thermal resistances and block capacitances, heatsink resistance and capacitance, connected to ambient temperature, C. simplified lumped model with only block normal resistances and capacitances connected directly to the chip temperature.

We model the thermal circuit as in Figure 3B. Each block dissipates a (different) power P_{block} and as a result will tend to have a (different) temperature T_{block}. Nearest neighbor blocks are connected together through "tangential" thermal resistances R_{tan} and each block is also connected through "normal" thermal resistances R_{norm} to the heatsink through the heat spreader. Each block also has a (different) thermal capacitance R_{block}. While silicon is not a very good thermal conductor, hence the possibility of hot spots and the necessity for finer grain modeling, the heat spreader and heatsink are designed to be very good conductors, and can be lumped into a single thermal resistance R_{heat} and capacitance C_{heat}.

4.3. Component Values for the Lumped Circuit

When determining the actual values for the lumped circuit, we observe two important aspects which allow us to further simplify the thermal model as in Figure 3C:

- The values of R_{tan} are much larger than R_{norm}. This means that the spatial distribution of the hot spots is dominated by R_{norm} and the tangential values can be ignored for a first-order analysis.

- The RC time constants for the heatsink are orders of magnitude larger than for the individual blocks. This means that the temporal distribution of hot spots for short time periods is dominated by the block values and the heatsink can be considered at a constant temperature over short periods of time.

Here is how we determine the component values for the lumped circuit. For the individual blocks we first consider the material properties of silicon. Both the thermal capacitance and thermal resistance for silicon are variable with temperature, but the variation is small. From published data [12] for silicon, at target temperatures, we derived an approximate thermal capacitance $c = 10^6 J/m^3 K$, and an approximate thermal resistivity $\rho = 10^{-2} mK/W$. With these values we can easily derive the block thermal capacitances C_{block} as $c \cdot A \cdot t$, and the block normal thermal resistances R_{norm} as $\rho \cdot t/A$ where A is the block area and t the wafer thickness. For a wafer thickness of 0.1 mm, C_{block} becomes $100 \cdot A$ and R_{norm} becomes $10^{-6}/A$, with the block area A expressed in square meters.

Calculating R_{tan} is slightly more complex. We omit the details, but this can be computed for a silicon wafer of thickness 0.1mm to derive $R_{tan} = 100K/W$. Since this is orders of magnitude larger than on chip R_{norm} values we conclude that we can safely ignore R_{tan}.

The time constants associated with a block on the chip will be on the order of 10^{-4} seconds (see next section), which is much smaller than the time constants for the heatsink. We conclude that we can safely ignore the dynamic aspects of the heatsink for short time periods and consider the average heatsink temperature as a constant. When we compared observed temperatures and thermal-emergency events between our localized model and current chip-wide thermal modeling techniques, we found that almost all thermal-emergency events detected with the localized model failed to be observed by the chip-wide model. The reason for this is that localized heating is much faster than chip-wide heating.

We used the resulting model for computing actual temperatures at various locations on the chip, and use the same model as a proxy for what temperature sensors would observe as they drive our PID-DTM control system. The next section describes our simulation environment and how we derived the specific thermal R and C values used in the simulations.

The only other architecture-level modeling of which we are aware is the TEMPEST work by Dhodapkar *et al.* [6], which describes a multi-mode simulation package that models performance, power, and temperature. They use a similar RC model, but only for the microprocessor as a whole with a focus on the effects of thermal packaging. To the best of our knowledge, this is the first work to derive a thermal model for heating effects in individual architectural structures.

5. Simulation Technique and Metrics

5.1. Performance and Power Simulation

To model temperatures and controllers, we extend the DTM version of Wattch [3] used by Brooks and Martonosi. We use Wattch version 1.02, which is now widely used for research on power issues in architecture. Wattch in turn is based on the *sim-outorder* simulator of SimpleScalar [4] version 3.0. Wattch adds cycle-by-cycle tracking of power dissipation by estimating unit capacitances and activity factors. For Wattch, we chose a feature size of 0.18μ, a V_{dd} of 2.0V, and a clock speed of 1.5 GHz, which is roughly representative of values in contemporary processors.

We extended the simulators in several ways. Because most processors today have pipelines longer than five stages, our simulations extend the pipeline by adding three additional stages between decode and issue. These stages model the extra renaming and enqueuing steps found in many pipelines today, like the Alpha 21264 [10], and are necessary to properly account for branch-resolution latencies and extra mis-speculated execution. The extra stages are also included in the power model. We also improve the performance simulator by updating the fetch model to count only one access (of fetch-width granularity) per cycle. We improve the power simulation by using the improved access counts that result from these behavioral changes and by adding modeling of the column decoders on array structures like the branch predictor and caches [16]. These changes were straightforward, but were also validated by testing with microbenchmarks plus comparison with known results.

As a processor configuration, we approximately model the Alpha 21264, as shown in Table 2. The hybrid branch predictor [15] is SimpleScalar's slightly simplified version, using bimodal (plain 2-bit counter style) predictors as the chooser and as one of the components. The branch predictor is updated speculatively and repaired after a misprediction [20]. We do not model the register-cluster aspect of the 21264.

5.2. Temperature Modeling

Due to a lack of any published data on thermal properties for specific structures and a general lack of any information on per-structure areas (publicly available models for area are currently in development but not yet available), we were forced to derive thermal R_{block} and C_{block} values using estimates for area. We obtained these using one of the

Processor Core	
Instruction Window	80-RUU, 40-LSQ
Issue width	6 instructions per cycle
	(4 Int, 2 FP)
Functional Units	4 IntALU,1 IntMult/Div,
	2 FPALU,1 FPMult/Div,
	2 mem ports
Memory Hierarchy	
L1 D-cache Size	64 KB, 2-way LRU, 32 B blocks
L1 I-cache Size	64 KB, 2-way LRU, 32 B blocks
	both 1-cycle latency
L2	Unified, 2 MB, 4-way LRU,
	32B blocks, 11-cycle latency, WB
Memory	100 cycles
TLB Size	128-entry, fully assoc.,
	30-cycle miss penalty
Branch Predictor	
Branch predictor	Hybrid:
	4K bimod and 4K/12-bit/GAg
	4K bimod-style chooser
Branch target buffer	1 K-entry, 2-way
Return-address-stack	32-entry

Table 2. Configuration of simulated processor microarchitecture.

most recent die-photos that we could find with a floorplan, for the MIPS R10000 [7]. We scaled the resulting areas by two generations to 0.18μ and by architectural size, and then combined these with the values for c and ρ from the previous section. This approach is clearly unsatisfactory in terms of the approximations it requires, and we are in the process of generating new data with areas provided by Wilcox and Manne for the Alpha 21264 [23]. We feel, however, that different ratios and areas of structure sizes would not materially affect the main conclusions of this paper. The use of lumped thermal R and C values is a general approach for modeling temperature. And regardless of structure sizes and temperature thresholds, if DTM is used for thermal management, feedback control confers the advantage of fine-tuning the thermal response to the operating conditions.

To derive thermal properties, we assumed a die thickness of 0.1 mm. This implies a "thinned" wafer necessary for removing heat in high-performance processors. The areas and corresponding R_{block}, C_{block}, and RC_{block} values are presented in Table 3. For this paper, we explore the load-store queue, the instruction window (which includes physical registers for uncommitted instructions), the architectural register file, the branch predictor (including branch target buffer), the data cache, the integer execution unit, and the floating-point execution unit.

Temperature is computed on a cycle-by-cycle basis. First the SimpleScalar pipeline model determines the activity of each structure; then Wattch computes power dissipation for each of them (P_i); and finally our thermal model computes temperature based on the values of R_{block}, C_{block}, and the

power dissipation in the past clock cycle. The specific difference equation for computing each ΔT for each structure i is

$$\Delta T_i = \frac{P_i \cdot \Delta t}{C_i} + \frac{T_i \cdot \Delta t}{R_i \cdot C_i} \quad (4)$$

where Δt is one clock cycle, 0.667 nanosec. The simulation cost of computing this for each block of interest is minor compared to the pipeline and power modeling.

We observed local dynamic temperature variations of up to $13°$. This number is within the range that peak power $\cdot$ R_{block} suggests. Of course, these temperature changes slowly raise the surrounding IC temperature. Because chip-wide temperature variations are on the order of seconds to minutes in the presence of a heat sink and fan, chip-wide temperatures cannot be modeled in Wattch in any reasonable amount of time. Instead we choose a baseline heatsink temperature of $100°$ C based on the SIA roadmap [18]. We set the thermal emergency threshold at $108°$ C based on the localized temperature ranges in [25]. At $108°$, at least one of the benchmarks (if not controlled by DTM) puts each structure within $1°$ of thermal emergency for some period of time, while there exist some benchmarks that never experience thermal emergencies, and some that never put any structure within $1°$ of thermal emergency. This means that our benchmark set exhibits a range of thermal behavior.

Our metrics of success are the percentage of cycles spent in thermal emergency and percentage of the non-DTM IPC. Our rule is that the temperature for any structure must never exceed the emergency temperature. Because DTM slows down or turns off parts of the processor, IPC can never exceed the baseline value, and the benchmarks with extreme thermal behavior will necessarily engage DTM and experience some slowdown. We are unaware of any technique for modeling optimal DTM to obtain a lower bound on the induced performance loss, so we simply try to make the induced performance loss as small as possible.

5.3. DTM Mechanisms

As mentioned earlier, of the five DTM mechanisms Brooks and Martonosi propose, we selected fetch toggling, specifically toggle1, as the vehicle for applying adaptive control.

For the CT-DTM mechanisms, we assume the presence of dedicated hardware—an adder and a multiplier—to perform the controller computations. These need not be especially fast, reducing their already small cost, and they operate so infrequently that their contribution to power and temperature should be negligible. An alternative is to inject instructions directly into the pipeline to perform the controller computations. To avoid interrupting the pipeline, special instructions that access 2–3 special registers would be required. Because the controllers only execute at most every 1000 cycles, the impact of this too should be negligible. Indeed, we could likely have used a longer sampling interval without significantly affecting accuracy, since the

structure	area (m^2)	peak power (W)	R (K/W)	C (J/K)	RC (J/W = sec)
LSQ	5.0e-7	2.7	8	5.0e-5	400 us
inst. window	9.0e-7	10.3	0.9	9.0e-5	81 us
regfile	2.5e-7	5.5	4	2.5e-5	100 us
bpred	3.5e-7	5.3	1.4	3.5e-5	49 us
D-cache	1.0e-6	11.6	1	1.0e-4	100 us
int exec. unit	5.0e-7	4.3	2	5.0e-5	100 us
FP exec. unit	5.0e-7	6.7	2	5.0e-5	100 us
chip		112.9	0.34	340	115 sec

Table 3. Per-structure area and thermal-R and thermal-C estimates.
For comparison, a value for chip-wide thermal R and C is also provided for the chip as a whole with heatsink [5].

thermal time constants are on the order of tens to hundreds of microsec., which is much greater than 667 nanosec. Determining the best sampling interval and modeling the associated overhead of computing the controller in terms of both performance and power are areas for future work.

In applying the different controllers to fetch toggling, we assume that the controller can vary the degree of toggling among eight discrete values distributed evenly across the range from 0% to 100%.

To more clearly demonstrate the benefit of applying control theory to design adaptive controllers, we also manually developed a controller ("M") whose response is proportional to the temperature. This mechanism simply sets the toggling rate equal to the percentage error in temperature, where 107° and less represents 0, and 108° and above represents 100%. For example, a temperature of 107.5° would correspond to an error of 50% and toggle the pipeline every other cycle.

The DTM schemes proposed by Brooks and Martonosi use some *thermal trigger* temperature level, less than the emergency level, at which the DTM mechanism is engaged. The CT-DTM schemes we propose also require a similar trigger level, this time to use as the setpoint. For the non-CT schemes (toggle1 and M), we use a trigger level of 107°. We found that a level any closer to the emergency threshold caused toggle1 to fail to stop some emergencies. For the P controller, we used a setpoint of 107.5°, and a sensor range of 107.0° − 108.0°; in other words, the "trigger" threshold is 107.0, as with toggle1 and M. For the PI and PID controllers, on the other hand, their more robust control permitted us to use a setpoint of 107.9° for the PI and PID controllers, with a sensor range of 107.8° − 108.0°; in other words, the "trigger" threshold above which toggling starts to engage for these controllers is 107.8.

For all the DTM techniques, we also assume a direct microarchitectural technique for signaling temperature effects, avoiding the overhead of OS interrupts as Brooks and Martonosi suggested.

5.4. Benchmarks

We evaluate our results using benchmarks from the SPEC CPU2000 suite [21]. The benchmarks are compiled and statically linked for the Alpha instruction set using the Compaq Alpha compiler with SPEC *peak* settings and include all linked libraries. For each program, we skip the first 2 billion instructions to avoid unrepresentative behavior at the beginning of the program's execution, and then simulate 200 million (committed) instructions using the reference input set. Simulation is conducted using SimpleScalar's EIO traces to ensure reproducible results for each benchmark across multiple simulations.

Due to the extensive number of simulations required for this study, we used only 18 of the total 26 SPEC2k benchmarks. A mixture of integer and floating-point programs with low, intermediate, and extreme thermal demands were chosen. Table 4 provides a list of the benchmarks we study along with their basic performance, power, and thermal characteristics. More detailed tables giving the same data on a per-structure granularity can be found in an extended version of this paper [19].

In addition to the eight benchmarks that experience actual emergencies, several others spend significant amounts of time within 1° of the emergency threshold. Table 4 lists the percent of cycles spent above 108° as well as the percent of cycles spent above 107°. Of particular interest are programs like *mesa, facerec, eon*, and *vortex*, which spend as much as 98% of their time above 107°, yet spend almost no time in thermal emergency. Any successful DTM scheme should minimize the penalties for these programs, and indeed the CT-DTM techniques provide some of the best improvements for this category. The program *art*, on the other hand, has the opposite behavior. It spends only 6% of its time above 107°, but more than half of these cycles—4%—are spent in emergency, meaning that *art* has very bursty thermal behavior.

Using these two tables together, we break the set of benchmarks into four categories of thermal behavior: extreme, high, medium, and low, as shown in Table 5.

6. Effectiveness of Control-Theoretic Techniques for Thermal Management

We developed P, PI, and PID controllers for pipeline toggling, and compared them to both the static toggle1 policy

	Avg. IPC	Avg. pwr (W)	Avg. temp. °C	Above 108°	Above 107°
164.gzip	2.1	47.7	43.2	0.0	0.0
168.wupwise	2.0	46.0	42.6	0.0	0.0
175.vpr	1.7	45.0	42.3	0.0	0.0
176.gcc	2.0	52.7	44.9	81.9	99.2
177.mesa	2.4	50.7	44.2	0.5	46.4
179.art	1.2	39.0	40.3	3.9	5.9
183.equake	2.8	56.4	46.2	99.7	99.8
186.crafty	2.3	50.4	44.1	0.0	6.8
187.facerec	2.3	49.9	44.0	0.0	63.8
191.fma3d	2.6	48.0	43.3	99.6	99.7
197.parser	1.4	40.6	40.8	4.1	24.8
252.eon	2.3	52.2	44.8	0.0	98.7
253.perlbmk	2.8	47.3	43.1	48.4	48.5
254.gap	2.1	45.2	42.4	0.0	0.0
255.vortex	2.1	47.4	43.1	0.0	97.2
256.bzip2	2.0	46.6	42.8	13.3	61.7
300.twolf	1.5	40.3	40.7	0.0	0.0
301.apsi	0.9	33.6	38.4	0.0	0.2

Table 4. Average IPC, power, and temperature characteristics for each benchmark

"Avg. temp." assumes that the heatsink temperature is at an ambient of 27° C and uses the chip-wide thermal-R of 0.34 K/W. Percent of cycles spent in thermal emergency (above 108°) and in a level of thermal stress (above 107°) assume that the heatsink temperature has risen to 100° and use the per-structure thermal R/C values.

Extreme	High	Medium	Low
gcc	mesa	facerec	gzip
equake	art	eon	wupwise
fma3d	parser	vortex1	vpr
perlbmk	bzip2		crafty
			twolf
			apsi

Table 5. Categories of thermal behavior.

and the manually-derived feedback-control policy (M) that is not based on control theory but attempts to set the degree of toggling proportionally to the error. We also developed a PD controller, but its performance was slightly inferior to the PI and PID controllers and we omit it here. For more information, see [19]. As mentioned before, the sampling rate for all the controllers is set to 1000 cycles to match the policy delay for the toggle1 mechanism.

To make the PI and PID controllers effective at eliminating thermal emergencies, we did have to implement anti-windup. Otherwise, the PI and PID controllers failed to prevent thermal emergencies. This behavior was especially prevalent for *perlbmk*, which spends over half its time below the thermal trigger, accumulating a large negative integral. *Gcc*, on the other hand, does not have this problem, because

it spends almost 100% of its time with at least one structure above 107°.

Figure 4 therefore shows the performance of the non-CT toggle1 controller, the manually-derived proportional controller (M), and the CT-toggle controllers (with anti-windup for the PI and PID controllers). All were able to completely eliminate thermal emergencies, so the metric of interest is performance. Recall that DTM only slows or disables parts of the processor, so the best we can accomplish is to minimize the slowdown. The figure therefore plots the percentage *loss* in performance compared to the baseline case with no DTM.

The adaptive techniques are substantially better than the fixed toggle1 policy, with the PI and PID techniques cutting the performance loss by about 65% compared to toggle1, and by about 37% compared to the M controller. Even the P controller cuts the performance loss by 21% compared to the M controller. Furthermore, the CT-DTM techniques are always better than the toggle1 policy, and almost always better than the M controller except for *equake* and a tiny difference for *fma3d* in the case of the PI and PID controllers, and *gcc* and *equake* for the P controller.

The most dramatic gains for CT-DTM come from the benchmarks with extreme thermal demands and the "medium" benchmarks that operate very close to thermal emergency but rarely actually experience emergencies (*mesa, facerec, eon*, and *vortex*). This latter category is most severely penalized by a fixed policy, and benefits most from the integrating action of the PI and PID controllers because they permit a much higher setpoint, so that these "medium" benchmarks rarely or never engage any toggling.

It is interesting to note that if the PI and PID controllers use a setpoint of 107.5° instead of 107.9°, they are inferior to the P controller despite being more sophisticated. The reason for this is that these controllers are actually doing *too* good a job of holding temperature to the setpoint. The P controller allows temperatures to rise as high as 107.9°, and a setpoint any higher than 107.5° therefore fails to stop some emergencies. The PI and PID controllers on the other hand hold the temperature extremely close to the setpoint. Indeed, the temperature never exceeds the setpoint by more than 0.01° for PI and PID. This means that the setpoint for these controllers should be set to a higher temperature. Ideally, an analysis of maximum overshoot would use the maximum possible power dissipation in each structure, the thermal RC time constant, and the response time of the controller to identify the maximum value for setpoint that still *guarantees* no thermal emergencies. For example, if 0.01° were proven to be the maximum overshoot for the PID controller, then the setpoint could actually be placed at 107.99° while preserving the guarantee that the emergency level of 108° would never be exceeded. That analysis is beyond the scope of this paper. Instead, we simply used the maximum observed temperatures to conclude that a setpoint of 107.9° is safe for this workload.

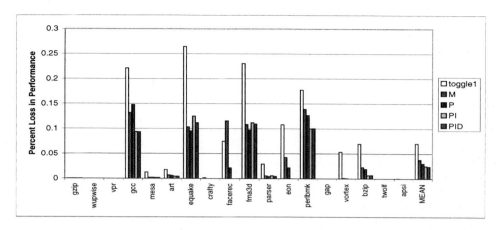

Figure 4. Performance loss for various DTM techniques relative to the IPC with no DTM.
The trigger threshold for the PI and PID controllers has been set to 107.8°. PD has been omitted in this graph. The mean reduction in performance loss compared to toggle1 is 64% for PI and 66% for PID.

Of course, such fine control over temperature may be overkill in an environment where the number of temperature sensors on chip is likely to be limited (perhaps four to eight at most), where thermal propagation and the intrinsic response of the sensors themselves imply a lag between heating at hot spots and the time at which this is detected by a sensor, and where imprecision in the sensor may mean accurate sensing and control to within fractions of a degree may be impossible.

Improved methods for distributed temperature sensing can remove most of these problems. But the main point of this paper is broader than the specific mechanisms described here. Rather, we used DTM as a vehicle to show that formal feedback control theory offers a variety of advantages for adaptive techniques in processor architecture, and the results presented here demonstrate that clearly.

7. Conclusions and Future Work

DTM pipeline toggling based on control-theoretic techniques is more effective than prior techniques at avoiding thermal emergencies while minimizing performance loss. Our CT-DTM techniques completely prevented thermal emergencies while reducing the loss in performance by 65% compared to the previously proposed "toggle1" technique and 36% over our own hand-designed proportional toggling technique. This shows that the benefits of CT-DTM come not just from their adaptivity, but that they also derive substantial benefit from the formal control theory from which they are derived.

Overall, this paper makes three contributions to the field of architecture-level dynamic thermal management.

1. We introduce the use of a new and more accurate thermal model that models temperature directly and is also computationally inexpensive.

2. We invoke DTM techniques in response to localized hot spots rather than chip-wide effects.

3. We apply control-theoretic techniques to control the thermal-management techniques. These controllers provide much more adaptive control of the temperature and thus minimize performance penalties.

We feel that the most important contribution of this work is our demonstration that formal feedback control theory offers compelling advantages. The control-theoretic techniques are effective because they engage only as much toggling as necessary, while holding the temperature so tightly to the setpoint that we were able to establish a setpoint of 107.9° but never exceed the emergency threshold of 108°. The controllers were also extremely easy to design, requiring almost no tuning.

More generally, our results suggest that applying control-theoretic techniques to other aspects of adaptive processor control is an extremely promising research area. The design of the controllers is itself a rich area for research, because in addition to choosing an overall controller algorithm, the controller parameters can be adjusted to formally determine the choice of thresholds and to guarantee settling times. This, for example, can be used to choose the highest possible setpoint that still guarantees successful regulation of temperature.

This work is just the first step in what we expect to be a long-range effort in thermal modeling and management. Our results so far suggests a variety of avenues for future work: more detailed thermal modeling to account for the second-order effects of thermal coupling among hot spots, thermal modeling and feedback control that account for the presence of only a limited quantity of temperature sensors and the associated sensor lag, validation of the thermal model against a circuit-based power model, new thermal management mechanisms, and application of control theory to other aspects of dynamic power and performance management.

We hope that the material presented here will provide the necessary foundation to help other architects perform more detailed thermal modeling and to help other architects apply control theory in the design of adaptive microarchitecture techniques.

Acknowledgments

This material is based upon work supported in part by the National Science Foundation under grant nos. CCR-0105626, CCR-0098269, MIP-9703440 (CAREER), and a grant from Intel MRL. We would like to thank George Cai, Margaret Martonosi, and David Brooks for their helpful comments; David Brooks for his extensive help in validating our DTM techniques within Wattch; Zhigang Hu for his help with the SimpleScalar EIO traces; and the anonymous reviewers for many helpful suggestions on how to improve this paper.

References

[1] S. Borkar. Design challenges of technology scaling. *IEEE Micro*, pages 23–29, Jul.–Aug. 1999.

[2] D. Brooks and M. Martonosi. Dynamic thermal management for high-performance microprocessors. In *Proceedings of the Seventh International Symposium on High-Performance Computer Architecture*, pages 171–82, Jan. 2001.

[3] D. Brooks, V. Tiwari, and M. Martonosi. Wattch: A framework for architectural-level power analysis and optimizations. In *Proceedings of the 27th Annual International Symposium on Computer Architecture*, pages 83–94, June 2000.

[4] D. C. Burger and T. M. Austin. The SimpleScalar tool set, version 2.0. *Computer Architecture News*, 25(3):13–25, June 1997.

[5] J. A. Chavez et al. Spice model of thermoelectric elements including thermal effects. In *Proceedings of the Instrumentation and Measurement Technology Conference*, pages 1019–1023, 2000.

[6] A. Dhodapkar, C. H. Lim, G. Cai, and W. R. Daasch. TEMPEST: A thermal enabled multi-model power/performance estimator. In *Proceedings of the Workshop on Power-Aware Computer Systems*, Nov. 2000.

[7] MIPS R10000 die photo. From website: CPU Info Center. http://bwrc.eecs.berkeley.edu/CIC/die_photos/#mips.

[8] N. Dragone, A. Aggarwal, and L. R. Carley. An adaptive on-chip voltage regulation technique for low-power applications. In *Proceedings of the 2000 International Symposium on Low Power Electronics and Design*, pages 20–24, July 2000.

[9] C. V. Hollot, V. Misra, D. Towsley, and W. Gong. A control theoretic analysis of RED. In *Proceedings of IEEE INFOCOM*, Apr. 2001.

[10] R. E. Kessler, E. J. McLellan, and D. A. Webb. The Alpha 21264 microprocessor architecture. In *Proceedings of the 1998 International Conference on Computer Design*, pages 90–95, Oct. 1998.

[11] Al Krum. Thermal management. In Frank Kreith, editor, *The CRC handbook of thermal engineering*, pages 2.1–2.92. CRC Press, Boca Raton, FL, 2000.

[12] F. J. De la Hidalga and M. J. Deen. Theoretical and experimental characterization of self-heating in silicon integrated devices operating at low temperatures. *IEEE Transactions on Electron Devices*, 47(5):1098–1106, May 2000.

[13] C. Lu, J. A. Stankovic, G. Tao, , and S. H. Son. Feedback control real-time scheduling: Framework, modeling, and algorithms. *Real-Time Systems Journal*, Mar.-Apr. 2002. To appear.

[14] S. Manne, A. Klauser, and D. Grunwald. Pipeline gating: speculation control for energy reduction. In *Proceedings of the 25th Annual International Symposium on Computer Architecture*, pages 132–41, June 1998.

[15] S. McFarling. Combining branch predictors. Tech. Note TN-36, DEC WRL, June 1993.

[16] D. Parikh, K. Skadron, Y. Zhang, M. Barcella, and M. Stan. Power issues related to branch prediction. In *Proceedings of the Eighth International Symposium on High-Performance Computer Architecture*, Feb. 2002.

[17] H. Sanchez et al. Thermal management system for high-performance PowerPC microprocessors. In *COMPCON*, page 325, 1997.

[18] SIA. *International Technology Roadmap for Semiconductors*, 1999.

[19] K. Skadron, T. Abdelzaher, and M. R. Stan. Control-theoretic techniques and thermal-RC modeling for accurate and localized dynamic thermal management. Technical Report CS-2001-27, University of Virginia Department of Computer Science, Nov. 2001.

[20] K. Skadron, D. W. Clark, and M. Martonosi. Speculative updates of local and global branch history: A quantitative analysis. *Journal of Instruction-Level Parallelism*, Jan. 2000. (http://www.jilp.org/vol2).

[21] Standard Performance Evaluation Corporation. SPEC CPU2000 Benchmarks. http://www.specbench.org/osg/cpu2000.

[22] D. C. Steere et al. A feedback-driven proportion allocator for real-rate scheduling. In *Proceedings of the Symposium on Operating System Principles*, Feb. 1999.

[23] K. Wilcox and S. Manne. Alpha processors: A history of power issues and a look to the future. In *Proceedings of the Cool Chips Tutorial: An Industrial Perspective on Low Power Processor Design*, pages 16–37, Nov. 1999.

[24] L. S. Y. Wong, S. Hossain, and A. Walker. Leakage current cancellation technique for low power switched-capacitor circuits. In *Proceedings of the 2001 International Symposium on Low Power Electronics and Design*, pages 310–15, Aug. 2001.

[25] T.-D. Yuan and B.-Z. Hong. Thermal management for high performance integrated circuits with non-uniform chip power considerations. In *Proceedings of the Seventeenth SEMI-THERM Symposium*, pages 95–101, Mar. 2001.

Energy-Efficient Processor Design Using Multiple Clock Domains with Dynamic Voltage and Frequency Scaling*

Greg Semeraro, Grigorios Magklis, Rajeev Balasubramonian,
David H. Albonesi, Sandhya Dwarkadas, and Michael L. Scott

Departments of Computer Science and of Electrical and Computer Engineering
University of Rochester

{semeraro, albonesi}@ece.rochester.edu
{maglis, rajeev, sandhya, scott}@cs.rochester.edu

Abstract

As clock frequency increases and feature size decreases, clock distribution and wire delays present a growing challenge to the designers of singly-clocked, globally synchronous systems. We describe an alternative approach, which we call a Multiple Clock Domain (MCD) *processor, in which the chip is divided into several (coarse-grained) clock domains, within which independent voltage and frequency scaling can be performed. Boundaries between domains are chosen to exploit existing queues, thereby minimizing inter-domain synchronization costs. We propose four clock domains, corresponding to the front end (including L1 instruction cache), integer units, floating point units, and load-store units (including L1 data cache and L2 cache). We evaluate this design using a simulation infrastructure based on SimpleScalar and Wattch. In an attempt to quantify potential energy savings independent of any particular on-line control strategy, we use off-line analysis of traces from a single-speed run of each of our benchmark applications to identify profitable reconfiguration points for a subsequent dynamic scaling run. Dynamic runs incorporate a detailed model of inter-domain synchronization delays, with latencies for intra-domain scaling similar to the whole-chip scaling latencies of Intel XScale and Transmeta LongRun technologies. Using applications from the MediaBench, Olden, and SPEC2000 benchmark suites, we obtain an average energy-delay product improvement of 20% with MCD compared to a modest 3% savings from voltage scaling a single clock and voltage system.*

1. Introduction

The continuing push for higher microprocessor performance has led to unprecedented increases in clock frequencies in recent years. While the Pentium III microprocessor broke the 1GHz barrier in 2000, the Pentium IV is currently shipping at 2GHz. At the same time, due to issues of reliability and performance, wire dimensions have been scaled in successive process generations more conservatively than transistor dimensions. The result of these frequency and dimensional trends is that microprocessor clock speeds have become increasingly limited by wire delays, so much so that some of the more recent microprocessors, *e.g.*, the Pentium IV [14], have pipeline stages solely dedicated to moving signals across the chip. Furthermore, a growing challenge in future systems will be to distribute the clock across a progressively larger die to increasing numbers of latches while meeting a decreasing clock skew budget. The inevitable conclusion reached by industrial researchers is that in order to continue the current pace of clock frequency increases, microprocessor designers will eventually be forced to abandon singly-clocked globally synchronous systems in favor of some form of asynchrony [8, 24].

Although purely asynchronous systems have the potential for higher performance and lower power compared to their synchronous counterparts, major corporations have been reluctant to fully migrate to asynchronous design methodologies. Two major reasons for this reluctance are the immaturity of asynchronous design tools relative to those in the synchronous domain, and the cost and risk of moving away from the mature design infrastructures that have been successfully used to create many generations of microprocessor products. Yet many existing synchronous designs do incorporate a limited amount of asynchrony. For example, several multiprocessor systems run the memory bus off of a different clock than the processor core in or-

---

*This work was supported in part by NSF grants CCR–9701915, CCR–9702466, CCR–9705594, CCR–9811929, EIA–9972881, CCR–9988361, and EIA–0080124; by DARPA/ITO under AFRL contract F29601-00-K-0182; and by an external research grant from DEC/Compaq.

der to allow a single system to accommodate processors of different frequencies. In such *dual clock domain* systems, the logic in each of the two clock domains is designed using conventional synchronous design methodologies. Well-known and highly-reliable techniques are used to *synchronize* communication between the two domains, albeit at the cost of extra delay.

An additional trend due to the wire scaling dilemma is to replace microarchitectural techniques requiring long global wires with alternatives requiring only local wiring. This approach improves both clock frequency and the scalability of the design in future process generations. For example, in several microprocessors including the Alpha 21164 and 21264 [11, 20] and the UltraSPARC III [17], the use of global wires to stall early pipeline stages has been replaced by the use of *replay traps* that cancel instructions and restart the pipeline. Although flushing the pipeline in this manner requires additional cycles for reloading, it results in a higher clock frequency and more scalable implementation due to the elimination of global wires. The designers of the UltraSPARC III fully embraced this approach by creating six functional blocks that run relatively independently of one another, with most long wires eliminated between units [17].

An approach that allows for aggressive future frequency increases, maintains a synchronous design methodology, and exploits the trend towards making functional blocks more autonomous, is a *multiple clock domain (MCD)* microarchitecture, which uses a *globally-asynchronous, locally-synchronous (GALS)* clocking style. In an MCD microprocessor each functional block operates with a separately generated clock, and synchronizing circuits ensure reliable inter-domain communication. Thus, fully synchronous design practices are used in the design of each domain. Although the inter-domain synchronization increases the number of clock cycles required to run a given application, an MCD microprocessor affords a number of potential advantages over a singly clocked design:

- The global clock distribution network is greatly simplified, requiring only the distribution of the externally generated clock to the local Phase Lock Loop (PLL) in each domain. The independence of each local domain clock implies no global clock skew requirement, permitting potentially higher frequencies within each domain and greater scalability in future process generations.

- The designers of each domain are no longer constrained by the speeds of critical paths in other domains, affording them greater freedom in each domain to optimize the tradeoffs among clock speed, latency, and the exploitation of application parallelism via complex hardware structures.

- Using separate voltage inputs, external voltage regulators, and controllable clock frequency circuits in each clock domain allows for finer grained dynamic voltage and frequency scaling, and thus lower energy, than can be achieved with single clock, single-core-voltage systems.

- With the ability to dynamically resize structures and alter the clock speed in each domain, the IPC/clock rate tradeoff can be tailored to application characteristics within each individual domain [1], thereby improving both performance and energy efficiency.

In this paper, we describe an initial implementation of an MCD microprocessor that is a straightforward extension of a singly-clocked synchronous dynamic superscalar design. By accurately modeling inter-domain synchronization, we characterize the performance and energy costs of the required synchronization circuitry. We then explore the potential benefits of per-domain dynamic voltage and frequency scaling. Our results demonstrate a 20% average improvement in energy-delay product for a set of benchmarks that includes both compute and memory-bound applications. Unlike rate-based multimedia applications, these benchmarks have not traditionally been candidates for voltage and frequency scaling.

The rest of the paper is organized as follows. In Section 2, we describe a microarchitecture with four separate clock domains, comprising the front end (including L1 instruction cache, rename, and reorder buffer), integer unit, floating-point unit, and load-store unit (including L1 data cache and L2 cache). We discuss the circuitry needed for cross-domain synchronization, and its performance costs. In Section 3, we describe the simulation infrastructure we used to evaluate this microarchitecture. The simulator, based on SimpleScalar and Wattch, includes detailed modeling of synchronization costs. We also describe an off-line analysis tool that we used in our experiments to identify promising points at which to reconfigure (scale) domains in various applications. Our performance and energy dissipation results, reported in Section 4, encompass applications from the MediaBench, Olden, and SPEC 2000 benchmark suites. Sections 5 and 6 contain additional discussion of related work and concluding remarks.

2. Multiple Clock Domain Microarchitecture

2.1. Division of Chip into Clock Domains

Matzke has estimated that as technology scales down to a $0.1\mu m$ feature size, only 16% of the die will be reachable within a single clock cycle [24]. Assuming a chip multiprocessor with two processors per die, each processor would need to have a minimum of three equal-size clock domains. Our design uses four domains, one of which includes the

L2 cache, so that domains may vary somewhat in size and still be covered by a single clock. In effect, we treat the main memory interface as a fifth clock domain, external to the MCD processor, and always running at full speed.

In choosing the boundaries between domains, we attempted to identify points where (a) there already existed a queue structure that served to decouple different pipeline functions, or (b) there was relatively little inter-function communication. Our four chosen domains, shown in Figure 1, comprise the front end (including instruction cache, branch prediction, rename, and dispatch); integer issue/execute; floating point issue/execute; and load/store issue/execute. Although we were initially concerned about the performance impact of implementing separate load/store and integer domains, we discovered that the additional synchronization penalty did not significantly degrade performance. Furthermore, because we discovered no energy savings from decoupling instruction fetch from rename/dispatch, we combined these regions into a single fetch/rename/dispatch domain to eliminate their inter-domain synchronization overhead. Finally, execution units of the same type (*e.g.*, integer units) were combined into a single domain to avoid the high cost of synchronizing the bypass and register file datapaths among these units. As a result of these divisions, there were no explicit changes to the pipeline organization of the machine. We also believe that these divisions would result in a physically realizable floorplan for an MCD processor.

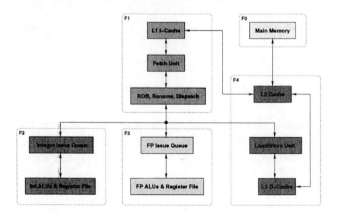

Figure 1. Multiple clock domain processor block diagram

2.2. Inter-Domain Synchronization

The primary disadvantage of an MCD processor is the performance overhead due to inter-domain synchronization. In this section, we discuss the circuitry required to perform this synchronization. We discuss how to model its performance cost in Section 4.

Some synchronization schemes restrict the phase relationship and relative frequencies of the clocks, thereby eliminating the need for hardware arbitration [27]. Unfortunately, these schemes impose significant restrictions on the possible choices of frequencies. In addition, the need to control the phase relationships of the clocks means that global clock synchronization is required. Our design specifically recognizes the overhead associated with independent clocks with no known phase relationship. We believe this overhead to be unavoidable in an MCD processor: one of the motivating factors for the design is the recognition that traditional global clock distribution will become increasingly difficult in the future.

The issue queues in the integer, floating point, and load/store domains (the Load/Store Queue within the Load/Store Unit), together with the Reorder Buffer (ROB) in the front end domain, serve to decouple the front and back ends of a conventional processor. Choosing these queues as inter-domain synchronization points has the advantage of hiding the synchronization cost whenever the queue is neither full nor empty (as described later in this section).

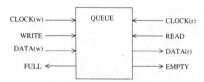

Figure 2. Queue structure

The general queue structure that we use for inter-domain communication is shown in Figure 2. The assertion of the *Full* flag indicates to the producer that it can no longer write to the queue until the flag is deasserted ($\overline{Full}$), while the *Empty* flag when asserted indicates that there is no valid data for the consumer to read from the queue. The consumer waits until *Empty* is deasserted before reading again.

The use of a full handshake protocol for this interface requires that the producer/consumer check the *Full/Empty* flag after every operation in order to avoid queue overruns on writes or reads from an empty queue. This requirement significantly slows down the interface thereby degrading performance. Rather, we assume that the *Full* and *Empty* flags are generated far enough in advance such that writes and reads can occur every clock cycle without over or underflowing the queue. In other words, the *Full* flag is generated early enough such that a burst of writes every cycle will terminate (due to recognition by the producer of the assertion of the *Full* flag) just as the last remaining queue entry has been written. An analogous situation exists for the consumer side of the queue, although our particular queues are different in this regard as we discuss later. Note that this scheme may result in underutilization of the queue under particular conditions. For example, if the write that initiates assertion of the *Full* flag is at the end of a burst, then there will be empty but unusable entries in the queue (because the *Full* flag will have been asserted) the next time the producer has data to write into the queue.

In order to avoid underutilization of the queues, we assume extra queue entries to buffer writes under worst-case conditions so that the original number of queue entries can be fully utilized. In the MCD design, the worst-case situation occurs when the producer is operating at the maximum frequency (max_freq) and the consumer at the minimum (min_freq). An additional complication occurs due to the need to compare queue head and tail pointers from different clock domains in order to generate the *Full* and *Empty* flags. Under these conditions, and assuming an additional cycle for the producer to recognize the *Full* signal, (max_freq/min_freq)+1 additional entries are required. Note that our results do not account for the performance advantage nor the energy cost of these additional entries.

Even with completely independent clocks for each interface, the queue structure is able to operate at full speed for both reading and writing under certain conditions. This concurrency requires a dual-ported SRAM structure where simultaneous read and write cycles are allowed to *different* SRAM cells. As long as the interfaces are designed to adhere to the protocol associated with the *Full* and *Empty* flags, the queue structure does not need to support simultaneous read and write access to the same SRAM cell. As long as the queue is not full (as described above) the producer can continue to write data on every rising edge of $Clock_w$ (Figure 3). Similarly, so long as the queue is not empty, the consumer can continue reading on every rising edge of $Clock_r$. Therefore, both interfaces operate at full speed so long as the queue is partially full, although newly written entries may not be recognized by the consumer until after a synchronization period. Once the queue becomes full, the queue state of $\overline{Full}$ can only result from data being read out of the queue on the read interface. When this event occurs, the queue pointer in the read domain must get synchronized with the write domain clock ($Clock_w$) in order to deassert *Full*. A similar synchronization delay occurs with the generation of the $\overline{Empty}$ condition due to a write to an empty queue.

Many of the queues that we use as synchronization points have a different interface than that described above. For the issue queue for example, each entry has *Valid* and *Ready* flags that the scheduler uses to determine if an entry should be read (issued). The scheduler by design will never issue more than the number of valid and ready entries in the queue. Note, however, that due to synchronization, there is a delay before the scheduler sees newly written queue data.

The delay associated with crossing a clock domain interface is a function of the following:

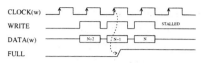

Figure 3. Full flag

- The synchronization time of the clock arbitration circuit, T_S, which represents the minimum time required between the source and destination clocks in order for the signal to be successfully latched at the destination. We assume the arbitration and synchronization circuits developed by Sjogren and Myers [28] that detect whether the source and destination clock edges are sufficiently far apart (at minimum, T_S) such that a source-generated signal can be successfully clocked at the destination. The destination clock is enabled only under these conditions. We assume a T_S of 30% of the period of the highest frequency.

- The ratio of the frequencies of the interface clocks.

- The relative phases of the interface clocks.

This delay can best be understood by examining a timing diagram (Figure 4), which shows source clock F_1 and destination clock F_2. Consider the case when the queue

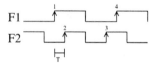

Figure 4. Synchronization timing

is initially empty. Data is written into the queue on the rising edge of F_1 (edge 1). Data can be read out of the queue as early as the next rising edge of F_2 (edge 2), if and only if $T > T_S$, *i.e.*, *Empty* has become false on the F_2 interface before the next rising edge of F_2. If $T \leq T_S$, the earliest that the data can be read is one F_2 period later (edge 3). This extra delay represents one source of performance degradation due to synchronization. The value of T is determined by the relative frequency and phases of F_1 and F_2, as well as the relative jitter of the clock sources, and may change over time. The cost of synchronization is controlled by the relationship between T and T_S, and to a lesser degree by the magnitude of T_S. The analogous situation exists when the queue is *Full*, replacing *Empty* with *Full*, edge 1 with edge 2, and edge 3 with edge 4 in the above discussion.

In our simulator, described in the next section, we accurately account for inter-domain overhead.

Table 1. Architectural parameters for simulated processor.

Branch predictor: comb. of bimodal and 2-level PAg
Level1	1024 entries, history 10;
Level2	1024 entries;
Bimodal predictor size	1024;
Combining predictor size	4096;
BTB	4096 sets, 2-way

Branch Mispredict Penalty	7
Decode Width	4
Issue Width	6
Retire Width	11
L1 Data Cache	64KB, 2-way set associative
L1 Instruction Cache	64KB, 2-way set associative
L2 Unified Cache	1MB, direct mapped
L1 cache latency	2 cycles
L2 cache latency	12 cycles
Integer ALUs	4 + 1 mult/div unit
Floating-Point ALUs	2 + 1 mult/div/sqrt unit
Integer Issue Queue Size	20 entries
Floating-Point Issue Queue Size	15 entries
Load/Store Queue Size	64
Physical Register File Size	72 integer, 72 floating-point
Reorder Buffer Size	80

Table 2. Benchmarks

Bench-mark	Suite	Datasets	Simulation window (instructions)
adpcm		ref	entire program
epic	Media-	ref	entire program
g721	Bench	ref	0–200M
mesa		ref	entire program
em3d		4K nodes, arity 10	70M–119M
health		4 levels, 1K iters	80M–127M
mst	Olden	1K nodes	entire program 199M
power		ref	0–200M
treeadd		20 levels, 1 iter	entire program 189M
tsp		ref	0–200M
bzip2		input.source	1000M–1100M
gcc	SPEC	166.i	1000M–1100M
mcf	2000 Int	ref	1000M–1100M
parser		ref	1000M–1100M
art	SPEC	ref	300M–400M
swim	2000 FP	ref	1000M–1100M

3. Simulation Methodology

Our simulation testbed is based on the SimpleScalar toolset [6] with the Wattch [5] power estimation extensions. The original SimpleScalar model supports out of order execution using a centralized Register Update Unit (RUU) [29]. We have modified this structure to more closely model the microarchitecture of the Alpha 21264 microprocessor [20]. Specifically, we split the RUU into separate reorder buffer (ROB), issue queue, and physical register file structures. A summary of our simulation parameters appears in Table 1.

We selected a mix of compute-bound, memory-bound, and multimedia applications from the MediaBench, Olden, and SPEC2000 benchmark suites. Table 2 specifies the benchmarks used along with the window of instructions simulated. We show combined statistics for the encode and decode phases of adpcm, epic, and g721, and for the mipmap, osdemo, and texgen phases of mesa.

For the baseline processor, we assume a 1GHz clock and 1.2V supply voltage, based on that projected for the forthcoming CL010LP TSMC low-power $0.1\mu m$ process [30]. For configurations with dynamic voltage and frequency scaling, we assume 32 frequency points spanning a linear range from 1GHz down to 250MHz. Corresponding to these frequency points is a linear voltage range from 1.2V down to 0.65V.[1] Our voltage range is tighter than that of XScale (1.65–0.75V), reflecting the compression of voltage

---

[1] In Wattch, we simulate the effect of a 1.2–0.65V voltage range by using a range of 2.0–1.0833V because Wattch assumes a supply voltage of 2.0V.

ranges in future generations as supply voltages continue to be scaled aggressively relative to threshold voltages. In addition, the full frequency range is twice that of the full voltage range. As we demonstrate in Section 4, these factors limit the amount of power savings that can be achieved with conventional dynamic voltage and frequency scaling.

We assume two models for dynamic voltage and frequency scaling: an *XScale* model and a *Transmeta* model, both of which are based on published information from the respective companies [10, 13]. For both of these models, we assume that the frequency change can be initiated immediately when transitioning to a lower frequency and voltage, while the desired voltage must be reached first before increasing frequency. For the Transmeta model, we assume a total of 32 separate voltage steps, at 28.6mV intervals, with a voltage adjustment time of $20\mu s$ per step. Frequency changes require the PLL to re-lock. Until it does the domain remains idle. We model the PLL as a normally distributed locking circuit with a mean time of $15\mu s$ and a range of 10–20μs. For the XScale model, we assume that frequency changes occur as soon as the voltage changes, *i.e.*, as the voltage is changed, the frequency is changed accordingly. There is no penalty due to a domain being idle waiting for the PLL: circuits execute through the change. To approximate a smooth transition, we use 320 steps of 2.86mV each, with $0.1718\mu s$ required to transition from one step to the next. Traversing the entire voltage range requires $640\mu s$ under the Transmeta model and $55\mu s$ under the XScale model.

Processor reconfiguration decisions (choices of times, frequencies, and voltages) could in principle be made in hardware, software, or some combination of the two, using information gathered from static analysis, on-line statistics, or feedback-based profiling. For the purposes of the current study we have attempted to identify the energy savings that might be achieved with good quality control algorithms, without necessarily determining what those algorithms should look like. More concretely, we employ an off-line tool that analyzes a trace collected during a full-speed run of an application in an attempt to determine the minimum frequencies and voltages that could have been used by various domains during various parts of the run without significantly increasing execution time. A list of these frequencies and voltages—and the times they should be applied—is then fed back into our processor simulator in the course of a second, dynamic scaling run, to obtain accurate estimates of energy and performance.

It is unclear whether this experimental methodology will overestimate or underestimate the benefits that might be achieved by realistic on-line control algorithms: our feedback-based system can in principle use future knowledge, but it is not provably optimal: a good on-line strategy might conceivably do better. What the methodology does provide is an existence proof: with the frequencies and voltages chosen by our analysis tool one could expect to realize the energy savings described in Section 4.

The two subsections that follow describe, respectively, our multiple clock domain simulator and the analysis tool used to choose reconfiguration points.

3.1. Simulating Multiple Clock Domains

The disadvantage of multiple clock domains is that data generated in one domain and needed in another must cross a domain boundary, potentially incurring synchronization costs as described in Section 2. In order to accurately model these costs, we account for the fact that the clocks driving each domain are independent by modeling independent jitter, the variation in the clock, on a cycle-by-cycle basis. Our model assumes a normal distribution of jitter with a mean of zero. The standard deviation is 110ps, consisting of an external Phase Lock Loop (PLL) jitter of 100ps (based on a survey of available ICs) and 10ps due to the internal PLL. These values assume a 1GHz on-chip clock generated from a common external 100MHz clock source. Despite the common use of the external clock, because the local clock sources are independent, the clock skew within individual domains is not a factor when calculating inter-domain penalties.

Our simulator tracks the relationships among all of the domain clocks on a cycle-by-cycle basis based on their scaling factors and jitter values. Initially, all the clocks are randomized in terms of their starting times. To determine the time of the next clock pulse in a domain, the domain cycle time is added to the starting time, and the jitter for that cycle (which may be a positive or negative value) is obtained from the distribution and added to this sum. By performing this calculation for all domains on a cycle by cycle basis, the relationship between all clock edges is tracked.

In this way, we can accurately account for synchronization costs due to violations of the $T > T_S$ relationship or to inter-domain clock rate differences.

For all configurations, we assume that all circuits are clock gated when not in use. We do not currently estimate the power savings or clock frequency advantage (due to reduced skew) from the absence of a conventional global clock distribution tree that supplies a low-skew clock to all chip latches.

3.2. Choosing Reconfiguration Points

To select the times and values for dynamic scaling in a given application, our reconfiguration tool begins by running the application on the simulator, at maximum speed. During this initial run we collect a trace of all primitive *events* (temporally contiguous operations performed on behalf of a single instruction by hardware in a single clock domain), and of the functional and data dependences among these events. For example, a memory instruction (load/store) is broken down into five events: fetch, dispatch, address calculation, memory access, and commit. Data dependences link these events in temporal order. Functional dependences link each event to previous and subsequent events (in different instructions) that use the same hardware units. Additional functional dependences capture the limited size of structures such as the fetch queue, issue queues, and reorder buffer. In the fetch queue, for example, event n depends on event $n - k$, where k is the size of the queue.

We use our trace information to construct a dependence directed acyclic graph (DAG) for each 50K cycle interval. (The length of this interval is chosen to be the maximum for which the DAG will fit in cache on our simulation servers.) Once the DAG has been constructed, we proceed through two additional analysis phases. The first phase uses the DAG as input, and confines its work to a single interval. Its purpose is to "stretch" (scale) individual events that are not on the application's critical execution path, as if they could, on an instruction-by-instruction basis, be run at a lower frequency. The final phase uses summary statistics from the first phase in order to cluster intervals into larger contiguous periods of time, with a uniform clock rate for each.

Whenever an event in the dependence DAG has two or more incoming arcs, it is possible—in fact likely—that one arc will constitute the critical path and that the others will have "slack". This slack indicates that the previous operation completed earlier than necessary. If all of the outgoing arcs of an event have slack, then we have an opportunity (assuming zero-cost scaling) to save energy by performing the event at a lower frequency and voltage. With each event in the DAG we associate a *power factor* whose initial value is based on the relative power consumption of the corresponding clock domain, as determined by parameters in Wattch. When we stretch an event we scale its power factor accordingly. Calculations are made on a relative basis, on the assumption that energy is proportional to the square of the clock frequency.

The stretching phase of our reconfiguration tool uses a "shaker" algorithm to distribute slack and scale edges as uniformly as possible. Since SimpleScalar, like any real processor, executes events as soon as possible subject to dependences and hazards, slack always appears at the ends of non-critical paths in the original execution trace. The shaker algorithm thus begins at the end of its 50K cycle interval and works backwards through the DAG. When it encounters an event whose outgoing edges all have slack, the shaker checks to see whether the power factor of the event exceeds a certain threshold, originally set to be slightly below the maximum power of any event in the graph. If so (this is a high-power event), the shaker scales the event until either it consumes all the available slack or its power factor drops below the current threshold. If any slack remains, the event is moved later in time, so that as much slack as possible is moved to its *incoming* edges.

When it reaches the beginning of the DAG, the shaker reverses direction, reduces its power threshold by a small amount, and makes a new pass forward through the DAG, scaling high-power events and moving slack to outgoing edges. It repeats this process, alternately passing forward and backward over the DAG, reducing its power threshold each time, until all available slack has been consumed, or until all events adjacent to slack edges have been scaled down to one quarter of their original frequency. When it completes its work for a given 50K cycle interval, the shaker constructs a summary histogram for each clock domain. Each histogram indicates, for each of the 320 frequency steps in the XScale model (being the maximum of the number of steps for the two models), the total number of cycles for the events in the domain and interval that have been scaled to run at or near that frequency.

Unfortunately, it turns out to be difficult to capture the behavior of the front end in terms of dependences among events. Unlike the time between, say, the beginning and the end of an add in the floating-point domain, the time between fetch and dispatch is not a constant number of cycles. In addition, experiments with manually selected reconfiguration points suggested that scaling of the front was seldom as beneficial as scaling of other domains. As a result, we have chosen to run the front at a steady 1GHz, and to apply the shaker algorithm to events in the other 3 domains only. Since the front end typically accounts for 20% of the total chip energy, this choice implies that any energy improvements we may obtain must come from the remaining 80%. Future attempts to address the front end may yield greater savings than are reported here.

The final, clustering phase of our off-line analysis tool recognizes that frequencies cannot change on an instantaneous, instruction-by-instruction basis. It also allows for a certain amount of performance degradation. Using the histograms generated by the shaker, we calculate, for each clock domain and interval, the minimum frequency f that would permit the domain to complete its work with no more than d percent time dilation, where d is a parameter to the analysis. More specifically, we choose a frequency (from among 32 possible values for Transmeta and from among 320 possible values for XScale) such that the sum, over all events in higher bins of the histogram, of the extra time required to execute those events at the chosen frequency is less than or equal to d percent of the length of the interval. This calculation is by necessity approximate. It ignores ILP within domains: it assumes that the dilations of separate events in the same domain will have a cumulative effect. At the same time it ignores most dependences across domains: it assumes that the dilations of events in different domains will be independent.[2] For most applications the overall time dilation estimate turns out to be reasonably accurate: the figures in Section 4 show performance degradation (with respect to the MCD baseline) that is roughly in keeping with d.

Whereas the shaker algorithm assumes that reconfiguration is instantaneous and free, the clustering algorithm must model reconfiguration times and costs. For each adjacent pair of intervals for a given domain, it merges histograms on a bin-by-bin basis and calculates the minimum frequency that would allow us to run the larger, combined interval at a single frequency. For the Transmeta power model we require that the time dilation of too-slow events *together with* the time required to reconfigure at interval boundaries not exceed d percent of total execution time. Since it eliminates one reconfiguration, merging intervals under the Transmeta model often allows us to run the combined interval at a lower frequency and voltage, thereby saving energy. Most mergers under the XScale model occur when adjacent intervals have identical or nearly identical target frequencies. The clustering algorithm continues to perform mergers, recursively, so long as it is profitable from an energy standpoint to do so.

When it is done performing mergers, the clustering algorithm calculates the times at which reconfiguration must begin in order to reach target frequencies and voltages at target times. If reconfiguration is not possible, for example, because of a large swing in frequency that would take longer (because of the time to reduce or increase voltage) than the available interval, it is avoided. Since transitions

---

[2]As an exception to this rule, we add the events of the load/store domain into the histogram of the integer domain. This special case ensures that effective address computations occur quickly when memory activity is high.

in the Transmeta model take $20\mu s$ per voltage level, this results in the inability to accommodate short intervals with a large frequency variance. The algorithm completes its work by writing a log file that specifies times at which the application could profitably have requested changes in the frequencies and voltages of various domains. This file is then read by the processor simulator during a second, dynamic configuration run.

4. Results

In this section, we compare the performance, energy, and energy-delay product of the MCD microarchitecture to that of a conventional singly clocked system. The *baseline* configuration is a single clock 1GHz Alpha 21264-like system with no dynamic voltage or frequency scaling. The *baseline MCD* configuration is split into four clock domains as described in Section 2 but with the frequency of all clocks statically set at 1GHz. This configuration serves to quantify the performance and energy cost of inter-domain synchronization. The *dynamic 1%* and *dynamic 5%* configurations are identical to *baseline MCD* except that they support dynamic voltage and frequency scaling within each clock domain, as described in Section 3. For the *dynamic 1%* case the clustering phase of our off-line reconfiguration tool (Section 3.2) uses a target of 1% performance degradation (beyond that of *baseline MCD*); for the *dynamic 5%* case it uses a target of 5%. Finally, the *global* configuration models the *baseline* configuration with the addition of dynamic scaling of its single voltage and frequency, and serves to quantify the benefits of multiple clock domains.

The frequency for the *global* case is set so as to incur an overall performance degradation equal to that of the *dynamic 5%* configuration, and its voltage is correspondingly reduced. The energy savings of *global* is calculated by running each application under SimpleScalar and Wattch using the reduced frequency and voltage values. This approach permits the energy savings of the MCD approach to be compared to that of conventional voltage and frequency scaling for the same level of performance degradation. We performed a sanity check of the energy results of the *global* configuration by comparing the Wattch results against a simple calculation of the energy of the *baseline* configuration scaled relative to the square of the voltage ratios and found the results to agree to within 2%.

Figures 5, 6, and 7 display the performance degradation, energy savings, and change in energy × delay of the *baseline MCD*, *dynamic 1%*, *dynamic 5%*, and *global* configurations with respect to the *baseline* configuration, under the XScale model of voltage and frequency scaling. The Transmeta model produced far less promising results than the XScale model. Because of the roughly $15\mu s$ required to re-lock the PLL under the Transmeta model, reconfigu-

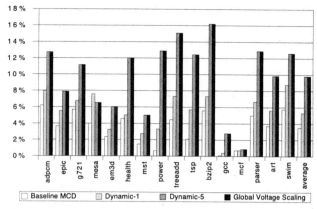

Figure 5. Performance degradation results

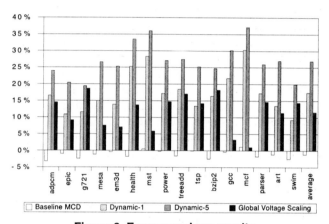

Figure 6. Energy savings results

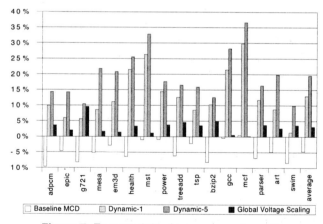

Figure 7. Energy-delay improvement results

rations are profitable much more rarely than they are under the XScale model, and energy improvements are much less. We will return to a comparison of the Transmeta and XScale models after discussing the XScale results in more detail.

The *baseline MCD* design, which simply uses multiple clock domains with no voltage or frequency scaling, shows an average performance degradation of less than

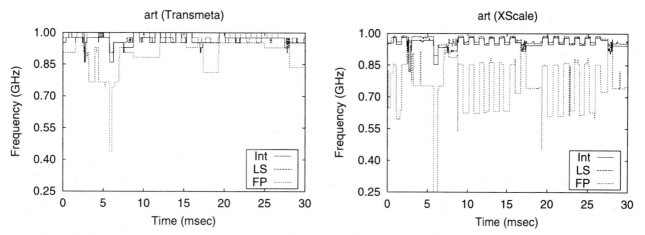

Figure 8. Frequency changes for *art* generated by our off-line algorithm for the *dynamic 1%* configuration.

4%, with average energy cost of 1.5%. The resulting impact on energy-delay product approaches −10% for *adpcm* and −5% overall. Note that any overheads introduced by the algorithms add directly to this *baseline MCD* overhead. For instance, the average *dynamic 5%* performance overhead is almost 10% or roughly what might be expected given the target degradation of 5% above the *baseline MCD*.

Our second observation is that the overall energy savings of the *global* approach is similar to its performance degradation, and averages less than 12% across the sixteen benchmarks. This result is somewhat counterintuitive, since when both frequency and voltage are reduced linearly by the same percentage, performance drops linearly with frequency, yet energy drops quadratically with voltage. Recall, however, that in our model a four-fold change in frequency (from 1GHz down to 250MHz) results in a less than two-fold change in voltage (from 1.2V down to 0.65V, modeled as 2.0V to 1.0833V in Wattch). As discussed in Section 1, this difference is due to the compression of voltage ranges relative to frequency ranges in successive process generations, as voltages are scaled down relative to threshold voltage, and frequencies are scaled up. The slope of the voltage curve has become much less steep than that of the frequency curve, greatly diminishing the quadratic effect on energy of a voltage reduction.

The MCD approaches, by contrast, achieve significant energy and energy × delay improvements with respect to the *baseline* configuration, with a comparatively minor overall performance degradation. For example, the *dynamic 5%* configuration achieves an average overall energy reduction of 27% and an energy × delay improvement of almost 20% relative to the *baseline* configuration, while incurring a performance degradation of less than 10% across the sixteen benchmarks under the XScale model. The *dynamic 1%* algorithm, which tries to more strictly cap the

performance degradation at the expense of energy savings, trades off a significant energy savings to achieve this goal, resulting in an energy × delay improvement of roughly 13%. Even so, this still far exceeds the 3% energy × delay improvement obtained with the *global* approach.

In several cases the opportunity to hide latency behind cache misses allows actual performance degradation to be significantly less than what one might expect from the frequencies chosen by the dynamic algorithm. In particular, the slack associated with L1 data cache misses often allows our reconfiguration tool to scale the integer and floating-point domains without significantly impacting overall performance (due to the fact that the available ILP is not sufficient to completely hide the miss latency), even when the utilization for these domains is high. The load/store domain, of course, must continue to operate at a high frequency in order to service the misses as quickly as possible, since the second level cache is in the same domain (unless we have a lot of level-two cache misses as well). The impact of misses can be seen in *gcc* (*dynamic 1%*), where the cache miss rate is high (12.5%) and the average frequency of the integer domain drops to approximately 920 MHz, but total performance degradation is less than 1%.

By contrast, branch mispredictions do *not* provide an opportunity for dynamic scaling: the dependence chain developed to resolve a branch precludes significant frequency reductions in the integer domain, and sometimes in the load/store domain as well. Applications that experience a high branch mispredict rate are likely to show performance degradation in accordance with frequency slowdown. This effect can be seen in *swim*, where the energy savings barely exceeds the performance degradation. (Here the floating point domain must also remain at a high frequency because of high utilization.)

The dynamic algorithm performs poorest with respect to global voltage scaling in *g721*. This is an integer bench-

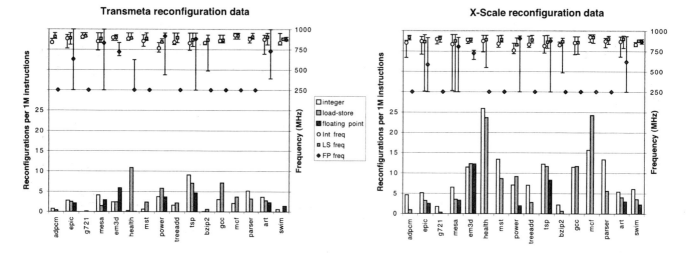

Figure 9. Summary statistics for intervals chosen by the off-line tool for the *dynamic 5%* configuration. Solid bars indicate, for the integer, load-store, and floating-point domains, the number of reconfigurations requested per 1 million instructions. Points above the bars indicate the average frequencies chosen for those domains. "Error bars", where shown, indicate the range of dynamic frequencies for the domain.

mark with a well balanced instruction mix, high utilization of the integer and load/store domains, a low cache miss rate, a low branch misprediction rate, and high *baseline MCD* overheads. Its IPC is relatively high (above 2), and the integer and load/store domains must run near maximum speed in order to sustain this. The floating point domain can of course be scaled back to 250MHz, but because of the high activity levels in the other domains, the resulting energy savings is a smaller fraction of total processor energy than it is in most of the other integer applications.

Comparing Figures 5–7 with corresponding results (not shown here) under the Transmeta scaling model, we found that the XScale model enables us to achieve significantly higher energy savings for a given level of performance degradation. The reasons for this result are illustrated in Figure 8, which displays the frequency settings chosen by our reconfiguration tool for a 30ms interval of the *art* benchmark, with a target performance degradation of 1%. In comparing the graphs in this figure, note that under the XScale model we are able both to make a larger number of frequency changes and to make those changes over a wider range of frequencies. In particular, while *art* is a floating-point intensive application, there are many instruction intervals during which we can safely scale back the floating-point domain. Because of its 10–20μs PLL relock penalty, the Transmeta model does not allow us to capture this comparatively short-term behavior.

Figure 9 presents summary statistics for the intervals chosen by our off-line reconfiguration tool in all 16 applications, under both the Transmeta and XScale models. While the average frequencies chosen for the integer, load-store,

and floating-point domains are similar in the two graphs, the total number of reconfigurations is much lower under the Transmeta model, and the frequency ranges are narrower.

Figures 8 and 9 both illustrate the value of using different frequencies in different clock domains: by controlling these frequencies independently we can maintain the required frequency in domains that are critical to performance, while aggressively scaling those domains that are less performance-critical. The floating-point domain in particular can be scaled back to the lowest available frequency in many applications, including some that include non-trivial numbers of floating-point operations. Note, however, that due to clock gating, the floating point domain is often not the largest source of energy dissipation for integer programs: the integer domain often is the largest source and thus even modest adjustments of its domain voltage yield significant energy savings. Furthermore, although one would expect dynamic scaling to reduce static power as well, we have not quantified the corresponding contribution to the energy savings. Dynamic voltage *gating* might achieve additional savings (given appropriate support for saving/restoring critical processor state), and would seem to be a promising avenue for future research.

5. Related Work

Several manufacturers, notably Intel [21] and Transmeta [16], have developed processors capable of global dynamic frequency and voltage scaling. Since minimum operational voltage is roughly proportional to frequency, and power is roughly proportional to the voltage squared, this dynamic scaling can be of major benefit in applications with real-time constraints for which the processor as a whole is over-designed: for example, video rendering. Marculescu [23] and Hsu et al. [18] evaluated the use of whole-chip dynamic voltage scaling with minimal loss of performance using cache misses as the trigger [23]. Other work [7, 26] has also begun to look at steering instructions to pipelines or functional units running statically at different speeds so as to exploit scheduling slack in the program to save energy. Our contribution is to demonstrate that a microprocessor with multiple clock domains provides the opportunity to reduce power consumption on a variety of different applications without a significant performance impact by reducing frequency and voltage in domains that do not contribute significantly to the critical path of the current application phase.

Govil et al. [15] and Weiser et al. [31] describe interval-based strategies to adjust the CPU speed based on processor utilization. The goal is to reduce energy consumption by attempting to keep the processor 100% utilized without significantly delaying task completion times. A history based on the utilization in previous intervals is used to predict the amount of work and thereby adjust speed for maximum utilization without work backlog. Pering et al. [25] apply a similar principle to real-time and multimedia applications. Similarly, Hughes et al. [19] use instruction count predictions for frame based multimedia applications to dynamically change the global voltage and frequency of the processor while tolerating a low percentage of missed frame deadlines. Bellosa [2, 3] describes a scheme to associate energy usage patterns with every process in order to control energy consumption for the purposes of both cooling and battery life. Cache and memory behavior as well as process priorities are used as input in order to drive the energy control heuristics. Benini et al. [4] present a system that monitors system activity and provides information to an OS module that manages system power. They use this monitoring system in order to demonstrate how to set the threshold idle time used to place a disk in low-power mode. Our work differs in that we attempt to slow down only those parts of the processor that are not on an application's critical path.

Fields et al. [12] use a dependence graph similar to ours, but constructed on the fly, to identify the critical path of an application. Their goal is to improve instruction steering in clustered architectures and to improve value prediction by selectively applying it to critical instructions only. We use our graph off-line in order to slow down non-critical program paths. Li et al. [22] explore the theoretical lower bound of energy consumption assuming that both the program and the machine are fully adjustable. Assuming equal energy dissipation in all hardware components, they show

that a program with balanced load on all components consumes less energy than one with significant variance.

Childers et al. [9] propose to trade IPC for clock frequency. The user requests a particular quality of service from the system (expressed in MIPS) and the processor uses an interval-based method to monitor the IPC and adjust the frequency and voltage accordingly. In their work, a process with high IPC will run at a low clock frequency while a process with low IPC will run at a high clock frequency, which is contrary to what is required for some applications (e.g., when low IPC is due to high miss rates). Our techniques work to achieve the exact opposite in order to provide maximum performance with minimum energy.

6. Conclusions

We have described and evaluated a *multiple clock domain (MCD)* microarchitecture, which uses a *globally-asynchronous, locally-synchronous (GALS)* clocking style along with dynamic voltage and frequency scaling in order to maximize performance and energy efficiency for a given application. Our design uses existing queue structures in a superscalar processor core to isolate the different clock domains in a way that minimizes the need for inter-domain synchronization.

Performance results for applications drawn from standard benchmark suites suggest that the division of the processor into multiple domains incurs an average baseline performance cost of less than 4%. At the same time, by scaling frequency and voltage in different domains dynamically and independently, we can achieve an average improvement in energy-delay product of nearly 20%. By contrast, global voltage scaling to achieve comparable performance degradation in a singly clocked microprocessor achieves an average energy-delay improvement of only 3%.

Our current analysis uses an off-line algorithm to determine the points in the program at which different domains should change frequency and voltage. Future work will involve developing effective on-line algorithms, including approaches for effective scaling of the front end. In addition, we will continue to investigate the circuit-level issues associated with being able to deliver tunable on-chip voltage and frequency with low latency.

References

[1] D. H. Albonesi. Dynamic IPC/Clock Rate Optimization. *Proceedings of the 25th International Symposium on Computer Architecture*, pages 282–292, June 1998.

[2] F. Bellosa. OS-Directed Throttling of Processor Activity for Dynamic Power Management. Technical Report TR-I4-3-99, C.S. Dept., University of Erlangen, Germany, June 1999.

[3] F. Bellosa. The Benefits of Event-Driven Energy Accounting in Power-Sensitive Systems. In *Proceedings of the 9th ACM SIGOPS European Workshop*, Sept. 2000.

[4] L. Benini, A. Bogliolo, S. Cavallucci, and B. Ricco. Monitoring System Activity for OS-directed Dynamic Power Management. In *Proceedings of the International Symposium on Low-Power Electronics and Design*, Aug. 1998.

[5] D. Brooks, V. Tiwari, and M. Martonosi. Wattch: A Framework for Architectural-Level Power Analysis and Optimizations. In *Proceedings of the 27th International Symposium on Computer Architecture*, June 2000.

[6] D. Burger and T. Austin. The Simplescalar Tool Set, Version 2.0. Technical Report CS-TR-97-1342, University of Wisconsin, Madison, Wisconsin, June 1997.

[7] J. Casmira and D. Grunwald. Dynamic Instruction Scheduling Slack. In *Proceedings of the Kool Chips Workshop, in conjunction with the 33rd International Symposium on Microarchitecture (MICRO-33)*, Dec. 2000.

[8] B. Chappell. The fine art of IC design. *IEEE Spectrum*, 36(7):30–34, July 1999.

[9] B. R. Childers, H. Tang, and R. Melhem. Adapting Processor Supply Voltage to Instruction-Level Parallelism. In *Proceedings of the Kool Chips Workshop, in conjunction with the 33rd International Symposium on Microarchitecture (MICRO-33)*, Dec. 2000.

[10] L. T. Clark. Circuit Design of XScale^{TM} Microprocessors. In *2001 Symposium on VLSI Circuits, Short Course on Physical Design for Low-Power and High-Performance Microprocessor Circuits*. IEEE Solid-State Circuits Society, June 2001.

[11] J. H. Edmondson et al. Internal Organization of the Alpha 21164, a 300-MHz 64-bit Quad–issue CMOS RISC Microprocessor. *Digital Technical Journal*, 7(1):119–135, 1995. Special Edition.

[12] B. Fields, S. Rubin, and R. Bodik. Focusing Processor Policies via Critical-Path Prediction. In *Proceedings of the 28th International Symposium on Computer Architecture*, July 2001.

[13] M. Fleischmann. Longrun^{TM} power management. Technical report, Transmeta Corporation, Jan. 2001.

[14] P. N. Glaskowsky. Pentium 4 (Partially) Previewed. *Microprocessor Report*, 14(8):1,11–13, Aug. 2000.

[15] K. Govil, E. Chang, and H. Wasserman. Comparing Algorithms for Dynamic Speed-Setting of a Low-Power CPU. In *Proceedings of the 1st ACM/IEEE International Conference on Mobile Computing and Networking*, pages 13–25, Nov. 1995.

[16] T. R. Halfhill. Transmeta breaks x86 low-power barrier. *Microprocessor Report*, 14(2), Feb. 2000.

[17] T. Horel and G. Lauterbach. UltraSPARC III: Designing Third-Generation 64-Bit Performance. *IEEE Micro*, 19(3):73–85, May/June 1999.

[18] C.-H. Hsu, U. Kremer, and M. Hsiao. Compiler-Directed Dynamic Frequency and Voltage Scaling. In *Proceedings of the Workshop on Power-Aware Computer Systems, in conjunction with the 9th International Conference on Architectural Support for Programming Languages and Operating Systems (ASPLOS-IX)*, Nov. 2000.

[19] C. J. Hughes, J. Srinivasan, and S. V. Adve. Saving Energy with Architectural and Frequency Adaptations for Multimedia Applications. In *Proceedings of the 34th Annual International Symposium on Microarchitecture (MICRO-34)*, Dec. 2001.

[20] R. E. Kessler, E. J. McLellan, and D. A. Webb. The Alpha 21264 Microprocessor Architecture. In *Proceedings of the International Conference on Computer Design*, pages 90–95, Austin, Texas, Oct. 1998. IEEE Computer Society.

[21] S. Leibson. XScale (StrongArm-2) Muscles In. *Microprocessor Report*, 14(9):7–12, Sept. 2000.

[22] T. Li and C. Ding. Instruction Balance, Energy Consumption and Program Performance. Technical Report UR-CS-TR-739, Computer Science Dept., University of Rochester, Dec. 2000. Revised February 2001.

[23] D. Marculescu. On the Use of Microarchitecture-Driven Dynamic Voltage Scaling. In *Proceedings of the Workshop on Complexity-Effective Design, in conjunction with the 27th International Symposium on Computer Architecture*, June 2000.

[24] D. Matzke. Will Physical Scalability Sabotage Performance Gains? *IEEE Computer*, 30(9):37–39, Sept. 1997.

[25] T. Pering, T. Burd, and R. W. Brodersen. The Simulation and Evaluation of Dynamic Voltage Scaling Algorithms. In *Proceedings of the International Symposium on Low-Power Electronics and Design*, Aug. 1998.

[26] R. Pyreddy and G. Tyson. Evaluating Design Tradeoffs in Dual Speed Pipelines. In *Proceedings of the Workshop on Complexity-Effective Design, in conjunction with the 28th International Symposium on Computer Architecture*, June 2001.

[27] L. F. G. Sarmenta, G. A. Pratt, and S. A. Ward. Rational Clocking. In *Proceedings of the International Conference on Computer Design*, Austin, Texas, Oct. 1995.

[28] A. E. Sjogren and C. J. Myers. Interfacing Synchronous and Asynchronous Modules Within A High-Speed Pipeline. In *Proceedings of the 17th Conference on Advanced Research in VLSI*, pages 47–61, Ann Arbor, Michigan, Sept. 1997.

[29] G. Sohi. Instruction Issue Logic for High-Performance Interruptible, Multiple Functional Unit, Pipelined Computers. *ACM Transactions on Computer Systems*, 39(3):349–359, Mar. 1990.

[30] TSMC Corp. TSMC Technology Roadmap, July 2001.

[31] M. Weiser, A. Demers, B. Welch, and S. Shenker. Scheduling for Reduced CPU Energy. In *Proceedings of the 1st USENIX Symposium on Operating Systems Design and Implementation*, Nov. 1994.

Speculative Multithreading

Eliminating Squashes Through Learning Cross-Thread Violations in Speculative Parallelization for Multiprocessors[*]

Marcelo Cintra[†]
Division of Informatics
University of Edinburgh

mc@dcs.ed.ac.uk

Josep Torrellas
Department of Computer Science
University of Illinois at Urbana-Champaign

torrellas@cs.uiuc.edu

ABSTRACT

With speculative thread-level parallelization, codes that cannot be fully compiler-analyzed are aggressively executed in parallel. If the hardware detects a cross-thread dependence violation, it squashes offending threads and resumes execution. Unfortunately, frequent squashing cripples performance.

This paper proposes a new framework of hardware mechanisms to eliminate most squashes due to data dependences in multiprocessors. The framework works by learning and predicting violations, and applying delayed disambiguation, value prediction, and stall and release. The framework is suited for directory-based multiprocessors that track memory accesses at the system level with the coarse granularity of memory lines. Simulations of a 16-processor machine show that the framework is very effective. By adding our framework to a speculative CC-NUMA with 64-byte memory lines, we speed-up applications by an average of 4.3 times. Moreover, the resulting system is even 23% faster than a machine that tracks memory accesses at the fine granularity of words – a sophisticated system that is not compatible with mainstream cache coherence protocols.

1 INTRODUCTION

Despite advances in compiler technology, compilers still fail to automatically parallelize many codes. Typically, compilers abstain from parallelizing codes with complex or unknown data dependences, such as those that contain pointer accesses, references to arrays with non-linear subscripts, very irregular control flow, or accesses across complicated procedure calling patterns.

To extract parallelism in such codes, speculative thread-level parallelization has been proposed [1, 4, 6, 7, 8, 10, 12, 18, 19, 20, 22, 23, 25, 26, 32]. In this approach, potentially dependent threads are speculatively executed in parallel, hoping not to violate dependences. If a cross-thread dependence is violated at run time, a corrective action is triggered to repair the state. Such an action often involves squashing one or several threads.

Proposed schemes for speculative parallelization differ in many ways. For example, some schemes rely on support code inserted by the compiler to check for dependence violations and to perform corrective actions [7, 19, 20]. Other schemes rely on special hardware to perform some or all of these operations [1, 4, 6, 8, 10, 12, 18, 22, 23, 25, 26, 32].

In most schemes, however, squashing a thread due to a dependence violation and restarting it is a costly operation. Typically, the cost includes the overhead of the squash operation itself, the loss of the work performed, and the cache misses necessary to reload state after restart. Squashes are especially costly in large multiprocessors, where the overhead of squashing distributed threads is high and the typical coarse grain of the threads likely implies more wasted work.

Unfortunately, squashes due to data dependence violations can be frequent. One reason is that the coherence protocol of multiprocessors typically operates at the granularity of memory lines. This is because word-based accesses usually exhibit suboptimal locality and result in increased traffic. However, line-based systems are subject to false sharing, which may appear to violate dependences.

Another reason for frequent dependence violations may be the early stage of development of compilation support for speculative parallelization [15, 16, 24, 28]. Specifically, compilers may occasionally make poor assessments of data dependences and attempt to speculatively parallelize codes with many dependences.

One approach to reduce the number of squashes is to attempt to learn at run time where the cross-thread dependence violations occur. Then, when we predict that one such violation is about to occur, we can prevent it from taking place. Past work has used these ideas to dynamically synchronize dependent load-store pairs in a uniprocessor [5, 21, 31], or even to dynamically synchronize dependent threads in a tightly-coupled multiscalar processor [14].

In this paper, we focus on how to eliminate squashes through run-time dependence learning in the distributed architecture of a directory-based CC-NUMA. Clearly, the problem that we address is different than the one addressed by previous work. Indeed, we cannot afford any centralized learning structure and there is no global context readily available. Moreover, we must largely rely on memory access information that is only available at the grain size of memory lines.

We propose a new framework of hardware mechanisms to eliminate most squashes due to data dependences in directory-based multiprocessors. The framework works by learning and predicting violations, and applying delayed disambiguation for false dependences, value prediction for same-word dependences, and stall and release for unpredictable, same-word dependences.

The framework works with multiprocessors that track system-level memory accesses at the coarse granularity of memory lines. Simulations of a 16-processor machine show that the framework is very effective. By adding the framework to a speculative CC-NUMA with 64-byte memory lines, we speed-up applications by an average of 4.3 times. Moreover, the resulting system is even 23% faster than a machine that tracks memory accesses at the fine granularity of words. Such fine-grain access tracking is not compatible with mainstream cache coherence protocols.

*This work was supported in part by the National Science Foundation under grants CCR-9970488, EIA-0081307, and EIA-0072102; by DARPA under grant F30602-01-C-0078; and by gifts from IBM and Intel.

†Work conducted in part while the author was with the Department of Computer Science at the University of Illinois at Urbana-Champaign.

This paper is organized as follows: Section 2 discusses background concepts; Section 3 presents the proposed framework; Section 4 outlines its implementation; Section 5 discusses the evaluation methodology; Section 6 evaluates the framework; Section 7 discusses related work; and Section 8 concludes the paper.

2 SPECULATIVE PARALLELIZATION

2.1 Basic Concepts

Speculative thread-level parallelization consists of extracting threads from sequential code and running them in parallel, hoping not to violate sequential semantics. Threads in a speculative system are typically classified into a single *non-speculative* thread and a set of *speculative* ones that can generate unsafe state. In speculative threads, stores generate speculative versions of variables, and loads that do not find a local version must get the most up-to-date one from a predecessor thread or memory. In such a system, a thread *commits* when it has finished its execution and is non-speculative. In the speculation protocol that we use in this paper, when a thread commits, it writes-back to main memory all the dirty lines in its cache [4]. Furthermore, a speculative thread becomes non-speculative only when all its predecessors have committed.

As execution proceeds, the system tracks memory accesses to identify any cross-thread data dependence violation. If one is found, the offending thread is *squashed*. Typically, to simplify the protocol, its successor threads are also squashed. Thread squash is a very costly operation. The cost is three-fold: overhead of the squash operation itself, loss of the work already performed by the offending thread and successors, and cache misses in the offending thread and successors needed to reload state after restarting. The latter overhead appears because, as part of the squash operation, the speculative state in the cache is invalidated. Figure 3a shows an example of a RAW violation across threads i and $i+j+1$. The consumer thread and its successors are squashed.

2.2 General Architectural Model

A few designs have been proposed to support speculative thread-level parallelization in directory-based architectures [4, 18, 23, 32]. In the discussion of our framework, we assume a model where a Speculation Module is added to the directory controller of the CC-NUMA machine (e.g., as in [4]). The module keeps track of the mapping of threads to processors and their ordering.

The speculation module is also responsible for detecting any data dependence violation. It does so by recording what data has been speculatively accessed by what thread with an exposed load or a store. An exposed load is a load to a location by a thread before the same thread has updated the location. If a violation is detected, the module squashes all the necessary threads [4].

2.3 Granularity of Access Tracking

Speculation protocols can be classified depending on whether they track speculative accesses with word or line granularity. Per-word protocols only need to squash threads in cross-thread RAW violations on the same word. However, they require costly per-word state support in caches, network messaging, and directory modules. They also tend to generate higher traffic.

Per-line protocols are more cost-conscious and are compatible with mainstream cache coherence protocols. However, they cannot disambiguate accesses at word level. Furthermore, they cannot combine different versions of a given line that have been updated in different words. Consequently, cross-thread RAW and WAW violations, on both the same and different words of a line, cause squashes.

A per-line protocol with per-word extensions in the cache hi-

erarchy is a compromise that effectively reduces squashing to the case of RAW violations on same or different words of a line. Each cache line is augmented with one *Store*, one *exposed Load*, and one *Valid* bit per word. The first bit indicates that the local thread has updated the word. The second bit, that the local thread has issued an exposed load to it. The Valid bits indicate which words of the line are valid and allow for invalidation of individual words. Line write-backs to memory piggy-back the Store bits of the line, so that the directory controller can successfully combine different versions of the line. Hence, all cross-thread WAW dependences are supported without causing squashes. Still, the directory state is kept per line. In this paper, we use this protocol as our baseline.

In all the protocols considered in this paper, we disable support for the forwarding of uncommitted dirty data between caches. We do this to simplify the implementation of the protocols. As a result, the violations described above include both out-of-order dependent accesses and in-order dependent accesses that need forwarding of uncommitted dirty data.

3 PROPOSED FRAMEWORK

Squashes due to cross-thread data dependence violations can cause major overheads under speculative parallelization in multiprocessors. One possible way to remove many such squashes is through learning where violations occur, predicting them, and then preventing them from taking place. The motivation for this general approach is that some form of learning, prediction, and synchronization of data dependences have been successfully used in uniprocessors and tightly-coupled chip multiprocessors [1, 5, 11, 13, 14, 21, 29, 30, 31].

In our work, we target directory-based CC-NUMA architectures. These architectures have distributed processors, caches, and directories, which require different solutions. In particular, we exploit the fact that, as indicated in Section 2.2, some speculative CC-NUMA designs have a speculation module in the directory controller (module 1 in Figure 1). Such a module can see all the accesses that are involved in dependence violations [4]. Consequently, we can build support for learning, predicting, and eliminating violations around that module.

In this section, we present a novel framework that uses these ideas. We first present an overview of the mechanisms (Section 3.1) and learning heuristics (Section 3.2) used. We then describe each mechanism in detail (Section 3.3) and some possible extensions (Section 3.4).

3.1 Overview of the Mechanisms

In conventional speculative systems, when the speculation module at the directory controller observes the two accesses involved in a RAW violation, it triggers a squash. In our framework, we try to eliminate such a squash with four mechanisms.

First, some squashes are unnecessary because there is no true data transfer between the threads involved: there is only false sharing. Since our baseline speculation protocol tracks accesses at the granularity of lines at the directory, false sharing causes squashes. To eliminate these squashes, we optimistically let the consumer thread proceed. However, before we allow the thread to commit, we use the per-word access bits in its cache hierarchy to check whether or not it was false sharing. We call this mechanism *Delay&Disambiguate*.

Secondly, even when there is true data transfer between threads, a squash can be avoided with effective use of value prediction. Specifically, we predict the value that the producer will produce, speculatively provide it to the consumer, and let the latter proceed. Before we allow the consumer to commit, we check whether or not the value used was correct. We call this mechanism *ValuePredict*.

In cases where value prediction fails, we can avoid the squash

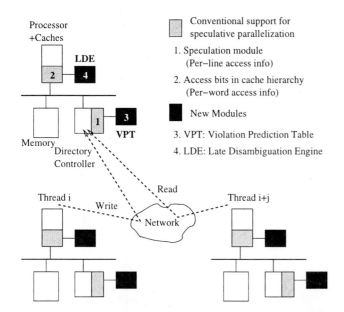

Figure 1: Model of speculative CC-NUMA used in this paper. The shaded areas are support that has been proposed elsewhere. The black areas are our proposed additions.

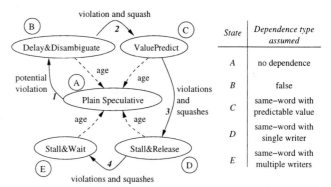

Figure 2: Finite state machine followed by the VPT for individual memory lines. Plain Speculative is the initial state.

by stalling the consumer thread until the producer has produced the value. At that point, the consumer reads the produced value and can resume. This case has two possible mechanisms. An aggressive approach is to release the consumer thread as soon as the first producer thread commits. In this case, if an intervening thread between the first producer and the consumer later writes the line, the consumer will be squashed. We call this mechanism *Stall&Release*. A more conservative approach is not to release the consumer thread until it becomes non-speculative. In this case, the presence of multiple predecessor writers will not squash the consumer. We call this mechanism *Stall&Wait*.

3.2 Learning and Prediction Heuristics

To learn and predict what memory accesses cause violations, we use the line address requested by the access. Specifically, we add an extension to each speculation module called the *Violation Prediction Table (VPT)* (module 3 in Figure 1). The VPT dynamically keeps the address and other information for the lines that have been involved in potential or actual violations in the past. When the VPT observes an access to one such line, it triggers one of our four mechanisms.

To decide what mechanism to use for a particular line, the VPT uses the finite state machine of Figure 2. Initially, a line accessed speculatively is in the Plain Speculative state in the VPT, and the VPT takes no action. When the line appears to be involved in a potential violation, the VPT transitions to the Delay&Disambiguate state for the line (transition 1 in Figure 2). This engages the mechanism for handling false dependences. Note that, by default, we predict that the dependence will turn out to be false. We make the assumption that, in line-based protocols, false dependences are more likely than same-word dependences.

If the dependence turns out to be a same-word dependence, a squash is triggered and the VPT transitions to the ValuePredict state for the line (transition 2 in Figure 2). This engages the mechanism for value prediction. If further same-word violations occur in the line, the VPT transitions to the Stall&Release state for the line (transition 3 in Figure 2). This engages the mechanism for consumer stall and restart as soon as the first producer commits.

Finally, if further violations occur in the line, the VPT transitions to the Stall&Wait state (transition 4 in Figure 2). This engages the mechanism for consumer stall and restart only when it becomes non-speculative. Any of these states can directly age back to the Plain Speculative state (dashed transitions in Figure 2).

3.3 Mechanisms Used

3.3.1 Delay&Disambiguate: False Dependences

For lines under the Delay&Disambiguate state, potential violations detected by the speculation module at the directory controller are assumed to be false. No squash is generated. Instead, the per-line speculation protocol operates mostly unaltered. Later, before the consumer thread is allowed to commit, access information from the producer and consumer threads are compared to perform word-address disambiguation.

Figures 3b and 3c show how a RAW violation is handled in this case. If the disambiguation shows the dependence to be false (Figure 3b), the consumer thread only sees a small overhead while the disambiguation is performed. However, if the dependence turns out to be for the same word (Figure 3c), the consumer thread and successors are squashed and restarted.

Implementing the Delay&Disambiguate mechanism requires the following: identifying potential violations that are likely to be false, remembering delayed unresolved violations, performing the delayed disambiguation, squashing threads when violations are confirmed, and learning which lines are involved in same-word violations.

This mechanism is triggered when the speculation module detects the second access of a RAW access pair to a line. At this point, the VPT checks if it has learned that the line has caused same-word dependences in the past. If it has not, the speculation module ignores the potential violation. At this point, the VPT transitions its state for the line to Delay&Disambiguate (Figure 2) and records the tag of the line involved and the ID of the consumer thread. The VPT also prepares a bit mask that will identify the words of the line that are actually written by predecessor threads. This mask is called the *Modified* mask, and is updated every time that a predecessor thread writes back the line to main memory at commit time. Recall that write-backs include bits that identify which words were written (Section 2.3).

When the consumer thread is about to become non-speculative, the Modified mask contains the record of the modifications by all the predecessor threads since the time of the potential violation. The VPT then sends the Modified mask to a new module associated with the cache hierarchy of the consumer node, along with a request for late disambiguation. Such a module is called the *Late Disambiguation Engine (LDE)* (module 4 in Figure 1). Before the

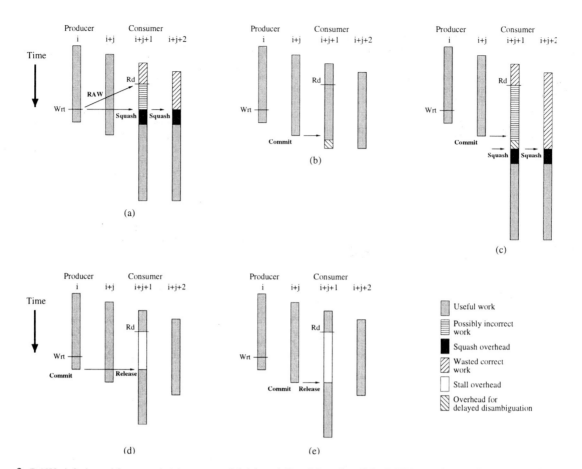

Figure 3: RAW violation with a squash (a); a successful delayed disambiguation (false RAW) or value prediction (b); a failed delayed disambiguation (same-word RAW) or value prediction (c); a stall with early release (d); and a stall with no early release (e).

consumer is allowed to commit, the LDE compares the Modified mask against the per-word Load and Store access bits of the corresponding line in the cache hierarchy of the consumer node (module 2 in Figure 1).

If there is an intersection between the Load bits and the mask, a same-word violation occurred and the thread is squashed. The VPT then transitions its state for the line to ValuePredict (Figure 2), effectively learning that the line exhibits same-word dependences. If no intersection is detected, the state in the VPT is kept as Delay&Disambiguate. Furthermore, any words in the line that both have the Store bit clear and are marked in the Modified mask, have become stale. Therefore, they are invalidated from the consumer cache hierarchy.

The effectiveness of Delay&Disambiguate is related to the fraction of delayed disambiguations that do not cause late squashes. We define such a fraction as the *selectivity* of the mechanism. Higher selectivity is better.

3.3.2 ValuePredict: Predicting Consumed Values

For lines under the ValuePredict state, the VPT provides a predicted value to the consumer thread on demand. The VPT remembers this value, which is finally compared with the correct value in the system when the consumer thread becomes non-speculative. If the prediction was correct the thread continues (Figure 3b). Otherwise, the thread and its successors are squashed (Figure 3c).

This mechanism requires: learning when to apply value prediction, predicting a value based on past observed values, comparing predicted consumed values with the actual values, and squashing

threads if necessary.

When Delay&Disambiguate identifies a same-word violation, a squash is triggered and the VPT transitions immediately to ValuePredict for the line. Alternatively, we could wait and observe the predictability of the values before attempting value prediction. The choice here depends on the history depth required by the prediction mechanism. In this paper, we only investigate an *approximate last-value* prediction, which allows for immediate transition.

We design the mechanism as follows. When a thread attempts to consume data from a line marked ValuePredict in the VPT, the VPT provides a predicted value of the line. For simplicity, in our implementation the predicted value of the line is the last value written-back to main memory. Consequently, the VPT provides the current version of the line in memory. This prediction technique has also been called *value reuse* or *silent store*. The VPT also records the line tag, the value of the line provided, and the ID of the consumer thread.

When the thread finally becomes non-speculative, the VPT compares the prediction it made to the final value of the line. Recall that, in our protocol, such a value is the one currently in memory (Section 2.1). For words whose values differ, the VPT sets the corresponding bit in the Modified mask described in Section 3.3.1. The VPT then sends the Modified mask to the LDE in the consumer node, which performs local late disambiguation as described in Section 3.3.1. The state of the line in the VPT remains in ValuePredict unless a squash is required and such a squash increases the squash count for the line over a certain threshold.

The effectiveness of the ValuePredict mechanism depends on

46

the predictability of the values and on the accuracy of the predictor used.

3.3.3 Stall&Release: Waiting for the First Writer

For lines under the Stall&Release state, the VPT stalls the consumer thread when it tries to load the line. Later, when the producer thread commits, the consumer thread finally gets the line and continues. Figure 3d shows how a potential RAW violation is handled under the Stall&Release mechanism.

This mechanism requires: identifying the lines that cause same-word violations where value prediction fails, stalling threads before they are allowed to consume unsafe data, and releasing threads when the data is considered safe.

Before transitioning to Stall&Release for a line, the VPT counts the number of squashes caused by the line under ValuePredict. When a threshold is exceeded, the VPT learns that violations cannot be successfully handled with value prediction. At that point, after the squash is complete, the VPT transitions the state of the line to Stall&Release (Figure 2) and issues cache invalidations for the line to all speculative threads. These invalidations are selective in that, in each cache, they only invalidate the words in the line that have no local modified version.

We can now see how the Stall&Release mechanism works. When a consumer thread issues an exposed read to one of the words in the line, the request misses in the cache and is propagated to the directory. Since the VPT knows that the line is in state Stall&Release, it buffers the request and does not reply. Therefore, the consumer thread will eventually stall when it runs out of instructions to execute.

The safe time to release a stalled thread is when it becomes non-speculative. However, releasing it earlier may speed-up execution. The earliest time when a line can be forwarded and the consumer released is when the producer thread commits and writes back the modified line to memory. At this time, the line can be forwarded provided that no other predecessor of the stalled consumer thread has created a newer version of the line in its cache. If no such version exists, the VPT releases the buffered request and allows it to proceed, therefore effectively releasing the stalled thread. This is shown in Figure 3d, where the consumer thread is released as soon as the producer thread commits. However, if any predecessor of the released thread now writes to the line, a squash will occur.

The effectiveness of Stall&Release is measured in terms of coverage and selectivity. *Coverage* is the fraction of the squashes that are successfully avoided. *Selectivity* is the fraction of the stalls that actually eliminate squashes. Ideally, both should be high.

3.3.4 Stall&Wait: Waiting for Multiple Writers

For lines under the Stall&Wait state, the VPT also stalls the consumer thread when it tries to load the line. However, the VPT does not allow the thread to resume until the thread becomes non-speculative. At that point, it is completely safe for the thread to resume. Figure 3e shows how a potential RAW violation is handled under the Stall&Wait mechanism.

For a given line, the VPT reaches Stall&Wait from Stall&Release. While in Stall&Release, the VPT counts the number of squashes caused by the line. Such squashes are nearly always due to premature early releases. Specifically, after the consumer has been released, other predecessor threads also write the line. If the number of such squashes reaches a certain threshold, the VPT transitions from Stall&Release to Stall&Wait for the line (Figure 2), effectively learning that the line has multiple writers.

We design the Stall&Wait mechanism like the Stall&Release one. The only difference is that the VPT keeps the consumer read buffered until the consumer thread becomes non-speculative.

3.4 Advanced Learning Heuristics

3.4.1 Violation Predictors

Our violation prediction heuristics are based on counting the number of violations caused by accesses to a particular memory line. Such a scheme is easy to implement in the memory subsystem of CC-NUMA multiprocessors, as it only requires monitoring in the directory controller the addresses of the accesses that cause violations.

Prediction of violations can instead be based on the addresses of the instructions causing the violations, as in [14]. However, this approach is a bit harder to implement in CC-NUMA multiprocessors as instruction addresses are not usually visible at the main memory system.

We have also experimented with more advanced prediction mechanisms based on history tables [17]. Such mechanisms can exploit correlation between related memory operations and thus predict violations better. However, our experiments showed little performance improvement. Due to the additional complexity of such predictors, we do not pursue them further.

3.4.2 Value Predictors

Our framework can accommodate more complex value predictors than the one investigated in this paper. Indeed, once a particular line has been identified as causing same-word violations, the VPT can keep a history of the actual values produced. This history can be updated every time that a thread commits and writes back to memory a new version of the line. Then, when the line is read, we can make a prediction based on this history.

Our experiments with a suite of floating-point applications (Section 5.1) show that values are either highly unpredictable or do not change because they are accessed by silent stores. For this reason, we do not pursue more complex value predictors. A more comprehensive investigation of value prediction under speculative parallelization for multiprocessors is beyond the scope of this paper.

4 IMPLEMENTATION

In this section, we show an implementation of the VPT and LDE modules. As an example, we implement them on top of the CC-NUMA speculation protocol and the speculation module presented in [4]. That module was called *Global Memory Disambiguation Table* (GMDT). In the following, we first describe the GMDT (Section 4.1) and then the VPT and LDE (Sections 4.2 and 4.3). We also outline implementations under other speculative CC-NUMA configurations (Section 4.4).

4.1 Global Memory Disambiguation Table (GMDT)

The GMDT tracks speculative accesses in a CC-NUMA somewhat like the directory tracks regular coherent accesses [4]. The GMDT is coupled with the directory and, like such, is physically distributed across nodes based on data address ranges. We show the GMDT as module 1 in Figure 1.

More specifically, the GMDT records the subset of lines that receive speculative exposed loads or stores from currently-active speculative threads (and stores from the non-speculative thread). The GMDT also knows about the relative ordering of the threads. While lines read speculatively can be displaced from caches, the GMDT cannot forget any of the exposed reads that took place. Unlike in [4], the GMDT design that we use tracks speculative accesses at the granularity of *lines*, not words.

The GMDT in a node is organized as a set-associative SRAM table where rows are dynamically allocated per memory line upon a speculative access (or a write by the non-speculative thread) [4]. This SRAM table is allowed to overflow into memory. Each row corresponds to a line (Figure 4). It contains a line address tag, a Valid bit, and a pair of Load and Store bits for the non-speculative thread and for each of the speculative threads that can be active at a time. The Load and Store bits indicate whether individual threads have issued an exposed load or a store, respectively, to the line. When a thread commits, all its cached dirty lines are written back to memory, and its GMDT bits are cleared and reassigned to another thread. If all Load and Store bits for an entire row become zero, the entry is deallocated.

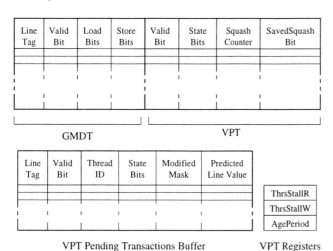

GMDT   VPT

VPT Pending Transactions Buffer   VPT Registers

Figure 4: Hardware structures for speculation (GMDT) and for learning (VPT, VPT Pending Transactions Buffer, and VPT Registers).

4.2   Violation Prediction Table (VPT)

The VPT is a table that keeps dynamic information on the memory lines that have recently been involved in potential or actual violations. The main VPT structure is an extension to every row of the GMDT (Figure 4). A VPT entry is allocated when its associated GMDT entry is allocated (Section 4.1). Initially, the VPT entry simply records that the line is in the Plain Speculative state of Figure 2. However, as potential or actual violations on the line occur, the VPT entry changes state as shown in Figure 2. The corresponding GMDT and VPT entries are routinely looked up when the directory controller receives a transaction that involves the line. Depending on the state of the VPT entry, the VPT triggers the actions discussed in Section 3.3. Finally, the associated GMDT and VPT entries are deallocated together, only when neither entry has any useful information. For the VPT entry, this occurs when the information about the involvement of the line in violations has aged out and the line is back in Plain Speculative state.

As shown in Figure 4, each row of the main VPT structure contains a *Valid* bit, 3 *State* bits that encode which state of Figure 2 the VPT entry is in, a *Squash* counter, and a *SavedSquash* bit. The last two will be described later. Overall, if we use 3 bits for the counter, a VPT row takes only 1 byte. We set the number of rows in the per-node GMDT and VPT to be 2048. Such a number was shown to be enough in [4], mostly because the compiler carefully marks the data that is accessed speculatively. As a result, the per-node VPT takes 2 Kbytes.

The VPT has two helper structures, namely the *VPT Registers* and the *VPT Pending Transactions Buffer* (Figure 4). The former contain three settable values called *ThrsStallR*, *ThrsStallW*, and

AgePeriod. They affect state transitions for VPT entries. We will discuss them later.

The VPT Pending Transactions Buffer allocates one entry for each exposed load in progress to a line that is in the VPT in state other than Plain Speculative. The entry contains temporary state for the transaction and is deallocated as soon as the transaction completes. Each entry effectively corresponds to one potential violation that has not yet been resolved. The buffer is implemented as a small SRAM table. When the buffer is full, accesses that can potentially cause violations cannot allocate entries and, therefore, are allowed to proceed unhindered. Fortunately, our experiments show that, at any time, only a few accesses that can potentially cause violations overlap with each other (Section 6).

In the following, we show how VPT entries change state, how Pending Transactions Buffer entries are allocated and deallocated, and how VPT entries age.

4.2.1   Changing State of VPT Entries

When a VPT entry is initially allocated, its State bits are set for the Plain Speculative state. As potential or actual violations on the line occur, possibly followed by squashes, the State bits in the entry change to follow the state diagram of Figure 2. At each state, the VPT entry triggers the corresponding actions discussed in Section 3.3.

Some of the state changes in Figure 2 depend on the number of squashes seen. For them, the VPT registers keep two squash thresholds, namely ThrsStallR and ThrsStallW (Figure 4). They keep the number of squashes that a line must cause before its VPT entry transitions from ValuePredict to Stall&Release, and from Stall&Release to Stall&Wait, respectively (Figure 2). At any time, the Squash counter in the VPT entry counts the number of squashes caused by the line. Consequently, when a VPT entry transitions to ValuePredict, the Squash counter is cleared. When the line causes a squash, the Squash counter is incremented and compared to ThrsStallR. If the counter exceeds the threshold, the VPT entry transitions to Stall&Release. A similar process occurs for ThrsStallW and the transition from Stall&Release to Stall&Wait.

4.2.2   Allocation & Deallocation of Buffer Entries

Every exposed load to a line that is in the VPT in state other than Plain Speculative triggers the allocation of an entry in the VPT Pending Transactions Buffer. The entry remains allocated until the transaction completes. As shown in Figure 4, an entry contains a line address tag, a *Valid* bit, the *Thread ID* of the consumer thread, 3 *State* bits for the state in Figure 2 that the corresponding VPT entry is in when the entry is allocated in the buffer, the *Modified Mask*, and the *Predicted Line Value*.

Consider first an entry in the buffer in state De-lay&Disambiguate. Every time that a predecessor commits and writes back to memory a dirty copy of the line, the Modified mask updates its bit-map according to the dirty words in the line. When the consumer thread is finally about to become non-speculative, the Modified mask contains a bit-map of all the modifications since the load. At this point, the mask is sent to the consumer node's LDE for late disambiguation and the buffer entry is deallocated.

When an entry in state ValuePredict is allocated in the buffer, the value of the line provided to the consumer is copied to the Predicted Line Value field. When the consumer thread is about to become non-speculative, the current value of the line in memory is compared to the value in the Predicted Line Value field. Words with mismatching values are marked in the Modified mask. The mask is then sent to the consumer node's LDE for late disambiguation like in Delay&Disambiguate and the buffer entry is deallocated.

An entry in state Stall&Release is kept in the buffer only until a committing predecessor writes back to memory a dirty copy of the line, and there are no other predecessors of the stalled thread with

48

dirty versions of the line in their caches. At that point, the entry is deallocated, allowing the original consumer load to proceed with the line read. Finally, an entry in state Stall&Wait is kept until the consumer thread is about to become non-speculative. Only then is the entry deallocated and the original consumer load allowed to proceed.

4.2.3 Aging VPT Entries

Given a VPT entry in state other than Plain Speculative, we want it to age back to Plain Speculative when the corresponding memory line is no longer involved in potential violations. The desired transitions are shown as dashed lines in Figure 2.

To support these transitions, we use the SavedSquash bit of each VPT entry (Figure 4). This bit is set every time that any of the mechanisms in our framework (Section 3.3) saves a violation on the corresponding line and, therefore, a squash. Consequently, at regular intervals, the directory controller scans all the local VPT entries. For a given entry, if the SavedSquash bit is clear, the state is set back to Plain Speculative. Otherwise, it means that at least one squash has been saved. In this case, the state is kept as it is and the SavedSquash bit is cleared. Note that, before doing this scanning pass, the directory controller checks the entries in the VPT Pending Transactions Buffer. Any memory lines that have entries there cannot have their VPT entries aged back to Plain Speculative state. The reason is that these buffer transactions are still pending under one mechanism.

The time interval between these scanning passes on the VPT is given by the value stored in the AgePeriod register. Such a value is given in terms of number of thread commits observed. The size of the interval determines how fast entries age.

We decide whether or not to set the SavedSquash bit every time that we deallocate an entry from the VPT Pending Transactions Buffer. At that point, an exposed load transaction is fully completed, and we can know whether our support indeed eliminated a squash relative to a plain speculative system. To know whether or not it did, we reuse the Modified mask of the buffer entry. Recall that, for entries in Delay&Disambiguate state, the mask records all the words in the line that are being updated by predecessors since the exposed load. To support aging, we simply use the Modified mask in the same way for all buffer entries, irrespective of their state. Then, right before the entry is about to be deallocated, we check the mask. If it is not clear, at least one predecessor wrote the line and, therefore, a squash would have been generated in a plain speculative system. Consequently, we set the SavedSquash bit. Otherwise, the bit is left unmodified. Note that, for entries in the ValuePredict state, after this operation is done, the mask is cleared and we proceed to use the mask as indicated in Section 4.2.2.

4.3 Late Disambiguation Engine (LDE)

The LDE is associated with the cache hierarchy of a node, although it is located outside the processor chip. It performs late disambiguation for exposed loads issued by the local node to lines that are in state Delay&Disambiguate or ValuePredict in their home VPT.

The LDE receives the Modified mask of any line for which it has to perform late disambiguation. The mask indicates what words in the line have potentially changed (in Delay&Disambiguate state) or indeed changed (in ValuePredict state) since the line was originally provided to the consumer thread. The LDE needs to compare the mask against the per-word exposed Load and Store bits that record the accesses of the consumer thread to the line. Such access bits are represented as module 2 in Figure 1 and are kept somewhere in the local cache hierarchy.

The LDE operation has two steps. First, it performs a bit-wise AND between the mask and the Load bits. If the result is not zero, the consumer has consumed incorrect data and has to be squashed. Second, the LDE performs a bit-wise AND between the mask and

the negated Store bits. If a resulting bit is set, the corresponding word was changed by predecessors and not overwritten by the consumer. Consequently, the word is stale and the LDE has to invalidate it from the local cache hierarchy.

While the LDE could perform the two AND operations as soon as it receives the mask, we choose a simpler implementation to minimize races with the local processor. Specifically, the LDE waits until the consumer thread finishes execution before performing the operations. After that, the thread can safely commit. Note that, in general, the access bits of a consumer thread need to be available after the thread has finished and until late disambiguation can be performed. In addition, the bits need to be accessible from outside the processor chip. To accomplish this, these bits may be temporarily buffered in the LDE.

4.4 Implementation Variations

The implementation that we have presented for our framework implicitly assumes the speculation protocol proposed in [4]. In this section, we briefly outline some changes necessary to accommodate the framework to other protocols.

Some scalable speculation protocols keep the speculation information only in the cache hierarchy of the processing nodes [23]. A thread communicates a commit or a squash operation only to its immediate successor. There is no speculation module attached to the directory controller such as the GMDT that knows about all such operations.

In such systems, the VPT will be coupled with the speculation engines in the cache hierarchies of the processing nodes. This VPT must be made to work with only the partial information available locally. For example, nodes that are not involved in the squash may not learn that the line is causing violations. Similarly, aging may be based on fairly limited information about the line's behavior. Consequently, our learning heuristics may have to change.

Other scalable protocols do not eagerly merge the state of committing threads with main memory. For example, dirty lines are not written back to main memory as the thread commits [18]. Instead, they are lazily merged with main memory on demand, often on a cache displacement. The implementation that we presented here relied on eager write-backs at commit time to quickly resolve pending exposed loads.

In such lazy systems, the VPT can be extended to proactively request write-backs from committing threads. These write-backs are for lines that have pending transactions in the VPT Pending Transactions Buffer and may be dirty in the cache of the committing thread. In this way, the few lines that are actively experiencing potential violations are written back eagerly at commit time, while all the other lines are written back lazily.

5 EVALUATION METHODOLOGY

5.1 Applications

To evaluate our framework, we choose one Perfect Club application (*TRACK*), two SPECfp2000 applications (*EQUAKE* and *WUPWISE*), and two HPF-2 applications (*EULER* and *DSMC3D*). The input sets used are the standard ones except for *EQUAKE* and *WUPWISE*, which use the *train* inputs. All applications spend a large fraction of their time on loops that cannot be fully analyzed by state-of-the-art compilers. The reason for the non-analyzability is that the dependence structure is either too complex or dependent on input data. Specifically, the codes often have array accesses with subscripted subscripts, procedure calls inside the loops, and complex control flow. Consequently, we use speculative parallelization for these loops. We use the Polaris parallelizing compiler [3] to identify and instrument such loops, mark the speculative variables, and privatize variables whenever safe and convenient. All the loops

Application	Loop to Parallelize	% of Seq. Time	Avg. Iterations per Invocation	RAW Dependences
TRACK	nlfilt_300	58	502	Same–word and False
DSMC3D	move3_100	41	758972	Same–word and False
EULER	dflux_[100,200] psmoo_20 eflux_[100,200,300]	90	2494	False
EQUAKE	smvp_1195	45	7294	Same–word
WUPWISE	muldeo_200' muldoe_200'	67	8000	Same–word and False

Table 1: Characteristics of the applications studied.

Processor Param.	Value
Issue width	4
Instruction window size	64
No. functional units (Int,FP,Ld/St)	3,2,2
No. renaming registers (Int,FP)	32,32
No. pending memory ops. (Ld,St)	8,16

Memory Param.	Value
L1,L2,VC size	32KB,1MB,64KB
L1,L2,VC assoc.	2–way,4–way, 8–way
L1,L2,VC line size	64B,64B,64B
L1,L2,VC latency	1,12,12 cycles
L1,L2,VC banks	2,3,2
Local memory latency	75 cycles
2–hop memory latency	290 cycles
3–hop memory latency	360 cycles
GMDT size	2K entries
GMDT assoc.	8–way
GMDT/VPT lookup	20 cycles
Pend. Trans. Buffer size	128 entries
Pend. Trans. Buffer scan	3 cycles/entry

Table 2: Parameters of the 16-processor CC-NUMA architecture modeled.

considered exhibit cross-iteration dependences, either to the same word or to different words of the same memory line (false dependences).

For each application, Table 1 shows the loops that we attempt to parallelize speculatively, the fraction of the sequential execution time taken by these loops on a Sun server excluding initialization and I/O, the average number of iterations executed per loop invocation, and the type of cross-iteration RAW dependences that exist.

These loops are dynamically scheduled into processors. The loops in *TRACK*, *DSMC3D*, *EULER*, and *EQUAKE* are unrolled three times to exploit data locality. In the case of *WUPWISE*, we obtain loops muldeo_200' and muldoe_200' by merging the three outer loops in loop nests muldeo_200 and muldoe_200, respectively. For that, it is necessary to hoist some induction variables and compute the loop indices appropriately, which is within the capabilities of compilers[1].

In Section 6, we present results and speedups for the loops in Table 1 only. We do not estimate overall application speedups because they are dependent on the efficiency of the parallel execution of the rest of the code.

5.2 Architecture Simulated

The evaluation is based on execution-driven simulations. Our simulation environment uses an extension to MINT [27] that includes a superscalar processor model [9], and supports dynamic spawn, squash, restart, and retire of light-weight threads. The processor model is a 4-issue dynamic superscalar with register renaming, branch prediction, and non-blocking memory operations. Some of its parameters are shown in the left portion of Table 2.

The memory system models the speculative CC-NUMA of Figure 1. However, as in [4], each node is a speculative chip multiprocessor (CMP). Each CMP includes 4 processors with their private L1 caches and an on-chip speculation engine that keeps speculation state at the granularity of words. This on-chip speculation engine only triggers squashes on same-word out-of-order RAW dependences inside the chip [4]. These squashes are beyond the control of the VPT and, therefore, not amenable to the mechanisms of our framework. Nevertheless, they are visible to the VPT and do increment the Squash counter like the squashes due to dependences across chips.

Each node in the machine has a CMP, an L2 cache, a victim cache (VC) for dirty lines evicted from L2, one local GMDT, VPT, and LDE module, a portion of the global memory and directory,

---
[1]Recently, as part of the SPEC OMP parallelization effort [2], loops similar to muldeo_200 and muldoe_200 have been parallelized with help from hand analysis. Such analysis is still beyond the capabilities of automatic parallelization alone.

and a network controller. The local cache hierarchy holds the per-word Load and Store access bits. However, it discards the Load access bits immediately when a thread finishes, in order to reallocate these bits to a newly-scheduled thread [4]. Thus, the local LDE is augmented to capture this information when a thread finishes, for possible disambiguation when the thread finally becomes non-speculative. We dynamically assign iterations to CMP nodes in chunks of four consecutive iterations [4]. In this way, the chunk appears to the GMDT and VPT as a single bigger thread, no different than if a single processor per node was used and assigned a block of unrolled iterations. The machine is equipped with a DASH-like directory-based cache coherence protocol and the GMDT-based speculation protocol outlined in Section 4.1 and discussed in [4]. For simplicity, when a thread is squashed, all its successors are also squashed.

The right part of Table 2 lists the main parameters used. L1, L2, VC, and memory latencies are round-trip times from the processor, without contention. Contention is modeled everywhere except in the interconnect, where a fixed time is assumed for each hop. We model all protocol transactions and messages in detail, as well as all GMDT, VPT, and LDE overheads. The GMDT and VPT Pending Transactions Buffer parameters in the table correspond to a single node. In all experiments, we use the same static round-robin page allocation policy across the nodes. Our *Baseline* system corresponds to a CC-NUMA with *per-line* speculation state in the GMDT. The machine has 4 CMPs, for a total of 16 processors. Unless otherwise indicated, we set ThrsStallR, ThrsStallW, and AgePeriod to 1, 4, and 4, respectively. Note that an AgePeriod of one corresponds to one commit seen by the VPT, which in our case is the commit of a chunk of 4 iterations.

6 EVALUATION

To evaluate the framework, we first examine the squash behavior of the applications. Then, we examine the mechanisms in the framework individually and in combination.

6.1 Squash Behavior

To assess the potential of the mechanisms in the framework, we characterize the squash behavior of the applications on the *Baseline* architecture. For each application, we count the number of squashes induced by each memory line. Squashes are classified based on their source: false dependences, same-word dependences where the store generates a new value (non-silent), and same-word dependences due to a silent store.

Figure 5 shows the squash counts. For each application, the figure groups the memory lines into those that generate 1, 2-10,

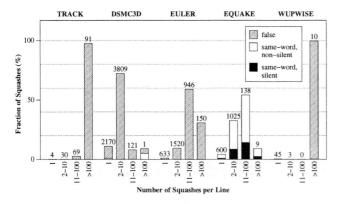

Figure 5: Distribution of the number of times that the same memory line causes a squash in *Baseline*. The numbers on top of the bars are the number of different lines in each bin.

11-100, and more than 100 squashes during the execution of the application. The actual number of lines in each bin is shown on top of each bar. The height of each bar is the fraction of total squashes in the application that fall in that bin. For example, in *TRACK*, 91 memory lines cause more than 100 squashes each, and their combined effect accounts for nearly 100% of the total squashes in the application.

The figure shows that, except in *EQUAKE*, the large majority of squashes are due to false dependences. Consequently, the Delay&Disambiguate mechanism has the potential to save many squashes. We also see that, of the squashes due to same-word dependences in *EQUAKE*, about one quarter are caused by silent stores. Consequently, the ValuePredict mechanism with the simple last-value prediction scheme that we use also has the potential to be beneficial. The figure also shows that, in general, individual memory lines cause many squashes. The best examples are *WUPWISE* and *TRACK*. Consequently, learning what lines cause squashes and then applying our mechanisms looks generally promising, the start-up cost of learning is likely to be amortized. Finally while it looks like the squashes are caused by a large number of lines, our experiments show that the squashes caused by a line are often clustered in time. Therefore, at any time, many fewer lines are actively involved in squashes. As a result, we may not need large VPT Pending Transactions Buffers.

6.2 Plain Speculation

We first compare a system with per-line speculation state in the GMDT and none of our mechanisms, to a system with full per-word speculation state in the GMDT. We call these systems *Baseline* and *Word*, respectively. Per-line schemes can suffer from false sharing. The latter can create false dependences and, therefore, squashes. However, per-word schemes tend to induce more traffic. Indeed, an invalidation or a dependence-checking message for one word does not usually eliminate the need for a similar message for another word in the same line.

The first two bars for each application in Figure 6 compare the execution time of the applications on these systems. For each application, the bars are normalized to *Baseline* and broken down into the following categories: execution of instructions and stall due to memory accesses (*Busy+Mem*); overhead associated with squash operations, including draining pending transactions and waiting for synchronization messages (*Squash*); other speculative execution overheads [4] plus conventional pipeline hazards (*Ovhd+Other*); and stall on exposed loads forced by our Stall&Release and Stall&Wait mechanisms (*Stall*). Note that the total cost of squashes shows up as *Squash* time and as additional *Busy+Mem* and *Ovhd+Other* time due to the reexecution of

threads. The numbers on top of the bars show the speedups over the sequential execution.

The figure shows that *Baseline* is usually much slower than *Word*. The large slowdowns of *Baseline* in *TRACK*, *DSMC3D*, *EULER*, and *WUPWISE* are mostly due to the additional squashes caused by false sharing. As shown in Figure 5, the squashes in these four applications come mostly from false dependences. Consequently, they appear in *Baseline* but not in *Word*. The higher traffic of *Word*, while probably slowing down the applications to some extent, has a much lower impact.

EQUAKE has only same-word violations and, therefore, the number of squashes in *Baseline* and *Word* is about the same. These squashes are very frequent and determine the execution time. Both *Baseline* and *Word* take the same time to execute, showing slowdowns with respect to sequential execution.

6.3 Individual Mechanisms

6.3.1 Delayed Disambiguation Only

We now augment *Baseline* with support for our Delay&Disambiguate mechanism only. The resulting system is called *Delay*. Such a system only implements states *A* and *B* in Figure 2. Specifically, once a VPT entry gets to Delay&Disambiguate state, it remains there unless it ages back to Plain Speculative state. For comparison, we also implement an ideal system called *Oracle_Delay*. Such a system is like *Delay* except that a VPT entry in Delay&Disambiguate state will not perform the actions for delayed disambiguation (Section 3.3.1) if the end result is that the thread will later get squashed anyway. Instead, it will trigger the squash immediately, as soon as the second access in the RAW dependence is received.

Figure 6 shows the performance of *Delay* and *Oracle_Delay*. We focus first on the applications with mostly false dependences (*TRACK*, *DSMC3D*, *EULER*, and *WUPWISE*). These applications are sped-up by *Delay* significantly. The reason is that the Delay&Disambiguate support eliminates practically all squashes. This can be seen from the negligible *Squash* time in *Delay*. As a result, *Delay* is much faster than *Baseline* and, typically, even faster than *Word*. It outperforms *Word* because it suffers no more squashes than *Word* and creates less traffic than it.

For these same applications, *Oracle_Delay* is no better than *Delay*. The reason is that most squashes come from false dependences and, therefore, *Oracle_Delay* will typically work as *Delay*.

For *EQUAKE*, *Delay* outperforms both *Baseline* and *Word*. This is unintuitive since all squashes in *EQUAKE* come from same-word dependences. We would expect *Delay* to be slower than *Baseline* because it delays the resolution of transactions that will cause squashes anyway.

In fact, in our architecture, delaying transaction resolution can help in applications with many dependences across threads. To see why, recall that our architecture uses CMP nodes and that dependences between threads running on different processors of the same CMP are not subject to our squash-removing mechanisms. Consequently, consider a thread with two dependences, one with a far-away thread in another CMP and one with a close-by thread in the same CMP. In *Baseline* and *Word*, as soon as the inter-chip dependence is detected, the thread is eagerly squashed. Then, the thread is re-started, only to be later squashed by the intra-chip violation. In *Delay*, the resolution of the inter-chip dependence is delayed. Eventually, the intra-chip violation will trigger a squash, therefore avoiding the need for the first squash. The result is fewer squashes and less overhead. This is why *Delay* outperforms both *Baseline* and *Word*. Note that *Delay* still has significant *Squash* time.

Oracle_Delay performs no different than *Delay* in *EQUAKE*. The reason is that inter-chip dependences do not end up causing

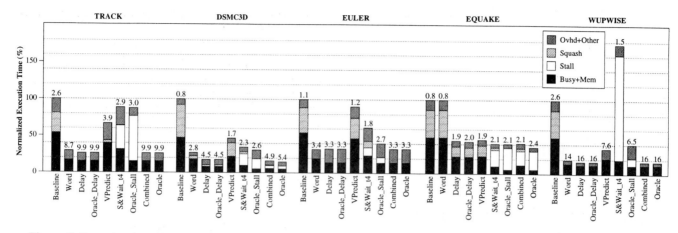

Figure 6: Execution time of the applications on different systems. The numbers on top of the bars are the speedups of the applications over the sequential execution.

Application	Delay&Disambiguate		Stall&Release (ThrsStallR=1)		
	Selectivity (%)	Buffer entries Avg. / Max.	Coverage (%)	Selectivity (%)	Buffer entries Avg. / Max.
TRACK	100.0	0.6 / 9	85.9	100.0	1.5 / 12
DSMC3D	99.8	0.9 / 14	89.3	97.1	1.8 / 12
EULER	100.0	4.1 / 77	74.2	100.0	0.7 / 12
EQUAKE	99.8	0.2 / 15	76.7	100.0	2.1 / 12
WUPWISE	99.1	0.2 / 3	97.8	100.0	3.3 / 15
Average	99.7	1.2 / 23.6	84.8	99.4	1.9 / 12.6

Table 3: Performance and usage statistics for different systems. The numbers for the VPT Pending Transactions Buffer are *per node*.

squashes and, as a result, *Oracle_Delay* follows *Delay*. Moreover, intra-chip squashes are outside the control of *Oracle_Delay*.

Finally, Table 3 shows some statistics that give insight into the behavior of *Delay*. The second column shows the selectivity of its Delay&Disambiguate mechanism. The selectivity is always close to 100%, which means that there are very few late squashes. This is consistent with the fact that *Delay* and *Oracle_Delay* have practically the same performance.

The third column in the table shows that the Delay&Disambiguate mechanism keeps very few entries in the VPT Pending Transactions Buffer at a time. On average, the buffer in a node keeps only 1.2 entries. This means that, at any given time, there are only very few concurrent transactions to lines being monitored for squashes.

6.3.2 Value Prediction Only

We augment *Baseline* with support for the ValuePredict mechanism only. Such a system only has states *A* and *C* in Figure 2. For a VPT entry to transition to the ValuePredict state, the VPT must first observe a squash to the line. As usual, the VPT entry remains in this state until it ages back to Plain Speculative. The resulting system is called *VPredict*.

Note that the simple value predictor that we use would not strictly need to squash to transition to ValuePredict: the value predicted is simply the current version of the line in memory and we can save it in the VPT Pending Transactions Buffer at the time that the potential violation is detected. However, we choose to need one squash to assess the impact of the start-up cost of a more realistic

value predictor. Such a predictor would need to see more than one value before predicting.

Figure 6 shows the performance of *VPredict*. In all the applications, *VPredict* performs better than *Baseline*. The reason is that it intrinsically supports delayed disambiguation of false dependences. However, it does not compare favorably to *Word* or *Delay*. The reason is that, in *VPredict*, each VPT entry needs one squash to transition out of the Plain Speculative state. These additional squashes make *VPredict* much slower than *Word* and *Delay* in *TRACK*, *DSMC3D*, *EULER*, and *WUPWISE*.

For the application with only true dependences and some silent stores (*EQUAKE*), *VPredict* performs much better than *Word*, but no faster than *Delay*. *VPredict* would be able to eliminate some squashes due to inter-chip dependences. However, it has little opportunity to succeed because threads are often squashed before the late disambiguation takes place. Its major effect, like *Delay*, comes from simply deferring the squashes due to inter-chip dependences until another squash occurs. Overall, therefore, we do not see any advantages of *VPredict* over *Delay* for our combination of applications and architecture.

6.3.3 Stall Only

We augment *Baseline* with support for the Stall&Release mechanism only, and with support for both the Stall&Release and Stall&Wait mechanisms. We call the former *S&Release* and the latter *S&Wait*. In these schemes, a VPT entry transitions from Plain Speculative to Stall&Release when the line has caused ThrsStallR squashes. In *S&Wait*, the entry further transitions to Stall&Wait when ThrsStallW additional squashes occur. For *S&Release*, we use a ThrsStallR of 1 and 4 (*S&Release_t1* and *S&Release_t4*). For *S&Wait*, we use a ThrsStallR of 1 and a ThrsStallW of 1 and 4 (*S&Wait_t1* and *S&Wait_t4*).

Figure 7 shows the execution times of the applications on these systems normalized to *Baseline*. We see that these systems eliminate most of the *Squash* time in *Baseline*. However, they trade it for the *Stall* category. This is because threads eliminate squashes by waiting. In general, these systems are faster than *Baseline* because many of the squashes have disappeared. However, in some cases such as *WUPWISE*, the performance is much worse. In *WUPWISE*, threads are very long, and the relative position of the conflicting loads and stores is such that trading off squashes for stall time hurts performance. Depending on the parameters used, stall-only mechanisms can backfire and lead to slowdowns compared to *Baseline*.

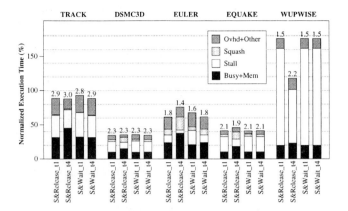

Figure 7: Performance of the Stall&Release and Stall&Wait mechanisms alone. The numbers on top of the bars are the speedups over sequential execution.

In general, these schemes tend to have good coverage and selectivity, and use the VPT Pending Transactions Buffer little. This is confirmed for *S&Release_t1* in the last three columns of Table 3.

Comparing the different schemes for the applications that improve, we see that they tend to have similar performance. However, *S&Wait* schemes tend to be faster than *S&Release*. Among the *S&Release* schemes, a low ThrsStallR (*S&Release_t1*) seems to be better. This suggests reacting fast to squashes as they initially occur. Among the *S&Wait* schemes, a high ThrsStallW (*S&Wait_t4*) seems to be better. This suggests aggressively releasing threads despite occasional squashes. Overall, therefore, *S&Wait_t4* seems to be best.

Finally, we place *S&Wait_t4* as the sixth bar in Figure 6. We can see that, in most applications, this system is not competitive with *Word* or *Delay*. Relative to these systems, *S&Wait_t4* suffers from much *Stall* time. The exception is *EQUAKE*, where *S&Wait_t4* is slightly faster than the other schemes. In applications with squashes due to same-word dependences, *S&Wait_t4* may have an edge over all the other schemes.

For comparison purposes, Figure 6 also includes an ideal stall-only system called *Oracle_Stall*. This is an oracle system that only stalls a thread when the exposed load would cause a squash (due to a false or a same-word dependence) and releases the thread as soon as the correct version is produced. Except in two applications, the performance of *S&Wait_t4* is close to this ideal system.

6.4 Combining all Mechanisms

Finally, we augment *Baseline* with support for our complete framework as shown in Figure 2. The resulting system is called *Combined*. For each application, it is shown as the last but one bar in Figure 6.

The figure shows that *Combined* is always as fast, or faster than, each of the systems with only a single mechanism. Furthermore, it successfully adapts to the behavior of the application. Indeed, consider first the applications with no or very few same-word dependences, namely *TRACK*, *EULER*, and *WUPWISE*. For these cases, VPT entries rarely transition to the ValuePredict and Stall states. The figure shows *Combined* to perform as well as *Delay*.

For applications with only same-word dependences where value prediction often fails, such as *EQUAKE*, VPT entries under *Combined* transition to the Stall&Wait state. As a result, Figure 6 shows that *Combined* performs as well as *S&Wait_t4*. More interestingly, consider applications with a mix of same-word and false dependences such as *DSMC3D*. In this case, VPT entries adapt to the dependence patterns, and *Combined* is shown to outperform both

Delay and *S&Wait_t4*.

Overall, to speed up a wide range of applications we recommend adding our complete framework to *Baseline*. For applications with mostly false dependences, the system will run as well as a system with only Delay&Disambiguate support. For applications with same-word dependences where value prediction often fails the system will run as well as with only Stall&Wait support. Finally, for applications that have mixed dependence patterns, the framework will adapt and perform better than all the other systems. On average, *Combined* runs the applications 4.3 times as fast as *Baseline*. Moreover, the average execution time of the applications is 23% lower than under *Word*.

Finally, the last bar of each application in Figure 6 (*Oracle*) corresponds to an ideal environment. This system is like *Combined* with full knowledge of all dependences. Therefore, *Oracle* can appropriately decide when to use delayed disambiguation, predict a silent store, stall a thread, and release a stalled thread. From the figure, we see that *Combined* always gets very close to *Oracle*. Consequently, we conclude that the performance of *Combined* is very close to its upper bound.

7 RELATED WORK

There are many proposals for architectures that support speculative thread-level parallelization [1, 4, 6, 8, 10, 12, 18, 22, 23, 25, 26, 32]. We focus on directory-based systems [4, 18, 23, 32].

While we use a framework of mechanisms to eliminate squashes under a per-line protocol, the other directory-based systems have tried other approaches to limit the impact of data dependence violations. Specifically, some systems provide per-word protocol support [4, 32], while another employs compiler-generated synchronization instructions plus some local per-word access information [23].

The system in [18] uses support for *high-level access patterns*. This support performs speculation at the per-line granularity when applications have no dependences. Consequently, under these conditions, it works like our system. However, when applications exhibit false dependences, the support in [18] simply reverts to a per-word protocol for lines exhibiting such dependences. Our system, instead, thanks to the Delay&Disambiguate mechanism, continues to operate with a per-line protocol even for these lines. While we save traffic over [18] for these lines, we do not expect our system to have a noticeable performance advantage unless many lines exhibit false dependences at the same time. However, our main advantage is that we only need to support a per-line protocol.

Dynamic prediction and synchronization of load-store pairs in a uniprocessor has been widely investigated in the past (e.g., [5, 21, 31]). Dynamic prediction and synchronization of cross-thread dependences has been investigated in the context of a tightly-coupled multiscalar processor in [14] and, concurrently with our work, in the context of a chip multiprocessor in [24]. Our solution and those of these two works are different. Indeed, we focus on a distributed directory-based multiprocessor. Moreover, while [14] uses learning mechanisms based on program counter values, we use mechanisms based on memory line addresses.

Value prediction within a single thread of control has been investigated in the past (e.g., [11, 29]). Value prediction in the context of multiple concurrent threads has been investigated in [1, 13, 24, 30]. These works have concentrated on integer applications and, except for [24], rely on little compiler support to eliminate largely statically-predictable values. We investigate value prediction for floating-point applications and use the compiler to eliminate easily-predictable values and to limit prediction to memory locations. We are then left with hard-to-predict floating-point values and our mechanism does not achieve the same level of gains as these other works.

8 CONCLUSIONS

We have proposed a new framework of hardware mechanisms to eliminate most squashes due to data dependences under speculative parallelization. The framework works by learning and predicting cross-thread violations. It is suited for directory-based multiprocessors with protocols that track speculative memory accesses at the system level with the coarse granularity of memory lines.

Simulations of a 16-processor machine showed that the framework is very effective. It can quickly and accurately track the violation behavior of applications and gets very close to an oracle system. We have taken a CC-NUMA that tracks memory accesses at the system level with the granularity of a 64-byte line and added our framework. The resulting system runs a set of applications with dependence violations on average 4.3 times faster. Moreover, the system is even 23% faster than a CC-NUMA that tracks accesses at the system level with the fine granularity of a word – a sophisticated system that is not compatible with mainstream cache coherence protocols.

For numerical applications with mostly false dependences such as ours, we found that the delayed disambiguation mechanism is responsible for most of the performance gains. Moreover, whenever same-word dependences occur, the stall and wait mechanism can complement it and improve performance. Finally, for our applications and architecture, a simple value prediction mechanism does not improve performance much.

REFERENCES

[1] H. Akkary and M. A. Driscoll. "A Dynamic Multithreading Processor." *Intl. Symp. on Microarchitecture*, pages 226-236, December 1998.

[2] V. Aslot, M. Domeika, R. Eigenmann, G. Gaertner, W. B. Jones, and B. Parady. "SPEComp: A New Benchmark Suite for Measuring Parallel Computer Performance." *Wksp. on OpenMP Applications and Tools*, pages 1-10, July 2001.

[3] W. Blume, R. Doallo, R. Eigenmann, J. Grout, J. Hoeflinger, T. Lawrence, J. Lee, D. Padua, Y. Paek, B. Pottenger, L. Rauchwerger, and P. Tu. "Advanced Program Restructuring for High-Performance Computers with Polaris." *IEEE Computer*, Vol. 29, No. 12, pages 78-82, December 1996.

[4] M. Cintra, J. F. Martínez, and J. Torrellas. "Architectural Support for Scalable Speculative Parallelization in Shared-Memory Multiprocessors." *Intl. Symp. on Computer Architecture*, pages 13-24, June 2000.

[5] G. Chrysos and J. Emer. "Memory Dependence Prediction Using Store Sets." *Intl. Symp. on Computer Architecture*, pages 142-153, June 1998.

[6] S. Gopal, T. Vijaykumar, J. Smith, and G. Sohi. "Speculative Versioning Cache." *Intl. Symp. on High Performance Computer Architecture*, pages 195-205, February 1998.

[7] M. Gupta and R. Nim. "Techniques for Run-Time Parallelization of Loops." *Supercomputing*, November 1998.

[8] L. Hammond, M. Wiley, and K. Olukotun. "Data Speculation Support for a Chip Multiprocessor." *Intl. Conf. on Architectural Support for Programming Languages and Operating Systems*, pages 58-69, October 1998.

[9] V. Krishnan and J. Torrellas. "A Direct-Execution Framework for Fast and Accurate Simulation of Superscalar Processors." *Intl. Conf. on Parallel Architectures and Compilation Techniques*, pages 286-293, October 1998.

[10] V. Krishnan and J. Torrellas. "A Chip-Multiprocessor Architecture with Speculative Multithreading." *IEEE Trans. on Computers, Special Issue on Multithreaded Architectures*, Vol. 48, No. 9, pages 866-880, September 1999.

[11] M. H. Lipasti and J. P. Shen. "Exceeding the Dataflow Limit via Value Prediction." *Intl. Symp. on Microarchitecture*, pages 226-237, December 1996.

[12] P. Marcuello and A. González. "Clustered Speculative Multithreaded Processors." *Intl. Conf. on Supercomputing*, pages 365-372, June 1999.

[13] P. Marcuello, J. Tubella, and A. González. "Value Prediction for Speculative Multithreaded Architectures." *Intl. Symp. on Microarchitecture*, pages 230-237, December 1999.

[14] A. Moshovos, S. E. Breach, T. N. Vijaykumar, and G. S. Sohi. "Dynamic Speculation and Synchronization of Data Dependences." *Intl. Symp. on Computer Architecture*, pages 181-193, June 1997.

[15] C.-L. Ooi, S. W. Kim, I. Park, R. Eigenmann, B. Falsafi, and T. N. Vijaykumar. "Multiplex: Unifying Conventional and Speculative Thread-Level Parallelism on a Chip Multiprocessor." *Intl. Conf. on Supercomputing*, pages 368-380, June 2001.

[16] J. Oplinger, D. Heine, and M. Lam. "In Search of Speculative Thread-level Parallelism." *Intl. Conf. on Parallel Architectures and Compilation Techniques*, pages 303-313, October 1999.

[17] S.-T. Pan, K. So, and J. T. Rahmeh. "Improving the Accuracy of Dynamic Branch Prediction Using Branch Correlation." *Intl. Conf. on Architectural Support for Programming Languages and Operating Systems*, pages 76-84, October 1992.

[18] M. Prvulovic, M. J. Garzaran, L. Rauchwerger, and J. Torrellas. "Removing Architectural Bottlenecks to the Scalability of Speculative Parallelization." *Intl. Symp. on Computer Architecture*, pages 204-215, June 2001.

[19] L. Rauchwerger and D. Padua. "The LRPD Test: Speculative Run-Time Parallelization of Loops with Privatization and Reduction Parallelization." *SIGPLAN Conf. on Programming Language Design and Implementation*, pages 218-232, June 1995.

[20] P. Rundberg and P. Stenström. "A Software Approach to Thread-Level Data Dependence Speculation for Multiprocessors." *Ninth ISCA Wksp. on Scalable Shared Memory Multiprocessors*, June 2000.

[21] Y. Sazeides and J. E. Smith. "The Predictability of Data Values." *Intl. Symp. on Microarchitecture*, pages 248-258, December 1997.

[22] G. Sohi, S. Breach, and T. Vijaykumar. "Multiscalar Processors." *Intl. Symp. on Computer Architecture*, pages 414-425, June 1995.

[23] J. G. Steffan, C. B. Colohan, A. Zhai, and T. C. Mowry. "A Scalable Approach to Thread-Level Speculation." *Intl. Symp. on Computer Architecture*, pages 1-12, June 2000.

[24] J. G. Steffan, C. B. Colohan, A. Zhai, and T. C. Mowry. "Improving Value Communication for Thread-Level Speculation." *Intl. Symp. on High-Performance Computer Architecture*, February 2002.

[25] M. Tremblay. "MAJC: Microprocessor Architecture for Java Computing." Presentation at *Hot Chips*, August 1999.

[26] J.-Y. Tsai, J. Huang, C. Amlo, D. Lilja, and P.-C. Yew. "The Superthreaded Processor Architecture." *IEEE Trans. on Computers, Special Issue on Multithreaded Architectures*, Vol. 48, No. 9, pages 881-902, September 1999.

[27] J. Veenstra and R. Fowler. "A Front End for Efficient Simulation of Shared-Memory Multiprocessors." *Intl. Wksp. on Modeling, Analysis, and Simulation of Computer and Telecommunication Systems*, pages 201-207, January 1994.

[28] T. N. Vijaykumar and G. Sohi. "Task Selection for a Multiscalar Processor." *Intl. Symp. on Microarchitecture*, pages 81-92, December 1998.

[29] K. Wang and M. Franklin. "Highly Accurate Data Value Prediction Using Hybrid Predictors." *Intl. Symp. on Microarchitecture*, December 1997.

[30] F. Warg and P. Stenström. "Limits on Speculative Module-Level Parallelism in Imperative and Object-Oriented Programs on CMP Platforms." *Intl. Conf. on Parallel Architectures and Compilation Techniques*, pages 221-230, September 2001.

[31] A. Yoaz, M. Erez, R. Ronen, and S. Jourdan. "Speculation Techniques for Improving Load Related Instruction Scheduling." *Intl. Symp. on Computer Architecture*, pages 42-53, May 1999.

[32] Y. Zhang, L. Rauchwerger, and J. Torrellas. "Hardware for Speculative Run-time Parallelization in Distributed Shared-Memory Multiprocessors." *Intl. Symp. on High-Performance Computer Architecture*, pages 161-173, February 1998.

Thread-Spawning Schemes for Speculative Multithreading

Pedro Marcuello and Antonio González

Departament d'Arquitectura de Computadors
Universitat Politècnica de Catalunya
Jordi Girona, 1-3 Mòdul D6
08034 Barcelona, Spain

{pmarcue,antonio}@ac.upc.es

Abstract

Speculative multithreading has been recently proposed to boost performance by means of exploiting thread-level parallelism in applications difficult to parallelize. The performance of these processors heavily depends on the partitioning policy used to split the program into threads. Previous work uses heuristics to spawn speculative threads based on easily-detectable program constructs such as loops or subroutines. In this work we propose a profile-based mechanism to divide programs into threads by searching for those parts of the code that have certain features that could benefit from potential thread-level parallelism.

Our profile-based spawning scheme is evaluated on a Clustered Speculative Multithreaded Processor and results show large performance benefits. When the proposed spawning scheme is compared with traditional heuristics, we outperform them by almost 20%. When a realistic value predictor and a 8-cycle thread initialization penalty is considered, the performance difference between them is maintained. The speed-up over a single thread execution is higher than 5x for a 16-thread-unit processor and close to 2x for a 4-thread-unit processor.

1. Introduction

Speculation is a well-known technique used to improve processor performance. These mechanisms have been widely used in order to reduce the penalties of both control and data dependences. Also, diminishing returns of instruction-level parallelism are boosting the use of alternative techniques to increase performance. Combining thread-level parallelism and instruction-level parallelism is an approach that has been considered by several processor vendors. These types of processors are usually referred to as multithreaded processors. The task of dividing programs into threads that will be executed in parallel is rather straight-forward for regular or numeric applications, and the current compiler technology can perform it efficiently. However, this task becomes hard for irregular and non-numerical programs; compilers usually fail to discover the potential thread-level parallelism that could be effectively exploited in this class of applications.

Speculative multithreading is a promising approach to solving this problem. In these systems, threads that may be control and data dependent on previous threads are speculatively spawned and executed. Relaxing the constraints to spawn a thread results in a significant increase of opportunities to exploit thread-level parallelism [2][15][16], even though, obviously, roll-back mechanisms are needed in case of misspeculations.

The performance of speculative multithreaded architectures is very sensitive to the policies that determine which parts of the code are executed by speculative threads and when they start execution. We refer to this criteria as the *thread-spawning policy*. In several architectures such as Multiscalar[5][21], the SPSM architecture[4] and the Superthreaded[24], the compiler is responsible for dividing the program into speculative threads. Alternatively, the Dynamic Multithreaded Processor[1] and the Clustered Speculative Multithreaded Processor[12][13] rely only on hardware techniques; programs are partitioned at run-time. The thread-spawning policies proposed so far for speculative multithreaded architectures are very simple. They are based on assigning speculative threads to common program constructs such as loop iterations, loop continuations and subroutine continuations.

A thread-spawning operation is identified by two instructions: 1) the spawning instruction that creates a new thread when it is reached, and 2) the spawned instruction where the speculative thread starts its execution. These instructions are referred to the spawning point and the control quasi-independent point, respectively.

In this paper we propose a general framework for identifying effective spawning and control quasi-independent points in any sequential program. Thus, a profile-based analysis is done in order to find the best sections of the code to create speculative threads depending on several requirements that they should match. This approach tries to identify pairs of spawning and control quasi-independent points in such a way that the execution of the control quasi-independent point is very likely once the spawning point is reached. Most of the instructions below the control quasi-independent point should be independent of the instructions between the spawning point and the control quasi-independent point. We show that this thread-spawning policy is more effective than previous schemes, which they are based on just exploiting common program constructs.

The rest of the paper is organized as follows. Section 2 reviews the related work. The profile analysis is described in Section 3. Section 4 shows the performance potential of the profile-based spawning scheme and evaluates it under realistic assumptions, and finally Section 5 summarizes the main conclusions of the work.

2.   Related Work

Several microarchitectural proposals for exploiting speculative thread-level parallelism have been recently proposed. The Expandable Split Window Paradigm [5] and its follow-up work, the Multiscalar Processor [21] were the pioneer works on this topic. In that architecture, the compiler is responsible for dividing the code into tasks. The policy used by the compiler is based on heuristics that try to minimize the data dependences among active threads or maximize the workload balance, among other compiler criteria [25].

In some other proposals such as the SPSM [4] and the Superthreaded [24] architectures, the compiler is also responsible for splitting the program into threads. But in both cases, threads are assumed to be loop iterations instead of the more complex analysis performed by the Multiscalar compiler.

On the other hand, some other architectures try to exploit thread-level parallelism speculating on threads dynamically created by the processor without any compiler assistance. The Speculative Multithreaded Processor [12] and the Clustered Speculative Multithreaded Processor [13] identify loops at run-time and simultaneously execute iterations in different thread units.

In the same way, the Dynamic Multithreaded Processor [1] relies only on hardware mechanisms to divide a sequential program into threads. In this case, it speculates on loop and subroutine continuations instead of loop iterations. Moreover, the architectural design of the processor allows for out-of-order thread creation which requires communication among all hardware contexts.

Trace Processors [17] also exploit certain kinds of speculative thread-level parallelism. The mechanism to partition a sequential program into almost fixed-length traces is specially suited to maximize the workload balance among the different thread units with the help of the trace cache [18].

A different proposal to divide the program into threads was done by Codrescu et al. The MEM-slicing [2] scheme is also based on profile analysis, but the spawning algorithm starts new threads at memory instructions.

Several other recent techniques are also based on identifying dynamic sequences of instructions that could potentially have a high impact on performance and assigns them to a speculative thread [3][11][26]. However, this thread identification technique relies on simple heuristics (e.g.; mispredicted branches and load misses are the most critical instructions).

In addition, several works on speculative thread-level parallelism on multiprocessor platforms have been performed [8][9][10][23]. In all cases, programs are split by the compiler using heuristics based on loop iterations or subroutine continuations.

Some works comparing different spawning policies have been performed for both an on-chip multiprocessor [2][16] and a Clustered Speculative Multithreaded Processor [15]. The spawning policies considered were based on assigning speculative threads to loop iterations, loop continuations and subroutine continuations. The reported results of these two works cannot be compared since the baseline architectures were totally different and in the case of an on-chip multiprocessor, the present interactions between fine and coarse-grain parallelism were not considered. Subroutine continuation shows the best thread spawning potential for an on-chip single-issue in-order multiprocessor, whereas for the Speculative Multithreaded Processor spawning at loop iterations is the most effective scheme.

The importance of value prediction in such architectures has been pointed out elsewhere [14][15]. Predicting thread input values allows the processor to execute speculative threads as if they were independent. In some previous proposals (e.g., the SPSM [4] or the Superthreaded [24] architecture) no mechanisms for value prediction was considered. This implies that for each inter-thread dependent pairs of instructions the consumer must wait until the producer has been executed. On the other hand, the Dynamic Multithreaded [1] processor uses a very simple value prediction scheme; the register values of the spawned thread are predicted to be the same as those of the spawning thread at spawn time. More effective prediction schemes are proposed in the Trace Processors [17] and the Clustered Speculative Multithreaded architecture [13].

3.   Speculative Thread-Level Parallelism

A thread spawning operation is identified by two instructions in the dynamic instruction stream that we refer to as the spawning and the control quasi-independent points. Each pair of points is referred to as a *spawning pair*. The spawning point is the instruction that, when reached by

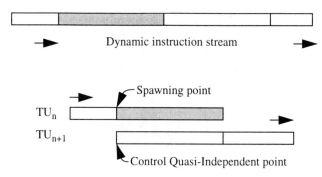

Figure 1: Spawning and Control Quasi-Independent Points.

the processor, it fires the creation of a new thread. The control quasi-independent point is where the new spawned thread starts. The spawning and the control quasi-independent points can be conventional instructions in the instruction set, denoted with special marks or special instructions such as fork and spawn. Figure 1 shows how speculative multithreaded processors work. Thread Unit n executes the instruction stream in the same way as a conventional superscalar processor until it reaches a spawning point. At this point, the processor identifies a future instruction (the control quasi-independent point) which will very likely be executed in the near future. Then, Thread Unit n+1 spawns a new thread speculatively starting at the control quasi-independent point while Thread Unit n continues executing instructions up to the control quasi-independent point which also becomes the join point between threads. That is, the join point of a thread is a control quasi-independent point of an on-going speculative thread.

It is obvious that the best instructions to be considered as spawning and control quasi-independent points are those where the speculative and the non-speculative thread were control and data independent, in such a way that the processor would be able to execute them concurrently. Unfortunately, these kind of threads are not common in some programs, especially in non-numerical codes, and thus, their potential thread-level parallelism may be rather low.

Effective spawning pairs should satisfy some requirements. First, the probability of reaching the control quasi-independent point after visiting the spawning point should be very high in order to conserve resources (executing instructions that will never be reached). Second, the distance[1] between the spawning point and the control quasi-independent point should not be too small or too large to keep the thread size within a certain limit. Small threads result in too much overhead and large threads may result in

work imbalance. Third, instructions after the control quasi-independent point should have few dependences with instructions above it or alternatively, the values that flow through such dependences should be predictable.

Previous thread-spawning policies basically focused on the first criterion:

- Loop iterations: considers the first instruction in static order of a loop (the target of a backward branch) as both the spawning and the control quasi-independent point. Note that once an iteration is started, a further iteration is very likely regardless of the outcome of the branches inside the loop body.

- Loop continuation: considers the first instruction in static order of a loop as the spawning point and the instruction following the backward branch in static order that closes the loop as the control quasi-independent point. Note that after starting a loop, the instruction at the control quasi-independent point is very likely to be executed regardless of the control-flow inside the loop.

- Subroutine continuation: considers a subroutine call as the spawning point and the instruction following the subroutine call in static order (e.g., the point where the subroutine will return) as the control quasi-independent point. Note again that after the call, this latter instruction is very likely to be executed regardless of the path followed inside the call.

3.1. Profile-Based Thread-Spawning Scheme

We are interested in identifying speculative threads that meet the three criteria discussed above. Threads are not necessarily associated with a particular program construct (e.g. loop iteration) and any instruction can be a spawning point or a control quasi-independent point.

The technique proposed here to identify spawning pairs is based on a profile-based analysis of the properties of any potential section of code. For this purpose, a dynamic control flow graph of the program is built. Each node of the graph represents a basic block and edges represent possible control flows among blocks. Edges are weighted with the frequency that the corresponding control flow has been followed during the profiling. Besides, to reduce the size of the graph, we prune the least frequently executed basic blocks. Thus, basic blocks are ordered by execution count and they are chosen from highest to lowest count until 90% of the total executed instructions are covered. However, in order not to lose information about possible control flows, whenever a node is pruned, any edge from a predecessor to it is transformed to a series of edges from that predecessor to their successors, and any edge from it to a successor is transformed to a series of edges from every predecessor to

---

[1] We refer to distance as the average number of instructions executed between the spawning point and the control quasi-independent point.

that successor. During this transformation, if an edge is transformed into multiple edges, its original weight is proportionally split across the new edges.

Once the reduced control flow graph is generated, the probability to reach any basic block after executing any other else is computed. We will refer to these probabilities as *reaching probabilities*. These probabilities are stored in a two-dimensional square matrix that has as many rows and columns as nodes in the control flow graph. Each element of the matrix represents the probability to execute the basic block represented by the column after executing the basic block represented by the row. This probability is computed as the sum of the different frequencies for all the different sequences of basic blocks that exist from the source node to the destination node. In order to simplify the computation, the only constraint taken into account for these sequences is that the source and the destination nodes can only appear once in the sequence of nodes as the first and the last nodes respectively (obviously, when the reaching probability of execute a basic block after executing itself is computed, that basic block appears twice, the former as source node and the later as destination node). Anyway, this constraint does not restrict any other basic block from appearing more than once in the sequence.

Once all these probabilities are computed, pairs of nodes are evaluated to become spawning and control quasi-independent points (in fact, the spawning and the control quasi-independent point will be the first instructions of the basic blocks selected). Thus, the previous constraint, in addition to simplifying the computation of the reaching probability matrix, it reduces the control logic of the processor since otherwise, the identification of the starting and ending points of each thread would become quite cumbersome.

Then, a prune of those pairs of nodes that do not accomplish the minimum requirements to be considered as good candidates to spawning pairs must be done. Those requirements were mentioned in the previous subsection. The first property that must be satisfied by each of these pairs is that their associated reaching probability should be very high, i.e. higher than a given threshold; that is, the probability to reach the control quasi-independent point after the spawning point is higher than a given threshold.

The second requirement that the spawning pairs must satisfy is that a minimum average number of instructions between the spawning point and the control quasi-independent point should exist in order to reduce the relative overhead of thread creation. Consequently, while the reaching probability is being computed, additional calculation regarding the average number of instructions between the source node and the destination node is performed. The average is calculated as the sum of the number of instructions executed by each sequence of basic blocks multiplied by their frequency. Thus, good candidates

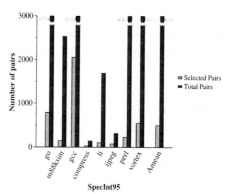

Figure 2: Number of pairs of basic blocks selected and number of selected pairs that have different spawning points.

to be considered as spawning pairs are those pair of basic blocks whose reaching probability is higher than a threshold and the average number of instructions between them is larger than a minimum size.

It is possible that for a given spawning point, there are several good candidates for its associated control quasi-independent point (i.e. for a given row of the probability matrix, there are more than one element that exceeds the minimum probability and the minimum size). Figure 2 shows the total number of pairs of basic blocks obtained for the SpecInt95 benchmarks, which is on average 6218, but only 499 have different spawning points. The minimum distance between the spawning point and the control quasi-independent point considered is 32 instructions and the minimum probability is 0.95.

When the processor reaches the spawning point it will start a speculative thread at only one control quasi-independent point. Thus, the alternative quasi control-independent points associated to each spawning point must be ordered according to the expected benefit. Three alternative criteria have been considered to produce such an ordering: a) maximizing the distance between the spawning and the control quasi-independent point - this is an estimation of the size of the corresponding speculative thread if we assume that the spawning thread and the spawned thread have the same instruction throughput -; b) the number of instructions of the spawned thread that are independent of previous instructions - again assuming a size of the thread equal to the distance between the spawning and the control quasi-independent point -; and c) maximizing the number of instructions of the spawned thread that are either independent of or dependent on a predictable value generated outside the thread. We initially consider the first criterion and we later present results for the other two.

Finally, all return point pairs (pairs of subroutine calls and the return point) are added to the list of spawning and control quasi-independent points if they satisfy the minimum size constraint, since some of them may not have been selected by the previous algorithm. In particular, if a subroutine is called from multiple locations, it will have multiple predecessors and multiple successors in the control-flow graph. If all the calls are executed a similar number of times, the reaching probability of any pair call and return point will be low since the graph will have multiple paths with similar weights.

4. Performance Evaluation

In this section we evaluate the performance of the proposed thread-spawning policy and compare it with previous proposals. For this evaluation we assume a particular speculative multithreaded processor, namely the Clustered Speculative Multithreaded Processor [12][13], but most of the results can be extrapolated to other architectures. We just focus on irregular applications (SpecInt95) for which compilers typically fail to exploit thread-level parallelism.

4.1. Experimental Framework

A Clustered Speculative Multithreaded Processor is made up of several thread units, each one being similar to a superscalar processor core. Communications among clusters occur for both memory and register values and a fully-interconnected topology is considered. Further details of the processor can be obtained elsewhere [12][13].

Performance statistics were obtained through trace-driven simulation of the whole SpecInt95 benchmark suite. The programs were compiled with the Compaq compiler for an AlphaStation 600 5/266 with full optimization (-O4) and instrumented by means of the Atom tool[22]. For the statistics, we have executed each to completion using training input data.

The baseline speculative multithreaded processor has a parameterized number of thread units (from 4 to 16) and each thread unit has the following features:

- Fetch: up to 4 instructions per cycle or up to the first taken branch, whichever is shorter.

- Issue bandwidth: 4 instructions per cycle

- Physical Registers: 64.

- Functional Units (latency in brackets): 2 simple integer (1), 2 load/store units (1 for address calculation plus the latency of accessing the cache), 1 integer multiplication (4), 2 simple FP (4), 1 FP multiplication (6), and 1 FP division (17).

- Reorder buffer: 64 entries.

- Local branch predictors: 10-bit gshare. Local predictors are not initialized when a new thread is spawned at a thread unit; instead, it will use the previous contents of such tables.

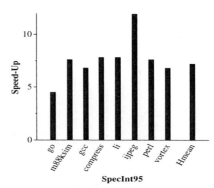

Figure 3: Speed-up over a single-threaded execution using the profile-based spawning scheme with 16 Thread Units and perfect value prediction.

- 32 KB non-blocking, 2-way set-associative, local, first-level data cache with an 32-byte block size and up to 4 outstanding misses. The L1 latencies are 3 cycles for a hit and 8 cycles for a miss.

Initially, we assume a perfect register value prediction (i.e., input register values are available when the speculative thread is started) and no thread creation overhead. Later, the impact of a realistic register value predictor is analyzed as well the impact of considering a realistic thread creation penalty.

Dependent values through memory locations are not predicted. The cost for forwarding data values from the producer thread unit to the consumer has been set to be 3 cycles. Memory dependence violations are detected by means of a cache coherence protocol based on the Speculative Versioning Cache [7].

In figures 3 to 12, spawning pairs are obtained from the profile-based analysis discussed in the previous section being the minimum reaching probability 0.95 and the minimum distance 32 instructions.

4.2. Performance Figures

Figure 3 shows the speed-up obtained by a Clustered Speculative Multithreaded Processor with 16 thread units over a single-threaded execution. We are using our profile-based spawning policy and assume a perfect value predictor for inter-thread register dependences. The average speed-up is 7.2 (harmonic mean) and it is quite important for all benchmarks. This shows the effectiveness of the proposed scheme for exploiting thread-level parallelism in irregular applications. For some programs such as ijpeg, which is the most regular program in the set, the speed-up reaches 11.9.

Figure 4 shows the average number of active threads for each program. As it can be expected the average number of active threads is closely related to the speed-up. On average, the average number of active threads is 7.5 and for

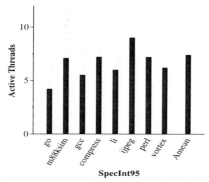

Figure 4: Average number of active threads

the program with the highest speed-up, ijpeg, it is 9.0. The additional speed-up achieved to that produced by thread-level parallelism is due to value prediction. Even though the effectiveness of our profile-based spawning policy is quite high, there are still about half of the processor resources that are wasted on average. This may be due to the application's features but also to some limitations in the spawning policy. We show below how some of these limitations can be overridden.

Since threads must commit in program order, thread units become available in the same order and thus, workload balancing may be a critical issue for performance. Threads that are being executed for long periods of time alone, or in parallel with very few other threads while the other thread units have finished the execution and are waiting for the completion of such threads to commit their respective threads, are undesirable. Thus, we extend the spawning scheme with a dynamic mechanism that monitors how much time a thread is executing alone. If it is above a certain threshold, the corresponding spawning pair is removed so that this thread is not created in the future[1]. This removal of spawning pairs can be done either the first time the above situation is observed or after the above situation has been repeated for a number of times. Figure 5a shows the performance when spawning pairs are never removed, when they are removed after executing 50 cycles alone, or when they are removed after executing 200 cycles alone. It can be observed that in general, the most aggressive spawning removal policy results in significant improvement, except for compress, whose performance dramatically drops when a small number of cycles is considered. This is due to the small number of selected spawning pairs in this program (only 30), when left to an aggressive removal mechanism leaves the program with too few spawning pairs. On average, the speed-up achieved for 200 cycles is higher than 8 over a single-threaded execution and represents a 10% improvement compared with the non spawning removal scheme.

---

[1] We have also evaluated a policy that considers again a removed thread after a certain period of time but we observed very small improvements.

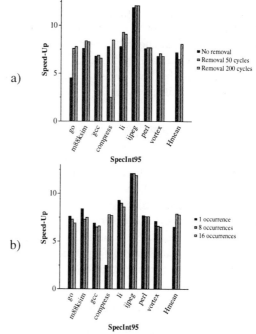

Figure 5: Speed-ups achieved by the different spawning pair removal scheme for a) different number of cycles executing alone and b) different number of occurrences before cancelling for the 50-cycle removal scheme.

An alternative way to temper the removal mechanism is to hold off cancelling a spawning pair until the speculative thread that is executing alone a minimum of occurrences. Figure 5b shows the performance for a cancelling policy with 50 cycle alone scheme when the number of occurrences is 8 and 16. On average, delaying the removal decision results in an improvement, but it is basically due to the huge improvement achieved by compress. In fact, the rest of the programs suffer a small performance loss. Although not shown in the graphs, we have also evaluated the delayed removal policy for the 200 cycle alone scheme and we have observed a small performance drop for all programs. We have also evaluated a policy that removes a spawning pair whenever the corresponding thread is executing with just a few threads instead of just one. This resulted in a small improvement on average, although most of the benefit came from three programs (compress, m88ksim and gcc).

Figure 2 shows that the number of candidate spawning pairs is much higher than the final number of selected pairs. Remember that only one spawning pair for a given spawning point is considered according to the criteria introduced in section 3.1. Also, whenever a thread reaches a spawning point and finds another more speculative thread already started in that control quasi-independent point, it does not spawn a new thread. An alternative policy may be considered. That says whenever a spawning point is

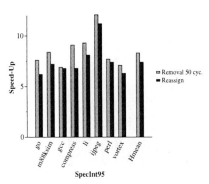

Figure 6: Speed-up of the reassign spawning policy compared with the 50-cycle removal policy (for compress, 200 cycles).

reached, if a thread cannot be spawned at the most convenient control quasi-independent point, the next control quasi-independent point is tried according the previously mentioned criteria. Likewise, whenever a spawning pair is removed we may consider the next most convenient pair with the same spawning point. We refer to this policy as the *reassign* spawning policy since it re-assigns a spawning point to a different control quasi-independent point. The result of these modifications are shown in Figure 6, together with the previous policy that just considers a single spawning pair per spawning point. It can be observed that the results are a bit worse for the reassign policy. One reason for this performance degradation is the fact that whenever a control quasi-independent point cannot be chosen, the next control quasi-independent point is usually too close and this results in generating very small threads as well introducing more spawning pairs, and does not necessarily imply better performance.

Figure 7a shows the average thread size performing spawning pair removal and with no reassign. We refer to *thread size* as the number of instructions executed in a thread unit starting when a speculative thread is assigned to this thread unit until it reaches a control quasi-independent point of an on-going thread, that is, a join point. It can be observed that the thread size for most of the benchmarks is smaller than 32, which was the minimum size we considered when selecting a spawning pair. This is due to the overlapped execution of speculative threads. Figure 7b shows the performance when a minimum size for the threads is enforced, in such a way that the spawning pairs whose associated threads are smaller than a minimum size are removed. It can be observed that the speed-up achieved is 10% over the conventional removal policy (a 50-cycle threshold is considered for all the benchmarks, except for `compress`, which is set to 200 cycles).

4.2.1. Comparison with traditional heuristics

In a previous study [15], a comparison among basic thread spawning heuristics for a Clustered Speculative

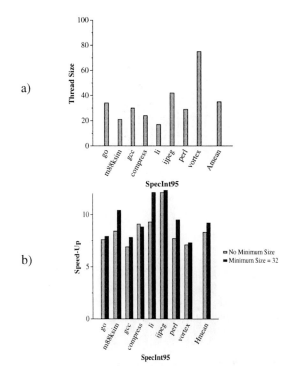

Figure 7: a) Average thread size b) Speed-up achieved when a minimum thread size is considered to spawn new speculative threads.

Multithreaded Processor was done. Although the best individual results were reported for the loop-iteration spawning scheme, it was pointed out that the best spawning policy may be a combination of all of them.

In Figure 8, the spawning policy proposed here and a combination of loop-iteration, subroutine-continuation and loop-continuation spawning schemes are compared. Results are reported as speed-ups achieved by the profile-based spawning scheme over the traditional heuristics. It can be observed that on average the improvement is close to 20%, being quite high for `vortex` and more than 10% for the rest of the benchmarks (except for `perl`, which suffers a slight slow-down (8%)). This fact is due to the work imbalance present in this benchmark based on our profile-based spawning policy.

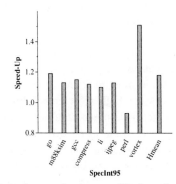

Figure 8: Speed-up of the profile-based spawning policy over the traditional heuristics.

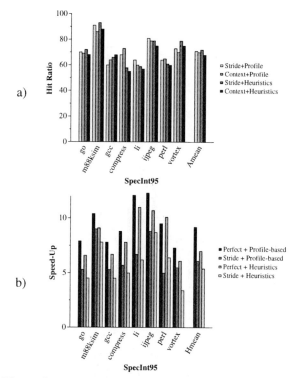

a)

b)

Figure 9: a) Value prediction accuracy and b) Speed-ups for the stride value predictor.

4.3. Critical Issues on the Clustered Speculative Multithreaded Processors

Next, the impact of a realistic value predictor, the thread creation overhead and a the number of thread units is studied.

4.3.1. Value Prediction

The importance of value prediction for speculative multithreaded architectures has been previously shown [15]. In this subsubsection, we present performance figures that show the impact of different value predictors on the performance of a Clustered Speculative Multithreaded processor with the propose profile-based spawning policy. A study regarding how value predictors work in speculative multithreaded architectures has been presented in [14]. The size of the value predictor has been fixed to 16KB for the two value predictors analyzed: the stride [6][19] and the context-based (FCM) [20] value predictors.

Figure 9a shows the prediction accuracy of the different value predictors for both spawning policies, the profile-based and the heuristic-based schemes. It can be observed that there are no significant differences in prediction accuracy for the different spawning policies and value predictors. On average, the hit ratio is around 70% (note that only thread input values are predicted). Prediction tables are indexed by hashing 3 values, the program counter of both the spawning point and the control quasi-

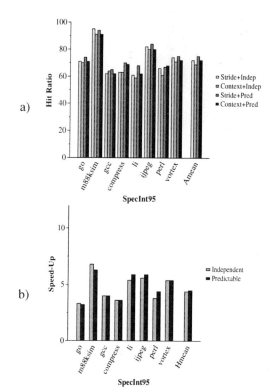

a)

b)

Figure 10: a) Value prediction accuracy and b) Speed-up achieved by the independent and predictable spawning policies.

independent point and the identifier of the register being predicted.

Figure 9b shows the speed-ups achieved by both spawning policies compared with the single-threaded execution, when a stride predictor is considered. Results for the FCM value predictor are very similar and are not present in the figure. It can be observed that the speed-ups reported are still quite high: the traditional heuristics obtain a speed-up close to 5.5, and the profile-based higher than 6, even though the gap between them has been reduced to only 13%. Moreover, note that the loss in performance when a realistic value predictor is considered is in both cases higher than 25% (30% for the traditional heuristics and 34% of slow-down for our proposed profile-based scheme).

For a realistic value predictor, alternative criteria to choose among the different control quasi-independent points for a given spawning point may be considered. Instead of choosing the point that results in the largest sized thread, we have evaluated a scheme that selects the point that maximizes the number of independent instructions between the spawning and the spawned thread. We have also considered a third scheme that selects the control quasi-independent point that maximizes the number of instructions either predictable or independent. We refer to these two new policies as *independent* and *predictable* spawning policies. For this study we have considered the

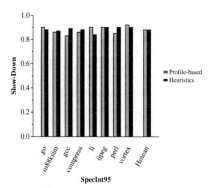

Figure 11: Slow-down suffered when an overhead penalty is considered

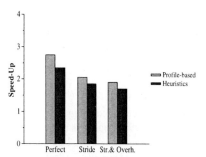

Figure 12: Average speed-ups for the spawning policies for 4 Thread Units.

stride predictor since it provides the best value prediction accuracy.

Figure 10a shows the prediction accuracy achieved by the value predictors when these new policies are applied. The first two bars correspond to the independent policy and the last two bars to the predictable policy. As expected, the policy oriented to predict values achieves the best value prediction hit ratio. It correctly predicts 75% of the values.

Nevertheless, a better value predictor accuracy does not imply a better overall performance. In Figure 10b it can be observed that for a stride predictor, the speed-ups achieved by these two new spawning policies are 35% lower than the obtained by the original one, which maximizes the distance between the spawning and the control quasi-independent point. This is due to the smaller sized threads created by these two spawning schemes. For perfect value prediction (not shown in the figures), the slow-down of the new spawning policies is somewhat lower (21% on average).

4.3.2. Overhead Considerations

Starting a new thread requires several operations that may take some non-negligible time. These operations include the prediction of the *live-in values*[1] for a thread. We refer to the penalty associated with all these operations as initialization overhead. In this section, we evaluate the impact of the initialization overhead for a penalty of 8 cycles, since it is known that the number of live-in values is relatively small. Penalty overhead is only suffered by the new spawned thread. Figure 11 shows the slow-down due to this overhead when a stride value predictor is considered. The slow-down is 12% on average for both cases and it ranges from 16% to 8% for all the benchmarks.

4.3.3. 4 Thread Units

Finally, in order to evaluate the scalability of the architecture with our spawning policy, the performance of

the profile-based spawning policy is evaluated for a 4-thread-unit configuration. Figure 12 shows the average speed-ups achieved by both spawning policies for a perfect register value predictor, a stride predictor without overhead penalty and a stride predictor with an initialization overhead of 8 cycles. It can be observed that the speed-up obtained is quite high, 2.75 for perfect value prediction, slightly higher than 2 for a stride predictor without initialization overhead and about 1.9 for a stride predictor with a 8-cycle thread initialization overhead. Note that the degradation in performance between perfect and realistic value predictors is about the same for 4 and 16 thread units.

The bottomline of this study is that a speculative multithreaded processor with a relatively low number of thread units, a simple value predictor and reasonable thread initialization overhead can achieve a significant speed-up for irregular applications such as the SpecInt95. The performance of the scheme scales reasonable well for 16 thread units, where the average speed-up is higher than 5 for a stride predictor and a 8-cycle thread initialization overhead.

5. Conclusions

In this work a new approach to spawn speculative threads in a sequential program has been presented. This technique is based on a profile-based analysis to detect which are the best instructions to spawn new threads and where the spawned thread has to start.

We have shown that the potential benefits of this spawning policy are quite high, reporting speed-ups close to 7x. Avoiding the creation of threads that will be executed alone and enforcing a minimum size can increase these speed-ups up to 9.4. The performance achieved by the profile-based spawning policy outperforms the best combination of traditional heuristics such as loop-iteration, loop-continuation and the subroutine-continuation spawning schemes by almost 20%.

When realistic assumptions are considered, the performance obtained is diminished but the results are still quite promising. With a realistic 16-KB stride predictor and an 8-cycle thread creation penalty, the speed-up achieved

---

[1] Live-in values are those register values that will be read in a speculative thread before they were written and they are produced by a previous thread[14].

by the profile-based scheme is still higher than 5, which is almost 15% better than the obtained by the traditional heuristics.

Acknowledgements

This work has been supported by grant CICYT TIC 511/98, The research described in this paper has been developed using the resources of the European Center for Parallelism of Barcelona (CEPBA). The authors would also thank Professor David Kaeli his comments in the realization of the camera ready of this paper.

6.   References

[1]   H. Akkary and M.A. Driscoll, "A Dynamic Multithreading Processor", in *Proc. 31st. Ann. Int. Symp. on Microarchitecture,* 1998.

[2]   L. Codrescu and D. Wills, "On Dynamic Speculative Thread Partitioning and the MEM-Slicing Algorithm", on Proc. of the Int. Conf. on Parallel Architectures and Compilation Techniques, pp. 40-46, 1999

[3]   J. Collins et al., "Speculative Precomputation: Long Range Prefetching of Delinquent Loads", in *Proc. of the 28th. Int. Symp. on Computer Architecture*, 2001.

[4]   P.K. Dubey, K. O'Brien, K.M. O'Brien and C. Barton, "Single-Program Speculative Multithreading (SPSM) Architecture: Compiler-Assisted Fine-Grained Multithreading", in *Proc. of the Int. Conf on Parallel Architectures and Compilation Techniques*, pp. 109-121, 1995.

[5]   M. Franklin and G. Sohi, "The Expandable Split Window Paradigm for Exploiting Fine Grain parallelism", in *Proc. of the Int. Symp. on Computer Architecture*, pp. 58-67, 1992.

[6]   F. Gabbay and A. Mendelson, "Speculative Execution Based on Value Prediction", *Technical Report #1080, Technion*, 1996.

[7]   S. Gopal, T.N. Vijaykumar, J. E. Smith and G. S. Sohi, "Speculative Versioning Cache", in *Proc. 4th Int. Symp. on High-Performance Computer Architecture*, 1998.

[8]   L. Hammond, M. Willey and K. Olukotun, "Data Speculation Support for a Chip Multiprocessor", in *Proc. of Int. Conf. on Architectural Support for Prog. Lang. and Operating Systems,* 1998

[9]   G. A. Kemp and M. Franklin, "PEWs: A Decentralized Dynamic Scheduler for ILP Processing", in *Proc. of the Int. Conf. on Parallel Processing*, pp. 239-246, 1996.

[10]   V. Krishnan and J. Torrellas, "Hardware and Software Support for Speculative Execution of Sequential Binaries on a Chip-Multiprocessor", in *Proc. of ACM Int. Conf. on Supercomputing,* pp. 85-92, 1998

[11]   C. Luk, "Tolerating Memory Latency through Software-Controlled Pre-Execution in Simultaneous Multithreading Processors", in *Proc. of the 28th. Int. Symp. on Computer Architecture*, pp. 40-51, 2001.

[12]   P. Marcuello, A. González and J. Tubella, "Speculative Multithreaded Processors", in *Proc. of the 12th Int. Conf. on Supercomputing*, pp. 77-84, 1998.

[13]   P. Marcuello and A. González, "Clustered Speculative Multithreaded Processors", in *Proc. of the 13th Int. Conf. on Supercomputing*, pp. 365-372 1999.

[14]   P. Marcuello, J. Tubella and A. González, "Value Prediction for Speculative Multithreaded Architectures", in *Proc. of the 32th. Int. Conf. on Microarchitecture, pp.* 230-236, 1999.

[15]   P. Marcuello and A. González, "A Quantitative Assessment of Thread-Level Speculation Techniques", in *Proc. of the 15th. Int. Parallel and Distributed Processing Symposium*, 2000.

[16]   J. Oplinger, D. Heine and M. Lam, "In Search of Speculative Thread-Level Parallelism", *Proc. of the Int. Conf. on Parallel Architectures and Compilation Techniques*, pp. 303-313, 1999.

[17]   E. Rotenberg, Q. Jacobson, Y. Sazeides and J.E. Smith, "Trace Processors", in *Proc. of the 30th. Int. Symp. on Microarchitecture*, pp. 138-148, 1997.

[18]   E. Rotenberg, S. Bennett and J.E. Smith, "Trace Cache: a Low Latency Approach to High Bandwidth Instruction Fetching", in *Proc. of 29th Int. Symp. on Microarchitecture*, 1996.

[19]   Y. Sazeides, S. Vassiliadis and J.E. Smith, "The Performance Potential of Data Dependence Speculation & Collapsing", in *Proc. of the 29th. Int. Symp on Microarchitecture*, Dec. 1996.

[20]   Y. Sazeides and J.E. Smith, "Implementations of Context-Based Value Predictors", Technical Report #ECE-TR-97-8, University of Wisconsin-Madison, 1997.

[21]   G. Sohi, S.E. Breach and T.N. Vijaykumar, "Multiscalar Processors", in *Proc. of the Int. Symp. on Computer Architecture*, pp. 414-425,1995.

[22]   A.Srivastava and A.Eustace,"ATOM: A system for building customized program analysis tools", in *Proc.of the Int. Conf. on Programming languages Design and Implementation*, 1994

[23]   J. Steffan and T. Mowry, "The Potential of Using Thread-Level Data Speculation to Facilitate Automatic Parallelization", in *Proc. 4th Int. Symp. on High-Performance Computer Architecture*, pp. 2-13, 1998

[24]   J.Y. Tsai and P-C. Yew, "The Superthreaded Architecture: Thread Pipelining with Run-Time Data Dependence Checking and Control Speculation", in *Proc. of the Int. Conf. on Parallel Architectures and Compilation Techniques*, pp. 35-46, 1996.

[25]   T.N. Vijaykumar, "Compiling for the Multiscalar Architecture", Ph. D. Thesis, University of Wisconsin-Madison, 1998.

[26]   C. Zilles and G. Sohi, "Execution-Based Prediction using Speculative Slices", in *Proc. of the 28th. Int. Symp. on Computer Architecture*, pp. 2-13, 2001.

Improving Value Communication for Thread-Level Speculation

J. Gregory Steffan, Christopher B. Colohan, Antonia Zhai, and Todd C. Mowry

Computer Science Department
Carnegie Mellon University
Pittsburgh, PA 15213
{steffan,colohan,zhaia,tcm}@cs.cmu.edu

Abstract

Thread-Level Speculation (TLS) allows us to automatically parallelize general-purpose programs by supporting parallel execution of threads that might not actually be independent. In this paper, we show that the key to good performance lies in the three different ways to communicate a value between speculative threads: speculation, synchronization, and prediction. The difficult part is deciding how and when to apply each method.

This paper shows how we can apply value prediction, dynamic synchronization, and hardware instruction prioritization to improve value communication and hence performance in several SPECint benchmarks that have been automatically-transformed by our compiler to exploit TLS. We find that value prediction can be effective when properly throttled to avoid the high costs of misprediction, while most of the gains of value prediction can be more easily achieved by exploiting silent stores. We also show that dynamic synchronization is quite effective for most benchmarks, while hardware instruction prioritization is not. Overall, we find that these techniques have great potential for improving the performance of TLS.

1 Introduction

Microprocessors which can simultaneously execute multiple parallel threads are becoming increasingly commonplace. Processors such as the Sun MAJC [34], IBM Power4 [18], and the Sibyte SB-1250 [8] are *single-chip multiprocessors* (CMPs), while the Alpha 21464 was designed to support *simultaneous-multithreading* [36]. Using this multithreaded hardware to improve the throughput of a workload is straightforward, but improving the performance of a single application requires parallelization.

How can we parallelize all of the applications that we care about? Writing parallel software can be a daunting task; we would much rather have the compiler parallelize our code for us. Traditionally, compilers have parallelized by proving that potential threads are independent [3, 17, 33]—but this is extremely difficult if not impossible for many general purpose programs due to their complex data structures and control flow, and use of pointers and runtime inputs. One promising alternative for overcoming this problem is *Thread-Level Speculation* (**TLS**) [2, 7, 14, 15, 16, 20, 23, 26, 32, 35] which allows the compiler to create parallel threads without having to prove that they are independent.

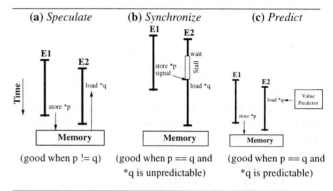

Figure 1. A memory value may be communicated between two epochs (E1 and E2) through (a) speculation, (b) synchronization, or (c) prediction.

1.1 The Importance of Value Communication for Thread-Level Speculation

In the context of TLS, value communication refers to the satisfaction of any true (read-after-write) dependence between *epochs* (sequential chunks of work performed speculatively in parallel). From the compiler's perspective, there are two ways to communicate the value of a given variable. First, the compiler may speculate that the variable is not modified (Figure 1(a)). However, if at run-time the variable actually *is* modified then the underlying hardware ensures that the misspeculated epoch is re-executed with the proper value. This method only works well when the variable is modified infrequently, since the cost of misspeculation is high. Second, if the variable is frequently modified, then the compiler may instead synchronize and forward[1] the value between epochs (Figure 1(b)). Since a parallelized region of code will contain many variables, the compiler will employ a combination of speculation and synchronization as appropriate.

To further improve upon static compile-time choices between speculating or synchronizing for specific memory accesses, we can exploit dynamic run-time behavior to make value communication more efficient. For example, we might exploit a form of *value prediction* [2, 13, 22, 24, 28, 29, 37], as illustrated in Figure 1(c). To get a sense of the potential upside of enhancing value communication under TLS, let us briefly consider the ideal case. From a performance perspective, the ideal case would correspond to a value predictor that could perfectly predict the values of any inter-thread dependences. In such a case, speculation

---

[1] This is also known as *doacross* [10, 27] parallelization.

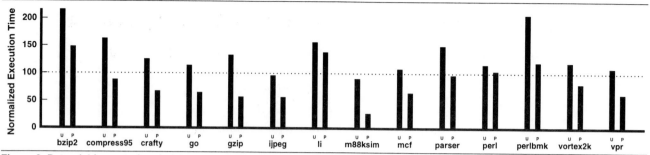

Figure 2. Potential impact of optimizing value communication. Relative to the normalized, original sequential version, U shows the unoptized speculative version and P shows perfect prediction of all inter-thread data dependences.

would never fail and synchronization would never stall. While this perfect-prediction scenario is unrealistic, it does allow us to quantify the potential impact of improving value communication in TLS. Figure 2 shows the impact of perfect prediction on several speculatively-parallelized SPECint [9] benchmarks, running on a 4-processor CMP that implements our TLS scheme [32] (details are given later in Section 3.2). Each bar shows the total execution time of all speculatively-parallelized regions of code, normalized to that of the corresponding original sequential versions of these same codes. As we see in Figure 2, efficient value communication often makes the difference between speeding up and slowing down relative to the original sequential code. Hence this is clearly an important area for applying compiler and hardware optimizations.

1.2 Techniques for Improving Value Communication

Given the importance of efficient value communication in TLS, what solutions can we implement to approach the ideal results of Figure 2? Figure 1 shows the spectrum of possibilities: i.e. speculate, synchronize, or predict. In our baseline scheme, the compiler synchronizes dependences that it expects to occur frequently (by explicitly "forwarding" their values between successive epochs), and speculates on everything else. How can we use hardware to improve on this approach? Hardware support for efficient *speculation* has already been addressed in a number of papers on TLS [2, 6, 14, 15, 16, 20, 23, 26, 32, 35]. Therefore our focus in this paper is how to exploit and enhance the remaining spectrum of possibilities (i.e. *prediction* and *synchronization*) such that they are complementary to speculation within TLS. In particular, we explore the following techniques:

Value Prediction: We can exploit *value prediction* by having the consumer of a potential dependence use a predicted value instead, as illustrated in Figure 1(c). After the epoch completes, it will compare the predicted value with the actual value; if the values differ, then the normal speculation recovery mechanism will be invoked to squash and restart the epoch with the correct value. We explore using value prediction as a replacement for both *speculation* and *synchronization*. In the former case (which we refer to later as *"memory value prediction"*), successful value prediction avoids the cost of recovery from an unsuccessful speculative load. In the latter case (which we refer to later as

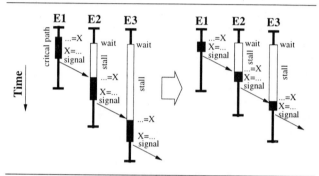

Figure 3. Reducing the critical forwarding path.

"forwarded value prediction"), successful prediction avoids the need to stall waiting for synchronization. Because the implementation issues and performance impact differ for these two cases, we evaluate them separately.

Silent Stores: An interesting program phenomenon that was recently discovered [21] is that many stores have no real side-effect since they overwrite memory with the same value that is already there. These stores are called *silent stores*, and we can exploit them when they occur to avoid failed speculation. Although one can view silent stores as a form of value prediction, the mechanism to exploit them is radically different from what is shown in Figure 1(c) since the changes occur with the *producer* of a communicated value, rather than the consumer.

Hardware-Inserted Dynamic Synchronization: In cases where the compiler decided to speculate that an ambiguous store/load dependence between speculative threads was not likely to occur, but where the dependence does in fact occur frequently and the communicated value is unpredictable, the best option would be to explicitly synchronize the threads (Figure 1(b)) to avoid the full cost of failed speculation. However, since the compiler did not recognize that such synchronization would be useful, another option is for the *hardware* to automatically switch from speculating to synchronizing when it dynamically detects such bad cases.

Reducing the Critical Forwarding Path: Once synchronization is introduced to explicitly forward values across epochs, it creates a dependence chain across the threads that may ultimately limit the parallel speedup. We can potentially improve performance in such cases by using scheduling techniques to reduce the critical path between the first use and last definition of the dependent value, as illustrated in Figure 3. We implement both compiler and hardware methods for reducing the critical forwarding path.

1.3 Contributions and Overview

This paper makes the following contributions. First, we evaluate a comprehensive set of techniques for enhancing value communication within a system that supports thread-level speculation, and demonstrate that many of them can result in significant performance gains. While we evaluate these techniques within the context of our own implementation of TLS, we expect to see similar trends within other TLS environments since the results are largely dependent on application behavior rather than the details of how speculation support is implemented. Second, and perhaps most importantly, we evaluate these techniques *after* the compiler has eliminated obvious data dependences and scheduled any critical forwarding paths, thereby removing the "easy" bottlenecks to achieving good performance. This leads us to very different conclusions than previous studies on exploiting value prediction within TLS [24, 26]. Third, we demonstrate the importance of throttling back value prediction to avoid the high cost of misprediction, and propose and evaluate techniques for focusing prediction on the dependences that matter most. Fourth, we present the first exploration of how *silent stores* can be exploited within TLS; compared with using traditional value prediction mechanisms to predict speculative memory loads, our silent stores approach yields comparable (if not better) performance while requiring considerably less hardware support. Finally, we evaluate two novel hardware techniques for enhancing the performance of synchronized dependences across speculative threads, but find mixed or disappointing results compared with what our compiler can do to optimize such cases in software.

The remainder of this paper is organized as follows. In Section 2 we describe our approach to TLS support, including our hardware implementation and compiler infrastructure. We take a closer look at the potential for improving value communication in Section 3, and show that our compiler optimizations have a large impact. In Section 4 we investigate techniques for improving value prediction, and explore methods to improve synchronization. Finally, in Section 5 we evaluate the combination of all techniques, and conclude in Section 6.

2 Our Support for Thread-Level Speculation

This section describes the goals of our approach, how we implement support for TLS in hardware, our compiler support, and our experimental framework. While this study is within the context of our approach to TLS support [31, 32], the techniques that we suggest for improving value communication are applicable to other approaches as well.

2.1 Goals of Our Approach

Before we begin our investigation of value communication for TLS, it is important to understand the philosophy behind our approach. First and foremost, our goal is to parallelize general-purpose programs. Our scheme supports parallelization of scientific codes, but for now we focus on the more difficult problem of parallelizing integer applications. Second, we want to keep the hardware support simple and minimal: we avoid large structures that are specialized for speculation, and preserve the performance of non-TLS workloads. Third, we take full advantage of the compiler which selects the regions of code to speculatively parallelize, eliminates data dependences where possible, and otherwise inserts synchronization and schedules the critical paths.

2.2 Underlying Hardware Support

Our scheme [31, 32] is applicable to shared-cache architectures, but for now we focus on single-chip multiprocessors where each processor has its own physically-private first-level data cache, connected to a unified second-level cache by a crossbar switch. TLS hardware support must implement two important features: buffering speculative modifications from regular memory, and detecting and recovering from failed speculation. In our scheme we implement this support by using the data caches and an extended version of standard invalidation-based cache coherence.

In a nutshell, our coherence scheme works by tracking which cache lines have been speculatively loaded or modified, and piggybacking a sequence number on coherence messages to detect when an epoch has violated a data dependence. We buffer speculative modifications from regular memory by ensuring that speculatively-modified cache lines are not evicted[2] so that only committed, non-speculative modifications are visible to the rest of the memory hierarchy. We also provide support for *multiple writers*, where two epochs can each speculatively modify their own copy of the same cache line: the coherence mechanism uses the sequence numbers to properly combine the cache lines when they are committed.

2.3 Compiler Support

In contrast with hardware-only approaches to TLS, we rely on the compiler to define where and how to speculate. Our compiler infrastructure is based on the Stanford SUIF 1.3 compiler system [33], and performs the following phases when compiling an application to exploit TLS.

Deciding Where to Speculate: For this paper, we focus solely on loops. With the help of automatically-gathered profile information, the compiler selects loops to maximize coverage while meeting heuristics for epoch size and loop trip counts: each loop must comprise at least 0.1% of overall execution time and have an average of at least 1.5 epochs per instance, as well as an average of at least 15 instructions per epoch. Once the key loops are selected, the compiler automatically applies loop unrolling to small loops to help amortize the overheads of speculative parallelization.

Transforming to Exploit TLS: Once speculative regions are chosen, the compiler inserts new TLS-specific instructions into the code that interact with the TLS hardware to create and manage the speculative threads (aka "epochs") [31]. We must also satisfy register dependences between speculative threads; to accomplish this, the compiler "forwards" register values between successive epochs by accessing a

---

[2] If a speculative cache line must be evicted, we simply cause speculation to fail for the corresponding epoch.

special portion of the stack called the *forwarding frame* which allows hardware to manage synchronization and communication for these values. Before the first use of a forwarded value, the compiler inserts a `wait` instruction, and then reads the value from the forwarding frame. After the last definition, the value is written back to the forwarding frame and a `signal` instruction allows the next epoch to proceed.

Optimization: Without optimization, execution can be unnecessarily serialized by synchronization (through `wait` and `signal` operations). A pathological case is a `"for"` loop in the C language where the loop counter is used at the beginning of the loop and then incremented at the end of the loop—if the loop counter is synchronized and forwarded then the loop will be serialized. However, scheduling can be used to move the `wait` and `signal` closer to each other, thereby reducing this critical path. Our compiler schedules these critical paths by first identifying the computation chain leading to each `signal`, and then using a dataflow analysis which extends the algorithm developed by Knoop [19] to schedule that code in the earliest safe location. We can do even better for any loop induction variable that is a linear function of the loop index; the scheduler hoists the associated code to the top of the epoch and computes that value locally from the loop index, avoiding any extra synchronization altogether. These optimizations have a large impact on performance, as we show later in Section 3.1.

Code Generation: Our compiler outputs C source code which encodes our new TLS instructions as in-line MIPS assembly code using gcc's "asm" statements. This source code is then compiled with gcc v2.95.2 using the "-O3" flag to produce optimized, fully-functional MIPS binaries with TLS instructions.

2.4   Experimental Framework

We evaluate our support for TLS through detailed simulation. Our simulator models 4-way issue, out-of-order, superscalar processors similar to the MIPS R10000 [38]. Register renaming, the reorder buffer, branch prediction, instruction fetching, branching penalties, and the memory hierarchy (including bandwidth and contention) are all modeled, and are parameterized as shown in Table 1. We simulate up to the first billion instructions[3] of SPECint95 and SPECint2000 benchmarks [9].[4]

3   A Closer Look at Improving Value Communication

In this section, we evaluate the impact of compiler optimization on performance and then show the potential for further improvement by hardware techniques.

3.1   Impact of Compiler Optimization

---

[3] Since the sequential and TLS versions of each benchmark are compiled differently, the compiler instruments them to ensure that they terminate at the same point in their executions relative to the source code.

[4] At the time of publication, our infrastructure could not yet handle GCC, TWOLF, GAP, nor EON.

Table 1. Simulation parameters.

Pipeline Parameters	
Issue Width	4
Functional Units	2 Int, 2 FP, 1 Mem, 1 Branch
Reorder Buffer Size	128
Integer Multiply	12 cycles
Integer Divide	76 cycles
All Other Integer	1 cycle
FP Divide	15 cycles
FP Square Root	20 cycles
All Other FP	2 cycles
Branch Prediction	GShare (16KB, 8 history bits)

Memory Parameters	
Cache Line Size	32B
Instruction Cache	32KB, 4-way set-assoc
Data Cache	32KB, 2-way set-assoc, 2 banks
Unified Secondary Cache	2MB, 4-way set-assoc, 4 banks
Miss Handlers	16 for data, 2 for insts
Crossbar Interconnect	8B per cycle per bank
Minimum Miss Latency to Secondary Cache	10 cycles
Minimum Miss Latency to Local Memory	75 cycles
Main Memory Bandwidth	1 access per 20 cycles

Table 2. Benchmark statistics.

Application Name	Portion of Dynamic Execution Parallelized (Coverage)	Number of Unique Parallelized Regions	Average Epoch Size (dynamic insts)	Average Number of Epochs Per Dynamic Region Instance
BZIP2	98.1%	1	251.5	451596.0
CRAFTY	36.1%	34	30.8	1315.7
GZIP	70.4%	1	1307.0	2064.8
MCF	61.0%	9	206.2	198.9
PARSER	36.4%	41	271.1	19.4
PERLBMK	10.3%	10	65.1	2.4
VORTEX2K	12.7%	6	1994.3	3.4
VPR	80.1%	6	90.2	6.3
COMPRESS95	75.5%	7	188.2	68.4
GO	31.3%	40	2252.7	56.2
IJPEG	90.6%	23	1499.8	33.8
LI	17.0%	3	176.4	124.9
M88KSIM	56.5%	6	840.4	50.2
PERL	43.9%	4	137.3	2.2

We begin by analyzing the performance impact of our compiler on TLS execution. Table 2 shows some statistics on our benchmarks. We observe that our *coverage* (i.e. the portion of dynamic execution time that has been parallelized using TLS) is reasonably good for most benchmarks: 51.4% on average, and as high as 98.1%. Figure 4 shows the performance on a single-chip, 4-processor multiprocessor. For each application in Figure 4, the leftmost bar (*S*) is the original sequential version of the code, and the next bar (*T*) is the TLS version of the code run on a single processor. For each experiment, we show region execution time normalized to the sequential case (*S*); hence bars that are less than 100 are speeding up, and bars that are larger than 100 are slowing down, relative to the sequential version. Comparing the TLS version run sequentially (*T*) with the original sequential version (*S*) isolates the overhead of TLS transformation. In all cases, this is roughly 10%. When we run the TLS code in parallel, it must overcome this overhead in order to achieve an overall speedup.

Each bar in Figure 4 is broken down into six segments explain-

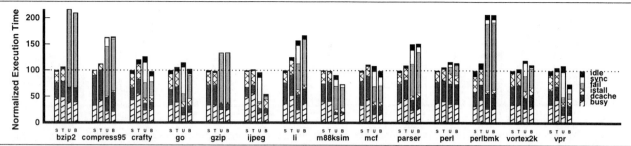

Figure 4. Performance impact of our TLS compiler. For each experiment, we show normalized region execution time scaled to the number of processors multiplied by the number of cycles (smaller is better). S is the sequential version, T is the TLS version run sequentially. There are two versions of TLS code run in parallel: U and B are without and with compiler scheduling of the critical forwarding path, respectively. Each bar shows a detailed breakdown of how time is being spent.

ing what happened during all potential graduation slots.[5] The *fail* segment represents all slots wasted on failed thread-level speculation, and the remaining five segments represent slots spent on successful speculation. The *busy* segment is the number of slots where instructions graduate; the *dcache* segment is the number of non-graduating slots attributed to data cache misses; the *sync* portion represents slots spent waiting for synchronization for a forwarded location; the *istall* segment is all other slots where instructions cannot graduate; the *idle* segment represents slots where the reorder buffer is empty.

We consider two versions of TLS code running in parallel: the B case includes all of the compiler optimizations described earlier in Section 2.3, and the U case is the same minus the aggressive compiler scheduling to reduce the critical forwarding path. In nearly every case, the "unoptimized"[6] version (U) slows down with respect to the sequential version. The additional impediments include decreased data cache locality, synchronization, and failed speculation. Many benchmarks spend a significant amount of time synchronizing on forwarded values (as shown by the *sync* portion). Some benchmarks suffer from non-negligible *idle* segments; in general, this indicates load imbalance and in many cases it is due to regions that have fewer epochs than there are processors. If the compiler optimizes forwarded values by removing dependences due to certain loop induction variables and scheduling the critical path (B, our baseline), we observe that the performance of several benchmarks (CRAFTY, GO, IJPEG, M88KSIM, MCF, VORTEX2K, and VPR) improves substantially through decreased synchronization (*sync*), indicating that this is a crucial optimization.

3.2 The Potential for Further Improvement by Hardware

To illustrate that the performance of many of our benchmarks is limited by the efficiency of value communication, we show in Figure 5 the impact of ideal prediction on performance. First, in the F experiment we see the impact of perfect prediction of forwarded values. In effect, this means that there will be no time spent waiting for synchronization of forwarded values. Most benchmarks

improve slightly, while M88KSIM, MCF, and PARSER show a substantial improvement: this makes sense since the baseline experiment (B) shows these benchmarks to be somewhat limited by synchronization. All benchmarks except for IJPEG and VPR suffer from a significant amount of failed speculation in the B and F experiments.

In the M experiment, we measure the impact of perfect memory value prediction, which means that no epoch will suffer from failed speculation. In this case, we see a great improvement in most benchmarks. CRAFTY, MCF, and PARSER show a significant synchronization portion for the M experiment, indicating that synchronization is still a limiting factor for these benchmarks.

Finally, in the P experiment we evaluate the impact of perfect prediction of both memory and forwarded value values. In this case, MCF and PARSER show a significant benefit compared with perfect memory value prediction alone, while the other benchmarks show only modest improvements. Evidently, avoiding failed speculation is the main bottleneck to good performance, while improving synchronization may still be important for some benchmarks. Also, if we cannot fully eliminate failed speculation then improving synchronization will still be important. Note that BZIP2, LI, PERL, and PERLBMK do not speed up, even with perfect prediction of memory and forwarded values. For these four benchmarks, the decreased data cache locality of executing on four processors is the limiting factor. IJPEG will not speed up further even under perfect prediction of both forwarded and memory values (P).

4 Evaluation of Techniques for Improving Value Communication

In this section we first focus on the benefits of predicting values for TLS: we describe the issues related to value prediction in the midst of speculation, describe how to predict memory values and how to predict forwarded values, and then discuss how to apply the technique of optimizing silent stores. Then, we focus on improving synchronization and automatically applying synchronization when speculation and prediction are ineffective.

4.1 Techniques for When Prediction Is Best

Value prediction in the context of a uniprocessor is fairly well understood [13, 22, 29, 37], while value prediction for thread-speculative architectures is relatively new. Gonzalez *et al.* [24]

---

[5] The number of graduation slots is the product of: (i) the issue width (4 in this case), (ii) the number of cycles, and (iii) the number of processors.

[6] Note that the "unoptimized" case still includes the `gcc` "`-O3`" flag, and is optimized in every way except for the aggressive critical forwarding path scheduling.

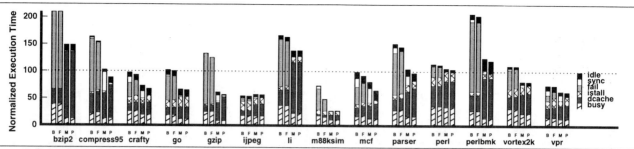

Figure 5. Potential for improved value communication. For each experiment, we show normalized region execution time (smaller is better). B is the baseline TLS version run speculatively in parallel, M shows perfect prediction of memory values, F shows perfect prediction of forwarded values, and P shows perfect prediction of both forwarded and memory values.

evaluated the potential for value prediction when speculating at a thread-level on the innermost loops from SPECint95 [9] benchmarks, and concluded that predicting synchronized (forwarded) register dependences provided the greatest benefit, and that predicting memory values did not offer much additional benefit. The opposite is true of our results for two reasons. First, our compiler has correctly scheduled easily-predictable but frequently-synchronized loop-induction variables so that they cannot cause dependence violations, and has also scheduled the code paths of forwarded values to minimize the impact of synchronization on performance. Second, we have selected much larger regions of code to speculate on, resulting in a greater number of memory dependences between threads. Concurrent with our work, Cintra *et al.* [7] investigated the impact of value prediction after the compiler has optimized loop induction variables in floating-point applications. Several other works evaluate the impact of value prediction without such compiler optimization. Oplinger *et al.* [26] evaluate the potential benefits to TLS of memory, register, and procedure return value prediction, and Akkary *et al.* [2] and Rotenberg *et al.* [28] also describe designs that include value prediction.

Predicting values for TLS has similar issues to predicting values in the midst of branch speculation, but at a larger scale. With branch speculation, we do not want to update the predictor for loads on the mispredicted path. Also, when a value is mispredicted we need only squash a relatively small number of instructions, so the cost of misprediction is not large. Similarly, in TLS we only want to update the predictor for values predicted in successful epochs, but this will require either a larger amount of buffering or the ability to back-up and restore the state of the value predictor. Furthermore, the cost of a misprediction is high for TLS: the entire epoch must be re-executed if a value is mispredicted because a prediction cannot be verified until the end of the epoch when all modifications by previous epochs have been made visible.[7] Finally, for TLS we require that each epoch has a logically-separate value predictor. For SMT or other shared-pipeline speculation scheme, this does not mean that each requires a physically separate value predictor, but that the prediction entries must be kept separate by incorporating the epoch context identifier into the indexing function. This is necessary since multiple epochs may need to simultaneously predict different versions of the same location.

For this paper, we model an aggressive hybrid predictor that combines a $1\text{K}\times 3$-entry context predictor with a 1K-entry stride

predictor, using 2-bit, up/down, saturating confidence counters to select between the two predictors. We found that the number of mispredictions can be minimized by simply predicting only when the prediction confidence is at the maximum value. Finding the smallest and simplest predictor that produces good results is beyond the scope of this paper. It is important to note that we also model misprediction by re-executing any epoch that has used a mispredicted-value. A misprediction is not detected until the end of the epoch when the prediction is verified.

4.1.1 Memory Value Prediction

One potential way to eliminate data dependence violations between speculative threads is through the prediction of memory values. But which loads should we predict? A simple approach would be to predict every load for which the predictor is confident. Previous work [4, 11] shows that focusing prediction on critical path instructions is important for uniprocessor value prediction when modeling realistic misprediction penalties. Similarly, the cost of misprediction in TLS is very high, so we instead want to focus only on the loads that can potentially cause misspeculation. Fortunately, this information is available from the speculative cache line state: only loads that are *exposed*[8] can cause speculation to fail. Since our scheme tracks which words have been speculatively-modified in each cache line, we can decide whether a given load is exposed.

Table 3 shows some statistics for the prediction of exposed loads using the predictor described above. M88KSIM and PERL are quite predictable, while the remaining benchmarks also provide a significant fraction of correct predictions. We see that the amount of misprediction is quite small—fewer than 4% of predictions are incorrect for all benchmarks. Hence we expect memory value prediction to work well.

In Figure 6, the E experiment shows the impact of predicting all exposed loads for which the predictor is confident. In almost every case, performance is worse due to an increased amount of failed speculation caused by misprediction. The problem is that it only takes a single misprediction to cause speculation to fail.

Rather than predict all exposed loads, we can be more selective by only predicting loads that are likely to cause dependence violations. We can track these loads with the following two devices. First, we keep a 16-entry table (called the *exposed load table*) that is indexed by the cache line tag, and stores the PC of the

---

[7] Some schemes support selective-squashing of instructions that have used a mispredicted value [2], but this requires a large amount of buffering.

[8] A load that is not proceeded in the same epoch by a store to the same location is considered to be exposed [1].

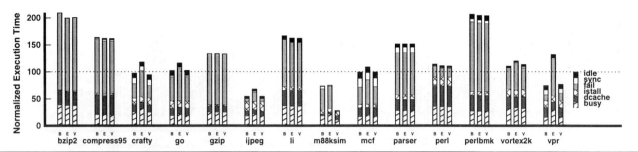

Figure 6. Performance with memory value prediction. B is the baseline experiment, E predicts all *exposed* loads, and V only predicts loads that have caused violations.

Table 3. Memory Value Prediction statistics.

Application	Avg. Exposed Loads per Epoch	Incorrect	Correct	Not Confident
BZIP2	9.5	0.2%	63.4%	36.3%
CRAFTY	4.5	3.0%	48.6%	48.3%
GZIP	66.6	1.4%	52.8%	45.7%
MCF	2.5	1.7%	34.9%	63.3%
PARSER	3.6	3.2%	48.7%	48.0%
PERLBMK	1.6	0.9%	17.9%	81.0%
VORTEX2K	25.4	2.8%	64.9%	32.2%
VPR	6.3	3.6%	49.8%	46.4%
COMPRESS95	12.0	0.3%	31.8%	67.9%
GO	7.0	2.5%	41.2%	56.2%
IJPEG	4.4	1.6%	35.4%	62.8%
LI	2.3	2.1%	50.8%	46.9%
M88KSIM	7.5	1.2%	90.9%	7.7%
PERL	12.3	1.1%	79.7%	19.1%

Table 4. Forwarded Value Prediction statistics.

Application	Incorrect	Correct	Not Confident
BZIP2	0.0%	0.0%	0.0%
CRAFTY	5.5%	24.6%	69.7%
GZIP	0.2%	98.0%	1.6%
MCF	2.5%	48.5%	48.9%
PARSER	2.8%	11.6%	85.5%
PERLBMK	2.9%	61.7%	35.2%
VORTEX2K	2.2%	81.9%	15.7%
VPR	2.8%	26.4%	70.7%
COMPRESS95	3.7%	31.2%	65.1%
GO	3.7%	28.3%	67.9%
IJPEG	5.8%	72.4%	21.6%
LI	1.0%	18.7%	80.1%
M88KSIM	5.4%	91.0%	3.4%
PERL	1.5%	91.4%	7.0%

corresponding exposed load. Subsequent exposed loads simply overwrite the appropriate entry—hence we track the most recent exposed loads. Second, whenever a dependence violation occurs it is associated with a cache line, so we can use the cache line tag to index the exposed load table and retrieve the PC of the offending load. Hence we can keep a list of load PCs which have caused violations (the *violating loads list*), and can now use this list to decide which loads we should predict. In Figure 6, the V experiment shows the impact of predicting only loads that have caused violations, as given by the violating loads list. Compared with the baseline B, we see that every benchmark either improves slightly or at least remains unchanged, except for VORTEX2K which degrades slightly, and M88KSIM which improves significantly by eliminating much failed speculation. Hence with proper throttling, memory value prediction can be used to improve the performance of some applications.

Having explored value prediction for the sake of avoiding failed speculation, we now turn our attention to using value prediction to mitigate the performance impact of explicit synchronization.

4.1.2 Prediction of Forwarded Values

Recall that forwarded values are those that are frequently modified and so they are synchronized between epochs by the compiler. Just as we did with memory values, we can also predict forwarded values. However, while we predict memory values to decrease the amount of failed speculation, we predict forwarded values to

decrease the amount of time spent synchronizing. Table 4 shows some statistics for the prediction of forwarded values. We see that the fraction of incorrect predictions is somewhat higher than for memory values, and the fraction of correct predictions is not as high.

In Figure 7, the F experiment shows the impact of predicting forwarded values: MCF improves by 4.2%, GZIP by 6.0%, and M88KSIM by 43.6%. The remaining benchmarks are not greatly affected, except for CRAFTY and VPR which become slightly worse due to mispredictions. In an attempt to remedy this problem, we applied a similar technique to that used in memory value prediction: we track which forwarded loads that cause the pipeline to stall waiting for synchronization, and only predict those values. The S bars shows the results of this experiment, which maintains the performance of the F experiment in every benchmark, and solved the problem for CRAFTY but not for VPR. In summary, the prediction of forwarded values is an effective way to reduce the amount of time spent synchronizing for some applications.

4.1.3 Silent Stores

Often, a store does not actually modify the value of its target location. In other words, the value of the location before the store is the same as the value of the location after the store. This occurrence is known as a *silent store* [21], and was first exploited to reduce coherence traffic. A store that is expected to be silent is replaced with a load, and the loaded value is compared with the value to be stored. If they are not the same, then the store is executed after all, otherwise we save the coherence traffic of gain-

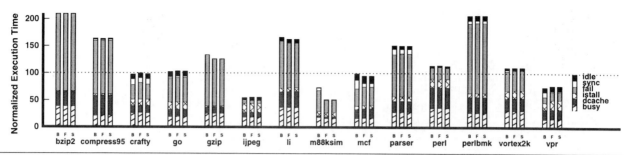

Figure 7. Performance of forwarded value prediction. B is the baseline experiment, F predicts all forwarded values S predicts forwarded values that have caused stalls.

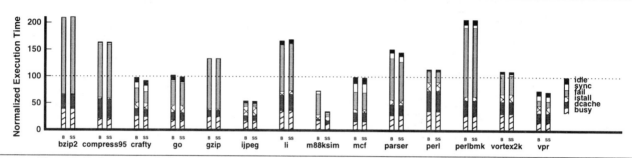

Figure 8. Performance of silent stores optimization. B is the baseline experiment, and SS optimizes silent stores.

Table 5. Percent of Dynamic, Non-Stack Stores That Are Silent.

Application	Dynamic, Non-Stack Silent Stores
BZIP2	11%
CRAFTY	16%
GZIP	4%
MCF	19%
PARSER	12%
PERLBMK	7%
VORTEX2K	84%
VPR	26%
COMPRESS95	80%
GO	16%
IJPEG	31%
LI	19%
M88KSIM	57%
PERL	36%

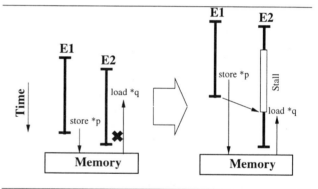

Figure 9. Dynamic synchronization, which avoids failed speculation (left) by stalling the appropriate load until the previous epoch completes (right).

ing exclusive access to the cache line and eliminate future update traffic. This same technique can be applied to TLS to avoid data dependence violations so that a dependent store-load pair can be made independent if the store is silent.

In Table 5 we see that silent stores are abundant, ranging from 4% to 80% of all dynamic non-stack stores within speculative regions. However, what matters is whether the stores which cause dependence violations are silent. Figure 8 shows that optimizing silent stores results in a slight improvement for most benchmarks, and a large improvement in M88KSIM; only LI performs slightly worse when optimizing silent stores. Compared with using value prediction to avoid potential memory dependences (as we explored earlier in Section 4.1.1), this silent stores approach yields similar if not better performance, but requires significantly less hardware support (e.g., no value predictor is needed). Hence this appears to be a very attractive technique for enhancing TLS performance.

4.2 Techniques for When Synchronization Is Best

We now turn focus on the scenarios when synchronization is the right thing to do. We investigate techniques for dynamic synchronization of dependences, and prioritization of the critical path.

4.2.1 Hardware-Inserted Dynamic Synchronization

For many of our benchmarks, failed speculation is a significant performance limitation; and as we observed in Section 4.1, prediction alone cannot eliminate all dependence violations. For dependences with unpredictable values that occur frequently, the only remaining alternative is to synchronize. Our compiler has already inserted synchronization for local variables. Still many dependences remain, as demonstrated in Section 3.2, which can be synchronized dynamically by hardware.

Dynamic synchronization has been applied to both uniprocessor and multiprocessor domains. Chrysos *et al.* [5] present a

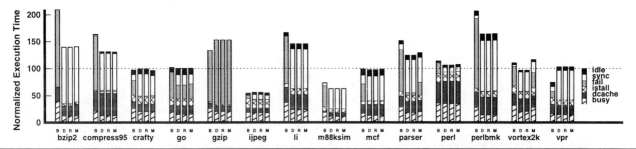

Figure 10. Performance of dynamic synchronization. B is the baseline experiment, D automatically synchronizes all violating loads, R builds on D by periodically resetting the violating loads list, and M builds on R by requiring a load to have caused at least 4 violations since the last reset before synchronizing it.

design for dynamically synchronizing dependent store-load pairs within the context of an out-of-order issue uniprocessor pipeline, and Moshovos *et al.* [25] investigate the dynamic synchronization of dependent store-load pairs in the context of the Multiscalar architecture [12, 30].

Both of these works differ from ours because they have the ability to forward a value directly from the store to the load in a dynamically-synchronized store-load pair: this is trivial in a uniprocessor since the store and load issue from the same pipeline; for a multiprocessor like the Multiscalar, this requires that the memory location in question is implicitly forwarded from the producer to the consumer—functionality that is provided by the Multiscalar's *address-resolution buffer* [12]. Our scheme does not provide this support because it would require the memory coherence protocol to perform complex version management.

Figure 9 illustrates how we dynamically synchronize. When a load is likely to cause a dependence violation, we can prevent speculation from failing by instead stalling the load until the previous epoch is complete: at that point, all modifications by previous epochs will be visible and the load can safely issue. We can use the *violating loads list* described in Section 4.1.1 to identify the loads most likely to cause a violation that should therefore be synchronized.

In Figure 10, experiment D shows the performance of dynamic synchronization where we have synchronized every load in the violating loads list. By inspecting both result graphs, we see that failed speculation has been replaced with synchronization as expected, resulting in improved performance for 10 of the 14 benchmarks. However, CRAFTY, GZIP, and VPR are now over-synchronized: we have unwittingly replaced successful speculation with synchronization as well. In an attempt to mitigate this effect, we periodically reset the violating loads list in experiment R, and build on that in experiment M by requiring that a load be responsible for at least 4 violations since the last reset before synchronizing. The M experiment solves the problem for CRAFTY but not for VPR, and performance is degraded for PARSER and VORTEX2K. Overall, this technique has a greater benefit than cost (an average improvement of 9%), and is a promising technique for improving the performance of TLS.

4.2.2 Prioritizing the Critical Path

In Section 4.1.2 we observed that even after aggressive prediction of forwarded values, synchronization is still an impediment

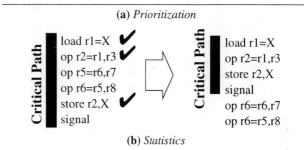

(a) *Prioritization*

(b) *Statistics*

Application	Issued Insts That Are High Priority and Issued Early	Improvement in Avg. Start-to-Signal Time (cycles)		
		Unprioritized	Prioritized	Speedup
BZIP2	0.0%	0.0	0.0	0.0
CRAFTY	6.8%	118.5	117.7	0.99
GZIP	3.6%	1622.6	1636.2	1.00
MCF	9.9%	86.7	80.2	0.92
PARSER	9.7%	110.9	105.6	0.95
PERLBMK	18.1%	45.5	44.0	0.96
VORTEX2K	3.6%	304.8	290.4	0.95
VPR	4.7%	81.8	79.7	0.97
COMPRESS95	7.1%	136.7	135.9	1.01
GO	12.9%	70.2	70.4	1.00
IJPEG	11.2%	28.1	26.0	0.92
LI	27.5%	37.4	33.1	0.88
M88KSIM	9.1%	212.8	218.4	1.02
PERL	16.6%	42.4	44.5	1.04

Figure 11. Prioritization of the critical path. We show (a) our algorithm, where we mark the instructions on the input chain of the critical store and the pipeline's issue logic gives them high priority; (b) some statistics, namely the fraction of issued instructions that are given high priority by our algorithm and issue early, and also the improvement in number of cycles from the start of the epoch until each signal.

to good speedup for some benchmarks. We call the instructions between the first use and the last definition of a forwarded value the *critical path*. A possibility for improving performance when it is not possible to eliminate synchronization is to instead prioritize instructions to help reduce the size of the critical forwarding path. Our compiler already performs this optimization to the best of its ability, but there may be more that can be done dynamically by hardware at run-time.

Our hardware prioritization algorithm works as shown in Figure 11(a). We mark all instructions with registers on the input-chain of the critical store. We also track the critical path through memory, so that a critical load also depends on the store which

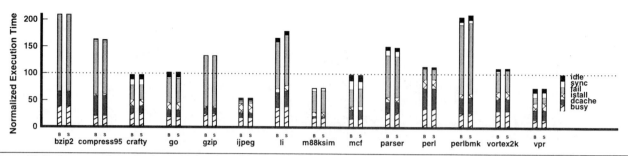

Figure 12. Performance impact of prioritizing the critical path: B is the baseline experiment, and S prioritizes the critical path.

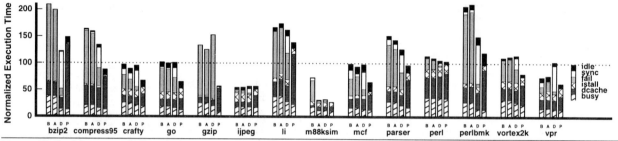

Figure 13. Performance of all techniques combined. B is the baseline experiment, A performs all optimizations except dynamic synchronization, D performs all optimizations, and P is the perfect prediction result from Section 3.2 for comparison.

produced the value for the given memory location. Ideally, we would also mark any instructions on the input-chain of an unpredictable conditional branch as being on the critical path, but this beyond the scope of this paper. The pipeline issue logic then gives priority to marked instructions so that the associated signal may be issued as early as possible. This algorithm could be implemented using techniques described by Fields *et al.* [11], but for now we focus on the potential impact.

The impact of prioritizing the critical path is shown in Figure 12. Note that we model a 128-entry reorder buffer (see Table 1), so the issue logic has significant opportunity to reorder prioritized instructions. Despite this fact, all benchmarks remain relatively unchanged, while MCF and PARSER improve slightly, and the performance of LI and PERLBMK degrades slightly. To clarify whether our prioritization has had any impact, Figure 11(b) shows the fraction of issued instructions that are given high priority by our algorithm and also issue early. This is between 4% and 28% of issued instructions, an average of 10.8% across all benchmarks with the exception of BZIP2 (which does not have forwarded values). Figure 11(b) also shows the change in the average number of cycles from the start of an epoch to the issue of each signal, for which the results are mixed: COMPRESS95, M88KSIM, and PERL have improved somewhat, GZIP and GO are unchanged, and the remaining benchmarks have slowed-down slightly. Given the potential complexity for implementing this technique and the resulting uncompelling performance, we do not advocate the use of this technique.

5 Combining the Techniques

In this Section, we evaluate the impact of all of our techniques combined. Most techniques are orthogonal in their operation with the exception of memory value prediction and dynamic synchronization: we only want to dynamically synchronize on memory

values that are unpredictable. This cooperative behavior is implemented by having the dynamic synchronization logic check the prediction confidence for the load in question, and synchronizing only when confidence is low.

Figure 13 shows the performance of all techniques combined, where A performs all optimizations except dynamic synchronization, D performs all optimizations, and P is the perfect prediction result from Section 3.2 for comparison. We achieve very close to the ideal speedup for M88KSIM, and we have improved CRAFTY and MCF significantly. After all of our optimizations, we observe that failed speculation remains a problem for many benchmarks. For BZIP2 the D experiment shows how some techniques can be complementary since its performance is better than that of any one technique alone.[9] Since including dynamic synchronization (D) degrades performance for more than half of the benchmarks, we do not advocate this technique in its current form.

6 Conclusions

We have shown that improving value communication in TLS can yield large performance benefits, and examined the techniques for taking advantage of this fact. Our analysis provides several important lessons. First, we discovered that prediction cannot be applied liberally when the cost of misprediction is high: predictors must be throttled to target only those dependences that limit performance. We observed that silent stores are prevalent, and squashing them can greatly improve the performance of TLS execution. We found that dynamic synchronization improves performance for many applications but can degrade performance for others—this technique requires further throttling before it can be

---

[9] The D bar out-performs the perfect prediction estimate (P) because that estimate does not account for the coherence traffic savings of memory value prediction and silent stores—only for the savings in failed speculation.

applied liberally. We also found that hardware prioritization to reduce the critical forwarding path does not work well, even though a significant number of instructions can be reordered. Finally, we have shown that compiler transformations can impact conclusions about hardware TLS support, and demonstrated that the compiler can be quite effective at improving the performance of TLS.

7 Acknowledgments

This research is supported by grants from Compaq, IBM, and NASA. Todd C. Mowry is partially supported by an Alfred P. Sloan Research Fellowship. We thank Joel Emer for his many helpful comments regarding this work.

References

[1] A. V. Aho, R. Sethi, and J. D. Ullman. *Compilers: Principles, Techniques and Tools.* Addison Wesley, 1986.

[2] H. Akkary and M. Driscoll. A Dynamic Multithreading Processor. In *MICRO-31*, December 1998.

[3] W. Blume, R. Doallo, R. Eigenmann, J. Grout, J. Hoeflinger, T. Lawrence, J. Lee, D. Padua, Y. Paek, B. Pottenger, L. Rauchwerger, and P. Tu. Parallel programming with polaris. *IEEE Computer*, 29(12):78–82, 1996.

[4] B. Calder, G. Reinman, and D. Tullsen. Selective value prediction. In *International Symposium on Computer Architecture*, 1999.

[5] G. Chrysos and J. Emer. Memory dependency prediction using store sets. June 1998.

[6] M. Cintra, J. F. Martínez, and J. Torrellas. Architectural Support for Scalable Speculative Parallelization in Shared-Memory Multiprocessors. In *Proceedings of ISCA 27*, June 2000.

[7] M. Cintra and J. Torrellas. Learning cross-thread violations in speculative parallelization for multiprocessors. In *HPCA02*, 2002.

[8] Broadcom Corporation. The Sibyte SB-1250 Processor. http://www.sibyte.com/mercurian.

[9] Standard Performance Evaluation Corporation. The SPEC Benchmark Suite. Technical report. http://www.spechbench.org.

[10] R. Cytron. Doacross: Beyond vectorization for multiprocessors. In *International Conference on Parallel Processing*, 1986.

[11] Brian A. Fields, Shai Rubin, and Rastislav Bodik. Focusing processor policies via critical-path prediction. In *ISCA 2001*, 2001.

[12] M. Franklin and G. S. Sohi. ARB: A Hardware Mechanism for Dynamic Reordering of Memory References. *IEEE Transactions on Computers*, 45(5), May 1996.

[13] F. Gabbay and A. Mendelson. Speculative execution based on value prediction. Technical Report EE Department TR #1080, Technion–Israel Institute of Technology, 1996.

[14] S. Gopal, T. Vijaykumar, J. Smith, and G. Sohi. Speculative Versioning Cache. In *Proceedings of the Fourth International Symposium on High-Performance Computer Architecture*, February 1998.

[15] M. Gupta and R. Nim. Techniques for Speculative Run-Time Parallelization of Loops. In *Supercomputing '98*, November 1998.

[16] L. Hammond, M. Willey, and K. Olukotun. Data Speculation Support for a Chip Multiprocessor. In *Proceedings of ASPLOS-VIII*, October 1998.

[17] Seema Hiranandani, Ken Kennedy, and Chau-Wen Tseng. Preliminary experiences with the Fortran D compiler. In *Supercomputing '93*, 1993.

[18] J. Kahle. Power4: A Dual-CPU Processor Chip. *Microprocessor Forum '99*, October 1999.

[19] Jens Knoop and Oliver Ruthing. Lazy code motion. In *Proc. ACM SIGPLAN 92 Conference on Programming Language Design and Implementation*, 92.

[20] V. Krishnan and J. Torrellas. The Need for Fast Communication in Hardware-Based Speculative Chip Multiprocessors. In *International Conference on Parallel Architectures and Compilation Techniques (PACT)*, October 1999.

[21] Kevin M. Lepak and Mikko H. Lipasti. On the value locality of store instructions. In *Proceedings of ISCA 27*, June 2000.

[22] Mikko H. Lipasti and John Paul Shen. Exceeding the dataflow limit via value prediction. In *International Symposium on Microarchitecture*, 1996.

[23] P. Marcuello and A. Gonzlez. Clustered Speculative Multithreaded Processors. In *Proc. of the ACM Int. Conf. on Supercomputing*, June 1999.

[24] P. Marcuello, J. Tubella, and A. Gonzalez. Value prediction for speculative multithreaded architectures. In *International Symposium on Microarchitecture*, November 1999.

[25] A. Moshovos, S. Breach, T. Vijaykumar, and G. Sohi. Dynamic speculation and synchronization of data dependences. June 1997.

[26] J. Oplinger, D. Heine, and M. S. Lam. In Search of Speculative Thread-Level Parallelism. In *Proceedings of the 1999 International Conference on Parallel Architectures and Compilation Techniques (PACT'99)*, October 1999.

[27] D. Padua, D. Kuck, and D. Lawrie. High-speed multiprocessors and compilation techniques. *IEEE Transactions on Computing*, September 1980.

[28] E. Rotenberg, Q. Jacobson, Y. Sazeides, and J. Smith. Trace processors. In *Proceedings of Micro 30*, 1997.

[29] Y. Sazeides and J. E. Smith. The Predictability of Data Values. *Proceedings of Micro 13*, pages 248–258, December 1997.

[30] G. S. Sohi, S. Breach, and T. N. Vijaykumar. Multiscalar Processors. In *Proceedings of ISCA 22*, pages 414–425, June 1995.

[31] J. G. Steffan, C. B. Colohan, and T. C. Mowry. Architectural Support for Thread-Level Data Speculation. Technical Report CMU-CS-97-188, School of Computer Science, Carnegie Mellon University, November 1997.

[32] J. G. Steffan, C. B. Colohan, A. Zhaia, and T. C. Mowry. A Scalable Approach to Thread-Level Speculation. In *Proceedings of ISCA 27*, June 2000.

[33] S. Tjiang, M. Wolf, M. Lam, K. Pieper, and J. Hennessy. *Languages and Compilers for Parallel Computing*, pages 137–151. Springer-Verlag, Berlin, Germany, 1992.

[34] M. Tremblay. MAJC: Microprocessor Architecture for Java Computing. *HotChips '99*, August 1999.

[35] J.-Y. Tsai, J. Huang, C. Amlo, D.J. Lilja, and P.-C. Yew. The Superthreaded Processor Architecture. *IEEE Transactions on Computers, Special Issue on Multithreaded Architectures*, 48(9), September 1999.

[36] D. M. Tullsen, S. J. Eggers, and H. M. Levy. Simultaneous Multithreading: Maximizing On-Chip Parallelism. In *Proceedings of ISCA 22*, pages 392–403, June 1995.

[37] Kai Wang and Manoj Franklin. Highly accurate data value prediction using hybrid predictors. In *International Symposium on Microarchitecture*, 1997.

[38] K. Yeager. The MIPS R10000 superscalar microprocessor. *IEEE Micro*, April 1996.

Panel

What Will Have the Greatest Impact in 2010: The Processor, the Memory, or the Interconnect?

Moderator
Timothy Mark Pinkston, University of Southern California

Panelists
Anant Agarwal, Massachusetts Institute of Technology
Bill Dally, Stanford University
José Duato, Univèrsitat Politècnica de València, Spain
Bob Horst, Horst Technology Research
Yale Patt, The University of Texas at Austin
T. Basil Smith, IBM T.J. Watson Research Center

Potpourri

Reverse Tracer:
A Software Tool for Generating Realistic Performance Test Programs

Mariko Sakamoto[*], Larry Brisson[†],
Akira Katsuno[*], Aiichiro Inoue[‡], and Yasunori Kimura[*]

[*]Fujitsu Laboratories Ltd.   [†]Sun Microsystems Inc.[(*1)]   [‡]Fujitsu Ltd.

{s.mariko, katsuno.akir-02,   Lawrence.Brisson@sun.com   inoue.aiichiro@jp.fujitsu.com

ykimura}@jp.fujitsu.com

Abstract

During the development of high-performance processors, software performance models are used to get performance estimates. These models are not cycle-accurate, so their results can have significant errors, leading to performance surprises after hardware is built.

Some performance tests can run directly on the logic simulators, to get more accurate results, but those simulators cannot run large interactive workloads with I/O and much Operating System code. So the accurate performance estimates from logic simulators are only available for application code, and are not adequate for evaluation of powerful server systems that will primarily run large interactive workloads.

We discuss a software tool system, the "Reverse Tracer" that generates executable performance tests from an instruction trace of the workload. The generated performance tests retain the essential performance characteristics of multi-user I/O-intensive workloads without doing any real I/O, so they can run in logic simulation to measure performance accurately before hardware is built.

1. Introduction

During the development of high-performance processor systems, hardware designers often use software simulators to get performance estimates. Later, when performance tests can be run on the real machine, in spite of all the performance simulation, performance problems are discovered. Often it's too late to implement improvements. The problems arise because the designers don't have a way to estimate final performance accurately before hardware is built. The software simulators are required to be developed rather quickly and to be quite flexible.

Given those requirements, it is very difficult to create a model that is also a cycle-accurate representation of the design. Therefore, performance models are likely to have errors of unknown magnitude.

Once the hardware design is complete, the hardware design simulator can be used to run performance tests to get more accurate results. Some performance tests can be run directly on the simulators, but those simulators practically cannot run large multi-user interactive workloads, which have a lot of I/O and asynchronous activity, and execute much Operating System code. So the accurate performance estimates from hardware simulators are only available for application code, and are not adequate for evaluation of powerful server systems that will primarily run large interactive workloads at present. There was no way to create tests that could run on such a hardware simulator environment and still capture the characteristics of a realistic interactive workload.

We focused our research on a method to obtain accurate performance estimates for powerful server systems before hardware is built. We propose to generate performance test programs that can be run on logic simulator and that include both application and OS code and have characteristics very similar to customers' large-scale interactive workloads. These can be used directly to estimate the ultimate system performance in the real world, and any performance problems observed in running such realistic programs are clearly important because they will affect real customer workloads.

In this paper, we present research leading to the development of a software tool system called the "Reverse Tracer" that allows us to generate realistic performance tests for interactive workloads by starting with an instruction trace of the workload. We created a test program with the Reverse Tracer, and report an evaluation that we did for a mainframe computer using that test program. Some key features of the generated performance tests are that they run deterministically, and they retain the essential performance characteristics of multi-user

---

[(*1)] Brisson did this work while he was at Amdahl corp.

I/O-intensive workloads without doing any real I/O, making it possible to run the tests in environments with little or no I/O support.

2. Our Approach and Goal

Our goal is to get accurate performance estimates of powerful server systems in an early phase of hardware development. We approach the goal by creating performance test programs that have these features:
* They should run on the logic simulator, a truly accurate representation of the design.
* They should accurately reflect realistic customer multi-user interactive workload characteristics.
* Ideally, they should also be able to run on real hardware. This means that the test program should not require special support from external software that might be available in logic simulation but not on the real hardware.

Our approach is to start with instruction traces. We already had tracing software that was capable of getting representative instruction traces of large-scale interactive workloads running in steady state. There were also tools and methods in place to check trace characteristics and validate them. Using such methods, we could obtain good traces from many workloads.

Given the existence of good traces, we developed "Reverse Tracer" software to transform an instruction trace into a binary program that, when executed, reproduces the execution sequence represented by the original trace.

Figure 1 illustrates the Reverse Tracer methodology.

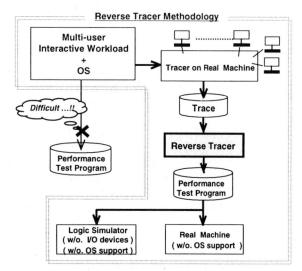

* **Difficult** to create performance tests that mimic the behavior of powerful sever systems based on knowledge of user workload and OS.

Figure 1: Proposed methodology.

We create traces of a system running a multi-user interactive workload in steady state under a normal OS. Each trace includes every instruction and interrupt, plus the contents of registers and memory. The Reverse Tracer reads such a trace and outputs a performance test program that can run both on a logic simulator and a real machine.

3. Problems that Reverse Tracer Covers

Given the goal of creating executable performance tests as described above, it is natural to consider the idea of using a memory dump, that is making the workload run on an existing machine, letting it reach steady state, halting the machine, and dumping the contents of memory and registers. One might load this entire architectural state into the simulator and let it run, in the hope that the program would behave like the real workload following that point. Unfortunately, there are a number of problems with this approach, and understanding those problems will help in understanding the algorithms and tools we have developed.
* The first, and probably most severe, problem is I/O. The dumped system image will very soon attempt to do I/O operations, and it is impractical for the simulation environment to support all the required I/O devices, and to have every device loaded with exactly the data that will be needed for the performance test to run properly.
* The next problem is asynchronous interrupts, which occur due to I/O operations and for timer functions. Because it is impossible to make the timing of I/O and timer interrupts in simulation match the original hardware machine, these asynchronous events will happen at times in simulation that may not be realistic, and can distort workload behavior. For example, if an I/O interrupt happens too soon in simulation relative to the instruction sequence, a process that does I/O and would normally have to wait for it, while other processes run, may get control back immediately in simulation, resulting in less process switching activity.
* In general, there may be a number of special instructions that cannot execute properly in the simulation environment. This is similar to the problem of I/O instructions but may apply to other types of instruction, depending on the architecture.
* Another problem arises because real systems use a Time of Day clock for various timing functions, and make decisions related to time, such as limiting execution time of a process to an allowed time-slice. It is difficult to force timers in simulation to match those in the real hardware, and failing to do so will affect the way the test program behaves, possibly making it unrealistic, and maybe even making it fail.

4. Prior Work

System level performance evaluation is a historical research field. Software performance models are developed for this purpose, some of which process traces while others directly interpret executable binary programs. Such simulation methodologies really consist of two kinds of model: models of the processor design, and models of workloads. It is important for both of these models to be reasonably accurate. References [1], [2], [3], and [4] are examples of current research that stress the importance of using representative workloads, having accurate performance models, and doing extensive performance simulation early in the design process.

The idea of generating performance tests using a Reverse Tracer first arose at Amdahl in 1992. Subsequently, over the next few years, a performance test program known as REVBUP was generated from one of Amdahl's traces. The traces available at that time had incomplete information about memory contents, so a general software tool for generating programs from traces could not be developed. Much of the generating work was manual, and much ad-hoc code was created to handle the specific problems in the trace. In REVBUP, many parts of the original trace could not be included, and there were frequent branches into fixup code. As a result, REVBUP was not very representative of real workloads, and the method of its creation was hard to apply to any new traces. Nevertheless, REVBUP was found to be very useful in spite of its limitations, and it demonstrated the potential value of a more general Reverse Tracer.

5. The Reverse Tracer

5.1. Overview

When this project began, we already had access to an instruction Tracer developed by Amdahl over a period of many years. The Amdahl Tracer ran on machines supporting the IBM ESA/390 architecture[6], and could trace workloads designed to run on the same architecture. This Tracer uses certain features of the IBM architecture, including SIE and PER, to execute the workload and to get control after each instruction in order to trace it. The Amdahl Tracer created a "virtual machine" in which to run the traced workload, similar to the way IBM's VM operating system works, but the Tracer was developed from scratch at Amdahl and is not based on VM.

In support of the Reverse Tracer project, we modified the original Tracer so it creates new records containing blocks of memory data used by the executing instructions. The new traces therefore contain the contents of every memory location that is actually used, directly or indirectly, by the traced workload.

The Reverse Tracer software is partitioned into two major parts: "MIMIC" (Initial Memory Image Creator,) and "MIP" (Memory Image Polisher).

MIMIC processes trace records and creates an executable memory image that includes all the instructions and other data that were used in the trace, plus some extra code and data needed to handle certain problems. We call this binary image the "PMI" (Primary Memory Image,) since it consists of the entire memory image needed to begin execution. The PMI can be run on a logic simulator or a real machine by loading it into memory and setting the Program Counter to the starting instruction address.

MIP is a software tool that helps to verify that the PMI runs correctly. MIP interfaces with an architectural simulator that runs the PMI, executing one instruction at a time, while MIP reads the original trace and checks that the execution of the PMI matches the trace, except for certain expected differences.

Figure 2 presents an outline of the Reverse Tracer. A trace is created for a workload running in a normal OS environment in steady state. In order to be sure each trace contains a realistic frequency of interrupts and diverse sample of activity, the trace consists of many separate intervals taken at times that were separated by "gaps" of several seconds of running the system without tracing. Each trace interval is a continuous sequence of instructions.

When MIMIC creates MO1 in Figure 2, the main focus is to process memory content records for instructions and data that are fetched. MIMIC keeps track of which bytes of memory have a known value, and builds a data

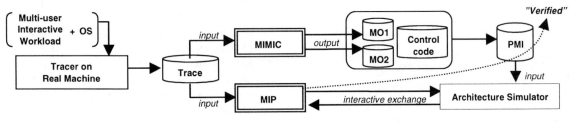

MO1 : Re-created memory space that is occupied by the original system.   MO2 : Fixup code. & Data for fixup and emulate.

Figure 2: Outline of Reverse Tracer.

structure that holds the first data value observed for every location actually fetched in the trace.

Some data, such as translation tables, is not explicitly accessed by instructions, but is nevertheless implicitly used. The Tracer creates memory records for all such table data that is actually used. As a result, to create the proper translation tables, MIMIC only needs to process the memory records, as it does for all other memory contents.

MO1 is similar to a dumped system image but it only includes the memory data that is actually used during PMI execution, and the rest of memory is simply left with zero values. As a result, the memory image, MO1, looks quite different from a dumped image of a real system filled with OS and application code and data, but it has all the data in the correct locations for the PMI to execute properly.

MO2 in Figure 2 includes data and code for problem solving, which we call "fixup code".

"Control code" in Figure 2 is a hand-written general routine that figures out which specific fixup code and data to use when a SVC interrupt occurs. There is a table in MO2 that maps the specific SVC interrupt to its corresponding fixup code.

We show a general PMI image in Figure 3. The PMI includes memory space (workload's space) that is occupied by the original system, and EXTRA space. The Workload's space is made of MO1 in Figure 2 and is the same size as the real memory that was used when the original workload was traced. EXTRA space includes "control code", "fixup code" and "fixup data" and is made of MO2 and Control Code in Figure 2. To help explain certain PMI features, we use comparison with dumped image, again. They are close, with some important differences:

* The PMI only includes the memory data that is actually used during its execution.
* The PMI includes some extra "fixup code" and data to handle problems.
* The Reverse Tracer inserts fixup-SVCs and emulate-SVCs in the workload's space.

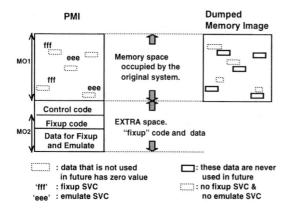

: data that is not used in future has zero value
'fff' : fixup SVC
'eee' : emulate SVC

: these data are never used in future
: no fixup SVC & no emulate SVC

Figure 3: Primary memory image (PMI).

* Some of the interrupt vectors in the original memory image are modified to invoke fixup code routines.

Figure 4 illustrates the basic idea for problem solving. MIMIC inserts a control transfer instruction in place of an instruction 'X' that corresponds to a point in the trace where a problem occurred. We used a "Supervisor Call (SVC)" instruction for this purpose. When the PMI runs, the fixup code executes instead of 'X' in Figure 4 and emulates the replaced instruction, updating memory data and updating register contents as needed. At the end of the fixup code, it branches to the proper address to continue normal execution.

.... : Code for problem solving (Not exists in original trace).
'X' : Problem place in trace.
Replaced with Control transfer inst.

Figure 4: Basic idea for problem solving.

Fixup code is used for the following four problems:

i. **Asynchronous Interrupts** Where asynchronous interrupts occur in the trace, we must force interrupts to occur when the PMI is run. To do this precisely, we insert a "fixup SVC" at the precise point in the PMI code, and "fake" the interrupt. As a result of this replacement, real I/O and Timer interrupts never happen in the performance test, but the fixup SVC makes the system act as if such interrupts did occur at exactly the same points in every run. The SVC is placed in the static code of the PMI, and it might be executed several times before the time when the asynchronous interrupt is supposed to happen. The fixup code therefore keeps a counter of how many times the SVC is executed, and the interrupt is simulated only at the proper time, with all other times being treated as no-ops.

ii. **Special Instructions** I/O instructions and some others not supported by the logic simulator must be emulated. We create an emulation routine in the fixup code area, and replace the instruction with an SVC of a type we call an "emulate-SVC".

iii. **Timer Related Instructions** The timers in logic simulation and on real hardware will run at different speeds than the clocks during tracing. This can cause problems unless we make it appear that clock values are exactly the same as when the trace was made. In the traced system, there are processes that compare Time of Day clock values with previously saved time values and use the comparison to make decisions. To avoid taking the wrong branch path, we emulate the clock related instructions and make all stored clock values appear exactly as they were in the trace. We also use a "fixup-SVC" to solve this problem.

iv. Gaps between Trace Intervals A Gap is similar to an interrupt because it is a point where we must change many values in registers and memory and force the execution path to jump to a different place. Therefore, MIMIC inserts a fixup SVC at the last instruction prior to the gap.

Synchronous interrupts, e.g. Page Faults, will occur naturally at the correct points, because the PMI uses the same data and addresses as were in the trace. Table 1 summarizes MIMIC's management of interrupt types.

Interrupt name	In PMI
I/O	Force interrupt to appear by SVC.
External	Force interrupt to appear by SVC.
SVC	Trace original form.
Program	Trace original form.
Machine check	(Not exist in trace).

Table 1: MIMIC interrupts handling.

5.2. MIMIC Algorithm

The fundamental idea of the MIMIC algorithm for creating the PMI is to process the trace, keeping track of the first data value ever fetched from each memory location that is ever used. The PMI will consist of all the bytes of physical memory, with correct initial values set in all bytes actually used when the workload runs, and most unused memory locations set to zero. To implement this algorithm, MIMIC keeps two arrays, each one equal in size to the entire physical memory to be used. One array will hold the actual data values that belong in memory; the other array has a status byte for each data byte. Initially, all bytes in both arrays are zero.

As the trace is processed, values are found that need to go in memory. These values include the binary instruction images themselves, operand data, and data for translation tables. Each time a data value is processed, it is stored into the data array only if the status byte is still zero, and the status byte for that location is then set to '1'.

We illustrate the basic algorithm of MIMIC with an example. In Figure 5, instructions 'i.1' to 'i.4' form a loop. These same four instructions repeat twice until 'i.5' to 'i.8'. Figure 5 shows some of the memory-related information present in the trace for each instruction. "Raddr" means

inst. #	inst. mnemonic.	inst (Raddr. Len. Image)	op2 (Raddr. Len. Data)
i1	l 5, 0x0(1,4)	0x6000 4 01514000	0x1100 4 0x8
i2	a 1, 2	0x6004 2 0212	- - -
i3	cl 5, 0x0(0,4)	0x6006 4 03504000	0x1000 4 0x10
i4	bc c, 0x54(0,3)	0x600a 4 04c03054	0x6000 4 0x01514000
i5	l 5, 0x0(1,4)	0x6000 4 01514000	0x1110 4 0x10
i6	a 1, 2	0x6004 2 0212	0x1000 4 -
i7	cl 5, 0x0(0,4)	0x6006 4 03504000	0x6000 4 0x10
i8	bc c, 0x54(0,3)	0x600a 4 04c03054	0x1004 4 0x01514000
i9	st 1, 0x4(0,4)	0x600e 4 09104004	- - -

Figure 5: MIMIC algorithm (Instructions).

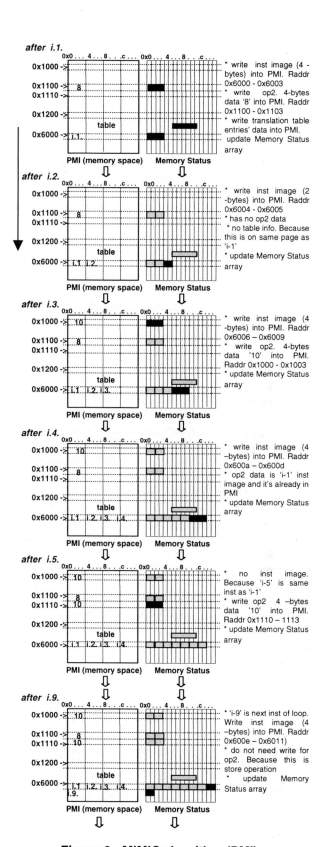

Figure 6: MIMIC algorithm (PMI).

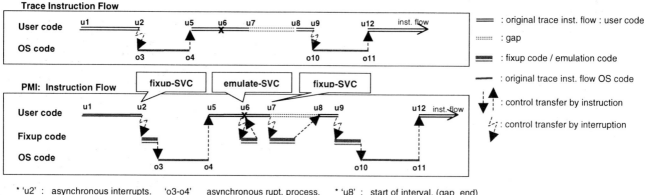

Trace Instruction Flow

* 'u2' : asynchronous interrupts.   'o3-o4' asynchronous rupt. process.   * 'u8' : start of interval. (gap end)
* 'u6' : instruction to be emulated.   * 'u9' : synchronous interrupts. 'o10-o11' synchronous rupt. process.
* 'u7' : end of interval. (gap start)

Figure 7: Trace instruction flow and PMI instruction flow.

Real Address, "Len" means memory data length, "Image" means the binary image of the instruction itself. "Data" means the contents of a memory operand.

In this example, inst. 'i.1' is the first one in the trace and the PMI starts out with all zero values in the data array.

Figure 6 shows a sequence of transformations of the "PMI (memory space)" data array and the "Memory Status" array.

In Figure 6, data values placed into the data array are shown as hex values, while the bytes in the status array start out blank and become shaded when the corresponding data has been stored.

For inst. 'i.1', inst. real address is 0x6000. From the status array, MIMIC can see that no value has been set for these bytes yet. MIMIC puts the inst. image into the proper location of the data array and marks the status array, as shown in Figure 6 at 'after i.1'. Inst. 'i.1' is a Load, so MIMIC also writes its memory operand data into the data array at the proper address, and sets the corresponding status bytes. Execution of this Load instruction also required use of one or more translation table entries, which are provided in the trace records, so they are also stored in the data array.

Similarly, inst. 'i.2' which is an Add, is processed. This Add instruction has no memory operands, so only the inst. image is placed in the data array. The instruction is on the same page as the previous one, so there are no new translation table entries to process. In Figure 6 'after i.2', you can see that the data area for locations 0x6004 and 0x6005 are updated along with the corresponding bytes of the status array.

When MIMIC reaches inst. 'i.5', which repeats 'i.1', the instruction image is not stored since it is already in the data array and the status bytes are set. However, the operand address is different this time, so operand data is stored at location 0x1110. Processing continues in this way. When the end of the trace is reached, every memory location that was referenced in any way in the trace will

have the correct initial data value present in the data array. Subsequently, a few locations will need to be modified by MIMIC to create the Fixup Code that is needed in certain cases, which are described below.

5.3. PMI Instruction Flow

Figure 7 illustrates instruction flow when the PMI is run. "Trace Instruction Flow" shows the instruction execution sequence when the trace was created, while "PMI Instruction Flow" shows the corresponding flow in the PMI. Interrupts occur at 'u2' and 'u9'. 'u2' is an asynchronous interrupt, so in the PMI a fixup-SVC causes a control transfer at that point. A special instruction is executed at 'u6', which is replaced by an emulate-SVC that leads to emulation logic, which finally branches back to the next normal instruction. 'u7' is the end of interval, so another fixup-SVC is executed in the PMI, and after all updating of memory data and register contents, the first instruction of the next interval, 'u8', would be executed. 'u9' is a synchronous interrupt, which occurs in the PMI exactly as it did in the trace.

5.4. Fixup Code and History Tables

MIMIC creates fixup code, invoked by fixup-SVCs inserted in the PMI in place of original instructions. MIMIC produces history tables and fixup code in 2 passes of the input trace. Each emulate and fixup-SVC has an entry that indicates what specific logic and data are needed. MIMIC creates these data structures during the 1st pass and adds more data during the 2nd pass, after which the tables and fixup code are completed.

In Figure 8, we show the form of the fixup data, a linked list of structures. The list elements are linked in order of execution sequence. The logic is described below in more detail.

1st pass. MIMIC creates a list member for the first asynchronous interrupt in the trace at the start of processing (before reaching the interrupt), and determines which static instruction in the PMI to replace with the needed fixup-SVC. Each time MIMIC reaches another asynchronous interrupt record, MIMIC creates a new member and links it to the previous one. MIMIC repeats these steps until the end of the trace.

2nd pass. In case an instruction replaced by a fixup-SVC is in a loop, the SVC would be executed several times before the time when the fixup is needed. We call these early extra executions of a fixup-SVC "Pre-Visits". For each member in the fixup list, MIMIC gathers the following additional data:

* The number of Pre-visits.
* Data for pre-visit to emulate the replaced instruction in fixup code.
* Register contents for pre-visit to modify register value(s).
* Program Counter for pre-visit to return.
* Data for fixup to modify memory area with fixup code.
* Register contents for fixup.
* Program Counter value to return to after fixup.
* Interrupt related info to modify fixed storage area.

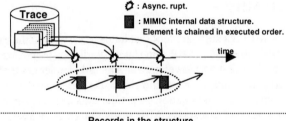

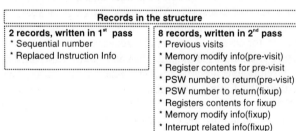

Records in the structure	
2 records, written in 1st pass * Sequential number * Replaced Instruction Info	**8 records, written in 2nd pass** * Previous visits * Memory modify info(pre-visit) * Register contents for pre-visit * PSW number to return(pre-visit) * PSW number to return(fixup) * Registers contents for fixup * Memory modify info(fixup) * Interrupt related info(fixup)

Figure 8: Asynchronous rupt. control.

In the second pass, we put a fixup-SVC into the PMI in the place where it is needed only for the first fixup in the list. The system is designed so there is only one fixup-SVC in memory at a time, and when that fixup occurs, it automatically removes that fixup-SVC, restoring the original instruction, and stores the next fixup-SVC at the place where it will be needed. We show this in Figure 9. Instruction 'i.a' in Figure 9 is currently replaced with an SVC (it was replaced when the previous fixup was completed). In this example, 'i.a' is executed three(3) times after it was changed to an SVC and before it arrives

at our fixup target. During the three pre-visits, the fixup-code just emulates the execution of 'i.a', and then on the 4th time, the fixup code stores the original instruction 'i.a' back in place, stores a fixup-SVC in place of instruction 'i.b', the next one on the fixup list, and does the rest of the real fixup logic as needed. This logic minimizes the number of times fixup-SVCs need to be executed without really doing a useful fixup.

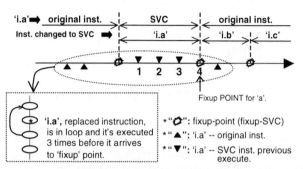

Figure 9: fixup-SVC in memory.

After the 2nd pass, MIMIC has filled in all the data needed in the fixup list, including data for changes needed in memory. MIMIC generates fixup logic that uses the

```
async.rupt "X" {
    if ( current visit is NOT "4" ) {
        Load registers' contents recorded in trace into registers.
        Give control flow to next instruction of "X"
    }
    else {                    /* asynchronous interrupt point */
        Write interrupt related info. in trace into suitable area in page-0.
        Update memory ( if necessary )
        Replace current "SVC" inst. with original inst. in trace.
        Fixup-SVC visit counter += 1.
        Write "SVC" opcode on specific memory area for next fixup-SVC.
        Load registers' contents recorded in trace into registers.
        Give control to OS interrupt handler code, as it was in the trace.
    }
}
```

Figure 10: Outline of typical fixup-SVC code.

fixup list data structures. We show an outline of typical fixup code in Figure 10.

5.5. Fixup Code for emulate-SVCs

MIMIC uses similar logic for emulate-SVCs. The only difference is that all emulate-SVCs always stay in memory because the replaced instructions must be emulated every time.

5.6. Control Code Operation

We create our own interrupt handlers to control all interrupts when the PMI is run. When SVC interrupts occur, the interrupt state is analyzed and the list data structures are used to determine the logic needed. This logic is illustrated in Figure 11.

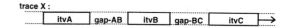

Figure 12: Intervals and gaps in traceX.

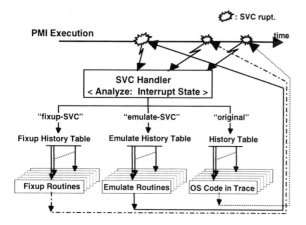

Figure 11: SVC interrupt handling.

External (Timer) and I/O interrupts are not expected to occur while the PMI is running, since we have arranged to fake them with carefully placed SVC's and fixup code. However, if the simulation environment happens to generate an occasional External or I/O interrupt, it is ignored. MIMIC modifies the interrupt vectors for these interrupts to go to simple code that counts them and returns to the interrupted point as if nothing happened.

If an unexpected Program interruption occurs, the logic treats it as an error, and stops. Table 2 summarizes how each interrupt type is handled when the PMI is run.

Interrupt name		handlings
SVC	(fixup)	SVC handler : fixup process routine
SVC	(emulate)	SVC handler : emulate process routine
SVC	(trace)	SVC handler : back to trace OS code
I/O, External		EXT, I/O handler : ignores (back to caller)
Program (trace)		Program handler : back to trace OS code
Program (not trace)		Error : stop !!
Machine check		Error : stop !!

Table 2: PMI interrupt handling.

5.7. Gap Fixup

We designed MIMIC to create one PMI from a trace that includes many intervals. The PMI runs all instructions in the trace. Gaps are handled like asynchronous interrupts except for the logic in pass 2 of MIMIC to figure out what memory values must be changed in the gap fixup.

In the following explanation, we use the example illustrated in Figure 12. In the figure, 'traceX' includes three intervals, 'itvA', 'itvB', and 'itvC' in that order, with gaps in between.

Consider how MIMIC figures out what memory data to modify in the fixup for gap-AB. While processing itvA, MIMIC keeps track of the memory contents with two arrays, each of them equal in size to the real memory where the workload ran, one having one byte to hold the data value for every known byte in the workload memory,

and the other array having a control byte for every data byte, to keep track of the state of the data bytes. At the start of pass 2, the data bytes contain the first value observed for every byte ever referenced in the entire trace. While MIMIC processes itvA (or any other interval), it updates this data array for any stores that execute. After processing itvA, MIMIC knows the contents of all of memory at the end of that interval.

To handle gap-AB fixup, MIMIC resets all control bytes to indicate that they have not yet been referenced in itvB, but leaves the data values as they were at the end of itvA. We construct the fixup data for gap-AB while processing itvB, by examining the first access to each byte used in itvB. If the first access is a fetch, and if the value shown in the trace for that byte is different from the value currently in the data array, then the byte must be modified in the gap fixup, so the address and value are added to the list of gap fixup data. When the end of itvB is reached, the gap fixup data for gap-AB is complete. Whenever a byte is accessed in itvB, its control byte is updated to show that an access has occurred.

5.8. MIP

MIP is a software tool that helps to verify that the PMI runs correctly. MIP interfaces with an architectural simulator that was developed at Amdahl. Under control of MIP, the simulator would load the PMI and run it, executing one instruction at a time and exchanging data with MIP. Meanwhile, MIP reads the original trace and checks that the execution of the PMI matches the trace, except for certain expected differences.

For example, if the trace has an I/O interrupt, the PMI will really execute a fixup-SVC, which will lead to a code path in the fixup routine that does not exist in the trace. MIP has logic to ignore the fixup code in the PMI, and continue matching the execution path again after the fixup code returns to the normal traced code.

MIP checks for correct execution by comparing all types of architectural data, including the Program Counter, instruction image, operand virtual and real addresses, register contents, and memory contents. If a discrepancy is found, MIP pauses and writes useful messages about the type of error, so the researcher can examine any details needed to find the cause of the error. The user can then patch in a temporary fix and tell MIP to continue, or can terminate the run. Either way, once the problem is understood, we needed to fix the problem in MIMIC, so future versions of the PMI would be generated correctly and automatically.

5.9. Iterations

For use on real machines, it is useful if a performance test can be run for long periods of time. Therefore, one of the design goals of our performance tests was to make it possible to iterate the test a large number of times, with each iteration following the same original execution path with essentially the same performance. This was implemented by adding some special fixup code that gets executed at the end of one entire iteration. If additional iterations are requested, this code modifies the contents of memory and registers to match the correct beginning state, and then branches back to start the next iteration.

5.10. A Tricky Problem

There are a few areas of the workload memory that must be modified in the PMI to implement our system. For example, some instructions are replaced by SVCs, and the interrupt vectors of the workload's OS are changed to execute fixup code. We found that a few places in OS code fetched values from those interrupt vectors, and found incorrect data there (because of our changes). We developed logic in MIMIC to detect such cases and replace the instruction that fetches the modified data with an emulate-SVC, which would supply the correct original data.

6. Evaluation

The Reverse Tracer was used to create a PMI named TBUP. We then compared various statistics relating to TBUP with similar statistics for the original trace. Obviously, the fixup code in TBUP would have different characteristics than the trace, but our goal was for the non-fixup code to be a good match. Many characteristics (e.g. opcode frequencies, dependencies) are guaranteed to match because the MIP tool confirmed that the non-fixup code matches the instruction sequence of the trace. It is more difficult to be sure that cache and TLB miss rates are similar.

The trace was made on a uni-processor mainframe system running an interactive workload in steady state. In the trace, there are 6 intervals, a total of 547,727 instructions, 94 SVC interrupts, 16 program interrupts, 6 I/O interrupts and 3 external (timer) interrupts. There were 173 special instructions, which would be replaced with emulate-SVCs. 78% of all instructions executed in supervisor mode.

In Figure 13, we show TBUP details. TBUP runs iteratively, and 732K instructions run in each iteration. 75% of them are from the original trace, gap fixup code is 2.6%, and other fixup code comprises 22.4% of the total in TBUP.

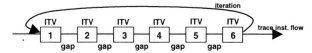

Instruction # in one iteration of TBUP.

Inst. from Trace dynamic #	547,727	(74.78%)
SVC inst. dynamic #	1,210	(0.17%)
Fixup code dynamic #	164,454	(22.45%)
Gap fixup inst. dynamic #	19,030	(2.60%)

TOTAL# 732,421
(Include iteration preparation.)

Figure 13: TBUP details.

Machine configuration		
Instruction TLB	2 way	2K entry
Operand TLB	2 way	2K entry
Instruction 1st cache	2 way	128 KB
Operand 1st cache	2 way	128 KB
Shared 2nd cache	4 way	2 MB
Memory size	---	2 GB

Table 3: GS8900 configuration.

We measured TBUP on Fujitsu: GS8900, whose configuration is in Table 3, using performance hardware counters to measure miss rates. We set up a software simulator to match the GS8900 configuration, so we could process the trace and predict its miss rates for such hardware. We had already verified the simulator's accuracy high.

Table 4 presents measured cache and TLB miss rates, from the trace-driven software model and TBUP on GS8900. Keep in mind that the hardware counters cannot distinguish fixup code from other code, so they show total miss rates, which are likely to be higher than normal because of jumping between normal code and fixup code.

Results on GS89000	miss rate (%)	
	TBUP	Orig. Trace
Instruction TLB	0.03	0.01
Operand TLB	1.48	0.15
Instruction 1st cache	2.44	2.14
Operand 1st cache	5.28	3.92
Shared 2nd cache	0.88	0.79

Table 4: Results on GS8900.

Table 4 reveals:
* TBUP operand TLB miss rate is nearly 10 times larger than original-trace's rate,
* TBUP instruction TLB miss rate is 3 times larger,
* TBUP 1st-cache operand miss rate is 1.3 times larger,
* TBUP 2nd-cache miss rate is slightly larger.

The largest differences are observed for the TLB miss rates. We have reason to expect these miss rates to be especially high in TBUP because of synonyms. We execute fixup code under control of a dynamic address translation table (DAT table) in which the mapping is set up so each translated real address is equal to the logical address. In fixup code, we copy data from the "fixup code and data area (ref. Figure 1)" to the "Trace Memory Data area". In the normal workload code in the PMI, most addresses have very different DAT table mappings, which means the same page has different logical addresses, or synonyms, which lead to a high TLB miss rate. In a future version of the Reverse Tracer, we plan to change the translations used in fixup code to avoid use of synonym addresses, and presumably reduce the TLB miss rate.

Although the cache miss rates do not match exactly, they are fairly close considering that the hardware measurements include fixup code. We suspect that many of the extra cache misses actually occur in fixup code. If so, we can avoid having the cost of those misses count in the final performance numbers if we make the fixup code self-timing, as discussed below, and subtract that time from the overall execution time, to get a performance number that only applies to the original code, not the fixup code. At the moment, the characteristics of TBUP are close enough to a normal workload to be useful, but we expect to improve its accuracy as explained below.

7. Current State and Future work

We have demonstrated that we can generate performance test programs from traces, including both OS and User/application code. We developed a set of software tools and methodology that should allow the creation of many more such programs with minimal manual effort. Our goals for further research include the following:

*   **Accuracy Improvement** Our goal is to estimate accurately the performance of processors in development. In the current implementation, there are several things that limit accuracy, and we think they can be improved.

    -   Improve TLB miss accuracy by changing the DAT table for fixup code to avoid generation of artificial synonyms.

    -   Reduce the impact of fixup code by hand-coding the main routines in assembler code.

    -   Improve accuracy by making the fixup code measure its own execution time and exclude that time in computing the final performance numbers. The fixup code could do this easily by saving the current time upon entry and exit, and accumulating the total time spent in fixup code.

    -   Improve accuracy by avoiding the distortion from cold-start periods: At the beginning of each trace interval, especially the first one, any computer design is likely to get an unusually high number of cache and TLB misses. We have a plan to add another special type of SVC to the generated PMI's that will interrupt the code for each new trace interval after

some number of instructions of that interval have executed. This new SVC will execute when enough activity has executed in that interval so that the caches are reasonably 'warm' with current data, and the cache miss rates should be more like steady state. When this is implemented, the cold start periods prior to reaching that SVC will be excluded from the measurement; i.e. those instructions are not counted in the execution count, and their execution time is excluded like the fixup code time is excluded. Using this method, the test program should be able to compute a very accurate performance number at the end of the run when running on real systems.

*   **Other Architectures** This approach is not limited to the currently targeted mainframe architecture. We would like to develop a similar system on a new architecture. In general, it is most efficient if the target architecture of the new processor is compatible with the architecture of the existing machine that runs the Tracer. However, it is possible to develop a tracer that runs on an existing architecture and simulates a new target architecture. With such a tracer, the Reverse Tracer methodology can be used to create performance test programs for new target architectures that do not yet exist in hardware.

*   **MP Systems** Another important goal for the future is to create performance test programs for MP systems. However, there are some problems in applying our methodology to MP systems. We don't think it will be possible to make all CPU's of an MP system execute in a deterministic way relative to each other, and that leads to the possibility that the performance test will follow unexpected paths and not function properly. We need to do more research to discover the best way to create MP performance tests.

8. Conclusion

Estimating performance of developing hardware before hardware logic is fixed can have a strong impact on final system performance, and our ability to predict it accurately. Before this project, we had no way to create practical test programs with multi-user interactive workload behavior that can run on logic simulators and in early hardware bringup. The test programs we had were inferior, and although they sometimes helped us find and fix performance problems, we could not use them to estimate performance with confidence, and there was a danger of optimizing the wrong things.

We took an approach of generating realistic performance tests from instruction traces that were made while a real system was running an interactive workload in steady state.

We demonstrated that we could create a performance test program from a trace:

* We developed a software system we called the Reverse Tracer that processed the trace, and
* generated an executable program from it that would mimic the execution path and data access patterns of the original workload that was traced, with a modest amount of extra 'fixup' code.
* We also created a tool that verifies the test program by running it on an architecture simulator and dynamically comparing its execution with the original trace records.

The result is that we have successfully generated one performance test that is useful, and have developed a set of software tools and a methodology that should allow creation of many more such tests.

Although this research is "work in progress", we have been able to create some performance test programs using the methodology and tools we developed. The performance test programs have been used at Fujitsu by the processor development group, and have been found to be truly valuable. One value is that the designers can be confident that when they make design changes to improve performance, the improvements seen with the performance test are real and will have a real impact on customer workloads. In the future, after our work for accuracy improvement, the tests will directly result in estimates of final system performance, and as the design evolves, the tests will provide a historical track of performance changes. The fact that the test is deterministic and repeatable makes it very easy to use in studying possible performance problems, trying solutions, and measuring the changes. The test program is designed so it can be iterated any number of times, with similar behavior and performance all the time, making it helpful for runs on real hardware on which a single iteration would be done in a small fraction of a second.

We would like to create more of these test programs to represent a variety of workloads, and we hope to generate larger ones, which execute millions of instructions in each iteration. The tools developed at this point were targeted for mainframe processors. In the future, we hope to create a corresponding set of tools for the UNIX server.

9. Acknowledgements

We thank Kuniki Morita, Chung-yen Chang, Hiroshi Takao and Yoshimasa Nomura for contributions to this research. Alberto Poggesi and his staff, who worked for Amdahl, supported us by developing functions that we requested in their architecture simulator. Eizo Ninoi, Noriyuki Toyoki, Mark Nielson, Hiromu Hayashi, Hiroshi Muramatsu, Akira Asato supported us working on this research. We would like to thank our colleagues for many insightful comments on this work.

We would like to mention John Andoh and Ron Hilton. They did the prior work at Amdahl.

Finally, the first author would like to express gratitude to Makoto Kobayashi and Saburo Kaneda for their words of encouragement, which were very helpful to me.

10. Reference

[1] Elaine J. Weyuker, Filippos I. Vokolos, "Experience with Performance Testing of Software Systems: Issues, and Approach, and Case Study," IEEE Transactions on Software Enginnering, Vol.26, No.12, December 2000.

[2] S.R.Kunkel, R.J.Eichemeyer, M.H.Lipasti, T.J.Mullins, B.O'Krafka, H.Rosenberg, S.P.VanderWiel, P.L.Vitale, L.D.Whitley, "A performance methodology for commercial server," IBM J. Res. Develop. Vol.44, 851-872, November 2000.

[3] Jeff Gibson, Robert Kunz, David Ofelt, Mark Horowitz, John Hennesy, Mark Heinrich, "FLASH vs. (Simlated) FLASH: Closing the Simulation Loop," Proceedings of the Ninth International Conference on Architecture Support for Programming Languages and Operating Systems, November 2000, pp.37-48.

[4] Ashwini Nanda, Kwok-Ken Mak, Krishnan Sugavanam, Ramendra K. Sahoo, Vijayaraghavan Soundararajan, T.Basil Smith, "MemorIES: A Programmable, Real-Time Hardware Emulation Tool for Multiprocessor Server Design," Proceedings of the Ninth International Conference on Architecture Support for Programming Languages and Operating Systems, Novemeber 2000, pp.49-58.

[5] Ferrari, D., "Computer Systems Performance Evaluation," Prentice-Hall, 1978.

[6] IBM Corp., "Enterprise Systems Architecture/390 Principles of Operation," 1996.

[7] Fuijtsu LTD., "FACOM OS IV/F4 MSP Supervisor Functions," 1983.

Tuning Garbage Collection in an Embedded Java Environment

G. Chen†, R. Shetty†, M. Kandemir†, N. Vijaykrishnan†, M. J. Irwin†, and M. Wolczko‡ *

† Microsystems Design Lab   ‡ Sun Microsystems, Inc.
The Pennsylvania State University   Palo Alto, CA
University Park, PA

Abstract

Java is being widely adopted as one of the software platforms for the seamless integration of diverse computing devices. Over the last year, there has been great momentum in adopting Java technology in devices such as cell-phones, PDAs, and pagers where optimizing energy consumption is critical. Since, traditionally, the Java virtual machine (JVM), the cornerstone of Java technology, is tuned for performance, taking into account energy consumption requires re-evaluation, and possibly re-design of the virtual machine. This motivates us to tune specific components of the virtual machine for a battery-operated architecture. As embedded JVMs are designed to run for long periods of time on limited-memory embedded systems, creating and managing Java objects is of critical importance. The garbage collector (GC) is an important part of the JVM responsible for the automatic reclamation of unused memory. This paper shows that the GC is not only important for limited-memory systems but also for energy-constrained architectures. In particular, we present a GC-controlled leakage energy optimization technique that shuts off memory banks that do not hold live data. A variety of parameters, such as bank size, the garbage collection frequency, object allocation style, compaction style, and compaction frequency, are tuned for energy saving.

1 Introduction

Java is becoming increasingly popular in embedded/portable environments. It is estimated that Java-enabled devices such as cell-phones, PDAs and pagers will grow from 176 million in 2001 to 721 million in 2005 [20]. One of the reasons for this is that Java enables service providers to create new features very easily as it is based on the abstract Java Virtual Machine (JVM). Thus, it is currently portable to 80 to 95 percent of platforms and lets developers design and implement portable applications without the special tools and

libraries that coding in C or C++ normally requires [17]. In addition, Java allows application writers to embed animation, sound, and other features within their applications easily, an important plus in web-based portable computing.

Running Java in an embedded/portable environment, however, is not without its problems. First, most portable devices have very small memory capacities. Consequently, the memory requirements of the virtual machine should be reduced and, accordingly, the application code should execute with a small footprint. Second, along with performance and form factor, energy consumption is an important optimization parameter in battery-operated systems. Since, traditionally, the virtual machine is tuned for performance, taking into account energy consumption requires re-evaluation, and possibly re-design of the virtual machine from a new perspective. Third, the JVM in a portable environment is not as powerful as the JVM in a general-purpose system as many native classes are not supported. All these factors motivate us to tune specific components of the JVM (e.g., garbage collector, class loader) for a portable environment.

As embedded JVMs are designed to run for long periods of time on limited-memory embedded systems, creating and managing Java objects is of critical importance. The JVM supports automatic object reclamation, removing objects that are no longer referenced. Existing embedded JVMs such as Sun's KVM [2] and HP's ChaiVM [3] are already finely tuned to conform with three important requirements of embedded systems: soft real-time, limited memory, and long-duration sessions. However, currently, there is little support for analyzing and optimizing energy behavior of such systems. This is of critical importance for more widespread adoption of this technology in battery-constrained environments. In particular, the energy consumption in the memory system is a significant portion of overall energy expended in execution of a Java application [22]. Thus, it is important to consider techniques to optimize memory energy consumption. There are two important components of memory energy: dynamic energy and leakage energy. Dynamic energy is consumed whenever a memory array is referenced or

---

*This work was supported in part by NSF grants CAREER 0093082, CAREER 0093085, 0073419 and a grant from Sun Microsystems.

precharged. Recent research has focused on the use of memory banking and partial shutdown of the idle banks in order to reduce dynamic energy consumption [8]. However, leakage energy consumption is becoming an equally important portion as supply voltages and thus threshold voltages and gate oxide thicknesses continue to become smaller [4]. Researchers have started to investigate architectural support for reducing leakage in cache architectures [23, 16]. In this paper, we show that it is possible to also reduce leakage energy in memory by shutting down idle banks using an integrated hardware-software strategy.

The garbage collector (GC) [13] is an important part of the JVM and is responsible for automatic reclamation of heap-allocated storage after its last use by a Java application. Various aspects of the GC and heap subsystems can be configured at JVM runtime. This allows control over the amount of memory in the embedded device that is available to the JVM, the object allocation strategy, how often a GC cycle is triggered, and the type of GC invoked. We exploit the interaction of these tunable parameters along with a banked-memory organization to effectively reduce the memory energy (leakage and dynamic) consumption in an embedded Java environment. Since garbage collection is a heap-intensive (i.e., memory-intensive) operation and directly affects application performance, its impact on performance has been a popular research topic (e.g., see [13] and the references therein). In an embedded/portable environment, however, its impact on energy should also be taken into account. This is important not because the garbage collector itself consumes a sizeable portion of overall energy during execution, but because it influences the energy consumed in memory during application execution. The GC can take the banked nature of main memory into account and (i) turn off unused memory banks and (ii) move objects (in memory) in a bank-sensitive manner so as to maximize energy reduction.

This paper studies the energy impact of various aspects of a mark-and-sweep (M&S) garbage collector (commonly employed in current embedded JVM environments) in a multi-bank memory architecture. The experiments are carried out using two different (compacting and non-compacting) collectors in Sun's embedded JVM called KVM [2]. Further, the virtual machine is augmented to include features that are customized for a banked-memory architecture. We also measure the sensitivity of energy behavior to different heap sizes, cache configurations, and number of banks. In order to investigate the energy behavior, we gathered a set of thirteen applications frequently used in hand-held and wireless devices. These applications include utilities such as calculator and scheduler, embedded web browser, and game programs.[1] We observe that the energy consumption of an embedded Java application can be significantly more if the GC parameters are not tuned appropriately. Further, we notice that the object allocation pattern and the number of memory banks available in the underlying architecture are limiting factors on how effectively GC parameters can be used to optimize the memory energy consumption.

The remainder of this paper is organized as follows. The next section summarizes the K Virtual Machine and its GCs. Section 3 explains the experimental setup used for our simulations. Section 4 gives the energy profile of the current KVM implementation and discusses the impact of dividing memory into multiple banks. This section also investigates the energy impact of different features of our garbage collectors from both the hardware and software perspectives. Section 5 discusses related work. Finally, Section 6 concludes the paper by summarizing our major contributions.

2 KVM and Mark-and-Sweep Garbage Collector

K Virtual Machine (KVM) [2] is Sun's virtual machine designed with the constraints of inexpensive embedded/mobile devices in mind. It is suitable for devices with 16/32-bit RISC/CISC microprocessors/controllers, and with as little as 160 KB of total memory available, 128 KB of which is for the storage of the actual virtual machine and libraries themselves. Target devices for KVM technology include smart wireless phones, pagers, mainstream personal digital assistants, and small retail payment terminals. The KVM technology does not support Java Native Interface (JNI). The current implementation is interpreter-based and does not support JIT (Just-in-Time) compilation.

An M&S collector makes two passes over the heap. In the first pass (called mark pass), a bit is marked for each object indicating whether the object is reachable (live). After this step, a sweep pass returns unreachable objects (garbage) to the pool of free objects. As compared to other garbage collectors such as reference counting and generational collectors [13], the M&S collector has both advantages and disadvantages. For example, unlike reference counting GC, M&S collector handles reference cycles naturally without any extra mechanism. Also, no pointer arithmetic is necessary during object assignments. As compared to generational collector, it has less information to maintain during garbage collection, is easier to implement, and has a simpler user interface.

The KVM implements two M&S collectors, one without compaction and one with compaction. In the non-compacting collector, in the mark phase, all the objects pointed at by the root objects, or pointed at by objects that are pointed at by root objects are marked *live*. This is done by setting a bit in the object's header called MARK BIT. In the sweep phase, the object headers of all objects in the heap are checked to see if the MARK BIT was set during the mark phase. All unmarked objects (MARK BIT=0) are added to the free list

---

[1]Our applications and GC executables are publicly available from www.cse.psu.edu/~gchen/kvmgc/

and for the marked objects (MARK BIT = 1), the MARK BIT is reset. While allocating a new object, the free list is checked to see if there is a chunk of free memory with enough space to allocate the object. If there is not, then garbage collector is called. After garbage collection (mark and sweep phases), object allocation is tried again. If there is still not any space in the heap, an out-of-memory exception is thrown. Note that since this collector does not move objects in memory, the heap can easily get fragmented and the virtual machine may run out of memory quickly.

In an embedded environment, this heap fragmentation problem brings up two additional issues. First, since the memory capacity is very limited, we might incur frequent out-of-memory exceptions during execution. Second, a fragmented heap space means more active banks (at a given time frame) and, consequently, more energy consumption in memory. Both of these motivate for compacting live objects in the heap. Compacting heap space, however, consumes both execution cycles and extra energy which also need to be accounted for.

In the compacting mark-and-sweep collector, permanent objects are distinguished from dynamic objects. A certain amount of space from the end of the heap is allocated for permanent objects and is called *permanent space*. This is useful because the permanent space is not marked, swept, or compacted (since it contains permanent objects which will be referenced until the end of execution of program). The mark and sweep part of this collector is same as the non-compacting collector. Compaction takes place on two occasions:

- after the mark and sweep phase if the size of the object to be allocated is still bigger than the largest free chunk of memory obtained after sweeping;

- when the first permanent object is allocated, and, as needed, when future permanent objects are allocated. Space for a permanent object is always allocated in steps of 2KB. If the object needs more space, then another 2KB-chunk is allocated, and so on until its space requirement is satisfied.

During compaction, all live objects are moved to one end of the heap. While allocating a new dynamic object, the free list is checked to see whether there is a chunk of free memory with enough space to allocate the object. If there is not, then the garbage collector is called. During garbage collection (after sweep phase), it is checked whether the largest free chunk of memory (obtained after sweep phase) satisfies the size to be allocated. If not, then the collector enters compaction phase. After compaction, object allocation is attempted again. If there still is not any space, an out-of-memory exception is signaled.

The default compaction algorithm in KVM is a Break Table-based algorithm[24]. Advantages of this algorithm are

that no extra space is needed to maintain the relocation information, objects of all sizes can be handled, and the order of object allocation is maintained. The disadvantage is that both sorting the break table and updating the pointers are costly operations both in terms of execution time and energy.

In the rest of the paper, we will refer to these compacting and non-compacting collectors as M&S and M&C, respectively. It should be noted that both the collectors are not optimal in the sense that they do not reclaim an object immediately after the object becomes garbage (as an object is not officially garbage until it is detected to be so).

Figure 1 shows the operation of garbage collection and compaction in our banked memory architecture that contains four banks for the heap. Each step corresponds a state of the heap after an object allocation and/or garbage collection/compaction. Step 0 corresponds to initial state where all banks are empty (turned off). In Step 1, object A is allocated and in Step 10, two more objects (B and C) are allocated. In Step 50, object B becomes garbage and three new objects (D, E, and F) are allocated. In Step 100, both D and E become garbage and G is allocated. Note that at this point all the banks are active despite the fact that Bank 2 holds only garbage. In Step 200, the garbage collector is run and objects B, D, and E are collected (and their space is returned to free space pool). Subsequently, since Bank 2 does not hold any live data, it can be turned off. In Step 500, object C in Bank 1 becomes garbage. Finally, Step 1000 illustrates what happens when both garbage collection and compaction are run. Object C is collected, live objects A, G, and F are clustered in Bank 0, and Banks 1 and 3 can be turned off. Two points should be emphasized. Energy is wasted in Bank 2 between steps 100 and 200 maintaining dead objects. Thus, the gap between the invocation of the garbage collection and the time at which the objects actually become garbage is critical in reducing wasted energy. Similarly, between steps 500 and 1000, energy is wasted in Banks 1 and 3 because the live objects that would fit in one bank are scattered in different banks. This case illustrates that compaction can bring additional energy benefits as compared to just invoking the garbage collector.

3 Experimental Setup

3.1 Banked Memory Architecture

The target architecture we assume is a system-on-a-chip (SoC) as shown in Figure 2. The processor core of the system is based on the microSPARC-IIep embedded processor. This core is a 100MHz, 32-bit five-stage pipelined RISC architecture that implements the SPARC architecture v8 specification. It is primarily targeted for low-cost uniprocessor applications. The target architecture also contains on-chip data and instruction caches that can be selectively enabled.

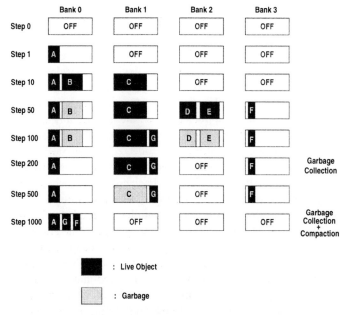

Figure 1. Operation of garbage collector and compactor.

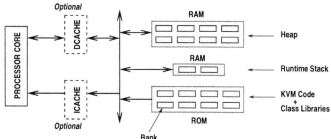

Figure 2. Major components of our SoC. Note that cache memories are optional.

Further, it contains an on-chip ROM and an on-chip SRAM. Figure 2 also shows both logical and physical views of the portion of the memory system of interest. This portion is divided into three logical parts: the KVM code and class libraries, the heap that contains objects and method areas, and the non-heap data that contains the runtime stack and KVM variables. Typically, the KVM code and the class libraries reside in a ROM. The ROM size we use is 128 KB for the storage of the actual virtual machine and libraries themselves [2]. The heap (a default size of 128KB) holds both application bytecodes and application data, and is the target of our energy management strategies. An additional 32KB of SRAM is used for storing the non-heap data. We assume that the memory space is partitioned into banks and depending on whether a heap bank holds a live object or not, it can be shutdown. Our objective here is to shutdown as many memory banks as possible in order to reduce leakage and dynamic energy consumption. Note that the operating system is assumed to reside in a different set of ROM banks for which no optimizations are considered here. Further, we assume a system without virtual memory support that is common in many embedded environments [12].

3.2 Energy Models

For obtaining detailed energy profiles, we have customized an energy simulator and analyzer using the Shade [6] (SPARC instruction set simulator) tool-set and simulated the entire KVM executing a Java code. Shade is an instruction-set simulator and custom trace generator. Application programs are executed and traced under the control of a user-supplied trace analyzer. Current implementations run on SPARC systems and, to varying degrees, simulate the SPARC (Versions 8 and 9) and MIPS I instruction sets.

Our simulator tracks energy consumption in the processor core (datapath), on-chip caches, and the on-chip SRAM and ROM memories. The datapath energy is further broken into energy spent during execution and energy spent during GC. The GC energy, itself, is composed of the energy spent in mark phase, sweep phase, and compaction phase (if used). Similarly, the memory energy is divided into three portions: energy spent in accessing KVM code and libraries, energy spent in accessing heap data, and energy spent in accessing the runtime stack and KVM variables. The simulator also allows the user to adjust the various parameters for these components. Energies spent in on-chip interconnects are included in the corresponding memory components.

The energy consumed in the processor core is estimated by counting (dynamically) the number of instructions of each type and multiplying the count by the base energy consumption of the corresponding instruction. The energy consumption of the different instruction types is obtained using a customized version of our in-house cycle accurate energy simulator [21]. The simulator is configured to model a five-stage pipeline similar to that of the microSPARC-IIep architecture. The energies consumed by caches are evaluated using an analytical model that has been validated to be highly accurate (within 2.4% error) for conventional cache systems [15]. All energy values reported in this paper are based on parameters for 0.10 micron, 1V technology. The dynamic energy consumption in the cache depends on the number of cache bit lines, word lines, and the number of accesses. In this paper, we model the SRAM-based memory using energy models similar to those used for caches. The number of banks and size of the banks in the SRAM-based memory are parameterizable.

In our model, a memory bank is assumed to be in *one of three modes (states)* at any given time. In the *read/write mode*, a read or write operation is being performed by the memory bank. In this mode, dynamic energy is consumed due to precharging the bitlines and also in sensing the data for a read operation. For a write operation, dynamic energy is consumed due to the voltage swing on the bitlines and in writing the cells. In the *active mode,* the bank is active (i.e., holds live data) but is *not* being read or written. In this mode, we consume dynamic precharge energy as there is no read or write into the bank. In addition, leakage energy is consumed in both these modes. Finally, in the *inactive mode,* the bank does not contain any live data. Thus, the bank is not precharged. Further, in this mode, we assume the use of a leakage control mechanism to reduce the leakage current. Thus, a bank in this mode consumes only a small amount of leakage energy and no dynamic energy.

In optimizing leakage current, we modify the voltage down converter circuit [14] already present in current memory chip designs to provide a gated supply voltage to the memory bank. Whenever the *Sleep* signal is high, the supply to the memory bank is cut off, thereby essentially eliminating leakage in the memory bank. Otherwise, the *Gated V_{DD}* signal follows the input supply voltage (V_{DD}). The objective of our optimization strategy is to put as many banks (from the heap portion of memory) as possible into the inactive mode (so that their energy consumption can be optimized). This can be achieved by compacting the heap, co-locating objects with temporal affinity, invoking the garbage collector more frequently, adopting bank-aware object allocation strategies, or a combination of these as will be studied in detail in Section 4. When a bank in the inactive mode is accessed to allocate a new object, it incurs a penalty of 350 cycles to service the request. The turn-on times from the inactive mode are dependent on the sizing of the driving transistors. Note that the application of this leakage control mechanism results in the data being lost. This does not pose a problem in our case as the leakage control is applied only to unused (inactive) banks.

The dynamic energy consumption for each of the modes is obtained by using scaled parameters for 0.10 micron technology from 0.18 micron technology files applying scaling factors from [1]. An analytical energy model similar to that proposed in [15] is used, and a supply voltage of 1V and a threshold voltage of 0.2V are assumed. We assume that the leakage energy per cycle of the entire memory is equal to the dynamic energy consumed per access. This assumption tries to capture the anticipated importance of leakage energy in future. Leakage becomes the dominant part of energy consumption for 0.10 micron (and below) technologies for the typical internal junction temperatures in a chip [4]. When our gated supply voltage scheme is applied, leakage energy is reduced to 3% of the original amount. This number is obtained through circuit simulation for 0.18 micron technology for a 64-bit RAM when using the scheme explained above with driver sizing to maintain the same read time.

3.3 Benchmark Codes and Heap Footprints

In this study, we used thirteen applications ranging from utility programs used in hand-held devices to wireless web browser to game programs. These applications are briefly described in Figure 3. The fourth column gives the maximum live footprint of the application; i.e., the minimum heap size required to execute the application without an out-of-memory error if garbage is identified and collected immediately. The actual heap size required for executing these applications are much larger using the default garbage collection mechanism without compaction. For example, Kwml requires a minimum heap size of 128KB to complete execution without compaction. The fifth column in the figure gives the effective live heap size; that is, the average heap size occupied by live objects over the entire duration of the application's execution. From detailed characterization, we observed that the size of the live heap varies across applications. Further, the live heap size varies with time even within a single application. For example, the Manyballs application exhibits an oscillating heap size requirement that increases and decreases periodically. The average live heap size of this application is only 62% of the maximum heap size. This indicates the potential for partially shutting down portions of the heap memory as the demand on the heap memory changes. The ability to exploit this potential depends on various factors. These factors include the bank size, the garbage collection frequency, object allocation style, compaction style, and compaction frequency as will be discussed in the next section.

4 Energy Characterization and Optimization

4.1 Base Configuration

Unless otherwise stated, our default bank configuration has eight banks for the heap, eight banks for the ROM, and two banks for the runtime stack (as depicted in Figure 2). All banks are 16KB. In this base configuration, by default, all banks are either in the active or read/write states, and *no* leakage control technique is applied. The overall energy consumption of this cacheless configuration running with M&S (GC without compaction) is given in the last column of Figure 3. The energy distribution of our applications is given in Figure 4. The contribution of the garbage collector to the overall datapath energy is 4% on average across the different benchmarks (not shown in the figure). We observe that the overall datapath energy is small compared to the memory energy consumption. We also observe that the heap energy constitutes 39.5% of the overall energy and 44.7% of the overall memory (RAM plus ROM) energy on the average.

Note that the memory energy consumption includes both the normal execution and garbage collection phases and is divided into leakage and dynamic energy components. On av-

Application	Brief Description	Source	Maximum Footprint	Effective Footprint	Base Energy (mJ)
Calculator	Arithmetic calculator	www.cse.psu.edu/~gchen/kvmgc/	18,024	14,279	0.68
Crypto	Light weight cryptography API in Java	www.bouncycastle.org	89,748	60,613	8.40
Dragon	Game program	comes with Sun's KVM	11,983	6,149	5.92
Elite	3D rendering engine for small devices	home.rochester.rr.com/ohommes/Elite/	20,284	11,908	3.67
Kshape	Electronic map on KVM	www.jshape.com	39,684	37,466	13.52
Kvideo	KPG (MPEG for KVM) decoder	www.jshape.com	31,996	14,012	1.52
Kwml	WML browser	www.jshape.com	57,185	49,141	34.97
Manyballs	Game program	comes with Sun's KVM	20,682	13,276	6.19
MathFP	Fixed-point integer math library routine	home.rochester.rr.com/ohommes/MathFP/	11,060	8,219	6.91
Mini	A configurable multi-threaded mini-benchmark	www.cse.psu.edu/~gchen/kvmgc/	31,748	16,341	1.46
Missiles	Game program	comes with Sun's KVM	26,855	17,999	4.28
Scheduler	Weekly/daily scheduler	www.cse.psu.edu/~gchen/kvmgc/	19,736	17,685	9.63
Starcruiser	Game program	comes with Sun's KVM	13,475	11,360	4.58

Figure 3. Brief description of benchmarks used in our experiments. The fourth and fifth columns are in bytes.

erage, 75.6% of the heap energy is due to leakage. The leakage energy is dependent on the duration of the application execution while the dynamic energy is primarily determined by the number of references. Considering this energy distribution, reducing the the heap energy through leakage control along with efficient garbage collection and object allocation can be expected to be very effective.

We also note from Figure 4 that overall ROM energy is less than the overall heap energy. This is mainly due to the following reasons. First, the dynamic energy for accessing a ROM is less than the corresponding value for a same size RAM. This difference results from the smaller capacitive load on the wordlines and bitlines. In the ROM, only the memory cells that store a value of zero contribute a gate capacitance to the wordline. Further, only these cells contribute a drain capacitance to the bitline [7]. In addition, the number of bitlines is reduced by half with respect to the RAM configuration and a single-ended sense amplifier is used for the ROM array as opposed to a differential sense amplifier in the RAM array. Our circuit simulations show that the per access energy of a RAM array can thus be as large as 10 times that of a ROM array. However, the difference is dependent on the actual bit pattern stored in the array. In our experiments, we conservatively used a dynamic energy cost for accessing the ROM to be half that of a corresponding RAM array access. Since the effective transistor width in the ROM array is also smaller than that in a correspondingly sized RAM array, the leakage energy of the ROM is also smaller. Another reason that the ROM energy is less than the heap energy is because of using a ROM configuration that implements a simple but effective energy optimization. In particular, we use a banked ROM configuration and activate the supply voltage selectively to only those banks that contain libraries that are accessed by the application. Note that this incurs a penalty at runtime when the bank is accessed the first time. However, we found this overhead to be negligible.

Another interesting observation is the relative leakage and dynamic energy consumption breakdowns in the heap memory and the ROM. We found that the dynamic energy of the

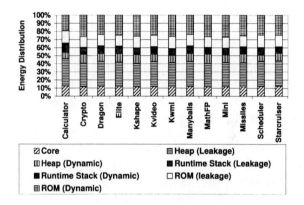

Figure 4. Energy distribution.

ROM is 63.7% of overall ROM energy which is much higher than the corresponding value in the heap. This difference is due to high access frequency of the ROM banks that contain the KVM code as well as class libraries.

4.2 Impact of Mode Control

Turning off a heap bank when it does not contain any live object can save energy in two ways. First, leakage energy is reduced as a result of the leakage reduction strategy explained earlier. Second, the precharge portion of dynamic energy is also eliminated when the bank is powered off. Figure 5 gives the heap energy consumption due to M&S when mode control (leakage control) is employed, normalized with respect to the heap energy due to M&S when no mode control is used (i.e., all partitions are active all the time). We observe from this figure that turning off unused banks reduces the heap energy consumption by 31% on the average (with savings ranging from 2% to 65%). On average, 90% of these savings come from leakage energy reduction.

Figure 5 also shows that the normalized runtime stack energy. This energy gain in runtime stack is achieved by not activating one of the banks of the runtime stack when it does not contain any useful data. Since we have two banks allo-

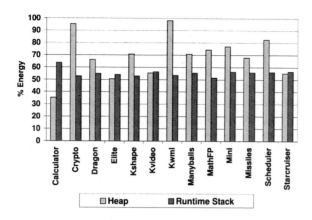

Figure 5. Normalized energy consumption in heap and runtime stack due to mode control (M&S).

cated to runtime stack (and the KVM variables) and many applications in our suite can operate most of the time with one bank only, on the average, we achieve around 50% energy saving on these banks.

These energy savings, however, do not come for free. As discussed earlier, accessing a powered off bank requires an extra 350 cycles for the supply voltage to be restored. During this time, a small amount of energy is also expended. However, we observed that the percentages of extra execution cycles and extra energy are no more than 3% and 5.2% respectively. Therefore, we can conclude that applying leakage control mechanism to the inactive heap banks can reduce energy consumption significantly without too much impact on execution time.

4.3 Impact of Garbage Collection Frequency

The M&S collector is called by default when, during allocation, the available free heap space is not sufficient to accommodate the object to be allocated. It should be noted that between the time that an object becomes garbage and the time it is detected to be so, the object will consume heap energy as a dead object. Obviously, the larger the difference between these two times, the higher the wasted energy consumption if collecting would lead to powering off the bank. It is thus vital from the energy perspective to detect and collect garbage as soon as possible. However, the potential savings should be balanced with the additional overhead required to collect the dead objects earlier (i.e., the energy cost of garbage collection).

In this subsection, we investigate the impact of calling the garbage collector (without compaction) with different frequencies. Specifically, we study the influence of a *k-allocation collector* that calls the GC once after every k object allocations. We experimented with five different values of k: 10, 40, 75, 100, and 250. The left graph in Figure 6

illustrates the heap energy (normalized with respect to M&S heap energy without mode control) of the k-allocation collector. The impact of pure mode control is reproduced here for comparison.

We clearly observe that different applications work best with different garbage collection frequencies. For example, the objects created by Dragon spread over the entire heap space very quickly. However, the cumulative size of live objects of this benchmark most of the time is much less than the available heap space. Consequently, calling the GC very frequently (after every 10 object allocations) transitions several banks into the inactive state and reduces heap energy by more than 40%. Reducing the frequency of the GC calls leads to more wasted energy consumption for this application. In Kvideo, we observe a different behavior. First, the energy consumption is reduced by reducing the frequency of collector calls. This is because each garbage collection has an energy cost due to fact that mark and sweep operations access memory. In this application, the overhead of calling GC in every 10 allocations brings an energy overhead that cannot be compensated for by the energy saving during execution. Therefore, calling the GC less frequently generates a better result. Beyond a point (k=75), however, the energy starts to increase as the garbage collections become so less frequent that significant energy is consumed due to dead but not collected objects. Applications like Mini, on the other hand, suffer greatly from the GC overhead and would perform best with much less frequent garbage collector calls. Overall, it is important to tune the garbage collection frequency based on the rate at which objects become garbage to optimize energy consumption.

The GC overhead also leads to increased energy consumption in the ROM, runtime stack, and processor core. The energy increase in the ROM is illustrated on the right graph of Figure 6. Each bar in this graph represents the energy consumption in the ROM normalized with respect to the energy consumption of the ROM with M&S with mode control. It can be observed that the case with $k = 10$ increases the energy consumption in ROM significantly for many of the benchmarks. On the other hand, working with values of k such as 75, 100, and 250 seems to result in only marginal increases, and should be the choice, in particular, if they lead to large reductions in heap energy. We also found that the energy overheads in the core and runtime stack were negligible and have less than 1% impact on overall energy excluding cases of $k = 10$. To summarize, determining globally optimal frequency demands a tradeoff analysis between energy saving in the heap and energy loss in the ROM. Except for cases when $k = 10$, the energy savings in the heap clearly dominate any overheads in the rest of the system.

A major conclusion from the discussion above is the following. Normally, a virtual machine uses garbage collector only when it is necessary, as the purpose of garbage collec-

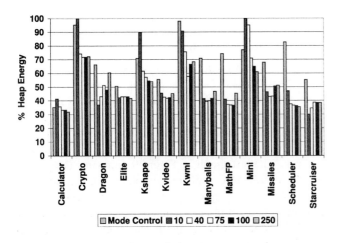
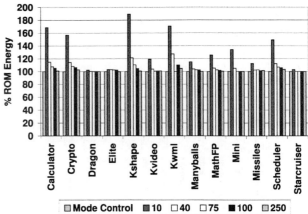

Figure 6. Normalized energy consumption in heap and ROM memory when M&S with mode control is used with different garbage collection frequencies.

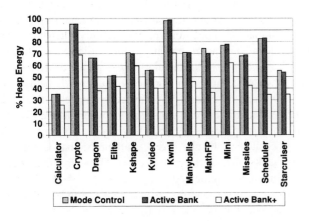

Figure 7. Normalized energy consumption in heap (active bank allocation versus default allocation).

tion is to create more free space in the heap. In an energy-sensitive, banked-memory architecture, on the other hand, it might be a good idea to invoke the collector even if the memory space is not a concern. This is because calling GC more frequently allows us to detect garbage *earlier*, and free associated space (and turn off the bank). This early detection and space deallocation might result in large number of banks being transitioned to the inactive state.

4.4 Impact of Object Allocation Style

M&S in KVM uses a global free list to keep track of the free space in the heap. When an object allocation is requested, this free list is checked, the first free chunk that can accommodate the object is allocated, and the free list is updated. While in a non-banked architecture, this is a very rea-

sonable object allocation policy, in a banked-memory based system it might be possible to have better strategies. This is because the default strategy does not care whether the free chunk chosen for allocation is from an already used (active) bank or inactive bank. It is easy to see that everything else being equal, it is better to allocate new objects from already active banks.

To experiment with such a strategy, we implemented a new bank allocation method where each bank has its own private free list. In an object allocation request, first, the free lists of active banks are checked and, only if it is not possible to allocate the space for the object from one of these lists, the lists of inactive banks are tried. This strategy is called the *active-bank-first allocation*.

Figure 7 gives the energy consumption for three different versions. M&S with leakage control (denoted Mode Control), active-bank-first allocation (denoted Active Bank), and a version that combines active-bank-first allocation with a strategy that activates the GC only when the new object cannot be allocated from an already active bank (denoted Active Bank+). All values in this figure are normalized with respect to the heap energy consumption of M&S without mode control. We see from these results that Active Bank does not bring much benefit over Mode Control in most cases (except that we observe a 6% heap energy improvement in MathFP).

This can be explained as follows. Objects with long life time are typically allocated early (before the first GC is invoked) and occupy the first few banks. The younger objects that occupy banks with higher addresses seldom survive the next garbage collection. From the the traces of bank occupation, we observe that after each GC, the banks with lower address are always occupied and the higher addresses are typically free. Consequently, the default allocation acts like active-bank-first allocation. MathFP is an exception to this

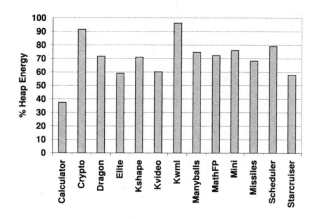

Figure 8. Energy consumption in heap due to mode control (M&C) normalized with respect to M&C without mode control.

allocation behavior. In `MathFP`, after each GC, the occupied banks are not always contiguous. In this case, active-bank-first allocation can save energy by postponing the turning on a new bank. In contrast, in benchmarks such as `Kwml` and `Scheduler`, the energy overhead of maintaining multiple free lists shows up as there is almost no gain due to the allocation strategy itself.

Thus, it is important to modify the default garbage collection triggering mechanism in addition to changing allocation policy to obtain any benefits. Active Bank+ combines the active-bank-first allocation mechanism along with a strategy that tries to prevent a new bank from being turned on due to allocation. As it combines an energy aware allocation and collection policy, Active Bank+ can lead to significant energy savings as shown in Figure 7. The causes for these savings are three-fold. First, Active Bank+ invokes the GC more frequently, and thus banks without live objects are identified and turned off early. Second, during allocation, it reduces the chances of turning on a new bank. Third, permanent objects are allocated more densely, thereby increasing the opportunities for turning off banks.

4.5 Impact of Compaction

As explained earlier in the paper, the compaction algorithm in KVM performs compaction only when, after a GC, there is still no space for allocating the object. In a resource-constrained, energy-sensitive environment, compaction can be beneficial in two ways. First, it might lead to further energy savings over a non-compacting GC if it can enable turning off a memory bank that could not be turned of by the non-compacting GC. This may happen as compaction tends to cluster live objects in a smaller number of banks. Second, in some cases, compaction can allow an application to run to completion (without out-of-memory error) while the non-

compacting algorithm gives an out-of-memory error. In this subsection, we study both these issues using our applications.

Let us first evaluate the energy benefits of mode control when M&C (the default compacting collector in KVM) is used. The results given in Figure 8 indicate that mode control is very beneficial from the heap energy viewpoint when M&C is employed. Specifically, the heap energy of the M&C collector is reduced by 29.6% over the M&C without mode control. The left graph in Figure 9 compares heap energy of M&S and M&C with mode control. Each bar in this graph represents heap energy consumption normalized with respect to M&S without mode control. It can be observed that M&C does not bring significant savings over M&S (denoted Mode Control in the graph). First, moving objects during compaction and updating reference fields in each object consumes energy. In addition, compacting may increase the applications running time, which also means more leakage energy consumption. Therefore, a tradeoff exists when compaction is used. In our implementation, to lessen the performance impact, compaction is performed only when the object to be allocated is larger than any of the available free chunks, or if it can turn off more banks. `Kwml` is one of the benchmarks where compaction brings some energy benefits over M&S with mode control. The execution trace of this code indicates that there are many scenarios where Mode Control does not turn off banks because all banks contain some small-sized permanent objects. M&C, on the other hand, turns off some banks after garbage collection due to the fact that it both compacts fragmented live objects with short life times and clusters permanent objects in a smaller number of banks. In some benchmarks such as `Dragon`, on the other hand, M&C does not create sufficient number of free banks to offset the extra energy overhead due to additional data structures maintained.

The original allocation policy in the compacting version distinguishes between permanent and dynamic objects as mentioned earlier. The default allocation policy always allocates dynamic objects from the first available bank while permanent objects from the last available bank. Thus this strategy requires activating at least two banks (The first one and the last one) when both permanent and dynamic objects are present. The active-bank-first strategy, on the other hand, always tries to allocate dynamic objects from the first active bank with enough space for the new object. Thus, until the total size of the allocated objects exceeds the bank size, only one bank is activated. Consequently, as opposed to the case without compaction, the Active Bank version (that is, allocating object from an already active bank if it is possible to do so) combined with M&C generates better results than M&C with default allocation, and consumes 10% less heap energy on the average. Finally, as before, the Active Bank+ outperforms other versions for most of the cases.

The right graph in Figure 9 compares heap energy con-

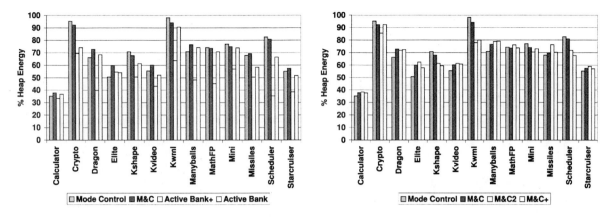

Figure 9. Left: Comparison of M&C and M&S. Right: Comparison of different compacting collectors.

sumption of three different compaction algorithms. M&C is the default compactor in KVM. The M&C+ version differs from M&C in that it performs compaction after each garbage collection (whether or not it is actually needed from the viewpoint of free space). Our results show that in some benchmarks such as Kshape and Scheduler, it generates better results than both M&S (denoted Mode Control in the figure) and M&C. This is due to the fact that, with M&C collector, objects are allocated linearly, which eliminates the cost for scanning and maintaining free list. M&C2, on the other hand, is a collector that uses the Lisp2 Algorithm, as opposed to the default Break Table-based algorithm in KVM. In the Lisp2 algorithm, during compaction, first, the new addresses for all objects that are live are computed. The new address of a particular object is computed as the sum of the sizes of all the live objects encountered until this one, and is then stored in an additional 'forward' field in the object's header. Next, all pointers within live objects which refer to other live objects are updated by referring to the 'forward' field of the object they point to. Finally, the objects are moved to the addresses specified in the "forward" field, and then the 'forward' field is cleared so that it can be used for the next garbage collection. The advantages of this algorithm are that it is can handle objects of varying sizes, it maintains the order in which objects were allocated, and it is a fast algorithm with an asymptotic complexity of $O(M)$, where M is the heap size. Its disadvantage is that it requires an additional four-byte pointer field in each object's header that increases the heap footprint of the application.

There are two potential energy benefits due to this compaction style. First, objects can be relocated accounting for temporal affinities and object lifetimes, instead of sliding-only compaction as in M&C. For example, clustering objects with similar lifetime patterns increases the potential for de-activating an entire bank (when the objects it holds die together). Secondly, reference fields can be updated more efficiently as compared to M&C and M&C+, where updating each reference field needs to look up the Break Table. Finally,

the extra forward field can be used as a stack in the marking phase to reduce the overhead during the scanning phase.

In case that the heap is severely fragmented, M&C2 will out perform M&C+ because it treats each object individually, and does not need to copy the Break Table (in this case, the Break Table will be large) when moving objects. On the other hand, when most live objects are placed contiguously, M&C+ will perform better because it can move objects in fewer chunks. Further, the smaller Break Table reduces the look up cost (whose time complexity increases logarithmically with respect to the Break Table size) when updating each reference field during compaction. Obviously, if the total number of reference fields is large, M&C+'s performance will suffer a lot during the updating phase.

Crypto is an example application with rather big heap footprint that benefits from M&C2's cheaper marking and updating. In contrast, Elite is an application with very small footprint. Due to the 4-byte's overhead in each objects, M&C2 turns on a new bank much earlier than M&C+. Specifically, M&C2 turns on the third bank about 5.6 seconds after program initialization while the corresponding value for M&C+ is 6.2 seconds. Initializing the forwarding fields of each objects also consumes some extra energy.

As we mentioned earlier, a compacting GC can run an application in a smaller heap memory than a corresponding non-compacting version. For example, Missiles can run using a 32KB heap when M&C is employed while requiring a minimum of 64KB heap when executing using M&S. Comparing the energy consumption for systems with these configurations, we found that the M&S that uses a 64KB heap with four 16KB-banks consumes a heap energy of 1.02mJ, which is much larger than 0.71mJ, the heap energy consumed by M&C2 when using a 32KB heap using two 16KB-banks. Similarly, Kwml can run using a 64KB heap when M&C is employed, while requiring a minimum of 128KB heap when executing using M&S. For this application, the M&S that uses a 128KB heap with eight 16KB-banks consumes a heap energy of 13.15mJ, which is much larger than 7.66mJ, the

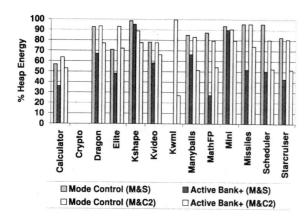

Figure 10. Impact of cache memory. All numbers are normalized with respect to the heap energy consumed using the same configuration with no mode control. Note that `Crypto` **does not run with 64KB heap. Also,** `Kwml` **cannot complete using the M&S GC.**

heap energy consumed by M&C2 when using a 64KB heap using four 16KB-banks.

4.6 Impact of Cache Memory

The presence of a cache influences the energy behavior in two ways. First, the number of references to the memory, both the ROM and RAM, are reduced. This reduces the dynamic energy consumed in the memory. In particular, we find that the heap energy reduces to 23% of the overall energy in the presence of the 4KB data and 4KB instruction caches. Note that embedded cores typically have small caches. Second, the cache can account for a significant portion of the overall system energy. In particular, the instruction cache is a major contributor as it is accessed every cycle. In the context of this work, it is important to evaluate how the cache influences the effectiveness of mode control strategy and the additional gains that energy-aware allocation and collection provide over pure mode control. Figure 10 shows the normalized heap energy in the presence of a 4K 2-way instruction cache and a 4KB 2-way data cache when a 64KB heap is used. Pure mode control with M&S reduces 15% of heap energy on the average across all benchmarks. An additional 28% heap energy saving is obtained through the energy-aware active bank allocation and garbage collection before new bank activation. The corresponding figures when M&C2 is used are 14% and 25%, respectively. These results show that the proposed strategies are effective even in the presence of a cache.

5 Related Work

Automatic garbage collection has been an active research area for the last two decades. The current approaches to garbage collection focus on locality-aware garbage collection (e.g., [5]), concurrent and hardware-assisted garbage collection (e.g., [11]), and garbage collection for Java among others. A comprehensive discussion of different garbage collection mechanisms can be found in [13]. All these techniques are geared towards improving performance rather than energy consumption. We showed in this paper that for an energy-aware collection, different GC parameters should be tuned. Diwan et al. [9] analyzed four different memory management policies from the performance as well as energy perspectives. Our work differs from theirs in that we focus on a banked-memory architecture, and try to characterize and optimize energy impact of different garbage collection strategies when a leakage control mechanism is employed.

Most of the Java-specific optimizations proposed so far focus on improving performance whereas we target improving energy consumption without unduly increasing execution time. Our work differs from these in that we specifically target embedded Java environments and focus mainly on exploiting leakage control mechanisms for reducing energy. We also illustrate how garbage collector can be tuned to maximize the effectiveness of leakage control. Flinn et al. [10] quantifies the energy consumption of a pocket computer when running Java virtual machine. In [22], the energy behavior of a high-performance Java virtual machine is characterized. In contrast to these, our work targets a banked-memory architecture and tunes garbage collector for energy optimization. Finally, numerous papers attempt to optimize energy consumption at the circuit and architectural levels. In particular, the leakage optimization circuit employed here tries to reduce leakage current and is similar to that used in [23, 16]. We employ a design that is a simple enhancement of existing voltage down converters present in current memory designs. Further, the circuit with the differential feedback stage helps to respond to load variations faster during normal operation.

6 Conclusions

As battery-operated Java-enabled devices continue to grow, it is becoming important to design resource-constrained Java virtual machines. Simply porting a desktop JVM to run on an embedded device can produce a large fixed memory overhead and result in a large energy consumption; both are unacceptable in most embedded products. Therefore, it is important to design virtual machines components afresh for embedded environments. In embedded environments, memory leaks combined with the limited memory capacity can be potentially crippling. Thus, garbage collection that automatically reclaims dead objects is a critical component. In this work, we characterized the energy impact of GC parameters built on top of Sun's embedded Java virtual machine, KVM. Further, we showed how the GC can be tuned to exploit the banked nature of memory architecture for saving energy.

References

[1] S. Borkar. Design challenges of technology scaling. *IEEE Micro.* pp.23-27, July-August 1999.

[2] CLDC and the K Virtual Machine (KVM). http://java.sun.com/products/cldc/.

[3] Chaivm for Jornado. http://www.hp.com/ products1/ embedded/jornada/index.html

[4] A. Chandrakasan, W. J. Bowhill, and F. Fox. *Design of High-Performance Microprocessor Circuits.* IEEE Press, 2001.

[5] T. M. Chilimbi and J. R. Larus. Using generational garbage collection to implement cache-conscious data placement. In Proc. *the International Symposium on Memory Management,* October 1998.

[6] B. Cmelik and D. Keppel. Shade: A Fast Instruction-Set Simulator for Execution Profiling. In Proc. *the ACM SIGMETRICS Conference on the Measurement and Modeling of Computer Systems,* pp. 128-137, May 1994.

[7] E. De Angel and E. E. Swartzlander. Survey of low-power techniques for ROMs. In Proc. *the International Symposium on Low Power Electronics and Design.* pp. 7-11, August 1997.

[8] V. Delaluz, M. Kandemir, N. Vijaykrishnan, A. Sivasubramaniam, and M. J. Irwin. DRAM energy management using software and hardware directed power mode control. In Proc. *the 7th International Conference on High Performance Computer Architecture,* Monterrey, Mexico, January 2001.

[9] A. Diwan, H. Li, D. Grunwald and K. Farkas. Energy consumption and garbage collection in low powered computing. http://www.cs.colorado.edu/~diwan. University of Colorado-Boulder.

[10] J. Flinn, G. Back, J. Anderson, K. Farkas, and D. Grunwald. Quantifying the energy consumption of a pocket computer and a Java virtual machine. In Proc. *International Conference on Measurement and Modeling of Computer Systems,* June 2000.

[11] T. Heil and J. E. Smith. Concurrent garbage collection using hardware assisted profiling. In Proc. *International symposium on Memory management,* October 2000.

[12] W-M. W. Hwu. Embedded microprocessor comparison. http://www.crhc.uiuc.edu/ IMPACT/ ece412/ public_html/ Notes/ 412_lec1/ ppframe.htm.

[13] R. Jones and R. D. Lins. *Garbage Collection: Algorithms for Automatic Dynamic Memory Management.* John Wiley and Sons. 1999.

[14] S. Jou and T. Chen. On-chip voltage down converter for low-power digital systems. *IEEE Transactions on Circuits and Systems-II: Analog and Digital Signal Processing,* Vol. 45, No. 5, May 1998, pp. 617–625.

[15] M. Kamble and K. Ghose. Analytical energy dissipation models for low power caches. In Proc. *the International Symposium on Low Power Electronics and Design,* page 143, August 1997.

[16] S. Kaxiras, Z. Hu, M. Martonosi. Cache Decay: Exploiting Generational Behavior to Reduce Cache Leakage Power. In Proc. *the 28th International Symposium on Computer Architecture,* June 2001.

[17] L. D. Paulson. Handheld-to-handheld fighting over Java. *IEEE Computer,* pp. 21, July 2001.

[18] R. Radhakrishnan, D. Talla and L. K. John. Allowing for ILP in an Embedded Java Processor. In Proc. *the International Symposium on Computer Architecture,* Vancouver, British Columbia, June 2000.

[19] M. L. Seidl and B. G. Zorn. Segregating heap objects by reference behavior and lifetime. In Proc. *8th International Conference on Architectural Support for Programming Languages and Operating Systems,* October 1998.

[20] D. Takahashi. Java chips make a comeback. *Red Herring,* July 12, 2001.

[21] N. Vijaykrishnan, M. Kandemir, M. J. Irwin, H. Y. Kim, and W. Ye. Energy-driven integrated hardware-software optimizations using SimplePower. In Proc. *the International Symposium on Computer Architecture,* Vancouver, British Columbia, June 2000.

[22] N. Vijaykrishnan, M. Kandemir, S. Tomar, S. Kim, A. Sivasubramaniam and M. J. Irwin. Energy Characterization of Java Applications from a Memory Perspective. In Proc. *the USENIX Java Virtual Machine Research and Technology Symposium,* April 2001.

[23] S. Yang, M. D. Powell, B. Falsafi, K. Roy, and T. N. Vijaykumar. An integrated circuit/architecture approach to reducing leakage in deep-submicron high-performance I-caches. In Proc. *the ACM/IEEE International Symposium on High-Performance Computer Architecture,* January 2001.

[24] B. K. Haddon and W. M. Waite. A compaction procedure for variable length storage elements. *Computer Journal,* 10:162-165, August 1967.

Memory-Aware Scheduling

Fine-grain Priority Scheduling on Multi-channel Memory Systems

Zhichun Zhu   Zhao Zhang   Xiaodong Zhang

Department of Computer Science

College of William and Mary

{zzhu, zzhang, zhang}@cs.wm.edu

Abstract

Configurations of contemporary DRAM memory systems become increasingly complex. A recent study [5] shows that application performance is highly sensitive to choices of configurations, and suggests that tuning burst sizes and channel configurations be an effective way to optimize the DRAM performance for a given memory-intensive workload. However, this approach is workload dependent. In this study we show that, by utilizing fine-grain priority access scheduling, we are able to find a workload independent configuration that achieves optimal performance on a multi-channel memory system. Our approach can well utilize the available high concurrency and high bandwidth on such memory systems, and effectively reduce the memory stall time of memory-intensive applications. Conducting execution-driven simulation of a 4-way issue, 2 GHz processor, we show that the average performance improvement for fifteen memory-intensive SPEC2000 programs by using an optimized fine-grain priority scheduling is about 13% and 8% for a 2-channel and a 4-channel Direct Rambus DRAM memory systems, respectively, compared with gang scheduling. Compared with burst scheduling, the average performance improvement is 16% and 14% for the 2-channel and 4-channel memory systems, respectively.

1 Introduction

As the performance gap between processor and DRAM memory continues to widen, the memory stall time of a typical memory-intensive application is becoming a dominant portion of the total execution time. On a multi-issue and multi-GHz processor, the latency of a single DRAM access could be equivalent to the time to execute hundreds of CPU instructions. Even for applications with low cache miss rates, the memory stall time due to a small percentage of DRAM accesses can easily exceed the CPU execution time. It is highly desirable to reduce memory stall times of memory-intensive applications.

Configurations of contemporary DRAM memory systems become increasingly complex. Modern memory systems, such as Direct Rambus DRAM systems, can support multiple memory channels, while each channel can connect multiple devices (chips). Each chip consists of multiple banks, where concurrent accesses to different banks can be pipelined. For memory-intensive applications running on contemporary computer systems, the occurrence of multiple outstanding memory requests is frequent. Memory access scheduling can reorder the sequence of concurrent accesses to reduce access latency and improve memory bandwidth utilization [12, 11, 7, 14, 15, 10]. In addition, a memory request for a cache miss can be further split into several sub-requests which can be processed separately. Normally, a cache miss results in a cache line fill request that fetches more data than what is immediately required to resume processor execution. This provides an opportunity to improve performance by splitting the request into multiple sub-requests with smaller sizes and serving the critical ones (containing immediately required data) first. On a multi-channel memory system, such a scheduling method requires a number of considerations, such as how to split a single reference, how to assign sub-requests to channels, and how to schedule concurrent accesses.

A recent study [5] finds that program performance is highly sensitive to the DRAM system configuration, and suggests that tuning burst (sub-block) sizes and channel configurations be an effective way to optimize the DRAM system performance for a given memory-intensive workload. Specifically, they evaluate the performance effect of sub-block size on burst ordering, where each cache block is split into multiple sub-blocks and critical sub-blocks are served before non-critical ones. In their study, all sub-blocks from a cache line are mapped to the same channel and the same page.

Thus, in order to exploit concurrency within a single channel, the choice of sub-block size becomes a trade-off between reducing latency of critical data access and lowering system overhead. They find that different applications have optimal performance on different sub-block sizes and the optimal sub-block sizes scale with the channel width.

In this study we show that, by utilizing fine-grain priority access scheduling, we are able to find a workload independent configuration that achieves optimal performance on a multi-channel memory system. In order to fully utilize the available bandwidth and concurrency, our approach splits a memory reference into sub-blocks with minimal granularity, and maps sub-blocks from a reference into different channels. All channels can be used to process a single cache line fill request. In order to increase the parallelism between processor execution and memory accesses, fine-grain priority scheduling is exploited. Sub-blocks that contain the desired data are marked as critical ones with higher priorities and are returned earlier than non-critical sub-blocks. This approach is similar to the method of "critical word first", but it also allows critical sub-blocks of one cache block to bypass non-critical sub-blocks from other cache blocks. By combining with existing DRAM scheduling policies, choosing the minimum sub-block size allows faster access to critical data without increasing the memory system overhead.

Figure 1 gives an example that shows the performance potential of fine-grain priority scheduling. In this example, a 4-channel memory system is processing four cache misses concurrently. Each cache block is split into eight sub-blocks, and the four critical sub-blocks are mapped to different channels. With fine-grain priority scheduling, all the critical sub-blocks finish earlier than non-critical sub-blocks, saving seven time units in fetching all critical data. In this example, the clustering of the four cache misses provides the scheduling opportunity. Our study will show that the cache miss clustering is frequent, i.e., the burstiness of cache misses is high. As a result, the queuing delay can be a major component of access time. Fine-grain priority scheduling can reduce the memory stall time by reducing the queuing delay of critical data.

In this study, we quantitatively investigate the miss burstiness for memory-intensive applications from the SPEC2000 benchmark suite on ILP processors with multi-channel Direct Rambus DRAM systems. We also analyze the combination of fine-grain priority scheduling with other DRAM access scheduling techniques, and compare the performance with that of gang scheduling [8] and burst scheduling [5]. Our study provides the following performance results and findings.

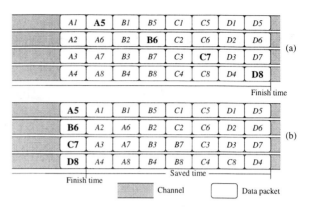

Figure 1. The order of transferring sub-blocks on a DRAM system with four memory channels: (a) without priority scheduling and (b) using fine-grain priority scheduling. The letters *A–D* represent cache blocks, each of which is split into eight sub-blocks. The boxes with bold letters represent the critical sub-blocks that contain the desired data.

- Fine-grain priority scheduling is effective in reducing memory stall time and increasing IPC (Instructions Per Cycle). Compared with gang scheduling that serves a single cache miss request with multiple channels grouped together, the IPC improvement is 13% on average (up to 34%) for fifteen selected SPEC2000 programs on a 2-channel Direct Rambus DRAM memory system, and 8% on average (up to 22%) on a 4-channel memory system. Compared with burst scheduling that serves multiple sub-requests of a single cache miss with one channel but critical sub-requests first, the average IPC improvement is 16% and 14% on the 2-channel and 4-channel memory systems, respectively. The processor is 2 GHz and 4-way issue.

- Combined with other scheduling policies, fine-grain priority scheduling is able to effectively utilize the memory system resource. For six of the programs, the 2-channel system with fine-grain priority scheduling can achieve performance comparable to that on the 4-channel system with gang scheduling or with burst scheduling.

- We suggest that a DRAM system configuration and its optimization be emphasized on access scheduling and DRAM mapping schemes. Taking this approach, we are able to find an optimal memory configuration that is workload independent.

We briefly introduce the background in the next section. In Section 3, we discuss the issues in fine-grain priority scheduling and its combination with other DRAM scheduling policies. The design complexity of fine-grain priority scheduling is discussed in Section 4. The experimental methodology is described in Section 5. The results are presented in Section 6. Finally, we conclude our work in Section 7.

2 Memory System Considerations

2.1 Memory Access Scheduling

Contemporary DRAM memory systems can serve multiple accesses concurrently. Memory access scheduling can reduce access latency and improve bandwidth utilization by re-arranging the order and issue time of DRAM operations for a group of concurrent requests [12, 11, 7, 14, 15, 10]. At a given time, a request may require one of the following operations, depending on the state of the bank to be accessed.

- *Precharge*: when the row buffer contains valid but not the desired data. This request is called a row buffer miss.

- *Row access*: when the bank is already *precharged*.

- *Column access*: when the row buffer contains the desired data. This request is called a row buffer hit.

Different operations required by concurrent memory requests may contend for the control bus, the data bus, or the DRAM banks. The contentions can be resolved by prioritizing the requests based on the request type (read or write), the arrival time, or an explicit priority information [15]. For example, *read-bypass-write policy* gives read requests higher priorities than write requests, considering that read requests will block the related load instructions. *In-order scheduling* gives the oldest request the highest priority. This can be combined with the read-bypass-write policy to prioritize old read requests. *Explicit priority scheduling* assigns an explicit priority to each request, giving the processor the opportunity to specify critical requests.

When a bank is activated (the row buffer contains valid data), it is possible that one request to the bank requires a column access while another request asks for a precharge. The column access is usually prioritized over the precharge so as to improve the memory bandwidth utilization [7, 15]. This policy is called *hit-first* in this paper. Operations to different banks may contend for the address bus and the data bus. To increase parallelism at the DRAM side (thus increase the bandwidth utilization), precharges can be prioritized over

row accesses, and row accesses can be prioritized over column accesses.

Another scheduling issue is to decide the time to precharge a bank when it has no pending requests. There are two strategies: *close page* and *open page*. The close page strategy issues the precharge immediately after the current column access finishes. The next access to the bank will require a row activation and a column access. In contrast, the open page strategy delays the precharge to hope that the next access is a row buffer hit, thus only the column access is needed. However, if the next access is a row buffer miss, it will require all the three operations. Which strategy performs better depends on the row buffer hit rate.

2.2 Multi-channel Memory Systems

Multi-channel memory systems have been used with high performance processors that require high bandwidth DRAM memories. Each channel can be scheduled independently. Direct Rambus DRAM is such a representative memory system. A Direct Rambus DRAM system generally consists of multiple channels, where each channel supports 1.6 GB/s bandwidth. Each channel has its own row control bus, column control bus, and two-byte wide data bus. The separation of row and column control buses eliminates the contention in the address bus between row operations (precharges and row activations) and column accesses. The bus clock rate is 400 MHz and the data is transfered on both edges of the clock. The row and column addresses/commands and the data are transfered in packets, each taking four bus cycles. The minimal data packet length is 16-byte. Each channel can connect multiple devices (chips). Each device can have 32 banks and 33 half-page row buffers (this may be different according to the configuration). Those banks may be operated independently, which provides high concurrency at the bank level. The Intel Pentium 4 processor supports two channels, and the Compaq Alpha 21364 processor supports up to eight channels.

2.3 DRAM Mapping Scheme

DRAM mapping scheme determines how to map a physical address to a location in the DRAM system. The choice of DRAM mapping scheme directly affects the row buffer hit rate and the memory system performance [20].

A word in a Direct Rambus DRAM system is addressed by the channel index, the device index, the bank index, the row address, and the column address. The first mapping consideration is on how to map the sub-blocks in a cache line onto multiple channels. We use a method interleaving the sub-blocks onto all channels, which is the same as that used in [8]. This interleaving scheme allows the aggregate bandwidth of all channels to be used to transfer a single cache line (assume the number of sub-blocks in a cache line is no less than the number of channels). The mapping scheme in [5] maps all cache lines in a DRAM page-sized block on a single channel. The requests on different channels are scheduled independently. However, this scheme cannot fully utilize the available bandwidth of all channels for a single cache line fill request. In addition, program access locality within the DRAM page-sized block may cause unbalanced usage of memory channels. In contrast, our method groups channels together to serve each cache line fill request, but schedules operations on each channel independently to return critical sub-blocks earlier.

Another mapping consideration is on how to map continuous addresses to multiple banks. Our approach interleaves page-sized blocks onto banks using the XOR-based page-interleaving scheme [20, 8]. It maps a continuous DRAM page-sized block onto a DRAM bank to exploit the locality in the row buffer, and XOR-es two portions of address bits (conventional bank index and cache tag) to permute the mapping of pages to banks. Consequently, accesses causing row buffer conflicts in the conventional page-interleaving scheme are distributed to different banks without changing the locality in the row buffer. The studies in [20, 8] show that the scheme can significantly improve the row buffer hit rate.

3 Fine-grain Priority Scheduling

3.1 Granularity of Scheduling

Current ILP processors have the ability to generate multiple cache misses before stalling. This provides an opportunity for performance improvement by scheduling the concurrent memory requests for those cache misses. In general, only a portion of a cache line contains the currently required data (although other portions may be needed in the near future). The fine-grain priority scheduling tries to exploit this opportunity. It issues multiple DRAM requests for a single cache miss, where each request fetches a *sub-block* of the cache line. Sub-blocks that contain the desired data are *critical sub-blocks*. The requests for critical sub-blocks are given higher priority over those requests for non-critical ones.

Each DRAM system has a limit on the minimal request length. Thus, the sub-block size should be no less than that minimal length. Using smaller sub-block size allows the current request to finish faster and makes newly arrived requests to be issued earlier. However, it is a concern that a small sub-block size may reduce the burst length of DRAM accesses thus increase the system overhead [5]. Nevertheless, we will show that if fine-grain priority scheduling is combined with other scheduling techniques and suitable mapping schemes, the overhead will not exceed that of coarse-grain scheduling on the Direct Rambus DRAM platform. For this reason, we choose the smallest granularity available for Direct Rambus DRAM system as the sub-block size, which is 16-byte, in this study.

3.2 Scheduling Policies

In this paper, we discuss three scheduling policies: fine-grain priority scheduling, gang scheduling, and burst scheduling. Each term actually represents a combination of several basic access scheduling policies, a channel configuration, a DRAM mapping scheme, and a choice of scheduling granularity. We assume a scheduler architecture similar to that presented in [15] (see Section 4) is used to enforce the three policies.

- Pending requests on a DRAM bank are queued in a bank scheduler. Each bank scheduler has an arbiter to determine the next operation on the associated bank.

- Each independent channel has a channel scheduler, which includes a row arbiter and a column arbiter. The row arbiter selects a precharge or a row access (if any) to use the row control bus. The column arbiter selects which column access (if any) to use the column control bus and the data bus.

All the three scheduling policies are combined with four basic scheduling policies that are enforced in the following order: *read-bypass-write*, *hit-first*, *explicit priority*, and *in-order*. For example, a non-critical read request that requires a column access is issued first even when there is another critical read request that requires a precharge to the same bank. The hit-first policy is enforced before the explicit priority scheduling so that fine-grain priority scheduling would not cause severe row buffer thrashing when multiple requests are mapped onto the same bank. In contrast, enforcing only the explicit priority scheduling may cause more precharges when bank conflicts occur.

There are three levels of explicit priorities for read requests, namely *critical priority*, *load priority*, and *store priority*, from highest to lowest. The critical priority is assigned to critical sub-blocks of read misses, and load priority is assigned to non-critical sub-blocks of read misses. The store priority is assigned to read requests for write misses, as a write-back and write-allocate L2 cache is used in this study.

In fine-grain priority scheduling, each L2 cache miss results in multiple DRAM requests that are mapped to multiple channels evenly; each DRAM request is associated with an explicit priority; and concurrent requests are scheduled based on the policies discussed above. It uses a fixed 16-byte as the sub-block size, which is the smallest granularity with current Direct Rambus technology. Each physical channel is configured as an independent unit and has its own channel scheduler. Instructions stalled for a critical sub-block are resumed when the data of the sub-block is returned.

Gang scheduling uses the cache block size as the burst size. All channel are grouped together as one logical channel, and there is only one channel scheduler. Instructions stalled for a missed block are resumed when the whole block is returned.

In burst scheduling, each L2 cache miss results in multiple DRAM requests that are mapped to the same independent channel; each DRAM request is associated with an explicit priority. In this study, the sub-block size is set to 32-byte. For a 2-channel system, each physical channel is an independent channel. For a 4-channel system, two physical channels are grouped together. There are two channel schedulers in both cases.

When a miss on a cache block happens, the sub-block containing the desired data is marked critical. Due to program locality, it is very likely that when the requests of this miss are being processed, more misses happen on other sub-blocks of the same cache block. In this case, the sub-blocks containing the newly arrived requests become critical ones and gain higher priority. Both fine-grain priority scheduling and burst scheduling will consider this change and update the priority information dynamically.

The read-bypass-write and hit-first policies not only improve the performance by themselves but also help fine-grain priority scheduling avoid the potential increase of system overhead. There is one case that the system overhead may still increase. When the number of banks is very small, the bank conflicts can be severe thus fine-grain priority scheduling may cause more precharges than burst scheduling. Fine-grain priority scheduling always balances the utilization of multiple channels, however, which scheduling performs better will depend on application access patterns. In practice, Direct Rambus memory systems have a sufficient number of banks to avoid severe bank conflicts. SDRAM memory systems usually have large size row buffers which lead to less precharges when the locality in row buffer is good. In addition, large size SDRAM mem-

ory systems may also have enough number of banks to avoid severe bank conflicts. The DRAM mapping scheme used in our study produces high row buffer hit rates. Thus, open page mode is used in our experiments.

4 Complexity Analysis

4.1 Complexity inside Processor

Cache and Cache Controller One concern on fine-grain priority scheduling is that it might change L2 cache and/or its controller, because data returns from the memory in a unit of sub-block instead of cache block. Such a change is definitely undesirable. Fortunately, there are existing mechanisms on high-performance processors that can address this issue. For example, the MIPS R10000 has a four-entry incoming buffer that can accept returning data at any rate and at any order [19]. Up to four outstanding read requests to memory are supported, thus each outstanding request is guaranteed to have one allocated incoming buffer entry. The Power-PC 604 has a similar line-fill buffer [16]. The incoming buffer can be used to merge out-of-order returning sub-blocks with only trivial changes. Future high-performance processors that support multiple outstanding memory requests will likely to have such kind of mechanisms.

Address Path to Memory Controller There will be additional lines for transferring priority information. Priority information can be transfered as a bitmap or the position index of a sub-block. Using a bitmap requires more additional lines, but allows priotizing multiple sub-blocks simultaneously, which helps the case when multiple cache misses happen to the same cache line at the same cycle.

Priority Updates The MSHR needs to send priority update to the memory controller when a read miss happens on a non-prioritized sub-block of a cache block that is already missed. A bitmap can be used with each MSHR entry to memorize which sub-blocks have been prioritized[1].

4.2 Complexity in Memory Controller

The basic function of memory controller is to issue DRAM operations (precharge, row activation, or column access) to DRAM banks under the DRAM timing constraints for DRAM access requests. With high-performance processors and high-bandwidth memory

---

[1]We assume that the MSHR implementation in [6] is used.

systems, the memory controller must have the access scheduling ability to order DRAM operations for multiple outstanding requests. Without this ability, the opportunity to exploit the memory access concurrency allowed by the processor and the memory system will be wasted, and the performance penalty is unacceptable for memory-intensive applications.

A *memory access scheduler architecture* is proposed in [15], which can enforce a number of scheduling policies. Fine-grain priority scheduling policy can be implemented on that architecture. The scheduler architecture organizes incoming requests by DRAM banks. Each bank has its own arbiter to determine its next operation. A global arbiter determines which bank gets the shared resources, such as the address bus and the data bus. This scheduler architecture can be adapted to work with Direct Rambus memory systems. Each independent channel needs a channel scheduler, and each channel scheduler needs two arbiters, one for row control bus and the other for column control bus. Although Direct Rambus memory systems can have a large number of banks, the bank schedulers can be assigned to busy banks dynamically, thus only a limited number of bank schedulers are needed.

With fine-grain priority scheduling on an n-channel system, n channel schedulers are needed. In comparison, with gang scheduling, there is only one independent channel thus one channel scheduler. On the other hand, fine-grain priority scheduling does not complicate the structure of each individual bank scheduler or channel scheduler. Another change is that the memory controller may split one memory reference request into multiple requests onto those channels, and need to accept priority updates. In this aspect, burst scheduling has almost the same complexity as fine-grain priority scheduling.

5 Experimental Environment

We use SimpleScalar 3.0b [3] to simulate an out-of-order execution processor. An event-driven simulation of a multi-channel Direct Rambus DRAM system is incorporated into the original simulator. Table 1 gives the key parameters of the processor model.

We use the parameters of 256 Mbit Direct Rambus DRAM [13] as the parameters of DRAM memory system simulated in our experiments. Table 2 describes the key parameters of this DRAM. We configure the simulated system as 2-channel and 4-channel systems, where each channel has four devices.

We use the pre-complied SPEC CPU2000 Alpha binaries in [18]. Fifteen programs (five integer programs and ten floating point ones) are selected, which have relatively large memory access demands. For all the

Speed	2GHz, 4-way issue
RUU size	64
LSQ size	32
MSHR size	16
write buffer size	8
L1 cache	4-way 64KB inst./data, 2-cycle hit latency, 64B cache line, write-back
L2 cache	unified 4-way 1MB, 8-cycle hit latency, 128B cache line, write-back

Table 1. Key processor parameters.

Parameters	Values
Precharge delay	8 bus cycles
Row access delay	8 bus cycles
Column access delay	8 bus cycles
Length of packets	16 bytes
Banks per device	32
Page size	2KB
Row buffer	33 half-page size

Table 2. Key parameters of the Direct Rambus DRAM used in the simulation. The bus cycle time is 2.5 ns (400 MHz).

applications, we fast-forward 4000M instructions and collect program execution statistics on the next 200M instructions.

6 Experimental Results

6.1 Burstiness in Miss Streams

We first measure the fraction of program execution time with bursty memory accesses. Figure 2 shows the fraction of program execution time with two or more outstanding memory references on a 2-channel system with gang scheduling for the selected SPEC2000 programs. We can see that the fraction of bursty phase is highly application dependent, which ranges from about 6% to 90%.

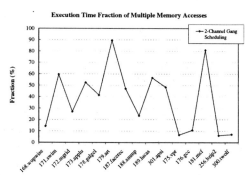

Figure 2. Fractions of bursty phase in execution for SPEC2000 programs.

Figure 3 further presents the distribution of the

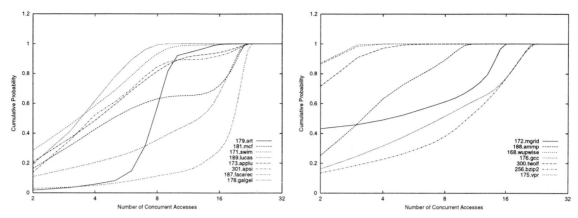

Figure 3. Distribution of the number of concurrent accesses.

number of concurrent accesses in the bursty phase. The left figure contains programs with the fraction of bursty phase higher than 40%; and the right one contains programs with the lower bursty phase fraction. Most programs have high burstiness in the bursty phase. In general, programs with a higher fraction of bursty phase tend to have higher probability on large number of concurrent accesses. For all the programs presented in the left figure, more than 40% of bursty references are grouped with at least three other references. Even for some programs with a small bursty phase fraction, the burstiness inside the bursty phase is still high. For example, program *256.bzip2* only spends 6% of its execution time in the bursty phase, however, more than 60% of concurrent accesses are clustered as groups with at least eight references.

6.2   Potentials of Fine-grain Priority Scheduling

Fine-grain priority scheduling targets at reducing the latency for critical sub-blocks by serving the critical ones before the non-critical ones. However, if all sub-blocks are critical, fine-grain priority scheduling will not make any difference. To evaluate the potential of fine-grain priority scheduling, we measure the percentage of critical sub-blocks in a cache line when the whole cache line fill request completes. Our experiments indicate that on the 2-channel system, for the fifteen programs, this percentage ranges from 15.3% to 57.7%. On average, 33.8% of sub-blocks are critical ones. This indicates that there is a large space left for fine-grain scheduling to reorder requests based on their priorities.

Figure 4 shows the waiting time distribution of critical sub-blocks and non-critical sub-blocks of read misses. We can see that critical sub-blocks have much shorter queuing delay than non-critical ones. Due to space limitation, we use two programs *179.art* and *256.bzip2* as examples here. Program *179.art* has very high bursty phase fraction (about 90%) and high

burstiness within the bursty phase. For this application, the waiting time is a significant portion of the total access time. Fine-grain priority scheduling effectively reduces the waiting time for critical sub-blocks. Compared with burst scheduling, the average waiting time for critical sub-blocks reduces from 133 cycles to 104 cycles, and the average waiting time for non-critical load sub-blocks reduces from 1157 cycles to 1070 cycles. With fine-grain priority scheduling, 60% of critical sub-blocks have waiting time less than 36 cycles. In comparison, with burst scheduling, 40% of critical sub-blocks have waiting time longer than 80 cycles. Compared with gang scheduling, the average waiting time for critical sub-blocks reduces from 557 cycles to 104 cycles, but the average waiting time for non-critical load sub-blocks increases from 557 cycles to 1070 cycles. *256.bzip2* has low bursty phase fraction (only 6%) but high burstiness in the bursty phase. Compared with gang scheduling and burst scheduling, the average waiting time for critical sub-blocks is reduced from 42 cycles and 32 cycles, respectively, to 27 cycles.

Figure 5 shows the probability that multiple critical sub-blocks are mapped to the same channel under fine-grain priority scheduling. We can see that for most programs, fine-grain priority scheduling can evenly distribute critical requests to different channels. However, for applications with high burstiness, it is still possible that multiple critical requests are mapped to the same channel. The existence of multiple critical requests in the same channel indicates that fine-grain priority scheduling can reduce the processor waiting time for currently required data.

6.3   Performance Improvement of Fine-grain Priority Scheduling

Figure 6 presents the performance improvement of fine-grain priority scheduling in terms of IPC for 2-channel and 4-channel Direct Rambus DRAM systems.

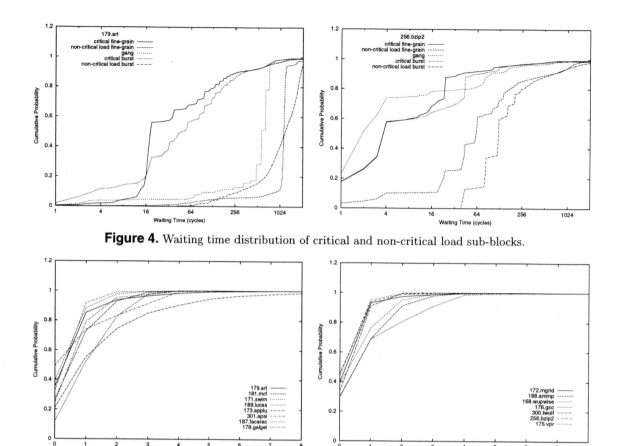

Figure 4. Waiting time distribution of critical and non-critical load sub-blocks.

Figure 5. Probabilities of multiple critical sub-blocks mapping to the same channel.

In this figure, the base IPC of each application is the IPC on a system with the perfect DRAM configuration that has the latency of L2 cache hit and an infinite bandwidth. The base IPC reflects the ideal performance after eliminating the memory stall time.

Compared with gang scheduling, fine-grain priority scheduling can increase the IPC by up to 34.2% for the 2-channel DRAM system. For the fifteen selected programs, the average IPC increase is 12.5%. Four programs (*172.mgrid, 173.applu, 181.mcf,* and *300.twolf*) have performance improvement higher than 15%. This implies that fine-grain priority scheduling effectively increases the parallelism between processor execution and DRAM accesses by reducing the latency for critical accesses.

Compared with burst scheduling, fine-grain priority scheduling can increase the IPC by 16.3% on average (up to 38.7%) for the 2-channel DRAM system. This indicates that fine-grain priority scheduling can better utilize the available concurrency of DRAM systems by spreading requests evenly onto multiple channels.

Fine-grain priority scheduling is especially effective for applications with a relative large memory stall por-

tion, modest memory bandwidth demand[2], and high burstiness in miss streams. For applications with small memory bandwidth demand and relatively fewer cache misses, the performance improvement from fine-grain priority scheduling is modest. For example, the memory bandwidth demand of *256.bzip2* is only 0.8 GB/s, the fraction of bursty phase is only 6%, and the number of L2 cache misses per 100 instructions is only 0.11. For this application, the memory stall time is not a significant portion of the total execution time. The fine-grain priority scheduling improves the performance modestly by 4.6% and 3.1% compared with gang scheduling and burst scheduling, respectively.

For applications with extremely high memory bandwidth demands, such as *179.art*, fine-grain priority scheduling improves performance modestly (6.0%) compared with gang scheduling. This is not surprising. The bandwidth demand of the program is so high (64.0 GB/s) compared with the available bandwidth (3.2 GB/s). Returning critical data earlier does not provide a large improvement in this case. Com-

---

[2]We use the memory bandwidth achieved by the application on the perfect DRAM system as the bandwidth demand of the application.

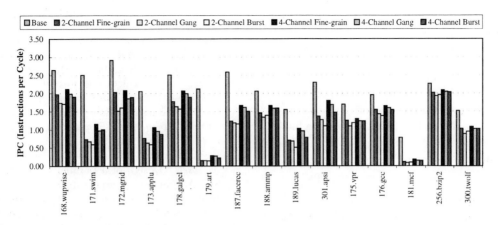

Figure 6. IPC on 2-channel and 4-channel Direct Rambus DRAM systems.

pared with burst scheduling, the performance improvement is promising (13.2%). This indicates that fine-grain priority scheduling can better utilize the available bandwidth and concurrency by evenly distributing subrequests to multiple channels.

As the number of channels increases to four, the congestion at the main memory system is reduced because of the increasing bandwidth and concurrency. As expected, the speedup by using fine-grain priority scheduling drops for most applications. For the fifteen programs, fine-grain priority scheduling increases the IPC by 7.8% on average (up to 22.3%) compared with gang scheduling. However, the speedup for some programs with high memory bandwidth demands increases. For example, the performance improvement for *171.swim* increases from 9.1% to 18.8% as the number of channels doubles. It indicates that, when the bandwidth pressure is alleviated for bandwidth-bounded applications, the performance potential of fine-grain priority scheduling increases. Compared with burst scheduling, the average performance improvement of the fifteen programs is 13.9%.

It is interesting to observe that for six of the fifteen programs, the performance on the 2-channel DRAM system after applying fine-grain priority scheduling is comparable or even better than that on the 4-channel DRAM system with gang scheduling. For *168.wupwise, 176.gcc*, and *256.bzip2*, the IPC on the 2-channel DRAM system with fine-grain priority scheduling is within 3% lower than that on the 4-channel DRAM system with gang scheduling. For *172.mgrid, 175.vpr*, and *300.twolf*, the IPC on the 2-channel DRAM system with fine-grain priority scheduling is higher than that on the 4-channel DRAM system with gang scheduling

by up to 10%. Compared with burst scheduling on the 4-channel DRAM system, fine-grain priority scheduling gains comparable or better performance on the 2-channel DRAM system for these six programs.

Compared with the 2-channel system, the 4-channel system not only doubles the available bandwidth, but also doubles the number of memory chips. Fine-grain priority scheduling can better utilize the existing resources and achieve performance comparable to that on a system with much higher cost. Of course, for those applications whose performance is limited by the available bandwidth, paying more cost to increase the bandwidth is the most effective way to improve performance.

For all applications on both the 2-channel and the 4-channel systems, fine-grain priority scheduling always achieves the best performance. In comparison, for gang scheduling and burst scheduling, which one performs better is application and configuration dependent.

7 Conclusion

Although careful tuning of DRAM parameters can effectively improve memory performance, its workload dependent feature may limit its usage in practice. In order to address this limit, we present a workload independent approach by focusing on optimizing fine-grain priority scheduling, and show its effectiveness using SPEC2000 benchmark programs. In addition to supporting workload independent configurations, fine-grain priority scheduling can increase the parallelism between processor execution and DRAM memory accesses, and improve the resource utilization of the memory system.

Hardware or software prefetching [17] is an effective approach to increase the parallelism between processor execution and DRAM operations. Recently, an increasing number of studies have been done on precomputation-based prefetching techniques [1, 2, 4, 9, 21]. By using speculative execution threads to detect future cache misses, those techniques not only increase memory access concurrency but also provide priority information on the prefetched data. However, the prefetch lookahead time is usually limited so that returning critical data early is desirable. We believe fine-grain priority scheduling can make an effective match for those techniques.

Acknowledgment:
We thank the anonymous referees for their constructive comments and insightful suggestions. This work is supported in part by the National Science Foundation under grants CCR-9812187, EIA-9977030, and CCR-0098055. This work is also a part of an independent research project sponsored by the National Science Foundation for program directors and visiting scientists.

References

[1] M. M. Annavaram, J. M. Patel, and E. S. Davidson. Data prefetching by dependence graph precomputation. In *Proceedings of the 28th Annual International Symposium on Computer Architecture*, pages 52–61, June 2001.

[2] R. Balasubramonian, S. Dwarkadas, and D. H. Albonesi. Dynamically allocating processor resources between nearby and distant ILP. In *Proceedings of the 28th Annual International Symposium on Computer Architecture*, pages 26–37, June 2001.

[3] D. C. Burger and T. M. Austin. The SimpleScalar Tool Set, Version 2.0. Technical Report CS-TR-1997-1342, University of Wisconsin, Madison, June 1997.

[4] J. D. Collins, H. Wang, D. M. Tullsen, C. Hughes, Y.-F. Lee, D. Lavery, and J. P. Shen. Speculative precomputation: Long-range prefetching of delinquent loads. In *Proceedings of the 28th Annual International Symposium on Computer Architecture*, pages 14–25, June 2001.

[5] V. Cuppu and B. Jacob. Concurrency, latency, or system overhead: Which has the largest impact on uniprocessor DRAM-system performance? In *Proceedings of the 28th Annual International Symposium on Computer Architecture*, pages 62–71, June 2001.

[6] K. I. Farkas, P. Chow, N. P. Jouppi, and Z. Vranesic. Memory-system design considerations for dynamically-scheduled processors. In *Proceedings of the 24th Annual International Symposium on Computer Architecture*, pages 133–143, June 1997.

[7] S. I. Hong, S. A. McKee, M. H. Salinas, R. H. Klenke, J. H. Aylor, and W. A. Wulf. Access order and effective bandwidth for streams on a Direct Rambus memory. In *Proceedings of the Fifth International Symposium on High-Performance Computer Architecture*, pages 80–89, Jan. 1999.

[8] W. F. Lin, S. Reinhardt, and D. Burger. Reducing DRAM latencies with an integrated memory hierarchy design. In *Proceedings of the Seventh International Symposium on High Performance Computer Architecture*, pages 301–312, Jan. 2001.

[9] C.-K. Luk. Tolerating memory latency through software-controlled pre-execution in simultaneous multithreading processors. In *Proceedings of the 28th Annual International Symposium on Computer Architecture*, pages 40–51, June 2001.

[10] B. K. Mathew, S. A. McKee, J. B. Carter, and A. Davis. Design of a parallel vector access unit for SDRAM memory systems. In *Proceedings of the Sixth International Symposium on High-Performance Computer Architecture*, pages 39–48, Jan. 2000.

[11] S. A. McKee and W. A. Wulf. Access ordering and memory-conscious cache utilization. In *Proceedings of the First International Symposium on High-Performance Computer Architecture*, pages 253–262, Jan. 1995.

[12] S. A. Moyer. *Access Ordering and Effective Memory Bandwidth*. PhD thesis, University of Virginia, Department of Computer Science, Apr. 1993. Also as TR CS-93-18.

[13] Rambus Inc. *256/288-Mbit Direct RDRAM (32 Split Bank Architecture)*, 2000. http://www.rambus.com.

[14] S. Rixner, W. J. Dally, U. J. Kapasi, B. Khailany, A. López-Lagunas, P. R. Mattson, and J. D. Owens. A bandwidth-efficient architecture for media processing. In *Proceedings of the 31st Annual ACM/IEEE International Symposium on Microarchitecture*, pages 3–13, Nov. 1998.

[15] S. Rixner, W. J. Dally, U. J. Kapasi, P. Mattson, and J. D. Owens. Memory access scheduling. In *Proceedings of the 27th Annual International Symposium on Computer Architecture*, pages 128–138, June 2000.

[16] S. P. Song, M. Denman, and J. Chang. The PowerPC-604 RISC microprocessor. *IEEE Micro*, 14(5):8–17, Oct. 1994.

[17] S. P. Vanderwiel and D. J. Lilja. Data prefetch mechanisms. *ACM Computing Surveys*, 32(2):174–199, June 2000.

[18] C. Weaver. http://www.simplescalar.org. *SPEC2000 binaries*.

[19] K. C. Yeager. The MIPS R10000 superscalar microprocessor: Emphasizing concurrency and latency-hiding techniques to efficiently run large, real-world applications. *IEEE Micro*, 16(2):28–40, Apr. 1996.

[20] Z. Zhang, Z. Zhu, and X. Zhang. A permutation-based page interleaving scheme to reduce row-buffer conflicts and exploit data locality. In *Proceedings of the 33rd Annual IEEE/ACM International Symposium on Microarchitecture*, pages 32–41, Dec. 2000.

[21] C. Zilles and G. Sohi. Execution-based prediction using speculative slices. In *Proceedings of the 28th Annual International Symposium on Computer Architecture*, pages 2–13, June 2001.

A New Memory Monitoring Scheme for Memory-Aware Scheduling and Partitioning

G. Edward Suh, Srinivas Devadas, and Larry Rudolph
Laboratory for Computer Science
MIT
Cambridge, MA 02139
{suh,devadas,rudolph}@mit.edu

Abstract

We propose a low overhead, on-line memory monitoring scheme utilizing a set of novel hardware counters. The counters indicate the marginal gain in cache hits as the size of the cache is increased, which gives the cache miss-rate as a function of cache size. Using the counters, we describe a scheme that enables an accurate estimate of the isolated miss-rates of each process as a function of cache size under the standard LRU replacement policy. This information can be used to schedule jobs or to partition the cache to minimize the overall miss-rate. The data collected by the monitors can also be used by an analytical model of cache and memory behavior to produce a more accurate overall miss-rate for the collection of processes sharing a cache in both time and space. This overall miss-rate can be used to improve scheduling and partitioning schemes.

1. Introduction

We present a low-overhead, on-line memory monitoring scheme that is more useful than simple cache hit counters. The scheme becomes increasingly important as more and more processes and threads share various memory resources in computers using SMP [2, 7, 8], Multiprocessor-on-a-chip [3], or SMT [21, 10, 4] architectures.

Regardless of whether a single process executes on the machine at a given point in time, or multiple processes execute simultaneously, modern systems are *space-shared* and *time-shared*. Since multiple processes or threads[1] can interfere in memory or caches, the performance of a process can depend on the actions of other processes. Despite the importance of optimizing memory performance for multi-tasking situations, most published research focuses only on improving the performance of a single process.

Optimizing memory usage between multiple processes is virtually impossible without run-time information. The processes that share resources in the memory hierarchy are only known at run-time, and the memory reference characteristic of each process heavily depends on inputs to the process and the phase of execution. But, hardware cache monitors in commercial, general-purpose microprocessors (e.g., [22]) only count the total number of misses which is useful for performance monitoring of a single application.

To determine how many and which jobs should execute simultaneously, it is often necessary to know how an application would perform for various cache sizes. The cache "footprint" for each application usually does not help since footprints for several applications executing simultaneously are likely to exceed the cache size for small caches. For example, consider the miss-rate curves for three different processes from SPEC CPU2000 [6] shown in Figure 1. For a cache of size 50, A and B could execute together but C should execute alone. Miss-rates as a function of cache size give much more information than a single footprint number and this information can be very relevant in scheduling and partitioning the cache among processes.

The memory monitoring scheme presented in this paper requires small modifications to the TLB, L1, and L2 cache controllers and the addition of a set of counters. Despite the simplicity of the hardware, these counters provide isolated miss-rates of each running process as a function of cache size under the standard LRU replacement policy[2]. Moreover, the monitoring information can be used to dynamically reflect changes in process' behavior by properly weighting counters' values.

In our scheduling and partitioning algorithms (Section 3, 4), we use marginal gains rather than miss-rate curves. The

---

[1]We use the term "process" in the paper to potentially include any execution context, such as threads. Too bad there is no consistent use of these terms.

[2]Previous approaches only produce a single number corresponding to one memory size.

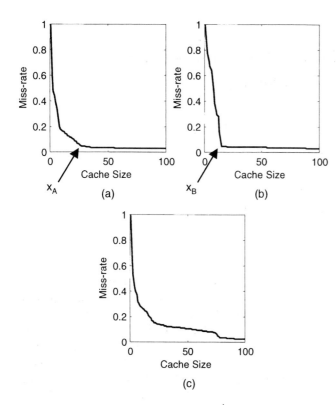

Figure 1. (a) Miss-rate curve for process A (gcc). **(b) Miss-rate curve for process** B (swim). **(c) Miss-rate curve for process** C (bzip2).

marginal gain of a process, namely $g(x)$, is defined as the derivative of the miss-rate curve [3] $m(x)$ properly weighted by the number of references for a process (ref);

$$g(k) = (m(k-1) - m(k)) \cdot ref. \qquad (1)$$

Therefore, we directly monitor marginal gains for each process rather than miss-rate curves. Using marginal gains, we can derive schedules and cache allocations for jobs to improve memory performance. If needed, miss-rate curves can be computed recursively from marginal gains.

We show how the information from the memory monitors is analyzed using an analytical framework, which models the effects of memory interference amongst simultaneously-executing processes as well as time-sharing processes (Section 5). The counter values alone only estimate the effects of reducing cache space for each process. When used in conjunction with the analytical model, they can provide an accurate estimate of the overall miss-rate of a set of processes time-sharing and space-sharing a cache.

---

[3]the miss-rate of a process using x cache blocks when the process is isolated without competing processes.

The overall miss-rate provided by the model can drive more powerful scheduling and partitioning algorithms.

The rest of this paper is organized as follows. In Section 2, we describe the counter scheme and its implementation. Section 3 and 4 validate our approach by targeting memory-aware scheduling and cache partitioning, respectively. We describe a simple algorithm for each problem, and then provide experimental results. Section 5 describes the analytical model which incorporates cache contention effects due to space-sharing and time-sharing. Related work is discussed in Section 6. Finally, Section 7 concludes the paper.

2. Marginal-Gain Counters

Memory monitoring schemes should provide information to estimate the performance of a given level of the memory hierarchy under different configurations or allocations to be useful when optimizing that level's performance. This section proposes an architectural mechanism using a set of counters to obtain the *marginal-gain* in cache hits for different sizes of the cache for a process or set of processes. Such information is used by memory-aware scheduling and partitioning schemes.

For fully-associative caches, the counters simply indicate the marginal gains, but for set-associative caches, the counters are mapped to marginal gains for an equivalent sized fully-associative cache. It is much easier to work with fully-associative caches and experimental results show that this works well in practice. For example, the contention between two processes sharing a fully-associative cache is a good approximation to the contention between the two processes sharing a set-associative cache.

2.1. Implementation of Counters

We want to obtain marginal gains for a process for various cache sizes without actually changing the cache configuration. In cache simulations, it has been shown that different cache sizes can be simulated in a single pass [15]. We emulate this technique in hardware to obtain multiple marginal gains while executing a process with a fixed cache configuration.

In any situation where the exact LRU ordering of each cache block is known, computing the marginal gain $g(x)$ simply follows from the following set of counters:

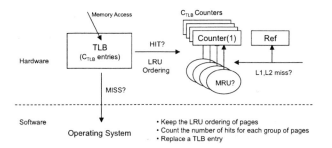

Figure 2. The implementation of memory monitors for main memory.

To compute the marginal gain curve for each process, a set of counters is maintained for each process. In a uniprocessor system, the counters are saved/restored during context switches, and when processes execute in parallel, multiple sets of counters are maintained in hardware. We thus subscript the counters with their associated process id. The marginal gain $g_i(x)$ is obtained directly by counting the number of hits in the xth *most recently used* block ($counter(x)$). The counters plus an additional one, ref_i, that records the total number of cache references for process i, are used to convert marginal gains to miss-rates for analytical models (Section 5).

2.1.1 Main Memory

Main memory can be viewed as a fully-associative cache for which on-line marginal gain counters could be useful. That is, we want to know the marginal gain to a process as a function of physical memory size. For main memory, there are two different types of accesses that must be considered: a TLB hit or a TLB miss. Collecting marginal gain information from activity associated with a TLB hit is important for processes that have small footprints and requires hardware counters in the TLB. Collecting this information when there is a TLB miss is important for processes with larger footprints and requires mostly software support.

Assuming the TLB is a fully-associative cache with LRU replacement, the hardware counters defined above can be used to compute marginal gains for the C_{TLB} most recently used pages, where C_{TLB} is the number of TLB entries, Figure 2. The counters are only increased if a memory access misses on both L1 and L2 caches. Therefore, counting accesses to main memory does not introduce additional delay on any critical path. If the TLB is set-associative we use the technique described in the next subsection.

On a TLB miss, a memory access is serviced by either a hardware or software TLB miss handler. Ideally, we want to maintain the LRU ordering for each page and count hits per page. However, the overhead of per-page counting is too high and experimentation shows that only dozens of data points are needed for performance optimization such as scheduling and partitioning. Therefore, the entire physical memory space can be divided into a few dozen groups and we count the marginal gain per group. It is easy for software to maintain the LRU information. All of a process' pages in physical memory form a linked list in LRU ordering. When the page is accessed, its group counter is updated, its position on the linked list is moved to the front, and all the pages on group boundaries update their group. Machines that handle TLB misses in hardware need only insert the referenced page number into a buffer and software can do the necessary updates to the linked list on subsequent context switches. The overhead is minor requiring only several bytes for each page whose size is of the order of 4-KB, and tens of counters to compute marginal gains.

2.1.2 Set-Associative Caches

In set-associative caches, LRU ordering is kept only within each set. (We call this LRU ordering within a set as *way LRU ordering*.) Although we can only estimate marginal gains of having each *way*, not each cache block, it turns out to often be good enough for scheduling and partitioning if the cache has reasonably high associativity.

Figure 3 (a) illustrates the implementation of this hardware counters for 2-way associative caches. It is also possible to have counters associated with each set of a cache.

Set-Counters for a Set-Associative Cache:
There is one counter for each set of the cache. LRU information for all sets is maintained. A hit to any block within the MRU set updates $counter(1)$. A hit to any block within the LRU set updates $counter(S)$, assuming S sets in the cache. There is an additional counter, ref, recording all the accesses to the cache.

To obtain the most detailed information, we can combine both *way-counters* and *set-counters*. There are $D \cdot S$ counters, one for each cache block. A hit to a block within the ith MRU set and the jth MRU way updates $counter(i, j)$. We refer to these as *DS-counters*.

In practice, we do not need to maintain LRU ordering on a per cache set basis. Since there could be thousands of cache sets, the sets are divided into several groups and the LRU ordering is maintained for the groups. Figure 3 (b) illustrates the implementation of DS-counters with two set groups.

2.2. Computing fully-associative marginal gain from set-associative counters

The marginal gain for a fully-associative cache can be approximated from the way-counters as follows:

$$counter_i(k) = \sum_{x=(k-1)\cdot S+1}^{k \cdot S} g_i(x) \qquad (2)$$

where S is the number of sets.

With a minimum monitoring granularity of a *way*, high-associativity is essential for obtaining enough information for performance optimization; our experiments show that 8-way associative caches can provide enough information for partitioning. Content-addressable-memory (CAM) tags are attractive for low-power processors [23] and they have higher associativity; the SA-1100 StrongARM processor [9] contains a 32-way associative cache.

If the cache has low associativity, the information from the way LRU ordering alone is often not enough for good performance optimization. For example, consider a 2-way associative cache shown in Figure 4 (a). For cache partitioning, the algorithm would conclude that the process needs a half of the cache to achieve a low miss-rate from two given

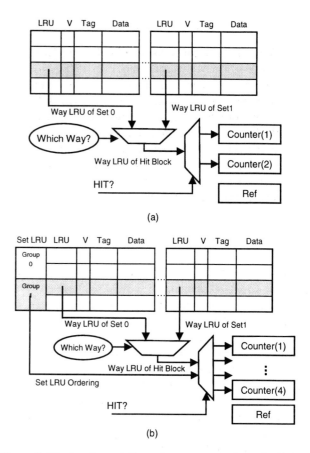

(a)

(b)

Figure 3. The implementation of memory monitors for 2-way associative caches. On a cache access, the LRU information is read for the accessed set. Then the counter is incremented based on this LRU information if the access hits on the cache. The reference counter is increased on every access. (a) The implementation that only uses the LRU information within a set. (b) The implementation that uses both the way LRU information and the set LRU information.

points, even though the process only needs one tenth of the cache space.

To obtain finer-grained information, we use either *Way-Counter* with *Set-Counters* or *DS-Counters* for low-associative caches. For example, Figure 4 (b) shows the miss-rate curve obtained using DS-Counters. As shown in the figure, we can obtain much more detailed information if we keep the set LRU ordering for 8 or 16 groups. Way-Counters with Set-Counters, which provide $D + S$ counter values, can also be used instead of DS-Counters. In this case, the value in each set-counter is distributed over the ways (D software counters) based on the values in the way-counters to generate $D \cdot S$ values.

There are several strategies for converting the $D \cdot S$ counter values into full-associative marginal gain information. In Figure 4 (b), we used *sorting* as a conversion method. First, $D \cdot S_{group}$ counter values are obtained from the hardware counters, where S_{group} represents the number of set groups. Then, these counters are sorted in decreasing order and assigned to marginal gains. This conversion is based on the assumption that the marginal gain is monotonically decreasing function of cache size. We are also investigating other conversion methods; column-major conversion, binomial probability conversion, etc.

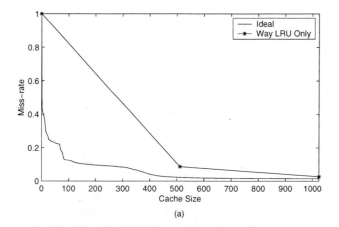

(a)

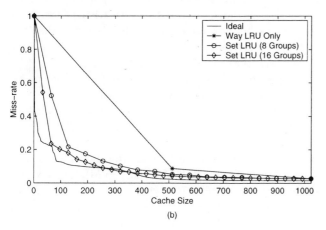

(b)

Figure 4. The estimated miss-rate curves using the set-associative cache monitor. The cache is 32-KB 2-way associative, and the benchmark is `vpr` from SPEC CPU2000. The ideal curve represents the case when you know the LRU ordering of all cache blocks. (a) Approximation only using the way LRU information. (b) Approximation using both the way LRU information and the set LRU information.

Since characteristics of processes change dynamically, the estimation of $g_i(x)$ should reflect the changes. But we also wish to maintain some history of the memory reference characteristics of a process, so we can use it to make decisions. We can achieve both objectives, by giving more

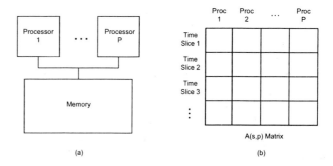

Figure 5. (a) A shared memory multiprocessor system with P processors. (b) Space-sharing and Time-sharing in multiprocessor system.

weight to the counter value measured in more recent time periods.

When a process begins running for the first time, all its counter values are initialized to zero. At the beginning of each time quantum that process i runs, the operating system multiplies $counter_i(k)$ for all k and ref_i by $\delta = 0.5$. As a result, the effect of hits in the previous time slice exponentially decays, but we maintain some history.

3. Memory-Aware Scheduling

When a scheduler has the freedom to select which processes execute in parallel, knowing the memory requirements of each process can help produce a better schedule. In particular, this section demonstrates how the marginal gain counters can be used to produce a memory-aware schedule. First, we begin with the problem definition and assumptions. Then, a scheduling algorithm based on marginal gains of each process is briefly explained. Finally, we validate our approach by simulations for main memory.

3.1. Scheduling Problem

We consider a system where P identical processors share the memory and N processes are ready to execute, see Figure 5 (a). The system can be a shared-memory multiprocessor system where multiple processors share the main memory, or it can be a chip multiprocessor system where processors on a single chip share the L2 cache.

Since there are P processors, a maximum of P processes can execute at the same time. To schedule more than P processes, the system is time-shared. We will assume processes are single-threaded, and all P processors context switch at the same time as would be done in gang scheduling [5]. These assumptions are not central to our approach, rather for the sake of brevity, we have focused on a basic scheduling scenario. There may or may not be constraints in scheduling the ready processes. Constraints will merely affect the search for feasible schedules.

A schedule is a mapping of processes to matrix elements, where element $A(s,p)$ represents the process scheduled on processor p for time slice s, see Figure 5 (b). A matrix with S non-empty rows indicates that S time slices are needed to schedule all N processes. In our problem, $S = \lceil \frac{N}{P} \rceil$.

Our problem is to find the optimal scheduling that minimizes processor idle time due to memory misses. The number of memory misses depends on both contention amongst processes in the same time slice and contention amongst different time slices. In this section, we only consider the contention within the time slice. Considering contention amongst time slices is briefly discussed in Section 5. For a more general memory-aware scheduling strategy, see [18].

3.2. Scheduling Algorithm

For many applications, the miss rate curve as a function of memory size has a knee (See Figure 1). That is, the miss rate quickly drops and then levels off. To minimize the number of misses, we want to schedule processes so that each process can use more cache space than the ordinate of its knee.

The relative footprint for process i is defined as the number of memory blocks allocated to the process when the memory with $C \cdot S$ blocks is partitioned among all processes such that the marginal gain for all processes is the same. C represents the number of blocks in the memory, and $C \cdot S$ represents the amount of available memory in S time slices. Effectively, the relative footprint of a process represents the optimal amount of memory space for that process when all processes execute simultaneously sharing the total memory resource over S time slices [4]. Intuitively, relative footprints corresponds to a knee of the miss-rate curve for a process.

We use a simple $C \cdot S$ step greedy algorithm to compute relative footprints. First, no memory block is allocated to any process. Then, for each block, we allocate the block to the process that obtains the maximum marginal gain for an additional block. After allocating all $C \cdot S$ blocks to processes, the allocation for each process is the relative footprint of the process. We limit the number of blocks assigned to each process to be less than or equal to C.

Once the relative footprints are computed, assigning processes to time slices is straightforward. In a greedy manner, the unscheduled process with the largest relative footprint is assigned to a time slice with the smallest total relative footprint at the time. We limit the number of processes for each time slice to be P.

---

[4]Stone, Turek, and Wolf [14] proved the algorithm results in the optimal partition assuming that marginal gains monotonically decrease as allocated memory increases.

Name	Description	FP (MB)
bzip2	Compression	6.2
gcc	C Compiler	22.3
gzip	Compression	76.2
mcf	Combinatorial Optimization	9.9
vortex	Object-oriented Database	83.0
vpr	FPGA Placement and Routing	1.6

Table 1. The descriptions and Footprints of benchmarks used for the simulations. All benchmarks are from SPEC CPU2000 [6].

3.3. Experimental Results

A trace-driven simulator demonstrates the importance of memory-aware scheduling and the effectiveness of our memory monitoring scheme. Consider scheduling six processes, randomly selected from SPEC CPU2000 benchmark suite [6] on the system with three processors sharing the main memory. The benchmark processes have various footprint sizes (See Table 1), that is, the memory size that a benchmark requires to achieve the minimum miss-rate. Processors are assumed to have 4-way 16-KB L1 instruction and data caches and a 8-way 256-KB L2 cache. The simulations concentrate on the main memory varying over a range of 8 MB to 256 MB with 4-KB pages.

All possible schedules are simulated. For various memory sizes, we compare the average miss-rate of all possible schedules with the miss-rates of the worst schedule, the best schedule, and the schedule by our algorithm. The simulation results are summarized in Table 2 and Figure 6. In the table, a corresponding schedule for each case is also shown except for the 128-MB and 256-MB cases where many schedules result in the same miss-rate. A schedule is represented by two sets of letters. Each set represents a time slice, and each letter represents a process: A-bzip2, B-gcc, C-gzip, D-mcf, E-vortex, F-vpr. In the figure, the miss-rates are normalized to the average miss-rate.

The results demonstrate that process scheduling can have a significant effect on the memory performance, and thus the overall system performance. For 16-MB memory, the best case miss-rate is about 30% better than the average case, and about 53% better than the worst case. Given the very large penalty for a page fault, performance is significantly improved due to this large reduction in miss-rate. As the memory size increases, scheduling becomes less important since the entire workload fits into the memory. However, note that smart scheduling can still improve the miss-rate by about 10% over the worst case even for 256-MB memory that is larger than the total footprint size from Table 1. This happens because the LRU policy does not allo-

Memory Size (MB)		Average of All Cases	Worst Case	Best Case	Algorithm
8	Miss-Rate(%)	1.379	2.506	1.019	1.022
	Schedule		(ADE,BCF)	(ACD,BEF)	(ACE,BDF)
16	Miss-Rate(%)	0.471	0.701	0.333	0.347
	Schedule		(ADE,BCF)	(ADF,BCE)	(ACD,BEF)
32	Miss-Rate(%)	0.187	0.245	0.148	0.157
	Schedule		(ADE,BCF)	(ACD,BEF)	(ABD,CEF)
64	Miss-Rate(%)	0.072	0.085	0.063	0.066
	Schedule		(ABF,CDE)	(ACD,BEF)	(ACF,BDE)
128	Miss-Rate(%)	0.037	0.052	0.029	0.029
	Schedule		(ABF,CDE)	(ACD,BEF)	(ACD,BEF)
256	Miss-Rate(%)	0.030	0.032	0.029	0.029
	Schedule		(ABF,CDE)	(ACD,BEF)	(ACD,BEF)

Table 2. The performance of the memory-aware scheduling algorithm. A schedule is represented by two sets of letters. Each set represents a time slice, and each letter represents a process: A-bzip2, B-gcc, C-gzip, D-mcf, E-vortex, F-vpr. For some cases multiple schedules result in the same miss-rate.

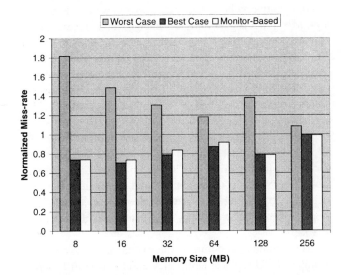

Figure 6. The comparison of miss-rates for various schedules: the worst case, the best case, and the schedule decided by the algorithm. The miss-rates are normalized to the average miss-rate of all possible schedules for each memory size.

cate the memory properly.

The results also illustrate that our scheduling algorithm can effectively find a good schedule, which results in a low miss-rate. In fact, the algorithm found the optimal schedule when the memory is larger than 64-MB. Even for small memory, the schedule found by the algorithm shows a miss-rate very close to the optimal case.

Finally, the results demonstrate the advantage of having marginal gain information for each process rather than one value of footprint size. If we schedule processes based on the footprint size, executing gcc, gzip and vpr together and the others in the next time slice seems to be natural since it balances the total footprint size for each time slice. However, this schedule is actually the *worst* schedule for memory smaller than 128-MB, and results in a miss-rate that is over 50% worse than the optimal schedule.

Memory traces used in this experiment have footprints smaller than 100 MB. As a result, the scheduling algorithm could not improve the miss-rate for memory which is larger than 256 MB. However, many applications have very large footprints, often larger than main memory. For these applications, the memory size where scheduling matters should scale up.

4. Cache Partitioning

Just like knowing memory requirements can help a scheduler, it can also be used to decide the best way to dynamically partition the cache among simultaneous processes. A partitioned cache explicitly allocates cache space to particular processes. In a partitioned cache, if space

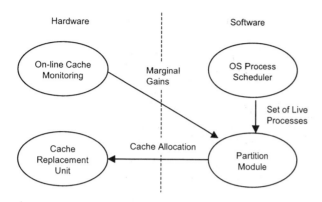

Figure 7. The implementation of on-line cache partitioning.

Name	Process	Description
Mix-1	art	Image Recognition/Neural Network
	mcf	Combinatorial Optimization
Mix-2	vpr	FPGA Circuit Placement and Routing
	bzip2	Compression
	iu	Image Understanding
Mix-3	art1	Image Recognition/Neural Network
	art2	
	mcf1	Combinatorial Optimization
	mcf2	

Table 3. The benchmark sets simulated. All but the Image Understanding benchmark are from SPEC CPU2000 [6]. The Image Understanding is from DIS benchmark suite [12].

is allocated to one process, it cannot be used to satisfy cache misses by other processes. Using trace-driven simulations, we compare partitioning with normal LRU for set-associative caches.

4.1. The Partitioning Scheme

The standard LRU replacement policy treats all cache blocks in the same way. For multi-tasking situations, this can often result in poor allocation of cache space among processes. When multiple processes run simultaneously and share the cache as in simultaneous multithreading and chip multiprocessor systems, the LRU policy blindly allocates more cache space to processes that generate more misses even though other processes may benefit more from increased cache space.

We solve this problem by explicitly allocating cache space to each process. The standard LRU policy still manages cache space within a process, but not among processes. Each process gets a certain amount of cache space allocated explicitly. Then, the replacement unit decides which block within a set will be evicted based on how many blocks a process has in the cache and how many blocks are allocated to the process.

The overall flow of the partitioning scheme can be viewed as a set of four modules: on-line cache monitor, OS processor scheduler, partition module, and cache replacement unit (Figure 7). The scheduler provides the partition module with the set of executing processes that shares the cache at the same time. Then, the partition module uses this scheduling information and the marginal gain information from the on-line cache monitor to decide a cache partition; the module uses a greedy algorithm to allocate each cache block to a process that obtains the maximum marginal gain by having one additional block. Finally, the replacement unit maps these partitions to the appropriate parts of the cache. Since the characteristics of processes change dynam-

ically, the partition is re-evaluated after every time slice. For details on the partitioning algorithm, see [17].

4.2. Experimental Results

This section presents quantitative results using our cache allocation scheme. The simulations concentrate on chip multiprocessor systems where processors (either 2 or 4) share the same L2 cache. The shared L2 cache is 8-way set-associative, whose size varies over a range of 256 KB to 4 MB. Each processor is assumed to have its own L1 instruction and data caches, which are 4-way 16 KB. Due to large space and long latency to main memory, our scheme is more likely to be useful for an L2 cache, and so that is the focus of our simulations. We note in passing, that we believe our approach will work on L1 caches as well if L1 caches are also shared.

Three different sets of benchmarks are simulated, see Table 3. The first set (Mix-1) has two processes, art and mcf both from SPEC CPU2000. The second set (Mix-2) has three processes, vpr, bzip2 and iu. Finally, the third set (Mix-3) has four processes, two copies of art and two copies of mcf, each with a different phase of the benchmark.

The simulations compare the overall L2 miss-rate of a standard LRU replacement policy and the overall L2 miss-rate of a cache managed by our partitioning algorithm. The partition is updated every two hundred thousand memory references ($T = 200000$), and the counters are multiplied by $\delta = 0.5$ (cf. Section 2.2). Carefully selecting values of T and δ is likely to give better results. The hit-rates are averaged over fifty million memory references and shown for various cache sizes (see Table 4).

The simulation results show that the partitioning can improve the L2 cache miss-rate significantly: for cache sizes between 1 MB to 2 MB, partitioning improved the miss-

Size (MB)	L1 %Miss	L2 %Miss	Part. L2 %Miss	Abs. %Imprv.	Rel. %Imprv.
art + mcf					
0.2		84.4	84.7	-0.3	-0.4
0.5		82.8	83.6	-0.8	-0.9
1	28.1	73.8	63.1	10.7	14.5
2		50.0	48.9	1.1	2.2
4		23.3	25.0	-1.7	-7.3
vpr + bzip2 + iu					
0.2		73.1	77.9	-0.8	-1.1
0.5		72.5	71.8	0.7	1.0
1	4.6	66.5	64.2	2.3	3.5
2		40.4	33.7	6.7	16.6
4		18.7	18.5	0.2	1.1
art1 + mcf1 + art2 + mcf2					
0.2		88.0	87.4	0.6	0.7
0.5		85.8	85.7	0.1	0.1
1	28.5	83.1	81.0	2.1	2.5
2		73.4	65.1	8.3	11.3
4		49.5	48.7	0.8	1.6

Table 4. Hit-rate Comparison between the standard LRU and the partitioned LRU.

rate up to 14% relative to the miss-rate from the standard LRU replacement policy. For small caches, such as 256-KB and 512-KB caches, partitioning does not seem to help. We conjecture that the size of the total workloads is too large compared to the cache size. At the other extreme, partitioning cannot improve the cache performance if the cache is large enough to hold all the workloads.

The results demonstrate that on-line cache monitoring can be very useful for cache partitioning. Although the cache monitoring scheme is very simple and has a low implementation overhead, it can significantly improve the performance for some cases.

5. Analytical Models

Although the straightforward use of the marginal gain counters can improve performance, it is important to know its limitation. This section discusses analytical methods that can model the effects of memory contention amongst simultaneously-running processes, as well as the effects of time-sharing, using the information from the memory monitoring scheme. The model estimates the overall miss-rate when multiple processes execute simultaneously and concurrently. Estimating an overall miss-rate gives a better evaluation of a schedule or partition. First, a uniprocessor cache model for time-shared systems is briefly summarized. Then, the model is extended to include the effects of mem-

ory contention amongst simultaneously-running processes. Finally, a few examples of using the model with the monitoring scheme are shown.

5.1. Model for Time-Sharing

The time-sharing model from elsewhere [16] estimates the overall miss-rate for a fully-associative cache when multiple processes time-share the same cache (memory) on a uniprocessor system. There are three inputs to the model: (1) the memory size (C) in terms of the number of memory blocks (pages), (2) job sequences with the length of each process' time slice (T_i) in terms of the number of memory references, and (3) the miss-rate of each process as a function of cache space ($m_i(x)$). The model assumes that the least recently used (LRU) replacement policy is used, and there are no shared data structures among processes.

5.2. Extension to Space-Sharing

The original model assumes only one process executes at a time. In this subsection, we describe how the original model can be applied to multiprocessor systems where multiple processes can execute simultaneously sharing the memory (cache). We consider the situation where all processors context switch at the same time. More general cases where each processor can context switch at a different time can be modeled in a similar manner.

To model both time-sharing and space-sharing, we apply the original model twice. First, the model is applied to processes in the same time slice and generates a miss-rate curve for a time slice considering all processes in the time slice as one big process. Then, the estimated miss-rate curves are processed by the model again to incorporate the effects of time-sharing.

What should be the miss-rate curve for each time slice? Since the model for time-sharing needs *isolated* miss-rate curves, the miss-rate curve for each time-slice s is defined as the overall miss-rate of all processes in time slice s when they execute together without context switching using memory of size x. We call this miss-rate curve for a time slice as a combined miss-rate curve $m_{combined,s}(x)$. Next we explain how to obtain the combined miss-rate curves.

The simultaneously executing processes within a time slice can be modeled as time-shared processes with very short time slices. Therefore, the original model is used to obtain the combined miss-rate curves by assuming the time slice is $ref_{s,p}/\sum_{i=1}^{P} ref_{s,i}$ for processor p in time-slice s. $ref_{s,p}$ is the number of memory accesses that processor p makes over time slice s.

Now we have the combined miss-rate curve for each time-slice. The overall miss-rate is estimated by using the original model assuming that only one process executes for a time slice whose miss-rate curve is $m_{combined,s}(x)$.

5.3. Model-Based Optimization

The analytical model can estimate the effects of both time-sharing and space-sharing using the information from our memory monitors. Therefore, our monitoring scheme with the model can be used for any optimization related to multi-tasking. For example, more accurate schedulers, which consider both time-sharing and space-sharing can be developed. Using the model, we can also partition the cache among concurrent processes or choose proper time quanta for them. In this subsection, we provide some preliminary examples of these applications.

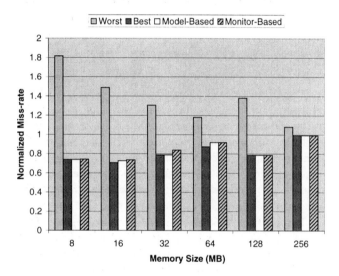

Figure 8. The comparison of miss-rates for various schedules: the worst case, the best case, the schedule based on the model, and the schedule decided by the algorithm in Section 3.

We applied the model to the same scheduling problem solved in Section 3. In this case, however, the model evaluates each schedule based on miss-rate curves from the monitor and decides the best schedule. Figure 8 illustrates the results. Although the improvement is small, the model-based scheduler finds better schedules then the monitor-based scheme for small memories.

The model is also applied to partition the cache space among concurrent processes. Some part of the cache is dedicated to each process and the rest is shared by all. Figure 9 shows the partitioning results when 8 processes (`bzip2`, `gcc`, `swim`, `mesa`, `vortex`, `vpr`, `twolf`, `iu`) are sharing the cache (32 KB, fully associative). The partition is updated every 10^5 cache references. The figure demonstrates

that time-sharing can degrade cache performance for some mid-range time quanta. Partitioning can eliminate the problem.

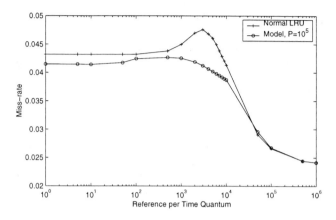

Figure 9. The results of cache partitioning among concurrent processes.

6. Related Work

Several early investigations of the effects of context switches use analytical models. Thiébaut and Stone [19] modeled the amount of additional misses caused by context switches for set-associative caches. Agarwal, Horowitz and Hennessy [1] also included the effect of conflicts between processes in their analytical cache model and showed that inter-process conflicts are noticeable for a mid-range of cache sizes that are large enough to have a considerable number of conflicts but not large enough to hold all the working sets. However, these models work only for long enough time quanta, and require information that is hard to collect on-line.

Mogul and Borg [11] studied the effect of context switches through trace-driven simulations. Using a time-sharing system simulator, their research shows that system calls, page faults, and a scheduler are the main sources of context switches. They also evaluated the effect of context switches on cycles per instruction (CPI) as well as the cache miss-rate. Depending on cache parameters, the cost of a context switch appears to be in the thousands of cycles, or tens to hundreds of microseconds in their simulations.

Snavely and Tullsen [13] proposed a scheduling algorithm considering various resource contention for simultaneous multithreading systems. Their algorithm runs samples of possible schedules to identify good schedules. While this approach is shown to be effective for a small number of jobs, random sampling is unlikely to find a good schedule for a large number of jobs. The number of possible schedules increase exponentially as the number of jobs increases. Our monitoring scheme with cache models can estimate cache miss-rates for all possible schedules without running all schedules. Therefore, our mechanism enables a scheduler to identify good schedules without a long sampling phase when the major resource contention is in caches. When there are many resources shared by processes (threads), the cache monitor can help the sampling scheme by suggesting good candidates with low cache contention.

Stone, Turek and Wolf [14] investigated the optimal allocation of cache memory between two competing processes that minimizes the overall miss-rate of a cache. Their study focuses on the partitioning of instruction and data streams, which can be thought of as multitasking with a very short time quantum. Their model for this case shows that the optimal allocation occurs at a point where the miss-rate derivatives of the competing processes are equal. The LRU replacement policy appears to produce cache allocations very close to optimal for their examples. They also describe a new replacement policy for longer time quanta that only increases cache allocation based on time remaining in the current time quantum and the marginal reduction in miss-rate due to an increase in cache allocation. However, their policy simply assumes the probability for a evicted block to be accessed in the next time quantum as a constant, which is neither validated nor is it described how this probability is obtained.

Thiébaut, Stone and Wolf applied their partitioning work [14] to improve disk cache hit-ratios [20]. The model for tightly interleaved streams is extended to be applicable for more than two processes. They also describe the problems in applying the model in practice, such as approximating the miss-rate derivative, non-monotonic miss-rate derivatives, and updating the partition. Trace-driven simulations for 32-MB disk caches show that the partitioning improves the relative hit-ratios in the range of 1% to 2% over the LRU policy.

An analytical model for time-sharing effects in fully-associative caches was presented in [16] (cf. Section 5.1). Partitioning methods based on off-line profiling were presented. Here, we have focused on on-line monitors to drive a partitioning scheme that better adapts to changes of behavior in processes. Further, we have extended the model to include the effects of memory contention amongst simultaneously-executing processes (Section 5.2). We have also addressed the memory interference issue in scheduling problems, and presented a memory-aware scheduling algorithm. An earlier version of this scheduling work has presented at the Job Scheduling Workshop for Parallel Processing [18].

7. Conclusion

The effects of memory contention are quite complex and vary with time. Current cache-hit counters and other profiling tools are geared to single job performance when executed in isolation. We have developed a methodology to solve certain scheduling and partitioning problems that optimize memory usage and overall performance, for both time-shared and space-shared systems.

Marginal gain information is collected for each process separately using simple on-line hardware counters. Rather than simply counting the number of hits to the cache, we propose to count the number of hits to the most recently, second most recently, etc., items in a fully-associative cache. For set-associative caches, a similar set of counters are used to approximate the values of counters had the cache been fully associative. A small amount of hardware instrumentation enables main memory to be similarly monitored.

This information can be used to either schedule jobs or partition the cache or memory. The key insight is that by knowing the marginal gains of all the jobs, it is then possible to predict the performance of a subset of the jobs executing in parallel or the performance from certain cache partitioning schemes.

The isolated miss-rate curves for each job can be computed from the marginal gain information and the miss-rate versus cache size curves are fed to an analytical model which combines the running processes' miss-rates to obtain an overall miss-rate curve for the entire set of running processes. The model includes the effects of space-sharing and time-sharing in producing the overall miss-rate, which is the quantity that we wish to minimize. Therefore, we can apply search algorithms that repeatedly compute the overall miss-rate for different sets of processes or cache sizes to determine which configuration is best. In some cases, the model-based approach outperforms the monitor-based approach.

The overhead associated with our methodology is quite low. We require hardware counters in a number that grows with the associativity of hardware caches, L1 or the TLB. Other counters are implemented in software. Our model is quite easy to compute, and is computed in schedulers or partitioners within an operating system. Alternately, in multi-threaded applications, *schedulers* can be modified to incorporate the model.

Our results justify collecting additional information from on-line monitoring beyond the conventional total hit and miss counts. Our framework will apply to other problems in memory optimization, including prefetching, selection of time quanta, etc.

Acknowledgments

Funding for this work is provided in part by the Defense Advanced Research Projects Agency under the Air Force Research Lab contract F30602-99-2-0511, titled "Malleable Caches for Data-Intensive Computing". Thanks also to E. Peserico, D. Chiou, D. Chen, and especially to P. Portante.

References

[1] A. Agarwal, M. Horowitz, and J. Hennessy. An analytical cache model. *ACM Transactions on Computer Systems*, 7(2), May 1989.

[2] Compaq. Compaq AlphaServer series. http://www.compaq.com.

[3] W. J. Dally, S. Keckler, N. Carter, A. Chang, M. Filo, and W. S. Lee. M-Machine architecture v1.0. Technical Report Concurrent VLSI Architecture Memo 58, Massachusetts Institute of Technology, 1994.

[4] S. J. Eggers, J. S. Emer, H. M. Levy, J. L. Lo, R. L. Stamm, and D. M. Tullsen. Simultaneous multithreading: A platform for next-generation processors. *IEEE Micro*, 17(5), 1997.

[5] D. G. Feitelson and L. Rudolph. Evaluation of design choices for gang scheduling using distributed hierarchical control. *Journal of Parallel and Distributed Computing*, 1996.

[6] J. L. Henning. SPEC CPU2000: Measuring CPU performance in the new millennium. *IEEE Computer*, July 2000.

[7] HP. HP 9000 superdome specifications. http://www.hp.com.

[8] IBM. RS/6000 enterprise server model S80. http://www.ibm.com.

[9] Intel. *Intel StrongARM SA-1100 Microprocessor*, April 1999.

[10] J. L. Lo, J. S. Emer, H. M. Levy, R. L. Stamm, D. M. Tullsen, and S. J. Eggers. Converting thread-level parallelism to instruction-level parallelism via simultaneous multithreading. *ACM Transactions on Computer Systems*, 15, 1997.

[11] J. C. Mogul and A. Borg. The effect of context switches on cache performance. In *the fourth international conference on Architectural support for programming languages and operating systems*, 1991.

[12] J. Munoz. *Data-Intensive Systems Benchmark Suite Analysis and Specification*. http://www.aaec.com/projectweb/dis, June 1999.

[13] A. Snavely and D. M. Tullsen. Symbiotic jobscheduling for a simultaneous multithreading processor. In *Ninth International Conference on Architectural Support for Programming Languages and Operating Systems*, 2000.

[14] H. S. Stone, J. Turek, and J. L. Wolf. Optimal partitioning of cache memory. *IEEE Transactions on Computers*, 41(9), Sept. 1992.

[15] R. A. Sugumar and S. G. Abraham. Set-associative cache simulation using generalized binomial trees. *ACM Transactions on Computer Systems*, 1995.

[16] G. E. Suh, S. Devadas, and L. Rudolph. Analytical cache models with application to cache partitioning. In *the 15th international conference on Supercomputing*, 2001.

[17] G. E. Suh, S. Devadas, and L. Rudolph. Dynamic cache partitioning for simultaneous multithreading systems. In *Thirteenth IASTED International Conference on Parallel and Distributed Computing System*, 2001.

[18] G. E. Suh, L. Rudolph, and S. Devadas. Effects of memory performance on parallel job scheduling. In *7th International Workshop on Job Scheduling Strategies for Parallel Processing (in LNCS 2221)*, pages 116–132, 2001.

[19] D. Thiébaut and H. S. Stone. Footprints in the cache. *ACM Transactions on Computer Systems*, 5(4), Nov. 1987.

[20] D. Thiébaut, H. S. Stone, and J. L. Wolf. Improving disk cache hit-ratios through cache partitioning. *IEEE Transactions on Computers*, 41(6), June 1992.

[21] D. M. Tullsen, S. J. Eggers, and H. M. Levy. Simultaneous multithreading: Maximizing on-chip parallelism. In *22nd Annual International Symposium on Computer Architecture*, 1995.

[22] M. Zagha, B. Larson, S. Turner, and M. Itzkowitz. Performance analysis using the MIPS R1000 performance counters. In *Supercomputing '96*, 1996.

[23] M. Zhang and K. Asanović. Highly-associative caches for low-power processors. In *Kool Chips Workshop in 33rd International Symposium on Microarchitecture*, 2000.

Energy and Thermal Management II

The Minimax Cache: An Energy-Efficient Framework for Media Processors[*]

Osman S. Unsal, Israel Koren, C. Mani Krishna, Csaba Andras Moritz

Department of Electrical and Computer Engineering, University of Massachusetts, Amherst, MA 01003
E-mail: {*ounsal,koren,krishna,moritz*}@*ecs.umass.edu*

Abstract

This work is based on our philosophy of providing inter-layer system-level power awareness in computing systems [26, 27]. Here, we couple this approach with our vision of multipartitioned memory systems [18, 19, 25], where memory accesses are separated based on their static predictability and memory footprint and managed with various compiler controlled techniques.

We show that media applications are mapped more efficiently when scalar memory accesses are redirected to a minicache. Our results indicate that a partitioned 8K cache with the scalars being mapped to a 512 byte minicache can be more efficient than a 16K monolithic cache from both performance and energy point of view for most applications. In extensive experiments, we report 30% to 60% energy-delay product savings over a range of system configurations and different cache sizes.

1. Introduction

The caching subsystem in the recently introduced low-power media/embedded processors consume a significant portion of the total processor power: 42% and 23% in StrongARM 110[17] and Power PC[2], respectively. Therefore, if we save on the data cache energy consumption, the overall energy consumption will also be considerably reduced. We firmly believe that the unique characteristics of multimedia applications dictate media-sensitive inter-layer architectural and compiler approaches to reduce the power consumption of the data cache. Our previous work extracted these characteristics; here we leverage this information to form our energy-saving Minimax cache framework.

Simply put, the Minimax cache is a regular L1 data cache with an additional small memory area. This small memory area is implemented as a statically managed *minicache*. While the size of the minicache is kept to a *minimum*, we employ it to get *maximum* energy-performance benefits. This organization leverages the fact that many accesses have very small footprints but they are frequently accessed. In our previous work, we have determined that scalar accesses exhibit this behavior for media applications[25]. We therefore redirect the scalar memory accesses to the minicache. Statically diverting the scalar and non-scalar accesses to the minicache and the regular L1 data cache, respectively, not only eliminates the cache interference but also saves power by only accessing a small minicache instead of a much larger data-array. In our previous work [25], we examined the interference issues. Here, we concentrate on the power aspect. Our results for a range of media applications indicate a 30% to 60% improvement in the energy-delay product.

The research spans the compiler and architectural layers. Our compiler-level analysis separates scalars from non-scalars and we map them to separate cache partitions. Existing cache partitioning schemes are driven by architectural features; examples are partitioning along instructions/data or along stack/heap accesses. The unique aspect of our Minimax cache partitioning scheme is the fact that it is driven by an application feature: scalar accesses. This is not only a finer granularity scheme but also one that blurs the compiler/architecture interface. By taking cache partitioning closer to the application layer, we are shifting caching from a hardware concern to a hardware/compiler one.

Briefly, our contributions in this paper are:

- Introduction of a new compiler-level scheme to partition scalars into a separate, much smaller cache area: the *minicache*. The scalars in the minicache and the non-scalars in the regular cache form the Minimax cache framework.

- Presentation of extensive experimental results on media applications and demonstrating that the Minimax cache organization is substantially more energy efficient while exhibiting high performance.

- Analyzing the energy impact of varying the register file size on media applications. We use register file sizes of 16 and 32.

---

[*]This research was supported in part by the National Science Foundation under grant EIA-0102696

131

Note that the Minimax cache approach is different from techniques to reduce energy dissipation that are based on placing a small cache in *front* of the L1 cache and managing it dynamically. Those approaches can come with a significant performance degradation relative to a conventional cache due to an increase in the access time on a miss in the small cache. Kin et al.[10] study a small L0 cache, called the *filter* cache, that saves energy while reducing performance by 29%.

The rest of this paper is organized as follows: We provide an analysis of related work in Section 2. Section 3 discusses our approach in more detail and provides our motivation. In Section 4 we introduce our experimental methodology. The results are given in Section 5. We conclude with a brief summary and a synopsis of future work in Section 6.

2. Previous Work

Previous cache partitioning research focused more on performance issues rather than energy. Providing architectural support to improve memory behavior include vertical cache partitioning schemes such as the selective cache ways proposed by Albonesi[1]. Panda et al.[20] propose use of a scratchpad memory in embedded processor applications. Kin et al.[10] study a small L0 cache that saves energy while reducing performance by 21%. Lee and Tyson [14] use the mediabench benchmarks and have a coarse-granularity partitioning scheme: they opt for dividing the cache along OS regions for energy reduction. A recent paper by Huang et al. [8] has a separate partition for the stack, they also address compiler implementation concerns as well.

Combined compiler/architectural efforts toward increasing cache locality [16] have exclusively focused on arrays. A recent memory behavior study for multimedia applications has also primarily targeted array structures [12]. Another recent paper by Delazuz et al. [7] discusses energy-directed compiler optimizations for array data structures on partitioned memory architectures; they use the SUIF compiler framework for their analysis. One previous work that also targeted multimedia systems, has considered dynamically dividing caches into multiple partitions [22], using the Mediabench benchmark in the performance analysis, with comments on compiler controlled memory. Cooper and Harvey [6] look at compiler-controlled memory. Their analysis includes spill memory requirements for some Spec '89 and Spec '95 applications. Sanchez et al. [23] introduce a compiler interference analysis and use a dual data cache for programs that have a high conflict miss ratio.
The fusion of the above research provided the motivation for this work. We consider scalar memory accesses, not only array or spill memory accesses, and we target multimedia systems running a suite of media applications. Compared to other cache partitioning approaches, we adopt a compiler-managed, application-driven finer granularity scheme: we direct scalar memory accesses to a minicache. To be fair, we do an execution time analysis of our minicache-added caching framework with a larger cache.

3. Background and Motivation

Our focus in this paper is multimedia architectures, but the methodology described can be applied to other classes of applications. We use the recently developed Mediabench benchmarks [13] in our experiments. Mediabench is a collection of popular embedded applications for communications and multimedia. See Table 1 for a short description of the benchmarks included in our analysis.

In our previous work [25], we implemented a compiler/architectural level scalar/non-scalar partitioning scheme through the use of a minibuffer. We define scalar accesses to be original and compiler-introduced scalar variables that couldn't be register promoted. One conclusion that was drawn in that study was that the scalars in media applications have a very low memory footprint and high access frequency. They also have considerable interference with non-scalar accesses. For the sake of clarity, we replicate the results for scalar static memory footprint upper bound using a 32 register configuration, see Table 2. Depending on the application, the actual memory footprint can be much smaller: addresses associated with variables that are no longer live could be reused, dead code sections could be eliminated, and so on. A compiler algorithm to compute the actual footprint requires inter-procedural analysis and a complex data-flow extraction. We have devised an effective compiler-level approximation for this purpose, the details and results are in [25].

The Minimax cache framework uses the same partition-

Application	(In Bytes)
ADPCM	0
EPIC	321
G721	48
GSM	202
JPEG	502
MESA	2191
MPEG	2125
RASTA	618

Table 2. The Memory Size Requirements.

ing scheme, however we map into a minicache instead of a

Benchmark	Description
ADPCM	Adaptive differential pulse code modification audio coding
EPIC	Image compression coder based on wavelet decomposition
G721	Voice compression coder based on G.711, G.721 and G.723 standards
GSM	Rate speech transcoding coder based on the European GSM standard
JPEG	A lossy image compression decoder
MESA	OpenGL graphics clone: using Mipmap quadrilateral texture mapping
MPEG	Lossy motion video compression decoder
RASTA	Speech recognition front-end processing

Table 1. Applicable Mediabench benchmarks. We do not include GHOSTSCRIPT since it is more amenable to embedded systems than multimedia. We also do not include the public key encryption schemes, PGP and PEGWIT, for similar reasons.

minibuffer and we conduct an extensive energy analysis.

3.1. Compiler and Architectural Implementation

Many embedded and media processors already have a scratchpad minibuffer or a minicache. The difference between the two organizations is that the minibuffer approach would require explicit management at compile-time of the memory accesses that are mapped into it, a conservative approach because compile-time analysis typically would need to overestimate the footprint to match exactly the size of the minibuffer, while the minicache could be a fully associative cache where the compile-time estimated footprint could be larger than the cache size. In practice, the dynamic memory footprint of memory accesses mapped into the small area is likely to be smaller than the static estimate, resulting in a high hit-rate in the minicache even if its size is chosen somewhat smaller than the static footprint size. Additionally, this latter approach could be used together with a simpler compiler analysis that gives a larger lower bound on the dynamic footprint. The minibuffer approach would require an exact bound on the footprint size to guarantee program execution correctness but, if that is successfully done would consume somewhat less power than the minicache. Coherence between the L1 data and minicache is guaranteed through type information based partitioning. In case one would want to add other data accesses to the minicache then alias analysis should be used. The output of the alias analysis would determine if there is any overlap in between the different memory accesses. If there is overlapping, mapping to the minicache should be avoided.

As far as implementation is concerned, no architectural modifications are necessary if the media processor is equipped with a minicache. An example is the recently introduced Intel StrongARM SA-1110 [9] which has a

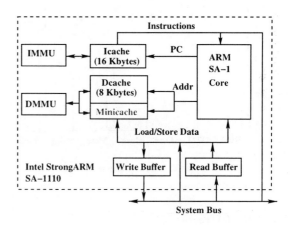

Figure 1. Intel Strongarm SA-1110 Architecture.

512 byte minicache, see Figure 1. This processor is very similar to our baseline. If the media processor is not equipped with any kind of minicache mechanism, then assembler annotations can be used to devise special load/store instructions which would channel the scalar data to a separate, smaller cache area.

3.2. Feasibility Study

The minibuffer approach[25] requires sophisticated compiler-level analysis. Our new framework, the Minimax cache, avoids most of this complexity. Since the footprint of scalars is low, we expect the Minimax cache to be as efficient as the minibuffer approach. One way of ascertaining this is to analyze how well the scalars are mapped into the separate cache area. In Figure 2, we present the minicache miss rates. The associated experimental setup is described in Section 4. We provide the results for both a 16 register and a 32 register processor, the smaller register file increases the number of scalar memory accesses. Note that a very small minicache size of 128 bytes can hold the working set of the scalar data for most applications. The working set of the 16 register configuration is higher due to the additional spills. However, even for a 16 register combination a size of 512 bytes is sufficient.

These results verify the promise of our approach. Although the Minimax cache requires some additional chip area compared to the monolithic cache, the impact is negligible since the minicache sizes used in this work are very small. Moreover, our comparative performance study of the

Minimax Cache with a much larger monolithic cache indicate that Minimax cache can even outperform the larger cache: see Section 5.

4. Experimental Methodology

Figure 3 shows a block diagram of our framework. We needed a detailed compiler framework that would give us sufficient feedback, is easy to understand, and allows us to change the source code for our modifications. With this in mind, we chose the SUIF/Machsuif suite as our compiler framework. SUIF [24] does high-level passes while Machsuif [15] makes machine specific optimizations. First, all the source files are converted into SUIF format and merged into one SUIF file. Next, we run this SUIF file through the Machsuif passes. We modified Machsuif passes to annotate all the scalar accesses and to vary the machine register file size. The modifications are propagated using the SUIF annotation mechanism. We amend the resulting assembler code by inserting NOP-like instructions around the annotated scalars, thus *marking* them.

We then used the Wattch [4] tool suite to run the bina-

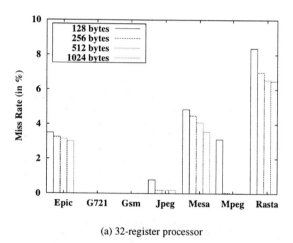

(a) 32-register processor

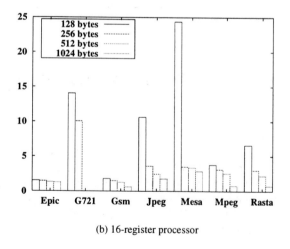

(b) 16-register processor

Figure 2. Miss Rates for different minicache sizes.

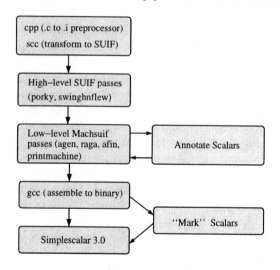

Figure 3. The Experimental Setup Block Diagram

ries and collect the energy results. Wattch is based on the Simplescalar [5] framework. The simulators has been modified to recognize the annotations in the *marked* code.

Our baseline machine model is an ARM-like single-issue in-order processor. Lee et. al. [14] use an identical configuration in their power dissipation analysis of region-based caches for embedded processors. We use the activity sensitive conditional clocking power model in Wattch, i.e., the cache consumes power when it is accessed. We modified Wattch to calculate the energy consumption of the addi-

Processor	L1 Cache	L2 Cache
ARM ARM10	32K	None
Transmeta Crusoe TM3200	32K	None
Transmeta Crusoe TM5400	64K	256K
Intel StrongARM SA-110	16K	None
Equator Map-CA	32K	None
Intel StrongArm 110	16K	None
Intel StrongARM 1100	8K	None

Table 3. Cache configurations for typical media processors.

tional minicache. To determine the baseline architecture, we did a survey of current media processors. As Table 3 indicates, the trend is towards larger caches. Therefore we have selected a 64Kbyte 2-way cache as our baseline, see Table 4. To be fair, we also examine 8K caches as well. The table also indicates that media processors do not typically have L2 data caches. Therefore, we only have L1 caches in our baseline architecture. However, some recent media processors have L2 data caches, the Transmeta Crusoe TM5400 is one example. So we also include an analysis of energy-delay impact of L2 caches. Here a concern might be the issue of consistency between the L2 cache and the L1 data + minicache. Namely, the block fetched from L2 into the L1 caches could contain a mix of scalar/non-scalar data. We avoid this problem by keeping the block sizes same across the caches. If the block sizes were different, then the issue could be addressed by clustering the scalar data to the beginning of the address space and padding them appropriately to the size of the L2 cache block size and boundary.

Processor Speed	1GHz
Issue	In-order Single-issue
L1 D-cache	64Kb, 2-way associative
Minicache	256bytes, fully-associative
L1 I-cache	32Kb, 2-way associative
L2 cache	None
L1 D-cache hit time	2 cycles
Minicache hit time	1 cycle
L2 cache hit time	20 cycles
Main memory hit time	100 cycles

Table 4. Baseline Parameters.

5. Results

Separating frequently-accessed low-footprint scalars from non-scalars by mapping them into separate cache

areas decreases cache interference. This leads to a more efficient use of the available caches. To underscore that intuition and to be fair, we next show that a much smaller 8Kbyte+512 byte Minimax cache can outperform a 16Kbyte monolithic cache for media applications, only for a few applications the larger cache is better, see Figure 4. The analysis is done for configurations with and without an L2 cache. We only include the execution time results here since the energy efficiency of the smaller Minimax cache is trivially obvious. The implication is that compiler-level schemes can result in saving chip real-estate by partitioning application accesses.

When introducing energy saving methods we need

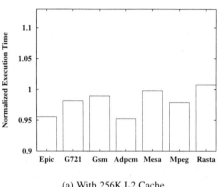

(a) With 256K L2 Cache

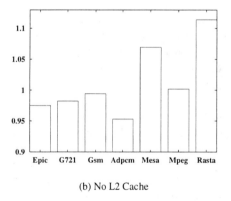

(b) No L2 Cache

Figure 4. Depending on benchmark, a Minimax Cache of much smaller size can be better than a monolithic cache of larger size. Here the results are the normalized execution time of an 8Kbyte Minimax cache with a 512 byte minicache. They are normalized with respect to the execution time of a 16Kbyte monolithic cache. To be fair, configurations with and without an L2 level cache are shown.

to be conscious of performance impacts of the proposed

method: we might save energy but this can come at the expense of performance. We therefore use the energy-delay product as our metric in our experiments. Here the delay is expressed as the total execution time. Figure 5 after the References shows the energy-delay product results in terms of *microJoules · second* for the L1 caching subsystem for the mediabench applications. We take the most challenging configuration for the Minimax cache: 16 register processor without L2 cache to penalize Minimax cache capacity misses. The results compare 8K and 64K monolithic caches with the same size Minimax cache with a minicache size of 128, 256, 512 and 1024 bytes. We get significant savings for the 64K cache: close to 30% for the worst case. For some applications with a very small footprint but frequent scalar accesses the savings are even more pronounced, 60% for the Epic benchmark for a minicache size of 128 bytes. The sensitivity of the results to the minicache size exhibits some interesting behavior. For some benchmarks the energy-delay product decreases as we increase the minicache size and then starts increasing as the size is further increased. This is due to the complex interplay between energy and performance: for those benchmarks small minicache sizes incur more scalar misses affecting performance, as the minicache size is increased the working set of the scalars fit in the cache and there is an *optimum* point beyond which the energy-delay product starts to increase with the increased energy consumption dominating the product. For some applications such as the Mesa or Rasta, a 128 byte minicache size has a higher energy-delay product than the monolithic cache since the working set of the scalars does not fit in 128 bytes. However, even for those applications a minicache of either 256 or 512 bytes gives substantial savings.

As the main memory to processor speed discrepancy grows, L3 caches have become feasible for general purpose processors[21]. Following the same trend, some recent media processor designs have started to include on-chip L2 caches, see Table 3. The rationale for this is the widening memory-gap as much as multiprogramming related causes. This motivates us to look into the combined energy-delay signature of the L1 data cache together with the L2 cache. We use a 256Kbyte 4-way associative L2 cache for this study. Figure 6 shows the results. Note that the energy-delay issues related with scalar data not fitting in the minicache for such benchmarks as Mesa or Rasta has been masked by the L2 cache. Comparison of Figure 6 with Figure 5 provides other interesting insights: note that the L1+L2 combination is more energy-delay effective for most benchmarks than L1 only configuration, even with the additional energy consumption of the L2 cache taken into account. This observation implies that future media processors can benefit from an on-chip L2 cache.

There is another aspect of scalar access related energy

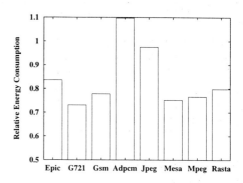

Figure 7. Relative energy consumption of the register files. The results give the register related energy consumption of a 16-register processor relative to that of a 32-register processor.

consumption: the register file. Since we model a media processor that is akin to the ARM architecture, we have used a register file size of 16 in our experiments. We now extend our analysis to register related energy impact of scalars and vary the register file size. Compared to the 32-register processor, average power per register access is lower for the 16-register case. This might imply that register file energy consumption of the 16-register processor would be less than 32-register processor for most applications. However, Figure 7 shows a counter-intuitive result: a 16-register processor consumes more register related energy than a 32-register processor for the Adpcm application. This is because all scalars for the Adpcm application fit in 32 registers and there are no scalar related memory accesses, see Table 2. However, the 16 register file is too small for the scalars to fit in and some scalars spill to memory. The energy impact of those additional scalar related data transfers between the registers and memory cause the 16-register processor to consume more register-related energy than 32-register one. This phenomenon offers the following insight: compiler/architecture coupling is becoming stronger and should be considered at the design stage.

In summary we consider an example of a media application mix. In particular, we would like to concentrate on a business videophone application. The application mix consists of an Mpeg decoder for video, Gsm encoder for voice transmission over telco lines, and Rasta speech recognition for minutes of meeting purposes. We weigh the applications as follows: Mpeg 60%, Gsm 20%, and Rasta 20%. We normalize the energy-delay products against the baseline monolithic cache case, and weigh them accordingly for a combined energy-delay product. See Figure 8 for the results. Minicaches of 512 bytes and 256 bytes give the best results for the L1 data cache only and with L2 cache, respectively. In both cases, we get 30% savings. Ideally, one should also take into account the interplay for multiple applications existing in the same system: issues such as context switches or L2 issues come to mind. We note those issues in the next Section.

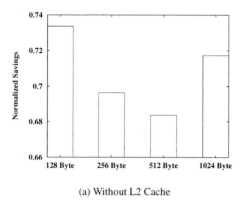

(a) Without L2 Cache

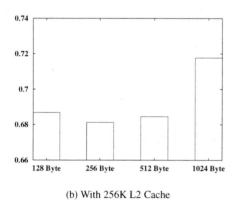

(b) With 256K L2 Cache

Figure 8. Relative energy savings for the videophone application for 64K L1 data cache. The minicache energy-delay product is normalized with respect to the monolithic cache.

6. Conclusions

We introduced our Minimax Cache framework for media processors. This framework further blurs the architecture/compiler interface. We discussed the architectural/compiler implementation issues of our approach. We demonstrated that statically mapping frequently used low footprint data such as the scalars in media applications to a separate cache partition is from 30% to 60% energy-delay efficient.

In the future, we would like to extend our analysis to multiple applications residing on the same media processor. This requires an extension to Wattch so that multiple processes and context-switches could be simulated.

In case of the instruction cache, one idea would be to map frequently accessed basic blocks from the secondary task, or interrupt handlers, into the minicache. This would reduce the interference between primary and secondary tasks in multimedia systems, that is a significant source of execution time variability [11]. Alternatively, if frequently accessed basic blocks are mapped, then energy savings could be obtained, similar to the Bellas et al. approach [3].

References

[1] Albonesi D. H., "Selective Cache Ways: On-Demand Cache Resource Allocation," *Journal of Instruction Level Parallelism*, May 2000

[2] Bechade R. et al., "A 32b 66MHz 1.8W Microprocessor," *Proceedings of the International Solid-State Circuits Conference*, 1994

[3] Bellas N. E., Hajj I. N., Polychronopoulos C. D., "Using Dynamic Cache Management Techniques to Reduce Energy in General Purpose Processors", *IEEE Transactions on Very Large Scale Integration (VLSI) Systems*, Vol. 8, No. 6, December 2000

[4] Brooks D., Tiwari V., Martonosi M., "Wattch: A Framework for Architectural-Level Power Analysis and Optimizations," *Proceedings of the 27th International Symposium on Computer Architecture, ISCA'00*, Vancouver, Canada, June 2000

[5] Burger D., Austin T. D., "The Simplescalar Tool Set, Version 2.0," *University of Wisconsin-Madison Computer-Sciences Department Technical Report #1342*, June 1997

[6] Cooper K. D., Harvey T. J., "Compiler-Controlled Memory," *Proceedings of the Eighth International Conference on Architectural Support for Programming Languages and Systems (ASPLOS)* October, 1998

[7] Delaluz V., Kandemir M., Vijaykrishnan N., Irwin M. J.,"Energy-Oriented Compiler Optimizations for Partitioned Memory Architectures," *Proceedings International Conference on Compilers, Architectures, and Synthesis for Embedded Systems CASES00*, San Jose, CA, November 2000.

[8] Huang M., Reanu J., Torellas J., "L1 Cache Decomposition for Energy Efficient Processors," *International Symposium on Low-Power Electronics and Design, ISLPED'01*, Huntington Beach, CA, August 2001

[9] *Intel StrongARM SA-1110 Microprocessor Brief Datasheet*, April 2000

[10] Kin J., Gupta M., Mangione-Smith W. H., "The Filter Cache: An Energy Efficient Memory Structure," *Proceeedings of the 30th Annual Symposium on Microarchitecture, MICRO'97*, 1997

[11] Koopman P.J.Jr.,"Perils of the PC Cache," *Embedded Systems Programming*, 6(5), May 1993

[12] Kulkarni C., Catthoor F., H. De Man, "Advanced Data Layout Organization for Multi-media Applications," *Workshop on Parallel and Distributed Computing in Image Processing, Video Processing, and Multimedia (PDIVM 2000)*, Cancun, Mexico, May 2000

[13] Lee C., Potkonjak M., Mangione-Smith W. H., "Mediabench: A Tool for Evaluating and Synthesizing Multimedia and Communications Systems," *Proceedings of the 30th Annual International Symposium on Microarchitecture*, December 1997

[14] Lee S. H., Tyson G. S., "Region-Based Caching: An Energy Efficient Memory Architecture for Embedded Processors," *Proceedings of PACM (CASES'00)*, San Jose, CA, November 2000

[15] http://www.eecs.harvard.edu/hube/software/software.html

[16] Memik G., Kandemir M., Haldar M., Choudhary A., "A Selective Hardware/Compiler Approach for Improving Cache Locality," *Northwestern University Technical Report CPDC-TR-9909-016*, 1999

[17] Montanaro J., Witek R. T., et al., "A 160MHz 32b 0.5W CMOS RISC Microprocessor," *IEEE International Solid-State Circuits Conference*, February 1994, vol. 39

[18] Moritz C. A., Frank M., Lee W., Amarasinghe S., "Hot Pages: Software Caching for Raw Microprocessors," *MIT-LCS Technical Memo LCS-TM-599*, Aug 1999

[19] Moritz C. A. , Frank M., Amarasinghe S.,"FlexCache: A Framework for Compiler Generated Data Caching," *To appear in Lecture Notes in Computer Science, Springer-Verlag*, 2001

[20] Panda P. R., Dutt N. D., Nicolau A., "Efficient Utilization of Scratch-Pad Memory in Embedded Processor Applications," *Proceedings of European Design and Test Conference*, Paris, France, 1997

[21] Poff D. E., Banikazemi M., Saccone R., Franke H., Abali B., Smith T. B., "Performance of Memory Expansion Technology," *Workshop on Memory Performance Issues, 28th International Symposium on Computer Architecture, ISCA'01*, Goteborg, Sweden, June 2001

[22] Ranganathan P., Adve S., Jouppi N. P., "Reconfigurable Caches and Their Application to Media Processing," *Proceedings of the 27th International Symposium on Computer Architecture ISCA'00*, Vancouver, Canada, June 2000

[23] Sanchez F. J., Gonzalez A., Valero M., "Static Locality Analysis for Cache Management," *Proceedings of the 1997 Conference on Parallel Architectures and Compilation Techniques PACT'97*, 1997

[24] http://suif.stanford.edu

[25] Unsal O. S., Wang Z., Koren I., Krishna C. M., Moritz C. A.,"On Memory Behavior of Scalars in Embedded Multimedia Systems," *Workshop on Memory Performance Issues, 28th International Symposium on Computer Architecture, ISCA'01*, Goteborg, Sweden, June 2001

[26] Unsal O. S., Koren I., Krishna C. M., "Power-Aware Replication of Data Structures in Distributed Embedded Real-Time Systems," *Lecture Notes in Computer Science, LNCS2000 Springer-Verlag*, May 2000

[27] Unsal O. S., Koren I., Krishna C. M., "Application Level Power-Reduction Heuristics in Large Scale Real-Time Systems," *Proceedings of the IEEE International Workshop On Embedded Fault-Tolerant Systems*, Washington, DC, September 2000

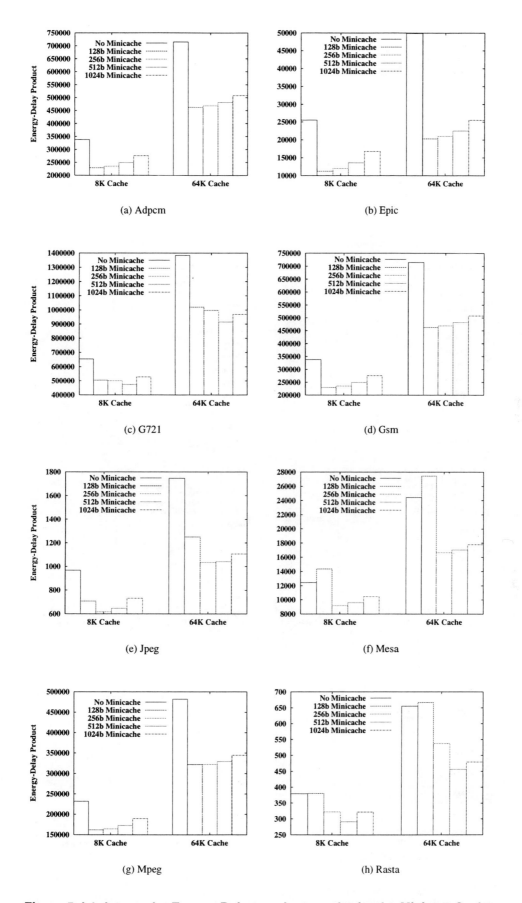

Figure 5. L1 data cache Energy-Delay product results for the Minimax Cache.

139

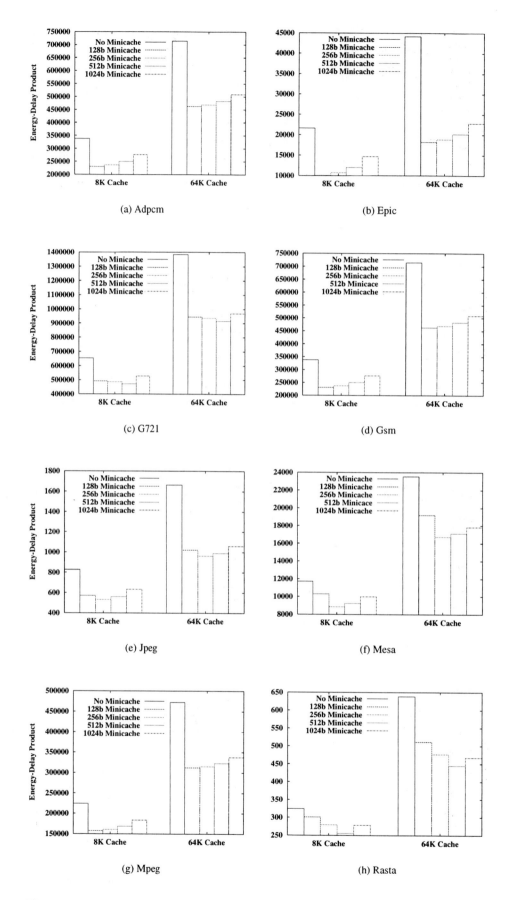

Figure 6. L1+L2 Cache Energy-Delay product results for the Minimax Cache.

140

Using Complete Machine Simulation for Software Power Estimation: The SoftWatt Approach

Sudhanva Gurumurthi   Anand Sivasubramaniam   Mary Jane Irwin   N. Vijaykrishnan

Mahmut Kandemir

Dept. of Computer Science and Engineering

The Pennsylvania State University, University Park, PA 16802

{gurumurt,anand,mji,vijay,kandemir}@cse.psu.edu

Tao Li   Lizy Kurian John

Dept. of Electrical and Computer Engineering

University of Texas at Austin, Austin, TX 78712

{tli3,ljohn}@ece.utexas.edu

Abstract

Power dissipation has become one of the most critical factors for the continued development of both high-end and low-end computer systems. The successful design and evaluation of power optimization techniques to address this vital issue is invariably tied to the availability of a broad and accurate set of simulation tools. Existing power simulators are mainly targeted for particular hardware components such as CPU or memory systems and do not capture the interaction between different system components. In this work, we present a complete system power simulator, called SoftWatt, that models the CPU, memory hierarchy and a low-power disk subsystem and quantifies the power behavior of both the application and operating system. This tool, built on top of the SimOS infrastructure, uses validated analytical energy models to identify the power hotspots in the system components, capture relative contributions of the user and kernel code to the system power profile, identify the power-hungry operating system services and characterize the variance in kernel power profile with respect to workload. Our results using Spec JVM98 benchmark suite emphasize the importance of complete system simulation to understand the power impact of architecture and operating system on application execution.

1 Introduction

Performance optimization has long been the goal of different architectural and systems software studies, driving technological innovations to the limits for getting the most out of every cycle. This quest for performance has made it possible to incorporate millions of transistors on a very small die, and to clock these transistors at very high speeds. While these innovations and trends have helped provide tremendous performance improvements over the years, they have at the same time created new problems that demand immediate consideration. An important and daunting problem is the power consumption of hardware components, and the resulting thermal and reliability concerns that it raises. As power dissipation increases, the cost of power delivery to the increasing number of transistors and thermal packaging for cooling the components goes up significantly [3, 33]. Cooling systems need to be designed to tackle the peak power consumption of any component. These factors are making power as important a criterion for optimization as performance in commercial high end systems design.

Just as with performance, power optimization requires careful design at several levels of the system architecture [13]. At the circuit level, several techniques such as clock gating, supply voltage scaling and supply voltage gating have been proposed to reduce both dynamic and leakage power [5]. Architectural level power saving techniques typically detect idleness of components not being used and appropriately transition them to a lower power consuming mode. Even the software - the operating system (OS), compiler and the application - has an important role to play in power efficient systems design. The operating system, which plays the role of hardware manager, can schedule jobs [23], allocate and manage memory [19], and control peripherals [20] to reduce overall system power. The compiler can generate code and data transformations to increase idleness of hardware components so that they can be transitioned to low power modes more effectively [7] Finally, algorithmic transformations in the application have been shown to give significant power savings [30].

The successful design and evaluation of such optimization techniques is invariably tied to a broad and accurate set of rich tools that are available for conducting these studies. The crucial role of design and evaluation tools for performance optimization has been well illustrated by several studies over the years, and the community at large is currently expending a lot of effort in the development of similar tools for power estimation and optimization. There are tools to facilitate this at the circuit [1], gate [32], and architectural [4, 35, 29] levels. However, power estimation and optimization tools at the architectural and software levels are still in their infancy. These tools are also not well-integrated enough to study several issues all at one, or to see how one optimization affects the complete system behavior and not just the target of the optimization. For instance, with today's tools, one could try out a compiler loop transformation technique by using tools such as SUIF [11] to conduct source-to-source transformations, run the output through gcc to get binaries, and run them on a simulator such as Wattch [4] to evaluate the power savings. This could help us study the impact of the optimization on the datapath, cache and memory power concurrently. However, this still does not tell us how the TLB behavior changes, and how the OS execution is affected as a result. Further, this does not provide us with the complete picture since there are still several other hardware components (e.g. the disk) that could be affected.

A similar observation was made a few years back in the context of performance, leading to a consideration of the complete system in the evaluation. Instrumentation/measurement or hardware profiling using performance counters on an actual platform is one way of complete system performance evaluation [16, 15]. However, we do not have access to all the relevant hardware events for accurate power calculations in complete system power profiling on today's systems. This approach also makes it difficult to perform detailed software and hardware profiling of several components at the same time without significant intrusion. Instead, a simulation based strategy can do the same without the intrusion, albeit at a high simulation cost. This is the strategy adopted in the SimOS [28] tool, which performs a complete system performance simulation of applications running on a multi-issue superscalar processor together with an actual commercial operating system (IRIX 5.3).

With the goal of conducting complete system power profiling (from the hardware and software viewpoint), we have extended SimOS to include power models for different hardware components (the processor datapath, caches, memory, and disk). Consequently, we have a powerful tool that can give us detailed performance and power profiles for different hardware and software components over the course of execution of real applications running on a commercial operating system. While there have been some previous endeavors in building complete system power estimation tools [26, 6, 2, 18, 22], most of these are limited to either specific environments/applications or have targeted embedded platforms. SoftWatt, the tool that is discussed in this paper, is the first one to target complete system power profiles of high end systems, that can be used for design and evaluation of power optimization techniques. Such a tool can help us answer several important issues that are explored in this paper:

- How does the power consumption of the complete system vary during the execution of a program? Does it remain constant, or are there variations/spikes? Are these variations, if any, due to user or kernel activity, and what hardware components are being exercised at those times? Even if the overall power consumption does not vary too much, are there changes between the relative proportions of user, kernel, and idle mode power consumption over time?

- What is the major contributor for power consumption from the software angle? Is it the kernel instructions, user instructions or the idle process (idling in a lot of commercial OS including IRIX is done by busy-waiting and is not necessarily a low power consumer)? What hardware components are the dominant power consumers in the user and kernel modes?

- Within the kernel, what OS services are the dominant power consumers? Why? Do performance and power profiles go hand-in-hand for all these results?

- What is the variation in energy consumption for a kernel service from one invocation to another? i.e., Is the per-invocation energy consumption of a kernel service very data dependent? If not, then from the simulation angle, there can be reasonable simulation speedups to be gained by not getting into the details of simulating kernel services.

- From the detailed hardware and software power profiles, can we make suggestions where future work needs to be directed for significant gains? What kind of hardware/software optimizations are suggested by the power profiles?

This paper examines several of these questions using our tool, SoftWatt, by experimenting with different Spec JVM98 benchmarks [31] together with the Java Virtual Machine (JVM) runtime system executing on IRIX 5.3. The performance and power profiles are given for different hardware components such as the processor datapath, L1 and L2 I/D caches, memory and disk.

The rest of this paper is organized as follows. Section 2 describes the simulation framework. Section 3 presents the power characterization of the Spec JVM98 benchmark suite Section 4 presents the impact of disk power-management to the system power consumption and performance. Section 5 discusses the characterization results and concludes the paper.

2 Simulator Design

The first step towards a comprehensive study of the power consumption of a computer system is the development of a suitable simulation infrastructure. SimOS, which provides a very detailed simulation of the hardware so as to be able to run the IRIX 5.3 operating system, is our base simulator. SimOS also provides interfaces for event-monitoring and statistics collection. The simulator has three CPU models, namely, *Embra*, *Mipsy*, and *MXS*. Embra employs *dynamic binary translation* and provides a rough-characterization of the workload. Mipsy provides emulation of a MIPS R4000-like architecture. It consists of a simple pipeline with blocking caches. MXS emulates a MIPS R10000-like [36] superscalar architecture. The overall design of the energy simulator is given in figure 1.

We modified MXS CPU and the memory-subsystem simulators to instrument accesses to their different components. This enables us to analyze our simulations using the Timing Trees [12] mechanism provided by SimOS. The MXS CPU simulator does not report detailed statistics about the memory subsystem behavior. Due to this limitation in SimOS, we use Mipsy for obtaining this information.

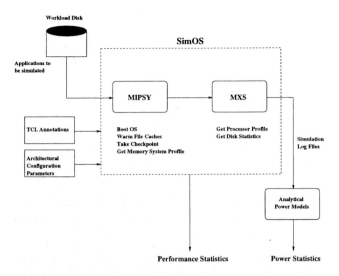

Figure 1. Simulator Design

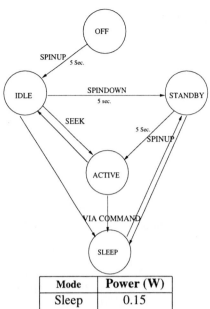

Mode	Power (W)
Sleep	0.15
Idle	1.6
Standby	0.35
Active	3.2
Seeking	4.1
Spin up	4.2

Figure 2. MK3003MAN Operating Modes State Machine and Power Values

MXS is used to obtain detailed information about the processor.

We also incorporated a disk-power model into SimOS for studying the overall system power consumption. SimOS models a HP97560 disk. This disk is not state-of-the art and does not support any low-power modes. We therefore incorporated a layer on top of the existing disk model to simulate the TOSHIBA MK3003MAN [34] disk, a more representative modern disk that supports a variety of low-power modes. The operating-modes state-machine implemented for this disk is shown in figure 2. The disk transitions from the IDLE state to the ACTIVE state on a seek operation. The time taken for the seek operation is reported by the disk simulator of SimOS. This timing information is used to calculate the energy consumed when transitioning from the IDLE to the ACTIVE state. In the IDLE state, the disk keeps spinning. A transition from the IDLE state to the STANDBY state involves spinning down the disk. This operation incurs a performance penalty. In order to service an I/O request when the disk is in the STANDBY state, the disk has to be spun back up to the ACTIVE state. This operation incurs both a performance and energy penalty. The SLEEP state is the lowest-power state for this disk. The disk transitions to this state via an explicit command.

We assume that the spin up and spin down operations take the same amount of time, and that the spin down operation does not consume any power. Our model also assumes that transition from the ACTIVE to the IDLE state takes zero time and power, as in [20]. Currently, we do not utilize the SLEEP state. We suitably modified the timing modules of SimOS to accurately capture mode-transitions. While it is clear that modeling a disk is important from the energy perspective, the features of a low-power disk can also influence the operating system routines such as the idle process running on the processor core. Hence, a disk model helps to characterize the processor power more accurately. During the I/O operations, energy is consumed in the disk. Further, as the process requesting the I/O is blocked, the operating system schedules the idle process to execute. Therefore, energy is also consumed in both the processor and the memory subsystem.

SoftWatt uses analytical power models. A post-processing approach is taken to calculate the power values. The simulation data is read from the log-files, pre-processed, and is input to the power models. This approach causes the loss of per-cycle information, as data is sampled and dumped to the simulation log-file at a coarser granularity. However, there is no slowdown in the simulation time beyond that incurred by SimOS itself. This is particularly critical due to the time-consuming nature of MXS simulations. The only exception to this rule is the disk-energy model, where energy-consumption is measured during simulation to accurately account for the mode-transitions. This measurement incurs very little simulation overhead. SoftWatt models a simple conditional clocking model. It assumes that full power is consumed if any of the ports of a unit is accessed; otherwise no power is consumed.

The per-access costs of the cache-structures are calculated based on the model presented in [17, 4]. The clock generation and distribution network is modeled using the technique proposed in [9], which has an error-margin of 10%. The associative structures of the processor are modeled as given in [25, 4]. In order to validate the entire CPU model, we configured SoftWatt to calculate the maximum CPU power of the R10000 processor. In comparison to the maximum power dissipation of 30 W reported in the R10000 data sheet [27], SoftWatt reports 25.3 W. As detailed circuit-level information is not available at this level,

Parameter	Value
Instruction Window Size	64
Register File	34 INT, 32 FP
Load/Store Queue	32
Fetch Width per Cycle	4
Decode Width per Cycle	4
Issue Width per Cycle	4
Commit Width per Cycle	4
Functional Units	2 Ints,2 FP
Branch History Table	1024
Branch Target Address Table	1024
Return Address Stack	32
Memory Size	128 MB
Cache Hierarchy	2-Level with L1 D- and I-Cache and Unified L2 Cache
Instruction Cache Size	32KB
Instruction Cache Line Size	64B
Instruction Cache Associativity	2
Data Cache Size	32 KB
Data Cache Line Size	64B
Data Cache Associativity	2
L2 Cache Size	1MB
L2 Cache Line Size	128B
L2 Cache Associativity	2
Unified TLB (fully assoc) entries	64
Feature Size	0.35 um
Vdd	3.3 V
MHz	200

Table 1. System Model

generalizations made in the analytical power models result in an estimation error.

3 Power Characterization of Spec JVM98 Benchmarks

3.1 System Configuration and Benchmarks

Table 1 gives the baseline configuration of SoftWatt that was used for our experiments. We chose the Spec JVM98 benchmarks [31] for conducting our characterization study. A description of these benchmarks is given in [10]. We chose this benchmark suite for two reasons. First, Java is becoming an increasingly popular language in many power-critical applications. Second, Java applications are also known to exercise the operating system more than traditional benchmark suites [21]. Thus, they form an interesting suite to characterize for power using our complete system power simulator, which includes the operating system as well. We excluded the mpegaudio benchmark from our characterization study, as it failed to execute on the MXS simulator. For all other Spec JVM98 benchmarks, the just-in-time (JIT) compilation mode was employed, and the s10 dataset was used. This dataset exercises the Java garbage-collector and the simulation also completes in a reasonable amount of time. On the average, the s10 dataset took 30 hours per application to complete on a 400 MHz Sun Sparc. All the benchmarks were initially run on the relatively fast Mipsy simulator. The file-caches were warmed and a checkpoint was taken before the program was loaded. Then, the benchmarks were run on the Mipsy simulator to get statis-

tics about the memory system behavior, and then on MXS to get processor statistics. For all the benchmarks, the profiled period consists of all the phases of the Java application execution until the program exits and returns to the shell-prompt.

In our characterization of the benchmarks, we use two metrics, namely, *power* and *energy*. We focus on the *average* power consumption. In the presence of dynamic thermal management techniques, a system can be designed accounting for average power consumption instead of peak power [3]. Our tool can also be used to obtain the peak power consumption from the profiles. Energy consumption is an important metric when considering battery life in high-performance mobile systems such as laptop computers. We also use an additional metric, namely, the *Energy-Delay Product (EDP)*, which captures the tradeoffs in design decisions for energy versus that for performance. Unless explicitly mentioned, the term "power consumption" refers to the power consumed in the processor datapath and the memory subsystem only.

3.2 Characterization

Figures 3 and 4 give the performance and power profiles of the jess benchmark, for four different phases (modes) of execution: user mode, kernel mode, kernel synchronization and idle. The profiles for the other benchmarks is given [10]. The kernel execution is split into the portion where instructions are executed and the portion where synchronization operations are performed. Idle refers to the idle times during the workload's execution. In Figure 3, the first two profiles, from the left, were obtained by executing them on Mipsy. The third profile was obtained by configuring MXS to be a single-issue processor. It is clear that the average power of the memory subsystem is more than twice that of the processor datapath. Therefore optimizing the memory subsystem is very important to reduce the overall power consumption in a single issue machine. The processor profiles in figure 4 were obtained on MXS. In the power profiles, the influence of clock-loading is not shown.

The bulk of the time is spent executing user-instructions. Also, the benchmarks show a greater percentage of operating system activity in the superscalar machine compared to that of the single-issue configuration. On the average, the percentage of kernel activity increases from 14.28% in a single-issue processor to 21.02% in the superscalar processor. This is because kernel code has a lower IPC (Instructions Per Cycle) and worse branch-prediction accuracy compared to the user code [21]. In all the power profiles, it is observed that the idle-mode initially dominates the power consumption, and then significantly decreases. The same trend can be seen in the execution profile as well. The initial idle-periods are due to the loading of the Java class files from the disk when executing the benchmarks. After this period, the required data is found in the file-cache most of the time. Further, it is observed that the memory subsystem energy increases steeply at the beginning of the profiled period. This is because of the cold-start misses in the caches, which cause several memory accesses. As the L2 cache and memory have a high per-access cost, the average power is high at the beginning. After the initial period, both the profiles even out, with the subsystems consuming a more or less constant amount of power.

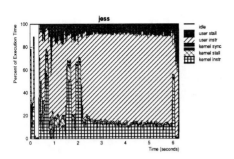
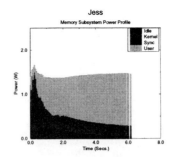
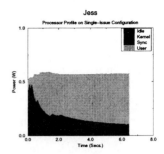

Figure 3. Profile of Memory Subsystem Behavior

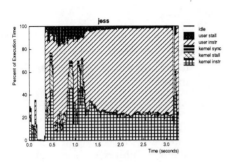
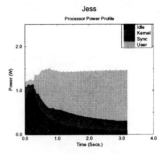

Figure 4. Profile of Processor Behavior

Figure 5 presents the overall power budget of the system, including the disk. Here, the breakdown is presented over all the modes of execution combined, and is averaged over all the benchmarks. The term "conventional" disk refers to a disk without any mode transitions. We assume that the disk can perform read/write, seek, or just keep spinning consuming the power as if it were in the ACTIVE mode. This model is the baseline disk configuration and gives an upper bound of its power consumption. It can be observed that, when no power-related optimizations are done, the disk is the single largest consumer of power in the system. Therefore, not considering this component when evaluating the power-consumption of a system does not give us the complete picture. However, the bulk of the power is still consumed in the processor datapath and memory system components. Therefore, these components are also an important target for power optimizations.

Now, we investigate the power consumption in the processor, caches, and memory. For the sake of clarity, the load-store queue, issue-window, register renaming unit, resultbus, register file, and ALUs have been clubbed together as the "datapath" in all the graphs. The graphs with the breakdown of the datapath components is given in [10]. Table 2 gives the breakdown of percentage of the cycles executed and the energy consumed for all the benchmarks. The largest fraction of the execution time is spent in the user-mode. This holds from the energy angle as well. However, the user-mode accounts for a larger proportion of the energy consumption than the fraction of the cycles. Thus, the proportion of the energy consumption for the kernel is lower than that of its execution fraction. Similarily, the idle-times consume a slightly lesser fraction of the energy than execution cycles. These variations can be explained by consider-

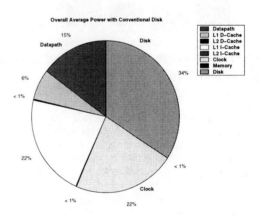

Figure 5. Overall Power Budget with A Conventional Disk - The slices of the pie are in an anti-clockwise order of the entries in the legend. The disk contributes 34% to the average power.

ing the average power (shown in figure 6). The user-mode accounts for the highest average power. The main contributor to the user-mode power consumption is the L1 I-cache. As observed from table 3, the user code has the highest number of (L1) instruction cache references per cycle. This is because, user-code exhibits higher instruction-level parallelism (ILP) compared to kernel code. Consequently, the effective fetch-width of the user code is higher than that of the kernel code. Power consumption of the data-caches is the highest for user-code, again due to its higher ILP. Similarly, the ALU-use per cycle is 0.76 for the user code which is much larger than that of the other phases (0.42 for the kernel, 0.59 for Synchronization and 0.26 for the Idle mode).

Focusing on the kernel synchronization mode, it is observed that synchronization operations are expensive in terms of power consumption. More specifically, they are found to intensely exercise the L1 I-cache and the ALUs, as compared to the other activities in the kernel mode [10]. This is because synchronization operations perform comparison and increment/decrement operations, within a tight loop. However, synchronization operations constitute less than 1% of the overall energy consumption of the benchmarks. Overall we observe that, the main power-hungry units are still the L1 caches and the clock, even when considering kernel code.

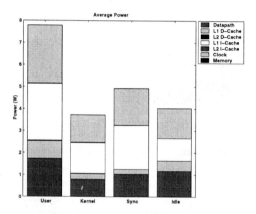

Figure 6. Average Power (averaged over all the benchmarks)

By including the IDLE state in the disk configuration, the dominance of the disk in the power budget decreases from 34% to 23%. This is shown in figure 7. This optimization provides significant power-savings, and also alters the overall picture. Now the L1 I-cache and the clock dominate the power profile.

3.3 Kernel Behavior

In this section, we give a detailed power/energy characterization of the operating system. We breakdown the kernel activity into services and compare the energy behavior of key kernel services with their performance in an attempt to answer the following questions:

- Do the services that account for the bulk of the kernel cycles also constitute the bulk of the energy consumption?

- Is their per-invocation energy consumption data-dependent? If so, how can this information be used to accelerate the simulation process?

As observed in the previous subsection, the operating system itself can be a significant consumer of energy (up to

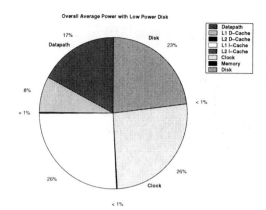

Figure 7. Percentage Contribution of the Disk with the IDLE state to the Power Consumption - The disk contributes 23% to the average power

17% in jack, for kernel instructions and synchronization operations combined). Table 4 gives the results for the services that account for the bulk of the kernel execution-time and compares the the execution cycles to their relative energy consumption contributions for each of the benchmarks. MIPS architectures have a software-managed TLB. The operating system handles the misses by doing the required address translation, reloads the TLB, and then restarts the user process. These operations are done by the *utlb* service. *demand_zero* zeroes out a newly allocated page and the *cacheflush* routine flushes the I-/D-caches. *vfault* is the validity-fault handler.

From the table, it is clear that those services that account for the bulk of the kernel execution time also account for the bulk of the energy consumption. However, the percentage of energy consumed for *utlb* is proportionately smaller compared to its execution time. As *utlb* accounts for the bulk of the operating system activity in these benchmarks, its behavior reflects on the kernel as a whole. Again, this trend can be explained by considering the average power of the services. Figure 8 shows the average power of four key kernel services. The power numbers presented have been averaged over all the invocations of the service over the entire profiled period, and then averaged over all the benchmarks.

Clearly, *utlb* has a much lower average power than the other services considered. The handler is not data-intensive, and therefore, does not exercise the data caches and the load/store queue. As these units are not accessed, the clock power is lower as well, leading to a smaller average power.

Table 5 shows how much variation there actually exists between the invocations of the services across the benchmarks. The variation is measured using the coefficient of deviation and is expressed as a percentage. The services presented can be roughly categorized as those being completely internal to the kernel (*utlb, demand_zero, cacheflush*) and those that are invoked by an user-program (*read, write, open*). The internal OS services show very small deviation in their energy behavior per invocation. On the other hand, the other externally-invoked services, which

Benchmark	User		Kernel Inst.		Kernel Sync.		Idle	
	Cycles	Energy	Cycles	Energy	Cycles	Energy	Cycles	Energy
compress	88.24	93.74	7.95	4.18	0.2	0.14	3.61	1.94
jess	63.69	77.15	24.57	15.12	0.86	0.68	10.88	7.05
db	66.1	81.19	24.28	13.22	0.75	0.54	8.87	5.05
javac	64.2	78.47	27.54	15.98	0.55	0.44	7.71	5.11
mtrt	80.62	90.07	14.8	7.44	0.26	0.17	4.32	2.32
jack	69.02	81.36	27.91	16.43	0.63	0.51	2.44	1.7

Table 2. Percentage Breakdown of Energy and Cycles

Benchmark	User		Kernel Inst.		Kernel Sync.		Idle	
	iL1Ref	dL1Ref	iL1Ref	dL1Ref	iL1Ref	dL1Ref	iL1Ref	dL1Ref
compress	2.0088	0.6833	1.1203	0.2080	1.5560	0.1745	0.7612	0.3546
jess	1.9861	0.6217	1.1143	0.2164	1.5956	0.1775	0.8267	0.3851
db	2.0911	0.6699	1.0602	0.1892	1.5240	0.1832	0.7244	0.3375
javac	1.9685	0.5604	1.0346	0.1835	1.5355	0.1720	0.8110	0.3778
mtrt	2.1105	0.6473	1.085	0.1908	1.5177	0.1697	0.7524	0.3505
jack	1.8465	0.5869	1.041	0.1931	1.5585	0.1708	0.8718	0.4061

Table 3. Cache References Per Cycle

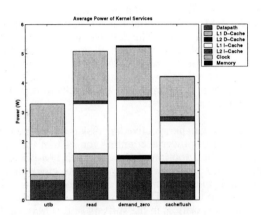

Figure 8. Average Power of Operating System Services

are I/O system calls, show a greater coefficient of deviation. This is because the energy consumed per invocation depends on factors such as the data transfer-size, whether the data is available in the file-cache etc. This result suggests that, given a trace of the number of invocations of the various kernel-services for a given workload, it is possible to get a rough estimate, with an error margin of about 10%, of the kernel energy consumption, without actually performing a detailed simulation. Such traces can be obtained using tools such as prof and truss, which are common in many Unix-based systems. Further, we found that, the per-cycle processor and memory-system access-behavior of the idle-process can be accurately predicted and is independent of the workload. We used this property in our disk model, where spin ups/spin downs could be simulated by just fast-forwarding the simulation by the requisite number of cycles rather than actually simulating it. This eliminates any additional cycles incurred in the simulation (and thus longer simulation time) due to the full use of the disk model.

4 Disk Power Management

As seen in section 3, the disk is the single most power-hungry unit in the computer system. The power consumption of the disk becomes paramount for large server machines, such as web-servers and file-servers, which perform a large amount of I/O [14]. This problem is tackled by using disk power management schemes [8, 24]. Modern-day disks are designed to support a variety of low-power modes. The disk transitions to one of these modes during inactive periods. We investigated the benefit of employing such a disk using the Toshiba disk model. We considered four different disk configurations for our study, namely:

1. The baseline disk used in section 3.

2. A disk that supports the IDLE low-power mode but no STANDBY mode.

3. A disk that supports the STANDBY mode with a spin down threshold of 2 seconds, in addition to the IDLE mode.

4. A disk that supports the STANDBY mode with a spin down threshold of 4 seconds, in addition to the IDLE mode.

Disk configuration 2 models a disk where there is a transition to the IDLE mode immediately after a read/write operation completes. The disk keeps spinning while in the IDLE mode and transitions back to the ACTIVE state when a seek operation is to be performed. In disk configurations 3 and 4, the disk spins down to the STANDBY mode after a fixed period of inactivity (with respect to the disk), called the Spin down Threshold. We chose a spin down threshold of 2 seconds for configuration 3 based on the results given in [20]. Figure 9 gives the results of our study for all the benchmarks.

For this study, we use energy as the metric instead of power, as we wish to evaluate designs which depend on periods of activity rather than a single processor cycle. The

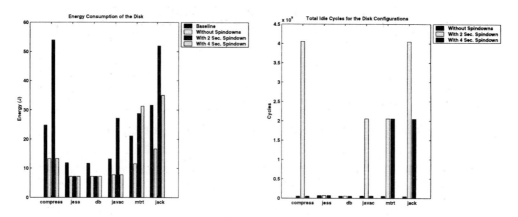

Figure 9. Energy-Performance Tradeoffs for the Disk Configurations

bar graphs in Figure 9 give the energy consumption of just the disk for the four configurations and the variation in the number of idle-cycles. As mentioned in section 2, the cycles due to disk activity are accounted for as idle-cycles in the execution profile.

Transitioning to the IDLE mode after a read or write provides significant energy benefit for all the benchmarks. Further, since transitions to the IDLE mode take zero time, there is no performance degradation, and an energy-benefit is always obtained. Therefore, the baseline disk configuration is not considered when comparing the configurations for their performance. jess and db are unaffected by using configuration 3 because of their short running times. For compress, javac, mtrt, and jack, there is severe energy and performance degradation. Their execution time and energy consumed (in the absence of spindowns) is a much smaller fraction to that of the spin-operations, and a large amount of energy and time is consumed to spin the disk back up. During the execution of compress and jack, the disk spins up and down multiple times, leading to a large increase in the number of idle-cycles and the overall energy consumption. This is reflected clearly in the performance graph. When we go from a spin down time of 2 seconds to 4 seconds, we see that the overall energy and performance behavior of compress, and javac becomes that of configuration 2. For jack, there is a 33% improvement in the energy-efficiency and there is also a significant reduction in the number of idle-cycles. This is because the longer spin down timeout value eliminates a pair of spin down and spin-up. However, it is interesting to observe that the energy consumption actually *increases* for mtrt, though the number of idle-cycles remains unaffected. That is because, for both configurations 3 and 4, two spindowns and spin-ups are performed. In configuration 3, the disk spins down to the STANDBY mode earlier than in configuration 4. As the STANDBY mode has a lesser power-cost than the IDLE mode, configuration 3 consumes lesser energy. From the above results, we make the following important observation: Disk spindowns should be done only if the time between consecutive disk accesses is much larger than the spin down and spin-up time.

5 Discussion and Conclusion

SoftWatt provides a simulation infrastructure for carrying out detailed studies about the power and performance behavior of applications. The detailed architecture and operating system simulation of SimOS coupled with the analytical power models make SoftWatt an ideal vehicle for conducting research in power-efficient design at several levels of the system. We summarize the results of our characterization study as follows:

- From a system perspective, the disk is the single largest consumer of power accounting for 34% of the system power. The adoption of the disk with low-power features shifts this power hotspot to the clock distribution and generation network and the on-chip first level instruction cache. The setting of the disk spin down threshold is critical in the shifting of this hotspot. Further, for single-issue processor configurations, we find that the memory subsystem has a higher average power than the processor core.

- Among the four different software modes, the user mode consumes the maximum power. Among the other modes, the kernel synchronization operations are expensive in terms of their power consumption. However, their contribution to overall system energy is small due to the infrequent synchronization operations when executing the Spec JVM98 benchmarks. Though the kernel mode has the least power consumption overall, due to the frequent use of kernel services, it accounts for 15% of the energy consumed in the processor and memory hierarchy. Thus, accounting for the energy consumption of the kernel code is critical for estimating the overall energy budget. This estimate is particularly important for high-performance mobile environments such as laptops.

- Among the kernel services, the *utlb* and *read* services are the major contributers to system energy. However, the frequently used *utlb* routine has a smaller power consumption as compared to *read* as it exercises fewer components. Further, the per-invocation of the kernel services is fairly constant across different applications. Thus, it is possible to estimate the energy consumed by

Benchmark	Service	Num	% Cycles	% Energy
compress				
	utlb	7132786	76.2862	64.2989
	read	5863	9.46498	13.7241
	demand_zero	3080	4.46058	6.91512
	cacheflush	1558	1.33649	1.39134
	open	192	1.04054	1.18379
	vfault	972	0.84626	1.12367
	write	71	0.82243	0.0.74204
	tlb_miss	12209	0.716817	0.917478
jess				
	utlb	8351936	64.8216	53.7089
	read	14902	16.5106	20.7921
	BSD	18066	4.15149	5.53606
	demand_zero	2585	3.20818	4.19697
	tlb_miss	92554	2.93511	4.329
	open	327	1.4382	1.63077
	cacheflush	2371	1.42624	1.52855
	vfault	1017	0.638494	0.826016
db				
	utlb	9311336	75.6565	66.6431
	read	6289	7.04481	10.1373
	write	698	5.12059	5.22395
	demand_zero	2172	2.57247	3.86259
	tlb_miss	53764	1.75243	2.82191
	du_poll	4066	1.08423	1.22557
	cacheflush	1540	0.981458	1.10068
	open	188	0.76878	0.913507
javac				
	utlb	12815956	78.782	71.6722
	read	6205	5.47241	7.96247
	demand_zero	3402	3.70849	4.86183
	tlb_miss	134265	3.33207	5.51917
	open	434	1.58547	2.09804
	cacheflush	2802	1.33713	1.65195
	xstat	142	0.627263	0.879387
	vfault	1054	0.517107	0.739405
mtrt				
	utlb	11871047	81.3054	72.199
	read	6400	6.35944	8.87615
	demand_zero	2868	3.23787	4.40053
	tlb_miss	84966	2.43972	3.65625
	cacheflush	1681	0.929139	1.03098
	open	210	0.739026	0.880839
	write	88	0.623178	0.582169
	vfault	1039	0.57036	0.792793
jack				
	utlb	30131127	71.0119	64.0483
	read	40079	16.7512	18.9097
	BSD	68612	6.6143	7.36693
	tlb_miss	204529	1.8767	3.03969
	demand_zero	3484	1.43321	1.88598
	cacheflush	2039	0.386741	0.44586
	open	239	0.292891	0.35692
	clock	963	0.265881	0.235892

Table 4. Breakdown of Kernel Computation by Service - Cycles vs. Energy

Service	Energy Per Invocation	
	Mean	Coefficient of Deviation (%)
utlb	2.1276×10^{-07}	0.13971
demand_zero	5.408×10^{-05}	1.4927
cacheflush	2.1606×10^{-05}	2.4698
read	4.8894×10^{-05}	6.615
write	0.00025351	10.6632
open	0.00015586	10.0714

Table 5. Variation in Behavior of Operating System Services

kernel code with an error margin of about 10% without detailed energy simulation.

- Whenever the operating system does not have any process to run, it schedules the idle-process. Though this has no performance implications, over 5% of the system energy is consumed during this period. This energy consumption can be reduced by transitioning the CPU and the memory-subsystem to a low-power mode or by even halting the processor, instead of executing the idle-process.

While the simulation results in this work were presented using the Spec JVM98 benchmarks, this tool will be invaluable in analyzing other workloads such as database workloads. The characterization and energy optimization of such workloads is becoming a major issue as power-hungry web hosters can consume as much as 10 to 30 Megawatts. We also plan to investigate acceleration of energy simulation using fast forward techniques without significant loss in accuracy.

Acknowledgements

This research has been supported in part by several NSF grants: 0073419, 0093082, 0093085, 0103583, 0097998, 9701475, 9988164, Sun Microsystems, Gigascale Silicon Research Center, and equipment grant EIA-9818327.

References

[1] Avant! Star-Hspice. http://www.avanticorp.com/products.

[2] K. Baynes, C. Collins, E. Fiterman, C. Smit, T. Zhang, and B. Jacob. The performance and Energy Consumption of Embedded Real-Time Operating Systems. Technical Report UMD-SCA-TR-2000-04, University of Maryland, November 2000.

[3] D. Brooks and M. Martonosi. Dynamic thermal management for high-performance microprocessors. In *Proceedings of the Seventh International Symposium on High-Performance Computer Architecture (HPCA-7)*, January 2001.

[4] D. Brooks, V. Tiwari, and M. Martonosi. Wattch: A Framework for Architectural-Level Power Analysis and Optimizations. In *Proceedings of the 27th International Symposium on Computer Architecture*, June 2000.

[5] A. Chandrakasan, W. J. Bowhill, and F. Fox. *Design of High-Performance Microprocessor Circuits*. IEEE Press, 2001.

[6] T. L. Cignetti, K. Komarov, and C. S. Ellis. Energy Estimation Tools for the Palm. In *Proceedings of ACM MSWiM 2000: Modeling, Analysis and Simulation of Wireless and Mobile Systems*, August 2000.

[7] V. Delaluz, M. Kandemir, N. Vijaykrishnan, A. Sivasubramaniam, and M. J. Irwin. DRAM Energy Management Using Software and Hardware Directed Power Mode Control. In *Proceedings of the 7th International Conference on High Performance Computer Architecture*, January 2001.

[8] F. Douglis and P. Krishnan. Adaptive disk spin-down policies for mobile computers. *Computing Systems*, 8(4):381–413, 1995.

[9] D. Duarte, N. Vijaykrishnan, M. J. Irwin, and M. Kandemir. Formulation and Validation of an Energy Dissipation Model for the Clock Generation Circuitry and Distribution Networks. In *Proceedings of the 2001 VLSI Design Conference*, 2001.

[10] S. Gurumurthi, A. Sivasubramaniam, M. J. Irwin, N. Vijaykrishnan, M. Kandemir, T. Li, and L. K. John. Using Complete Machine Simulation for Software Power Estimation: The SoftWatt Approach. Technical Report CSE-01-029, The Pennsylvania State University, November 2001.

[11] M. W. Hall, J. M. Anderson, S. P. Amarasinghe, B. R. Murphy, S.-W. Liao, E. Bugnion, and M. S. Lam. Maximizing multiprocessor performance with the SUIF compiler. *IEEE Computer*, 29(12):84–89, 1996.

[12] S. A. Herrod. *Using Complete Machine Simulation to Understand Computer System Behavior*. PhD thesis, Stanford University, February 1998.

[13] M. Irwin, M. Kandemir, N. Vijaykrishnan, and A. Sivasubramaniam. A Holistic Approach to System Level Energy Optimization. In *Proceedings of the International Workshop on Power and Timing Modeling, Optimization, and Simulation*, September 2000.

[14] J. Jones and B. Fonseca. Energy Crisis Pinches Hosting Vendors. http://iwsun4.infoworld.com/articles/hn/xml/01/01/08/010108hnpower.xml.

[15] R. Joseph, D. Brooks, and M. Martonosi. Runtime Power Measurements as a Foundation for Evaluating Power/Performance Tradeoffs. In *Proceedings of the Workshop on Complexity Effectice Design*, June 2001.

[16] I. Kadayif, T. Chinoda, M. Kandemir, N. Vijaykrishnan, M. J. Irwin, and A. Sivasubramaniam. vEC: Virtual Energy Counters. In *Proceedings of the ACM SIGPLAN/SIGSOFT Workshop on Program Analysis for Software Tools and Engineering (PASTE'01)*, June 2001.

[17] M. B. Kamble and K. Ghose. Analytical Energy Dissipation Models for Low Power Caches. In *Proceedings of the International Symposium on Low-Power Electronic Design*, pages 143–148, August 1997.

[18] M. Lajolo, A. Raghunathan, S. Dey, L. Lavagno, and A. Sangiovanni-Vincentelli. Efficient Power Estimation Techniques for HW/SW Systems. In *Proceedings of IEEE Volta*, 1999.

[19] A. R. Lebeck, X. Fan, H. Zeng, and C. S. Ellis. Power Aware Page Allocation. In *Proceedings of the 9th International Conference on Architectural Support for Programming Languages and Operating Systems (ASPLOS IX)*, November 2000.

[20] K. Li, R. Kumpf, P. Horton, and T. E. Anderson. Quantitative Analysis of Disk Drive Power Management in Portable Computers. Technical Report CSD-93-779, University of California, Berkeley, 1994.

[21] T. Li, L. K. John, N. Vijaykrishnan, A. Sivasubramaniam, J. Sabarinathan, and A. Murthy. Using Complete System Simulation to Characterize SPECjvm98 Benchmarks. In *Proceedings of the International Conference on Supercomputing (ICS) 2000*, May 2000.

[22] J. R. Lorch. A complete picture of the energy consumption of a portable computer. Master's thesis, University of California, Berkeley, December 1995.

[23] J. R. Lorch and A. J. Smith. Scheduling Techniques for Reducing Processor Energy Use in MacOS. *Wireless Networks*, 3(5):311–324, October 1997.

[24] Y.-H. Lu and G. D. Micheli. Adaptive hard disk power management on personal computers. In *Proceedings of the IEEE Great Lakes Symposium*, March 1999.

[25] S. Palacharla, N. P. Jouppi, and J. E. Smith. Complexity-Effective Superscalar Processors. In *Proceedings of the 24th International Symposium on Computer Architecture*, 1997.

[26] R. P.Dick, G. Lakshminarayana, A. Raghunathan, and N. K. Jha. Power Analysis of Embedded Operating Systems. In *Proceedings of the 37th Conference on Design Automation*, pages 312–315, 2000.

[27] R10000 Microprocessor User's Manual. http://www.sgi.com/processors/r10k/manual/t5.ver.2.0.book_4.html.

[28] M. Rosenblum, S. A. Herrod, E. Witchel, and A. Gupta. Complete Computer System Simulation: The SimOS Approach. *IEEE Parallel and Distributed Technology: Systems and Applications*, 3(4):34–43, 1995.

[29] T. Simunic, L. Benini, and G. D. Micheli. Cycle-Accurate Simulation of Energy Consumption in Embedded Systems. In *Proceedings of the Design Automation Conference*, June 1999.

[30] A. Sinha, A. Wang, and A. Chandrakasan. Algorithmic Transforms for Efficient Energy Scalable Computation. In *Proceedings of the IEEE International Symposium on Low-Power Electronic Design (ISLPED' 00)*, August 2000.

[31] Spec JVM98 Benchmark Suite. http://www.spec.org/osg/jvm98/.

[32] Synopsys Power Compiler. http://www.synopsis.com/products/power/power.html.

[33] V. Tiwari, D. Singh, S. Rajgopal, G. Mehta, R. Patel, and F. Baez. Reducing Power in High-Performance Microprocessors. In *Proceedings of the Design Automation Conference*, June 1998.

[34] Toshiba Storage Devices Division. http://www.toshiba.com/.

[35] W. Ye, N. Vijaykrishnan, M. Kandemir, and M. Irwin. The Design and Use of SimplePower: A Cycle-Accurate Energy Estimation Tool. In *Proceedings of the Design Automation Conference (DAC)*, June 2000.

[36] K. C. Yeager. The MIPS R10000 Superscalar Microprocessor. *IEEE Micro*, 16(2):28–40, April 1996.

Exploiting Choice in Resizable Cache Design
to Optimize Deep-Submicron Processor Energy-Delay

Se-Hyun Yang, Michael D. Powell[†], Babak Falsafi, and T. N. Vijaykumar[†]

Computer Architecture Laboratory
Carnegie Mellon University
{sehyun,babak}@ece.cmu.edu

[†]School of Electrical and Computer Engineering
Purdue University
{mdpowell,vijay}@ecn.purdue.edu

Abstract

Cache memories account for a significant fraction of a chip's overall energy dissipation. Recent research advocates using "resizable" caches to exploit cache requirement variability in applications to reduce cache size and eliminate energy dissipation in the cache's unused sections with minimal impact on performance. Current proposals for resizable caches fundamentally vary in two design aspects: (1) cache organization, where one organization, referred to as selective-ways, varies the cache's set-associativity, while the other, referred to as selective-sets, varies the number of cache sets, and (2) resizing strategy, where one proposal statically sets the cache size prior to an application's execution, while the other allows for dynamic resizing both within and across applications.

In this paper, we compare and contrast, for the first time, the proposed design choices for resizable caches, and evaluate the effectiveness of cache resizings in reducing the overall energy-delay in deep-submicron processors. In addition, we propose a hybrid selective-sets-and-ways cache organization that always offers equal or better resizing granularity than both of previously proposed organizations. We also investigate the energy savings from resizing d-cache and i-cache together to characterize the interaction between d-cache and i-cache resizings.

1 Introduction

The ever-increasing level of on-chip integration in CMOS technology has enabled phenomenal improvements in microprocessor performance but has also caused an increase in energy dissipation in a chip. High energy dissipation diminishes the utility of portable systems and reduces reliability, requires sophisticated cooling technology, and increases cost in all segments of the computing market including high-end servers [11]. In state-of-the-art microprocessor designs, cache memories account for a significant fraction of total power/energy dissipation. For instance, 16% of total power in Alpha 21264 [3] and 21% in Pentium Pro [6] is dissipated in on-chip caches.

Current circuit techniques to reduce energy dissipation in caches typically trade off speed for lower energy dissipation in less performance-critical cache structures.

Instead of solely relying on circuit techniques, recent research also advocates using "resizable" caches to reduce energy dissipation especially in high-performance caches [1,13]. Resizable caches are based on the observation that cache utilization varies *within and across* application execution. These caches allow hardware/software to customize the cache size to fit an application's demands. By eliminating energy dissipation in the cache's unused sections, resizable caches significantly improve energy-efficiency with *minimal* impact on application performance.

Current proposals for cache resizing fundamentally differ in cache organization, resizing framework, and how they exploit variability in applications' cache utilization to save energy. One proposal [1] advocates a *selective-ways* cache organization which allows for varying the cache's set-associativity. Another proposal [13] advocates *selective-sets* cache organization which varies the number of cache sets. These cache organizations differ in (1) the offered range of cache sizes, (2) the offered resizing granularity — i.e., the distance between two adjacent offered sizes, (3) the allowable set-associativity at various resizings, and (4) the hardware complexity. The effectiveness of either organizations to reduce size and energy depends on the one hand on the application's demand for a specific size and set-associativity and on the other hand the cache's ability to meet the demands.

The two proposals also differ in the cache resizing strategy of "when" to resize. The proposal for selective-ways [1] advocates *static resizing* by setting the cache size prior to an application's execution, and exploits variation in cache utilization only across applications. The proposal for selective-sets [13] advocates a *dynamic resizing* based on monitoring cache miss ratio and resizes the cache to react to varying demand for cache size both within and across applications. The two resizing strategies differ in two respects: (1) the ability to resize the cache during an application's execution, and (2) the design complexity. The effectiveness of dynamic resizing depends on both the resizing opportunity within applications and the ability of the dynamic resizing mechanisms to seize the opportunity.

The previous studies on resizable caches focused on a single cache design of interest, and did not compare and contrast the design choices for resizable caches. In this paper we identify the opportunity for cache resizing in a spectrum of applications, exploit the various design choices for both instruction and data resizable caches, and evaluate their effectiveness in reducing the *overall* energy dissipation in processors. We use Wattch [3] and SPEC benchmarks to simulate and model energy-delay for state-of-the-art processors and their cache hierarchies. We present results for optimal energy-delay, but show that the impact on overall performance is less than 3% in most of the experiments and less than 6% in all of the experiments.

The contributions of this paper are:

- **Resizing organization:** Selective-sets allows for maintaining set-associativity while resizing and offers superior energy-delay over selective-ways for caches with set-associativity of less than or equal to four. Selective-ways offers a better range of sizes and benefits caches with set-associativity of eight and higher. We propose a *hybrid selective-sets-and-ways* organization that always equals or improves energy-delay over the best of selective-sets or selective-ways alone.

- **Resizing strategy:** On average, static resizing captures most of the opportunity for resizing and reducing processor energy-delay in applications as compared to a miss-ratio based dynamic resizing framework while simplifying design. Dynamic resizing exhibits clear advantages over static resizing *only* in two scenarios: (1) when cache misses directly lie on the execution's critical path — e.g., instruction cache misses or blocking data cache misses — and the application exhibits varying working set sizes benefiting from resizing at runtime, or (2) the application's required cache size lies in between two sizes offered by the organization; unlike static resizing, dynamic resizing switches between two sizes and "emulates" the required size.

- **Resizing both d-cache and i-cache:** Our results indicate that resizing L1 d-cache and i-cache simultaneously has minimal impact on the application's footprint in L2 and therefore the cache resizing and energy-delay savings from the two caches are "additive". In a four-way out-of-order processor with 32K 2-way static selective-sets d-cache and i-cache and a 512K L2 cache, we measure an overall processor energy-delay savings of 20%.

The rest of the paper is organized as follows. Section 2 describes the design space of resizable caches, and in Section 3, we present energy dissipation in state-of-the-art cache memories and energy savings of resizable caches. In Section 4, we describe the experimental methodology and results. Section 5 presents an overview of the related work. Finally, we conclude the paper in Section 6.

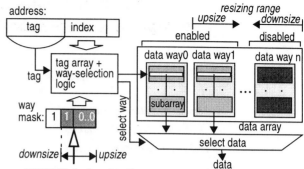

FIGURE 1: A selective-ways organization.

2 Resizable Caches

Resizable caches exploit the variability in cache size requirements in applications to save energy dissipation with minimal performance impact. Resizable caches save energy by enabling/disabling portions of the cache. To enable/disable cache sections, resizable caches exploit the cache subarrays, found in modern high-performance implementations. To optimize for cache access speed, cache designers divide the array of blocks into multiple subarrays of SRAM cell rows [12]. Resizing electrically isolates cache sections in multiple subarrays to save energy [1]. We will describe the details of energy savings in Section 3.

The basic cache organizations we study in this paper are derived from conventional RAM-tag caches, in which the tag and data arrays are organized as RAM structures. While CAM-tag caches (e.g., StrongARM [7]) have been shown to be more energy-efficient, they are typically limited to low-performance designs. While resizing in general is also applicable to CAM-tag caches, a study of resizable CAM-tag caches is beyond the scope of this paper.

Based on how they exploit the cache resizing opportunity in applications, resizable caches primarily differ in two respects: (1) cache resizing organization, dictating "which" cache dimensions are adjustable, and (2) resizing strategy (or time), dictating "when" the caches readjust these dimensions. In the rest of this section, we look at resizing organization and strategy one by one and also propose a hybrid organization.

2.1 Cache Resizing Organization

There are two proposals for resizable cache organizations, which we call *selective-ways* [1] and *selective-sets* [13]. Selective-ways allows enabling/disabling each individual associative way. Figure 1 depicts the basic structure of a selective-ways resizable cache. As in conventional set associative caches, at the higher level the data array is organized into cache ways. Each cache way consists of a number of subarrays. A *way-mask* allows enabling/disabling all the subarrays in a given way. Hardware or soft-

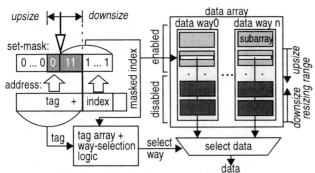

FIGURE 2: A selective-sets organization.

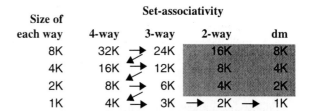

Size of each way	Set-associativity			
	4-way	3-way	2-way	dm
8K	32K →	24K	16K	8K
4K	16K ←	12K	8K	4K
2K	8K →	6K	4K	2K
1K	4K ←	3K →	2K →	1K

Table 1: Enhanced resizing granularity using hybrid.

ware can adjust the number of ways the cache uses by setting the way-mask. The cache access logic uses the way-mask to identify which cache ways to access.

Alternatively, selective-sets allows enabling/disabling cache sets. Figure 2 depicts the anatomy of a selective-sets cache organization. In a conventional cache, the number of cache sets and the cache block size dictate the set of *index* and *tag* bits used to look up a cache block. Therefore, changing the number of cache sets changes both the required index and tag bits. Selective-sets provides a *set-mask* to allow varying the number of cache sets and the used index bits. Because enabling/disabling occurs in multiples of subarrays (Section 3), the minimum number of sets achievable is a single subarray per cache way.

There are fundamental differences between these organizations in their complexity and effectiveness. First, the two organizations differ in applicability and the range of cache sizes offered. Selective-ways changes cache size linearly in multiples of cache ways maintaining a constant resizing granularity. However, in high-performance caches (optimized for access time) which are often direct-mapped or use limited set-associativity, selective-ways is either not applicable or ineffective. Alternatively, selective-sets offers a better spectrum of sizes with low set-associativity. However selective-sets is limited when set-associativity is high, and is not applicable to fully associative caches.

Moreover, cache sizes offered by selective-sets are powers of two (due to the index-based set-mapping in conventional caches) allowing for fine-grain resizing only at smaller cache sizes. Therefore, selective-sets may be suboptimal when application working sets are large. Moreover, selective-ways changes set-associativity along with size and may miss the significant opportunity for resizing for memory reference streams with small working sets but high conflict miss rates. Selective-sets maintains set-associativity upon resizing increasing the opportunity for resizing for reference streams with high conflict miss rates.

A key advantage of selective-ways is its design simplicity. Selective-ways only requires an additional way-mask with corresponding logic. In contrast, selective-sets

increases design complexity beyond the addition of a set-mask and its logic. Because resizing changes the number of tag bits, with smaller caches requiring a larger number of tag bits, selective-sets must use a tag array as large as that required by the smallest size offered. Therefore, using selective-sets, a cache of a given size requires a larger tag array which may be slower and dissipate more energy than selective-ways of the same size and set-associativity. Moreover, selective-ways does not change the set-mapping of cache blocks and as such obviates the need for flushing blocks in the enabled subarrays upon resizing. Selective-sets not only requires flushing modified blocks of disabling arrays, but also all blocks (clean or modified) for which set-mappings change upon enabling subarrays.

2.1.1 A Hybrid Organization

In this paper, we also propose and evaluate a hybrid selective-sets-and-ways organization for resizable caches. The key motivation behind a hybrid organization is that each of the resizable cache organizations offers a spectrum of cache sizes neither of which is a superset of the other. Selective-ways offers a spectrum of sizes that are multiples of a cache way size. Selective-sets offers a spectrum of sizes that are powers of two. A hybrid organization exploits the resizing granularity advantages of both organizations offering a richer spectrum of sizes than either organization alone, thereby optimizing energy savings by providing a size closest to the required demand for size by the application.

Table 1 illustrates cache size and set-associativities offered by a hybrid selective-ways-and-sets cache. For a 32K 4-way set associative cache and a subarray size of 1K, a hybrid cache offers all of 32K, 24K, 16K, 12K, 8K, 6K, 4K, 3K, 2K, and 1K sizes. Whereas, a selective-ways cache would only offer 32K, 24K, 16K, and 8K sizes (indicated by the first row) and a selective-sets cache would provide 32K, 16K, 8K, and 4K (indicated by the 4-way column). The table also depicts our simple resizing scheme. All the sizes between 32K and 3K simply go in steps between a 4-way and a 3-way configuration. For sizes less than 3K, the only configurations offered are those that further reduce set-associativity. This scheme follows the intuition that at higher cache sizes, capacity plays a bigger role than set-associativity while at lower cache sizes, set-associativity can significantly impact cache performance [5]. Downsizing from a 4-way 32K, our cache opts for a larger 24K size with a lower set-associativity of 3 ways rather than selecting a 4-way 16K cache as selective-sets would. Such an approach increases the resizing opportunity for applications with working set sizes closer to 24K than 16K.

Table 1 also indicates that a hybrid cache offers redundant sizes (shaded gray in the table). For instance, a 32K 4-way hybrid cache offers 16K with any of 4-way and 2-way set-associativities. In such cases, the hybrid cache offers the highest set-associativity to minimize miss ratio and optimize the utilization of block frames.

2.2 Cache Resizing Strategy

Besides organization, a key design choice in resizing is the strategy of "when" to resize. There are two proposals for resizing strategy. *Static resizing* [1] allows cache resizing prior to application execution, exploiting cache size variability across applications. Static resizing requires profiling an application's execution with different (static) cache sizes to determine the cache size with minimal energy dissipation and performance degradation. In static resizing, the application provides a cache size which the operating system loads into a programmable size mask (i.e., the way- or set-mask) prior to application's execution or upon a context switch.

Dynamic resizing [13] reacts to application demand for resizing to customize cache size and optimize energy savings during an application execution. Dynamic resizing uses extra hardware to monitor an application's execution and dynamically estimate performance and energy dissipation. When opportunity for resizing arises, dynamic resizing uses the cache size masks to resize the cache. In this paper, we evaluate a simple miss-ratio based dynamic resizing framework proposed in [13]. Hardware monitors the cache in fixed-length intervals measured in number of cache accesses. A miss counter counts the number of misses in each interval. At the end of each interval, hardware determines the need for cache resizing depending on whether the miss counter is higher or lower than a preset value, referred to as the *miss-bound*. To avoid thrashing, the framework prevents the cache from downsizing beyond a preset size, the *size-bound*. As in static resizing, the parameters are extracted offline through profiling.

Much like cache organization, there are fundamental differences in resizing strategy. Static resizing's key advantage is that it minimizes design complexity by fixing the size during an application's execution. When the application exhibits a fixed working set size, static resizing obviates the need for hardware monitoring and may achieve optimal energy reduction. Also, when cache miss latency is not exposed to the performance, regardless of

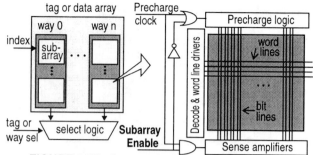

FIGURE 3: Modern cache implementation and energy saving technique.

the existence of working set size variation, the performance impact of misses created by static resizing's fixed size choice can be small and acceptable. Therefore, static resizing can downsize aggressively and save energy.

However, when there is working set variation within an application and the latency of additional misses directly affects performance, static resizing often fails to seize the opportunity and is suboptimal. In such a case, dynamic resizing may help optimize the energy savings and capitalize on its ability to capture the variation in working set size. Moreover, when the cache size required by an application lies between two sizes offered by the organization, dynamic resizing switches between the two sizes and emulates the required sizes with minimal impact on performance. Dynamic resizing, however, increases complexity and may require sophisticated hardware mechanisms to monitor and react to an application's change in behavior.

Dynamic resizing's effectiveness in reducing energy depends on the accuracy and timeliness of the mechanisms to react to an application behavior. In general, online estimation of opportunity for resizing is difficult when miss latency can be hidden and performance is *not* sensitive to simple cache performance metrics such as miss ratio. Inaccurate resizing may incur a large performance degradation due to large increases in the miss ratio. Dynamic resizing also incurs an increase in the miss ratio from flushing some of the cache blocks in the disabled/enabled subarrays upon resizing (Section 2.1). Furthermore, disabled subarrays may have included part of an application's primary working set, resulting in an increase in the miss ratio to bring the blocks back into the new enabled subarrays.

3 Energy Savings in Resizable Caches

In today's CMOS technology, the dominant source of power/energy is the switching energy dissipated in charging and discharging capacitive loads on bitlines. An increasingly important source of power/energy dissipation is the subthreshold leakage energy in future CMOS circuits [2] that aggressively scale down the transistor threshold voltage to reduce switching energy while maintaining high switching speeds. In this paper, we primarily focus on

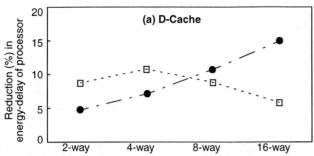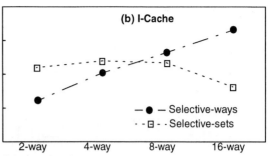

FIGURE 4: Resizable cache organizations and energy-delay reductions.

cache resizing as a technique to reduce switching energy dissipation. Because leakage energy dissipation is proportional to cache size [9], the results in this paper are also directly applicable to reducing leakage energy dissipation. However, a detailed analysis of the impact of cache resizing on leakage is beyond the scope of this paper.

Figure 3 depicts the structure of a modern cache implementation and the anatomy of a cache subarray. To optimize for access speed, cache designers divide the tag and data arrays into multiple subarrays of SRAM cell rows, each containing one or more cache blocks [12]. Modern high-performance cache designs precharge *all* the subarrays prior to a cache access, to overlap the precharging time with the address decode and wordline assertion. Unfortunately, in deep-submicron designs, precharged bitlines of *all* subarrays discharge through the pass transistors, even though only a small number of subarrays (equal to the cache's set-associativity) are actually accessed, leading to low energy efficiency. Precharging *only* the accessed subarrays to save energy requires either predicting the subarray to be accessed [8] or delaying the precharging until the address is available [4,7]. The latter, however, increases access time by as much as 30% as per CACTI simulations [12]. In this paper, we assume that all subarrays are precharged prior to access as modeled by Wattch [3]. A detailed study of techniques to trade off access time for energy is beyond the scope of this paper.

Instead, resizable caches select the appropriate cache size, disable the unused subarrays (Figure 3), and reduce switching energy by precharging only the enabled subarrays. Resizable caches are also able to eliminate unneces-

sary clock propagation to the disabled subarrays, achieving additional energy saving. Cache downsizing and (dynamic resizing's) block flushing between sense intervals increase activity in L2 and its energy consumption. However the increase is insignificant because energy per L2 access, that is less critical than L1 access, can be managed to be small using the techniques like delayed precharge. Additionally for selective-sets, L1 energy increases due to the extra resizing tag bits. This is also insignificant because the number of resizing tag bits is small (usually between 1 and 4) compared to the number of bit lines in a cache block (e.g., 256). In the result section, we report the energy consumption for the entire processor, so that we take all these factors into account.

4 Results

In this section, we present the results in the comparisons of resizable cache's resizing organizations and strategies. We use Wattch 1.0 [3], which is an architecture-level power analysis tool built on top of SimpleScalar 3.0. Wattch reports both the execution time and the power/energy consumption of simulated processors. Table 2 shows our base system configuration parameters. We assume a 0.18μ technology and 1K subarray for L1 caches. Our base system has a power rating of 40.1W from Wattch.

We run SPEC benchmarks using reference inputs. We use *ammp, vortex,* and *vpr* from SPEC2000 and nine applications from SPEC95. For *gcc, ijpeg, m88ksim, su2cor, and tomcatv,* we simulate the entire runs; for the other applications we skip one billion instructions and run the next two billion instructions to reduce simulation turnaround time. On average, with our base configuration, d-cache accounts for 18.5% of total energy consumption for all these applications and i-cache accounts for 17.5%. Note that, unlike our average numbers here, reports on the power breakdown of commodity processors typically do not take into account activity factors of structures in the processors. Because there exist many structures that have smaller activity factors than caches, such as floating-point execution units, our average energy for overall cache structure appears larger than the numbers from such reports (e.g. 16% in Alpha 21264 [3].) With no activity

Issue/decode width	4 intrs per cycle
ROB / LSQ	64 entries / 32 entries
Branch predictor	combination
writeback buffer / mshr	8 entries / 8 entries
Base L1 i-caches	32K 2-way; 1 cycle
Base L1 d-cache	32K 2-way; 1 cycle
L2 unified cache	512K 4-way; 12 cycles
Memory access latency	(80 + 5 per 8 bytes) cycles

Table 2: Base system configuration.

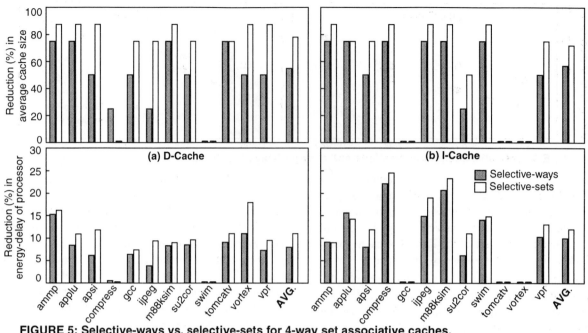

FIGURE 5: Selective-ways vs. selective-sets for 4-way set associative caches.

factor taken into consideration, our experiments also show that overall cache structure in the base system configuration accounts for only 18% of total processor power.

We use the energy-delay product of a processor to present the results because it is a well-established metric used in low-power research and ensures that both energy reduction and accompanying performance degradation are taken into account. For each design point, the relative energy-delay is obtained by normalizing its energy-delay with respect to that of the non-resizable cache with the same size and set-associativity. We always present the lowest energy-delay product achieved for each application regardless to the performance degradation. Nevertheless, all the lowest energy-delay products presented in this section are achieved within 6% of performance degradation and most of them, over 90% of the results presented, are achieved within 3% of degradation. Other configuration parameters are specified as they are varied in each section.

4.1 Cache Resizing Organization

In this section, we compare two resizing organizations, selective-ways and selective-sets. Based on our discussion in Section 2, we expect selective-sets to achieve the best relative energy-delay for high-performance low set associative caches by maintaining set-associativity for the applications with high conflict miss rate and by providing smaller minimum sizes for the applications with small size requirement. However, applications requiring finer granularity around the maximum size and having low conflict miss rate can benefit from selective-ways. Moreover, for highly associative caches, selective-ways provides larger

spectrum of cache sizes in entire range and therefore is expected to achieve better energy-delay.

Figure 4 shows the reductions in processor's relative energy-delays of static selective-ways and selective-sets averaged for all the applications. Set-associativities of base caches range from 2-way to 16-way to include all the meaningful comparisons between two organizations of 32K size with 1K subarray. For d-caches, selective-ways reduces the energy-delays by 5% for 2-way, 8% for 4-way, 11% for 8-way and 15% for 16-way set associative cache, and selective-sets reduces by 9%, 11%, 9% and 6% in the same order. For i-caches, the numbers are 6%, 10%, 13% and 17% for selective-ways and 11%, 12%, 11% and 8% for selective-sets. The results indicate for both d-cache and i-cache that selective-sets achieves more reduction than selective-ways at low associativity but for 8-way or higher set associative caches, selective-ways is more effective.

Note that selective-sets achieves the best reduction at 4-way set associative cache, not at 2-way, although 2-way offers the best spectrum of cache sizes to this organization. It is well known that lower set associative caches produce more misses than higher set associative caches and the gap increases as the cache size decreases. Therefore, downsizing in higher set associative caches creates smaller number of misses, resulting in less performance impact and more aggressive downsizing. As far as the organization provides enough resizing granularity, higher set associative cache can downsize and save energy better, but selective-sets beyond 4-way does not offer enough granularity.

Also note that selective-sets on 2-way associative cache does not save as much energy as selective-ways on

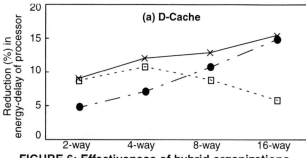 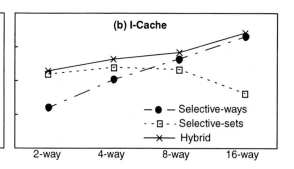

FIGURE 6: Effectiveness of hybrid organizations.

16-way cache does, although these two configurations have the best size spectrum on their own organizations. It is mainly due to different resizing granularity of two organizations. While selective-ways on 32K 16-way cache offers fine resizing granularity of 2K in entire range, selective-sets on 2-way offers fine grain resizing only at small sizes; no cache size is offered between 32K and 16K. Therefore, applications requiring cache sizes between 32K and 16K work more successfully with selective-ways. For instances, *compress* and *swim* for d-cache and *gcc*, *tomcatv* and *vortex* for i-cache belong to this type.

To investigate the resizing characteristics of each application on each organization, we present the reduction in cache sizes achieved by static selective-ways and selective-sets for 32K 4-way d- and i-caches in Figure 5. We include the average values at the end of each graph. To show the impact to the overall processor energy, we also present the reduction in processor's relative energy-delays. We use 4-way set associative cache because it provides a reasonable resizing granularity for both organizations. Specifically, selective-sets provides smaller minimum size (4K), while selective-ways offers better granularity between 32K and 16K. Note that although two applications have the same average cache size, their energy-delays would be different due to the difference in cache's energy contribution and resizing's performance impact.

In d-caches, for ten applications out of twelve, selective-sets shows better energy-delay reduction than selective-ways. Six applications, *apsi*, *gcc*, *ijpeg*, *su2cor*, *vortex* and *vpr*, mainly benefit from selective-sets' ability to maintain set-associativity and prevent conflicts. Three applications, *ammp*, *applu* and *m88ksim*, require small cache sizes and take advantage of the smaller minimum size offered by selective-sets. For *compress*, selective-ways shows better energy-delay reduction than selective-sets, because the application requires granularity at large cache sizes offered by selective-ways but not by selective-sets. For *swim*, downsizing creates large amount of misses and large performance degradation, resulting in no downsizing for both organizations. *Tomcatv* reduces the cache size equally for both, but incurs larger performance impact with selective-ways due to more conflict misses.

For i-caches, *ammp*, *compress*, *ijpeg*, *m88ksim*, and *swim* require small cache sizes throughout execution and take advantage of the small minimum size available in selective-sets. *Apsi*, *su2cor* and *vpr* require set-associativity rather than cache size to keep the performance. Therefore, selective-sets exhibits better energy-delay reduction for them. For *applu*, selective-sets chooses the same cache sizes as selective-ways, but selective-ways dissipates less energy because lower set associative caches read fewer subarrays on each access (as many as set-associativity). *Gcc* and *tomcatv* have no cache downsizing because their working sets are larger than 32K and downsizing incurs large performance degradation.

4.1.1 Hybrid Organization

In this section, we investigate and evaluate hybrid organization. Figure 6 presents the average reduction in energy-delays for all three organizations including hybrid organization. The figure presents the set-associativities from 2-way to 16-way. The results show that hybrid organization achieves equal or better energy-delay reduction than both selective-ways and selective-sets in any set-associativities. On average, hybrid's energy-delay reductions for d-cache are 9% for 2-way, 12% for 4-way, 13% for 8-way and 15% for 16-way, and for i-cache, the numbers are 11%, 13%, 14% and 17%.

As we forecasted, there are two situations for which hybrid organization saves better than both the selective-ways and selective-sets. We do not show the result of each individual application, but for instances, for the applications like *compress*, *ijpeg*, *gcc*, *su2cor* in 4-way d-cache and *apsi*, *su2cor*, *ammp*, *swim*, *apsi* in 4-way i-cache, its better granularity plays a role and reduces energy-delays better. Hybrid offers better resizing granularity than either of selective-ways or selective-sets and therefore provides cache sizes closer to the actual cache size demand of the applications. The cache sizes utilized by these applications in the hybrid organization are supported by neither selective-ways nor selective-sets. Second, hybrid resizing offers small sizes less than the minimum sizes of selective-sets or selective-ways. For example, *ammp*, *applu*, and *m88ksim*, for 4-way d-cache, *ammp*, *compress*, *ijpeg*, *m88ksim*, and *swim* for 4-way i-cache exploit the smaller sizes.

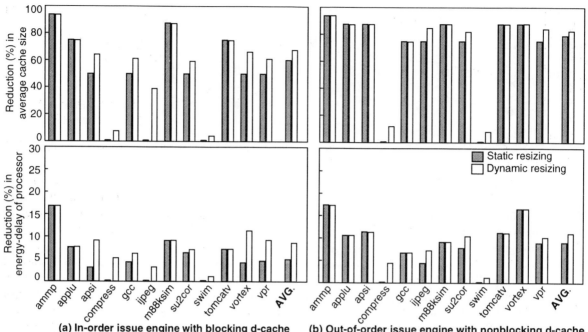

FIGURE 7: D-cache resizing in two processor configurations.

(a) In-order issue engine with blocking d-cache   (b) Out-of-order issue engine with nonblocking d-cache

4.2 Cache Resizing Strategy

In this section, we investigate static and dynamic resizing strategies based on two different processor configurations. Dynamic resizing presented here is a miss-ratio based strategy proposed in [13], implementation detail of which is described in Section 2.2. As we described, dynamic resizing is, in general, beneficial for applications with large variation in cache size requirement. Also, dynamic resizing has an advantage of emulating the cache sizes not offered by the organization.

Especially when miss latency is exposed to critical path of execution, suboptimal size chosen by static resizing that creates large number of misses during the execution incurs large performance degradation. Therefore, in this case, static resizing does not encourage cache downsizing. Instead, more accurate detection of working set variation, or using dynamic resizing, is required to achieve better energy savings without degrading performance.

However, when miss latency is hidden or has relatively less impact on performance, the cache resizing is more aggressive and downsizing is encouraged. Although static resizing incurs more misses from the program phases requiring larger cache sizes, these misses might not degrade performance significantly, therefore even static resizing downsizes aggressively, without hurting the performance. It, in turn, leaves smaller opportunity for dynamic resizing, and the effectiveness of dynamic resizing over static resizing is not as significant as when miss latency is highly exposed. Moreover, due to the misses possibly overlapped, miss ratio is not a good indicator of

performance, and our miss-ratio based strategy is less effective to capture the cache size requirement.

To highlight the effect of miss latency exposure to the cache resizing, we compare cache resizings on two types of processor configuration: in-order issue engine with blocking d-cache and out-of-order issue engine with nonblocking d-cache. The former exposes d-cache miss latency to performance. Here, i-cache misses are relatively less critical to performance. However, the latter can highly exploit the instruction parallelism existing in applications to hide d-cache miss latency. Unlike d-cache, i-cache miss latency impacts the performance more directly in this configuration, being highly exposed to performance.

4.2.1 Resizing Data Caches

Figure 7 shows the reductions of energy-delay and average cache size by static and dynamic selective-sets for 2-way set associative d-cache on both types of processor configuration. We present only selective-sets because both organizations show similar results in this comparison. On average, with in-order issue processor, static resizing reduces 5% of total energy-delay, while dynamic resizing reduces 9%. Meanwhile, static resizing reduces 9% with out-of-order issue processor, and dynamic achieves 11%. In d-cache, cache resizing with out-of-order issue processor is more aggressive and achieves larger reductions.

With in-order issue engine and blocking d-cache, dynamic resizing exhibits larger reductions in cache sizes and energy-delays than static resizing, for eight applications. For these applications, the gap of average cache sizes between dynamic and static resizings is 16% on aver-

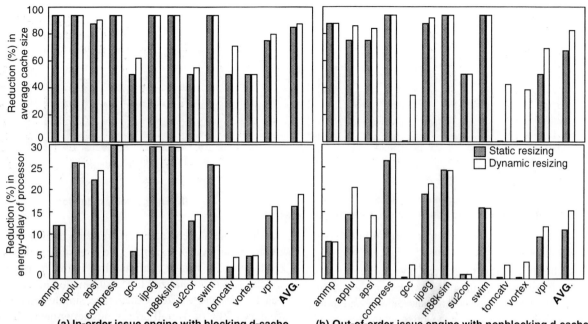

FIGURE 8: I-cache resizing in two processor configurations.

(a) In-order issue engine with blocking d-cache

(b) Out-of-order issue engine with nonblocking d-cache

age with maximum of 38% in *ijpeg*. Also, the gap between energy-delays is 6% on average and as large as 8% in *vortex*. In this processor type, high exposure of d-cache miss latency to performance requires accuracy in capturing working set size variation. For *apsi*, *vortex* and *vpr* in in-order issue processor, static resizing achieves comparable cache size reduction to dynamic resizing — less than 15% gap between two but, interestingly, its energy-delay reductions are much less than half of dynamic resizing's results. It is because static resizing incurs relatively high performance impact that is close to 6%. It increases "delay" parts of the energy products relatively large, ending up with no significant reductions in energy-delay.

In contrast to the former processor type, the results with out-of-order issue engine and nonblocking d-cache show that dynamic resizing does not achieve significantly better savings. Aggressive superscalar engine with nonblocking d-cache exploits the parallelism between instructions and takes a lot of d-cache misses off of the critical path of application execution. As we mentioned, in such a case, aggressive downsizing is encouraged and static resizing possibly performs as good as dynamic resizing. We see even for the applications requiring variable cache sizes such as *apsi*, *gcc* and *vortex*, static resizing achieves as good reductions as dynamic resizing.

According to the dynamic resizing behavior, we group applications into three types. The simplest is those that have a constant size during the execution. For these applications, static and dynamic resizings show almost the same reductions. *Ammp*, *applu*, *m88ksim*, and *tomcatv* exhibit constant sizes. The next type of applications exhib-

its variation in working set size, indicated by changes in cache resizing behavior over many intervals. Examples of working-set variation in d-caches are *compress*, gcc, *vortex*, and *vpr*. *Su2cor* is an example of periodic variation in working set size as execution phases repeat. Dynamic resizing takes advantage of working-set size variation within these applications, especially with in-order issue engine and blocking d-cache.

The third type is unavailable-size emulation, which occurs when the cache size required by the application is not offered. This type includes *apsi*, *compress*, *ijpeg*, and *swim* in in-order issue engine with blocking d-cache, and *compress* has the property of both second and third types. For the third type of applications, the resizable cache chooses cache sizes above and below the required size to achieve emulation. Unavailable-size emulation occurs because there is too much performance degradation at a smaller size but little degradation at a larger size. Unlike static resizing, dynamic resizing may be able to amortize the degradation by spending a while at the larger size. Additional sizes might be captured by using a hybrid selective-sets/selective-ways organization, but dynamic resizing's granularity is not limited by the organizations.

4.2.2 Resizing Instruction Caches

Figure 8 shows the reductions for 2-way set associative i-cache. With in-order issue engine and blocking d-cache, static resizing exhibits 16% of energy-delay reduction, while dynamic resizing reduces 18%. With out-of-order issue engine and nonblocking d-cache, static resizing reduces 11% of total energy-delay and dynamic reduces

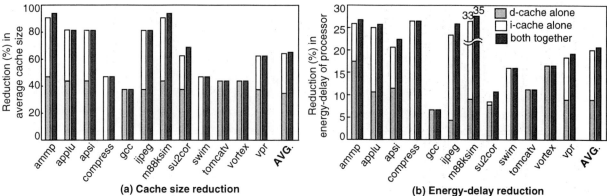

(a) Cache size reduction   (b) Energy-delay reduction

FIGURE 9: Decoupled resizings on d-cache and i-cache.

by 15%. For i-cache, cache resizing with in-order issue processor achieves larger reductions.

In i-cache, in contrast to d-cache, dynamic resizing's ability to capture the working set size variation plays more important role with out-of-order issue engine and non-blocking d-cache, because i-cache miss latency is more exposed to performance when the processor exploits more parallelism on d-cache accesses. We see in out-of-order issue engine with nonblocking d-cache, dynamic resizing exhibits larger reductions in cache sizes and energy-delays than static resizing for seven applications. For these seven applications, the gap of average cache sizes between dynamic and static resizings is 31% on average and as large as 38% of *ijpeg*. Static resizing in in-order processor performs comparable to dynamic resizing, because i-cache misses in in-order processor exhibit less performance impact. Therefore static resizing can be aggressive and leaves smaller opportunity for dynamic resizing. Like d-cache resizing, i-cache resizing has three different types. The first type that exhibits a constant cache size throughout execution includes *ammp*, *compress*, *m88ksim*, *su2cor* and *swim*. For the second type, *applu*, *apsi* and *ijpeg* indicate periodic variation in i-cache working set size. The third type of behavior, unavailable size emulation, occurs in *gcc*, *tomcatv*, *vortex* and *vpr*.

Note that the same average cache size can result in different energy-delay reductions for two processor types because they have different breakdowns of the energy contribution. On average, energy contribution of i-cache in in-order issue processor is 21.5%, 4% larger than out-of-order issue processor.

4.3 Resizing Both Data and Instruction Caches

We have studied different aspects of resizable caches separately on d-cache and i-cache so far. In this section, we investigate the interaction between d-cache and i-cache resizings and the results of resizing them simultaneously.

In Figure 9, we present the reductions in average cache size and processor energy-delay achieved by resizing d-

cache alone, i-cache alone and resizing both caches at the same time. As an example, we use static selective-sets with our base system configuration. In this figure, average cache size is normalized to the summation of base case d-cache and i-cache sizes. On average, simultaneous resizing reduces 20% of overall processor energy-delay. By stacking up the reductions from d-cache and i-cache resizings in one bar next to the result from simultaneous resizing, we easily see the additivity property; when we resize both caches together, the overall reductions in cache size and energy-delay are close to the summation of the reductions achieved by resizing each cache alone. Resizing both at the same time exhibits larger performance degradation, up to 10% but mostly less than 5%.

Moreover, there exist several applications exhibiting larger reduction from resizing both together than the sum of the reductions from resizing each individually. Downsizing one cache has an effect of shifting the bottleneck of overall performance close to itself, due to the additional misses in the cache. Therefore, the other cache can be downsized more aggressively resulting in less performance degradation with same downsizing than the case of downsizing itself alone.

Additivity property implies d-cache and i-cache resizings are decoupled from each other and we can study them separately expecting the additive energy savings when we apply resizing techniques for both at the same time.

5 Related Work

A number of previous studies have focused on architectural/microarchitectural techniques to reduce the energy dissipation in cache memories. Among them, recently there have been three proposals for cache resizing [1,10,13] two of which focus on reducing energy dissipation. Ranganathan, et al. [10], propose a statically resizing selective-ways d-cache and use it to partition the cache and use the unused part as auxiliary storage for instruction reuse information to increase performance. Albonesi [1] proposes a statically resizing a selective-ways cache, and evaluates the cache's effectiveness in reducing switching energy. Yang, et al. [13], propose a dynamically resizing selective-sets i-cache, and evaluate its effectiveness to reduce leakage energy dissipation. In this paper, we draw *key* resizing architectural design aspects from Albonesi's and Yang, et al.'s proposals, to evaluate effectiveness of and opportunity for cache resizing to reduce energy dissipation. We also consider overall energy dissipation including both switching and leakage energy, and propose a hybrid cache organization and that exploits advantages of both selective-ways and selective-sets.

6 Conclusions

Using a cycle-accurate performance and energy simulation tool, we studied and compared the merits of the resizable cache's two design aspects: cache resizing organization and resizing strategy. For organization, our results showed that selective-sets offers better energy-delay over selective-ways for caches with set-associativity of less than or equal to four, by maintaining set-associativity upon resizing. Meanwhile, selective-ways benefits caches with set-associativity of eight and higher. We proposed a hybrid selective-sets-and-ways organization that always equals or improves energy-delay over the best of selective-sets or selective-ways alone.

For cache resizing strategy, we showed that on average, static resizing captures most of the opportunity for resizing and reducing processor energy-delay in applications as compared to a miss-ratio based dynamic resizing framework with minimal design complexity incurred. Dynamic resizing exhibits clear advantages over static resizing only in two scenarios: (1) when cache misses directly lie on the execution's critical path and the application exhibits varying working set sizes benefiting from resizing at runtime, or (2) the application's required cache size lies in between two offered sizes by the cache organization; unlike static resizing, dynamic resizing switches between the two sizes and emulates the required size.

Our results also indicated that resizing L1 d-cache and i-cache simultaneously has minimal impact on L2's footprints and therefore the cache resizing and energy-delay savings from the two caches are uncorrelated and additive. In a four-way out-of-order processor with 32K 2-way static selective-sets d-cache and i-cache and a 512K L2 caches, we measured an overall processor energy-delay savings of 20% on average.

Acknowledgments

This research is supported in part by SRC under contract 2000-HJ-768. We would like to thank Yuen Chan and the anonymous reviewers for their useful comments.

References

[1] D. H. Albonesi. Selective cache ways: On-demand cache resource allocation. In *Proceedings of the 32nd Annual IEEE/ACM International Symposium on Microarchitecture (MICRO 32)*, pages 248–259, Nov. 1999.

[2] S. Borkar. Design challenges of technology scaling. *IEEE Micro*, 19(4):23–29, July 1999.

[3] D. Brooks, V. Tiwari, and M. Martonosi. Wattch: A framework for architectural-level power analysis and optimizations. In *Proceedings of the 27th Annual International Symposium on Computer Architecture*, pages 83–94, June 2000.

[4] J. H. Edmondson, et al. Internal organization of the Alpha 21164, a 300-MHz 64-bit quad-issue CMOS RISC microprocessor. *Digital Technical Journal*, 7(1), 1995.

[5] M. D. Hill. A case for direct-mapped caches. *IEEE Computer*, 21(12):25–40, Dec. 1988.

[6] S. Manne, A. Klauser, and D. Grunwald. Pipeline gating: Speculation control for energy reduction. In *Proceedings of the 25th Annual International Symposium on Computer Architecture*, pages 132–141, June 1998.

[7] J. Montanaro, et al. A 160-MHz, 32-b, 0.5-W CMOS RISC microprocessor. *IEEE Journal of Solid-State Circuits*, 31(11):1703–1714, 1996.

[8] M. D. Powell, A. Agrawal, T. Vijaykumar, B. Falsafi, and K. Roy. Reducing set-associative cache energy via selective direct-mapping and way prediction. In *Proceedings of the 34th Annual IEEE/ACM International Symposium on Microarchitecture (MICRO 34)*, Dec. 2001.

[9] M. D. Powell, S.-H. Yang, B. Falsafi, K. Roy, and T. N. Vijaykumar. Gated-V_{dd}: A circuit technique to reduce leakage in cache memories. In *Proceedings of the 2000 International Symposium on Low Power Electronics and Design (ISLPED)*, pages 90–95, July 2000.

[10] P. Ranganathan, S. Adve, and N. P. Jouppi. Reconfigurable caches and their application to media processing. In *Proceedings of the 27th Annual International Symposium on Computer Architecture*, pages 214–224, June 2000.

[11] D. Singh and V. Tiwari. Power challenges in the internet world. Cool Chips Tutorial in conjunction with the 32nd Annual International Symposium on Microarchitecture, November 1999.

[12] S. J. E. Wilson and N. P. Jouppi. An enhanced access and cycle time model for on-chip caches. Technical Report 93/5, Digital Equipment Corporation, Western Research Laboratory, July 1994.

[13] S.-H. Yang, M. D. Powell, B. Falsafi, K. Roy, and T. N. Vijaykumar. An integrated circuit/architecture approach to reducing leakage in deep-submicron high-performance i-caches. In *Proceedings of the Seventh IEEE Symposium on High-Performance Computer Architecture*, Jan. 2001.

Latency Tolerance and Caches

Non-vital Loads

†Ryan Rakvic, †Bryan Black, ‡Deepak Limaye, & †John P. Shen

†*Microprocessor Research Lab*
Intel Labs
{ryan.n.rakvic,bryan.black,john.shen}@intel.com

‡*Electrical and Computer Engineering*
Carnegie Mellon University
dlimaye@ece.cmu.edu

Abstract

As the frequency gap between main memory and modern microprocessor grows, the implementation and efficiency of on-chip caches become more important. The growing latency to memory is motivating new research into load instruction behavior and selective data caching. This work investigates the classification of load instruction behavior. A new load classification method is proposed that classifies loads into those vital to performance and those not vital to performance. A limit study is presented to characterize different types of non-vital loads and to quantify the percentage of loads that are non-vital. Finally, a realistic implementation of the non-vital load classification method is presented and a new cache structure called the Vital Cache is proposed to take advantage of non-vital loads. The Vital Cache caches data for vital loads only, deferring non-vital loads to slower caches.

Results: *The limit study shows 75% of all loads are non-vital with only 35% of the accessed data space being vital for caching. The Vital Cache improves the efficiency of the cache hierarchy and the hit rate for vital loads. The Vital Cache increases performance by 17%.*

1 Introduction

The latency to main memory is quickly becoming the single most significant bottleneck to microprocessor performance. In response to long-latency memory, on-chip cache hierarchies are becoming very large. However, the first-level data cache (DL1) is limited in size by the short latency it must have to keep up with the microprocessor core. For an on-chip cache to continue as an effective mechanism to counter long latency memory, DL1 caches must remain small, fast and become more storage efficient.

A key problem is that microprocessors treat all load instructions equally. They are fetched in program order and executed as quickly as possible. As soon as all load source operands are valid, loads are issued to load functional units for immediate execution. All loads access the first level of data cache and advance through the memory hierarchy until the desired data is found. Treating all loads equally implies that all target data are vying for positions in each level of the memory hierarchy regardless of the importance (vitality) of that data.

As demonstrated by Srinivasan and Lebeck [22] not all loads are equally important. In fact, many have significant tolerance for execution latency. Our work proposes a new classification of load instructions and a new caching method to take advantage of this load classification. We argue that load instructions should not be treated equally because many loads need not be executed as quickly as possible.

This work presents two contributions. 1) We perform a limit study analyzing the classification of load instructions as vital (important) or non-vital (not important). Vital loads are loads that must be executed as quickly as possible in order to avoid performance degradation. Non-vital loads are loads that can be delayed without impacting performance. 2) We introduce a new cache called the Vital Cache to selectively cache data only for vital loads. The vital cache improves performance by increasing the efficiency of the fastest cache in the hierarchy. The hit rate for vital loads is increased at the expense of non-vital loads, which can tolerate longer access latencies without impacting performance. Performance is also increased by processing (scheduling) the vital loads ahead of non-vital loads.

2 Previous Work

In [1] the predictability of load latencies is addressed. [15] showed some effects of memory latencies, but it was [21][22] to first identify the latency tolerance of loads exhibited by a microprocessor. These works show that loads leading to mispredicted branches or to a slowing down of the machine are loads that are critical. This work is built on the same concept as [21][22]. In fact, part of our classification (lead to branch, see Section 4) is taken from this previous research. This work further identifies additional classes of loads and uses a different classification algorithm. Furthermore, we introduce a new caching mechanism to take advantage of them.

The work in [21] introduced an implementation based on the non-critical aspect of loads. They implemented two different approaches: using a victim critical cache, and prefetching critical data. Neither seemed to show much performance benefit. The work in [7] also introduced a buffer containing non-critical addresses. The implementation in Section 5 is based on the same spirit of [7][21], but is done in accordance with non-vital loads.

Section 5 introduces a form of selective vital caching. This selective caching is similar in concept to [9][10][14][19][25]. The goal of selective caching is to improve the efficiency of the cache. [9][10] cached data based on temporal reuse. [25] selectively cached data based on the address of loads. In particular, loads which typically hit the cache are given priority to use the cache. We also propose caching data based on the address of loads. However, we cache data based on the vitality or importance of the load instruction.

The non-vital concept should not be confused with "critical path" [24] research. Non-vital loads may or may not be on the critical path of execution. Non-vital loads become non-vital based on resource constraints and limitations. Therefore, a load that is considered "non-vital" may be on the critical path, but its execution latency is not vital to overall performance. [6] introduced a new insightful critical path model that takes into account resource constraints. [6] used a token-passing method to try to identify instructions that are critical to performance. On the other hand, our approach attempts to identify the loads that are not critical to performance and therefore do not need DL1 cache hits to maintain high performance.

Other popular research tries to design a DL1 that maintains a high hit rate with very low latency[8]. One approach used streaming buffers, victim caches [13], alternative cache indexing schemes [20], etc. [10]. Another approach attempts to achieve free associativity. Calder et al. [4], following the spirit of [12][11][2][17], proposed the predictive sequential associative cache (PSA cache) to implement associative caches with a serial lookup. The aim of their work was to reduce the miss rate of direct mapped caches by providing associativity in such a way that the cache access latency was the same as a direct mapped cache. They achieved in-

creased hit rate and thereby performance through a sequential lookup of a direct mapped cache.

[3][5][11][23][26] focused on providing bandwidth and speed by distributing the cache accesses. Cho et al. [5] provided high-speed caches by decoupling accesses of local variables. Neefs et al. [16] also provided high bandwidth high speed cache memories. Their solution utilized a general multi-banked scheme interleaved based on data address. [18] provided high bandwidth and high speed by partitioning the DL1 into subcaches based on temporality use. Our implementation (Section 5) is similar in spirit, but is built around the non-vital concept.

3 Simulation Model

A cycle accurate simulator is used to gather all the data presented. The machine model employs eight instruction wide fetch, dispatch, and completion. The instruction window size is 128 instructions and the Load-Store Queue has 64 entries. The first level data cache (DL1) has 32KB and is a dual-ported 4-way set-associative cache with 32-byte blocks and 3-cycle latency. The second level unified cache is 256KB, with a 10 cycle access latency. There is a 32-entry store buffer, and the ports are assumed to be read/write. There are ten functional units that execute instructions out-of-order. A hybrid branch predictor using both a bimodal and a 2-level predictor is used. The instruction cache is set at 32KB and is also single cycle. The fetch unit is capable of fetching eight instructions or one basic block per cycle. We propose this as a relatively realistic machine.

Seven integer (compress, gcc, go, ijpeg, li, m88ksim, perl) and seven floating point (applu, apsi, fpppp, mgrid, swim, tomcatv, wave5) benchmarks from the Spec CPU95 suite are used for this study. Unless otherwise noted, numbers presented represent harmonic means of all benchmarks.

4 Non-vital Loads

This section examines the classification of non-vital loads. A classification method is presented along with a limit study that shows how many loads are non-vital. Section 5 outlines an implementation that leverages the non-vital load classification to improve IPC by increasing the efficiency of the data cache.

4.1 Classification

Loads are classified into two categories: vital and non-vital. Vital loads are loads that must be executed as quickly as possible in order to maximize performance. Non-vital loads are loads that are less vital to program execution and for various reasons do not require immediate execution in order to maximize performance. Figure 1 illustrates the classification of load instructions into vital or non-vital. We

Non-vital	Vital
Unused	
Store forwarded	
Lead to store	
Not instantly used	Instantly used
Lead to correctly predicted branch	Lead to mispredicted branch

Figure 1 Classification of loads as Non-vital and Vital.

do note that the non-vital loads are not of equal vitality, but we do not present an ordering.

Unused: A load is classified as non-vital if its result is not used before the destination register is redefined. A load can go unused when the compiler hoists it above a branch that does not branch to the basic block that consumes the load's result.

Store forwarded: Another type of non-vital loads is a load that receives its data from the store buffer via store forwarding. Such a load is classified as non-vital because the data access does not reach the cache hierarchy. Hence, the load's data value need not reside in the first level cache.

Lead to store: Store instructions are by nature non-vital. As a result any data flow leading to a store's address or data source is also non-vital. When all dependents of a load ultimately lead to a store and the data flow terminates at the store, the load can be classified as non-vital.

Instantly Used: Instructions dependent on a load's result may be in the instruction window when the load finishes

execution. However, other resource or data hazards can cause the dependent instruction to defer execution for some time. If a load's dependent is immediately ready for execution when the load finishes, the load is considered vital, due to the critical demand of the dependent. If the dependent instruction is not ready for execution as the load finishes then the load is non-vital.

Lead to branch: As demonstrated in [22], loads that lead to predictable branches are non-vital. Every data flow path beginning with the load must terminate at a predictable branch for the load to be considered non-vital. If a branch is not predicted correctly or not all paths lead to a predictable branch then the load is classified as vital.

4.2   Limit Study of Non-vital Loads

This section presents the results of a limit study on the classification of non-vital loads. Realistic hardware implementation for the load classification, outlined in Section 4.1, is described in Section 5. To properly classify non-vital loads, as per the classification in Section 4.1, a complete

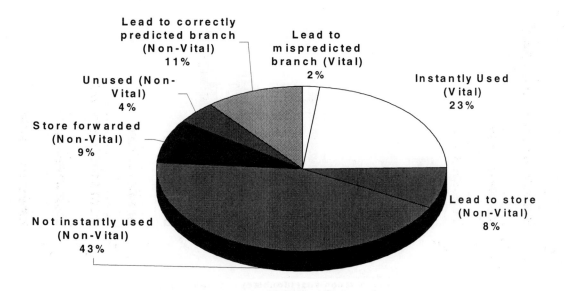

Figure 2 Load classification.

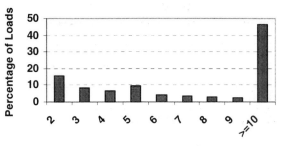

Figure 3 Dependence distance from loads.

dependency chain beginning with each load is constructed. Dependency chains are required to determine if a load leads to a store or branch. Each dependency chain begins with a load and is constructed and maintained only while the load is in the machine. Once the load completes it is classified as either vital or non-vital, and the dependency chain is discarded.

The pie chart in Figure 2 shows a complete break down of all loads and their classification as vital or non-vital. Astoundingly only 25% of loads in the SPEC95 benchmarks are vital. On the vital loads, 2% are leading to mis-predicted branches and 23% are vital due to instant demand from dependent instructions. The remaining 75% of loads are classified as non-vital. Of the five categories of non-vital loads, loads that lead to not-instantly-used instructions make up 43% of all loads. 8% of loads ultimately lead to stores, while 9% receive their data from the store buffer via store forwarding. Another 11% of loads lead to a correctly predicted branch and 4% of loads are unused.

To further analyze the 43% of loads with not instantly using dependents, Figure 3 illustrates the number of cycles between a load's execution and its dependent's execution. If the dependent executes immediately, the load is considered vital. If the dependent instruction does not execute immediately after the load, then the load is classified as non-vital. Figure 3 shows that almost 50% of the time, a load's dependent instruction executes 10 or more cycles after the load. The >=10 bar lumps all cases in which the dependent instruction did not execute within 10 cycles of the load's execution. If the dependent instruction is not in the machine at the time of load completion its execution is considered more than 10 cycles after the load. One cause of this delay is when a load precedes a mispredicted branch but the dependent instruction is following the mispredicted branch, and is stalled by the misprediction recovery.

4.3 Verification of Non-vital Load Classification

To verify the classification results in Section 4.2, the benchmarks are executed with doubling the execution latency of all loads classified as non-vital. If there is little or no performance impact then these loads are truly non-vital, otherwise they are incorrectly classified. Performance loss from increasing non-vital loads' latency can be due to resource constraints. For example, if a non-vital load's latency is increased, it may cause the Re-order Buffer (ROB) to fill up. The ROB fill-up may in turn cause instruction fetch to stall and overall performance reduction. Similarly, functional unit unavailability can also cause performance degradation. Vital loads, however suffer performance loss due to various reasons. For example, vital loads that lead to a mispredicted branch cause instruction fetch to continue down the wrong path for extra cycles.

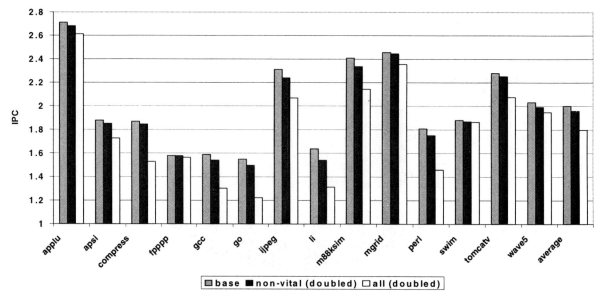

Figure 4 Performance impact of load access latency.

168

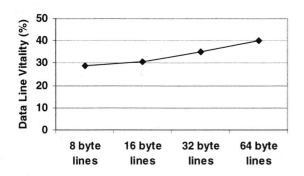

Figure 5 Data vitality relative to cache line sizes.

Figure 4 presents IPC results comparing a baseline model (base) with a model that doubles the DL1 latency for all loads (all) and a model that doubles the DL1 latency only for loads classified as non-vital. Across all benchmarks, there is little performance degradation (~2%) when the non-vital load access latency is doubled. However, an average performance loss of 10% is observed when the latency of all loads are doubled.

When considering new caching mechanisms based on load vitality it is not enough to consider just execution latency. For instance, if a vital load accesses a data line, then the line is considered vital and the data must be stored in the fastest cache. This data vitality is vital to any implementation that is designed to take advantage of non-vital loads. If all data are vital then load classification is uninteresting. Figure 5 presents the percentage of unique data that are vital as a function of cache line size. As expected, as the line size increases, the probability that a vital load will access a data element within the line increases. If any vital load accesses a data line at any point within the program execution, the line is considered and remains vital; hence as the line size increases, the data vitality increases. The data vitality ranges from 28%-40% as the line size is varied from 8 bytes to 64 bytes. For a 32-byte cache line, the average data vitality is only ~35%.

This limit study shows that 75% of all loads in the SPEC95 benchmarks are non-vital and only 35% of the accessed data space is vital. The next section outlines a new caching strategy that takes advantage of non-vital loads and data vitality to improve performance.

5 Vital Cache - An Application of Non-vital Loads

There is much pressure on the first level cache (DL1) of the memory hierarchy in today's microprocessors. Section 4.3 (data vitality) shows that not all data that are brought into the DL1 are vital to processor performance. There is the po-

tential of taking advantage of non-vital loads. One application is to redesign the data cache hierarchy. This section introduces the Vital Cache (VC). The vital cache is a realistic cache implementation that takes advantage of non-vital loads. Vital cache caches only data of vital loads. Section 5.1 describes the implementation while Section 5.2 shows initial results and their analysis.

5.1 Implementation

As discussed in Section 4.1 there are five types of non-vital loads: unused, lead to store, lead to correctly predicted branch, store forwarded, and not instantly used. Some of these types are more difficult to determine than others. In order to maintain a realistic implementation, this section will focus only on the most dominant and easiest to identify non-vital loads, the not instantly used.

We present a scheme that 1) identifies which loads are not instantly used, 2) stores this information on a per load basis, and 3) uses this information to process the load instructions. We highlight three structures needed for this scheme: 1) vitality classification via rename register file; 2) vitality storage via instruction cache; and 3) the vital cache. The following sections describe these in detail.

5.1.1 Vitality Classification via Rename Register File

As stated, we only need to identify the case when the load's value is not used immediately following its execution. We only identify the not-instantly-used non-vital loads because they constitute the largest portion of non-vital loads, and are easy to identify (the other non-vital loads can also be identified, but are left for future work). The rename register file (RRF) can collect this information (see Figure 6). Two extra bits are added to each renamed register. These bits are originally in an initial state (00). They are set to a new state (01) upon a write by a load to the renamed register. If the register is not read in the next cycle, then they go to a final state of non-vital (10). Otherwise, they go to a final state of vital (11). After identification, the vitality information is used to update the instruction cache for each static load. Every dynamic occurrence of a load causes it to be re-identified.

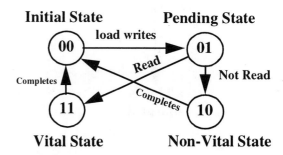

Figure 6 State machine for vitality classification.

5.1.2 Vitality Storage via Instruction Cache

The instruction cache is used to store the vitality information for each static load. Each load has only one bit that represents if it is vital or not. This added bit should not impact fetch latency, and can be attached to the instruction cache or kept in a separate table. The separate table can be accessed after decode, and indexed by the instruction pointer of the load. This bit is sent with the load to the memory hierarchy. It determines the updating of the data caches.

5.1.3 Vital Cache

The heart of our non-vital load implementation is the vital cache (VC) in the memory hierarchy (see Figure 7). We propose adding a level of cache above the DL1. This cache (DL0) should be a small cache that can be clocked in one cycle. The vital cache is only allocated/updated by vital loads; whereas the DL0 will update the cache for every load on a miss (see Figure 7). The goal is to have the non-vital loads retrieve their data from the DL1, while the vital loads get their data faster from the VC. A VC configuration also provides a port advantage by prioritizing vital loads access. For example, if a vital load is ready to execute in a given cycle, the vital load is given the available VC port (the DL0/VC is assumed to be write-through and single ported, and the DL1 is assumed to have 2 overall ports for both configurations). Prioritizing (separating) vital loads provides another performance advantage for the VC scheme.

5.2 Results

As stated in Section 3, we assume that the 32KB cache has multi-cycle latency. Therefore, we will show that it is advantageous to add a smaller, faster data cache (DL0) to the

memory hierarchy. Instead of treating all loads equally like the DL0, the VC gives priority to vital loads. We begin by comparing the overall performance impact that a non-vital load implementation can have. Figure 8 shows IPC results for each individual benchmark for three different configurations: 1) DL1 with 3 cycle latency (DL1); 2) DL1 and a 256B DL0 (DL1+DL0); and 3) DL1 and 256B vital cache (DL1+VC). As graphed, adding a small (256B) single-cycle cache to the hierarchy (DL1+DL0) adds performance for almost all the benchmarks, averaging a 4% increase in overall performance. But by using a vital cache configuration, we gain an additional 12% compared to the DL0 configuration. The IPC performance gain is noticeably higher for the floating point benchmarks. The vital cache does present a performance gain for all the benchmarks, and averages a 17% increase over the configuration with just the DL1.

The performance gain is derived from an increase in the efficiency of the highest level cache (DL0 or VC) and by prioritizing the processing of vital loads (allocating the VC port to vital loads). However, increasing the latency of non-vital loads by pushing their access time to that of the slower DL1 may also have a negative effect on performance (see Figure 4). If the ROB (or other resource constraints) is strained by the increased load latency, then the machine may stall, and overall performance is reduced. But the IPC results in show that this negative effect of the vital cache is more than compensated for by the increase in priority for the vital loads.

The percentage of loads (non-vital) that do not update the vital cache is high and is shown in Figure 9. Recall: 43% of

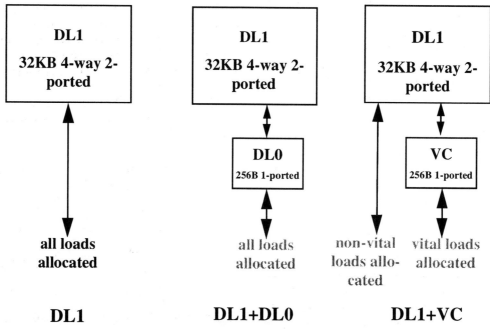

Figure 7 Different cache configurations.

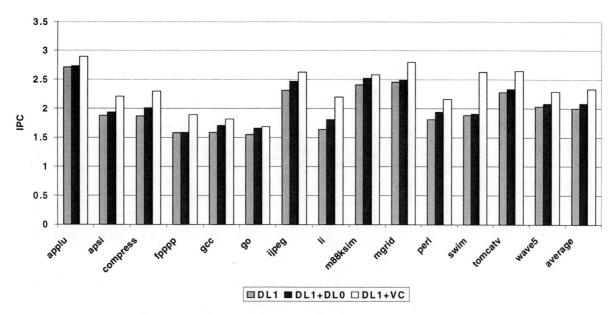

Figure 8 Implementation performance comparison.

all loads are classified as not instantly used. But this number changes as the cache hierarchy management changes. For example, when a non-vital load's data does not move to the vital cache, the load (with higher latency) may actually become a vital load. The interactions and changing of vital/non-vital loads is outside the scope of this paper and left for future work. For some of the benchmarks there is correlation be-tween this percentage (loads not updated), and the overall IPC performance impact that is shown in Figure 6. For example, mgrid has a high percentage of loads which do not update the vital cache (in theory making it more efficient), and the IPC's positive impact reflects this.

Hardware identification of a load's vitality is done via prediction and is described in Section 5.1. The scheme pre-

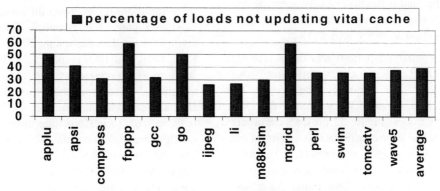

Figure 9 Loads that do not update the vital cache.

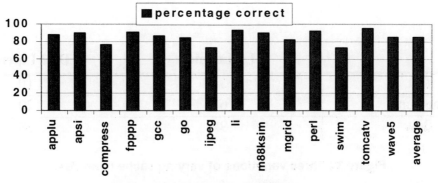

Figure 10 Vitality predictability.

171

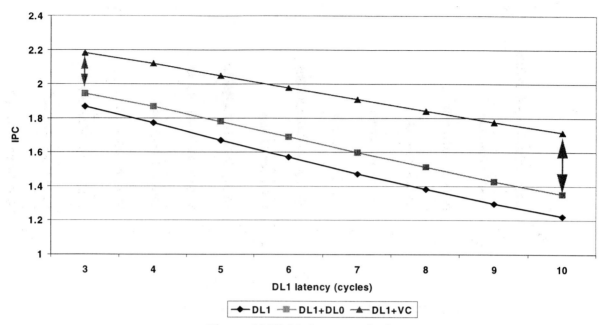

Figure 11 DL1 latency analysis.

sented is a simple initial scheme, and implements a last-value prediction algorithm, i.e. if a static load is identified as non-vital the last time it executed, then we will predict that it will be non-vital the next time it executes. A simple last-value prediction mechanism is accurate and the results are illustrated in Figure 10. Figure 10 graphs the results for the prediction of the not-instantly-used loads. A misprediction is counted if the load is fluctuating between vital and non-vital. The vitality of this class of loads is predictable, with the mean prediction accuracy above 85%.

The 32KB 4-way associative 2-ported cache that acts as the DL1 is assumed to be 3 cycles in all simulation results so far. As microprocessor clock frequency increases, the latency of DL1 will also increase. We now vary the DL1 from 3 cycles to 10 cycles. Figure 11 presents harmonic means of the IPC for the three configurations again. As the DL1's latency becomes greater, the impact of the vital cache becomes greater (slope of the vital cache configuration is not as steep as the other configurations). Assuming 10-cycle DL1 latency, a VC configuration outperforms the

DL0 configuration by 27% and a DL1-only configuration by 40%.

Preceding simulation results had the DL0/VC fixed at 256B. We now present simulation results varying the size of this highest-level cache from 256B to 8KB (assuming single cycle DL0/VC for all cases). Figure 13 compares the performance between a DL0 and VC configuration for three variations representing different DL1 and DL2 latencies: see Figure 12. For example, for medium-DL0, the latencies for the data caches are 20, 6, and 1 cycle(s) for the DL2, DL1, and DL0 respectively. These variations (fast, medium, slow) represent cache latency scaling with future anticipated microprocessor clock frequencies (DL2 and DL1 are scaled by the same factor). As the size of the DL0 is increased, the performance difference between the VC configuration and a normal DL0 configuration is reduced. The efficiency of the VC becomes less of a factor as the size of the cache is increased. However, for the three different schemes, a 1KB VC consistently outperforms an 8KB DL0.

	DL1 Latency	**DL2 Latency**
fast	3	10
medium	6	20
slow	9	30

Figure 12 Three variations of varying cache latencies.

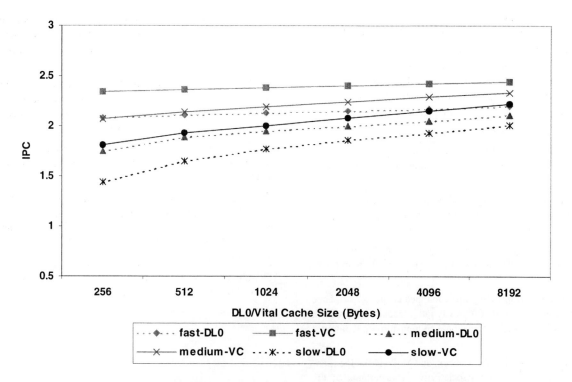

Figure 13 DL0 vs. vital cache with varying cache latencies.

Figure 13 also shows that as the latencies of the caches become greater, the importance of VC becomes greater. For example, assuming "slow" caches, a 256B VC outperforms a 256B DL0 by 26%. It can also be noted that a slow-VC configuration performs equivalent to a fast-DL0 configuration. As microprocessor clock frequencies continue to increase, the importance of the VC will also increase.

6 Conclusion

In this paper, a new load classification method is proposed, that classifies loads as those vital to performance and those not vital to performance. A study is presented that analyzes different types of non-vital loads and quantifies the percentage of loads that are non-vital. 75% of all loads are non-vital with only 35% of the accessed data space being vital. A realistic implementation of the non-vital load classification method is presented and a cache called the vital cache is proposed that makes use of the non-vital load classification. The vital cache is designed to cache data for vital loads only, deferring non-vital loads to slower caches. The vital cache improves the efficiency of the cache hierarchy and hit rate for vital loads. The vital cache increases performance by 17%, relative to a design without the vital cache.

As microprocessors continue to push towards even higher frequencies, the efficiency of the first and second level caches will become more and more critical. In order to make more efficient use of these caches, we must leverage the dynamic behavior of memory accessing instructions. This paper has shown that the vitality attribute of load instructions can be effectively leveraged to enhance cache efficiency and hence overall processor performance.

References

[1] S.G. Abraham, R.A. Sugamar, B.R. Rau and R. Gupta, "Predictability of Load/Store Instruction Latencies", Proc. 26th International Symposium on Microarchitectures, Dec 1993, 139--152.

[2] A. Agarwal and S. D. Pudar. "Column-associative caches: A technique for reducing the miss rate of direct-mapped caches", In Proceedings of the 20th International Symposium on Computer Architecture, pages 169--178, San Diego, CA, May 1993.

[3] T. Alexander and G. Kedem. "Distributed Prefetch-buffer/Cache Design for High Performance Memory Systems", In Proceedings of the 2nd International Symposium on High-Performance Computer Architecture, pages 254--263, February 1996.

[4] B. Calder, D. Grunwald, and J. Emer, "Predictive sequential associative cache," in Proceedings of the Second International Symposium on High-Performance Computer Architecture, Feb. 1996.

[5] S. Cho, P. Yew, and G. Lee. "Decoupling Local Variable Accesses in a Wide-Issue Superscalar Processor," Proc. of the 26th Int'l Symp. on Computer Architecture.

[6] Brian A Fields, Shai Rubin and Rastislav Bodik. "Focusing Processor Policies via Critical-Path Prediction", In proceedings of 28th International Symposium on Computer Architecture.

[7] B. Fisk and I. Bahar. "The Non-Critical Buffer: Using Load Latency Tolerance to Improve Data Cache Efficiency", In IEEE International Conference on Computer Design, October 1999.

[8] M. D. Hill. "A Case for Direct-Mapped Caches," IEEE Computer, pp. 25 - 40, Dec. 1988.

[9] Johnson, Connors, Merten, & Hwu. "Run-Time Cache Bypassing", in IEEE Transactions on Computers, Vol. 48, No.12, December 1999.

[10] L. John and S. A. "Design and performance evaluation of a cache assist to implement selective caching." In International Conference on Computer Design.

[11] T. Juan, T. Lang, and J. Navarro. "The Difference-bit Cache." Proc. of the 30th Annual Int'l Symp. on Microarchitecture.

[12] N. P. Jouppi. "Improving direct-mapped cache performance by the addition of a small fully-associative cache and prefetch buffers." In 17th Annual International Symposium on Computer Architecture.

[13] R. E. Kessler, R. Jooss, A. Lebeck, and M. D. Hill. "Inexpensive implementations of set-associativity," Proceedings of the 16th Annual International Symposium on Computer Architecture, 17(3):131--139, 1989.

[14] Kin, Gupta, and Mangione-Smith. "The Filter Cache: An Energy Efficient Memory Structure", International Symposium on Microarchitecture, 1997.

[15] L. Kurian, P. T. Hulina, and L. D. Coraor. "Memory latency effects in decoupled architectures." IEEE Transactions on Computers, 43(10):1129--1139, October 1994.

[16] H. Neefs, H. Vandierendonck, and K. De Bosschere. "A Technique for High Bandwidth and Deterministic Low Latency Load/Store Accesses to Multiple Cache Banks," Proceedings of the 5th International Symposium on High-Performance Computer Architecture.

[17] B. Rau. "Pseudo-Randomly Interleaved Memory," 18th International Symposium on Computer Architecture, May 1991.

[18] J. A. Rivers, G. S. Tyson, E. S. Davidson, and T. M. Austin. "On High-Bandwidth Data Cache Design for Multi-Issue Processors," Proc. of the 30th Annual Int'l Symp. on Microarchitecture, pp. 46 - 56, Dec. 1997.

[19] Sanchez, Gonzalez, & Valero. "Static Locality Anlysis for Cache Management", In the Proceedings of PACT, November 11-15, 1997.

[20] A. Seznec. "A case for two-way skewed-associative caches." In 20th Annual International Symposium on computer Architecture.

[21] Srinivasan , Ju, Lebeck, & Wilkerson, "Locality vs. Criticality", in Proceedings of the 28th International Symposium on Computer Architecture, 2001.

[22] Srinivasan and A. Lebeck, "Load latency tolerance in dynamically scheduled processors.", in Proceedings of the Thirty-First International Symposium on Microarchitecture, pp. 148--159, 1998.

[23] G. S. Sohi and M. Franklin. "High-Bandwidth Data Memory Systems for Superscalar Processors," Proc. of the Fourth Int'l Conf. on Architectural Support for Programming Languages and Operating Systems, pp. 53 - 62, April 1991.

[24] Tune, Liang, Tullsen, Calder. "Dynamic Prediction of Critical Path Instructions". In the Proceedings of the 7th High Performance of Computer Architecture.

[25] Gary Tyson, Matthew Farrens, John Matthews, and Andrew R. Pleszkun. "A modified approach to data cache management." In Proceedings of the 28th Annual ACM/IEEE International Symposium on Microarchitecture, pages 93--103, December 1995.

[26] K. M. Wilson and K. Olukotun. "Designing High Bandwidth On-Chip Caches," Proc. of the 24th Int'l Symp. on Computer Architecture, pp. 121 - 132, June 1997.

Let's Study Whole-Program Cache Behaviour Analytically

Xavier Vera[†]
Institutionen för Datateknik
Mälardalens Högskola
Västerås, Sweden
xavier.vera@mdh.se

Jingling Xue
School of Computer Science and Engineering
University of New South Wales
Sydney, NSW 2052, Australia
jxue@cse.unsw.edu.au

Abstract

Based on a new characterisation of data reuse across multiple loop nests, we present a method, a prototyping implementation and some experimental results for analysing the cache behaviour of whole programs with regular computations. Validation against cache simulation using real codes shows the efficiency and accuracy of our method. The largest program we have analysed, Applu from SPECfp95, has 3868 lines, 16 subroutines and 2565 references. In the case of a 32KB cache with a 32B line size, our method obtains the miss ratio with an absolute error of about 0.80% in about 128 seconds while the simulator used runs for nearly 5 hours on a 933MHz Pentium III PC. Our method can be used to guide compiler locality optimisations and improve cache simulation performance.

1. Introduction

Data caches are a key component to bridge the increasing performance gap between processor and main memory speeds. However, caches are effective only when programs exhibit sufficient data locality in their memory access patterns. Optimising compilers attempt to apply loop transformations such as tiling [3, 6, 14, 24, 26] and data transformations such as padding [12, 13, 17, 18] to improve the cache performance of a program. The models guiding these transformations (in making an appropriate choice of parameter values such as tile and pad sizes) are mostly heuristic or approximate. Memory system designers often use cache simulators to evaluate alternative design options. In both cases, a fast and accurate assessment of a program's cache behaviour at compile time is useful in guiding compiler locality optimisations and improving cache simulation performance.

In the past few years, some progress has been made in the development of compile-time analytical methods for predicting cache behaviour. These include the Cache Miss Equations (CMEs) [11], the probabilistic method described in [9] and the Presburger-formulas-based method described in [4]. The underlying idea is to set up mathematical formulas to provide a precise characterisation of the cache behaviour of a program in the hope that, if these formulas can be solved or manipulated efficiently, then the information gathered such as the number of cache misses and their causes can be exploited for various performance-enhancing purposes. However, the CMEs [11] and the probabilistic method [9] are limited to analysing perfect loop nests with straight-line assignments. The Presburger-formulas-based method [4], which is capable of handling multiple nests and IF conditionals, has been applied only to loop nests of small problem sizes with a few references. Its feasibility in analysing larger loop nests of realistic problem sizes remains to be seen. Neither of these methods can handle call statements.

This paper presents an analytical method for predicting the cache behaviour of complete programs with regular computations. By building primarily on and extending Wolf and Lam's framework [24] for quantifying reuse and the CMEs for characterising cache misses, we make the following contributions:

Reuse Analysis and Representation. By generalising traditional concepts such as iteration vectors and uniformly generated references for perfect loop nests, we introduce reuse vectors for quantifying reuse between references contained in multiple nests. Our reuse represen-

[†]This work was carried out during the 1st author's visit to the 2nd author at the University of New South Wales.

tation includes Wolf and Lam's reuse vectors [24] as a special case, allowing potentially existing reuse-driven optimisations to be applied to multiple nests.

Whole-Program Analysis. We can handle programs with regular computations consisting of subroutines, call statements, IF statements and arbitrarily nested loops. In order to predict a program's cache behaviour *statically*, these programs must be free of data-dependent constructs such as variable loop bounds, data-dependent IF conditionals, indirection arrays and recursive calls.

Prototyping Implementation. Our prototyping system consists of components on normalising loop nests, inlining calls (abstractly), generating reuse vectors, sampling memory accesses and forming and solving the equations for cache misses. The inlining component has not been implemented. In our experiments, the calls in all programs (if any) are inlined by hand.

Validation and Experimental Results. We have validated our method against cache simulation using programs from SPECfp95, Perfect Suite, Livermore kernels, Linpack and Lapack. We include the results for three kernels and three whole programs. The largest program we have analysed, Applu from SPECfp95, has 3868 lines of FORTRAN code, 16 subroutines and 2565 references. Assuming a 32KB (direct-mapped, 2-way and 4-way, resp.) cache with a 32B line size, our method obtains the miss ratios with absolute errors (0.78%, 0.82% and 0.84%, resp.) in about 128 seconds while the cache simulation runs for nearly 5 hours on a 933MHz Pentium III PC. In comparison with the three recent compile-time analytical methods reported in [4, 9, 11], our method is the only one capable of analysing this scale of programs efficiently with accuracy.

The rest of this paper is organised as follows. Section 2 defines the cache architectures used. Section 3 describes our program model, with a particular emphasis on our new representation of reuse vectors for multiple nests and our technique for abstract call inlining. Section 4 outlines two algorithms for cache behaviour analysis. Section 5 describes the structure of our prototyping implementation. Section 6 presents our experimental results. Section 7 discusses the related work. Section 8 concludes the paper and discusses future work.

2. Cache model

We assume a uniprocessor with a k-way set-associative data cache using LRU replacement. In the case of write misses, we assume a fetch-on-write policy so that writes and reads are modelled identically. In a k-way set-associative cache, a cache set contains k distinct cache lines. C_s and L_s denote the cache size and line size (in array elements), respectively.

A *memory line* refers to a cache-line-sized block in the memory while *a cache line* refers to the actual block in which a memory line is mapped.

3. Program model

Presently, we restrict ourselves to analysing FORTRAN programs with regular computations. We can handle programs made up of subroutines consisting of possibly IF statements, call statements and arbitrarily nested loops. In order to predict at compile time a program's cache behaviour, the following restrictions are imposed. All loop bounds and array subscript expressions must be affine in terms of the enclosing loops. All IF conditionals must be expressions consisting of loop indices and compile-time known constants. The base addresses of all non-register variables including actual parameters (scalars or arrays) must be known at compile time. The sizes of an array in all but the last dimension must be known statically.

Our program model excludes all and only data-dependent constructs, which include, for example, variable loop bounds, data-dependent IF conditionals, indirection arrays and recursive calls.

3.1. Loop nest normalisation

We normalise all loop nests to put a program into a suitable form for analysis. During normalisation, we apply loop sinking to move all statements into their respective innermost loops by adding IF conditionals appropriately [24, 25]. After normalisation, all loop nests are n-dimensional, and, in addition, all loop variables at depth k are normalised to I_k.

3.2. Iteration vectors

A particular instance of a statement S (known as an *iteration* or *iteration point*) of the enclosing (n-dimensional) loop nest is identified by a $2n$-dimensional *iteration vector* of the form $\vec{i} = (\ell_1, I_1, \ell_2, I_2, \ldots, \ell_n, I_n)$, where

- $\vec{L} = (\ell_1, \ell_2, \ldots, \ell_n)$ is the *loop label* (*vector*) for the innermost loop containing S, and

- $\vec{I} = (I_1, I_2, \ldots, I_n)$ is the *index vector* consisting of the indices of the n loops enclosing S.

Figure 1 lists the iteration vector for each statement in an example. It is not difficult to see how the iteration vectors are derived in general.

REAL*8 B(N,N)	Iteration Vector
DO $I_1 = \cdots$	
DO $I_2 = \cdots$	
S_1: $B(I_2 - 1, I_1) = \cdots$	$(1, I_1, 1, I_2)$
DO $I_2 = \ldots$	
S_2: $\cdots = B(I_2, I_1)$	$(1, I_1, 2, I_2)$
DO $I_1 = \cdots$	
DO $I_2 = \cdots$	
S_3:$B(I_1, I_2) = \cdots$	$(2, I_1, 1, I_2)$

Figure 1. Iteration vectors for statements.

As usual, the set of all iterations for a particular n-dimensional perfect loop nest in the program is called the *iteration space* of that nest.

In a sequential execution, all iteration points are executed in lexicographical order. The usual lexicographic order operators $\prec$, $\preceq$, $\succ$ and $\succeq$ are used in the normal manner.

3.3. Reference iteration spaces

The *reference iteration space (RIS)* of a reference R, denoted RIS_R, is defined as the set of iteration points where the reference is accessed. If a reference is not guarded by a conditional, its RIS is the entire iteration space of the enclosing loop nest. Otherwise, the RIS can be a subspace of that iteration space.

We can handle any IF conditionals involving loop indices and compile-time constants. For a dedicated treatment of IF statements, we refer to [21].

3.4. Uniformly generated references

After the loop nest normalisation, $\vec{I} = (I_1, I_2, \ldots, I_n)$ is the index vector of all n-dimensional loop nests. The concept of uniformly generated references for perfect loop nests [10, 24, 26] can be carried over to multiple nests. There are two uniformly generated reference sets in Figure 1: $\{B(I_2 - 1, I_1), B(I_2, I_1)\}$ and $\{B(I_1, I_2)\}$. Note that the two references in the first set are not enclosed in the same innermost loop (i.e., not contained in the same perfect nest).

3.5. Reuse vectors

We generalise Wolf and Lam's reuse framework [24, 26] to calculate reuse vectors for multiple nests. We also add additional spatial reuse vectors to capture the reuse spanning two adjacent columns of an array (where the elements are co-located in a common memory line).

Let R_p and R_c be two uniformly generated references (p stands for producer and c for consumer), which may be contained in different nests. Let R_p be the producer $A(M\vec{I} + \vec{m}_p)$ nested inside the innermost loop labelled by $(\ell_1^p, \ell_2^p, \ldots, \ell_n^p)$ and R_c be the consumer $A(M\vec{I} + \vec{m}_c)$ nested inside the innermost loop labelled by $(\ell_1^c, \ell_2^c, \ldots, \ell_n^c)$, where $\vec{I} = (I_1, I_2, \ldots, I_n)$. For both the producer $A(M\vec{I} + \vec{m}_p)$ and the consumer $A(M\vec{I} + \vec{m}_c)$, the index vector $\vec{I}$ is confined in the iteration space of the respective enclosing loop nest. These constraints are ignored during the derivation of reuse vectors and are enforced in the equations for cache misses (Section 4).

Let $\vec{x} = (x_1, x_2, \ldots, x_n)$ be a solution to:

$$M\vec{x} = \vec{m}_p - \vec{m}_c \qquad (1)$$

and

$$\vec{r_t} = (\ell_1^c - \ell_1^p, x_1, \ell_2^c - \ell_2^p, x_2, \ldots, \ell_n^c - \ell_n^p, x_n)$$

such that $\vec{r_t} \succeq 0$. Then $\vec{r_t}$ is a *temporal reuse vector* from R_p to R_c. In addition, $\vec{r_t}$ represents *self* reuse if R_p and R_c are identical and *group* reuse otherwise.

There are two kinds of spatial reuse vectors depending on whether they span a single array column or not. Their derivations are discussed below.

The spatial reuse vectors confined within a single array column are derived algebraically just like temporal reuse vectors. In FORTRAN, arrays are column-major. Let $\vec{y} = (y_1, y_2, \ldots, y_n)$ be a solution to:

$$\begin{aligned} M'\vec{y} &= \vec{m}_p' - \vec{m}_c' \\ |M_1\vec{y}| &< L_s \end{aligned} \qquad (2)$$

but not a solution to (1), where M_1 is the first row of M and every primed term is obtained from its corresponding term in (1) with its first row or entry removed. Let

$$\vec{r_s} = (\ell_1^c - \ell_1^p, y_1, \ell_2^c - \ell_2^p, y_2, \ldots, \ell_n^c - \ell_n^p, y_n)$$

such that $\vec{r_s} \succeq 0$. Then $\vec{r_s}$ is a *spatial reuse vector* from R_p to R_c. In addition, $\vec{r_s}$ represents *self* reuse if R_p and R_c are identical and *group* reuse otherwise.

If a memory line spans two adjacent columns of an array, we will add spatial reuse vectors to capture such reuse. The spatial reuse vectors of this second kind are added individually depending on the iteration space shapes and cache parameters used. In some real programs, an array can have a column with less than $L_s - 1$ elements. The spatial reuse vectors that span multiple columns in this case are derived similarly. Every cross-column spatial reuse vector from R_p to R_c has the form $\vec{r_s} = (r_1, r_2, \ldots, r_{2n})$, where $(r_1, r_3, \ldots, r_{2n-1}) = (\ell_1^c - \ell_1^p, \ell_2^c - \ell_2^p, \ldots, \ell_n^c - \ell_n^p)$.

Let us derive reuse vectors for the first two references to B in Figure 1. Let R_p be $B(I_2 - 1, I_1)$ nested in the inner loop labelled by $\vec{L_p} = (1, 1)$ and R_c be $B(I_2, I_1)$ nested inside the inner loop labelled by $\vec{L_c} = (1, 2)$. The subscript expressions for both references are affine:

$$M\vec{I} + \vec{m_p} = \begin{bmatrix} 0 & 1 \\ 1 & 0 \end{bmatrix} \begin{bmatrix} I_1 \\ I_2 \end{bmatrix} + \begin{bmatrix} -1 \\ 0 \end{bmatrix}$$
$$M\vec{I} + \vec{m_c} = \begin{bmatrix} 0 & 1 \\ 1 & 0 \end{bmatrix} \begin{bmatrix} I_1 \\ I_2 \end{bmatrix} + \begin{bmatrix} 0 \\ 0 \end{bmatrix}$$

In this case, the equation (1) becomes:

$$\begin{bmatrix} 0 & 1 \\ 1 & 0 \end{bmatrix} \begin{bmatrix} x_1 \\ x_2 \end{bmatrix} = \begin{bmatrix} -1 \\ 0 \end{bmatrix}$$

which has the unique solution $(0, -1)$. Thus, the unique temporal reuse vector from $B(I_2 - 1, I_1)$ to $B(I_2, I_1)$ is $(0, 0, 1, -1)$. To find the spatial reuse vectors spanning a single column of B, we solve:

$$\begin{bmatrix} 1 & 0 \end{bmatrix} \begin{bmatrix} y_1 \\ y_2 \end{bmatrix} = 0$$
$$\begin{bmatrix} 0 & 1 \end{bmatrix} \begin{bmatrix} y_1 \\ y_2 \end{bmatrix} < L_s$$

which is the instance of the equation (2) for this case. Thus, all these spatial reuse vectors have the form $(0, y_2)$. Our reuse vector generator produces the following spatial reuse vectors $(0, 0, 1, -2), (0, 0, 1, -3), \ldots, (0, 0, 1, -(L_s-1))$. Note that $(0, 0, 1, -1)$, which is also a solution to the above group spatial reuse equation, is regarded as a temporal rather than spatial reuse vector.

Finally, our reuse vector generator will generate $(0, 1, 1, -N), (0, 1, 1, 1-N), \ldots, (0, 1, 1, L_s - N - 2)$ to capture all possible reuse for the elements at the end of one array column and the beginning of the next column (assuming that $N \geqslant L_s - 1$). The derivation of $(0, 1, 1, -N)$ is illustrated in Figure 2.

These reuse vectors collectively represent the fact that $B(I_2, I_1)$ for a fixed (I_1, I_2) may reuse a cache line touched when $B(I_2 - 1, I_1)$ was accessed previously along one of these directions.

If a reference is guarded by an IF conditional, its RIS may not be the entire iteration space of the enclosing loop nest. This causes complications only in the derivation of group reuse vectors. The self

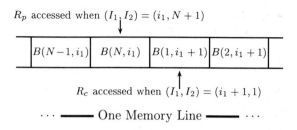

Figure 2. The derivation of the spatial reuse vector $(0, 1, 1, -N)$ across two columns.

temporal and spatial reuse vectors for a reference are defined and derived without a need to refer to its RIS. As for the group (temporal or spatial) reuse vectors from R_p to R_c, there can be infinitely many from some facets of RIS_{R_p} to some facets of RIS_{R_c}. In these worst cases, our implementation will generate only a subset of all reuse vectors. Our extensive validation reported in [21] confirm that an overestimation of cache misses thus caused is negligible since (a) we overestimate only on some facets of RIS_{R_c} and (b) R_c may reuse on the facets along other (usually self) reuse vectors.

3.6. Call statements

In FORTRAN, all arguments are passed by reference. To analyse a program that contains call statements, we perform an *abstract inlining* for a call whenever possible. We do not actually generate the inlined code. We only need to obtain the information required for analysing the inlined code. Each subroutine is associated with an *abstract function* consisting of the information about the memory accesses to the run-time stack, its code body (i.e., its loop nests with references), and local variable and formal parameter declarations. As shown in Figure 3, every call to a subroutine is abstractly inlined by replacing the call with the information in the abstract function associated with that subroutine. The calling conventions used for a program are compiler- and architecture-dependent. What is shown in the figure is one such a convention for a 32 bit machine. *Stack* denotes the run-time stack modelled as a one-dimensional array of an infinite size. If BP is 0 initially, its value is known at compile time at every call site due to the absence of recursion. The base address of *Stack*, if unknown at compile time, has to be obtained at run time. Then *Stack* is treated just like an ordinary array reference. For large programs, the impact of these stack accesses on the miss ratio should be negligible.

```
                          . . .
                  Stack[BP] = RetAddr
                  Stack[BP + 4] = BaseAddr(A)
                  Stack[BP + 8] = BaseAddr(B)
   . . .          . . . = Stack[BP − 4]
CALL f(A, B) ⇒    . . . = Stack[BP − 8]
   . . .          f's code body (with the formals
                  replaced by actuals or renamed)
                  RetAddr = Stack[BP − 12]
                          . . .
```

Figure 3. Abstract inlining of a call.

Program	Actual Parameters			Calls	
	Total	P-able	R-able	Total	A-able
Tomcatv	0	0	0	0	0
swim	0	0	0	5	5
su2cor	590	503	87	150	150
hydro2d	141	122	0	82	82
mgrid	103	68	0	23	2
applu	79	79	0	23	23
apsi	1811	1601	0	186	118
fppp	86	83	0	17	16
turb3D	834	759	0	111	86
wave5	703	591	2	171	127
CSS	2497	2489	0	965	965
LWSI	159	140	0	28	18
MTSI	188	186	0	63	63
NASI	473	236	0	75	41
OCSI	668	620	0	244	209
SDSI	256	189	18	129	103
SMSI	362	321	0	53	38
SRSI	418	242	0	50	13
TFSI	228	137	0	44	13
WSSI	970	836	127	185	179
TOTAL	10566	9202	234	2604	2251
%	100	87.09	2.21	100	86.44

Table 1. Analysability of actual parameters and calls in SPECfp95 and Perfect.

Not every call can be inlined according to Table 1. To analyse a call exactly, our method needs to know at compile time the base addresses of all its actual parameters. Let AP be an actual parameter that is either a scalar or an array variable or a subscripted variable with an affine data access expression and FP be its matching formal parameter.

AP is *propagateable* if, after inlining, every reference to FP can be replaced by a reference to AP. Such a replacing reference can be analysed statically if it has an affine subscript expression. A propagateable AP allows the reuse to AP both in the caller and in all the callees to be potentially exploited. In Column "P-able", we consider AP as propagateable if FP is a scalar, a one-dimensional array or if both AP and FP are arrays of the same dimensionality with matching sizes in all but the last dimension.

AP is *renameable* if, after inlining, every reference to FP can be replaced by a reference to a new array AP' such that (a) AP and AP' have the same base address and (b) AP' inherits the same declaration as FP. Such a replacing reference can be analysed statically if it has an affine subscript expression. The propagateable actuals are not also classified as renameable. In Column "R-able", we consider AP as renameable if the sizes of all but the last dimension for AP and FP are known statically. This still allows the reuse between the references to FP in a common subroutine to be exploited.

A call can be abstractly inlined, i.e., is potentially *analysable*, if all its actuals are either propagateable or renameable. A parameterless call is regarded as being analysable. Analysable calls are represented in Column "A-able", which shows that 86.44% of calls from SPECfp95 and Perfect benchmarks can be inlined. These statistics are obtained by examining only a call and its callee in isolation.

Figure 4 serves to illustrate the inlining of a code segment (which may have out of array bound accesses if loop bounds are not chosen properly). This example also demonstrates how the subscript expressions of replacing references are computed. The inlined code does not compile but can be analysed by our method. Hence, the name abstract inlining.

Finally, system calls (to I/O subroutines and intrinsic functions) are not inlined. The memory accesses inside are not accounted for. Theses calls can be inlined if their abstract functions are known.

4. Cache behaviour analysis

There are two kinds of miss equations: *compulsory or cold (miss) equations* and *replacement (miss) equations*. *Cold* misses represent the first time a memory line is touched while *replacement* misses are those accesses that result in misses because the cache lines that would have been reused were evicted from the cache before they get reused.

4.1. Forming equations

Let $\vec{r}$ be a reuse vector from the producer reference R_p to the consumer reference R_c. We want to find out if R_c at iteration $\vec{\imath}$ can reuse the cache line accessed by R_p at $\vec{\imath} - \vec{r}$. Let R_i be an *intervening*

```
REAL*8 X, A, B
DIMENSION A(10, 10), B(20, 20)
DO I₁ = ...
   DO I₂ = ...
      A(I₁, I₂) = ···
      CALL f(X, A, B, B(I₁, I₂))
      CALL g(A(I₁, I₂), A(1, I₂), A, B)

SUBROUTINE f(Y, C, D, S)
REAL*8 Y, C, D, S
DIMENSION C(10, 10), D(400), S(10, 10, *)
DO I₃ = ...
   DO I₄ = ...
      C(I₃, I₄ − 1) = Y + D(I₃ − 1 + 20 * (I₄ − 1))
      S(I₃, I₄, 2) = ···

SUBROUTINE g(E, F, G, T)
REAL*8 E, F, G, T
DIMENSION E(10, 10), F(10), G(10, 10), T(100, 4)
DO I₃ = ...
   DO I₄ = ...
      E(I₃, I₄) = F(I₄) − T(I₃, I₄)
      G(I₃, I₄) = ···
```

```
REAL*8 X, A, B, B1, B2
DIMENSION A(10, 10), B(20, 20)
C THE FOLLOWING LINE DOES NOT COMPILE
DIMENSION B1(10, 10, *), B2(100, 4)
DO I₁ = ...
   DO I₂ = ...
      A(I₁, I₂) = ···
      DO I₃ = ...
         Do I₄ = ...
            A(I₃, I₄ − 1) = X + B(I₃ − 1 + 20 * (I₄ − 1))
            B1(I₁ + 20 * (I₂ − 1) + I₃ − 1, I₄, 2) = ···
      DO I₃ = ...
         Do I₄ = ...
            A(I₁ + I₃ − 1, I₂ + I₄ − 1) = A(I₄, I₂) − B2(I₃, I₄)
            A(I₃, I₄) = ···
```

Figure 4. Propagation and renaming of actual parameters. All actuals but the last are propagated. The last actuals in both calls are renamed to $B1$ and $B2$, respectively. After inlining, B, $B1$ and $B2$ share the same base address.

reference such that the access of R_i at some iteration point $\vec{j}$ between $\vec{\imath} - \vec{r}$ and $\vec{\imath}$ may be mapped to the same cache set as the access of R_p at $\vec{\imath} - \vec{r}$. If that happens, a *set contention* occurs between the access of R_p at $\vec{\imath} - \vec{r}$ and the access of R_i at $\vec{j}$. In a k-way set-associative cache, it takes k distinct set contentions to evict the cache line touched by the access of R_p at $\vec{\imath} - \vec{r}$.

We give below the miss equations that can be analysed to determine if the access of R_c at $\vec{\imath}$ is a miss or hit, assuming the single reuse vector $\vec{r}$ from R_p to R_c and the single intervening reference R_i.

$Mem\_Line_R(\vec{\imath})$ ($Cache\_Set_R(\vec{\imath})$) denotes the memory line (cache set) to which the memory

address accessed by reference R at iteration $\vec{\imath}$ is mapped.

Cold equations. The cold equations for R_c along $\vec{r}$ represent the iteration points where the memory lines are brought to the cache for the first time:

$$\vec{\imath} \in RIS_{R_c}$$
$$\text{and}$$
$$(\vec{\imath} - \vec{r} \notin RIS_{R_p}$$
$$\text{or}$$
$$Mem\_Line_{R_c}(\vec{\imath}) \neq Mem\_Line_{R_p}(\vec{\imath} - \vec{r}))$$

If $\vec{r}$ is temporal, the inequality is false and thus redundant.

Replacement equations. The *replacement equations* for R_c along $\vec{r}$ are to investigate if R_c at iteration $\vec{\imath}$ can reuse the cache line that R_p accessed at iteration $\vec{\imath} - \vec{r}$ subject to the set contentions caused by the memory accesses from R_i at all intervening points executed between $\vec{\imath} - \vec{r}$ and $\vec{\imath}$:

$$Mem\_Line_{R_c}(\vec{\imath}) = Mem\_Line_{R_p}(\vec{\imath} - \vec{r})$$
$$\vec{\imath} \in RIS_{R_c}$$
$$\vec{\imath} - \vec{r} \in RIS_{R_p}$$
$$Cache\_Set_{R_c}(\vec{\imath}) = Cache\_Set_{R_i}(\vec{\jmath})$$
$$\vec{\jmath} \in J_{R_i}$$

where J_{R_i} denotes the set of all these intervening iteration points, called the *interference set* for R_c along $\vec{r}$, and is specified precisely by:

$$J_{R_i} = \{\vec{\jmath} \in RIS_{R_i} \mid \vec{\jmath} \in \ll \vec{\imath} - \vec{r}, \vec{\imath} \gg\}$$

where '$\ll$' is '[' if R_i is lexically after R_p and '(' otherwise and '$\gg$' is ']' if R_i is lexically before R_c and ')' otherwise. As shown in Figure 6, the lexical order between two references is deduced from an intermediate representation of the original program.

4.2. Solving equations

Figure 5 gives two algorithms for obtaining the cache misses from a looping construct consisting of multiple references and reuse vectors. Both *Find-Misses* and *EstimateMisses* analyse each reference by going through its reuse vectors in lexicographical order $\prec$. If an iteration point is a solution to the cold equations along the current reuse vector $\vec{r}$, its behaviour is indeterminate and will be examined further using the other reuse vectors later in the list. Otherwise, the iteration point is classified either as a hit or a miss using the replacement equations along $\vec{r}$. After all reuse vectors have been

```
Algorithm MissAnalyser                              Algorithm FindMisses
for each reference R                                for each reference R (in no particular order)
    Sort its reuse vectors in increasing order ≺        S(R) = RIS_R // analyse all points
    H_R = ∅        // Hits for R                    MissAnalyser
    RM_R = ∅       // Replacement misses for R
    CM_R = S(R) // Cold misses for R initially      Algorithm EstimateMisses
    for each reuse vector r⃗ of R in the sorted list c is the confidence percentage from the user
        CM'_R = solutions of R's cold miss along r⃗ w is the confidence interval from the user
        for each i⃗ ∈ (CM_R − CM'_R)                 for each reference R (in no particular order)
            if i⃗ is a "replacement" hit along r⃗       compute the volume of RIS_R
                H_R = H_R ∪ {i⃗}                         if RIS_R is too small to achieve (c, w)
            else                                            if RIS_R is large enough to achieve
                RM_R = RM_R ∪ {i⃗}                               the default (c', w') = (90%, 0.15)
        CM_R = CM'_R                                             S(R) = a sample (c', w') of RIS_R
    Miss_Ratio(R) = |CM_R|+|RM_R| / |S(R)|                  else
    Loop_Nest_Miss_Ratio = Σ_R |RIS_R|×Miss_Ratio(R) / Σ_R |RIS_R|     S(R) = RIS_R // analyse all points
                                                        else
                                                            S(R) = a sample (c, w) of RIS_R
                                                    MissAnalyser
```

Figure 5. Two algorithms for computing cache misses from cold and replacement equations.

tried, the remaining indeterminate iteration points are cold misses.

Our replacement equations represent only cache set contentions. In a k-way set-associative cache, it takes k distinct cache set contentions to cause a cache line to be evicted from the cache set. There will be a cache miss only when k distinct solutions are found [11, 21].

FindMisses analyses all iteration points in a RIS and is practical only for programs of small sizes [11, 21]. *EstimateMisses* analyses a sample of a RIS and is capable of analysing programs significantly more efficiently with a controlled degree of accuracy. For technical details regarding c and w, see [7, 20].

We compute the volume of a RIS using an algorithm discussed in [21]. Other methods for computing the volume of convex polytopes exist [5, 16].

5. Prototyping implementation

Figure 6 depicts the structure of our prototyping system for finding cache misses and validating the accuracy of our method against a cache simulator. The component *Opts* optimises the program and allocates variables to registers or memory. The reuse vectors, the base addresses of variables and the relative access order of memory references are obtained from a load-store lower-level IR, which is produced from the Polaris IR [8] of the program using Ictineo [1]. The inlining component is not yet functioning. The same information obtained is fed to both our algorithms and the cache simulator used.

6. Experiments

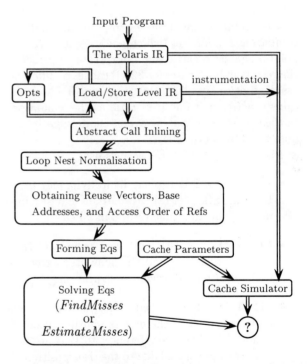

Figure 6. A framework for analysis and evaluation.

We present our results for three isolated kernels and three whole programs. For a detailed evaluation of codes consisting of IF statements, we refer to [21].

As Figure 6 shows, the same load/store level IR

Program	Cache	#Cache Misses		%Loop Nest Miss Ratio		Abs. Error	Execution Time (secs)
		Simulator	*FindMisses*	Simulator	*FindMisses*		
Hydro (KN=JN=100)	direct	52603	52603	14.12	14.12	0.00	1.07
	2-way	52603	52603	14.12	14.12	0.00	1.35
	4-way	42703	42703	11.47	11.47	0.00	1.64
MGRID (M=100)	direct	1518879	1518879	9.49	9.49	0.00	91.29
	2-way	1424038	1424038	8.90	8.90	0.00	99.45
	4-way	1424038	1424038	8.90	8.90	0.00	100.70
MMT (N=BJ=100 & BK=50)	direct	145671	147075	4.82	4.87	0.05	43.09
	2-way	171647	172592	5.68	5.71	0.03	47.06
	4-way	246980	247744	8.18	8.20	0.02	57.44

Table 2. Cache misses for 32KB caches with a 32B line size from *FindMisses* **and a simulator.**

is fed to both our method and a simulator. In our experiments, all scalars in the IR are assumed to be register-allocated and are thus not included in our analysis and simulation.

Unless otherwise specified, we assume a 32KB cache with a 32B line size. The execution times are all obtained on a 933MHz Pentium III PC.

6.1. Multiple loop nest kernels

We evaluate the accuracy of our method by comparing *FindMisses* (which analyses all iteration points) against a cache simulator. Table 2 presents the results in both cases for 32KB caches of different associativities. In all but one case, our method obtains exactly the same miss ratio as the simulator. In the exceptional case, we overestimate slightly the miss ratio by up to 0.05%.

Figure 7 gives the three kernels used.

- **Hydro** is a 2-D explicit hydrodynamics from Livermore (kernel 18). *FindMisses* and the simulator yield the same results in all cases.

- **MGRID** is a 3-D loop nest from MGRID. Again *FindMisses* and the simulator agree on their results in all cache configurations.

- **MMT** is a 3-D blocked loop nest taken from [9] that computes the matrix multiplication of A and B^T. The two references to WB are not uniformly generated due to the transposition of B. Being unable to exploit their reuse, *FindMisses* over-estimates the cache miss ratios in all three cases slightly. Due to transposition, the degree of reuse between these two references is rather minimal. The inaccuracy lies in the incompleteness of reuse information rather than our method iself.

Program	Cache	Abs. Error	Execution Time (secs)
Hydro (KN=JN=100)	direct	0.05	0.27
	2-way	0.05	0.32
	4-way	0.05	0.36
MGRID (M=100)	direct	0.36	0.19
	2-way	0.32	0.22
	4-way	0.32	0.22
MMT (B=BJ=100 & BK=50)	direct	0.23	0.10
	2-way	0.37	0.10
	4-way	0.37	0.11

Table 3. Cache misses from *EstimateMisses* **for 32KB caches with a 32B line size (**$c = 95\%$ **and** $w = 0.05$**).**

Table 2 indicates that *FindMisses*, while being capable of finding exactly cache miss numbers, does so at the expense of large execution times.

Table 3 shows the accuracy and efficiency of *EstimateMisses* using a 95% confidence with an interval of 0.05 for all references in the program. In all cases, the absolute errors are less than 0.40% and the execution times less than half a second. Note that *EstimateMisses* yields only the miss ratio for a program. The actual miss ratio for each kernel can be found from Table 2.

6.2. Whole programs

We evaluate *EstimateMisses* against a simulator using three programs from SPECfp95. Table 4 presents the results for 32KB caches of different associativities. For each program, we have succeeded in abstractly inlining all the calls and obtained one loop nest for the program. In addition, all actual parameters are propagateable, meaning that the references to every actual can be potentially exploited across calls. Since our inlining component is not

```
PROGRAM Hydro
REAL*8 ZA, ZP, ZQ, ZR, ZM, ZB, ZU, ZV, ZZ
DIMENSION ZA(jn+1,kn+1), ZP(jn+1,kn+1), ZQ(jn+1,kn+1), ZR(jn+1,kn+1), ZM(jn+1,kn+1))
DIMENSION ZB(jn+1,kn+1), ZU(jn+1,kn+1), ZV(jn+1,kn+1), ZZ(jn+1,kn+1)
T= 0.003700D0
S=0.004100D0
DO k= 2,KN
  DO j= 2,JN
    ZA(j,k)=(ZP(j-1,k+1)+ZQ(j-1,k+1)-ZP(j-1,k)-ZQ(j-1,k))*(ZR(j,k)+ZR(j-1,k))/(ZM(j-1,k)+ZM(j-1,k+1))
    ZB(j,k)= (ZP(j-1,k)+ZQ(j-1,k)-ZP(j,k)-ZQ(j,k))*(ZR(j,k)+ZR(j,k-1))/(ZM(j,k)+ZM(j-1,k))
  ENDDO
ENDDO
DO k= 2,KN
  DO j= 2,JN
    ZU(j,k)= ZU(j,k)+S*(ZA(j,k)*(ZZ(j,k)-ZZ(j+1,k))-ZA(j-1,k)*(ZZ(j,k)-ZZ(j-1,k))
          -ZB(j,k)*(ZZ(j,k)-ZZ(j,k-1))+ZB(j,k+1) *(ZZ(j,k)-ZZ(j,k+1)))
    ZV(j,k)= ZV(j,k)+S*(ZA(j,k)*(ZR(j,k)-ZR(j+1,k))-ZA(j-1,k) *(ZR(j,k)-ZR(j-1,k))
          -ZB(j,k) *(ZR(j,k)-ZR(j,k-1))+ZB(j,k+1) *(ZR(j,k)-ZR(j,k+1)))
  ENDDO
ENDDO
DO k= 2,KN
  DO j= 2,JN
    ZR(j,k)= ZR(j,k)+T*ZU(j,k)
    ZZ(j,k)= ZZ(j,k)+T*ZV(j,k)
  ENDDO
ENDDO
END
```

```
PROGRAM MGRID
REAL*8 U,Z
DIMENSION U(M,M,M), Z(M,M,M)
DO 400 I3=2,M-1
  DO 200 I2=2,M-1
    DO 100 I1=2,M-1
      U(2*I1-1,2*I2-1,2*I3-1)=U(2*I1-1,2*I2-1,2*I3-1)
      +Z(I1,I2,I3)
100 CONTINUE
    DO 200 I1=2,M-1
      U(2*I1-2,2*I2-1,2*I3-1)=U(2*I1-2,2*I2-1,2*I3-1)
      +0.5D0*(Z(I1-1,I2,I3)+Z(I1,I2,I3))
200 CONTINUE
  DO 400 I2=2,M-1
    DO 300 I1=2,M-1
      U(2*I1-1,2*I2-2,2*I3-1)=U(2*I1-1,2*I2-2,2*I3-1)
      +0.5D0*(Z(I1,I2-1,I3)+Z(I1,I2,I3))
300 CONTINUE
    DO 400 I1=2,M-1
      U(2*I1-2,2*I2-2,2*I3-1)=U(2*I1-2,2*I2-2,2*I3-1)
      +0.25D0*(Z(I1-1,I2-1,I3)+Z(I1-1,I2,I3)
      +Z(I1, I2-1,I3)+Z(I1, I2,I3))
400 CONTINUE
STOP
```

```
PROGRAM MMT
REAL*8 A, B, D, WB
DIMENSION A(N,N), B(N,N), D(N,N), WB(N.N)
DO J2 = 1,N,BJ
  DO K2 = 1,N,BK
    DO J=J2,J2+BJ-1
      DO K=K2,K2+BK-1
        WB(J-J2+1,K-K2+1)=B(K,J)
      ENDDO
    ENDDO
    DO I = 1,N
      DO K=K2,K2+BK-1
        RA=A(I,K)
        DO J=J2,J2+BJ-1
          D(I,J)=D(I,J)+
          WB(J-J2+1,K-K2+1)*RA
        ENDDO
      ENDDO
    ENDDO
  ENDDO
ENDDO
END
```

Figure 7. Three kernels.

	Tomcatv	Swim	Applu
#lines	190	429	3868
#subroutines	1	6	16
#call-statements	0	6	27
#references	79	52	2565

Table 4. Three whole programs.

working yet, all calls were inlined by hand. Each program is analysed using the reference input data. Thus, the variables in all READ statements are initialised from the reference data and then treated as compile-time constants.

Table 5 presents the experimental results obtained. For a scale of programs such as Applu, *EstimateMisses* obtains close to real miss ratios in about 128 seconds. This translates into a three orders of magnitude speedup over the cache simulator used!

Program	Cache	Miss Ratio		Abs.	Sim.T	Exe.T
		Sim.	*E.M*	Err	(secs)	(secs)
Tomcatv	direct	10.90	10.94	0.04	3676.20	0.30
	2-way	10.89	10.92	0.03	3750.34	0.37
	4-way	11.88	11.82	0.06	3860.23	0.58
Swim	direct	7.26	7.01	0.25	8136.01	2.47
	2-way	6.98	6.73	0.25	8281.10	2.63
	4-way	7.24	6.97	0.27	8425.80	3.23
Applu	direct	6.95	7.73	0.78	17089.03	127.31
	2-way	6.60	7.42	0.82	17155.20	127.60
	4-way	6.56	7.40	0.84	17278.19	127.50

Table 5. Cache misses from *EstimateMisses* (E.M) for 32KB caches with a 32B line size ($c = 95\%$ and $w = 0.05$).

Our results are further discussed below.

Tomcatv. This example is used to demonstrate the capability of our method in analysing real codes. The number of iterations of the outermost loop is data-dependent. For the reference input data used, the outermost loop runs for 750 iterations. The only data-dependent IF conditional in the program is always false. In our analysis, the memory accesses contained in this conditional are included but those contained inside the IF body are ignored.

Swim. This example demonstrates that we can analyse codes consisting of call statements. All calls are parameterless. After inlining, the outermost loop is an *IF-GOTO* construct, which has been converted into a *DO* construct.

Applu. This example shows that our method is capable of analysing this scale of programs efficiently with a good degree of accuracy. All actual parameters are propagateable. In subroutine SSOR, there are some data-dependent constructs. All but one are guarded by an IF branch that is false at compile time and are thus ignored. The remaining one is a WRITE statement for a register-allocated scalar. The memory accesses in this IF conditional are included in our analysis.

Table 6 evaluates *EstimateMisses* further for three more different cache configurations.

Program	Cache	Miss Ratio		Abs.	Sim.T	Exe.T
		Sim.	*E.M*	Err	(secs)	(secs)
Tomcatv	$C\#1$	19.84	19.91	0.07	4151.67	0.31
	$C\#2$	43.41	43.44	0.03	4428.01	0.40
	$C\#3$	9.92	9.97	0.05	4153.00	0.32
Swim	$C\#1$	13.37	13.26	0.11	8404.03	3.10
	$C\#2$	26.66	26.60	0.06	8605.37	3.50
	$C\#3$	6.71	6.59	0.12	8325.20	3.00
Applu	$C\#1$	14.18	15.10	0.92	17301.46	222.98
	$C\#2$	28.04	29.20	1.16	17524.20	230.30
	$C\#3$	6.96	7.92	0.96	17303.11	224.20

$C\#1$: $(C_s, L_s, k) = $ (64KB, 16B, direct)
$C\#2$: $(C_s, L_s, k) = $ (32KB, 8B, 2)
$C\#3$: $(C_s, L_s, k) = $ (128KB, 32B, 2)

Table 6. Cache misses from *EstimateMisses* (E.M) for three different cache configurations ($c = 95\%$ and $w = 0.05$).

7. Related work

We review the three recent compile-time analytical methods for predicting cache behaviour [4, 9, 11]. For a survey on trace-driven simulation, see [19]. Recently, Weikle *et al* [22] introduce a trace-based idea of viewing caches as filters. Their framework can potentially handle any programs consisting of any pattern of memory references.

Ghost *et al* [11] present their seminal work on using the CMEs to analyse statically a program's cache behaviour. This framework is targeted at isolated perfect nests consisting of straight-line assignments by exploiting only the reuse vectors between uniformly generated references in the same nest. They show that the CMEs can provide insights in choosing appropriate tile and pad sizes. Since analysing all iteration points is costly, an efficient implementation of the CMEs based on polyhedral theory and statistical sampling techniques is discussed in [2, 20].

N	BJ	BK	C_s	L_s	k	Δ_P	Δ_E
200	100	100	16	8	2	6.23	0.10
200	100	100	256	16	2	2.73	0.50
200	200	100	32	8	1	6.88	0.06
200	200	100	128	8	2	2.86	0.05
200	200	100	128	32	2	44.25	16.00
200	50	200	16	4	1	4.62	0.05
200	100	200	32	8	2	12.51	0.10
200	100	200	64	16	1	3.31	0.40
400	100	100	16	8	2	4.48	0.03
400	100	100	256	16	2	4.26	0.50
400	200	100	32	8	1	2.65	0.40
400	200	100	128	8	2	5.82	0.05
400	200	100	128	32	2	44.68	16.00
400	50	200	16	4	1	2.02	0.05
400	100	200	32	8	2	5.55	0.06
400	100	200	64	16	1	7.12	0.30

Table 7. Comparison with Fraguela et al's probabilistic method using MMT. Δ_p denotes the relative error between the estimated and real miss ratios for the probabilistic method and Δ_E for *EstimateMisses*.

Fraguela *et al* [9] rely on a probabilistic analytical method to provide a fast estimation of cache misses. While allowing multiple nests, they exploit only the reuse between references contained in the same nest (as can also be done in the CMEs.) These references differ by constants in their matching dimensions, forming a subset of uniformly generated references considered in the CMEs. Their experimental results using three examples indicate that their method can achieve a good degree of accuracy in estimating cache misses for perfect nests. Their two perfect nest examples can be analysed by the CMEs and are not compared here. The other one is a 3-D blocked imperfect nest computing AB^T (named MMT in Figure 7). Table 7 compares their method with ours. Our *EstimateMisses* produces better results in all cases. The two largest relative errors are due to the fact that the total number of misses is small in each case.

Chatterjee *et al* [4] present an ambitious method for *exactly* modelling the cache behaviour of loop nests. They use Presburger formulas to specify a program's cache misses, the Omega Calculator [15] to simplify the formulas, PolyLib [23] to obtain an indiscriminating union of polytopes, and finally, Ehrhart polynomials to count the number of integer points (i.e. misses) in each polytope [5]. They can formulate Presburger formulas for a looping structure consisting of imperfect nests, IF statements, references with affine accesses and non-linear data

layouts. That is, they are not restricted to uniformly generated references and linear array layouts. When solving their formulas, they provide only the cache miss numbers for 20×20 and 21×21 matrix multiplication without giving detailed execution times. In the case of matrix-vector product, they have derived the Presburger formulas for $N = 100$ but did not solve them.

Exact analysis is undoubtedly useful but can be too costly for realistic codes to be of any use in guiding compiler optimisations to improve performance. *FindMisses* can be exact if all necessary reuse vectors are used. Our current implementation exploits only the reuse among uniformly generated references. One future work is to derive systematically the reuse vectors for non-uniformly generated references and study their impact on miss analysis.

Neither of the three methods discussed above can handle call statements. In comparison with these existing techniques, our method can analyse complete regular programs efficiently with accuracy.

8. Conclusions

We have introduced a new characterisation of reuse vectors for quantifying reuse across multiple nests. Based on these reuse vectors, we have developed an analytical method for statically predicting the cache behaviour of complete programs with regular computations. We outlined two algorithms for computing cache misses. *FindMisses* analyses all iteration points and can predict exactly the cache misses for programs of small problem sizes. *EstimateMisses* analyses a sample of all memory accesses and can achieve close to real cache miss ratios in practical cases efficiently. The experimental results obtained for three kernels and three whole programs (one of which is Applu from SPECfp95 with 3868 lines, 16 subroutines and 2565 references) show that our method can analyse programs efficiently with a controlled degree of accuracy. Our method can be used to guide compiler locality optimisations and improve the speeds of cache simulators.

While this work represents a useful step towards an automatic analysis of whole programs, data-dependent constructs such as variable bounds, data-dependent IF conditionals and indirection arrays are still not analysable. We plan to investigate techniques for their analysis. To go beyond FORTRAN, we need to cope with pointers and recursive calls.

9. Acknowledgements

The authors would like to thank the referees for their helpful comments and suggestions. This work has been supported by an Australian Research Council Grant A10007149.

References

[1] E. Ayguadé, C. Barrado, A. González, J. Labarta, J. Llosa, D. López, S. Moreno, D. Padua, F. Reig, Q. Riera, and M. Valero. Ictineo: a tool for research on ILP. In *Supercomputing '96*, 1996. Research Exhibit "Polaris at Work".

[2] N. Bermudo, X. Vera, A. González, and J. Llosa. Optimizing cache miss equations polyhedra. In *4th Workshop on Interaction between Compilers and Computer Architectures (INTERACT-4)*, 2000.

[3] S. Carr and K. Kennedy. Compiler blockability of numerical algorithms. In *Supercomputing '92*, pages 114–124, Nov. 1992.

[4] S. Chatterjee, E. Parker, P. J. Hanlon, and A. R. Lebeck. Exact analysis of the cache behavior of nested loops. In *ACM SIGPLAN '01 Conference on Programming Language Design and Implementation (PLDI'01)*, pages 286–297, 2001.

[5] P. Clauss. Counting solutions to linear and nonlinear constraints through Ehrhart polynomials. In *ACM International Conference on Supercomputing (ICS'96)*, pages 278–285, Philadelphia, 1996.

[6] S. Coleman and K. S. McKinley. Tile size selection using cache organization and data layout. In *ACM SIGPLAN '95 Conference on Programming Language Design and Implementation (PLDI'95)*, pages 279–290, Jun. 1995.

[7] M. DeGroot. *Probability and statistics*. Addison-Wesley, 1998.

[8] K. A. Faigin, J. P. Hoeflinger, D. A. Padua, P. M. Petersen, and S. A. Weatherford. The Polaris internal representation. *International Journal of Parallel Programming*, 22(5):553–586, Oct. 1994.

[9] B. B. Fraguela, R. Doallo, and E. L. Zapata. Automatic analytical modeling for the estimation of cache misses. In *International Conference on Parallel Architectures and Compilation Techniques (PACT'99)*, 1999.

[10] D. Gannon, W. Jalby, and K. Gallivan. Strategies for cache and local memory management by global program transformations. *Journal of Parallel and Distributed Computing*, 5:587–616, 1988.

[11] S. Ghosh, M. Martonosi, and S. Malik. Cache miss equations: a compiler framework for analyzing and tuning memory behavior. *ACM Transactions on Programming Languages and Systems*, 21(4):703–746, 1999.

[12] S. C. V. V. Jain, A. R. Lebeck, S. Mundhra, and M. Thottethodi. Nonlinear array layout for hierarchical memory systems. In *ACM International Conference on Supercomputing (ICS'99)*, pages 444–453, Rhodes, Greece, Jun. 1999.

[13] M. Kandemir, A. Choudhary, P. Banerjee, and J. Ramanujam. A linear algebra framework for automatic determination of optimal data layouts. *IEEE Transactions on Parallel and Distributed Systems*, 10(2):115–135, Feb. 1999.

[14] M. Lam, E. E. Rothberg, and M. E. Wolf. The cache performance of blocked algorithms. In *4th International Conference on Architectural Support for Programming Languages and Operating Systems (ASPLOS'91)*, Apr. 1991.

[15] W. Pugh. The Omega test: A fast and practical integer programming algorithm for dependence analysis. *Communication of the ACM*, 35(8):102–114, Aug. 1992.

[16] W. Pugh. Counting solutions to Presburger formulas: how and why. In *ACM SIGPLAN '94 Conference on Programming Language Design and Implementation (PLDI'94)*, pages 121–134, 1994.

[17] G. Rivera and C.-W. Tseng. Data transformations for eliminating conflict misses. In *ACM SIGPLAN '98 Conference on Programming Language Design and Implementation (PLDI'98)*, pages 38–49, 1998.

[18] O. Temam, E. Granston, and W. Jalby. To copy or not to copy: A compile-time technique for accessing when data copying should be used to eliminate cache conflicts. In *Supercomputing '93*, pages 410–419, 1993.

[19] R. A. Uhlig and T. N. Mudge. Trace-driven memory simulation: a survey. *ACM Computing Surveys*, 29(3):128–170, Sept. 1997.

[20] X. Vera, J. Llosa, A. González, and N. Bermudo. A fast and accurate approach to analyze cache memory behavior. In *European Conference on Parallel Computing (Europar'00)*, 2000.

[21] X. Vera and J. Xue. Analysing cache behaviour for programs with IF statements. Technical Report UNSW-CSE-TR0107, University of New South Wales, May 2001.

[22] D. A. B. Weikle, K. Skadron, S. A. McKee, and W. A. Wulf. Cache as filters: a unifying model for memory hierarchy analysis. Technical Report CS-2000-16, University of Virginia, Jun. 2000.

[23] D. Wilde. A library for doing polyhedral operations. Technical Report 785, Oregon State University, 1993.

[24] M. E. Wolf and M. S. Lam. A data locality optimizing algorithm. In *ACM SIGPLAN '91 Conference on Programming Language Design and Implementation (PLDI'91)*, pages 30–44, Toronto, Ont., Jun. 1991.

[25] J. Xue. Unimodular transformations of nonperfectly nested loops. *Parallel Computing*, 22(12):1621–1645, 1997.

[26] J. Xue and C.-H. Huang. Reuse-driven tiling for data locality. *International Journal of Parallel Programming*, 26(6):671–696, 1998.

Memory Latency-Tolerance Approaches for Itanium Processors: Out-of-Order Execution vs. Speculative Precomputation

Perry H. Wang, Hong Wang, Jamison D. Collins[†], Ed Grochowski, Ralph M. Kling, and John P. Shen

Microprocessor Research Lab
Intel Labs, Intel Corporation
2200 Mission College Blvd
Santa Clara, CA 95052
http://www.intel.com/research/mrl/research/arch.htm

Abstract

The performance of in-order execution Itanium[TM] processors can suffer significantly due to cache misses. Two memory latency tolerance approaches can be applied for the Itanium processors. One uses an out-of-order (OOO) execution core; the other assumes multithreading support and exploits cache prefetching via speculative precomputation (SP). This paper evaluates and contrasts these two approaches. In addition, this paper assesses the effectiveness of combining the two approaches. For a select set of memory-intensive programs, an in-order SMT Itanium processor using speculative precomputation can achieve performance improvement (92%) comparable to that of an out-of-order design (87%). Applying both OOO and SP yields a total performance improvement of 141% over the baseline in-order machine. OOO tends to be effective in prefetching for L1 misses; whereas SP is primarily good at covering L2 and L3 misses. Our analysis indicates that the two approaches can be redundant or complementary depending on the type of delinquent loads that each targets. Both approaches are effective on delinquent loads in the loop body; however only SP is effective on delinquent loads found in loop control code.

1. Introduction

As the speeds of processors and memory systems continue to diverge, the performance of a processor depends more heavily on its ability to hide memory latency. In-order execution processors, such as the current Itanium[TM] processor designs [18], may suffer an expensive stall when servicing data cache misses. This problem is exacerbated in programs exhibiting hard-to-predict memory accesses. To effectively hide the latency for in-order execution processors, microarchitecture enhancements as well as software optimizations can be applied. For example, caches can be implemented as non-blocking caches to avoid unnecessary processor stalls, or the compiler can insert prefetch hints into the program. This paper evaluates and compares two memory latency tolerance microarchitecture approaches for the future Itanium processors. One approach is to implement an out-of-order execution core. The other approach retains in-order execution, but adds SMT [24] capability to the processor, enabling the use of speculative precomputation [4]. The primary goal of this study is to quantify how effective these two different techniques are in tolerating memory latency. In partiuclar, we are motivated to gain insights on benefits of combining both techniques in future Itanium processor designs.

Out-of-order (OOO) execution allows the processor to dynamically schedule the code and adapt to the run-time behavior of the program. Its major objectives are to prevent unnecessary stalls and to hide memory latency. Due to explicit support to control speculation and data speculation provided in the Itanium architecture [12], the advanced compiler can potentially achieve performance comparable to out-of-order execution through effective instruction scheduling. However, in applications with complex memory access patterns and very short load-to-use distances, it is difficult for the compiler to reduce the impact of cache misses for such applications. An out-of-order Itanium core can discover independent instructions dynamically and overlap their execution with the unpredictable outstanding cache misses, thereby effectively hiding the miss latency.

Speculative precomputation (SP) assumes an SMT machine and leverages SMT resources to aggressively prefetch for single-threaded applications. The SP approach targets a small set of delinquent loads that incur most of the cache

---

† Jamison D. Collins is currently a Ph.D. student in the Department of Computer Science and Engineering at the University of California, San Diego

187

misses, and generates a precomputation slice (p-slice) targeting each delinquent load. The early spawning and execution of a p-slice as a speculative thread in a separate thread context effectively prefetches for the corresponding delinquent load. Speculative precomputation threads can be spawned from either the original main thread (basic triggers) or from other speculative threads (chaining triggers) [4].

This paper presents our in-depth study of both approaches on a research Itanium processor pipeline. The paper is organized as follows. Section 2 describes related work. Section 3 presents the motivation and an overview of the two approaches. Section 4 compares the effectiveness of each approach in hiding latency at different levels of the memory hierarchy, as well as the tradeoffs for combining both. Section 5 provides detailed program analysis that explains why the two approaches may produce redundant latency-tolerance effort and how to judiciously integrate both techniques to achieve complementary benefits. Finally, Section 6 summarizes our key insights and concludes.

2. Related Work

In the past decade, OOO execution has become a de facto standard technology used in most high-end microprocessors [1, 9, 11], primarily due to its ability in latency tolerance [21]. Recently the possibility of incorporating OOO execution in Itanium processors has been explored [27], and two novel techniques were developed to facilitate the implementation of OOO execution for Itanium processors. In this paper, the OOO pipeline assumes the techniques described in [27].

Several recent research projects have considered leveraging simultaneous multithreading (SMT) [24] and chip multiprocessor (CMP) [14] resources to improve the performance of single-threaded applications. Recently, two forms of speculative precomputation using basic triggers and chaining triggers were studied for an SMT in-order Itanium research processor [4]. In [16], a technique called speculative data driven multithreading (DDMT), which is similar to using basic trigger, was studied for an OOO processor. In [5], Dundas et al. proposed pre-executing instructions under a cache miss. In [22], Sundaramoorthy et al. proposed Slipstream Processors in which a nonspeculative version of a program runs alongside a shortened speculative version to achieve performance gains. In [3], Chappell et al. proposed Simultaneous Subordinate Microthreading (SSMT) in which sequences of microcode are injected into the main thread to predict when certain events might occur. In [20], Song et al. proposed Assisted Execution in which tightly-coupled subordinate threads share fetch and execution resources on a dynamically scheduled processor to accelerate the main thread. In [26], Wallace et

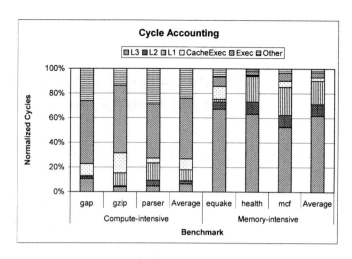

Figure 1. Breakdown of execution cycles of three compute-intensive benchmarks and three memory-intensive benchmarks on the in-order baseline Itanium processor.

al. proposed Threaded Multipath Execution which attempts to reduce performance loss due to branch mispredictions by forking speculative threads that execute both directions of a branch. As pointed out by Roth et al. in [17], these speculative multithreading approaches in effect are performing access execute decoupling as originally envisioned by Smith in [19] and further studied in [8, 13, 15]. However, unlike these past studies on access execute decoupling, recent studies on speculative multithreading, including this paper, does not assume any special hardware dedicated to decouple memory access. Instead, access and execute operations are decoupled as distinct speculative threads that can execute on different thread contexts in the general purpose SMT or CMP hardware.

3. Memory Latency Tolerance

3.1. Cache Miss Penalty Analysis

For memory-intensive programs, stalls due to L2 and L3 cache misses are often the biggest performance bottleneck. In contrast, compute-intensive programs presumably suffer cache miss penalties mostly from the L1 cache. In this paper, both categories of benchmarks are studied to provide a complete picture of the the benefit and limit of the latency-hiding techniques. One program set consists of three integer benchmarks *gap*, *gzip*, and *parser* from the CPU2000 suite [10]. These programs are compute-intensive and suffer relatively less memory access penalty. The other benchmark set comprises an integer benchmark *mcf*, a floating-point benchmark *equake*, both from the CPU2000 suite, and *health* from the Olden suite [2]. These benchmarks are known to suffer greatly from frequent L2 and L3 cache misses, thus resembling memory access behaviors of benchmarks like TPC-C. In particular, in these benchmarks, a set of very few static loads, called *delinquent loads* [4], are responsible for most cache penalty.

Figure 1 depicts where cycles are spent for these benchmarks running on a research in-order Itanium processor (see Section 4). The results are based on the execution of 200 million instructions from each benchmark. The total cycles are partitioned into six categories: *L3Cache*, *L2Cache*, *L1Dcache*, *Cache+Exec*, *Exec*, and *Other*. For each cycle of execution, if only one of L3, L2, L1-D is busy servicing a cache miss while no instruction is issued for execution, this cycle is attributed to the respective category in *L3Cache*, *L2Cache*, or *L1Dcache*. If more than one level of caches are busy servicing multiple cache misses concurrently, the current cycle is then attributed to one of these 3 levels in the priority of L1-D, L2, and L3, thus reflecting difference in criticality of these caches. If the processor issues an instruction to execution while none of the caches are busy servicing cache misses, the current cycle is accounted as *Exec*. If the cache hierarchy and instruction issue are both active in the same cycle, the cycle belongs to *Cache+Exec*. The *Other* category accounts for all other cycles, including the bubble cycles due to pipeline stall events, such as branch misprediction, instruction cache miss, and dependency induced stall like encountering compiler-inserted stop-bits. In essence, *L3Cache*, *L2Cache*, *L1Dcache* can characterize the sheer performance impact of memory access latency, while *Exec* measures cycles attributed to compute-intensive portion. The *Cache+Exec* measures the level of overlapping between memory access and execution.

To account for the trend towards multiple GHz clock frequencies and increasing memory latencies, we assume large penalties for cache misses in our simulation. While the L1-D hit is 2 cycles, the miss penalties for L1-D, L2, and L3 caches are 14, 30, and 230 cycles, respectively. So for a load that misses the L3 cache and having to accesses the memory, the total penalty of 230 cycles are split up and assigned as: 14 to *L1Dcache*, 16 to *L2Cache*, and the remaining 200 to *L3Cache*.

As shown in Figure 1, the first three benchmarks, *gap*, *gzip*, and *parser*, on average spend more than 70% of the time in computation or other non-cache activities. These compute-intensive benchmarks also spend less than 20% of the cycles in caches alone, and with another small portion of cache activities overlapping with instruction execution. This is primarily due to high L2 hit rates. However, for the other three benchmarks, the situation is very different. These benchmarks, *equake*, *health*, and *mcf*, on average suffer 90% of the execution time in L2 and L3 misses. The *L3Cache* cycles alone account for as much as 68% of the total time on *equake*. *Equake* spends about 25% of the

time on instruction execution, with less than 10% overlapping with memory operations. *Health* is even worse, spending only about 7% time on execution and the rest of processing time waiting for cache misses. Similarly, for *mcf*, 84% of the total time can be attributed to the cache miss latency. In summary, Figure 1 highlights quantititatively that these memory-intensive benchmarks suffer significant performance penalty due to cache misses in L2 and L3.

3.2. Latency Tolerance Techniques

To tackle the cache miss problems in these memory-intensive benchmarks, we evaluate two memory latency tolerance approaches, namely out-of-order execution and speculative precomputation. The OOO execution employs the use of a register renamer and reservation stations to dynamically schedule the in-flight instructions for execution. The latency tolerance of the OOO approach is achieved by finding and executing instructions independent from the missing loads while the misses are being served.

The latency tolerance of the SP approach is accomplished through the use of basic triggers and chaining triggers. The basic trigger is used by the main thread to spawn a speculative thread and initiate a prefetch stream, while the chaining trigger is used by a speculative precomputation thread to further spawn new speculative threads, thus sustaining the prefetch stream off the critical path of the main thread. Each speculative thread computes a slice of dependent instructions that lead to the prefetches for the delinquent loads, so that the data are brought into the cache before the main thread requests it. This is especially beneficial for pointer chasing code, where the addresses of the pointer-dereferencing loads are hard to predict.

As shown in [4], the use of chaining trigger can achieve impressive speedup due to two primary factors. First, using basic trigger alone will limit how far the spawned thread can run ahead of the main thread since the speculative thread of interest cannot be spawned unless the main thread encounters the trigger again. In addition, the overhead associated with thread spawning is often incurred on the main thread's critical path. In contrast, using chaining trigger allows speculative thread to be spawned from another speculative thread. This eliminates the overhead of thread spawning incurred directly on the critical path of the main thread. Second, chaining triggers allow the processor to better utilize available thread contexts. A p-slice in chaining trigger consists of three components: a prologue representing loop carried dependency computation, a chaining trigger, and then an epilogue representing non-loop-carried dependency computation leading to a delinquent load prefetch. As soon as the prologue has been executed, chaining triggers cause speculative threads to spawn additional threads before the epilogue computes the effective addresses for the delinquent load prefetches. If this prologue can be exe-

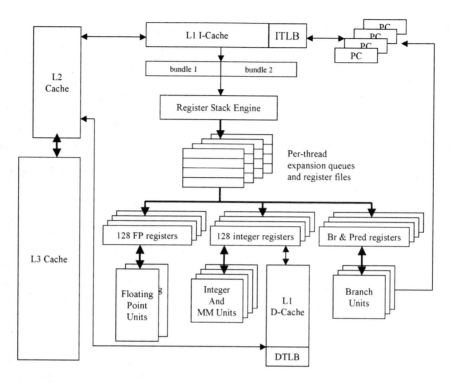

Figure 2. Pipeline organization of a research Itanium processor with SMT support

cuted quickly, speculative threads can be rapidly spawned to populate all available hardware thread contexts, leading to multiple concurrent prefetches that are serviced by the non-blocking caches. For the SP-enabled in-order configuration, we assume a rather conservative yet more realistic form of chaining triggers where speculative threads can only be spawned off at the retirement stage of the pipeline. Moreoever, the thread that spawns a speculative thread also incurs additional penalty including pipeline flush followed by the transfer time of the live-in states before the spawned thread can start.

Both OOO and SP aim to hide memory latency by overlapping instruction execution with the service to outstanding cache misses. OOO tries to overlap the outstanding cache miss cycles by finding instructions independent from the outstanding missing load in the instruction window and execute them as early as possible. SP prefetches for the delinquent loads far ahead of the non-speculative thread, thus overlapping future cache misses with the current execution of the non-speculative thread.

While both SP and OOO can reduce data cache miss penalty incurred on the program's critical path, they differ in the targeted memory access instructions and effectiveness for different levels of cache hierarchy. On one hand, while OOO can potentially hide miss penalty for all load and store instructions to all layers of cache hierarchy, it is most effective in tolerating L1 miss penalty. But for misses on L2 or L3, OOO may have difficulty in finding sufficient

independent instructions to execute and overlap the much longer cache access latency. On the other hand, SP by design only targets a small set of delinquent loads which incur cache misses all the way to the memory. More quantitative analysis will be presented in the next section.

4. Experiments

In this section, we begin with an introduction of our research Itanium processor pipelines and a description of the simulation environment. We then present in-depth analysis of performance data, show how OOO and SP distinctly achieve cache miss tolerance, and shed light on potential benefits of integrating both techniques.

4.1. Simulation Environment

Our experiments are carried out by using SMT-SIM/IPFsim, a version of SMTSIM simulator [23] adapted to work with Intel Itanium-related simulation environment [25]. This infrastructure is execution-driven and cycle-accurate. It simulates a variety of single-threaded and multithreaded Itanium research processor models, including in-order pipeline, out-of-order pipeline, and SMT support. It enables comprehensive evaluation of thread speculation techniques including speculative precomputation using chaining triggers and basic triggers.

In our study, the baseline in-order Itanium pipeline is a two-bundle wide, 12-stage microarchitecture. It resembles the microarchitectures in [18], albeit with a longer pipeline to account for higher core frequency. It supports SMT mechanism with 4 total hardware thread contexts. Compared to the baseline in-order pipeline, the OOO pipeline assumes two additional front-end pipe stages to account for the extra OOO complexity, and explicit OOO register rename stage and scheduler stage, for a total of 16 pipeline stages. Furthermore, the OOO pipeline incorporates the optimization techniques introduced in [27]. Non-blocking caches are assumed for both in-order and OOO models. Full details on the processor models are described in Table 1. The pipeline organization is depicted in Figure 2.

All benchmarks studied in this paper are compiled with the Intel Electron compiler [6, 7] using the advanced instruction-level parallelism compilation techniques, including aggressive use of control speculation, data speculation, predication, software pipelining and software prefetching. Extensive profile-feedback guided optimizations are also used to further improve the quality of these benchmark binaries.

4.2. Speedup Analysis

4.2.1. OOO vs SP. We first compare the speedups gained by the OOO processor and the SP-enabled in-order processor respectively over the baseline in-order processor. As indicated in Figure 1, the in-order baseline processor suffers significant performance losses due to the large number of cache misses incurred in the memory-intensive benchmarks. The in-order pipeline stalls when an instruction attempts to use the destination register of an outstanding load miss. The memory-intensive benchmarks often have extensive use of pointer de-references, which are translated into adjacent dependent loads with very short distances in between. Consequently, cache misses on the dependent loads will quickly induce pipeline stalls upon these nearly immediate uses. Figure 3 shows that the OOO processor can achieve an impressive speedup over the baseline in-order processor, with 87% average across the memory-intensive benchmarks. For the compute-intensive benchmarks, OOO can achieve on average 27% speedup over in-order due to OOO's ability to tolerate L1 cache misses.

The SP-enabled in-order processor, albeit only targeting the top 10 most delinquent loads that miss frequently in the L2 or L3 caches, can achieve an average speedup of 92% over the baseline in-order processor for the memory-intensive benchmarks. This speedup is slightly higher than the 87% speedup achieved by the OOO processor. Most noticeably, for *health*, the SP-enabled in-order processor actually outperforms the OOO processor by 40%. As shown in Figure 1, these three memory-intensive benchmarks suffer performance loss from cache misses at nearly all levels of the memory hierarchy. The SP approach can effectively initiate long range prefetches, attacking load miss latency far

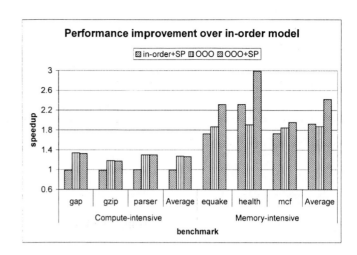

Figure 3. Speedups of in-order+SP, OOO, and OOO+SP over in-order

beyond the size of the OOO instruction window.

However, for the compute-intensive benchmarks, the SP-enabled in-order processor actually performs slightly worse than the baseline in-order processor, while the OOO processor outperforms the baseline in-order processor by an average of 27%. The explanation lies in the fact that these benchmarks, though incurring large amount of L1 misses, rarely miss in L2. So the timeliness of the SP prefetches for L1 misses is offset by the overhead incurred from spawning speculative threads. Worse yet, these SP threads can actually slow down the main thread due to increased resource contention. Obviously, the performance data suggest that the overhead of SP outweighs its benefit for the compute-intensive benchmarks.

4.2.2. Combination of OOO and SP. In perspective, OOO and SP can achieve effective tolerance for different memory latencies at different layers of the memory hierarchy. It is naturally of great interest to further investigate whether a combination of OOO and SP can achieve additive benefit that is greater than using either alone. To this end, we consider the integration of SP in an SMT OOO machine. Similar to the organization in [16], the cross-thread register communication can be implemented via sharing renaming table rather than through explicit copy between register files of different thread contexts. Specifically, if an input register of an instruction in one thread is dependent on an output register of an instruction in another thread, then both registers can be mapped to the same physical register via the register renaming table. Unlike [16] which only uses basic triggers to spawn precomputation threads, the SP considered in this integration also employs chaining triggers.

For all memory-intensive benchmarks, the SP-enabled OOO processor shows significant speedups over the base-

Pipeline Structure	In-order: 12 stage pipeline. Out-of-order: 16 stage pipeline.
Fetch	2 bundles from 1 thread, or 1 bundle from 2 threads
Branch Predictor	2K entry GSHARE 256 entry 4-way associative BTB
Expansion Queue	Private, per-thread, in-order 8 bundle queue
Register Files	Private, per-thread register files. 128 Integer Registers, 128 FP Registers, 64 Predicate Registers, 128 Control Registers
Execute Bandwidth	In-order: 6 instructions from 1 thread or 3 instructions from 2 threads Out-of-order: 6-bundle or 18 instruction schedule window
Cache Structure	L1 (separate I and D): 16K 4-way, 8 way banked, 2 cycle latency L2 (shared): 256K 4-way, 8 way banked, 14 cycle latency L3 (shared): 3072K 12-way, 1 way banked, 30 cycle latency Fill buffer (MSHR): 16 entries. All caches have 64 byte lines
Memory Latency	230 cycle latency, TLB Miss Penalty 30 cycles

Table 1. Details of the research Itanium processor

line in-order processor, with an average speedup of 141%. For *heath*, the SP-enabled OOO processor achieves an impressive speedup of 198%. For the compute-intensive benchmarks, the average speedup is 26%, slightly lower than the 27% speedup achieved by the OOO processor without SP.

How effective the two approaches work together depends on the benchmarks. For *health*, the OOO and SP approaches individually achieve about 131% and 90% speedup, respectively. Together the two approaches achieve a near additive speedup of 198%, demonstrating potential complementary effects between the two approaches. For this particular benchmark, most cache misses originate from one very tight loop. It consists of pointer chasing loads in the loop control, which computes loop carried dependency between consecutive iterations. The computation of the data deferenced from the pointers is in the loop body. While the SP expedites the pointer chasing in the loop control, the OOO execution can overlap cache accesses in the loop body from different iterations. In Section 5, a more thorough analysis of program behavior will be elaborated to guide judicious integration of SP and OOO.

Equake also benefits from the integration of OOO and SP. As shown in [4], *equake* has a large number of delinquent loads and the top 10 worst delinquent loads targeted by SP only account for about 60% of total cache misses. Thus for the SP-enabled OOO processor, there are plenty of opportunities for the OOO core to tolerate cache misses incurred by the rest of delinquent loads.

For *mcf*, the SP-enabled OOO processor shows less than 10% of improvement over the OOO processor, and just about 22% over the SP-enabled in-order processor. The primary reason is that, for the loop that causes the largest number of misses, OOO and SP redundantly cover the same set of delinquent loads in the loop body. Thus, their respective gains are not additive as seen in *health*.

For the compute-intensive benchmarks, SP does not bring about any speedup beyond using OOO alone. For the SP-enabled in-order processor, the overhead associated with thread spawning and increased resource contention from the SP threads often result in performance degration of the main thread. It is worthwhile to note that the degradation is rather limited. This is primarily due to the use of outstanding slice counter (OSC) [4] in SP that actively monitors and controls the progress of the speculative thread relative to that of the main thread. OSC ensures that the speculative thread would neither run behind the main thread nor too far ahead.

4.3. Cache Latency Reduction Analysis

To further understand the speedups achieved by OOO, SP and a combination of both techniques, we present in Figure 4 a detailed cycle breakdown for these techniques. All data are normalized to the execution cycle count of the baseline in-order shown in Figure 1.

4.3.1. OOO vs SP. Figure 4 shows how much miss penalty OOO and SP manage to reduce at different levels of the cache hierarchy. For *health*, while the *L3Cache* cycles account for 62% of the total execution time on the baseline in-order processor, on OOO, the *L3Cache* cycles drops to only 28%. The reduction in *L3Cache* cycles on the SP-enabled in-order processor is even more dramatic, a mere 9%. Clearly, SP is effective in reducing stalls due to L2 or L3 cache misses, even though only the top 10 delinquent loads are considered. However, for the compute-intensive benchmarks, SP degrades performance. The primary cause is that most cache accesses missing at L1 would hit in L2 and leave little headroom for the SP threads to run ahead and produce timely prefetches.

Unlike SP, the OOO processor handles all memory operations including those beyond the top 10 delinquent loads. In addition to its ability to tolerate cache misses, OOO can also tolerate long execution latency on functional units. For example, *parser*, when executing on an OOO processor, achieves a 10% reduction in L1 cache stall cycles, but

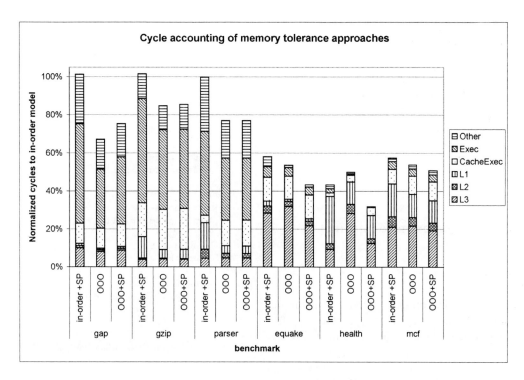

Figure 4. Cycle breakdown of in-order+SP, OOO, and OOO+SP

reaches an even larger 12% reduction in the execution cycles accounted by *Exec*. Furthermore, *Cache+Exec* shows an increase of 9%.

For the memory-intensive benchmarks, the OOO processor is very effective in hiding L1 cache misses. For *health*, the OOO processor reduces the *L1Dcache* cycles to only 12%. Similarly for *mcf*, the OOO processor reduces *L1Dcache* cycles to 12%. For *equake* where the worst 10 delinquent loads account for about 60% of total L1 cache misses, the OOO can benefit far more delinquent loads and reduce the *L1Dcache* cycles to a mere 2%.

4.3.2. Combination of OOO and SP. Figure 4 also shows how effectively a combination of both approaches, namely OOO+SP, can tolerate latency. For *health*, SP alone can reduce *L3Cache* cycles to 9% without improving *L1Cache*. (25%), and OOO alone can reduce *L1Cache* to 11% with relatively smaller reduction in *L3Cache* (28%). By attacking both L1 and L3 cache misses, SP and OOO in combination can achieve reduction to 12% for both *L1Cache* and *L3Cache*. This displays a complementary relationship between OOO and SP, where each covers misses at relatively disjoint levels of the cache hierarchy. Another interesting observation is that on the SP-enabled OOO processor, almost all instruction executions are overlapped with memory accesses, a desired effect of memory tolerance techniques.

For *equake*, OOO not only contributes to effectively hid-

ing latency for the L1 cache misses, it also helps substantially in reducing the L3 penalty in addition to the portion reduced by SP. This is primarily due to the inherient data parallelism among operations on the multi-dimentional arrays in *equake* algorithm. As soon as SP brings in sub-array data along the leading dimension, OOO execution can perform data accesses to multiple sub-arrays in other dimensions in parallel. So OOO is effective in tolerating L3 cache misses incurred on these parallel sub-array accesses, while the SP is effective in tolerating L3 misses incurred on traversing the leading dimension.

For *mcf*, the proportional reduction in cycle counts in each category does not vary as much, since most of the delinquent loads in the loop body are covered redundantly by the two approaches. This clearly indicates both approaches overlap the efforts to tolerate latency. However, as to be discussed in the next section, it is possible to judiciously apply SP only to selected part of the code, and minimize redundant efforts to achieve benefit complementary to OOO.

5. Program Behavior Analysis

To further understand why SP and OOO seem to be redundant in some cases and complementary in other cases, we further analyze program behavior to highlight the existence of two classes of delinquent loads that differ in criticality. Depending on how SP and OOO cover these delinquent loads, the effort can be redundant or complementary.

```
arc = arcs + group_pos;
for( ; arc < stop_arcs; arc += nr_group ) {
  if( arc->ident > BASIC ) {
    red_cost = arc->cost
             - arc->tail->potential
             + arc->head->potential;
    if(bea_is_dual_infeasible(arc,red_cost)){
      basket_size++;
      perm[basket_size]->a = arc;
      perm[basket_size]->cost = red_cost;
      perm[basket_size]->abs_cost =
                          ABS(red_cost);
    }
  }
}
```

Figure 5. First example from mcf

5.1. Loop Control

In the memory-intensive programs, frequent and unpredictable memory accesses that can cause severe performance loss are mostly observed in loops. Some loops perform stride-based array traversal. In other types of loops, the traversal is based on pointer chasing over linked data structure, where a pointer is de-referenced to obtain another data-accessing pointer for the next iteration. Regardless how the data structure is traversed, a subset of the instructions in a loop that computes the live-in registers for the next iteration can be identified as the *loop control*. The actual work done in each iteration is carried out by the rest of the instructions in the *loop body*. Loop control may include induction variable updates using stride or pointer derferences. Two examples from *mcf* are shown in Figure 5 and Figure 6. The instructions in loop control are highlighted in bold-faced. In Figure 5, the loop control consists of the stride reference code which, at every iteration, increments arc by a constant nr_group. Figure 6 shows two inner while loops as part of the outlier loop control, where the pointer node needs to be dereferenced in order to calculate the node for the next iteration of the outer loop. Loops in both examples have delinquent loads, which are shown in italic, and they occur in the loop body.

5.2. Criticality in Execution of Loops

Since the loop control instructions dictate the execution of the next iteration, the OOO processor cannot look beyond the current iteration without resolving the loop-carried dependency in the loop control first. Thus, cache misses triggered in the loop control could potentially stall the out-of-order execution, thereby lengthening the critical path.

Figure 7 illustrates the execution of three loop iterations on the OOO processor. The top portion of the figure shows the instruction execution with no cache misses in the loop control, while two delinquent loads from the loop body incur cache misses in each loop iteration.

```
while( node != root ) {
  while( node ) {
    if( node->orientation == UP )
      node->potential = node->basic_arc->cost
                      + node->pred->potential;
    else {
      node->potential = node->pred->potential
                      - node->basic_arc->cost;
      checksum++;
    }
    tmp = node;
    node = node->child;
  }
  node = tmp;
  while( node->pred ) {
    tmp = node->sibling;
    if( tmp ) {
      node = tmp;
      break;
    }
    else
      node = node->pred;
  }
}
```

Figure 6. Second example from mcf

A key benefit of out-of-order execution is the ability of the processor to look for independent instructions beyond the current executing instruction when its data sources are not available. Even when the delinquent loads in the loop body incur long cache miss latencies, the OOO processor is able to partially, if not completely, hide the latency by overlapping the misses, as indicated by the six cache miss bars in Figure 7. As long as the memory subsystem is not saturated, the misses can be serviced in parallel.

On the other hand, the execution of the loop carried dependency in loop control has to be serialized. The bottom part of Figure 7 illustrates the same execution as the top, except that the loop control execution is stretched out due to cache misses. Because of the loop-carried dependency, the OOO processor cannot effectively advance past the current iteration since it needs to wait for the pending cache misses. This prevents the OOO processor from finding independent instructions from the next iteration and beyond. If the loop control takes more time to finish, the overall execution time is in fact lengthened.

Therefore, for OOO execution, not all cache misses that occur in loops are equally important. Misses incurred in loop control may stall the OOO pipeline, thus deemed more critical than those incurred in loop body.

5.3. Redundant Efforts

When the targeted delinquent load is in the loop body, the SP approach could be prefetching for a cache miss that can be just as effectively covered by OOO execution. When these two latency-tolerance approaches are combined, the efforts to hide the cache miss latency of delinquent loads in

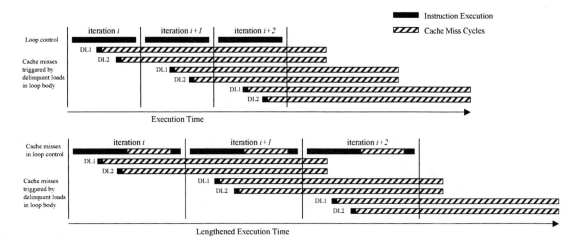

Figure 7. OOO Execution of loop control and loop body

the loop body may become redundant. For example, in Figure 5, the delinquent loads are in the loop body and the loop control is a simple stride based update of induction variable. The OOO processor needs not stall upon cache misses on the delinquent loads for these pointer dereferences, since during a pending cache miss, the OOO processor is able to compute induction variable update in the loop control rapidly, and run many iterations ahead.

Hence, the combination of OOO and SP applied to this loop cannot improve performance beyond what each of them can accomplish alone.

5.4. Combined Effectiveness

A key to effectively utilizing speculative precomputation on an OOO processor is to avoid overlapping the efforts of these two latency-tolerance approaches. As discussed in Section 5.2, lengthy loop control usually is on the critical path for the OOO execution. Thus, it is crucial for SP to target critical cache misses in the loop control. These cache misses may or may not come from the delinquent loads, but it is imperative for the SP thread to resolve them first so that the OOO processor can continue to advance as fast as possible.

When cache misses occur in the loop control, the triggering loads usually come from either stride-based reference or pointer dereference. Stride reference in the loop control can be predicted by the compiler or a hardware prefetcher. However, the addresses from pointer dereferences are hard to predict. Thus, the SP thread can be used to prefetch for the critical loads in loop control, while OOO execution can handle delinquent loads in the loop body.

When delinquent loads occur in the loop control, like the case in *health*, the combined benefits from OOO and SP are even greater. In *mcf* loop in Figure 6, even though the pointer dereferences, `node->child` and `node->pred`,

in the loop control are not among the top 10 delinquent loads, they still constitute a considerable number of cache misses. Thus, on an OOO processor, when SP are applied to this loop, the SP thread can contribute to speeding up the loop control consisting of the two inner `while` loops. Our data have shown that on *mcf*, a moderate amount of improvement can be achieved by using SP over using OOO alone.

Hence, by judiciously targeting SP to cache misses incurred in loop control, both OOO and SP can complement each other and further increase the program performance improvement from either approach alone.

6. Conclusion

In this paper we examine two approaches to reducing the impact of cache misses on the performance of Itanium processors, namely out-of-order (OOO) execution and speculative precomputation (SP). We also study the effectiveness of combining the two approaches. There are three major conclusions we can draw from this study. First, for the selected set of memory-intensive benchmarks, it appears that OOO and SP are equally effective in achieving comparable performance gains. This implies that if an Itanium machine already has the SMT mechanism, SP can be used to leverage the SMT resources to achieve single thread performance improvement comparable to that of an Itanium machine with an OOO execution core. Granted, the relative hardware complexity involved in implementing SMT vs. OOO is an issue that needs to be addressed. However, the SMT capability can potentially allow the machine to also achieve better throughput on threaded or multitasking workloads .

Second, there is a complex interaction between OOO execution and SP-based prefetching in terms of reducing the cache miss penalty. For some benchmarks, these two approaches overlap and their efforts are redundant, i.e. they target the same set of cache misses from the loop body. On the other hand, other benchmarks indicate that these two approaches have an additive effect in achieving overall performance gains. This means that the two approaches are targeting different sets of cache misses, i.e. SP prefetches for the loads in the loop control while OOO hides the cache misses in the loop body, and their effectiveness is complementary in achieving performance gains. Therefore, for certain memory-intensive programs, the application of SP on top of an OOO machine is justified.

Third, the use of chaining triggers in SP is effective in achieving performance gains even for an OOO machine. Previously reported speedups of SP [4] were very impressive. However, these speedups were relative to an in-order machine. This study has shown that, for a set of memory-intensive benchmarks, SP with chaining triggers can achieve on average an additional 55% speedup over an OOO baseline design. The SP performance data is based on prefetching for only the ten worst delinquent loads and spawning speculative threads at the instruction commit pipeline stage. With greater coverage of delinquent loads and more aggressive spawning, SP with chaining triggers will likely achieve additional speedups.

Acknowledgment

The authors would like to thank Justin Rattner and Dean Tullsen for their support, and the anonymous reviewers for their comments.

References

[1] D. P. Bhandarkar. *Alpha Implementations and Architecture.* Digital Press, Newton, MA, 1996.

[2] M. Carlisle. Olden: Parallelizing Programs with Dynamic Data Structures on Distributed-Memory Machines. Technical Report PhD Thesis, Princeton University Department of Computer Science, June 1996.

[3] R. Chappell, J. Stark, S. Kim, S. Reinhardt, and Y. Patt. Simultaneous Subordinate Microthreading. In *26th International Symposium on Computer Architecture*, May 1999.

[4] J. Collins, H. Wang, D. Tullsen, H. C, Y.-F. Lee, D. Lavery, and J. Shen. Speculative Precomputation: Long-range Prefetching of Delinquent Loads. In *28th International Symposium on Computer Architecture*, July 2001.

[5] J. Dundas and T. Mudge. Improving Data Cache Performance by Pre-Executing Instructions Under a Cache Miss. In *11th Supercomputing Conference*, July 1997.

[6] J. B. et al. The Intel IA-64 Compiler Code Generator. *IEEE Micro*, Sept-Oct 2000.

[7] R. K. et al. An Advanced Optimizer for the IA-64 Architecture. *IEEE Micro*, Nov-Dec 2000.

[8] M. K. Farrens, P. Ng, and P. Nico. A Comparison of Superscalar and Decoupled Access/Execute Architectures. In *26th International Symposium on Microarchitecture*, Nov 1993.

[9] J. Heinrich. *MIPS R10000 Microprocessor User's Manual.* MIPS Technologies Inc, September 1996.

[10] J. L. Henning. SPEC CPU2000: measuring CPU performance in the new millennium. *IEEE Computer*, July 2000.

[11] G. Hinton, D. Sager, M. Upton, D. Boggs, D. Carmean, A. Kyker, and P. Roussel. The Microarchitecture of the Pentium 4 Processor. *Intel Technology Journal*, Q1 2001.

[12] J. Huck, D. Morris, J. Ross, A. Knies, H. Mulder, and R. Zahir. Introducing the IA-64 Architecture. *IEEE Micro*, Sept-Oct 2000.

[13] G. P. Jones and N. P. Topham. A Limitation Study into Access Decoupling. In *The 3rd Euro-Par Conference*, Aug 1997.

[14] K. Olukotun, B. Nayfeh, L. Hammond, K. Wilson, and K. Chang. The Case for a Single-Chip Multiprocessor. In *7th International Conference on Architectural Support for Programming Languages and Operating Systems*, Oct 1996.

[15] S. Palacharla, N. Jouppi, and J. Smith. Complexity-Effective Superscalar Processors. In *24th International Symposium on Computer Architecture*, 1997.

[16] A. Roth and G. Sohi. Speculative Data-Driven Multithreading. In *7th IEEE International Symposium on High Performance Computer Architecture*, Jan 2001.

[17] A. Roth, C. B. Zilles, and G. S. Sohi. Microarchitectural Miss/Execute Decoupling. In *MEDEA Workshop*, Oct 2000.

[18] H. Sharangpani and K. Aurora. Itanium Processor Microarchitecture. *IEEE Micro*, Sept-Oct 2000.

[19] J. E. Smith. Decoupled Access/Execute Computer Architecture. In *9th International Symposium on Computer Architecture*, July 1982.

[20] Y. Song and M. Dubois. Assisted Execution. Technical Report CENG 98-25, Department of EE-Systems, University of Southern California, Oct 1998.

[21] S. Srinivasan and A. Lebeck. Load Latency Tolerance in Dynamically Scheduled Processors. In *31st International Symposium on Microarchitecture*, Nov 1998.

[22] K. Sundaramoorthy, Z. Purser, and E. Rotenberg. Slipstream Processors: Improving both Performance and Fault Tolerance. In *9th International Conference on Architectural Support for Programming Languages and Operating Systems*, Nov 2000.

[23] D. M. Tullsen. Simulation and Modeling of a simultaneous multithreaded processor. In *22nd Annual Computer Measurement Group Conference*, Dec 1996.

[24] D. M. Tullsen, S. J. Eggers, and H. M. Levy. Simultaneous Multithreading: Maximizing On-Chip Parallelism. In *22nd International Symposium on Computer Architecture*, Jun 1995.

[25] R. Uhlig, R. Rishtein, O. Gershon, I. Hirsh, and H. Wang. SoftSDV: A Presilicon Software Development Environment for the IA-64 Architecture. *Intel Technology Journal*, Q4 1999.

[26] S. Wallace, B. Calder, and D. Tullsen. Threaded Multiple Path Execution. In *25th International Symposium on Computer Architecture*, June 1998.

[27] P. Wang, H. Wang, R. Kling, K. Ramakrishnan, and J. Shen. Register Renaming and Scheduling for Dynamic Execution of Predicated Code. In *7th IEEE International Symposium on High Performance Computer Architecture*, Jan 2001.

Quantifying Load Stream Behavior

Suleyman Sair   Timothy Sherwood   Brad Calder

Department of Computer Science and Engineering
University of California, San Diego
{ssair,sherwood,calder}@cs.ucsd.edu

Abstract

The increasing performance gap between processors and memory will force future architectures to devote significant resources towards removing and hiding memory latency. The two major architectural features used to address this growing gap are caches and prefetching.

In this paper we perform a detailed quantification of the cache miss patterns for the Olden benchmarks, SPEC 2000 benchmarks, and a collection of pointer based applications. We classify misses into one of four categories corresponding to the type of access pattern. These are next-line, stride, same-object (additional misses that occur to a recently accessed object), or pointer-based transitions. We then propose and evaluate a hardware profiling architecture to correctly identify which type of access pattern is being seen. This access pattern identification could be used to help guide and allocate prefetching resources, and provide information to feedback-directed optimizations.

A second goal of this paper is to identify a suite of challenging pointer-based benchmarks that can be used to focus the development of new software and hardware prefetching algorithms, and identify the challenges in performing prefetching for these applications using new metrics.

1 Introduction

One of the most important impediments to current and future processor performance is the memory bottleneck. Processor clock speeds are increasing at an exponential rate, much faster than DRAM access time improvements [21]. Cache memory hierarchies and data prefetching are the two primary techniques used in current processors to try and hide or eliminate memory latency. Memory latency can be removed if data is found to be in the cache. For data not in the cache, data prefetching is used to hide the latency by beginning the fetch before it is needed.

Several models have been proposed for prefetching data to reduce or eliminate load latency. These range from inserting compiler-based prefetches to pure hardware-based data prefetching. Compiler-based prefetching annotates load instructions or inserts explicit prefetch instructions to bring data into the cache before it is needed to hide the load latency. These approaches use locality analysis to insert prefetch instructions, showing significant improvements [14]. Hardware-based prefetching approaches are able to dynamically predict address streams and prefetch down them in ways that may be hard to do using compiler analysis. In [18], we presented a prefetching architecture that uses a predictor-directed stream buffer to prefetch down data miss streams independent of the instruction stream being executed. Other hardware schemes attempt to pre-compute the computation kernel on a separate thread or co-processor to reduce the memory latency [1, 6, 12].

We first show how to classify load miss streams into different classes based on their miss access patterns. We show for a large number of programs what types of accesses are causing misses so that they may be targeted for future research. We further show how this classification can be done efficiently in hardware with a high degree of accuracy, so that architectural structures such as the caches or prefetching engines can be made access pattern aware. We classify these loads into four types of access patterns or streams – (1) next-line, (2) stride, (3) same-object (additional misses to a recently referenced heap object), or (4) pointer-based misses.

Out of these four types of cache miss streams, pointer-based streams can be the most difficult to eliminate using existing hardware and software prefetching algorithms. To better understand the behavior of these loads and their applications we examine two new metrics. The first metric, *Object Fan Out*, is used to quantify the number of pointers in an object that are transitioned and frequently miss in the cache. The second metric, *Pointer Variability*, quantifies how many pointer transitions are stable versus how many are frequently changing. A pointer transition is a load that loads a pointer. Pointer variability shows how many times a pointer transition for a given *address* loads a pointer different from the last pointer that was loaded from that address. Programs with low object fan out and pointer variability will be much easier to prefetch, in comparison to programs that have high object fan out and variability, and we show that a large percentage of misses in real programs fall into this second category.

An additional goal of this paper is to compare the behavior of Olden, SPEC 2000, and set of additional pointer-based benchmarks. This is to identify a suite of challenging pointer-based benchmarks that can be used to focus the

197

Program	Description
burg	A program that generates a fast tree parser using BURS technology. It is commonly used to construct optimal instruction selectors for use in compiler code generation. The input used was a grammar that scribes the VAX instruction set architecture.
deltablue	A constraint solution system implemented in C++. It has an abundance of short lived heap objects.
dot	Dot is taken from the AT&T's GraphViz suite. It is a tool for automatically making hierarchical layouts of directed graphs. Automatic generation of graph drawings has important applications in key technologies such as database design, software engineering, VLSI and network design and visual interfaces in other domains.
equake	Equake is from the SPEC 2000 benchmark suite. The program simulates the propagation of elastic waves in large, highly heterogeneous valleys, such as California's San Fernando Valley, or the Greater Los Angeles Basin. The goal is to recover the time history of the ground motion everywhere within the valley due to a specific seismic event. Computations are performed on an unstructured mesh that locally resolves wavelengths, using a finite element method.
mcf	Mcf is from the SPEC 2000 benchmark suite. It is a combinatorial optimization algorithm solving a minimum cost network flow problem.
sis	Synthesis of synchronous and asynchronous circuits. It includes a number of capabilities such as state minimization and optimization. The program has approximately 172,000 lines of source code and performs a lot of pointer arithmetic.
vis	VIS (Verification Interacting with Synthesis) is a tool that integrates the verification, simulation, and synthesis of finite-state hardware systems. It uses a Verilog front end and supports fair CTL model checking, language emptiness checking, combinational and sequential equivalence checking, cycle-based simulation, and hierarchical synthesis.

Table 1: Description of pointer-based benchmarks used.

development of new software and hardware prefetch algorithms.

2 Methodology

We make use of both profiling and detailed cycle accurate simulation in this study. When performing profiling we use Compaq's ATOM [20] tool, to gather miss rates and perform base line classifications.

The simulator used in this study was derived from the SimpleScalar/Alpha 3.0 tool set [2], a suite of functional and timing simulation tools for the Alpha AXP ISA. The timing simulator executes only user-level instructions, performing a detailed timing simulation of an aggressive 8-way dynamically scheduled microprocessor with two levels of instruction and data cache memory. Simulation is execution-driven, including execution down any speculative path until the detection of a fault, TLB miss, or branch mis-prediction.

To perform our evaluation we collected results from the complete SPEC 2000 integer benchmark suite, selected

SPEC 2000 floating point benchmarks, the popular programs from the Olden benchmark suite, and a set of other pointer intensive programs. The pointer intensive programs we will examine in detail are described in Table 1. All programs were compiled on a DEC Alpha AXP-21264 processor using the DEC FORTRAN, C or C++ compilers under OSF/1 V4.0 operating system using full compiler optimization (-O4 -ifo).

2.1 Baseline Architecture

Our baseline simulation configuration models a next generation out-of-order processor microarchitecture. We have selected the parameters to capture underlying trends in microarchitecture design. The processor has a large window of execution; it can fetch up to 8 instructions per cycle. It has a 128 entry re-order buffer with a 64 entry load/store buffer. To compensate for the added complexity of disambiguating loads and stores in a large execution window, we increased the store forward latency to 2 cycles.

To make sure that the load classification speedups we report are from eliminating those load memory latencies and not from compensating for a conservative memory disambiguation policy, we implemented perfect store sets [5]. Perfect store sets cause loads to only be dependent on stores that write to the same memory, i.e when they are actually dependent instructions. In this way loads will not be held up by false dependencies.

In the baseline architecture, there is an 8 cycle minimum branch mis-prediction penalty. The processor has 8 integer ALU units, 4-load/store units, 2-FP adders, 2-integer MULT, and 2-FP MULT/DIV. The latencies are: ALU 1 cycle, MULT 3 cycles , FP Adder 2 cycles, FP Mult 4 cycles, and FP DIV 12 cycles. All functional units, except the divide units, are fully pipelined allowing a new instruction to initiate execution each cycle. We use a McFarling gshare predictor [13] to drive our fetch unit. Two predictions can be made per cycle with up to 8 instructions fetched.

We rewrote the memory hierarchy in SimpleScalar to better model bus occupancy, bandwidth, and pipelining of the second level cache and main memory. The L1 instruction cache is a 32K 2-way associative cache with 32-byte lines. The baseline results are run with a 32K 2-way associative data cache with 32-byte lines. A 1 Megabyte unified 4-way L2 cache is simulated with 64-byte lines. The L2 cache has a latency of 12 cycles. The main memory has an access time of 120 cycles. The L1 to L2 bus can support up to 8 bytes per processor cycle whereas the L2 to memory bus can support 4 bytes per cycle.

3 Prefetching Focused at the Different Load Stream Classifications

In this section we categorize and describe prior software and hardware prefetching research into the classes of next-line, stride, same-object, and pointer traversals. This classification corresponds to an increasing implementation complexity of hardware prefetching techniques.

3.1 Next-Line

The simplest form of prefetching is to prefetch the next cache block that occurs after a given load. This form of prefetch is very accurate, since programs have a lot of spatial locality.

Next-Line Prefetching (NLP) was proposed by Smith [19], where each cache block is tagged with a bit indicating when the next block should be prefetched. When a block is prefetched, its tag bit is set to zero. When the block is accessed during a fetch and the bit is zero, a prefetch of the next sequential block is triggered and the bit is set to one.

Jouppi introduced *stream buffers*, as a high latency hiding form of a next-line prefetching architecture [9]. The stream buffers follow multiple streams prefetching them in parallel and these streams can run ahead independent of the instruction stream of the processor. They are designed as FIFO buffers that prefetch consecutive cache blocks, starting with the one that missed in the L1 cache. On subsequent misses, the head of the stream buffer is probed. If the reference hits, that block is transferred to the L1 cache.

3.2 Stride-based Prefetching

A logical extension of next-line prefetching is *stride-based prefetching*. This scheme allows the prefetcher to eliminate miss patterns that follow a regular pattern but access non-sequential cache blocks. This type of access frequently occurs in scientific programs using multidimensional arrays.

Palacharla and Kessler [15] suggested a *non-unit stride* detection mechanism to enhance the effectiveness of stream buffers. This technique uses a *minimum delta* non-unit detection scheme. With this scheme, the dynamic stride is determined by the minimum signed difference between the past N miss addresses. If this minimum delta is smaller then the L1 block size, then the stride is set to the cache block size with the sign of the minimum delta. Otherwise, the stride is set to the minimum delta.

Farkas et. al. [7] made an important contribution by extending this model to use a *PC-based* stride predictor to provide the stride on stream buffer allocation. The PC-stride predictor determines the stride for a load instruction by using the PC to index into a stride address prediction table. This differs from the minimum-delta scheme, since the minimum-delta uses the global history to calculate the stride for a given load. A PC-stride predictor uses an associative buffer to record the last miss address for N load instructions, along with their program counter values. Thus, the stride prediction for a stream buffer is based only on the past memory behavior of the load for which the stream buffer was allocated.

3.3 Same Object Prefetching

Programs make use of different types of data structures to accomplish their final goal. Often times, logically related data are grouped together into an *object* to enhance semantics. The amount of data located inside an object does not always fit into a single cache block, and accesses to various parts of the same object can cause multiple cache misses. To eliminate these incidental misses, one could trigger the prefetch of the whole object once a miss occurs to data within the object. This could require the prefetching algorithm to know/predict the size of an object.

Zhang and Torrellas [22] recognized the benefit of grouping together fields or objects that are used together, and prefetching these all together as a prefetch group of blocks. They examined using user added grouping instructions that allowed the user to group together fields/objects that should be prefetched together. These groupings are then stored in a hardware buffer, and as soon as one of them is referenced and misses, all the cache blocks in the group are prefetched.

3.4 Pointer-Based Prefetching

As logically related data is collected into an object, objects that are related are also connected to each other via pointers. *Pointer-based prefetching*, either predicts or accesses these pointer values to prefetch the next object that is likely to be visited after the current one.

The inherent dependency between neighbor objects limits the amount of latency that can be hidden by the prefetching algorithm. This is known as the *pointer-chasing problem* [10]. The imposed serialization of object accesses constrain the prefetcher from running enough ahead of the execution stream to hide the full memory latency.

Luk and Mowry [10] examined prefetching for Recursive Data Structures (RDS). They examined the phenomenon of using pointer chaining for prefetching to hide latency. Greedy Prefetching was used to prefetch down all the pointers in a given heap object. They also examine adding *jump-pointers* to hook up a heap object X to another heap object Y that occurs earlier in the pointer chain, by adding an explicit jump-pointer from Y to X. This approach can hide more latency than their demand based greedy algorithm, but comes at a cost of adding jump-pointers into their structures. In addition, this could potentially perform badly if the structure of the RDS changes radically between traversals over the structure.

Roth et. al. [16] propose analyzing the producer-consumer relationship among loads to alleviate the effects of the pointer-chasing problem. In this scheme, load instructions that produce object addresses are linked together to facilitate a prediction chain. Prefetches read address values from memory and initiate another prefetch using the value just prefetched as an address. They examine prefetching one iteration ahead of the current execution to reduce the number of useless prefetches. Furthermore, Roth and Sohi [17] extend the jump-pointer prefetching technique by providing hardware, software and cooperative schemes to facilitate linking objects together. These different techniques provide a variety of trade-off points between prefetch accuracy and prefetching overhead.

Markov prefetching has been proposed as an effective technique for correctly predicting pointer-based loads [8]. When a cache miss occurs, the miss address would index into a Markov prediction table that provides the next set of possible cache addresses that have followed that miss address in the past. After these addresses are prefetched, the prefetcher stays idle until the next cache miss.

Recently we proposed a decoupled architecture for prefetching pointer-based miss streams [18]. We extended the stream buffer architecture proposed by Farkas et. al. [7] to follow prediction streams instead of a fixed stride. Our *Predictor-Directed Stream Buffer* (PSB) architecture uses a Stride-Filtered Markov predictor to generate the next addresses to prefetch. Predictor-directed stream buffers are able to achieve timely prefetches, since the stream buffers can run independently ahead of the execution stream, filling up the stream buffer with useful prefetches. Different predictors can be used to direct this architecture making it quite adept at finding both complex array access and pointer chasing behavior over a variety of applications. The predictor-directed stream buffer achieved a 30% speedup on pointer-based applications using only a 4 Kilobyte Markov table along with a 256 entry stride prediction table.

4 Load Miss Stream Classification

In section 3 we described the types of misses we wish to classify and how they behave in relationship to prior prefetching research. In this section we start by defining the different load miss models and show how the misses for many different types of programs are classified into these models. We then present a hardware technique for quickly and efficiently classifying cache misses for the purpose of guiding dynamic prefetching.

4.1 Miss Classes Defined

As described in section 3, there are four major types of memory access behavior prevalent in most programs that can be captured by hardware. Listed in order of increasing complexity they are: next-line, stride, access within an object, and dereferencing of pointers.

Next-line accesses are the simplest to capture with hardware, a simple stream buffer is very efficient at capturing this type of behavior. The stream buffer can identify accesses to sequential cache blocks and use this information to fetch sequentially down the stream. While this type of access is very simple, it is also very common in a multitude of applications. We classify a cache miss as being a next-line access if it is an access to a cache block that is adjacent to a cache block that was recently fetched.

Stride accesses are the next easiest to capture in hardware and many different prefetching architectures exist to capture this type of behavior. Farkas et. al. [7] showed that the most efficient way to capture this sort of behavior is by examining access patterns on a per static load basis. We use this observation to help us define stride access behavior. We define a cache miss to be stride miss if the same stride has been seen twice in a row for the static load that performed the access.

So far we have concerned ourselves with regular access patterns, the type that may be commonly found in programs dominated by large multidimensional arrays. The next two classes may not fall into this category. The class of misses, which we call Same-Object, are non-sequential, non-striding accesses going within a single object. We define a *Same-Object* cache miss as a miss to an object that has already had a miss recently. These misses may possibly be prevented if whenever we access an object we fetch the whole object, or at least those cache blocks of the object that will soon be referenced. These misses can also be targeted by field reordering [4].

The final hardware classification that we make is the Pointer class. The *Pointer* class represents misses to objects that are accessed via the dereference of a pointer. Pointer misses can constitute a large portion of total cache misses due to the accesses having very little conventional spatial locality. This has led to many recent hardware and software schemes that attempt to capture their behavior for the purpose of prefetching. These misses can be targeted by the software techniques of object reordering [11], smart object placement [3], software prefetching [10], or hardware schemes such as jump pointer prefetching [16, 17] and predictor-directed stream buffers [18].

We classify all cache misses into one and only one of these categories. If there is a cache miss that can fit into more than one category, such as loads with a stride of 1, we classify them into the simplest category possible, which in this case would be next-line.

In the description of the classifications please note the use of the term "recently". In order to capture the recent behavior of the loads we use a profiling technique called *Windowing*. We build a window of the last cache misses and loads, and use only this information when classifying subsequent loads. Using windowing prevents all loads being classified as "next-line", since only a fixed amount of history is kept track of. The window models the recent working set of load misses that could potentially trigger a prefetch of the load that missed. The window size is limited, because the prefetched block could only reside in a prefetch buffer or cache without being used for a window of time before being evicted. For the results presented in this section we capture the last 200 cache misses and the last 500 loads for pointer tracking.

4.2 Miss Classification Results

The first thing to look at before we begin discussing the classification of loads is the cache miss rates for the various programs. Tables 2, 3, and 4 show the data input used to run each program, the L1 and L2 cache miss behavior, and the percent of loads executed by each program. The L1 and L2 cache misses are both in terms of the average number of cache misses that occurred per 1K of executed instructions.

The programs consist of the full set of SPEC 2000 integer programs, a subset of the SPEC 2000 floating point programs that have been used in recent prefetching and precomputation papers, the Olden benchmark suite, and a set of pointer intensive programs. We chose the Olden benchmarks that have shown performance improvements from prior prefetching papers.

We now show the results of applying the classification technique described above over several suites of programs. Figure 1 shows the classification of the loads that miss in the L1 cache for the SPEC 2000 benchmarks. The four programs of interest from the SPEC 2000 suite that have a significant amount of cache misses include art, ammp, equake and mcf, and all of these have 80% or more of their misses classified, with mcf having the largest pointer behavior of these applications.

The classification of the programs from the Olden suite can be seen in figure 2. Health has by far the largest miss rate of all the programs, and is also the most dominated by the pointer behavior. The other programs have less significant miss rates and are more balanced in the types of misses that they exhibit. The one counter example to this is treeadd which is dominated by next-line prefetchable structures. All treeadd does is allocate a tree in depth-first order, and then traverse the tree in depth-first order. This results in the tree being created where every left child is allocated in memory right after its parent node, and therefore almost all of the cache misses would be covered by next-line prefetching. For that reason, treeadd has almost no pointer misses.

Figure 3 shows the same classification technique applied to our own set of pointer intensive benchmarks. As the name suggests, the suite of applications that we have assembled are dominated by pointer behavior. However this pointer behavior is not the only form of misses. There is a mix of access patterns seen, from next-line to pointer behavior, stride and same-object. The benchmark with the highest miss

benchmark	input	L1 MissPer1kI	L2 MissPer1kI	% Loads
ammp	ref	14.14	8.42	8.29%
applu	ref	28.42	13.57	25.89%
apsi	ref	13.70	3.34	21.34%
art	110	15.04	0.01	4.84%
bzip2	graphic	4.49	0.90	17.48%
crafty	ref	6.08	0.03	22.32%
eon	cook	0.09	0.00	10.06%
equake	ref	44.76	16.29	31.91%
galgel	ref	24.14	2.39	21.64%
gap	ref	1.90	0.88	14.70%
gcc	200	10.30	0.81	21.65%
gzip	graphic	7.47	0.11	17.47%
lucas	ref	0.92	0.47	4.25%
mcf	ref	130.16	91.54	28.34%
mgrid	ref	21.81	6.13	29.34%
parser	ref	13.00	1.92	19.66%
perlbmk	diffmail	4.62	0.08	23.00%
swim	ref	45.31	17.23	19.73%
twolf	ref	19.81	2.45	20.26%
vortex	two	2.38	0.29	21.00%
vpr	place	12.77	1.21	20.81%
wupwise	ref	6.34	2.94	16.56%

Table 2: SPEC 2000 cache miss behavior. The L1 data cache is a 32K 2-way associative cache with 32 byte lines. The L2 is a unified 1 Meg 4-way associative cache with 64 byte lines.

benchmark	input	L1 MissPer1kI	L2 MissPer1kI	% Loads
burg	rrh-vax	15.82	0.89	17.63%
deltablue	long	56.12	1.11	27.93%
sis	markex	4.58	0.04	36.32%
vis	clma	7.67	2.17	19.91%
dot	small	90.03	68.85	32.91%

Table 3: Pointer-based programs cache miss behavior. The L1 data cache is a 32K 2-way associative cache with 32 byte lines. The L2 is a unified 1 Meg 4-way associative cache with 64 byte lines.

benchmark	input	L1 MissPer1kI	L2 MissPer1kI	% Loads
health	5 500 1 1	122.93	0.36	34.86%
mst	1024 1	9.63	5.53	18.19%
perimeter	12 1	13.58	9.42	17.60%
treeadd	20 1	9.20	4.56	21.30%
tsp	100000 1	1.53	0.65	6.94%

Table 4: Olden cache miss behavior. The L1 data cache is a 32K 2-way associative cache with 32 byte lines. The L2 is a unified 1 Meg 4-way associative cache with 64 byte lines.

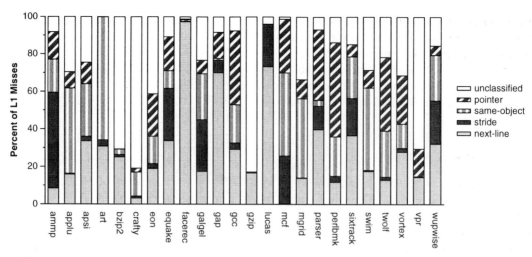

Figure 1: Classification of SPEC 2000 program load misses into the four prefetching models of next-line, stride, same-object, and pointer.

rate, `dot`, is also the program most dominated by pointer behavior. The programs `sis` and `vis` also show very strong pointer behavior.

The ability to do this classification in software is useful to quantify applications allowing researchers to find applications exhibiting certain behavior or to guide profile-directed optimizations. However, there are still some questions to be answered about those loads that are left unclassified.

4.3 Unclassified Loads

As can be seen in figure 1, some programs have a fair number of cache misses that do not fit into the categories of next-line, stride, same-object or pointer transition. These cache misses have arithmetic operations (not captured by stride) used to calculate their effective addresses. These classifications are not easily captured by existing hardware prefetchers. For these cache misses, we use three additional types of cache miss classifications. To determine the classification we search back over the dependency chain used to calculate the effective address.

We classify cache misses as *Recurrent* if there is an instruction that is inside of a loop that has the same logical register definition as one of its operands, and the operand register being defined has an address stored in it. A load whose effective address is calculated in this manner is producing its effective address each iteration of the loop off of the prior loop's address calculation. Cache misses that are classified as recurrent perform arithmetic operations to produce the effective address not captured by stride prefetching.

A cache miss is labelled as *Base Address* if there is an instruction in the load's dependency chain that uses the same address over and over again in a calculation to produce the load's effective address. This occurs when the calculation for the effective address is performed off of the same base

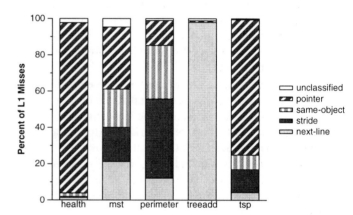

Figure 2: Classification of Olden program load misses into the four prefetching models of next-line, stride, same-object, and pointer.

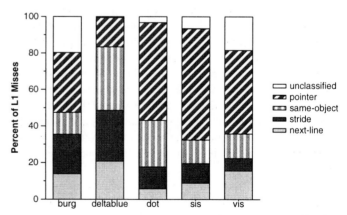

Figure 3: Classification of Pointer program load misses into the four prefetching models of next-line, stride, same-object, and pointer.

benchmark	% Unclassified Recurrent	% Unclassified Base Address	% Unclassified Complex
ammp	6.24%	0.94%	0.95%
applu	14.05%	1.00%	14.54%
apsi	7.91%	3.06%	13.56%
art	0.00%	0.06%	0.02%
bzip2	70.65%	0.03%	0.00%
crafty	79.45%	1.37%	0.01%
eon	23.75%	5.61%	11.85%
equake	10.60%	0.08%	0.02%
fma3d	0.19%	0.03%	1.01%
galgel	9.26%	0.19%	13.89%
gap	8.05%	0.21%	0.00%
gcc	6.52%	0.93%	0.07%
gzip	82.58%	0.13%	0.00%
lucas	1.88%	0.90%	1.08%
mcf	1.19%	0.01%	0.01%
mgrid	17.59%	0.20%	15.76%
parser	6.53%	0.21%	0.05%
perlbmk	12.24%	1.41%	0.09%
swim	13.85%	0.79%	0.11%
twolf	26.76%	0.67%	1.04%
vortex	20.00%	0.78%	0.82%
vpr	29.61%	1.63%	0.03%
vpr	57.53%	5.41%	7.56%
wupwise	1.51%	0.18%	13.77%
burg	19.45%	0.31%	0.00%
deltablue	0.49%	0.07%	0.00%
dot	3.23%	0.02%	0.00%
sis	5.69%	0.85%	0.03%
vis	17.16%	0.38%	0.86%
health	1.58%	0.64%	0.07%
mst	4.55%	0.08%	0.02%
perimeter	1.03%	0.00%	0.00%
treeadd	1.14%	0.01%	0.00%
tsp	0.31%	0.00%	0.25%

Table 5: Detailed classification of unclassified L1 misses.

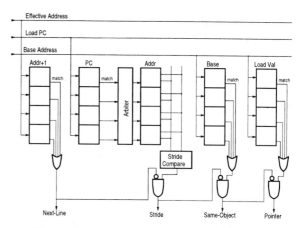

Figure 4: Load Miss Classification Hardware.

4.4 Hardware Classification

In order to take advantage of classification we need to provide a way for it to be done efficiently in hardware at run time. To accomplish this we make use of the windowing technique described in section 4.1, along with a very small fully associative buffer. The classification hardware keeps information in the buffer for the last N cache misses and then performs a lookup on its tables during a cache miss. Different types of matches mean different classifications for that load.

Figure 4 shows the proposed classification architecture. The basic structures in the architecture are small CAMs each with an update pointer. Every time there is a cache miss, the CAM is checked for hits for the four different models. This hit information is used to calculate the classification of the cache miss. The structure is then updated at the update pointer and the update pointer is incremented to the next entry. The structure is therefore accessed in two ways, a parallel lookup and a rotating register style update using the update pointer.

The structure to find next-line misses is a small CAM with a list of the past addresses that have missed with one block size added to them. Figure 4 is drawn showing a CAM with 4 entries, while each actual CAM has 32 entries in the architecture we modeled. Whenever a cache miss occurs, we simply check for a match in the CAM. A hit in any of the elements of the CAM indicates that the load was of the next-line type. Then after this information is computed we update the CAM with the most recent address information.

To find stride misses we add a structure that performs a parallel lookup as in the CAM before, but this time we attempt to match the PC of the load instruction rather than the address that is being loaded. If there is a hit in the CAM, the address seen in the slot is output and the two most recent addresses for that load are output and subtracted. The output of this subtraction is then added to the first address and a check for a match is done, with a match indicating a suc-

address every loop iteration.

Finally, a load is labelled as *Complex* if it is not recurrent nor base-address, and the load's effective address is calculated from a prior load in the dependency chain, and that prior load's value was an address. The address from that prior pointer load is used in an equation to produce the effective address that missed in the cache.

Table 5 presents a detailed look into load misses that go unclassified as described above. Most of the unclassified misses are recurrent pointer misses, potentially indicating that the loop induction variable is updated in a non-linear fashion. This makes these misses unclassifiable to next-line or stride predictors.

In the remainder of the paper we concentrate completely on the next-line, stride, same-object and pointer classifications, since these are captured by hardware prefetching techniques, and in the next section we will describe an approach for performing these four classifications in hardware.

cessful classification. This circuit is very similar in behavior to the arbiter used in the issue stage of an out of order processor, but much smaller. It is further simplified by the fact that the operation can be multicycle and pipelined.

Misses to the same heap object can be easily detected using the same type of structure used for next-line detection, but this time we store the base address rather than the possible next-line address. The base address from a cache miss is looked up in the CAM, and a hit indicates that this miss is classified as an access to the same object. On update, each cache miss stores its base address into this CAM.

To detect pointer based loads we add one last small structure, which is another CAM. This CAM is updated with the result of every load using the update pointer associated with that CAM. Because the result of all recent loads are stored in the CAM, loads to pointers are captured. When there is a cache miss we check the CAM to see if we can find the base address of the missing load. If there is a hit then we know that a prior load recently loaded the base pointer for the object that just missed and hence it is a pointer miss.

In using this classification scheme, the first miss to an object for a pointer-based application most likely will be classified as a pointer miss, and all subsequent misses to that same object would be classified as same object misses.

To test this the hardware scheme we compare it against the real classifications that were presented in section 4.2. We use a very small hardware window size, of $N=32$. This means that we only need 896 Bytes of storage to implement this architecture, and this could be further reduced to around 256 Bytes if partial tags are used with a small hash function.

To evaluate the classification hardware, we would like to predict what the *next* classification will be for a given load. To accomplish this we keep a small direct mapped table, which is indexed by the address of the load. In this table we store the last known classification of the load, as generated by the classification hardware. We then compare this value stored in this table to the true classification of the load. Figures 5 and 6 show the accuracy of this classification prediction mechanism over the pointer and Olden benchmark suites if a prediction table of size 128 is used.

The prediction accuracies show that by using the presented architecture we can correctly classify the majority of cache misses for the applications examined. The programs that the predictive classification had the most trouble with were `burg` and `sis`. For `burg` the predictor is caught jumping between stride and pointer classifications, this is because the application happened to allocate some of its' objects at a fixed stride from each other. This causes stride to be predicted when a stride is done, but pointer is the still the true access type. This is not a problem because either answer is really valid, but it could be fixed with the addition of a small amount of hysteresis. The classification for `Sis` is around 80% because the program performs pointer arithmetic to load some of its data, and these are not accurately

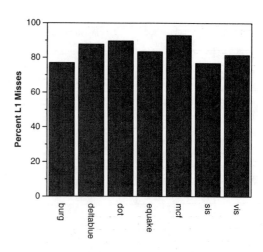

Figure 5: Classification prediction accuracy for the suite of pointer intensive applications.

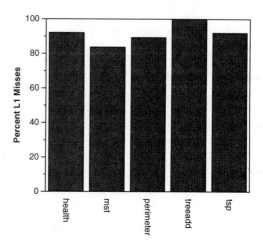

Figure 6: Classification prediction accuracy for the Olden benchmark suite.

classified.

4.5 Performance Results

In order to measure the potential benefit of applying our classification scheme, we ran detailed performance simulations using the SimpleScalar model described in section 2. The goal of these simulation results are to show the potential IPC performance if all of the cache misses are eliminated related to one or more of the prior four types of load miss classifications using the classification hardware presented in the prior section. Figures 7, 8, 9, and 10 show IPC results when we assume perfect load latency for these loads. The first bar shows IPC results for the baseline architecture. The next bar (NL) shows results when loads classified as next-line using our hardware classification architecture are given perfect L1 latency (they do not miss in the cache). The re-

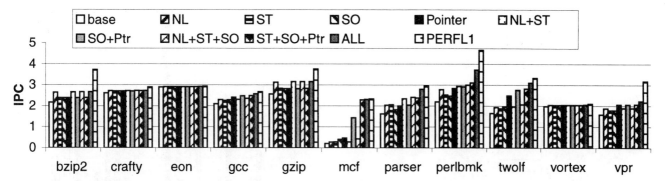

Figure 7: SPEC'CINT00 integer benchmark suite performance results when assigning perfect load latency for loads that match the different classifications.

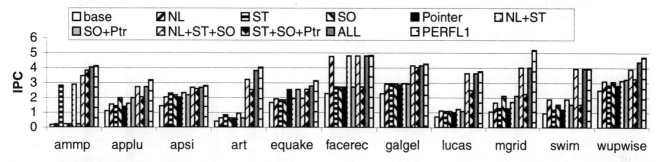

Figure 8: SPEC'CFP00 floating point benchmark suite performance results when assigning perfect load latency for loads that match the different classifications.

maining bars show the same optimization applied to loads classified as stride (ST), same-object access (SO), pointer accesses (Pointer), and combinations of different classes. The bar (All) shows the IPC where all loads classified (i.e. next-line, stride, same-object and pointer loads) are assumed to hit in the cache. The last bar (PerfL1) shows the IPC when there are no memory stalls. During simulation, each L1 cache miss is passed to the classification hardware. If the cache miss is classified as one of the types of misses we are eliminating, then the cache access is performed with no latency.

For all of the Olden benchmarks, a single load classification dominates the misses for `health` and `treeadd`. Applying a single optimization targeting specific loads achieves very good results. All of `Health`'s important load misses are pointer misses. All of the important misses in `treeadd` are captured by the next-line classification.

Figure 10 presents the results for a suite of pointer-intensive applications. No one particular load class dominates the accesses. In this regard, a prefetching algorithm needs to be able to handle all four of these different classes of loads at the same time in order to provide significant speedups. This is shown in `burg`, `deltablue`, `dot`, `mcf`, and `vis`. This is in stark contrast to most of the Olden benchmarks, in which handling just one of the classifications provides complete speedups.

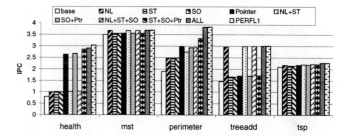

Figure 9: Olden benchmark suite performance results when assigning perfect load latency for loads that match the different classifications.

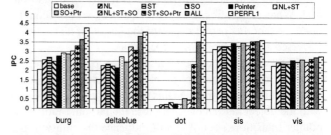

Figure 10: Pointer benchmark suite performance results when assigning perfect load latency for loads that match the different classifications.

5 Quantifying Object and Pointer Behavior

One of the most challenging types of access patterns to capture are pointer transition patterns. These are often also the

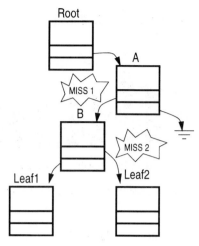

Figure 11: Fan Out Example

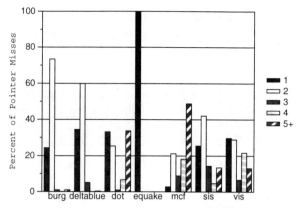

Figure 12: Object fan-out of the pointer-based programs. A histogram of object fan-out is shown for L1 cache misses classified as pointer transitions in section 4.

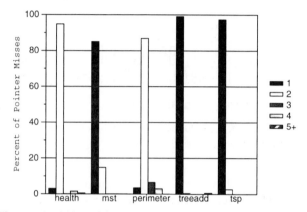

Figure 13: Object fan-out of the Olden benchmark suite. A histogram of object fan-out is shown for L1 cache misses classified as pointer transitions in section 4.

most critical to capture because of the high degree of dependence typically seen between pointer loads, and the poor spatial locality exhibited by this type of access.

There are two major factors that make capturing pointer behavior difficult. Pointer structures often have a high degree of fan out making the path to be traversed more difficult to choose. In addition, pointer transitions can be dynamic by their very nature and can change dramatically through the execution of the program via insertions or deletions to the data structure. Applications that have a high degree of fan-out and pointer transition variability will potentially be harder to accurately prefetch. In this section we provide an analysis of these two factors over our set of pointer based programs and the Olden benchmark suite.

5.1 Object Fan-Out

A given heap object that contains a set of n pointers to other objects, is said to have a *fan-out* of n. For example, a binary tree with a right and left child is said to have a fan-out of 2, while a tree with three child pointers is said to have a fan-out of 3. When calculating fan-out for an object, we only count a pointer to another object as part of the fan-out if it is actually traversed at least once during execution.

Since we are concerned with memory performance, we are interested in pointer transitions from object A to object B that result in a cache miss. In this example, we are concerned with the object fan-out of A, because the fan-out (number of pointer transitions) out of A will influence the ability of the hardware to prefetch the cache miss transition to B. Figure 11 shows an example of this. Suppose that we have the small tree, where A has one NULL child and one child transition to B, and node B has two real children. Now suppose that there is a cache miss when the program attempts to transition to node B, noted as $Miss1$ in the diagram. This cache miss will be classified as having a fan-out of 1, because it was the dereference of a pointer from an object (A) with a

fan-out of 1. Cache $Miss2$ on the other hand will be noted as having a fan-out of 2, because it comes from the dereference of node B, which has a fan-out of 2.

Now that we have this measure of fan-out, we wish to see how the misses are distributed across objects with different fan-outs. Figures 12 and 13 show the histogram of fan-out misses for both the pointer-based programs we have chosen and the Olden benchmarks. The fan-out results are shown for the L1 cache misses that are classified as pointer transitions in figures 1, 2 and 3. Looking at the graphs in figure 12, the fan-out for *equake* stands out. Equake has all of its misses coming from objects with a fan-out of 1, such as a simple linked list. The programs deltablue and burg are split between objects that have a fan-out 1 or 2 that transition to a miss, while dot, mcf, sis, and vis have misses from objects with many transitions to chose from. The dominate fan-out for dot and mcf is at 5 or greater.

This is in stark contrast to the behavior of the Olden benchmarks seen in Figure 13, where all of the programs are dominated by a single fan-out of either 1 or 2. This shows that the behavior of the Olden benchmarks is dominated by a single simple homogeneous data structure which is not representative of the complexity inherent in the other pointer based applications.

5.2 Variability

Another factor that makes prefetching of pointer structures difficult is the fact that the pointer transitions to other objects changes over the lifetime of the application. In order to understand how the pointer structures change over time we add a new metric called variability.

The *variability* of a pointer in a program is the number of different values (addresses) it has over the life time of the program. In order for a data structure to change, the pointers within the structure must point to different objects. Every time we see one of these changes, we record that it changed. After the program has completed running, we put all of the cache misses associated with a pointer address into a bucket based upon the number of different addresses stored in that pointer (the variability) during execution. From this we make a histogram, which can be seen in figures 14 and 15. This shows the percent of pointer classification L1 misses that had the different degrees of variability.

In analyzing figure 14, `equake` again shows that the pointer transitions do not change during the execution after the initial data structure has been set up. This correlates to the fan-out results in figure 12, which showed each object has only one outgoing edge creating misses and that transition retains its' value throughout the program. `Mcf`, `sis` and `vis` also are interesting to look at as most of the misses are caused by objects with high variability. These programs are difficult to accurately prefetch as the data stream is constantly changing and hence, is highly unpredictable.

Most of the Olden benchmarks data structures remain fairly static with little variability, making them suitable for software based prefetching techniques [10]. The one program that is, at least at the surface, counter to this characterization is `treeadd`. The reason why `treeadd` is shown to have a high degree of variability is that only 3% of all of its cache misses were classified as pointer misses as shown in Figure 2. These 3% of the misses came from a load in malloc which temporarily stores the address of newly allocated memory, and the pointer is overwritten repeatedly.

6 Summary

That gap between processor performance and memory latency continues to grow at an astonishing rate, and because of this the memory hierarchy continues to be the target of a great deal of architectural research. In this paper, we present both an analysis of cache miss behavior, to help guide researchers in future cache and prefetching research, and a dynamic hardware technique to perform classification on the

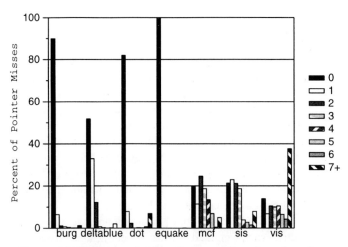

Figure 14: Pointer variability for the pointer-based applications. A histogram of pointer variability is shown for L1 cache misses classified as pointer transitions in section 4.

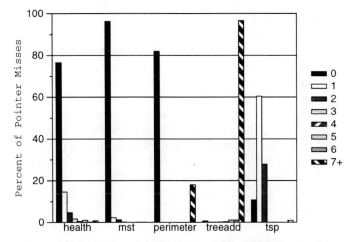

Figure 15: Pointer variability for the Olden benchmark suite. A histogram of pointer variability is shown for L1 cache misses classified as pointer transitions in section 4.

fly, which will enable architectural structures to be access pattern aware.

We classify load access patterns into one of four types, next-line, stride, same-object (additional misses that occur to a recently accessed object), and pointer-based transitions. These four access patterns account for more than 90% of all cache misses in the programs we examined. We then show a hardware technique that can detect this behavior using very little on-chip area. The dynamic classification technique presented can accurately predict more the 77% of cache misses as being of the correct type for all programs. On average across all programs, the technique correctly classifies 85% of all misses.

We also evaluate the potential benefit of correctly identifying load classes and the effect of removing their memory latency. This in effect simulates a perfect prefetcher for each class of loads. Our results show that a multi-pronged attack is needed to hide the majority of the memory latency. Prefetching only a single class of load does not provide noticeable benefits for the pointer-based collection of applications we examined. In contrast, removing the latency for only a single load stream classification achieved perfect results for a few of the Olden benchmarks.

In addition to the hardware classification technique presented, we further study those misses identified as pointer-based. Pointer-based misses have become the subject of a great deal of research in recent years and for future research it is important to understand their behavior.

To quantify the behavior of pointer loads, we examined two metrics each weighted by the number of cache misses for pointer-based loads. We use the fan-out metric of objects to quantify the branching factor that data structures have. For a set of programs that are actually used to solve real problems, the fan-out tends to be both large and non-uniform. In contrast, the Olden benchmark suite shows both a very regular and a very small fan-out.

In addition to fan-out, we also examine how often a pointer transition changes over the life time of the application. To track this we keep a list of every pointer in the program and note how many times the pointer's value changes over the execution. We found that while about half the programs simply build and then destroy a large data structure, the other half change their data structures around quite often. This can make prefetching techniques that are based on learning the access pattern much more difficult to implement. The Olden benchmarks showed very little variability in their pointer transitions.

Acknowledgments

We would like to thank Yuanfang Hu for her help in gathering the recurrent, base address, and complex pointer load classification results. In addition, we would like to thank the anonymous reviewers for providing useful comments on this paper. This work was funded in part by DARPA/ITO under contract number DABT63-98-C-0045, a grant from Compaq Computer Corporation, and an equipment grant from Intel.

References

[1] M Annavaram, J. Patel, and E. Davidson. Data prefetching by dependence graph precomputation. In *28th Annual International Symposium on Computer Architecture*, June 2001.

[2] D. C. Burger and T. M. Austin. The simplescalar tool set, version 2.0. Technical Report CS-TR-97-1342, University of Wisconsin, Madison, June 1997.

[3] B. Calder, C. Krintz, S. John, and T. Austin. Cache-conscious data placement. In *Proceedings of the Eighth International Conference on Architectural Support for Programming Languages and Operating Systems (ASPLOS-VIII)*, San Jose, October 1998.

[4] Trishul M. Chilimbi, Mark D. Hill, and James R. Larus. Cache-conscious structure layout. In *SIGPLAN Conference on Programming Language Design and Implementation*, pages 1–12, May 1999.

[5] G. Chrysos and J. Emer. Memory dependence prediction using store sets. In *25th Annual International Symposium on Computer Architecture*, June 1998.

[6] J. Collins, H. Wang, D. Tullsen, C. Hughes, Y.F. Lee, D. Lavery, and J.P. Shen. Speculative precomputation: Long-range prefetching of delinquent loads. In *28th Annual International Symposium on Computer Architecture*, June 2001.

[7] K. Farkas, P. Chow, N. Jouppi, and Z. Vranesic. Memory-system design considerations for dynamically-scheduled processors. In *24th Annual International Symposium on Computer Architecture*, June 1997.

[8] D. Joseph and D. Grunwald. Prefetching using markov predictors. In *24th Annual International Symposium on Computer Architecture*, June 1997.

[9] N. Jouppi. Improving direct-mapped cache performance by the addition of a small fully associative cache and prefetch buffers. In *Proceedings of the 17th Annual International Symposium on Computer Architecture*, May 1990.

[10] C.-K. Luk and T. C. Mowry. Compiler based prefetching for recursive data structures. In *Seventh International Conference on Architectural Support for Programming Languages and Operating Systems*, October 1996.

[11] Chi-Keung Luk and Todd C. Mowry. Memory forwarding: Enabling aggressive layout optimizations by guaranteeing the safety of data relocation. In *ISCA99*, pages 88–99, May 1999.

[12] C.K. Luk. Tolerating memory latency through software-controlled pre-execution in simultaneous multithreading processors. In *28th Annual International Symposium on Computer Architecture*, June 2001.

[13] S. McFarling. Combining branch predictors. Technical Report TN-36, Digital Equipment Corporation, Western Research Lab, June 1993.

[14] T.C. Mowry, M.S. Lam, and A. Gupta. Design and evaluation of a compiler algorithm for prefetching. In *Proceedings of the Fifth International Conference on Architectural Support for Programming Languages and Operating Systems (ASPLOS-V)*, October 1992.

[15] S. Palacharla and R. Kessler. Evaluating stream buffers as secondary cache replacement. In *21st Annual International Symposium on Computer Architecture*, April 1994.

[16] A. Roth, A. Moshovos, and G. Sohi. Dependence based prefetching for linked data structures. In *Eigth International Conference on Architectural Support for Programming Languages and Operating Systems*, October 1998.

[17] A. Roth and G. Sohi. Effective jump-pointer prefetching for linked data structures. In *26th Annual International Symposium on Computer Architecture*, May 1999.

[18] T. Sherwood, S. Sair, and B. Calder. Predictor-directed stream buffers. In *33rd International Symposium on Microarchitecture*, December 2000.

[19] J. E. Smith and W.-C. Hsu. Prefetching in supercomputer instruction caches. In *Proceedings of Supercomputing*, November 1992.

[20] A. Srivastava and A. Eustace. ATOM: A system for building customized program analysis tools. In *Proceedings of the Conference on Programming Language Design and Implementation*, pages 196–205. ACM, 1994.

[21] Wm. A. Wulf and Sally A. McKee. Hitting the memory wall: Implications of the obvious. Technical Report CS-94-48, 1, 1994.

[22] Z. Zhang and J. Torrellas. Speeding up irregular applications in shared-memory multiprocessors: Memory binding and group prefetching. In *22nd Annual International Symposium on Computer Architecture*, June 1995.

Speculation and Prediction

Modeling Value Speculation

Yiannakis Sazeides
Department of Computer Science
University of Cyprus
yanos@ucy.ac.cy

Abstract

Several studies of speculative execution based on values have reported promising performance potential. However, virtually all microarchitectures in these studies were described in an ambiguous manner, mainly due to the lack of formalization that defines the effects of value–speculation on a microarchitecture. In particular, the manifestations of value–speculation on the latency of microarchitectural operations, such as releasing resources and reissuing, was at best partially addressed. This may be problematic since results obtained in these studies can be difficult to reproduce and/or appreciate their contribution.

This paper introduces a model for a methodical description of dynamically–scheduled microarchitectures that use value–speculation. The model isolates the parts of a microarchitecture that may be influenced by value–speculation in terms of various variables and latency events. This provides systematic means for describing, evaluating and comparing the performance of value–speculative microarchitectures.

The model parameters are integrated in a simulator to investigate the performance of several value–speculation related events. Among other, the results show value–speculation performance to have non-uniform sensitivity to changes in the latency of these events. For example, fast verification latency is found to be essential, but when misspeculation is infrequent slow invalidation may be acceptable.

1 Introduction

Performance has been a driving force for microarchitecture research since the advent of the computer. One of the popular approaches used to improve performance is the application of hardware and software transformations to a program to increase its Instruction Level Parallelism (ILP). Fundamentally, true dependences limit the amount of ILP that can be extracted from a program. Two instructions exhibit a true dependence, or simply are *dependent*, when an output operand of one instructions is an input of another.

Dependences are typically divided into control and data dependences. Probably, the most primitive type of control dependence is the program counter (PC) dependence because every instruction depends on its predecessor's output program counter. However, most instructions modify the PC in a trivial fashion, i.e. they increment it by the instruction length. This length is fixed for many architectures (e.g. RISC) and for others is a function of the instruction type. In either case, the instruction length can be determined prior to execution. Processors effectively deal with the trivial PC–dependences by employing instruction caches that allow multiple consecutive instructions to be fetched simultaneously. This leaves control transfer instructions as the remaining control dependence problem.

For a control transfer instruction determining the next PC requires the execution of the instruction and this leads to a serialization in the execution. Prediction and speculation [4, 10, 36] have been proposed as a means for alleviating the impediments of control dependences by predicting the next PC of control transfer instructions and speculatively executing the instructions that follow them.

In addition to control dependences through the PC, there is also a serialization of execution due to data dependences through register and memory locations. These dependences were shown to be predictable [1, 22, 25] and suited to drive speculative execution [11, 22, 25, 35].

The predictability of register dependence values (value prediction) - the motivation for this work - and of other program information types (such as control and memory dependences) may suggest the existence of fundamental transformations that can reduce/eliminate predictable computation. The identification of such transformations represent promising directions for research. However, until such transformations are discovered and understood the performance of future processors may benefit by *value–speculation*: use of value prediction to drive speculative execution.

There is a plethora of work that reports on the promising performance potential of value–speculation. Value–speculation has been proposed and investigated for dynamically [3, 6, 8, 11, 13, 14, 17, 18, 21, 22, 28, 31, 42] and statically [7, 26] scheduled processors, for distributed microarchitectures [23, 27, 30, 43], and with compiler assistance [12, 16, 41].

Although the above and other related work represent a significant body of knowledge, its focus was mainly directed towards higher accuracy predictors and compiler support/transformations to facilitate more effective value prediction. We argue that there has been insufficient investigation of the microarchitectural implications of value speculation. This is evident by the imprecision with which microarchitectures are described in value–speculation work. This can be attributed to the lack of a formalization for describing such microarchitectures. What's more, the implications of value–speculation on the latency of microarchitectural operations such as releasing resources and reissue, are rarely addressed. This can be problematic because the obtained results may be difficult to reproduce and assess their significance. Although ambiguity is expected for a new research subject, the amount of research invested for value speculation justifies the need for formalization.

This paper introduces a model (the central theme of the paper) for a systematic description of dynamically–scheduled microarchitectures that use value–speculation. The model defines the design space of the microarchitecture influenced by value–speculation in terms of various *variables* and *latency events*. The model can therefore provide a method for accurate evaluation and comparison of the performance of value–speculative microarchitectures. The model parameters are integrated in a microarchitectural simulator to evaluate the performance with value–speculation for several latency events.

1.1 Motivation

The most problematic issue with value–speculation work is the timing of microarchitectural events. In general, to avoid unnecessary stalls in a pipelined processor, future events are scheduled based on (expected) deterministic latencies of currently executing events. For example, when a register–to–register add instruction is issued, the control logic of a processor **anticipates** that this operation will complete within a deterministic latency. Consequently, instructions dependent on the *add* can be scheduled (and possibly issued) prior to the completion of the *add*. The anticipation approach is employed almost in every stage of a pipelined processor. Meeting the timing constraints for anticipation at each stage is a critical design issue since uncertainty can compromise correct functionality and long paths can slow down clock. In practice, when the timing can not be met this may result in an additional pipe stage or a pipeline stall.

Value–speculation may increase the critical path of one or more anticipation mechanisms in a pipeline. Although one can be optimistic about how value–speculation influences

these latencies, it is important to study the performance as the latencies change. This view is not adopted in most previous value–speculation work since nearly all latencies are fixed. For instance, most papers assume one cycle minimum latency between misprediction and reissue. Furthermore, vague explanations are given for the assumptions and implications of the one cycle latency.

We believe it is paramount to establish how sensitive value–speculation performance is to the latency of various events and then consider mechanisms to achieve or approximate the desired performance. For motivation consider the example in Fig. 1 showing the pipelined execution of three instructions - *1*, *2* and *3* - with correct and incorrect prediction (the example is discussed in more detail in Section 4). Three execution models are considered - *Super*, *Great* and *Good* - each with different latencies for various events. The (in)sensitivity to the changing latencies is evident. This underlines the need for a methodical investigation of the microarchitectural events influenced by value–speculation: wakeup, selection, verification, invalidation, resource releasing, branch resolution and memory resolution. This paper attempts to propose a systematic framework for doing such exploration and examines the effect on performance for most of these events.

1.2 Outline

The microarchitecture used in the paper is described in Section 2. Section 3 discusses the design space of value speculation and reviews related work. Section 4 introduces a model for describing value–speculative microarchitectures. The experimental framework is outlined in Section 5. Results are discussed in Section 6. The conclusions are presented in Section 7.

2 Microarchitecture

This section describes a base-microarchitecture and then introduces the value–speculation microarchitecture used in the paper.

2.1 Base Microarchitecture

For baseline microarchitecture we consider an out-of-order superscalar processor based on the Register Update Unit [39] which unifies issue resources (reservation stations [40]) and retirement resources (reorder buffer entries [37]). In the text will refer to the unified issue/retirement structure as the instruction window. An entry in the instruction window will be referred as reservation station(RS).

As instructions are fetched, they are assigned entries in the instruction window according to the dynamic program order and remain in the window until they can be retired.

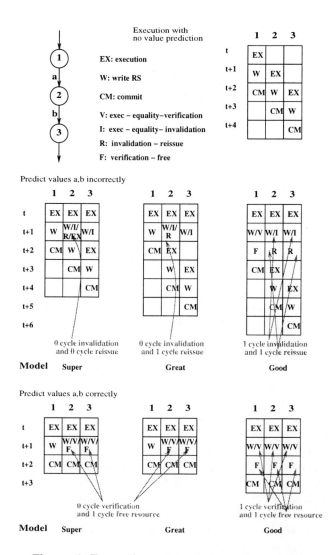

Figure 1. Execution example based on different Speculative Models

In1Ready	In1Tag	In1Value
In2Ready	In2Tag	In2Value
OutValue	Issued	Executed

The *ready* fields are used to indicate whether an input operand is available (*valid* or *invalid*). The *tags* are used to specify which results an instruction is waiting for. The *value* field holds the actual input value. The *outvalue* stores the output of an instruction that is eventually used for updating the processor state when the instruction retires. The two binary fields *issued* and *executed* are used to guide issue and retirement.

Wakeup and selection logic, in the instruction window, determines the instructions that get issued each cycle. *Wakeup* determines which instructions can be considered for issue in the next cycle. An instruction can *wakeup* when its *ready* fields are *valid* and has not issued already. *Selection* chooses which of these instructions to issue in the next cycle. The selection scheme used in this paper gives priority to branches and loads and then to the oldest instruction.

Memory instructions consist of two operations: address generation and memory access. Loads are executed when all preceding store addresses in the instruction window are known and hence no memory dependence violations can occur. A perfect load cache hit predictor is assumed, i.e. load dependent instructions are not issued when a load will miss in the cache. The only source of misspeculation in the base-processor is due to branch misprediction: when a branch is mispredicted all subsequent instructions in the window are squashed and fetching starts from the new target address.

2.2 Microarchitecture with Value Speculation

The base-processor is augmented with value–speculation as shown in Fig. 2. This is a similar microarchitecture to the one proposed in [21]. Essential to a processor supporting speculation are mechanisms that: (a) provide predictions (and confidence estimation for predictions), (b) verify predictions, and (c) invalidate misspeculated instructions. The integration of these mechanisms in a superscalar processor pipeline can lead to pervasive changes in the functionality and/or latency of different microarchitectural events.

One such change regards the handling of various values types. In particular, the use of value prediction introduces two additional types of values in the processor: *predicted* and *speculative*. A value is *predicted* if it is obtained directly from the value predictor, and is *speculative* if it is the result of computation(s) that included a predicted value. An input value is *valid* if it is read from the architected file or is the result of a computation that involved only valid inputs. Therefore, with value–speculation, an input operand may be: speculative, predicted, valid, and invalid.

Virtually all papers agree about the treatment of predicted, valid and invalid values, however there are two ap-

Values in this organization can exist in the following locations: register file, instruction window and functional units. The register file maintains architected state and is only updated when instructions retire. Instructions read any available input values from the register file before entering a reservation station in the instruction window. Instructions can also receive values through a bypassing network from predecessors in the window. Instructions with unresolved dependences monitor the results bus and capture their source operands as the producing instructions finish execution. The result of an executed instruction is also written in a field in its RS. When an instruction is the oldest in the window, it can commit its result in the register file or memory and release its entry in the window.

The important fields in a RS are shown below:

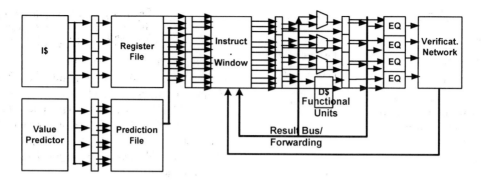

Figure 2. Pipeline With Value Prediction

proaches towards speculative values: one does not support forwarding of speculative values [31] whereas the other allows propagation of speculative values(the latter being the typical assumption in value speculation work). Although no forwarding can offer an implementation advantage, in this paper we choose to allow the forwarding of speculative values because it may represent the method with the highest potential.

To accommodate the new value types in the proposed microarchitecture, the ready fields in the RS are expanded to two bits. Another required change is for checking the correctness of output predictions: a field is added in the RS to indicate whether the output of an instruction is predicted and another field is used to contain the predicted output value. The modified RS incorporating the above changes is shown below (this is similar to the changes suggested by [31]):

In1Ready	In1Tag	In1Value
In2Ready	In2Tag	In2Value
OutValue	Issued	Executed
Predicted Value	*Predicted*	

The following section discusses the design space of various value speculation mechanisms and expands on the way the different RS flags can be used to guide various policies.

Although the rest of the paper emphasizes issues relevant to the microarchitecture outlined in this section, the discussion will often have a broader scope.

3   Design Space and Related Work

Value–speculation was proposed independently by Lipasti et al. and Gabbay and Mendelson [11, 22] as a performance enhancing method exploiting the predictability of values. Since then value–speculation has been a subject of a number papers. Although it is difficult to categorize published work, we divide value–speculation papers into two categories: those that address microarchitectural issues and those that do not. For example, a paper that introduces a value predictor may do so in a microarchitectural independent fashion. More relevant to this work are papers that

made microarchitectural contributions or were conducive in better understanding the microarchitectural implications of value speculation.

The fundamental microarchitectural contributions related to value speculation were made by Lipasti et al. [20, 21, 22]. The authors introduced all basic microarchitectural functions required by value–speculation, namely: providing predictions, verifying correctness and invalidating in case of misspeculation. The notion of selective invalidation was also introduced in their work. In addition some of the effects of value–speculation on the microarchitecture were described.

Follow-ups to the above work helped define the design space of value speculation more accurately. However, the microarchitectures were described in an ad-hoc manner with little justification for the choice of various parameters. We realize that simulation models in previous work may have been detailed enough, what this paper contends is that their descriptions were not.

Statically scheduled processors can also employ value–speculation [7, 26]. And such microarchitectures may be less problematic to describe because value–speculation related operations can be done in software. Issues related to statically scheduled value–speculation are beyond the scope of this paper.

The following sections consider the design space of value–speculation. The purpose of the discussion is to elucidate possible misconceptions, identify subtle to describe/distinguish microarchitectural features and give direction for future research. Several issues related to prediction and predictors, such as prediction model, tables configuration, number of ports, hash functions and replacement are not discussed due to limited space. The interested reader can consult [2, 6, 18, 20, 31, 32].

3.1   Invalidation

Invalidation is responsible for informing the direct or indirect successors of a mispredicted instruction that they have received incorrect operands. This is essential to recover from side effects caused by a misprediction. Invalidation latency can be crucial because it can determine how quickly a misspeculated instruction reissues. There are two basic invalidation models to consider: **complete** and **selective**.

Complete invalidation treats a value misprediction similar to a branch misprediction. Few papers [8, 41] compared the performance of selective and complete invalidation and observed smaller but still positive potential for complete invalidation. Complete invalidation may be practical to implement and beneficial in terms of performance if value mispredictions are rare and/or the potential of value–speculation is large. Value mispredictions can be made rare using confidence estimation[2, 8, 15].

Most papers adopt a hierarchical selective invalidation, that is an instruction can only invalidate its direct successors. The invalidated successors then invalidate their own successors. This process is repeated until all successors receive the invalidation. This may be build on top of the existing(or similar) tag broadcasting mechanism used to wakeup instructions[22, 30, 31, 42]. So far the only proposed design for selective invalidation requires instructions with speculative/predicted operands to remain in their reservation stations after they issue. This may be necessary as it is unclear how to perform selective actions in a pipeline otherwise. The following discussion assumes that invalidation is selective and all instructions with predicted/speculative operands remain in their RS after they are issued.

The invalidation mechanism with the highest performance potential is one that invalidates in parallel all direct and indirect successors. Selective parallel invalidation is effectively a flattened–hierarchical invalidation scheme. The model described in Section 4 considers invalidation as a distinct event that forces a misspeculated instruction to reissue.

3.2 Verification

When an instruction is predicted correctly, verification is responsible for informing the instruction's direct and indirect successors that their input operand(s) are valid. Since a verification mechanism has almost identical functionality with a selective–invalidation mechanism (Section 3.1), one mechanism may be sufficient to implement both.

Considering that an instruction may need to hold a resource until all its input operands become *valid*, then fast verification can be decisive for improving performance. Verification directly influences the release of *issue* resources (reservation stations) and *retirement* resources (reorder buffer entries).

Fast verification latency may also be relevant when it is desirable to resolve branch or memory instructions only with *valid* values. The problem with resolving branches using predicted/speculative values is that value prediction may be less accurate than branch prediction and hence may lead to additional branch mispredictions. Similarly, load instructions may be preferable to access memory with valid addresses to avoid store-load dependence violations. Slow verification may translate in a longer misprediction penalty for both branches and values.

There are at least four approaches for performing verification:

Hierarchical–Verification
With hierarchical–verification a correctly predicted instruction can validate only its direct successors. The verified successors will then verify their own successors. This process will be repeated until all successors get verified. Hierarchical–verification can be implemented using the existing, or similar, tag broadcasting mechanism used by processors to wakeup instructions. This verification approach can provide a performance improvement provided there are separate dependence chains in the instruction window. Otherwise, the increased execution parallelism from value–speculation will be nullified by the serialization in verification.

Retirement–Based Verification
It can be demonstrated that the retirement mechanism, used in dynamically–scheduled superscalar processor, can be used to *verify* in parallel multiple instructions. That is, verification can be overloaded to retirement. However, this approach may have two pitfalls:
(a) for each cycle only the w oldest instructions in the instruction window can be validated, where w is the retirement bandwidth of the processor. This may be undesirable if a younger instruction is otherwise valid but forced to hold needlessly a resource.
(b) the additional functionality may stress the critical path of the anticipation mechanism for releasing retirement resources. In particular, the condition for committing a value–predicted instruction requires an additional compare operation. If the latency of the comparison is on the critical path then resources may be freed with at least an extra cycle delay.

Hybrid Retirement–Based and Hierarchical Verification
This approach attempts to build on the strengths of the two previous approaches. *Retirement–based* verification is used for releasing resources faster whereas *hierarchical* verification is intended for faster detection of mispredictions.

Flattened–Hierarchical Verification
In this scheme all direct and indirect successors of a correctly predicted instruction are validated in parallel. This is analogous to **flattened–hierarchical** invalidation. The *flattened-hierarchical* verification represents the verification method with the highest performance potential, however it is also likely to be the method with the highest implementation cost.

It is noteworthy that a microarchitecture may require a

different verification approach depending on: (a) whether the issue and retirement resources are unified, and (b) whether branch and memory instructions are resolved with speculative/predicted values. Due to space limitations we do not elaborate on this important topic.

This work considers a microarchitecture with unified issue and retirement resources. Branches and memory instructions are allowed to execute only with *valid* operands. For verification(and invalidation) the functionality of a flattened–hierarchical tag broadcasting scheme is assumed. It is also assumed that at any given point any number of instructions can verify/invalidate their successors. This is referred as the *verification network*.

Although the functionality of the verification network is intuitive to understand, its implementation may present a significant challenge. The objective of this work is to assess whether such mechanism is essential to achieve high performance with value–speculation. It is unclear if any previous work considers such a scheme. The proposed model (Section 4) will be used to determine how important fast verification(invalidation) is and how critical it is to inform quickly branch and memory instructions about the state of their input operands (e.g. when predicted or speculative operands become *valid*).

Parallel–verification was assumed in a number of papers, however, no previous work discussed it in detail. Hierarchical–verification is explained in [31]. The first work to explore the effects of value–speculation on branches was presented by Sodani and Sohi [38]. The authors compared the performance when branches are resolved with speculative/predicted values and when resolved only with valid values. That work also considered the effects of 0 and 1 cycle validation latency. However, it is unclear how the assumed latencies affect various processor events (such as releasing resources). Also, it is unclear whether additional latency, to the verification latency, is considered when branches are not allowed to be resolved with speculative/predicted values. In previous work [19, 21, 29, 30] branches were resolved out-of-order only when their operands were known to be non-speculative. A third option for dealing with branches is to combine the two approaches examined in [38] based on confidence [9]. A recent study [28] considered the combination of address, value and dependence prediction for resolving speculative loads.

The above suggest that evaluation and design of different verification mechanisms present interesting directions for future research.

3.3 Equality

Equality is responsible for determining whether a value is predicted correctly or incorrectly. Equality can be performed by comparing the predicted value against the actual value (**value–equality**). As far as we know, value-equality is the approach used for checking predictions by all proposals that rely on prediction and speculation. Alternatives that do not require strict equality have been suggested but have not been explored[20, 32]. In the proposed microarchitecture (see Fig. 2) value-equality is performed in the write/verification stage using comparators (denoted EQ).

The latency for performing value–equality can be on the critical path of many microarchitectural operations, such as recovery from misspeculation and releasing resources, and hence is an important performance parameter. The proposed model (Section 4) considers the effects with increasing value–equality latency.

3.4 WakeUp

Without value–speculation an instruction can wakeup when it has not issued already and has received the tags for all its input operands – indicated by the ready fields being *valid* in its RS.

The use of value–speculation introduces additional choices for instruction wakeup. Wakeup may be useful to be seen as a filter that selects instructions for speculative execution. In particular, the wakeup function can consider the following information for an instruction: (a) the ready state of its inputs (ready fields of a RS), (b) issued state (issued field of a RS), (c) predicted state (predicted field of a RS), and (d) the speculative "state" of its inputs (this is a value that comes from the verification network and *roughly* corresponds to the next ready state for an input operand).

The options described above imply a number of possibilities as to when to wakeup instructions. Only one wakeup function is considered in this paper and allows for an instruction to wakeup only when its inputs are either valid and/or speculative and the instruction has not yet issued. Due to space limitation we do not report the precise function used.

Wakeup serves another purpose: nullifying the effects of a misprediction. The semantics for nullification are: (a) remove the effects of previous execution of an instruction, and (b) enable a future wakeup of the instruction. This is achieved by resetting the issued field in the RS whenever an instruction gets *invalidated*.

Note that the above policies ensure that instructions without predicted or speculative operands can wakeup as fast as on the base-processor.

Sodani and Sohi [38] performed a comparison of two wakeup schemes: wakeup each time a new value is reaching an instruction[30] or limiting the wakeup of an instruction to at most two executions[22]. The two approaches have a subtle but important difference, the former effectively ignores speculative status of the operands and hence may reissue faster a misspeculated instruction. This also implies that instructions may issue needlessly when they are not misspeculated.

Considering the numerous possibilities that exist for wakeup functions, future work should investigate their performance and design.

3.5 Selection

Selection with speculative execution presents new tradeoffs since instructions can be candidates for issue with: predicted, speculative and/or valid inputs. Therefore *selection* needs to consider additional information such as, how many speculative inputs an instructions has, confidence in those inputs and whether the instruction is on the critical path. Selection of which value–speculative instructions get issued based on confidence and critical path information was proposed by Calder et al.[8]. This was also addressed more recently by Larson and Austin[16].

A selection scheme combined with accurate confidence estimation can ignore the speculative state information of an operand since most of the time predictions will be correct. Alternatively, a selection with a poor confidence estimator may assign higher priority to all instructions with valid inputs and then consider instructions with speculative operands.

In this work we consider a selection scheme that assigns highest priority to branch and load instructions and prioritizes the rest based on dynamic program order - oldest first. Non-speculative instructions are preferred over speculative. Selection for speculative execution is an important research subject not explored in this paper.

3.6 Confidence

Accurate confidence estimation[15] may be necessary to reduce value misspeculation. A number of interesting possibilities for confidence estimation for value prediction are discussed in [2, 8]. Calder et al.[8] explored the use of confidence levels (low, medium and high) for resetting counters. They also proposed propagation of confidence to dependent instructions. They have shown that speculating on predictions with low confidence that lie on the critical path can improve performance. Bekerman et al.[2] suggested to associate with a mispredicted instruction part of the control flow history that lead to it. In the case of future match, a prediction is assigned low confidence. In this paper we compare the performance with oracle and realistic confidence (Section 6).

4 Model for Value Speculative Microarchitectures

The norm in previous work is to describe ambiguously the microarchitectural implications of value–speculation. It is also common not to state assumptions or offer rationale for a value of a design parameter. The discussion in Section 3 illustrated that value–speculation may cause pervasive changes on a microarchitecture. Furthermore, subtle to describe but distinct microarchitectural features - with possibly different cost and complexity - may represent quite different or similar performance points (Section 6). We interpret this as a call for more formalized approach for describing value speculation microarchitectures.

We propose the combining of different microarchitectural mechanisms(variables) that influence speculative execution under a single model called *speculative-execution model*. Consequently, when describing a speculative execution the following information should be provided:

- a specific list of variables and their values, and
- manifestations of speculative execution in terms of latency between different microarchitectural events.

Below we summarize the design space of speculative execution models in terms of model variables and some of their possible values. The value(s) determine a method for implementing the mechanism corresponding to a variable.

Model Variable	Values
WakeUp	ready fields, issue flag, predicted-state, confidence
Selection	ready fields, instruction type, confidence
Branch Resolution	speculative or valid operands
Memory Resolution	speculative or valid operands
Invalidation	complete, selective (hierarchical or parallel)
Verification	hierarchical, parallel (based on retirement or dedicated network)

A model manifests itself in terms of at least the following **latency variables** that describe the latency required between microarchitectural events influenced by speculative execution. The latency variables are defined from the end of the first event to the end of the second event and should be given in terms of cycles:

Execution – Equality, latency required to determine if the prediction and a computed value are equal assuming equality is performed immediately after an instruction finishes execution.

Equality – Invalidation, latency required for an instruction to be invalidated after it was determined that a predecessor's prediction was incorrect. This may not be a fixed number of cycles (for example, the latency of selective serial invalidation is a function of the dependence chain invalidated).

Equality – Verification, similar to the previous but for correct predictions.

Verification – Free issue resource, latency after an instruction is verified before it can release its reservation station entry.

Verification – Free retirement resource, latency after an instruction is verified before it can release its reorder buffer entry.

Invalidation – Reissue, latency after an instruction is invalidated before it can reissue.

Verification – Branch, latency after verification of the inputs of a branch before a branch can issue.

Verification Address – Memory Access, latency after verification of a speculative address generation before issue to memory.

These latencies are not all relevant to every speculative execution model. The latency for branch and memory instructions is pertinent if these instruction types are not allowed to be resolved based on speculative values. The verification – free issue resource latency is not relevant when instructions issued with predicted and/or speculative values do not retain their reservation station. We note that the latencies for the events need not be given separately, for example instead of reporting Execution – Equality and Equality – Verification with two separate values they can be combined as Execution – Equality – Verification and described by a single value.

It is worthwhile to note that no previous work identified all of these microarchitectural events. To our best knowledge, this is the first paper that breaks misspeculation into three events: Execution – Equality, Equality – Invalidation, Invalidation – Reissue. Typically, misspeculation was treated as a single event with one cycle latency. In general, previous work may have overlooked value speculation events that may be performance critical.

Although we do not claim that the above are complete for describing speculative execution precisely, we believe that this is a more systematic approach that can mitigate the problems mentioned before. In the next section, we present several speculative execution models and vary some parameters to illustrate how they influence execution.

4.1 Example Speculative Execution Models

This section considers few speculative execution models with the following values for the model variables: instructions can wakeup based on id-tags and state-tags; selection is based on instruction types and dynamic order and considers speculative state (i.e. considers whether operands are predicted/speculative or valid); branches are always resolved based on valid values; memory instructions are not allowed to access memory with speculative addresses; verification/invalidation is based on the verification network. The specific choices were described with more detail in Section 3.

Three models, denoted **super**, **great**, and **good** are considered and defined as follows:

Latency Variable	Super	Great	Good
Execution – Equality – Invalidation	0	0	1
Execution – Equality – Verification	0	0	1
Verification – Free Issue Resource	1	1	1
Verification – Free Retirement Res.	1	1	1
Invalidation – Reissue	0	1	1
Verification – Branch	0	1	1
Verification Address – Mem. Access	0	1	1

When computation does not include predicted values, all models have behavior identical to the base-processor. Recall that because we have a unified issue/retirement structure, the latency to free(release) issue and retirement resources is the same. Also note that in the proposed microarchitecture, resources cannot be free earlier than a cycle following the completion of an instruction.

The *super* model is the most optimistic and the *good* model the most pessimistic. The difference between the *good* and the *great* is in verification/invalidation latency, from one to zero cycle. The *super* model has zero cycle verification/invalidation, zero cycle reissue latency - that can enable mispredicted instructions to execute early - and zero cycle latency to inform branch and memory instructions when their inputs become valid.

Fig. 1 illustrates the pipelined execution of three instructions using the three speculative execution models with correct and incorrect prediction. The figure also shows the execution without value speculation. For all seven scenarios the common initial condition is that the three instructions are in the instruction window. The various pipeline latency events are defined in the figure (EX for execution, W for write to RS etc). The three instructions, labeled 1, 2 and 3, form a dependence chain: 2 depends on 1 and 3 depends on 2.

The base processor requires 5 cycles to retire all instructions. For the misprediction scenario it is assumed that the outputs of 1 and 2 are mispredicted. The figure shows that the more optimistic a model is the more activities are packed in a cycle. For instance, for the Super model, at the beginning of cycle t+1 it is detected (effectively with zero latency) that the outputs of instructions 1 and 2 were mispredicted. At the same time the successors of the two instructions get invalidated (that will be instructions 2 and 3). Also at t+1, instruction 2 that consumes the output of instruction 1 is scheduled for reissue and starts executing. Instruction 3 wakes-up at t+1 and is scheduled during cycle t+1 to execute at t+2. In contrast, the *good* model detects the mispredictions early in cycle t+1 and instructions 2 and 3 get invalidated by the end of the cycle. During t+2 is determined that instruction 2 can reissue. Instruction 2 gets executed during cycle t+3. At t+3 instruction 3 wakes up and is scheduled to execute at t+4.

The most important observation from the example is that execution behavior appears to be sensitive to the model event-latencies. Note that for the *good* model, unlike *super* and *great* models, instructions with predicted outputs, but not predicted or speculative inputs, still need to go through verification.

The models represent a spectrum of designs with variable degree of optimism regarding the different latencies and are only a *few* of numerous possible models. We believe that exploring the design space of different speculative execution models and understanding their requirements is essential for: (a) better comprehending how to design value–speculative processors, and (b) focusing research effort on performance critical issues. We evaluate the performance of the *super*, *great* and *good* models in Section 6.

5 Simulation Methodology

5.1 Parameters

To evaluate the performance of the different speculative execution models, a simulation study was performed for the microarchitecture presented in Section 2. The various model events were integrated in an out-of-order simulator. Provided the simulator is accurate, it offers the means to evaluate and compare the performance for various speculative execution models.

The simulator used in this work is a modified version of the out-of-order simplescalar simulator[5]. A gshare branch predictor[24] is used that hashes 16 bits of global branch history with the 16 lower bits of the branch PC to index a 64K prediction table. The branch predictor is updated with correct information following each prediction. Unconditional and direct jumps are always predicted correctly. Conditional branch targets are assumed to be predicted correctly as long as the branch direction is correct. The L1 instruction cache contains 64KB of instructions, with 32B per block, is 4-way associative and a hit requires 1 cycle. An ideal fetch engine is assumed: provided instruction references hit in the cache and branches are predicted correctly, then the fetch engine can read and align from multiple basic blocks in the same cycle. The L1 data cache has the same configuration as the instruction cache, however, has as many ports as half the issue width of the processor under consideration and its hit time is 2 cycles. A unified L2 cache that can hold 1MB of data and instructions is used. This L2 cache is 4-way associative, with 64B per block, 12 cycle hit and 36 cycle miss time. A load/store queue with size equal to the instruction window is used. Loads can receive a value from a preceding store in the queue in a single cycle. Wrong path instructions are executed and their side effects are modeled. There are no resource constraints except limited number of data cache ports. All simple integer instructions require one cycle to execute. Complex integer operations and floating point operations, depending on the type, require from 2 to 24 cycles.

Simulations were performed for all integer SPEC95

Benchmark	Input Flags	Dynamic Instr (mil)	Instructions Predicted (%)
compress	400000 e 2231	103	70.5
gcc	gcc.i	203	67.3
go	9 9	132	78.7
ijpeg	specmun.ppm	129	82.0
m88ksim	scrabbl.in	120	70.6
perl	modified train	40	63.9
vortex	modified train	101	61.9
xlisp	7 queens	202	61.7

Table 1. Benchmark Characteristics

benchmarks(Table 1). The benchmarks were compiled using the simplescalar *gcc* compiler with *-O3* optimization. Speedup was calculated as a ratio of the performance of a configuration with value prediction to an identical configuration without value prediction. For average speedup calculation harmonic mean was used. Arithmetic mean was used for reporting average prediction rates so each benchmark effectively contributes the same number of predictions.

5.2 Value Predictor and Confidence Estimation

This work considered the performance of value–speculation with a context-based value predictor[33, 34]. The predictor uses two tables. The first level (or history table) is indexed with the PC of the predicted instruction. An entry in the history table maintains the context - a hash of the most recent 4 values produced by the instructions that map to the entry. The context is used to index into the second table - prediction table - and read out a 32 bit prediction. We used direct mapped 64K entry history table and a 64K entry prediction table. Entries in the history table are always updated whereas the prediction table uses a one bit counter to guide replacement.

In addition to the tables used for prediction, a table is used for providing confidence estimation. A confidence table is indexed using the PC of the predicted instruction and contains resetting counters that are incremented by 1 on correct predictions and reset to 0 on incorrect predictions. A prediction is considered confident when the confidence value is at maximum. In the simulations we compare the performance of real confidence based on a confidence table and that of an oracle confidence. When real confidence is employed we assume a table with 64K entries with 3 bit resetting counters in each entry. No attempt is made to optimize the realistic confidence mechanism[2, 8], the intention is to observe general trends when in use. Future work should consider confidence in more detail.

One other predictor dimension considered is the effects of update timing on prediction. Results are presented when the value predictor is update immediately (I) after prediction with the correct value, or delay updated at retirement (D). When delayed updating is used, the history table of the predictor is updated speculatively with the prediction.

6   Results

This section reports on the performance of three speculative execution models: *good*, *great* and *super* discussed in Section 4.1. The performance of the models was measured for three processor configurations with issue width/window size: 4/24, 8/48 and 16/96. Each configuration was studied for real (R) and oracle (O) confidence using delayed (D) and immediate (I) update timing (D/R, I/R, D/O and I/O). We report averages and do not show the individual benchmark behavior due to space limitations - the individual benchmark behavior is similar to the overall.

Fig. 3 shows the average speedup for the various models and different configurations. As expected, and shown in a number of previous studies, value speculation has the potential to improve performance. The benefits are increasing with larger issue width and window size. As it was argued in[13], wider processors expose more dependences and hence increase the potential of value–speculation.

Several important observations can be made: (a) the *good* model behaves significantly worse as compared to the *great* and *super* models; in some cases having worse performance than the base configuration, (b) there is no significant difference between the *great* and *super* models, (c) performance is much more sensitive to confidence than to the timing of updates.

The first observation underlines the importance of fast verification latency. The verification latency for the *good* model was 1 cycle whereas for the *great* and *super* models was 0. If 0 cycle verification is infeasible, is imperative to explore speculative execution models where verification can be varied between 1 and 0. The criticality of fast verification latency is underlined by the fact that even under immediate update and oracle confidence the performance can be lower than the base.

The small performance difference between the *super* and *great* models indicates that a cycle delay (a) for informing speculative branches and memory instructions that their inputs are (not)valid, and (b) for reissuing following misspeculation, are not critical to performance. Recall that branch and memory instructions are not allowed to resolve speculatively. The reason that the cycle delay may not be so detrimental is that when these types of instructions are predicted correctly they enable useful speculative execution of other instructions and hence their additional delay is not usually exposed. Also, the real confidence method used in this study, as we show next, allows very few misspeculations. Thus the quick reissue provided by the *great* model is underutilized. An interesting direction of future research

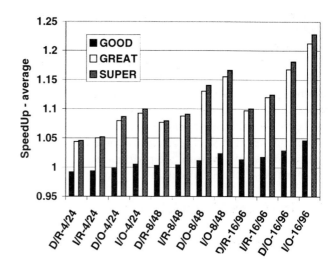

Figure 3. Speculative Execution Models Average Speedup

will be to study the above models with different confidence mechanisms. Specifically, we expect that with more frequent misspeculations, the relative difference of the *great* model will be more significant.

Another way to interpret the small performance difference between the *great* and *super* models is that accurate confidence can reduce the need for fast (and possibly complex) mechanisms for informing quickly speculative branch and memory instructions about the validity of their inputs. Recall that one of the reasons for using the verification network was to communicate quickly to the branch and memory instructions the speculative state (state-tag) of their inputs. The results indicate that this may not be important to performance. This fact, however, does not demonstrate that the verification network is not needed at all as it is also used to perform selective invalidation. An interesting direction of future research will be to investigate the relative importance of different verification schemes and determine how much additional benefit is provided by the verification network. Examples of schemes that can approximate the verification network include (in)validating successors up to a certain dependence chain depth, limiting the number of instructions that participate in a given (in)validation transaction, or limiting the period an instruction is not verified.

The data seem to support that confidence is a very significant performance parameter because moving from real confidence (X/R) to oracle confidence (X/O) provides a large performance increase (higher than the improvement achieved by immediate over delayed updating). This may indicate that either a lot of incorrect predictions are assigned high confidence and hence a lot of misspeculation, or many correct predictions are assigned low confidence and performance opportunity is lost. Prediction accuracy is considered

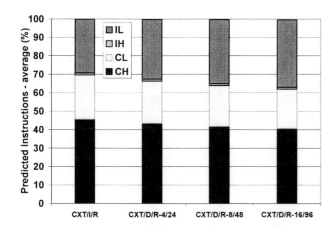

Figure 4. Average Prediction Accuracy

subsequently and reveals that the scheme based on 3–bit resetting counters performs poorly. This also suggests that one of the keys for realizing the potential of value prediction is accurate confidence predictors.

As for the effects of delayed updating on performance, the results suggest that more performance is lost, as compared to immediate updates, with increasing width/window. The reason is reduced prediction accuracy (discussed next).

Fig. 4 shows the average prediction accuracy for the great model. Predictions are divided into four sets, the set of predictions that were correct with high confidence (CH), correct predictions with low confidence (CL), incorrect predictions with high confidence (IH), and incorrect predictions with low confidence (IL). The total number of correct predictions is the sum of sets CH and CL. The results show that on the average 63% – 71% of the predictions are correct depending on the timing model and configuration used. The results suggest that context-based prediction is sensitive to timing and width/window size. Also it can be observed that with delayed updates and increasing width/window size prediction rate decreases.

One of the main reasons for lower accuracy, with increasing window size, is less constructive sharing of the prediction table among multiple instructions. With immediate updating, when two or more instructions produce identical sequences, one of the instructions can be mispredicted but is able to train the predictor immediately and, as a result, the other instructions get predicted correctly. Another reason for the sensitivity to update timing is any instruction that produces "almost" repeating sequences. Many of the correct predictions using context-based predictors are caused by instructions that are not 100% predictable. Immediately updating a predictor in the case of such instructions enables the context to point back to the correct sequence faster.

More interest to this work is the observation that the confidence method is successful in minimizing misspeculation (IH size is less than 1%), however this is done at the expense of a large set of correct predictions with low confidence (CL size is 20%–25% depending on the timing and configuration). This explains the large performance difference between real and oracle confidence and reinforces the importance of accurate confidence estimation for value prediction.

7   Conclusion

In this paper we argued that previous work did not describe systematically the effects of value speculation on a microarchitecture due to the lack of a formalized framework. We offer a discussion on the design space of value speculation to distinguish between subtle but possibly important design options, clarify misconceptions and provide research directions. The discussion is also used to underline the pervasive changes value speculation may require when integrated in a microarchitecture.

A model was introduced for a methodical description of microarchitectures that use value–speculation. The model isolates the parts of the microarchitecture that may be influenced by value speculation: wakeup, selection, verification, invalidation and resource releasing. The model describes the effect of value speculation on these parts of a microarchitecture in terms of various microarchitectural operations.

The model was integrated in a simulator that was used to investigate the performance of value–speculation. The results show value–speculation performance to have non-uniform sensitivity to changes in the latency of some events. For example, fast verification latency is found to be essential, but when misspeculation is infrequent slow invalidation may be acceptable.

8   Acknowledgments

James E. Smith is credited for supervising part of this work. Eric Rotenberg is acknowledged for influencing the author's views on microarchitectural issues. The original inspiration for this work was provided by Stamatis Vassiliadis. We thank the anonymous referees for their useful suggestions and constructive critique. Finally, the author is indebted to Pedro Trancoso and Toni Juan for proof–reading this manuscript and Francisco Jesus Sanchez for his comments on an earlier draft of the paper.

References

[1] J. L. Baer and T. F. Chen. An Effective on-chip Preloading Scheme to Reduce Data Access Penalty. In *Proceedings of Supercomputing*, pages 176–186, November 1991.
[2] M. Bekerman, S. Jourdan, R. Ronen, G. Kirshenboim, L. Rappoport, A. Yoaz, and U. Weiser. Correlated load-address predictors. In *Proceedings of the 26th Annual International Symposium on Computer Architecture*, June 1999.

[3] B. Black, B. Mueller, S. Postal, R. Rakic, N. Utamaphethai, and J. P. Shen. Load Execution Latency Reduction. In *Proceedings of the 12th International Conference on Supercomputing*, June 1998.

[4] W. Buchholz. *Planning a Computer System*. McGraw-Hill Book Company, NY, 1962.

[5] D. Burger, T. M. Austin, and S. Bennett. Evaluating Future Microprocessors: The SimpleScalar Tool Set. Technical Report CS-TR-96-1308, University of Wisconsin-Madison, July 1996.

[6] M. Burtcher and B. G. Zorn. Exploring Last n Value Prediction. In *International Conference on Parallel Architectures and Compilation Techniques*, 1999.

[7] M. J. C. Fu, S. Larin, and T. Conte. Value Speculation Scheduling for High Performance Processors. In *Proceedings of the 8th International Conference on Architectural Support for Programming Languages and Operating Systems*, October 1998.

[8] B. Calder, G. Reinman, and D. Tullsen. Selective value prediction. In *Proceedings of the 26th Annual International Symposium on Computer Architecture*, June 1999.

[9] Eric Rotenberg and Quinn Jacobson and James E. Smith. A study of control independence in superscalar processors. Technical Report CS-TR-98-1389, University of Wisconsin-Madison, December 1998.

[10] J. A. Fisher. Trace Scheduling: A Technique for Global Microcode Compaction. *IEEE Transactions on Computers*, 30(7):478–490, July 1981.

[11] F. Gabbay and A. Mendelson. Speculative Execution Based on Value Prediction. Technical Report (Available from http://www-ee.technion.ac.il/fredg), Technion, November 1996.

[12] F. Gabbay and A. Mendelson. Can Program Profiling Support Value Prediction? In *Proceedings of the 30th Annual ACM/IEEE International Symposium on Microarchitecture*, pages 270–280, December 1997.

[13] F. Gabbay and A. Mendelson. The Effect of Instruction Fetch Bandwidth on Value Prediction. In *Proceedings of the 25th Annual International Symposium on Computer Architecture*, pages 272–281, June 1998.

[14] J. Gonzalez and A. Gonzalez. The Potential of Data Value Speculation. In *Proceedings of the 12th International Conference on Supercomputing*, pages 21–28, June 1998.

[15] E. Jacobsen, E. Rotenberg, and J. E. Smith. Assigning Confidence to Conditional Branch Predictions. In *Proceedings of the 29th Annual ACM/IEEE International Symposium on Microarchitecture*, pages 142–152, December 1996.

[16] E. Larson and T. Austin. Compiler Controlled Value Prediction using Branch Predictor Based Confidence. In *Proceedings of the 33nd Annual ACM/IEEE International Symposium on Microarchitecture*, 2000.

[17] S. Lee, Y. Wang, and P. Yew. Decoupled Value Prediction on Trace Processors. In *HPCA9*, 2000.

[18] S. Lee and P. Yew. On Some Implementation Issues for Value Prediction on Wide-Issue ILP Processors. In *International Conference on Parallel Architectures and Compilation Techniques*, 2000.

[19] M. Lipasti. *personal communication*, 1999.

[20] M. H. Lipasti. Value Locality and Speculative Execution. Technical Report CMU-CSC-97-4, Carnegie Mellon University, May 1997.

[21] M. H. Lipasti and J. P. Shen. Exceeding the Dataflow Limit via Value Prediction. In *Proceedings of the 29th Annual ACM/IEEE International Symposium on Microarchitecture*, pages 226–237, December 1996.

[22] M. H. Lipasti, C. B. Wilkerson, and J. P. Shen. Value Locality and Data Speculation. In *Proceedings of the 7th International Conference on Architectural Support for Programming Languages and Operating Systems*, pages 138–147, October 1996.

[23] P. Marcuelo and A. Gonzalez. Value Prediction for Speculative Multithreaded Architectures. In *Proceedings of the 32nd Annual ACM/IEEE International Symposium on Microarchitecture*, 1999.

[24] S. McFarling. Combining Branch Predictors. Technical Report DEC WRL TN-36, Digital Western Research Laboratory, June 1993.

[25] A. Moshovos, S. E. Breach, T. J. Vijaykumar, and G. Sohi. Dynamic Speculation and Synchronization of Data Dependences. In *Proceedings of the 24th International Symposium on Computer Architecture*, pages 181–193, June 1997.

[26] Y. Nakra, R. Gupta, and M. L. Soffa. Value prediction in vliw machines. In *Proceedings of the 26th Annual International Symposium on Computer Architecture*, June 1999.

[27] J. Parcerisa and A. Gonzalez. Reducing Wire Delay Penalty through Value Prediction. In *Proceedings of the 33nd Annual ACM/IEEE International Symposium on Microarchitecture*, 2000.

[28] G. Reinman and B. Calder. Predictive Techniques for Aggressive Load Speculation. In *Proceedings of the 31st Annual ACM/IEEE International Symposium on Microarchitecture*, pages 127–137, December 1998.

[29] E. Rotenberg. *personal communication*, 1999.

[30] E. Rotenberg, Q. Jacobson, Y. Sazeides, and J. E. Smith. Trace Processors. In *Proceedings of the 30th Annual ACM/IEEE International Symposium on Microarchitecture*, pages 138–148, December 1997.

[31] B. Rychlik, J. Faistl, B. Krug, and J. P. Shen. Efficacy and Performance of Value Prediction. In *International Conference on Parallel Architectures and Compilation Techniques*, October 1998.

[32] Y. Sazeides. An Analysis of Value Predictability and its Application to a Superscalar Processor. *PhD Thesis, University of Wisconsin-Madison*, 1999.

[33] Y. Sazeides and J. E. Smith. Implementations of Context–Based Value Predictors. Technical Report ECE-TR-97-8, University of Wisconsin-Madison, Dec. 1997.

[34] Y. Sazeides and J. E. Smith. The Predictability of Data Values. In *Proceedings of the 30th Annual ACM/IEEE International Symposium on Microarchitecture*, pages 248–258, December 1997.

[35] Y. Sazeides, S. Vassiliadis, and J. E. Smith. The Performance Potential of Data Dependence Speculation & Collapsing. In *Proceedings of the 29th Annual ACM/IEEE International Symposium on Microarchitecture*, pages 238–247, December 1996.

[36] J. E. Smith. A Study of Branch Prediction Strategies. In *Proceedings of the 8th International Symposium on Computer Architecture*, pages 135–148, May 1981.

[37] J. E. Smith and A. R. Pleszkun. Implementing Precise Interrupts in Pipelined Processors. *IEEE Transactions on Computers*, 37(5):562–573, May 1988.

[38] A. Sodani and G. S. Sohi. Understanding the Differences between Value Prediction and Instruction Reuse. In *Proceedings of the 31st Annual ACM/IEEE International Symposium on Microarchitecture*, pages 205–215, December 1998.

[39] G. Sohi. Instruction Issue Logic for High Performance, Interruptible, Multiple Functional Unit, Pipelined Computers. *IEEE Transactions on Computers*, 39(3):349–359, March 1990.

[40] R. M. Tomasulo. An Efficient Algorithm for Exploiting Multiple Arithmetic Units. *IBM Journal of Research and Development*, 11:25–33, January 1967.

[41] D. M. Tullsen and J. S. Seng. Storageless value prediction using prior register values. In *Proceedings of the 26th Annual International Symposium on Computer Architecture*, June 1999.

[42] G. Tyson and T. Austin. Improving the Accuracy and Performance of Memory Communication through Renaming. In *Proceedings of the 30th Annual ACM/IEEE International Symposium on Microarchitecture*, December 1997.

[43] Y. Wu, D. Chen, and J. Fang. Better exploration of region-level value locality with integrated computation reuse and value prediction. In *Proceedings of the 28th Annual International Symposium on Computer Architecture*, May 2001.

The FAB Predictor: Using Fourier Analysis to Predict the Outcome of Conditional Branches

Martin Kampe, Per Stenström, and Michel Dubois[†]

Department of Computer Engineering
Chalmers University of Technology
SE–412 96 Göteborg, Sweden
{*mkampe,pers*}@*ce.chalmers.se*

[†]Department of Electrical Engineering - Systems
University of Southern California
Los Angeles, CA 90089-2562, USA
(213)-740-4475
Fax: (213)-740-7290
dubois@paris.usc.edu

Abstract

This paper proposes to transform the branch outcome history from the time domain to the frequency domain. With our proposed Fourier Analysis Branch (FAB) predictor, we can represent long periodic branch history patterns — as long as 2^{13} bits — with a realistic number of bits (52 bits).

We evaluate the potential gains of the FAB predictor by considering a hybrid branch predictor in which each branch is predicted using a static scheme, the 2-bit dynamic scheme, the PAp and GAp schemes, and our FAB predictor. By including our FAB predictor in the hybrid predictor, it is possible to cut the misprediction rate of integer applications in the SPEC95 suite by between 5 and 50% with an average of 20%. Besides evaluating its performance, this paper shows some key properties of our FAB predictor and presents some possible implementation approaches.

1 Introduction

One factor that limits further exploitation of instruction-level parallelism is the accuracy with which the outcome of conditional branch instructions can be predicted. Even if the prediction strategies proposed in the past achieve branch prediction accuracies in excess of 90%, small mispredictions can severely cut performance as future processors are expected to rely on more aggressive speculation mechanisms and on deeper pipelines [16].

There are two approaches to branch prediction: static and dynamic. In static schemes (e.g. [6, 3, 10]), high-level or profile information based on previous executions is used to predict the most likely outcome for each branch instruction. Static prediction schemes work well for branch instructions that are mostly taken or not-taken. However, since they do not exploit run-time information, they cannot adapt to changes in branch execution behavior at run-time.

Among the first dynamic schemes was the 2-bit scheme [17], where noise in the form of occasional changes in the outcome of the branch execution is filtered out. This schemes fails, however, when the branch outcome alternates between taken and not-taken, resulting in a 50% misprediction rate. As a remedy, Yeh and Patt [20, 21] introduced the Per-Address correlated branch prediction scheme, PAp. Conceptually this scheme acknowledges that an outcome of a branch execution may be correlated to the previous history *pattern* of the branch execution outcome, rather than just the last two outcomes as is the case in the 2-bit scheme. The PAp scheme can require a lot of storage bits depending on the size of the repeated outcome history pattern. Yeh and Patt also introduced the global correlation scheme, GAp, together with PAp. The GAp scheme exploits the fact that the outcome of a branch instruction may be correlated to the outcome of a previous branch instruction, hereby reducing the total number of history bits.

Even though the PAp and the GAp schemes significantly improve branch prediction accuracy, it still leaves the problem of predicting accurately the branch instructions that are not correlated to other branch instruction and whose branch history pattern exhibits periodic behavior with a long period resulting in a large number of history bits. Recent studies [2, 12, 22, 5] have demonstrated increased branch prediction accuracy if the size of the outcome history is increased significantly. This observation has triggered some research into methods to store the history information in a more condense manner. For example, in [5] it is proposed to apply a standard data compression algorithm to reduce the storage space needed for history information. Data in [5] shows that a storage reduction of 20% can be achieved. The questions motivating our research are: Which fraction of the branch execution patterns is lost with realistically sized branch history registers and how can we store these patterns in a more condense form so that they can fit in such registers.

We propose to represent branch history information in the frequency domain rather than in the time domain. We use Fourier analysis to transform the time function of branch execution outcomes for each conditional branch instruction into the frequency domain. We have observed that some branch instructions in the SPEC95 integer applications have periods that are much longer than the number of history bits typically used in dynamic branch predictors (i.e., 32 bits). Our first observation is that one would need *more than 2^{13} history bits* per branch instruction in order to accurately maintain the whole period of all branch execution patterns. By mapping the history into the frequency domain, we show that we can *reduce drastically the size of this history information*! Additionally, we show that the approach based on the Fourier transform can cut the branch misprediction rate of integer applications in the SPEC95 suite (which are known to reach fairly low branch prediction accuracies) by up to 50% and on average by 20% compared to state-of-the-art dynamic schemes. Besides representing histories with very long periods, the Fourier transform algorithm also acts as a very accurate noise filter, conceptually similar to the filter implemented by the 2-bit scheme.

The primary contribution of this paper is the observation that it is beneficial to view branch execution history in the frequency domain rather than in the time domain as currently done. Our approach here is static, but nothing indicates that this is not possible to do dynamically. A second contribution of this paper is to propose a new branch predictor – the FAB predictor. The FAB predictor is an addition to state-of-the-art static and dynamic schemes and it applies Fourier analysis to branch execution patterns that cannot realistically be handled by current schemes. Our intent is not to replace current schemes, but to aid these schemes when they do not work well. The FAB predictor is a novel hardware implementation that can be improved in the future.

The outline of the paper is as follows. In the next section, we present the performance of some of the most promising branch prediction schemes proposed so far which, in later sections, will be compared to our Fourier analysis based branch prediction. In Section 3, we describe how Fourier analysis can be applied to branch prediction. Section 4 is devoted to a conceptual presentation of FAB – our Fourier analysis based predictor – along with some key properties associated with it. Our experimental findings are reported in Section 5 after which we propose possible implementations of a predictor that combines the advantages of existing schemes with those of a FAB predictor. Section 7 compares it to other branch compression technique. Finally, we discuss the implications of our findings and future research in the last section of the paper.

2 Performance of Branch Prediction

In this section, we establish a framework to isolate branch instructions that cannot be predicted sufficiently well with existing branch prediction schemes. The outcome of each branch instruction is predicted by a set of branch predictors in parallel and, for each branch instruction, we choose the prediction that yields the best accuracy. To remove interferences caused by implementation idiosyncrasies that are irrelevant for the purpose of the study, we abstract away some of the limitations that would otherwise make existing branch prediction schemes perform poorly.

Bench-mark	Input data	#	# Miss	Below	Benchmark description
Comp	10k k 2131	34M	2.41M	5M	Compress text files.
Gcc	jump.i	23M	0.69M	3M	GNU C compiler.
Go	2stone9	62M	7.44M	15M	GO game.
Li	train	24M	1.18	3M	Xlisp interpreter.
M88k	dcrand	15M	0.31M	1M	Motorola 88100 sim.
Perl	scrabb	5M	0.09 M	0.5M	Perl interpreter.

Table 1: Benchmarks used and input data sets. '#' is the total number of executed branches. '# Miss' is the total number of executed branches that are mispredicted with standard predictors. 'Below' is the total number of executions of branch instructions that have less than 99.99% success rate with standard predictors.

The set of existing branch prediction schemes we consider are a static scheme [6, 3], the 2-bit dynamic scheme [17], and the PAp and GAp [20, 21] dynamic schemes. To measure the prediction rates of these schemes, we have developed a simulation platform based on the so called "safe" version in the SimpleScalar package [1]. SimpleScalar is an execution-driven simulator using a MIPS ISA derivative. We drive it with a set of integer applications from the SPEC95 [18] benchmark suite according to Table 1. The benchmarks are compiled with no optimization using the gcc compiler that comes with the SimpleScalar package.

We have extended the SimpleScalar simulator with an on-line process that tags each branch instruction with the misprediction rate for each of the prediction schemes used in this study. We now explain in details the different prediction schemes and the on-line tagging process.

2.1 Static Predictors

There are two approaches to static branch prediction. First, by using source-level information only it is possible to determine whether a conditional branch instruction has a higher probability to go either way [6]. The disadvantage with the compiler method is that programs can be heavily dependent on data input. The second approach is to run the program to gather run-time information that can be fed into the compiler to improve the prediction accuracy [3]. This profiling approach has some known drawbacks [6]: It is time consuming, some applications may not permit it (e.g., real-time applications), it may be dependent on data input, and all sections of the program must be executed during profiling. In this study we do not look at how to extract the static information, we simply assume that it is possible.

In the first on-line tagging step we compare each branch execution pattern to an always taken pattern and an always not-taken pattern. The branch prediction rates for these two static predictors are then stored for each branch instruction.

2.2 Dynamic Predictors

The second predictor in our on-line tagging process is an extended version of the SimpleScalar built-in 2-bit dynamic predictor. The predictor is extended with a virtually infinite-size branch table, which eliminates the aliasing problem altogether. In the 2-bit scheme, each branch instruction is associated with a four-state finite-state machine [17].

The SimpleScalar output is a trace containing all branch instructions tagged with the branch prediction rates for the static and the 2-bit prediction schemes and their total branch execution outcome history in the form of zeroes and ones, taken/not-taken, history pattern for each branch instruction.

In order to evaluate correlated branch prediction schemes, the trace also contains time information, to record the order in which all branch instructions were executed. The reason for evaluating the correlation prediction schemes off-line is that we found it easier to avoid hardware limitations than if we had done it on-line in SimpleScalar.

The first correlation scheme called Per-Address (PA) prediction [20] exploits the correlation between executions of the same branch instruction. PA predictors differ from the 2-bit predictor because a PA predictor makes a prediction based on a branch execution history *pattern* rather than just the last two executions of the branch. The idea behind PA predictors is that a branch execution has a pattern of length up to k that is repeated periodically OR that it has a branch execution outcome such that it is taken up to n times and then not-taken for up to m times. The n and m version of PAp is a compact representation of long periods for branch patterns with a regular behavior (n times taken and m times not-taken). The maximum values of the parameters k, n and m are set to 32, 256, and 256, respectively, and are the same as in Evers et al.[8]. In the k case we save 32 outcomes for each branch instruction and use this history to predict the next outcome by pattern matching. In the n and m case two counters are associated with each branch instruction and we save the lengths of the last streaks of taken and not-taken outcomes. For example, if a branch instruction is taken 20 times and then it is not-taken 10 times (n=20 and m=10), then we predict that the branch will be taken 20 times. Please observe that only one of the two PA schemes, can be used for each branch instruction at a time. The prediction success rates for these two PA schemes are stored for each branch instruction based on the actual outcome.

The second correlation scheme exploits the correlation between the current branch instruction and other branch instructions previously executed. It is called Global Address prediction, or GAp. The following example of source code that generates globally correlated branch instructions is drawn from Evers et al. [8]:

```
if(cond1) (first branch)
...
if(cond1 AND cond2) (correlated branch)
```

In a set of correlated branch instructions, the branch ex-

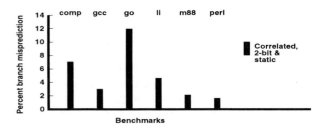

Figure 1: Misprediction with current branch predictors.

ecution history for the first branch instruction can be used to predict the outcome of the subsequent correlated branch executions. The scheme we model searches for the best correlated branch executions to each branch execution in the trace; thus, contrary to an actual implementation of the scheme, there is no restriction on how far apart these branch instructions can be in the program as long as the first branch instruction always executes before any correlated branch instruction. The prediction accuracy corresponding to the best matching branch instruction is selected.

2.3 Misprediction Rates

For each branch instruction, we have computed the minimum number of mispredictions across the four basic prediction schemes using the methodology described above. The resulting misprediction rates are displayed in Figure 1. It is interesting to note that, although we have eliminated implementation constraints, such as finite table sizes from this analysis, the misprediction rates for the aggressive hybrid scheme we model are still high and range from 2 to 12%.

Given the fact that we assume branch history tables with an infinite number of entries, the key remaining question is how much the misprediction rate is impacted by the limited size of each entry. If a branch instruction contributes largely to the misprediction rate and has a periodic branch history with a period longer than the size of the history entries, it cannot be predicted with the existing schemes above. We propose to apply a Fourier transform to map the branch history of these troublesome branch instructions to the frequency domain in the hope of representing them more compactly so that their history fits in a history register.

Fourier analysis is a time-consuming process. In order to reduce the amount of simulation work we did not apply the Fourier transform analysis to every branch. If a branch instruction is correctly predicted more than 99.99% of the time with any one of the four basic prediction schemes we did not run it through the Fourier transform. The number of branch executions evaluated with Fourier analysis is displayed in the "Below" column shown in Table 1. This threshold enables us to reduce the number of branch instructions on which we apply the Fourier analysis by 85%, on average. The main reason for this limit is that a large portion of the branch executions predicted with the four basic schemes end up in the interval of 99.99% to 100%. These branch executions can of course be evaluated too, but we believe it is unlikely that there is periodic behavior in these branches which is not already captured by current schemes.

3 Fourier Analysis of Branch Patterns

In this section we provide the basic background needed to understand how Fourier analysis works and how we can benefit from it in representing branch history patterns. For a more complete coverage of the fundamentals of Fourier analysis, please refer to e.g. [15]. Our idea to use Fourier analysis for branch execution prediction originated from a paper by Voldman and Hoevel [19], in which the authors applied Fourier analysis to predict cache misses.

Let $B_x(t)$ be a time series representing whether a branch instruction x is taken or not, where 1 denotes "taken" and 0 denotes "not-taken". Let the time t be the number of consecutive executions of a particular branch instruction. The Fourier transform, $F_x(\omega)$, for $B_x(t)$ is then:

$$F_x(\omega) = \int_{-\infty}^{\infty} B_x(t)e^{-j\omega t}\, dt$$

Since the function $B_x(t)$ is a discrete time series, we use the discrete Fourier transform. Then the integral above can be approximated by a sum of sine components (see e.g. [15] for more information.) The discrete Fourier transform routine used in this study was provided by FFTW [11] and computed with double precision in the complex dimension. Our goal is to detect repeated behavior in the branch history outcome, especially periodic behavior with very long periods. To illustrate this, let us consider some examples of branch execution patterns.

Let's assume first that we have a simple branch execution pattern that is taken every third time the branch is executed, i.e., $B_{x,f=3}(t) = 001001001001....$ The frequency spectrum of $B_{x,f=3}(t)$ is shown in Figure 2.

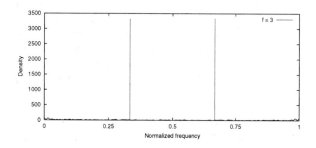

Figure 2: Frequency diagram of the branch execution pattern: 001001001...

The x-axis in Figure 2 is the normalized frequency and scales from 0 to 1. Please observe that the x-axis is mirrored around 0.5 due to a property of the discrete Fourier transform [15]. As the frequency is normalized to the total number of executions of a branch instruction, events occurring on every z reference are observed at $1/z$ on the x-axis. This normalization facilitates the comparison between branch instructions with different frequency of execution.

The y-axis displays the density of events: the more frequently an event occurs every z references the higher the density at $1/z$. The density can be interpreted as the probability that a branch is taken with a frequency of $1/z$. Figure 2 illustrates the case of a branch which is taken every third time it is executed and hence there is a sharp peak at 1/3 in the frequency spectrum. We can safely predict from the frequency spectrum that the branch is taken every third time it is executed. However, for this simple example, other schemes, such as PAp, are just as effective.

The frequency spectrum of the second example, $B_{y,f=5} = 0000100001...$, is shown in Figure 3.

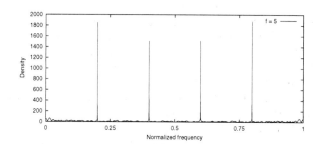

Figure 3: Frequency diagram of the branch execution pattern: 000010000100001...

The expected component for $B_{y,f=5}(t)$ is 0.2 (1/5). However it is accompanied by another component at normalized frequency 0.4. This added component is the first harmonic for the base frequency 0.2 and its frequency is obtained by adding the base frequency to itself, i.e., 0.2 + 0.2 = 0.4.

The branches with history patterns $B_{x,f=3}(t)$ or $B_{y,f=5}(t)$ could be easily predicted by, for instance, a PAp predictor. Let's assume however that the branch conditions of two branch instructions x and y affect the branch outcome of a third branch instruction b in such a way that if x or y are taken, then b is also taken. The taken/not-taken pattern of branch instruction b would then be:

$B_{x,fre=3}(t) = 001001001001001...$
$B_{y,fre=5}(t) = 000010000100001...$
==================
$B_{b,f=3\&5}(t) = 001011001101001...$

The Fourier transform of $B_{b,f=3\&5}(t)$ is displayed in Figure 4. The frequency spectrum in Figure 4 is not a simple merging of Figure 2 and 3. There is a third component at 0.066(=1/15) and then there are three other harmonics. Since 15 is the least common multiplier for 3 and 5, the component at 15 is redundant because every 15:th access, the value of either $B_{x,f=3}(t)$ or $B_{y,f=5}(t)$ is 1.

While a branch with the combined period given by $B_{b,f=3\&5}(t)$ can be predicted with PAp since the history length is only 15, it is easy to construct an example where the required history would be long in the time domain. Consider a branch such that $B_{z,f=7}(t)$ is added to $B_b(t)$, then the least common multiplier becomes $7*15 = 105$. Hence,

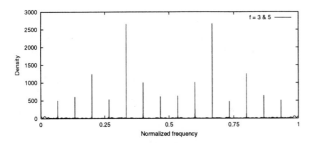

Figure 4: Frequency diagram of the branch execution pattern: 001011001101001....

a history of 105 bits is required to store this history pattern. By representing this pattern in the frequency domain using the Fourier transform, we are able to reduce the number of bits required, since we only need to keep track of three frequencies in this example (1/3, 1/5 and 1/7).

Please observe that the simple relation between the frequency spectrum and the branch execution time function $B(t)$ shown in Figure 2 to 4 is hardly the case in reality, as illustrated by the branch execution pattern from a real execution in Figure 5. If a branch execution function only consisted of simple events as seen in Figure 2 and 3, we would not need to keep the amplitude (A) in the representation of a frequency component. However, by adding the amplitude to the frequency we are able to represent much more complex patterns than for instance $B_{b,f=3\&5}(t)$ and take advantage of the superposition of frequency components. For example, the first 50 outcomes of execution for the branch instruction at address 0x425d68 in m88ksim is shown below. Using four Fourier components we are able to predict this branch correctly almost 100% of the time. By contrast, the best of the four existing schemes, the 2-bit scheme, only achieves a branch prediction accuracy of 60%. At first glance, the pattern looks simple, but the actual period is 562 and not 9, as a cursory look at the pattern might suggest.

01001000101001000101001000101 0
0100010100100010100 1...

The GAp predictor is ineffective for this branch because it does not correlate with any other branch. This particular branch instruction in m88ksim is used to decide whether a *simulated* instruction is a "branch" instruction or not. It is preceded by other branch instructions that select between other simulated instructions. If we always had a simulated "branch" instruction preceded by, let say, a simulated "add" we could take advantage of the correlation, since the branch instruction for the "add" would always be taken before the branch instruction for the "branch". Unfortunately this is not the case and the GAp predictor is mostly ineffective. The PAp predictor is also ineffective since the repeated execution pattern is of length 562 and the maximum values for k is 32. In addition, since the pattern does not contain contiguous series of ones or zeroes, it is not possible to represent it using PAp with m and n either. Finally, it is clear

that the execution pattern cannot be represented with a static value as there is neither a strong bias towards the taken nor the not-taken case.

The Fourier theorem states that any periodic waveform can be derived from the superposition of a series of frequency components. The square wave in Figure 6 can be constructed using a Fourier expansion of sine waves. The more frequency components are used, the better the approximation is.

The three curves in the figure show improvement of the square waveform with increased number of frequency components. In our case, the waveform would be the branch execution pattern that we are trying to predict. Representing correctly a sharp edge with a Fourier transform requires a large number of frequency components. This is illustrated in Figure 6, which shows the approximation of a square waveform with increasing numbers of frequency components. If we need a large number of frequency components to represent a branch execution pattern we also need a lot of space to store the frequency components, which is what we are trying to avoid. Fortunately, there is no need to represent accurately sharp waveform edges in the branch execution pattern as we will show in the next sections. As we will see, complex branch pattern waveforms can often be represented with just a few frequency components.

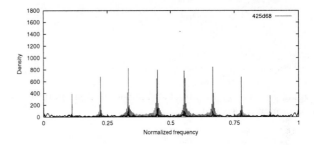

Figure 5: Frequency diagram for the branch in m88ksim at address 0x425d68.

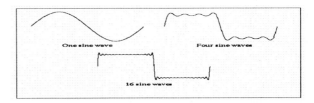

Figure 6: Superposition of sinusoidal waveforms to form a square wave.

4   FAB: Fourier Analysis Branch Predictor

We first propose a strategy for extracting the frequency components of a branch history pattern using the Fourier transform in Section 4.1. We also show how they can be used to predict future branches by transforming them back to the time domain. Then we discuss some key properties of FAB in Section 4.2.

4.1 Frequency Component Extraction

If a branch pattern history $B(t)$ is represented by n frequency components, $A_n * sin(\omega_n t)$, each frequency component contributes to the probability that the branch execution is taken. The maximum value each component can add to the total probability, $P_{tot}(t)$, is A_n. The probability that a branch is taken at time t is computed as the sum of all frequency components:

$$P_{tot}(t) = \sum_{n=1}^{N} A_n * sin(\omega_n t) / \sum_{n=1}^{N} A_n$$

Hence, in the FAB predictor, if $P_{tot}(t)$ exceeds a threshold TH at time t, the branch execution is predicted as taken. Through experimentation, we have found that a threshold of half of the sum of the amplitudes A_n yields the best prediction accuracy, i.e.,

$$TH = 0.5 \sum_{n=1}^{N} A_n$$

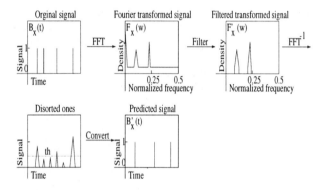

Figure 7: Strategy to extract and create FAB predictions for one branch instruction.

The process to construct a Fourier analysis based (FAB) predictor is displayed in Figure 7. The first step is to transform the stream of ones and zeros for each branch execution pattern into the frequency domain by using the Fourier transform, as shown by the first arrow in Figure 7. Among the created frequency components, we keep those with the highest peaks, as shown by the second arrow in Figure 7. In other words the components that contribute the most to the probability P_{tot} are kept, and the rest is discarded. This selection has the desirable effect of filtering out aperiodic events (i.e., noise) in the branch execution pattern, as they have a small amplitude (or probability) in the frequency spectrum. As mentioned in Section 2 we are only interested in periodic events, even if they have a long period. In other words, we filter the original frequency function $F_x(\omega)$ constructed from the actual branch execution pattern $B_b(t)$ for a branch instruction b and end up with a filtered frequency function $F_x'(\omega)$ that only contains the high peaks, as shown in the third diagram in Figure 7. These peaks are represented by an amplitude and a frequency and their time domain equivalent is then used as a predictor for the original branch execution pattern. These frequency components

$A_n * sin(\omega_n t)$ constitute the FAB predictor. To predict if a branch execution is taken or not at time t, all the frequency components are added together and if the sum exceeds the threshold TH, as seen in the fourth diagram in Figure 7, the branch is predicted as taken. Please observe that the inverse Fourier transformation, the FFT^{-1} arrow in Figure 7 corresponds to the summation of frequency components, $A_n * sin(\omega_n t)$, described above.

The aim of our FAB predictor is, as mentioned before, not to be better at already "well" predicted branch executions, but to aid in the cases where it is not easy to make a good prediction using existing predictors. Therefore, the FAB predictor can be viewed as an additional contribution in the context of branch classification [2, 12] for a certain type of branch instructions. These branch instructions are typically those which have (i) a longer period in their periodic execution pattern than afforded by the size of history registers, (ii) do not correlate to other branches, and (iii) for which static predictors do not work well because there is not a strong bias towards either the taken nor the not-taken case.

4.2 Properties of FAB

The major drawback of the FAB predictor is that it does not work well for branch execution patterns with a large deviation from a pattern with a 50-50 distribution of taken/not-taken outcomes. The reason is that a waveform edge requires a lot of frequency components to be accurately reconstructed as shown in Figure 6. As shown in Figure 8, a large number of frequency components on top of the base sine wave in the bottommost diagram is needed to reconstruct the square waveform in the topmost diagram with enough accuracy given the threshold used. Using a single frequency component, the base sine wave, will result in a taken rate that is much higher than that of the real branch execution function because of the width of the sine wave for the given threshold. In general, the bigger the deviation is from a 50-50 distribution of taken/not-taken the more frequencies are needed. For more information, please refer to texts on Fourier analysis (e.g., [15]).

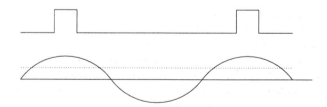

Figure 8: A branch execution pattern with a low fraction of taken outcomes. Representing the waveform with a small number of sine waves is subject to large prediction errors. In this example the single sine wave is above the threshold for a longer time than the time the branch is taken. The threshold is marked with a dotted line.

It would seem that the 50-50 restriction on the distribution limits the use of the FAB predictor, but it has been shown in previous studies such as [2, 12] that it is just for this kind of branches that current predictors experience difficulties. Figure 9 shows the histogram of the taken/not-taken distribution for the branches in the li and m88ksim benchmarks. For example, the 0-20% category corresponds to branches that are taken 0-20% of the time. In Figure 9 we can observe that a majority of the branches in the m88ksim benchmark are in the 41-60% category whereas, in the li benchmark, the branch instructions are spread across the entire range. This is probably why the FAB predictor improves the branch behavior of m88ksim much more than li.

In the next section, we show the extent to which the FAB predictor improves branch prediction for branches with which existing branch predictors have problems.

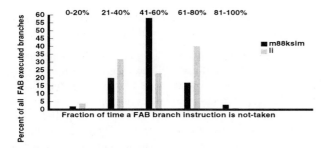

Figure 9: Distribution of taken / not-taken branches in the m88ksim and li benchmarks.

5 Experimental Results

In Section 5.1, we present simulation results for the base configuration of our FAB branch predictor. This configuration uses four frequencies. Section 5.2 evaluates the tradeoff between the number of frequencies in the Fourier representation and the branch prediction accuracy.

5.1 Base Case

To evaluate the performance of our FAB predictor, we compare it to the currently available predictors according to the methodology described in Section 2, which is extended as follows. We first tag the branch instructions with the misprediction rate of the four basic predictors described in Section 2. Then we apply the FAB predictor to the branch instructions yielding less than 99.99% accuracy and, if the FAB predictor has a lower misprediction rate than the others, we use it instead.

In Figure 10, we show the branch execution misprediction rate obtained with the four existing techniques as well as the misprediction rate obtained after adding the FAB predictor. To get the misprediction rate for the branch executions with the FAB predictor we compare the first diagram in Figure 7 with the last diagram in Figure 7. In other words we compare the $B(t)$ with the $B'(t)$ function.

As seen in Figure 10 misprediction reduction is close to 20 percent on average. We expect this reduction to improve performance significantly, especially for processors with wider instruction windows. The addition of the FAB predictor reduces the number of mispredicted dynamic branches

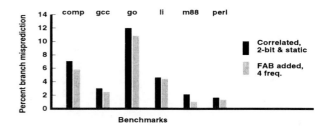

Figure 10: Branch misprediction rate for the four basic prediction schemes and for the four basic prediction schemes augmented with FAB (4-freq).

in Table 1 to 2.00 millions in compress, 0.51 million in gcc, 6.82 millions in go, 1.12 million in li, 0.15 million in m88ksim, and 0.05 million in perl. Two benchmarks exhibit very different misprediction reduction: m88ksim and li. m88ksim has a misprediction reduction of over 50 percents whereas, for li, we only observe a 5 percents misprediction reduction. The high misprediction reduction for m88ksim may be explained by the fact that the outcome of each FAB predicted branch instruction is affected by several factors and each factor is easy to detect with FAB. On the other hand, the reason for the small reduction in li is conjectured to be caused by the unbalanced distribution of taken/not-taken pattern as shown in Figure 9.

Today's branch prediction schemes could reap the same benefits as the FAB predictor provided history registers with very large number of bits are available. Figure 11 shows the distribution of the period length for the branch instructions predicted with FAB. To estimate the period length we simply compute the least common multiplier of the four frequencies used to build the branch execution pattern. However, please note that this is not a precise method. To illustrate this consider the following, with a repeating pattern of 010, except that every 10 times the pattern is 011:

010 010 010 010 010 010 010 010 010 011 ...

Whereas the whole period is 30, the prediction accuracy is only slightly affected if we used a period of three instead. Therefore, the values in Figure 11 should be interpreted as an indication of the period rather than a precise value. Figure 11 reveals that the length of the period of the branch execution patterns for branches successfully predicted with FAB is 2^{13} or more in most cases.

In order to understand the underlying behavior of branch instructions that work well with FAB we have randomly sampled 10 branch instructions in each benchmark and thoroughly evaluated them. All the sampled branches have in common that their branch behavior is affected by more than one branch condition variable, such as:

if(cond1 OR cond2 OR cond3)

A typical example of this kind of branch instructions is a branch in the m88ksim benchmark, which checks whether a simulated instruction is a branch. The instruction set of the m88k processor has a number of different types of branches

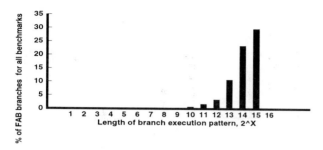

Figure 11: Number of history bits in the branch patterns targeted by FAB.

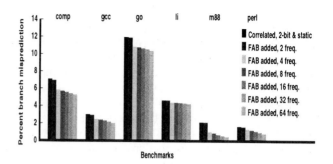

Figure 12: Effect of the number of frequencies used in FAB on the branch misprediction rate.

and each of these branches occurs in the simulated code with a fairly periodic behavior. However since there are a number of different branch types and each type has a different frequency the overall branch pattern is fairly complex.

Another example is drawn from the li benchmark. In li, the number of parameters of a lisp instruction is evaluated in the following loop:

while(..) {.. if(last parameter) jump; ..}

Since each lisp instruction usually has more than one parameter, the branch execution pattern may look like this:

0000100010010001....

The lisp instructions in this example have 4, 3, 2, and 3 parameters respectively. Even though the pattern can be repeated due to locality in the lisp instruction executions it is very difficult for a FAB predictor to take advantage of this. The reason is probably that a FAB predictor needs a close to 50% distribution of taken/not-taken outcomes in the pattern and, in most cases, a lisp instruction has more than 2 parameters, which leads to an uneven distribution. This uneven distribution characteristic of the li benchmark can also be observed in Figure 9.

5.2 Number of Frequencies vs. Accuracy in FAB

In Section 5.1 we used four frequencies for our FAB predictor. If we used all frequencies, (normally thousands) we would reach a 100% prediction accuracy, but a prohibitive amount of storage would then be needed. In Figure 12 we can see that that the misprediction rate drops abruptly until four frequencies and, for more than four frequencies, the improvement of the misprediction rate flattens out, which suggests that using four frequencies is a good choice.

6 Hardware implementation

In this section we discuss hardware implementations of the FAB predictor. In Section 5.1 we saw that the FAB predictor is intended for branch instructions that have more than one factor influencing their outcome. Determining whether a branch instruction has several factors affecting it can be carried out at compile time. The selected branches can then be profiled in order to confirm that they are well-suited for representation by a FAB predictor. The profiling step also serves a second purpose, namely to obtain the frequency components for the branches to be predicted with the FAB predictor. To achieve the best result, the input data in the profiling stage should be selected so that all the branch instructions in the program are executed.

We concluded in Section 5.2 that four frequencies is a good compromise and as will be explained subsequently, each frequency component needs 13 bits for its representation. The representation of each component, $A * sin(\omega t)$, comprises two parts. The first part is the amplitude A or the density as shown on the y-axis in Figure 2, 3, and 4. The density part needs 3 bits, which can represent 8 levels. From Figure 4 we see that there are more than 8 levels in the density scale. However, these density levels can easily be quantified to fit in 8 levels. We have run the FAB predictor with all levels as well as with only 8 levels and the misprediction rates in both cases are virtually the same. The second part in the frequency representation is the $sin(\omega t)$ component. ω can be constructed from the frequency f on the x-axis in Figure 2, 3, and 4, by using the formula: $\omega = 2 * \pi * f$. In our evaluations no frequency f exceeded 32; hence f can be represented by 5 bits. 5 additional bits are used as a counter, in order to know where in the sine-wave we presently are. The counter counts from f down to zero and, when zero is reached, it is reinitialized to f.

An inverse Fourier Transform must be computed dynamically to predict every branch, see Section 4. In other words the frequency components must be added together. To speed up this process, we propose to hard-code one period of a sinusoidal waveform in a table. (If storage space is an issue we can reduce the storage space by a factor four by only storing a fourth of a sine wave, since all needed information is present in that quarter. However this requires extra computation steps, such as inversion or negation, when the lookup is not done in the first quarter.) The key parameter of the sinusoidal function is ω rather than the frequency, but, since a table is used, we can scale entries by 2π and use f directly to index the table. To be able to get the value of a frequency component at a certain time we use the time in the counter t multiplied by f for the branch instruction to look up the sine table. This lookup provides the amplitude from the sine table, which must be multiplied by the A value of the frequency component. This procedure is then repeated

230

for the four frequencies for the branch and the components are summed up. If the sum is greater than a threshold, normally $0.5 * maximum value$, then the branch execution is predicted as taken. The procedure is shown in Figure 13, where the flow goes from top to bottom. Please observe that only one set of the hardware is required, since we only alter the Branch history entry in the hardware for different branches. Our sine table has 32 entries, since f can only have the maximum value of 32.

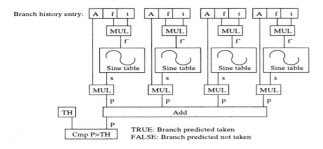

Figure 13: Hardware implementation. Flow goes from top to bottom.

In Figure 13 t is the counter value, f the frequency, and A the frequency components fc amplitude. f' is the equivalent of ω and used to lookup the hard-coded sine wave (sine table in Figure 13) and p_x is the probability for the x:th frequency component to be taken. These probabilities are added to the total probability P. As we use four frequency components the process is repeated four times in order to get the correct total probability P that a branch is taken. Please observe that this is executed in parallel in our implementation. When P is calculated we need to compare it to the threshold TH. The threshold TH can either be stored or calculated by dividing the sum of all amplitudes by two.

Please observe that these computations can be done in advance, before the next execution of a particular branch instruction. We can even predict branches in batches, reducing the workload even more. Let us assume we predict four outcomes of a branch execution pattern in one batch. We do not need to do the first two lookups in the frequency component entry, since f is the same and t is equal to the old t plus one. The multiplication is needed $f' = t * f$, since t changed and we also need a new lookup for s. The amplitude A is already known so we do not need its lookup, but the multiplication to get the frequency component value, $fc = A * s$ is needed since s has a new value. We also need to sum up the contributions of the frequency components. In summary we can reduce the computation per branch by three table lookups.

Instead of using hardware to compute the inverse Fourier Transform, we can use helper threads in the context of simultaneous multithreaded processors, as was previously proposed in papers by Chappell et al. [4] and by Song and Dubois [7]. There are two main advantages of using helper threads. First, complex schemes, like ours, can be written in microcode and hereby be less complex to implement in

hardware. Second, the scheme can be very flexible: We can for instance use different routines in different settings or turn the feature off completely. This is very suitable to our approach, since the FAB predictor is an add-on to other schemes. Each branch instruction may be preceded in the code by a SPAWN instruction that invokes the right predictor for this particular branch instruction. As mentioned before we can, at compile time, select the branch instructions benefiting from the FAB predictor. The branch instructions that work well with FAB will invoke a FAB routine while other will invoke a classical branch predictor such as gshare.

In this paper the FAB predictor is static. However it might be envisioned to use FAB predictors on the fly, especially if we have a large number of transistors [16] and if we are able to select the FAB branches at compile time.

One could argue that, if we have one billion transistor to waste on a chip, we might have enough storage space to store the branch patterns as is done today. However we have shown in Figure 11, that storing long branch patterns for all branches is not feasible, unless we can find some very effective compression method for the patterns.

7 Related Work

There has been research aiming to reduce the storage needed for branch history. Chen et al. [5] used a classical data compression algorithm to encode periodic branch execution patterns. One idea would be to use this compression algorithm in conjunction with a correlated scheme. However, our evaluations show that, using this compression technique, we still need 2^{10} bits to represent branch history patterns in addition to executing a compute-intensive algorithm (zip) each time we predict a branch execution.

Another idea presented by Federovsky et al. [9] is the context tree weighting algorithm. The branch execution is predicted by going through a tree where each tree branch represents a possible path for the branch execution. Each tree branch is weighted and the prediction is made by walking the path in the tree with the highest probability. The number of storage bits used in this method is reduced; however, whether this method can exploit the long branch execution patterns we aim for is questionable.

Jimenez and Lin [14] used perceptrons in order to reduce the number of storage bits. According to their evaluations, they can reduce the number of bits by one fourth. Even if this is a great achievement, it still requires large amount of storage for branch pattern periods that are 2^{13} bits long.

Finally, another interesting approach to reduce the length of the branch history is to encode a Boolean formula in the branch instruction, Jimenez, Hanson, and Lin [13]. By doing this the large branch prediction table is not needed. However the method requires N bits to be encoded in the branch instruction to be able to predict a branch history pattern of N bits. Therefore it is not possible to predict branches with long history patterns, since that would result in extremely long branch instructions.

8 Discussion and Conclusion

Accurate branch prediction is significant to overall processor performance [16]. The main contribution of this paper is to demonstrate the benefits of representing branch prediction histories in the frequency domain instead of in the time domain. By using the frequency domain the storage needed for branch patterns is dramatically reduced. We also show up to 50% reduction in branch misprediction as compared to correlated schemes such as PAp and GAp [20]. The branch instructions we target have a periodic history with a very long period that can not be affordably stored in an entry of a branch history table. We believe that the reason behind the long periods is that the outcomes of some branches depend on several factors in the program. Each of these factors taken independently has a short period, which explains the effectiveness of frequency based prediction.

Our approach here is static, since the main goal is to evaluate the FAB approach as a method. However we think it is possible to use FAB dynamically. As explained in Section 6, the FAB branches may be tagged at compile time.

The FAB method should be viewed as part of Branch Classification [2] [12] where different predictors are effective for different types of branches. The branches well predicted by FAB are typically branches that have a 50%-50% taken/not-taken rate and this is typically the type of branches where ordinary predictors do not do well [2].

In this paper we have also proposed hardware implementations of our scheme. We believe that the FAB idea will work best in an environment with a multithreaded processor, [7], using Simultaneous Subordinate Microthreading (SSMT) described by Chappell et al. [4]

The method of using frequency-based branch prediction is far from fully evaluated, especially the hardware implementation. Our future work will focus on implementation schemes as well as making it a dynamic method. Another important fact is that the basic approach used in FAB prediction is not limited to branch prediction; in fact most predictions can be made with this method, including the prediction of memory access patterns. Such prediction might lead to improved cache replacement and prefetching algorithms. To be successful however the 50%-50% distribution must be present in the pattern we try to predict.

Acknowledgments

Appreciations to J. Jeong, M. Karlsson, J. Lext, P. Rundberg, and X. Qiu for help in various ways. This research is supported by the Swedish Research Council on Engineering Science (TFR) (contract: 211-1997-593) and The Swedish Foundation for International Cooperation in Research and Higher Education (STINT) under the MECCA project. Sun Microsystems has generously provided an equipment grant to support this research. Michel Dubois is funded by NSF Grant #MIP-9223812.

References

[1] Doug Burger and M. Todd Austin. The SimpleScalar Tool Set, Version 2. Technical report, University of Wisconsin-Madison Computer Science Department, 1997.

[2] Po-Yung Chang, Eric Hao, Tse-Yu Yeh, and Patt Yale. Branch Classification: a New Mechanism for Improving Branch Predictor Performance. In *Proceedings of the 27th Annual International Symposium on Microarchitecture*, pages 22–31, Nowember 1994.

[3] Pohua P. Chang, Scott A. Mahlke, and Wen-mei W. Hwu. Using Profile Information to Assist Classic Code Optimizations. *Software - Practice and Experience (SPE)*, 21(12):1301–1321, 1991.

[4] Robert S. Chappell, Jared Stark, Sangwook P. Kim, Steven K. Reinhardt, and Yale N. Patt. Simultanious Subordinate Microthreading (SSMT). In *Proceedings of the 26th International Symposium on Computer Architecture*, pages 186–195, May 1999.

[5] I-Cheng K. Chen, John T. Coffey, and Trevor N. Mudge. Analysis of Branch Prediction via Data Compression. In *Proceedings of the ASPLOS VII*, pages 128–137, October 1996.

[6] Brian L. Deitrich, Ben-Chung Cheng, and Wen-mei W. Hwu. Improving Static Branch Prediction in a Compiler. In *Proceedings of the Parallel Architectures and Compilation Techniques*, pages 214–221, October 1998.

[7] Michel Dubois and Yong Ho Song. Assited Execution. Technical report, University of Southern California Department of Electrical Engineering, 1998.

[8] Marius Evers, Sanjay J. Patel, Robert S. Chappell, and Yale N. Patt. An Analysis of Correlation and Predictability: What Makes Two-Level Branch Predictors Work. In *Proceedings of the 25th International Symposium on Computer Architecture*, pages 52–61, June 1998.

[9] Eitan Federovsky, Meir Feder, and Shlomo Weiss. Branch Prediction Based on Universal Data Compression Algorithms. In *Proceedings of the 25th International Symposium on Computer Architecture*, pages 62–71, June 1998.

[10] Joseph A. Fisher and Stefan M. Freudenberg. Predicting Conditional Branch Directions From Previous Runs of a Program. In *Proceedings of the ASPLOS V*, pages 85–95, October 1992.

[11] Matteo Frigo and Steven G. Johnson. *FFTW User's Manual*. http://www.fftw.org/, November 1999.

[12] Michael Haungs, Phil Sallee, and Matthew Farrens. Branch Transition Rate: A New Metric form Improved Branch Classification Analysis. In *Proceedings of the 6th International Symposium on High-Performance Computer Architecture*, pages 241–250, January 2000.

[13] Daniel A. Jimenez, Heather L. Hanson, and Calvin Lin. Boolean Formula-based Branch Prediction for Future Technologies. In *Proceedings of the Parallel Architectures and Compilation Techniques*, pages 97–106, September 2001.

[14] Daniel A. Jimenez and Calvin Lin. Dynamic Branch Prediction with Perceptrons. In *Proceedings of the 7th International Symposium on High-Performance Computer Architecture*, Jannuary 2001.

[15] Alan V. Oppenheim, Alan S. Willsky, and Ian T. Young. *Signals and Systems*. Prentice-Hall International Inc., 1 edition, 1983.

[16] Yale N. Patt, Sanjay J. Patel, Evers Marius, Daniel H. Friendly, and Jared Stark. One BillionTransistors, One Uniprocessor, One Chip. *COMPUTER*, 30(9):51–57, 1997.

[17] Jim Smith. A Study of Branch Prediction Strategies. In *Proceedings of the 8th International Symposium on Computer Architecture*, pages 135–148, May 1981.

[18] The Standard Performance Evaluation Corporation (SPEC). *SPEC 95 Benchmarks*. http://www.spec.org/, August 1995.

[19] J. Voldman and Lee W. Hoevel. The software-cache connection. *IBM Journal of Research and Development*, 25(6):877–893, November 1981.

[20] Tse-Yu Yeh and Yale Patt. Two-Level Adaptive Branch Prediction. In *Proceedings of the 24th Annual ACM/IEEE International Symposium on Microarcitecture*, pages 51–61, November 1991.

[21] Tse-Yu Yeh and Yale Patt. Alternative Implementations of Two-Level Adaptive Branch Prediction. In *Proceedings of the 19th Annual International Symposium on Computer Arcitecture*, pages 124–134, December 1992.

[22] Tse-Yu Yeh and Yale N. Patt. A Comparison of Dymaic Branch Predictors that use Two Levels of Branch History. In *Proceedings of the 20th International Symposium on Computer Architecture*, pages 257–266, May 1993.

Power Issues Related to Branch Prediction

Dharmesh Parikh[†], Kevin Skadron[†], Yan Zhang[‡], Marco Barcella[‡], Mircea R. Stan[‡]
Depts. of [†]Computer Science and [‡]Electrical and Computer Engineering
University of Virginia
Charlottesville, VA 22904
{dharmesh,skadron}@cs.virginia.edu, {yz3w,mb6nj,mrs8n}@ee.virginia.edu

Abstract

This paper explores the role of branch predictor organization in power/energy/performance tradeoffs for processor design. We find that as a general rule, to reduce overall energy consumption in the processor it is worthwhile to spend more power in the branch predictor if this results in more accurate predictions that improve running time. Two techniques, however, provide substantial reductions in power dissipation without harming accuracy. Banking reduces the portion of the branch predictor that is active at any one time. And a new on-chip structure, the prediction probe detector (PPD), can use pre-decode bits to entirely eliminate unnecessary predictor and branch target buffer (BTB) accesses. Despite the extra power that must be spent accessing the PPD, it reduces local predictor power and energy dissipation by about 45% and overall processor power and energy dissipation by 5–6%.

1. Introduction

This paper explores tradeoffs between power and performance that stem from the choice of branch-predictor organization, and proposes some new techniques that reduce the predictor's power dissipation without harming performance. Branch prediction has long been an important area of study for micro-architects, because prediction accuracy is such a powerful lever over performance. Power-aware computing has also long been an important area of study, but until recently was mainly of interest in the domain of mobile, wireless, and embedded devices. Today, however, power dissipation is of interest in even the highest-performance processors. Laptop computers now use use high-performance processors but battery life remains a concern, and heat dissipation has become a design obstacle as it becomes more difficult to developing cost-effective packages that can safely dissipate the heat generated by high-performance processors.

While some recent work has explored the power-performance tradeoffs in the processor as a whole and in the memory hierarchy, we are aware of no prior work that looks specifically at issues involving branch prediction. Yet the branch predictor, including the BTB, is the size of a small cache and dissipates a non-trivial amount of power—10% or more of the total processor's power dissipation—and its accuracy controls how much mis-speculated execution is performed and therefore has a substantial impact on energy. For this reason, it is important to develop an understanding of the interactions and tradeoffs between branch predictor organization, processor performance, power spent in the predictor, and power dissipation in the processor as a whole.

Reducing power dissipated in the branch predictor can actually have harmful effects. If reducing the power spent in the predictor comes at the expense of predictor accuracy and hence program performance, this localized reduction may actually increase total power (*i.e.*, energy) dissipated by the processor by making programs run longer. Fortunately, not all the techniques that reduce localized power dissipation in the branch predictor suffer such problems. For example, breaking the predictor into banks can reduce power by accessing only one bank per cycle and hence reducing precharge costs, and banking need not have any effect on prediction accuracy. Eliminating some branch-predictor accesses altogether is an even more powerful way to reduce power.

Overall, there are four main levers for controlling the branch predictor's power characteristics:

1. *Accuracy*: For a given predictor size, better prediction accuracy will not change power dissipation within the predictor, but will make the program run faster and hence reduce total energy.

2. *Configuration*: Changing the table size(s) and can reduce power within the predictor but may affect accuracy.

3. *Number of Lookups*: Reducing the number of lookups into the predictor is an obvious source of power savings.

4. *Number of Updates*: Reducing the number of predictor updates is another obvious source, but is a less powerful lever because mis-speculated computation means that there are more lookups than updates, and we do not further consider it here.

Branch predictors predict conditional branches taken or not taken according to the outcome of the previous ones. This state must be kept in some sort of on-chip storage. All the tables used to store information—whether caches, branch predictors, or BTBs—consist of essentially the same structure: a memory core of SRAM cells accessed via row and column decoders. Correctly modeling such array structures is very important for accurate estimations of performance and power consumption.

1.1. Contributions

This work extends the Wattch 1.02 [3] power/performance simulator to more accurately model branch-predictor behavior, and then uses the extended system to:

- Characterize the power/performance characteristics of different predictor organizations. As a general rule, to reduce overall energy consumption it is worthwhile to spend *more* power in the branch predictor if it permits a more accurate organization that improves running time.

- Explore the best banked predictor organizations. Banking improves access time and cuts power dissipation at no cost in predictor accuracy.

- Propose a new method to reduce lookups, the *prediction probe detector* (PPD). The PPD can use compiler hints and pre-decode bits to recognize when lookups to the BTB and/or direction-predictor can be avoided. Using a PPD cuts power dissipation in the branch predictor by over 50%.

- Revisit and develop new techniques for speculation control via pipeline gating [16]. Even despite adaptive speculation control based on recent predictor accuracy, pipeline gating has little effect for today's more sophisticated and accurate predictors.

Although a wealth of dynamic branch predictors have been proposed, we focus on power issues for a representative sample of the most widely used predictor types: bimodal [23], GAs/gshare [17, 29], PAs [29], and hybrid [17]. We focus mostly on the branch predictor that predicts directions of conditional branches, and except for eliminating unnecessary accesses using the PPD, do not explore power issues in BTB. The BTB has a number of design choices orthogonal to choices for the direction predictor. Exploring these is simply beyond the scope of this paper. Please note that data for the "predictor power" includes power for both the direction predictor and the BTB.

Our goal is to understand how the different branch-prediction design options interact at both the performance and power level, the different tradeoffs that are available, and how these design options affect the overall processor's power/performance characteristics. Our hope is that these results will provide a road-map to help researchers and designers better find branch predictor organizations that meet various power/performance design goals.

1.2. Related Work

Some prior research has characterized power in other parts of the processor. Pipeline gating was presented by Manne *et al.* [16] as an efficient technique to prevent mis-speculated instructions from entering the pipeline and wasting energy while imposing only a negligible performance loss. Albonesi [1] explored disabling a subset of the ways in a set associative cache during periods of modest cache activity to reduce cache energy dissipation. He explores the performance and energy implications and shows that a small performance degradation can produce significant reduction in cache energy dissipation. Ghose and Kamble [10] look

at sub-banking and other organizational techniques for reducing energy dissipation in the cache. Kin *et al.* [15] and Tang *et al.* [26] describe filter caches and predictive caches, which utilize a small "L0" cache to reduce accesses and energy expenditures in subsequent levels. Our PPD performs a somewhat analogous filtering function, although it is not itself a branch predictor. Ghiasi *et al.* [9] reasoned that reducing power at the expense of performance is not always correct. They propose that software, including a combination of the operating system and user applications, should use a performance mechanism to indicate a desired level of performance and allow the micro-architecture to then choose between the extant methods that achieve the specified performance while reducing power. Finally, Bahar and Manne [2] propose an architectural solution to the power problem that retains performance while reducing power. The technique, called *pipeline balancing*, dynamically tunes the resources of a general purpose processor to the needs of the application by monitoring performance within each application.

The rest of this paper is organized as follows. The next section describes our simulation technique and our extensions to the Wattch power model. Section 3 then explores tradeoffs between predictor accuracy and power/energy characteristics, and Section 4 explores changes to the branch predictor that save energy without affecting performance. Finally, Section 5 summarizes the paper.

2. Simulation Technique and Metrics

Before delving into power/performance tradeoffs, we describe our simulation technique, our benchmarks, and the ways in which we improved Wattch's power model for branch prediction.

2.1. Simulator

For the baseline simulation we use a slightly modified version of the Wattch [3] version 1.02 power-performance simulator. Wattch augments the SimpleScalar [4] cycle-accurate simulator (*sim-outorder*) with cycle-by-cycle tracking of power dissipation by estimating unit capacitances and activity factors. Because most processors today have pipelines longer than five stages to account for renaming and en-queuing costs like those in the Alpha 21264 [14], Wattch simulations extend the pipeline by adding three additional stages between decode and issue. In addition to adding these extra stages to sim-outorder's timing model, we have made minor extensions to Wattch and sim-outorder by modeling speculative update and repair for branch history and for the return-address stack [20, 21], and by changing the fetch engine to recognize cache-line boundaries. A more important change to the fetch engine is that we now charge a predictor and BTB lookup for each *cycle* in which the fetch engine is active. This accounts for the fact that instructions are fetched in blocks, and that—in order to make a prediction by the end of the fetch stage—the branch predictor structures must be accessed before any information is available about the contents of the fetched instructions. This is true because the instruction cache, direction predictor, and BTB must typically all be accessed in parallel. Thus, even if the I-cache contains pre-decode bits, their contents are typically not available in time. This is the most straight-forward fetch-engine arrangement; a variety of other more sophisticated arrangements are possible, some of which we explore in Section 4.

Processor Core	
Instruction Window	RUU=80; LSQ=40
Issue width	6 instructions per cycle:
	4 integer, 2 FP
Pipeline length	8 cycles
Fetch buffer	8 entries
Functional Units	4 Int ALU, 1 Int mult/div,
	2 FP ALU, 1 FP mult/div,
	2 memory ports
Memory Hierarchy	
L1 D-cache Size	64KB, 2-way, 32B blocks, write-back
L1 I-cache Size	64KB, 2-way, 32B blocks, write-back
L1 latency	1 cycles
L2	Unified,2MB,4-way LRU
	32B blocks,11-cycle latency,WB
Memory latency	100 cycles
TLB Size	128-entry, fully assoc., 30-cycle miss
	penalty
Branch Predictor	
Branch target buffer	2048-entry, 2-way
Return-address-stack	32-entry

Table 1. Simulated processor configuration, which matches an Alpha 21264 as much as possible.

Unless stated otherwise, this paper uses the baseline configuration as shown in Table 1, which resembles as much as possible the configuration of an Alpha 21264 [14]. The most important difference for this paper is that in the 21264 there is no separate BTB, because the I-cache has an integrated next-line predictor [5]. As most processors currently do use a separate BTB, our work models a separate, 2-way associative, 2 K-entry BTB that is accessed in parallel with the I-cache and direction predictor.

To keep in line with contemporary processors, for Wattch technology parameters we use the process parameters for a $0.18\mu m$ process at V_{dd} 2.0V and 1200 MHz. All the results use Wattch's non-ideal aggressive clock-gating style ("cc3"). In this clock-gating model power is scaled linearly with port or unit usage, and inactive units still dissipate 10% of the maximum power.

We have also enhanced Wattch to account for power expenditures in column decoders and to better identify the best "square-ified" structure for the branch predictor. The column decoders increase power dissipation in the branch predictor by 10-15%, and this can be important when modeling changes that increase the size or numbers of decoders, such as with banking. Without a proper accounting for power expended in the column decoders, comparators and drivers, resulting conclusions might be incorrect. Accurate choice of the form factor of data arrays is important for similar

reasons. Although we are accustomed to thinking of array structures (branch predictors, caches etc.) with their logical dimensions, their implementations is different and is based on delay and energy considerations. The physical dimensions are typically as square as possible so that the bitline and wordline lengths are minimized. Details about these modifications can be found in an extended version of this paper [19].

2.2. Benchmarks

We evaluate the programs from the SPECcpu2000 [25] benchmark suite. Basic branch characteristics are presented in Table 2. Branch mispredictions also induce other negative consequences, like cache misses due to mis-speculated instructions, but we do not treat those second-order effects here. All benchmarks were compiled using the Compaq Alpha compiler with the SPEC *peak* settings, and the statically-linked binaries include all library code. Unless stated otherwise, we always use the provided reference inputs. We mainly focus on the programs from the integer benchmark suite because the floating point benchmarks have very good prediction accuracy and very few dynamic branches. We use Alpha EIO traces and the EIO trace facility provided by SimpleScalar for all our experiments. This ensures reproducible results for each benchmark across multiple simulations. *252.eon* and *181.mcf*, from SPECint2000, and *178.galgel* and *200.sixtrack*, from SPECfp2000, were not simulated due to problems with our EIO traces. All benchmarks were fast-forwarded past the first 2 billion instructions and then full-detail simulation was performed for 200 million instructions.

2.3. Metrics

The following metrics are used to evaluate and understand the results.

- Average Instantaneous Power: The total power consumed on a per-cycle basis. This metric is important as it directly translates into heat and also gives some indication of current-delivery requirements.

- Energy: Energy is equal to the product of the average power dissipated by the processor and the total execution time. This metric is important as it translates directly to battery life.

- Energy-Delay Product: This metric [11] is equal to the product of energy and delay (*i.e.*, execution time). Its advantage is that it takes into account both the performance and power dissipation of a microprocessor.

- Performance: We use the common metric of instructions per cycle (IPC).

3. Performance-Power Tradeoffs Related to Branch Prediction

3.1. Branch Predictors Studied

The bimodal predictor [23] consists of a simple *pattern history table* (PHT) of saturating two-bit counters, indexed by branch PC. This means that all dynamic executions of a particular branch site (a "static" branch) will map to the

	Dynamic Unconditional Branch Frequency	Dynamic Conditional Branch Frequency	Prediction Rate w/ Bimod 16K	Prediction Rate w/ Gshare 16K
gzip	3.05%	6.73%	85.87%	91.06%
vpr	2.66%	8.41%	84.96%	86.27%
gcc	0.77%	4.29%	92.03%	93.51%
crafty	2.79%	8.34%	85.88%	92.01%
parser	4.78%	10.64%	85.37%	91.92%
perlbmk	4.36%	9.64%	88.10%	91.25%
gap	1.41%	5.41%	86.59%	94.18%
vortex	5.73%	10.22%	96.58%	96.66%
bzip2	1.69%	11.41%	91.81%	92.22%
twolf	1.95%	10.23%	83.2%	86.99%
wupwise	2.02%	7.87%	90.38%	96.62%
swim	0.00%	1.29%	99.31%	99.68%
mgrid	0.00%	00.28%	94.62%	97.00%
applu	0.01%	0.42%	88.71%	98.95%
mesa	2.91%	5.83%	90.68%	93.31%
art	0.39%	10.91%	92.95%	96.39%
equake	6.51%	10.66%	96.98%	98.16 %
facerec	1.03%	2.45%	97.58%	98.70%
ammp	2.69%	19.51%	97.67%	98.31%
lucas	0.00%	0.74%	99.98%	99.98%
fma3d	4.25%	13.09%	92.00%	92.91%
apsi	0.51%	2.12%	95.24%	98.78%

Table 2. Benchmark summary.

same PHT entry. This paper models 128-entry through 16 K-entry bimodal predictors. The 128-entry predictor is the same size as that in the Motorola ColdFire v4 [27]; 4 K-entry is the same size as that in the Alpha 21064 [7] and is at the point of diminishing returns for bimodal predictors, although the 21164 used an 8 K-entry predictor [8]. The gshare predictor [17], shown in Figure 1a, is a variation on the two-level GAg/GAs global-history predictor [18, 29]. The advantage of global history is that it can detect and predict sequences of correlated branches. In a conventional global-history predictor (GAs), a history (the global branch history register or GBHR) of the outcomes of the h most recent branches is concatenated with some bits of the branch PC to index the PHT. Combining history and address bits provides some degree of anti-aliasing to prevent destructive conflicts in the PHT. In gshare, the history and the branch address are XOR'd. This permits the use of a longer history string, since the two strings do not need to be concatenated and both fit into the desired index width. This paper models a 4 K-entry GAs predictor with 5 bits of history; a 16 K-entry gshare predictor in which 12 bits of history are XOR'd with 14 bits of branch address (this is the configuration that appears in the Sun UltraSPARC-III [24]); a 32 K-entry gshare predictor, also with 12 bits of history; and a 32 K-entry GAs predictor with 8 bits of history. Instead of using global history, a two-level predictor can track history on a per-branch basis. In this case, the first-level structure is a table of per-branch history registers—the *branch history table* or BHT—rather than a single GBHR shared by all branches. The history pattern is then combined with some number of bits from the branch PC to form the index into the PHT. Figure 1b shows a PAs predictor. Local-history prediction cannot detect correlation, because—except for unintentional aliasing—each branch maps to a different entry in the BHT. Local history, however, is effective at exposing

patterns in the behavior of individual branches. The Intel P6 architecture is known to use a local-history predictor, although its exact configuration is unknown. This paper examines two PAs configurations: the first one has a 1 K-entry, 4-bit wide BHT and a 2 K-entry PHT; the second one has a 4 K-entry, 8-bit wide BHT and a 16 K-entry PHT. Both are based on the configurations suggested by Skadron *et al.* in [22].

Because most programs have some branches that perform better with global history and others that perform better with local history, a hybrid predictor [6, 17], Figure 1c combines the two. It operates two independent branch predictor components in parallel and uses a third predictor— the *selector* or *chooser*—to learn for each branch which of the components is more accurate and chooses its prediction. Using a local-history predictor and a global-history predictor as the components is particularly effective, because it accommodates branches regardless of whether they prefer local or global history. This paper models four hybrid configurations:

1. Hybrid_1: a hybrid predictor with a 4K-entry selector that only uses 12 bits of global history to index its PHT; a global-history component predictor of the same configuration; and a local history predictor with a 1 K-entry, 10-bit wide BHT and a 1 K-entry PHT. This configuration appears in the Alpha 21264 [14] and is depicted in Figure 1c. It contains 26 Kbits of information.

2. Hybrid_2: a hybrid predictor with a 1 K-entry selector that only uses 3 bits of global history to index its PHT; a global-history component predictor of 2K entries that uses 4 bits of global history; and a local history predictor with a 512 entry, 2-bit wide BHT and a 512 entry PHT. It contains 8 Kbits.

3. Hybrid_3: a hybrid predictor with an 8 K-entry selector that only uses 10 bits of global history to index its PHT; a global-history component predictor of 16K entries that uses 7 bits of

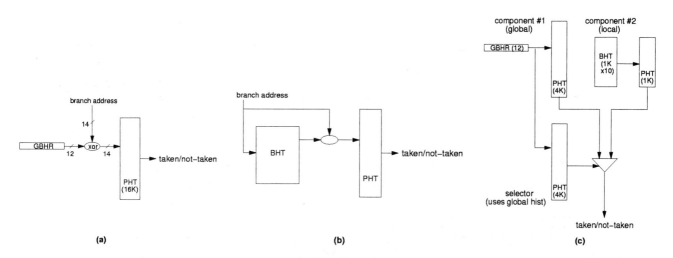

Figure 1. (a) A gshare global-history branch predictor like that in the Sun UltraSPARC-III. (b) A PAs local-history predictor. (c) A hybrid predictor like that in the Alpha 21264.

global history; and a local history predictor with a 1 K-entry, 8-bit wide BHT and a 4 K-entry PHT. It contains 64 Kbits.

4. Hybrid_4: a hybrid predictor with an 8 K-entry selector that only uses 6 bits of global history to index its PHT; a global-history component predictor of 16K entries that uses 7 bits of global history; and a local history predictor with a 1 K-entry, 8-bit wide BHT and a 4 K-entry PHT. It also contains 64 Kbits.

Hybrid_2, 3, and 4 are based on configurations found to perform well by Skadron *et al.* in [22].

3.2. Base Simulations for Integer Benchmarks

We now examine the interaction between predictor configuration, performance, and power/energy characteristics. In our discussion below, the term "average", wherever it occurs, means the arithmetic mean for that metric across all the benchmarks simulated.

Figure 2 (left) presents the average branch predictor direction accuracy for integer benchmarks, and Figure 2 (right) presents the corresponding IPC. For each predictor type (bimodal, GAs, gshare, hybrid, and PAs), the predictors are arranged in order of increasing size, and the arithmetic mean is superimposed on each graph as a thicker and darker curve. The trends are exactly as we would expect: larger predictors get better accuracy and higher IPC, but eventually diminishing returns set in. This is most clear for the bimodal predictor, for which there is little benefit to sizes above 4K entries. For the global-history predictors, diminishing returns set in at 16K entries. Among different organizations, gshare slightly outperforms GAs, and hybrid predictors are the most effective at a given size. For example, compare the 32 K-entry global predictors, hybrid_3 and 4, and the second PAs configuration: they all have 64 Kbits total area, but the hybrid configurations are slightly better on average and also for almost every benchmark.

Together Figure 3a and Figure 3b show that processor-wide energy is primarily a function of predictor *accuracy*

and not energy expended in the predictor. For example, although the energy spent locally in hybrid_3 and hybrid_4 is larger than for a gshare predictor of 16 K-entry, the chip-wide energy is almost the same. And the small or otherwise poor predictors, although consuming less energy locally in the predictor, actually cause substantially more chip-wide energy to be consumed. The hybrid_4 predictor, for example, consumes about 7% less chip-wide energy than bimodal-4K despite consuming 13% more energy locally in the predictor. This suggests that "low-power" processors (which despite their name are often more interested in long battery life) might be better off to use *large* and aggressive predictors if the die budget can afford it. The best predictor from an energy standpoint is actually hybrid_1, the 21264's predictor, which attains a slightly lower IPC but makes up for the longer running time with a predictor of less than half the size. Although hybrid_1 is superior from an energy standpoint, it shows less advantage on energy-delay; the 64 Kbit hybrid predictors (hybrid_3 and hybrid_4) seem to offer the best balance of energy and performance characteristics.

The power data in Figure 4 shows that power dissipation in the predictor is mostly a function of predictor size, and that unlike energy, power in the processor as a whole tracks predictor *size*, not predictor *accuracy*. This is because power is an instantaneous measure and hence is unaffected by program running time. Average activity outside the branch predictor is roughly the same regardless of predictor accuracy, so predictor size becomes the primary lever on overall power. Figure 4 also shows that if power dissipation is more important than energy, GAs_1_4K, gshare_16K, or one of the smaller hybrid predictors is the best balance of power and performance.

Finally, Figures 2, 3 and 4 also show data for individual benchmarks. It is clear that the group *crafty, gzip, vortex,* and *gap*, with high prediction rates, have high IPCs and correspondingly low overall energy and energy-delay despite higher predictor and total instantaneous power. The group

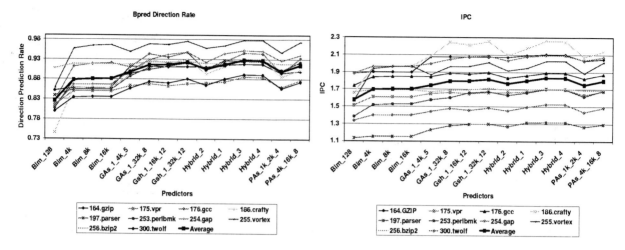

Figure 2. (a) Direction-prediction accuracy and (b) IPC for SPECint2000 for various predictor organizations. For each predictor type, the predictors are arranged in order of increasing size along the X-axis. The arithmetic mean is the dark curve in each of the graphs.

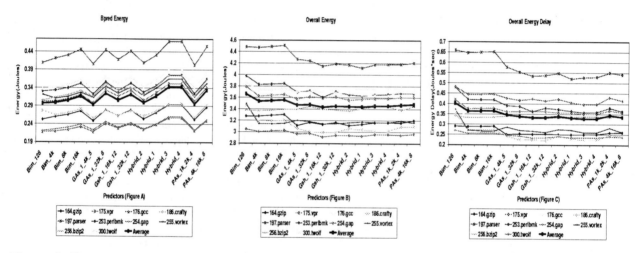

Figure 3. Energy expended in (a) the branch predictor and (b) the entire processor, and (c) energy-delay for the entire processor for SPECint2000.

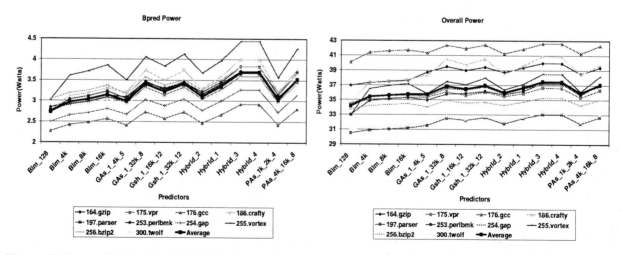

Figure 4. Power dissipation in (a) the branch predictor and (b) the entire processor for SPECint2000.

parser, twolf, and *vpr,* at the other extreme, have the exact opposite properties. This merely reinforces the point that almost always there would be no rise (and in fact usually a decrease) in total energy if we use larger branch predictors to obtain faster performance! We repeated these experiments for SPECfp2000. The trends are almost the same, with two important differences. First, because floating-point programs tend to be dominated by loops and because branch frequencies are lower, these programs are less sensitive to branch predictor organization. Second, because they are less sensitive to predictor organization, the energy curves for the processor as a whole are almost flat. Indeed, the mean across the benchmarks is almost entirely flat. This is because the performance and hence energy gains from larger predictors are much smaller and are approximately offset by the higher energy spent by larger predictors. Detailed plots can be found in an extended version of this paper [19].

4. Reducing Power That Stems from Branch Prediction

The previous section showed that in the absence of other techniques, smaller predictors that consume less power actually *raise* processor-wide energy because the resulting loss in accuracy increases running time. This section explores three techniques for *reducing* processor-wide energy expenditure without affecting predictor accuracy. All remaining experiments use only the integer programs because they represent a wider mix of program behaviors.We have chosen a subset of seven integer benchmarks: *gzip, vpr, gcc, crafty, parser, gap* and *vortex.* These were chosen from our ten original integer benchmarks to reduce overall simulation times but maintain a representative mix of branch-prediction behavior.

4.1. Banking

As shown by Jiménez, Keckler, and Lin [13], slower wires and faster clock rates will require multi-cycle access times to large on chip structures, such as branch predictors. The most natural solution to that is banking. We used a slightly modified version of Cacti [28] to determine the access times for a banked branch predictor. We assume that for any given access only one bank is active at a time; therefore banking not only saves us power spent in the branch predictor but also reduces access time, as shown in Figure 5. We plot cycle times normalized with respect to the maximum value, because achievable cycle times are extremely implementation-dependent and might vary significantly from the absolute numbers reported by Cacti. Banking might come at the cost of extra area, (for example due to extra decoders) but exploring area considerations is beyond the scope of this paper. The number of banks range from one in case of smaller predictors of size 2 Kbits or smaller to four in case of larger predictors of size 32 Kbits or 64 Kbits. The number of banks for different branch predictor sizes is given in Table 3.

Figures 6 and 7 show the average reduction in power and energy for the branch predictor and for the overall pro-

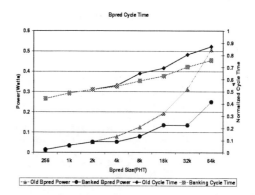

Figure 5. Cycle time for a banked predictor.

	No. of Banks
128bits	1
4Kbits	2
8Kbits	2
16Kbits	4
32Kbits	4
64Kbits	4

Table 3. Number of banks.

cessor with respect to the base simulation results. It can be observed that the largest decrease in predictor power comes for larger predictors. This is exactly as expected, since these predictors are broken into more banks. The large hybrid predictors do not show much difference, however, because they are already broken into three components of smaller sizes and banking cannot help much. Banking results in modest power savings in the branch predictor, but only reduces overall power and energy by about 1%.

4.2. Reducing Lookups Using a PPD

A substantial portion of power/energy in the predictor is consumed during lookups, because lookups are performed every cycle in parallel with the I-cache access. This is unfortunate, because we find that the average distance between control-flow instructions (conditional branches, jumps, etc.) is 12 instructions. Figure 8 shows that 40% of conditional branches have distance greater than 10 instructions, and 30% of control flow instructions have distance greater than 10 instructions. Jiménez *et al.* report similar data [13]. We also compared these results with gcc-compiled SimpleScalar PISA binaries. The results were similar, so these long inter-branch distances are not due to *nops* or predication.

This suggests that we should identify when a cache line has no conditional branches so that we can avoid a lookup in the direction predictor, and that we identify when a cache line has no control-flow instructions at all, so that we can eliminate the BTB lookup as well. If the I-cache, BTB, and direction predictor accesses are overlapped, it is not sufficient to store pre-decode bits in the I-cache, because they only become available at the end of the I-cache access, after the predictor accesses must begin.

Instead, we propose to store pre-decode bits (and possi-

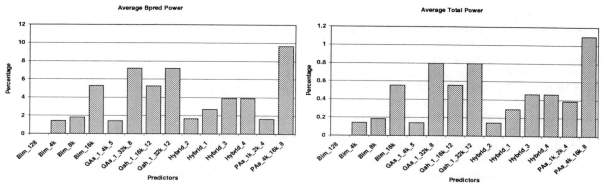

Figure 6. Banking results: percentage reduction in branch-predictor power (left) and overall power (right).

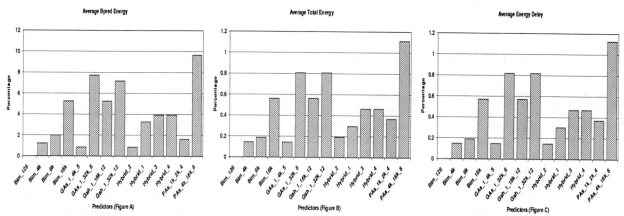

Figure 7. Banking Results: (a) Percentage reduction in branch-predictor energy, (b) overall energy, and (c) energy-delay.

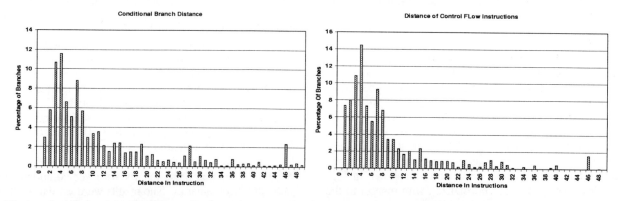

Figure 8. (a) Average distance (in terms of instructions) between conditional branches. (b) Average distance between control-flow instructions (conditional branches plus unconditional jumps).

bly other information) in a structure called the *prediction probe detector* (PPD). The PPD is a separate table with a number of entries exactly corresponding to I-cache entries. The PPD entries themselves are two-bit values; one bit controls the direction-predictor lookup, while the other controls the BTB lookup. This makes the PPD 4 Kbits for our processor organization. The PPD is updated with new pre-decode bits while the I-cache is refilled after a miss. A

schematic of the PPD's role in the fetch stage is shown in Figure 9a.

Because the PPD is an array structure and takes some time to access, it only helps if the control bits are available early enough to prevent lookups. A variety of timing assumptions are possible. Exploring fetch timings scenarios is a paper in its own right, so here we explore two extremes, shown in Figure 9b.

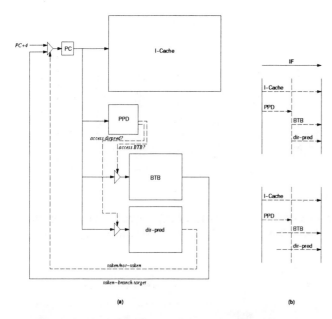

Figure 9. (a) A schematic of the PPD in the fetch stage. (b) The two timing scenarios we evaluate.

- Scenario 1: The PPD is fast enough so that we can access the PPD and then the BTB sequentially in one cycle. The BTB access must complete within one cycle; more flexibility exists for the direction predictor. The direction predictor is also accessed sequentially after the PPD; but either this access fits entirely within the same cycle, or as with the 21264, overlaps into the second cycle. The former case is reasonable for smaller predictors; the latter case applies to large predictors, as shown in both the 21264 and by Jiménez *et al.*.

- Scenario 2: We consider the other extreme also. Here the assumption is that the BTB and the direction predictor need to be accessed every cycle and these accesses take too long to place after the PPD access. Instead, we assume that the PPD access completes in time to stop the BTB/direction-predictor accesses after the bitlines (before column multiplexor). The savings here are clearly less, but the PPD is still able to save the power in the multiplexor and the sense-amps.

Now, instead of accessing the BTB and direction predictor every cycle, we must access the PPD every cycle. This means we must model the overhead in terms of extra power required for the PPD. If the PPD does not prevent enough BTB/predictor lookups, then introducing a PPD actually increases power dissipation. Fortunately, there are indeed a sufficient number of cache lines that need no BTB/predictor lookups that the PPD is substantially effective.

A further consideration that must be taken into account is whether the predictor is banked. If the predictor is banked, the PPD saves less power and energy (because some banks are already not being accessed), but the combination of techniques still provides significant savings.

Figures 10–11 show the effect of a PPD on a 32 K-entry GAs predictor. We chose this configuration in order to be able to include the effects of banking. Figure 10 shows the average reduction in power for the branch predictor and in the overall processor power. We observe a similar trend in Figure 11 for the energy metrics. The PPD is small enough and effective enough that spending this extra power on the small PPD brings us larger benefits overall. Since the PPD simply permits or prevents lookups, savings will be proportional for other predictor organizations. It can also be observed that the greater the average distance between branches for a benchmark, the more the savings we get from the PPD. For Scenario 2, the power savings are closely tied to our timing assumptions, and further work is required to understand the potential savings in other precharge and timing scenarios.

4.3. Pipeline Gating and Branch Prediction

Finally, we briefly explore the power savings that can be obtained using speculation control or "pipeline gating" originally proposed by Manne *et al.* [16]. The goal of pipeline gating is to prevent wasting energy on mis-speculated contribution. Pipeline gating is relevant because it is natural to expect that the more accurate the branch predictor, the less gating helps save energy: there is less mis-speculation to prevent. Indeed, even with a very poor predictor, we find that the the energy savings are quite small—smaller than previous work using the metric of "extra work" would suggest. Furthermore, under certain conditions, pipeline gating can even harm performance and *increase* energy.

Figure 12 shows the operation of pipeline gating. It uses a confidence estimator [12] to assess the quality of each branch prediction. A high-confidence estimate means the prediction of this branch is likely to be correct. A low-confidence estimate means the prediction of this branch is likely to be a misprediction and subsequent computation will be mis-speculated. These confidence estimates are used to decide when the processor is likely to be executing instruction that may not commit. The number of low-confidence predictions permitted, N, before gating is engaged is a design parameter. Once the number of in-flight low confidence branches, M, reaches the threshold N, we gate the pipeline, stalling the fetch stage.

We modified Watch to model pipeline gating and did an analysis of power vs. performance. We used the "both strong" estimation method [16] which marks a branch as high confidence only when both of predictors of the hybrid predictor have the same direction (taken or not taken). The "both strong" uses the existing counters of the branch predictor and thus has no additional hardware requirements. The drawback is that it only works for the hybrid predictor.

We simulated five different hybrid predictor configurations, adding a new, very small and very poor hybrid predictor: hybrid_0, which has a 256-entry selector, a 256-entry gshare component, and a 256-entry bimodal component. Hybrid_0 of course yields an artificially bad prediction accuracy, but we only include it to see the effect on pipeline gating in the extreme case of poor prediction. The results

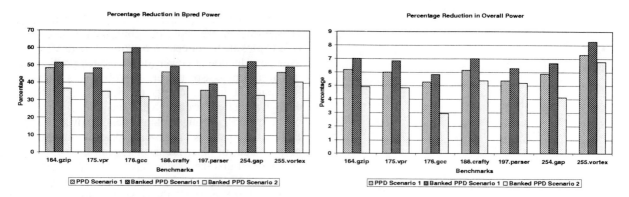

Figure 10. Net savings with a PPD for a 32 K-entry GAs predictor in terms of (a) power in the branch predictor and (b) overall processor power with a PPD. Scenarios 1 and 2 refer to two timing scenarios we model.

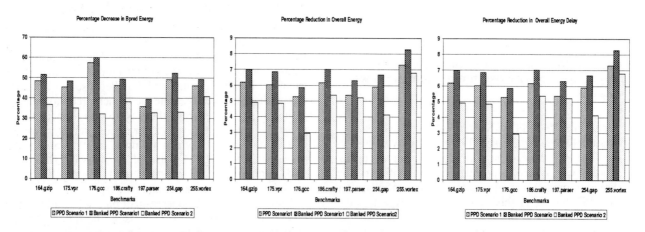

Figure 11. Net savings with a PPD for a 32 K-entry GAs predictor in terms of (a) energy expended in the branch predictor, (b) total energy, and (c) energy-delay.

of hybrid_1,hybrid_2,hybrid_3 and hybrid_4 are quite close. We therefore just show results of the smallest one, hybrid_0, and the largest one, hybrid_3 in Figure 13. For each metric, results are normalized to the baseline case with no gating.

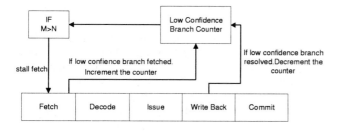

Figure 12. Schematic showing the operation of pipeline gating.

The results show that only the most aggressive pipeline gating, $N = 0$, has substantial effect. For the more relaxed thresholds, the reduction in IPC is small but so is the energy savings.

At threshold $N = 0$, for hybrid_0, the average number of the executed instructions is reduced by 8%; the total energy is reduced by 3.5%, and the IPC is reduced by 6.6%. There are two reasons why the reduction in energy is less than the reduction in instructions would suggest. One reason is that these reduced "wrong path" instructions will be squashed immediately when the processor detects the misprediction. Some mis-speculated instructions therefore spend little energy traversing the pipeline, so preventing these instructions' fetch saves little energy. A second reason is that errors in confidence prediction sometimes cause pipeline gating to stall the pipeline when the branch was in fact correctly predicted. This slows the program's execution and increases energy consumption.

For hybrid_3 and $N = 0$, the average number of total executed instructions is reduced by 6%; the total energy is reduced by 2.6%, and the IPC is reduced by 3.4%. This suggests that better branch prediction does indeed reduce the benefits of pipeline gating: fewer branches are marked as low confidence and pipeline gating occurs less frequently.

It may be that the impact of predictor accuracy on pipeline gating would be stronger for other confidence esti-

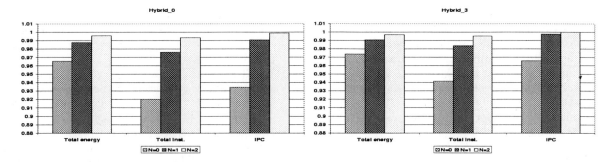

Figure 13. Pipeline gating: overall results of (a) hybrid_0 and (b) hybrid_3.

mators. While easy and inexpensive to implement, the accuracy of "both strong" confidence estimation is a function of the predictor organization. This is less true for other confidence estimators [12] that are separate from the predictor. This warrants further study.

Although not shown separately, the behavior of the benchmark *vortex* is especially interesting, because for $N = 0$ the total energy with pipeline gating is larger than without pipeline gating. Prediction accuracy is quite high for *vortex* (97%), so pipeline gating is likely to provide little benefit. Instead, confidence estimation is especially poor for vortex, causing many unnecessary pipeline-gating events. IPC drops 14%, slowing execution time and increasing energy expenditure.

Overall, our results show that pipeline gating can be modestly helpful in reducing energy but that (1) energy savings are substantially less than the previous metric of "extra work" suggests, and that (2) for benchmarks with already high prediction accuracies, pipeline gating may substantially reduce performance and increase energy.

5. Summary and Future Work

The branch predictor structures, which are the size of a small cache, dissipate a non-trivial amount of power—over 10% of the total processor-wide power—and their accuracy controls how long the program runs and therefore has a substantial impact on energy. This paper explores the effects of branch predictor organization on power and energy expended both locally within the branch predictor and globally in the chip as a whole.

In Section 2, we pointed out that array structures (including caches) should model not only the row but also the column decoders. Although the column decoders are not on the critical timing path, they do dissipate a non-trivial amount of power. We also pointed that the choice of how to square-ify a predictor has little effect on its power dissipation .

Section 3 then showed that for all the predictor organizations we studied, total energy consumed by the chip is affected much more strongly by predictor accuracy rather than energy consumed locally by the predictor, because more accurate predictors reduce the running time. We found that for integer programs, large but accurate predictors actually reduce total energy. For example, a large hybrid predictor uses 13% more energy than a bimodal predictor but actually yields a 7% savings in total, chip-wide energy. For floating-point programs, the energy curves are flat across the range of predictor organizations, but this means that choosing a large predictor to help integer programs should not cause harm when executing floating-point programs. This suggests that if the die budget can afford it, processors for embedded systems that must conserve battery life might actually be better off with large, aggressive branch predictors rather than lower-power but less accurate predictors.

Section 4 showed that there are some branch-prediction-related techniques that do save energy without affecting performance. Banking both reduces access time and saves power by accessing only a portion of the total predictor structure. A *prediction probe detector* (PPD) uses predecode bits to prevent BTB and predictor lookups, saving as much as 40–60% in energy expended in the predictor and 5–7% of total energy. Finally, we revisited pipeline gating and showed that it does offer modest energy savings on average, but at the risk of actually increasing energy consumption.

Overall, we hope that the data presented here will serve as a useful guide to help chip designers and other researchers better understand the interactions between branch behavior and power and energy characteristics, and help identify the important issues in balancing performance and energy when choosing a branch predictor design.

There are a wide range of avenues for future work. This paper has not considered optimizations specific to the BTB's organization, and this is worth further investigation. The tradeoff reported here between larger but more power-hungry structures and improved performance and energy dissipation are likely to apply to other on-chip structures like the caches and TLBs, and this tradeoff is important to understand. Finally, this paper only considered a few specific timing and precharge scenarios for the structures in the fetch stage. A more thorough characterization of this design space is needed to understand the range of benefits that a PPD might provide.

Acknowledgments

This material is based upon work supported in part by the National Science Foundation under grants nos. CCR-0082671 and CCR-0105626, NSF CAREER MIP-9703440, a grant from Intel MRL, and by an exploratory grant from the University of Virginia Fund for Excellence in Science and Technology. We would also like to thank John Kalamatianos for helpful discussions regarding branch-predictor design; Margaret Martonosi and David brooks for their assistance with Wattch and for helpful discussions on various power issues; Zhigang Hu for help with the EIO traces; and the anonymous reviewers for many helpful suggestions on how to improve the paper.

References

[1] D. H. Albonesi. Selective cache ways: On-demand cache resource allocation. In *Proceedings of the 32nd Annual ACM/IEEE International Symposium on Microarchitecture*, pages 248–59, Nov. 1999.

[2] R. I. Bahar and Srilatha Manne. Power and energy reduction via pipeline balancing. In *Proceedings of the 28th Annual International Symposium on Computer Architecture*, June 2001.

[3] D. Brooks, V. Tiwari, and M. Martonosi. Wattch: A framework for architectural-level power analysis and optimizations. In *Proceedings of the 27th Annual International Symposium on Computer Architecture*, pages 83–94, June 2000.

[4] D. C. Burger and T. M. Austin. The SimpleScalar tool set, version 2.0. *Computer Architecture News*, 25(3):13–25, June 1997.

[5] B. Calder and D. Grunwald. Next cache line and set prediction. In *Proceedings of the 22nd Annual International Symposium on Computer Architecture*, pages 287–96, June 1995.

[6] P.-Y. Chang, E. Hao, and Y. N. Patt. Alternative implementations of hybrid branch predictors. In *Proceedings of the 28th Annual International Symposium on Microarchitecture*, pages 252–57, Dec. 1995.

[7] Digital Semiconductor. *DECchip 21064/21064A Alpha AXP Microprocessors: Hardware Reference Manual*, June 1994.

[8] Digital Semiconductor. *Alpha 21164 Microprocessor: Hardware Reference Manual*, Apr. 1995.

[9] S. Ghiasi, J. Casmira, and D. Grunwald. Using IPC variation in workload with externally specified rates to reduce power consumption. In *Proceedings of the Workshop on Complexity-Effective Design*, June 2000.

[10] K. Ghose and M. Kamble. Reducing power in superscalar processor caches using subbanking, multiple line buffers and bit-line segmentation. In *Proceedings of the 1999 International Symposium on Low Power Electronics and Design*, pages 70–75, Aug. 1999.

[11] R. Gonzalez and M. Horowitz. Energy dissipation in general purpose microprocessors. *IEEE Journal of Solid-State Circuits*, 31(9), Sep. 1996.

[12] D. Grunwald, A. Klauser, S Manne, and A. Pleszkun. Confidence estimation for speculation control. In *Proceedings of the 25th Annual International Symposium on Computer Architecture*, pages 122–31, June 1998.

[13] D. A. Jiménez, S. W. Keckler, and C. Lin. The impact of delay on the design of branch predictors. In *Proceedings of the 33rd Annual IEEE/ACM International Symposium on Microarchitecture*, pages 67–77, Dec. 2000.

[14] R. E. Kessler, E. J. McLellan, and D. A. Webb. The Alpha 21264 microprocessor architecture. In *Proceedings of the 1998 International Conference on Computer Design*, pages 90–95, Oct. 1998.

[15] J. Kin, M. Gupta, and W. Mangione-Smith. The filter cache: An energy-efficient memory structure. In *Proceedings of the 30th Annual International Symposium on Microarchitecture*, pages 184–93, Dec. 1997.

[16] S. Manne, A. Klauser, and D. Grunwald. Pipeline gating: speculation control for energy reduction. In *Proceedings of the 25th Annual International Symposium on Computer Architecture*, pages 132–41, June 1998.

[17] S. McFarling. Combining branch predictors. Tech. Note TN-36, DEC WRL, June 1993.

[18] S.-T. Pan, K. So, and J. T. Rahmeh. Improving the accuracy of dynamic branch prediction using branch correlation. In *Proceedings of the Fifth International Conference on Architectural Support for Programming Languages and Operating Systems*, pages 76–84, Oct. 1992.

[19] D. Parikh, K. Skadron, Y. Zhang, M. Barcella, and M. R. Stan. Power issues related to branch prediction. Technical Report CS-2001-25, University of Virginia Department of Computer Science, Nov. 2001.

[20] K. Skadron, P. S. Ahuja, M. Martonosi, and D. W. Clark. Improving prediction for procedure returns with return-address-stack repair mechanisms. In *Proceedings of the 31st Annual ACM/IEEE International Symposium on Microarchitecture*, pages 259–71, Dec. 1998.

[21] K. Skadron, D. W. Clark, and M. Martonosi. Speculative updates of local and global branch history: A quantitative analysis. *Journal of Instruction-Level Parallelism*, Jan. 2000. (http://www.jilp.org/vol2).

[22] K. Skadron, M. Martonosi, and D. W. Clark. A taxonomy of branch mispredictions, and alloyed prediction as a robust solution to wrong-history mispredictions. In *Proceedings of the 2000 International Conference on Parallel Architectures and Compilation Techniques*, pages 199–206, Oct. 2000.

[23] J. E. Smith. A study of branch prediction strategies. In *Proceedings of the 8th Annual International Symposium on Computer Architecture*, pages 135–48, May 1981.

[24] P. Song. UltraSparc-3 aims at MP servers. *Microprocessor Report*, pages 29–34, Oct. 27 1997.

[25] Standard Performance Evaluation Corporation. SPEC CPU2000 Benchmarks. http://www.specbench.org/osg/cpu2000.

[26] W. Tang, R. Gupta, and A. Nicolau. Design of a predictive filter cache for energy savings in high performance processor architectures. In *Proceedings of the 2001 International Conference on Computer Design*, pages 68–73, Sept. 2001.

[27] J. Turley. ColdFire doubles performance with v4. *Microprocessor Report*, Oct. 26 1998.

[28] S. J. E. Wilton and N. P. Jouppi. Cacti: An enhanced cache access and cycle time model. *IEEE Journal of Solid-State Circuits*, 31(5):677–88, May. 1996.

[29] T.-Y. Yeh and Y. N. Patt. Two-level adaptive training branch prediction. In *Proceedings of the 24th Annual International Symposium on Microarchitecture*, pages 51–61, November 1991.

Keynote Speaker

Recovery Oriented Computing: A New Research Agenda for a New Century

David A. Patterson

Pardee Chair of Computer Science

University of California at Berkeley

Abstract

After 15 years of successfully improving cost-performance, it's time for new challenges for the systems research community.

As a result of the focus on cost-performance, the fabled five 9s of availability (99.999% uptime) looks to be much easier to achieve in advertising than in computers, and the cost of managing systems can be five times the cost of the hardware. In a Post-PC Era of wireless gadgets using services on the Internet, one new challenge is building services that really are dependable and much less expensive to maintain.

Traditional Fault-Tolerant Computing concentrates on tolerating hardware and operating system faults, ignoring faults by human operators and even applications. Recovery Oriented Computing (ROC) aims at improving Mean Time To Recover to both lower the cost of management and improve at the availability of whole system, including the people who operate it. We look to civil engineering and diplomacy to inspire principles for ROC design.

This talk outlines motivation for and proposed principles of ROC design, plus some concrete results in the area of benchmarking of availability.

Multiprocessor Systems

Bandwidth Adaptive Snooping

Milo M. K. Martin, Daniel J. Sorin, Mark D. Hill, and David A. Wood
Computer Sciences Department
University of Wisconsin-Madison
{milo, sorin, markhill, david}@cs.wisc.edu
http://www.cs.wisc.edu/multifacet/

Abstract

This paper advocates that cache coherence protocols use a bandwidth adaptive approach to adjust to varied system configurations (e.g., number of processors) and workload behaviors. We propose Bandwidth Adaptive Snooping Hybrid (BASH), a hybrid protocol that ranges from behaving like snooping (by broadcasting requests) when excess bandwidth is available to behaving like a directory protocol (by unicasting requests) when bandwidth is limited. BASH adapts dynamically by probabilistically deciding to broadcast or unicast on a per request basis using a local estimate of recent interconnection network utilization. Simulations of a microbenchmark and commercial and scientific workloads show that BASH robustly performs as well or better than the best of snooping and directory protocols as available bandwidth is varied. By mixing broadcasts and unicasts, BASH outperforms both snooping and directory protocols in the mid-range where a static choice of either is inefficient.

1 Introduction

Snooping and directory protocols are the two dominant classes of cache coherence protocols for hardware shared memory multiprocessors. In a snooping system, a processor broadcasts a request for a block to all nodes in the system to find the owner (which could be memory) directly. In a directory protocol, a processor unicasts a request to the home directory for the block, the directory forwards the request to the owner (trivial when the directory is the owner), and the owner responds to the requestor. Thus, snooping protocols can achieve lower latencies than directory protocols on sharing misses (a.k.a., cache-to-cache transfers or dirty misses) by avoiding the indirections incurred by directories.

By broadcasting to avoid indirections for sharing misses, snooping can outperform directories when bandwidth is plentiful, but directories outperform snooping when bandwidth is limited. In today's commercial workloads, sharing misses comprise a significant fraction of level two cache misses and correspondingly impact performance [3, 18].

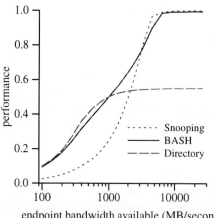

Figure 1. Performance vs. available bandwidth for a microbenchmark on 64 processors

Martin et al. [23] showed that snooping can outperform directories on a medium size (16 processor) system running commercial workloads, at the cost of additional bandwidth. In Figure 1, we plot performance versus available interconnection network bandwidth for a simple locking microbenchmark on 64 processors (described in Section 4). This graph reinforces the intuition that the relative performances of snooping and directories depend on available bandwidth. The point at which increasing bandwidth does not improve performance occurs at a bandwidth much greater (by a factor of 5) for snooping than for directories.

Designing a single protocol to provide high performance for many system configurations and workloads is difficult. Hennessy writes [14], "[W]e don't have a coherency scheme that does well under all these situations: from small to large processor counts, different levels of [software] optimization, and differing cache sizes." We advocate an adaptive approach to address this challenge.

There are two reasons why an adaptive scheme is desirable. First, due to the trend towards integrating the coherence protocol logic and the processor on the same die [7, 12, 30], a single protocol must suffice for multiple hardware configurations (processor counts, cache sizes, and interconnection networks). If the microprocessor is to be used in a scalable system, the protocol must also be scalable. For example, since Alpha 21364 [12] systems can scale to hundreds of

This work is supported in part by the National Science Foundation with grants EIA-9971256, CDA-9623632, and CCR-0105721, an IBM Graduate Fellowship (Martin), an Intel Graduate Fellowship (Sorin), two Wisconsin Romnes Fellowships (Hill and Wood), and donations from Compaq Computer Corporation, IBM, Intel, and Sun Microsystems.

processors, a directory protocol is currently the only option. However, many scalable system designs are used for smaller systems that could be better served by a snooping protocol. Even the vast majority of scalable systems sold are systems of moderate size. For example, a recent essay [24] estimated that, of the 30,000 Origin 200/2000 [20] systems shipped, less than 10 systems contained 256 or more processors (~0.03%), and less than 250 of the systems had 128 processors or more (~1%).

Second, statically choosing between a directory protocol and a snooping protocol is not desirable due to the varying behaviors of different workloads and the time-varying behavior within a workload. Our results show that for a given system size and configuration, some workloads perform better with snooping while other workloads are better served by a directory protocol. Further, a given workload's demand on system bandwidth varies dynamically over time. For example, different phases of behavior for a multiprocessor database workload have been observed with periods on the order of minutes [25]. During a phase of high cache miss rate, a broadcast request in a snooping protocol could further congest the system.

For these two reasons, an adaptive hybrid protocol that provides robust performance is preferable to a static choice of either snooping or directories. Our contribution is an adaptive mechanism (Section 2) and a hybrid protocol (Section 3) that leverages this mechanism to perform like snooping (by broadcasting requests) if bandwidth is plentiful and perform like a directory protocol (by unicasting requests) if bandwidth is limited. Our protocol, *bandwidth adaptive snooping hybrid (BASH)*, adapts dynamically to the available bandwidth to provide robust performance. Using a microbenchmark (shown in Figure 1 and further explored in Section 4) and commercial workloads (Section 5), we show that the performance of *BASH* tracks that of the directory protocol in the limited bandwidth case and tracks that of snooping in the plentiful bandwidth case. Moreover, in the mid-range where the performances of snooping and directories are similar, *BASH* outperforms both protocols.

2 A Bandwidth Adaptive Mechanism

In this section, we describe the mechanism each processor uses to decide dynamically whether a request should be broadcast or unicast.

2.1 Goal and Approach

BASH's goal is to minimize average miss latency. Given infinite bandwidth, broadcasting all requests would achieve this goal by avoiding all indirections for sharing misses. However, the finite bandwidth of interconnection networks can lead to congestion and queuing delays that outweigh the benefit of avoiding indirection. Nevertheless, mean queuing delay only dominates when the interconnect is highly utilized. Figure 2 illustrates this trade-off with a simple queuing

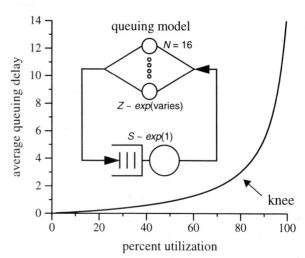

Figure 2. Average queuing delay vs. utilization for a sim-

network. Above the "knee" in the curve, increasing utilization dramatically increases response time.

The mechanism we propose for *BASH* uses feedback to keep the interconnect utilization below this critical level and thus mitigate queuing delays. Our mechanism uses a processor-local estimate of interconnect utilization to keep utilization below a pre-specified threshold by dynamically adjusting the probability of broadcasting. Feedback control theory suggests that the mechanism should adapt to changes in interconnect congestion, but not so quickly that it overshoots and leads to oscillation [19]. As described in Section 2.2, our mechanism avoids oscillation by adapting relatively slowly and using a probabilistic mechanism to decide whether or not to broadcast. In initial experiments, we tried a simpler mechanism that switched between always and never broadcasting, and we observed unstable behavior due to oscillation between these two extremes.

2.2 Implementation

Our bandwidth adaptive implementation uses a simple mechanism to estimate the interconnect utilization and adjust the rate of broadcast. The mechanism consists of three parts: (1) estimating interconnect utilization, (2) adjusting the probability of broadcasting, and (3) determining whether or not to broadcast a specific request.

First, a processor uses the utilization of its link to the interconnection network as a local estimate of global interconnect utilization. While this local information does not capture certain global effects, it is easy to obtain and correlates strongly with global interconnect utilization due, in part, to the broadcast nature of the requests that are most likely to cause contention. Each processor uses a simple, signed, saturating *utilization counter* to calculate if the link utilization is above or below a static threshold. Figure 3 illustrates the counter's operation assuming a target link utilization of 75%. For each cycle, the mechanism increments the counter by one if the link is utilized, and decrements it by

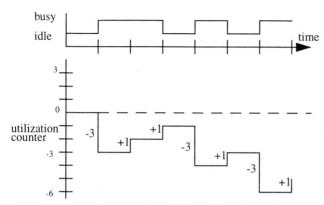

Figure 3. Example operation of the utilization counter

three otherwise. When the counter is sampled, a positive value means that the link was used more than the threshold, and a negative value means that the link was used less than the threshold. The counter is reset to zero after each sample. Since the link in Figure 3 was used 4 out of the previous 7 cycles (57%), the counter would be, as expected, negative ($4 \times 1 + -3 \times 3 = -5$).

Second, an unsigned, saturating *policy counter* averages the utilization information and determines the fraction of requests that should be broadcast. Our mechanism samples the utilization counter every n cycles (the sampling interval), and it increments/decrements the policy counter by one if the utilization was greater/less than the threshold. Thus, a larger value of the policy counter corresponds to a lower probability of broadcast.

Finally, a given request is unicast or broadcast with a probability proportional to the policy counter. For example, an 8-bit policy counter with the value of 100 implies that a request should be unicast with probability of 100/255 or 39%. For each out-going request, the processor compares the policy counter to a randomly generated integer the same size as the policy counter. The processor unicasts if the policy counter is smaller than the random number, and it broadcasts otherwise. Pseudo-random numbers can be generated easily by a linear feedback shift register [11]. Our mechanism generates random numbers and performs the comparison to the policy counter off the critical path, allowing the mechanism to have negligible impact on miss latency.

Through experimentation, we selected a utilization threshold of 75%, a sampling interval of 512 cycles, and a policy counter size of 8 bits. A smaller sampling interval and policy counter size would enable the mechanism to respond more rapidly to different workload phases, but they would make the mechanism more susceptible to oscillation. With these parameters, our adaptive mechanism can change from 100% unicast to 0% unicast (or vice versa) in $512 \times 255 = \sim130,000$ cycles in which the measured utilization is above/below the threshold. Since the uncontended round-trip latency for an L2 cache misses is around 125 cycles (for our target system), the mechanism can adapt over its entire range in ~1000 cache misses.

3 A Bandwidth Adaptive Snooping Protocol

BASH, our bandwidth adaptive snooping hybrid protocol, incorporates features of both snooping and directory protocols. While there are different ways to combine these two types of protocols to synthesize a hybrid, we choose to form *BASH* from an aggressive snooping protocol and a recently-published directory protocol. These two protocols have some (surprisingly) common features that we exploit in creating our hybrid protocol.

First, in Sections 3.1 and 3.2, we describe the two protocols used as the foundation of our hybrid. They will also serve as the base cases against which we will compare *BASH* for its evaluation in Sections 4 and 5. Second, in Section 3.3, we describe our synthesis of these two protocols. A key issue in this synthesis is reconciling the differences between the methods used by snooping and directories to enforce ordering between racing transactions. For each protocol described in this section, Figure 4 illustrates the operation of two typical protocol transactions, so as to highlight the similarities and differences between the protocols. Third, in Section 3.4, we discuss several issues relating to *BASH*, including livelock/deadlock, scalability, complexity, and verification.

All three protocols are write-invalidate, use the MOSI states [29], allow processors to silently downgrade from S to I, support several transactions (e.g., get an S copy, get an M copy, writeback an M or O copy), and interact with the processors to support a consistency model. Our results assume sequential consistency.

3.1 A Snooping Protocol

Traditional snooping protocols rely on a totally ordered delivery of coherence requests to (1) enable processors and memories to agree on the next owner and (2) obviate the need for explicitly acknowledging invalidations of shared blocks. Since racing transactions are totally ordered, a snooping cache controller can make a strictly local decision on each transaction and infer that other nodes will make compatible decisions. We base *BASH* on an aggressive MOSI snooping protocol (which we refer to as *Snooping*) that is loosely based on the Sun UE10000 [6].

We assume that our snooping protocol uses separate virtual networks for requests and responses. The request network must enforce a total order, but it need not ensure synchronous broadcast [23]. Modern snooping systems use address-interleaved hierarchical switches to achieve high throughput for ordered broadcasts [6]. The response network has no ordering requirements and can use any unordered switched interconnection network.

A processor broadcasts its requests to all other nodes on the request network, and all processors snoop all requests. The owner (potentially memory) sends data directly to the requestor over the response network. A requestor must also snoop its own request, which serves as a *marker* to indicate its place in the total order.

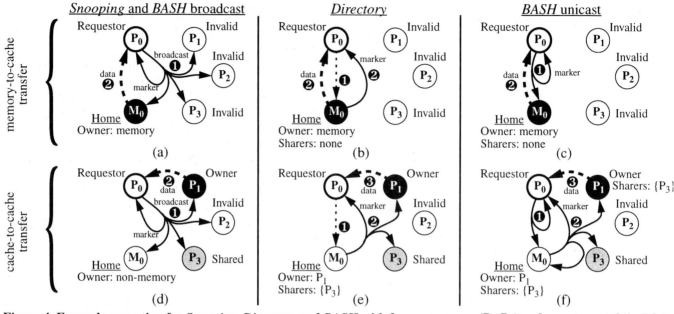

Figure 4. Example operation for *Snooping*, *Directory*, and *BASH* with four processors (P_0-P_3) and memory module (M_0). (a)-(c) illustrate a request by P_0 for exclusive access to a block that is satisfied by memory (a memory-to-cache transfer). (d)-(f) illustrate a similar request by P_0 where P_1 is the owner and P_3 is a sharer (a cache-to-cache transfer with an invalidation). Totally ordered messages are drawn with solid lines and unordered messages are drawn with dashed lines.

A memory controller behaves much like it does in a traditional snooping protocol, except for keeping one bit of state per block to indicate if it is the owner, similar to what was done in the Synapse N+1 [9]. This bit of state eliminates the need for a global owned snoop response. If memory is the owner, it responds with data.

3.2 A Directory Protocol

Traditional directory protocols rely on unordered or, at most, point-to-point ordered interconnection networks. While the lack of ordering facilitates building scalable interconnects, it requires the protocols to use explicit acknowledgment messages and transient states to enforce order between racing transactions.

A recent directory protocol, implemented in the AlphaServer GS320 [10], uses a totally ordered multicast interconnect to optimize the protocol and eliminate explicit acknowledgments. Like *Snooping*, the GS320 uses a marker on the ordered network to indicate a request's place in the total order. Below we describe a protocol (which we refer to as *Directory*) modeled after the GS320.

Directory uses three virtual networks: an unordered request network, a totally ordered network for requests forwarded by the directory to processors, and an unordered network for responses from processors and directories. The totally ordered forwarded request network supports multicasting and, as in *Snooping*, eliminates the need for acknowledgment messages. In the GS320, this totally ordered interconnect is implemented as an 8-way crossbar that connects to 4-processor nodes, supporting up to 32 processors.

Processors unicast all requests to the directory at memory. The memory controller maintains a directory with state about each block for which it is the home, including the owner and a superset of the sharers. Like all directory protocols, the memory controller responds directly when it has sufficient permissions and forwards the request when it does not. On a direct response, the memory controller sends the data on the unordered response network and a marker message on the forwarded request network. The latter indicates the request's place in the total order. Forwarded requests are sent via the totally ordered multicast network to the owner, sharers, and requestor. The marker sent to the requestor allows it to infer where the forwarded request occurs in the total order. The owner and sharers observing the same total order obviates the need for explicit acknowledgement messages.[1] Racing request messages are ordered at the directory, and they are either processed locally or forwarded on the ordered multicast network.

When a processor responds to a request that is forwarded to it by the directory, it does not need to send an explicit acknowledgment, since the forwarded request network is totally ordered. Processors also monitor the forwarded request network for the marker messages that indicate their request's place in the total order.

3.3 An Adaptive Hybrid Protocol

In this section, we describe how our hybrid protocol integrates *Snooping* and *Directory*, and we then discuss a number of issues that arise from the integration. The integration is possible because both protocols use a totally ordered net-

---

1. Along with the total order, the GS320 protocol guarantees that all forwarded requests can be processed at the target node, which is also necessary to eliminate explicit acknowledgments.

work to eliminate the need for explicit acknowledgments and preserve order between racing transactions. However, we must resolve a key discrepancy in how these protocols order racing transactions. In *Snooping*, racing request messages are ordered entirely by the request network. In *Directory*, the order of racing messages is determined by the order in which they are processed by the directory controller; the ordered multicast network simply preserves this order for forwarded requests. Resolving this difference requires subtle, but relatively simple, hardware. Our adaptive protocol handles these races similarly to Multicast Snooping [4, 28], and *BASH* can be considered a special case of this more general protocol.

Our hybrid protocol uses two virtual networks. Requests use a totally ordered multicast request network, but no restrictions are placed upon its topology or synchrony. As in *Snooping*, the total order of requests—necessary for correct coherence protocol behavior and enforcing a memory consistency model—is determined by their ordering on the request network. Responses travel on an unordered point-to-point data network.

From the requestor's point of view, *BASH* behaves similarly to *Snooping*, except that the cache controller must choose whether to broadcast or unicast each request. Our policy for deciding between broadcast and unicast was explained in Section 2.2. Writeback requests are always unicast. Since the request network is the ordering point, a *BASH* "unicast" request is actually a dualcast sent to both the home node and back to the requestor. Similar to *Snooping*, the return of the request acts as the marker and informs the requestor of the transaction's place in the total order. Processors respond to incoming requests as in *Snooping*, except processors must detect and ignore retried requests as discussed below.

Like *Directory*, *BASH*'s memory controller maintains the owner and a superset of the sharers for each block for which it is the home. The memory controller's basic operation is to compare the owner/sharer information from the directory against the set of nodes that received the request message to determine if the request was sent to a sufficient set of nodes.[2] If the request was sent to the owner and all necessary sharers, the memory controller updates the directory state and responds with data as necessary. For broadcast requests, a *BASH* memory controller behaves as in *Snooping*, with the addition of updating the directory state as needed. For unicast requests that find data at the home, the memory controller behaves as in *Directory*, immediately updating the state and responding with data. Unlike *Directory*, *BASH* need not send a marker message, since this was already sent with the original request.

When a processor issues a unicast for a block that is owned in a third node, the memory controller behaves as in

Directory, with two important differences. First, it does not update the directory state, because the request is not yet satisfied. Second, instead of forwarding the request on a separate forwarded request network, it *retries* the request as a multicast on the totally ordered request network. The multicast set for the retried request includes the memory controller in addition to the owner, sharers, and requestor. Assuming no racing transactions, the owner will satisfy the retried request.

More complex cases occur when broadcasts, unicasts, and multicast retries race for the same block. The memory controller has a "window of vulnerability" between when the original and retried requests are ordered on the request network. If a broadcast request for the same block is ordered during that window, the retried request's multicast set may be insufficient, forcing the request to be retried again. Since any non-broadcast request may require retries, there exist livelock and deadlock issues, discussed in Section 3.4.

3.4 Discussion

With *BASH*, as for any coherence protocol, one must address the issues of livelock/deadlock, scalability, complexity, and verification.

Livelock and deadlock. Retrying requests presents the twin problems of livelock and deadlock. Livelock could occur, for example, if a non-broadcast is competing with broadcasts for a heavily contended block; no matter how many times the memory controller retries a non-broadcast request, there is no guarantee that it will ever succeed. *BASH* avoids livelock by broadcasting—which is guaranteed to succeed—on its third retry.

Most multiprocessor systems avoid interconnection network deadlocks (in part) by accessing virtual networks in a strict order to avoid cyclic dependences. By retrying requests on the same virtual network, *BASH* introduces a circular dependence—and thus potential deadlock—because it may use the request network multiple times to process a single request. Rather than avoiding deadlock, *BASH* detects a potential deadlock and resolves it by sending a negative acknowledgment (nack) to the original requestor. Specifically, if the memory controller cannot allocate a network buffer for the retry, it sends a nack to the requestor on the data response network. The requestor can then reissue its request as a broadcast, which is guaranteed to succeed.

Scalability. *BASH* is more scalable than snooping protocols because it does not require all requests to be broadcast, yet it is less scalable than directory protocols that do not rely on a totally ordered interconnect [20, 21]. Fortunately, hierarchical switches can be used to make high-bandwidth totally ordered interconnects. Removing the broadcast-always behavior of snooping may allow the design of a well-balanced system of significantly larger size than would be possible with broadcast snooping. Examples of real systems with a large number of processors and an ordered intercon-

---

2. If a processor is the owner, it also tracks the sharer set and determines if the request was sufficient, so as to make a decision consistent with that of the memory controller.

nect include the AlphaServer GS320 [10], Sun's UE10000 [6], and Fujitsu's PRIMEPOWER 2000 [15], and these systems support 32, 64, and 128 processors, respectively. In addition, Martin et al. [23] recently proposed an approach for an ordered interconnect with no central bottleneck. This approach allows for more general, and perhaps more scalable, interconnect topologies that still maintain a total order.

Complexity. As a hybrid of two protocols, *BASH* is more complex than either protocol on which it is based, and the difficulty of verification is directly related to the complexity. However, complexity does not grow as much as one might expect because of the strong similarities between the underlying protocols. For example, *BASH* processors react identically to requests, regardless of whether they are unicasts, multicasts, or broadcasts. In fact, a broadcast in this system appears as though the directory simply specified an overly generous set of sharers to invalidate.

As a rough measure of the complexity of each protocol, Table 1 displays the numbers of states (both stable and transient), events, and state transitions for each controller. Compared to *Snooping* and *Directory*, we find *BASH* has a comparable number of states, but about 50% more events and double the number of transitions. While not all state/event combinations are equally difficult to verify, and the numbers of states and events depend somewhat on how one chooses to express a protocol, implementing *BASH* should be less difficult than including both a snooping and directory protocol in the same system.

Verification. To gain confidence in the correctness of *BASH*, we have used both random testing and formal methods. All three protocols—*Snooping, Directory,* and *BASH*—were tested using a stand-alone random tester. This tester uses false sharing, random action/check (store/load) pairs [33], and widely variable message latencies to force each protocol through a myriad of corner cases. We ran the tester through millions of coherence operations and uncovered numerous subtle race conditions. In the end, our tool reported full coverage for all state transitions with no detected errors.

In our experience, random testing is excellent at finding protocol errors even for complex protocols, but it is little help for finding deadlock, livelock, and memory consistency model errors. We have explored more formal methods, including model checking and Lamport clocks [26], to address these issues. A technical report [28] describes our experience verifying an enhanced version of the Multicast Snooping protocol [4].[3] Since *BASH* is based upon this enhanced protocol, this proof carries over directly to *BASH*.

---

3. The original Multicast Snooping protocol described in Bilir et al. [4] must nack insufficient requests. Sorin et al. [28] describe the important optimization of retries at the directory. This optimization allows an insufficient unicast in *BASH* to have the same latency as a request that must be forwarded by the directory.

Table 1. States, events, and transitions for *BASH*, *Snooping,* and *Directory*

Protocol	Total			Cache			Mem/Dir		
	States	Events	Trans.	States	Events	Trans.	States	Events	Trans.
BASH	21	23	114	17	14	94	4	9	20
Snooping	19	13	68	17	9	61	2	4	7
Directory	21	13	75	17	9	61	4	4	14

4 Microbenchmark Performance Evaluation

Before presenting performance results for commercial workloads using full-system simulation, we present results for a simple locking microbenchmark. The microbenchmark is easy to understand and allows us to explore the effects of system scaling and workload intensity. We start by describing our microbenchmark and simulation methods. We then explore the performance of *BASH* over a range of available bandwidths, utilization thresholds, system sizes, and workload intensities.

4.1 Microbenchmark

In the microbenchmark, each processor acquires and releases locks that are generally uncontended. After the release of one lock, a processor immediately attempts to acquire another lock. Each processor can have at most one outstanding request. Since we choose the number of locks to be approximately the number of lines per cache, the microbenchmark incurs sharing misses almost exclusively. While this is near the worst-case performance scenario for directory protocols, smaller fractions of sharing misses do not qualitatively change our conclusions, as shown in Section 5.

4.2 Simulation Methods

Before discussing our microbenchmark results, we describe our memory system simulator and timing assumptions. Our memory hierarchy simulator captures timing races and all state transitions (including transient states) of the coherence protocols in cache and memory controllers. We consider integrated processor/memory nodes connected via a single link to an interconnection network. Since *BASH*, *Snooping,* and *Directory* all require a total order of requests, but do not require a specific interconnection network topology, we abstract the details of the interconnect design by modeling a fixed latency crossbar with limited bandwidth and contention at the endpoints. All request, forwarded request, and retried request messages are 8 bytes, and data responses are 72 bytes (64 byte data block with an 8 byte header).

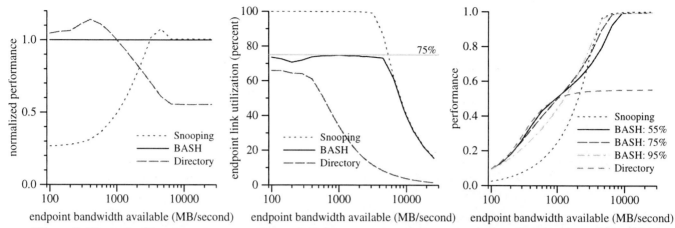

Figure 5. Normalized performance vs. available bandwidth for a micro-benchmark on 64 processors

Figure 6. Utilization vs. available bandwidth for a microbenchmark on 64 processors

Figure 7. Sensitivity to utilization threshold value for a microbenchmark on 64 processors

To approximate the published latencies of systems like the Alpha 21364 [12], we selected 50 ns for each interconnection network traversal (which includes wire propagation, synchronization, and routing) and 80 ns for memory DRAM access time. When a protocol request arrives at a processor or memory, it takes 25 ns or 80 ns, respectively, to provide data to the interconnect. These assumed latencies result in a 180 ns latency to obtain a block from memory in all three protocols, a 125 ns latency for a cache-to-cache transfer for both a *Snooping* and a broadcast *BASH* request, and a 255 ns latency for a cache-to-cache transfer for a *Directory* and a unicast *BASH* request.

For *Snooping* and successful *BASH* requests, the cache-to-cache transfer latency is smaller than the memory latency (~70% of memory latency: 125 ns vs. 180 ns). We assume that this scenario is carefully optimized, as is the case for the IBM NorthStar (RS64-II) SMPs [5], where a cache-to-cache transfer latency is ~55% of main memory latency [17]. The cache-to-cache transfer latency for *Directory* requests and for *BASH* requests that need to be retried is significantly higher than a fetch from memory, due to the indirection through the directory (memory controller). An indirected request incurs the latencies of a DRAM directory access, supplying the data from the cache, and three interconnect traversals. An SRAM directory or directory cache would mitigate the latency of accessing directory state. However, due to a third traversal of the interconnect, a *Directory* cache-to-cache transfer would still have a greater latency than that of a broadcast request.

4.3 Microbenchmark Results

We compare the microbenchmark performance (in units of normalized lock acquires per nanosecond) of *BASH* against *Snooping* and *Directory*. Figure 5 presents the same data as shown in Figure 1, except in Figure 5 performance is normalized to that of *BASH*. The graph shows that, for a 64-pro-

cessor system, *BASH* performs like *Directory* in the limited bandwidth case and like *Snooping* in the plentiful bandwidth case. At extremely low available bandwidths, *Directory* outperforms both other protocols; *BASH* is ~10% worse than *Directory* due to additional marker messages (shown in Figure 4(f)). In the middle range (near where the *Snooping* and *Directory* curves intersect), *BASH* outperforms both protocols by up to 25%. As the available bandwidth increases, *Snooping* outperforms *BASH*, because *BASH* conservatively reduces its rate of broadcast. As bandwidth becomes even more plentiful, *BASH* always broadcasts requests, and thus the performances of *BASH* and *Snooping* converge.

Interconnection network utilization. To further explain these performance results, we plot interconnection network endpoint utilization versus available bandwidth in Figure 6. *Snooping* uses large amounts of bandwidth and thus over-utilizes the network in the case of limited bandwidth, while *Directory* under-utilizes the network when bandwidth is plentiful. *BASH* achieves the desired 75% utilization (denoted by the horizontal line) until bandwidth is so plentiful that even by always broadcasting it does not reach 75% utilization. Figure 5 shows that this is also the point at which the performances of *BASH* and *Snooping* converge.

Utilization threshold selection. In Figure 7, we plot performance versus available bandwidth for three threshold values, and we observe that performance is not overly sensitive to the exact threshold value selected. Even for thresholds as high as 95% or as low as 55%, the qualitative performance of *BASH* remains similar. While we choose 75% for our experiments, we do not claim that 75% is the optimal threshold for this or any other workload. In practice, it has achieved good performance.

Adaptation to system size. To explore the potential benefits of *BASH* over a range of system sizes, we plot performance *per processor* versus available bandwidth for a range of pro-

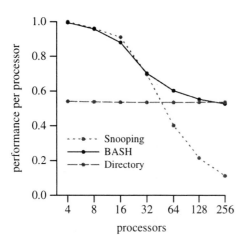

Figure 8. Impact of system size for a microbenchmark with 1600 MB/second endpoint bandwidth per processor

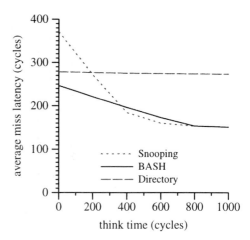

Figure 9. Average miss latency vs. think time for a micro-benchmark on 64 processors with 1600 MB/second endpoint bandwidth per processor

cessor counts in Figure 8. Endpoint link bandwidth per processor is fixed at 1600 MB/second, and the processor count is plotted logarithmically on the x-axis. We observe that the line for *Directory* is nearly flat, signifying near-perfect scalability. *BASH* performs as well as *Snooping* for small systems and as well as *Directory* for large systems. In the midrange, *BASH* outperforms both other protocols. For this specific design point, *Directory* far outperforms *Snooping* for processor counts above 64. Higher link bandwidth would help *Snooping*, but the figure illustrates why directory protocols are attractive for large-scale systems and why an adaptive scheme is desirable in general.

Adaptation to workload intensity. To explore the impact of workload behavior on performance, we adjust the intensity of the microbenchmark's memory traffic. The memory traffic's intensity is adjusted by adding a *think time* (i.e., the time between when a processor releases one lock and acquires another). Figure 9 plots average miss latency (lower is better) versus think time. Increasing think time corresponds to decreasing workload intensity. Our results show that, for a fixed system configuration (64 processors and 1600 MB/second endpoint link bandwidth), the choice between snooping and directories depends on workload intensity (i.e., think time or miss rate).

5 Workload Performance Evaluation

While microbenchmarks can provide insight into behavior and allow exploration of the design space, *BASH*'s performance on commercial workloads matters most. This section describes our benchmarks, target system assumptions, and simulation techniques for evaluating the performance of bandwidth adaptive snooping. We compare *BASH* against *Snooping* and *Directory* using full-system simulation of a 16-processor SPARC system running four commercial workloads and one scientific benchmark. Unfortunately, due to the complexities of full-system simulation and commercial workload setup and tuning, we are currently unable to obtain

results with more than 16 processors. To approximate *BASH*'s performance on larger systems, we also present simulation results for a 16 processor system in which the bandwidth cost of broadcasting is four times greater than normal.

5.1 Benchmarks

Table 2 describes our benchmarks. We concentrate on commercial workloads, such as database and web servers, but we also include one scientific application for comparison. We run all of the commercial workloads for a warm-up period to bring the system to a steady state before measurement. To simplify the simulations of our commercial workloads, the client does not model think time between requests, and the client and server are collocated on the same simulated machine.

5.2 Target System Assumptions

We evaluate 16-node SPARC systems running unmodified Solaris 8. Each node contains a processor core, level one caches, a unified level two cache (4 MB, 4-way set associative, 64-byte blocks), a cache controller, and a memory controller for part of the globally shared memory (2 GB total). We assume that a processor and level one caches would complete four billion instructions per second if the memory system beyond the level one caches was perfect. This could be accomplished, for example, with a 2 GHz processor that has a perfect-L2-cache IPC (instructions per cycle) of 2.

5.3 Simulation Methods

We simulate our target systems with the Simics full-system multiprocessor simulator [22], and we extend Simics with a memory hierarchy simulator (described in Section 4.2) to compute execution times. Simics is a system-level architectural simulator developed by Virtutech AB that is capable of booting unmodified commercial operating systems and running unmodified applications. We use Simics/sun4u, which simulates Sun Microsystems' SPARC v9 platform architecture (e.g., used for Sun E6000s). Simics

Table 2. Benchmark descriptions

On-Line Transaction Processing (OLTP): DB2 with a TPC-C-like workload. The TPC-C benchmark models the database activity of a wholesale supplier, with many concurrent users performing read/write transactions against the database. Our OLTP workload is based on the TPC-C v3.0 benchmark using IBM's DB2 v7.2 EEE database management system and an IBM benchmark kit to build the database and model users. Our experiments use a 1 GB 10-warehouse database stored on five raw disks and an additional dedicated database log disk. There are 128 simulated users (8 per processor). The database was warmed up for 10,000 transactions before taking measurements, and our results are based on runs of 1000 transactions.

Static Web Content Serving: Apache with SURGE. Web servers such as Apache have become an important enterprise server application. We use Apache 1.3.19 for SPARC/Solaris 8 configured to use pthread locks and minimal logging as the web server, and SURGE [2] to generate web requests. Our experiments used a repository of 2000 files (totalling ~50 MB). There are 160 simulated users (10 per processor). The system was warmed up for ~80,000 transactions, and our results are based on runs of 2,500 requests.

Java Server Workload: SPECjbb. SPECjbb2000 is a server-side java benchmark that models a 3-tier system, focusing on the "middleware" server business logic and object manipulation. We used Sun's HotSpot 1.4.0 Server JVM. The benchmark includes driver threads to generate transactions. Our experiments used 24 threads and 24 warehouses (with a data size of approximately ~500MB). The system was warmed up for 100,000 transactions, and our results are based on runs of 100,000 transactions.

Dynamic Web Content Serving: Slashcode. Our Slashcode benchmark is based on an open-source dynamic web message posting system used by slashdot.org. We use Slashcode 2.0, Apache 1.3.20, and Apache's `mod_perl` 1.25 module for the web server, and MySQL 3.23.39 as the database engine. A multithreaded user emulation program is used to simulate user browsing and posting behavior. The database is a snapshot of the slashcode.org site, and it contains ~3000 messages. There are 48 simulated users (3 per processor). The system was warmed up for 240 transactions before taking measurements, and our results are based on runs of 50 transactions.

Scientific application: Barnes-Hut from SPLASH-2. We selected one application from the SPLASH-2 benchmark suite [32]: *barnes-hut* with 64K bodies. The benchmark was compiled with Sun's WorkShop C compiler and uses the PARMACS shared-memory macros used by Artiaga et al. [1]. The macro library was modified to enable user-level synchronization through test-and-set locks rather than POSIX-thread library calls. We began measurement at the start of the parallel phase to avoid measuring thread forking.

is a functional simulator only, and it assumes that each instruction takes one simulated cycle to execute (although I/O may take longer), but it provides an interface to support our detailed memory hierarchy simulation. We use Simics to generate blocking requests to a unified single level cache. We use this simple processor model to enable tractable simulation times for full-system, multiprocessor simulation of commercial workloads.

Since full-system simulation captures kernel behavior and inter-processor timing, small changes in system timing can lead to significant variations in execution time. For example, we find that our operating system intensive workloads (OLTP, Slashcode, and Apache) exhibit more variation than workloads that are less operating system intensive (SPECjbb and Barnes-Hut). To overcome observed instabilities, we calculate the arithmetic mean and standard deviation of multiple simulations to estimate experimental uncertainty. We plot the mean and, if the coefficient of variation is greater than 1%, error bars at plus/minus one standard deviation for all data points. To gather multiple data points, we perturb our otherwise deterministic simulations by adding a small random delay to each request.

5.4 Results

We now present results for the workloads described in Table 2. Figure 10 illustrates the performances of the protocols over a range of bandwidths for 16 processors. For each benchmark, we plot performance—normalized to that of *Snooping* with unbounded bandwidth—as a function of available interconnect endpoint bandwidth. We also include

the results of our microbenchmark to allow for direct comparison. Our results show that, for a 16 processor system and a range of bandwidths, *Snooping* and *BASH* perform similarly, and both outperfom *Directory*. The macrobenchmark results look qualitatively similar to the microbenchmark, but the performance difference between *Snooping* and *Directory* is smaller for some of the benchmarks. This is due to a lower cache miss rate (Barnes and Slashcode) or a smaller fraction of sharing misses (SPECjbb).

To approximate *BASH*'s performance on a larger system, we increase the cost of broadcast by quadrupling the interconnect bandwidth used by any broadcast request. Figure 11 presents these results and shows that, for a range of bandwidths, *BASH* performs as well or better than both *Snooping* and *Directory*. We did not perform any macrobenchmark simulations with less than 600 MB/second endpoint bandwidth due to excessive simulation times. However, we expect the performance of *BASH* to closely track that of *Directory*, as was the case for the microbenchmark on 64 processors (shown in Figure 1).

While these results show that *BASH* can adapt to system configuration, one of *BASH*'s strengths is adaptation to varying behaviors between workloads. In Figure 12, we plot the 1600 MB/second data excerpted from Figure 11 normalized to the performance of *BASH*. For this configuration, *Snooping* outperforms *Directory* for Barnes-Hut and OLTP, but the reverse is true for SPECjbb. The performances of Slashcode and Apache are similar for *Snooping* and *Directory*. For this configuration, *BASH* matches or exceeds the performances of both other protocols for all five workloads.

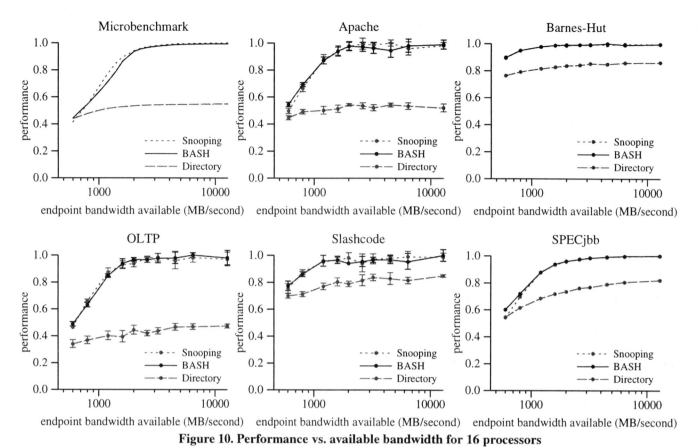

Figure 10. Performance vs. available bandwidth for 16 processors

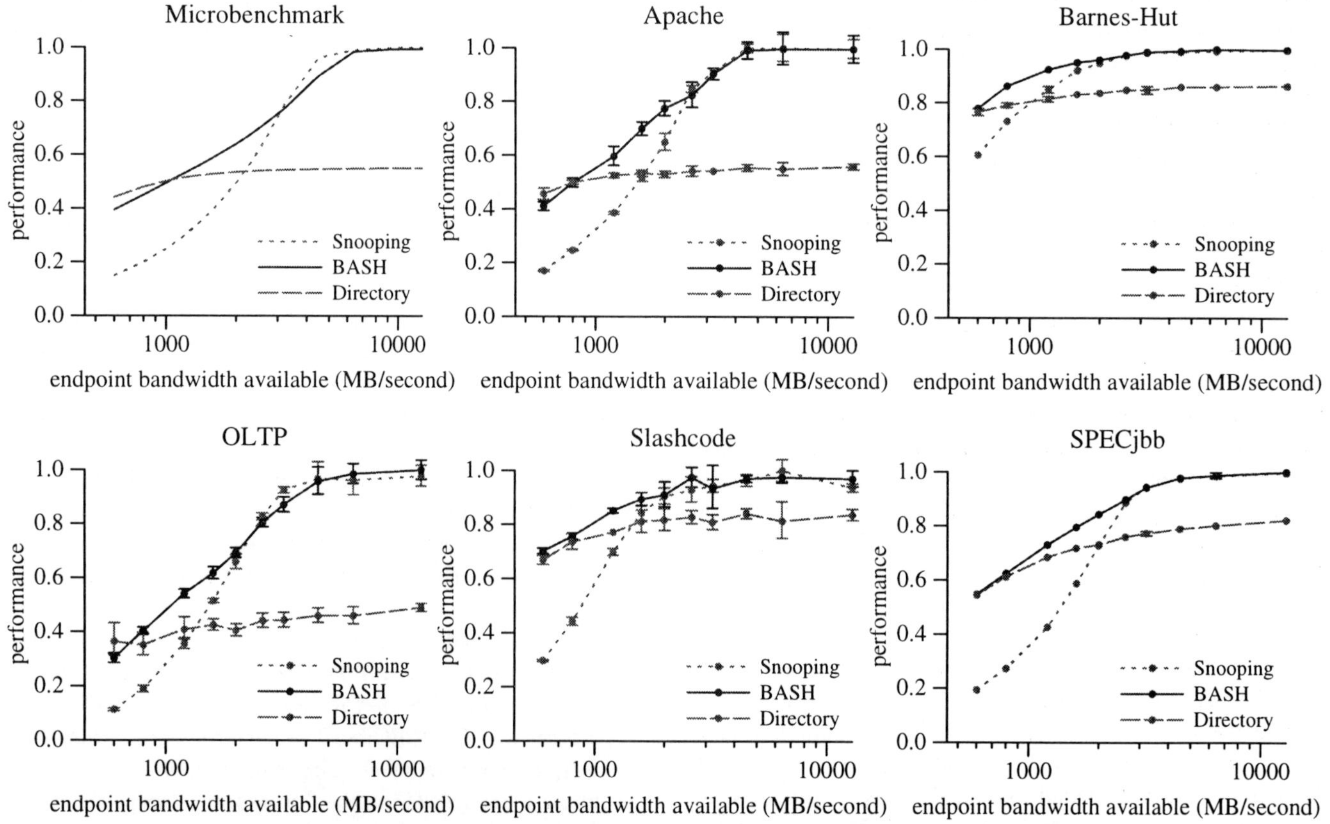

Figure 11. Performance vs. available bandwidth for 16 processors with 4x broadcast cost

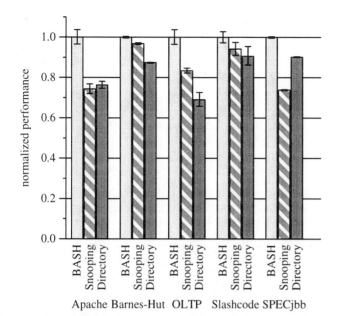

Figure 12. Adapting to workload intensity

Though increasing the relative cost of broadcasting does not capture other effects of increasing system sizes such as lock contention and changes to sharing patterns, we believe these results show that bandwidth adaptive coherence in general, and *BASH* in particular, enables robust system performance for a wide range of system configurations and workloads.

6 Related Work

Prior related research falls roughly into the two categories of protocols and networks.

Protocols. There is a great deal of research in protocols that adapt towards sharing patterns rather than network usage. Multicast Snooping protocols [4, 28] allow processors to multicast requests to those nodes that are suspected to need to observe the request, and the multicast mask is predicted based on observed sharing patterns. This differs from bandwidth adaptive snooping in that *BASH* only predicts two types of masks (unicast or broadcast) and chooses its multicast mask based on available bandwidth. Competitive snoopy caching adapts between an invalidate and an update protocol [16] to limit the overhead to within a factor of two of optimal. Additional research has pursued the idea of adaptive protocols, but none of which we are aware consider interconnection network utilization. Another class of adaptive protocols includes the COMA [9, 13] and R-NUMA [8] protocols. These protocols migrate data to where it is used, adaptively reducing communication and network traffic.

Networks. Scott and Sohi [27] proposed using network feedback to adaptively avoid tree saturation in multistage interconnection networks. They use feedback control theory

to adjust network usage to avoid performance degradation due to hot spots in memory access patterns. This work differs from bandwidth adaptive snooping in that it seeks to throttle requests from being issued, whereas *BASH* chooses between issuing a unicast or a broadcast.

Thottethodi et al. [31] have developed a scheme for using global network information to throttle requests before they can congest the network. At the cost of an additional network sideband for communication of contention effects, this scheme can adapt more accurately than a scheme that relies solely on local information. This work complements bandwidth adaptive snooping in that it could be used to estimate network utilization, and future work may adapt these techniques to improve our detection of network congestion. Other research has also explored techniques for estimating interconnect traffic (refer to the related work in [31]).

7 Conclusions and Future Work

We have developed a hybrid shared memory cache coherence protocol, and we have demonstrated the benefits provided by adaptivity. Moreover, the trend towards integration of the coherence protocol logic and the processor on the same die suggests a unified adaptive design. An adaptive approach allows a single highly integrated microprocessor design to be used in many system configurations (e.g., number of processors). Also, adaptivity allows the system to adjust to various workloads, including future workloads whose behaviors are unknown at hardware design time.

One area of future work is the exploration of additional mechanisms for deciding whether to unicast or broadcast. Particularly in the middle range of bandwidth where a decision based on available bandwidth is less obvious, it might be preferable to predict based on sharing patterns. There are many instances where the decision would be easy, such as the choice to unicast requests for misses due to instruction fetches. Moreover, integrating bandwidth adaptivity with multicast snooping [4]—rather than simply unicasting or broadcasting—might be worthwhile. Additionally, more sophisticated adaptive mechanisms, perhaps using global estimates of interconnection network utilization [31], could be employed.

Acknowledgments

We thank Virtutech AB for their support of Simics and the Condor group and Remzi Arpaci-Dusseau for providing additional computing resources. Alaa Alameldeen, Pacia Harper, and Min Xu contributed to the setup and tuning of our workloads. We also thank Adam Butts, Kourosh Gharachorloo, Anders Landin, Alvin Lebeck, Ravi Rajwar, Amir Roth, Craig Zilles and the Wisconsin Computer Architecture Affiliates for their comments on this work.

References

[1] E. Artiaga, N. Navarro, X. Martorell, and Y. Becerra. Implementing PARMACS Macros for Shared Memory Multiprocessor Environments. Technical report, Polytechnic University of Catalunya, Department of Computer Architecture Technical Report UPC-DAC-1997-07, Jan. 1997.

[2] P. Barford and M. Crovella. Generating Representative Web Workloads for Network and Server Performance Evaluation. In *Proceedings of the 1998 ACM Sigmetrics Conference on Measurement and Modeling of Computer Systems*, pages 151–160, June 1998.

[3] L. A. Barroso, K. Gharachorloo, and E. Bugnion. Memory System Characterization of Commercial Workloads. In *Proceedings of the 25th Annual International Symposium on Computer Architecture*, pages 3–14, June 1998.

[4] E. E. Bilir, R. M. Dickson, Y. Hu, M. Plakal, D. J. Sorin, M. D. Hill, and D. A. Wood. Multicast Snooping: A New Coherence Method Using a Multicast Address Network. In *Proceedings of the 26th Annual International Symposium on Computer Architecture*, pages 294–304, May 1999.

[5] J. Borkenhagen and S. Storino. 4th Generation 64-bit PowerPC-Compatible Commercial Processor Design. IBM Server Group Whitepaper, Jan. 1999.

[6] A. Charlesworth. Starfire: Extending the SMP Envelope. *IEEE Micro*, 18(1):39–49, Jan/Feb 1998.

[7] A. Charlesworth. The Sun Fireplane Interconnect. In *Proceedings of SC2001*, Nov. 2001.

[8] B. Falsafi and D. A. Wood. Reactive NUMA: A Design for Unifying S-COMA and CC-NUMA. In *Proceedings of the 24th Annual International Symposium on Computer Architecture*, pages 229–240, June 1997.

[9] S. J. Frank. Tightly Coupled Multiprocessor System Speeds Memory-access Times. *Electronics*, 57(1):164–169, Jan. 1984.

[10] K. Gharachorloo, M. Sharma, S. Steely, and S. V. Doren. Architecture and Design of AlphaServer GS320. In *Proceedings of the Ninth International Conference on Architectural Support for Programming Languages and Operating Systems*, Nov. 2000.

[11] S. W. Golumb. *Shift Register Sequences*. Aegean Park Press, revised edition, 1982.

[12] L. Gwennap. Alpha 21364 to Ease Memory Bottleneck. *Microprocessor Report*, Oct. 1998.

[13] E. Hagersten, A. Landin, and S. Haridi. DDM–A Cache-Only Memory Architecture. *IEEE Computer*, 25(9):44–54, Sept. 1992.

[14] J. Hennessy. The Future of Systems Research. *IEEE Computer*, 32(8):27–33, Aug. 1999.

[15] N. Izuta, T. Watabe, T. Shimizu, and T. Ichihashi. Overview of PRIMEPOWER 2000/1000/800 Hardware. *Fujitsu Scientific & Technical Journal*, 36(2):121–127, Dec. 2000.

[16] A. R. Karlin, M. S. Manasse, L. Rudolph, and D. D. Sleator. Competitive Snoopy Caching. *Algorithmica*, 3(1):79–119, 1988.

[17] S. Kunkel. Personal Communication, Apr. 2000.

[18] S. Kunkel, B. Armstrong, and P. Vitale. System Optimization for OLTP Workloads. *IEEE Micro*, pages 56–64, May/June 1999.

[19] B. C. Kuo. *Automatic Control Systems*. Prentice Hall, seventh edition, 1995.

[20] J. Laudon and D. Lenoski. The SGI Origin: A ccNUMA Highly Scalable Server. In *Proceedings of the 24th Annual International Symposium on Computer Architecture*, pages 241–251, June 1997.

[21] D. Lenoski, J. Laudon, K. Gharachorloo, W.-D. Weber, A. Gupta, J. Hennessy, M. Horowitz, and M. Lam. The Stanford DASH Multiprocessor. *IEEE Computer*, 25(3):63–79, Mar. 1992.

[22] P. S. Magnusson et al. SimICS/sun4m: A Virtual Workstation. In *Proceedings of Usenix Annual Technical Conference*, June 1998.

[23] M. M. K. Martin, D. J. Sorin, A. Ailamaki, A. Alameldeen, R. M. Dickson, C. J. Mauer, K. E. Moore, M. Plakal, M. D. Hill, and D. A. Wood. Timestamp Snooping: An Approach for Extending SMPs. In *Proceedings of the Ninth International Conference on Architectural Support for Programming Languages and Operating Systems*, pages 25–36, Nov. 2000.

[24] J. R. Mashey. NUMAflex Modular Design Approach: A Revolution in Evolution. Posted on comp.arch news group, Aug. 2000.

[25] A. Nanda, K.-K. Mak, K. Sugavanam, R. K. Sahoo, V. Soundararajan, and T. B. Smith. MemorIES: A Programmable, Real-Time Hardware Emulation Tool for Multiprocessor Server Design. In *Proceedings of the Ninth International Conference on Architectural Support for Programming Languages and Operating Systems*, Nov. 2000.

[26] M. Plakal, D. J. Sorin, A. E. Condon, and M. D. Hill. Lamport Clocks: Verifying a Directory Cache-Coherence Protocol. In *Proceedings of the Tenth ACM Symposium on Parallel Algorithms and Architectures*, pages 67–76, June 1998.

[27] S. Scott and G. Sohi. The Use of Feedback in Multiprocessors and its Application to Tree Saturation Control. *IEEE Transactions on Parallel and Distributed Systems*, 1(4):385–398, Oct. 1990.

[28] D. J. Sorin, M. Plakal, M. D. Hill, A. E. Condon, M. M. Martin, and D. A. Wood. Specifying and Verifying a Broadcast and a Multicast Snooping Cache Coherence Protocol. Technical Report 1412, Computer Sciences Department, University of Wisconsin–Madison, Mar. 2000.

[29] P. Sweazey and A. J. Smith. A Class of Compatible Cache Consistency Protocols and their Support by the IEEE Futurebus. In *Proceedings of the 13th Annual International Symposium on Computer Architecture*, pages 414–423, June 1986.

[30] J. M. Tendler, S. Dodson, S. Fields, H. Le, and B. Sinharoy. POWER4 System Microarchitecture. IBM Server Group Whitepaper, Oct. 2001.

[31] M. Thottethodi, A. R. Lebeck, and S. S. Mukherjee. Self-Tuned Congestion Control for Multiprocessor Networks. In *Proceedings of the Seventh IEEE Symposium on High-Performance Computer Architecture*, Jan. 2001.

[32] S. C. Woo, M. Ohara, E. Torrie, J. P. Singh, and A. Gupta. The SPLASH-2 Programs: Characterization and Methodological Considerations. In *Proceedings of the 22nd Annual International Symposium on Computer Architecture*, pages 24–37, June 1995.

[33] D. A. Wood, G. A. Gibson, and R. H. Katz. Verifying a Multiprocessor Cache Controller Using Random Test Generation. *IEEE Design and Test of Computers*, Aug. 1990.

CableS : Thread Control and Memory Management Extensions for Shared Virtual Memory Clusters

Peter Jamieson and Angelos Bilas

Department of Electrical and Computer Engineering
University of Toronto
Toronto, Ontario M5S 3G4, Canada
fjamieson,bilasg@eecg.toronto.edu

Abstract

*Clusters of high-end workstations and PCs are currently used in many application domains to perform large-scale computations or as scalable servers for I/O bound tasks. Although clusters have many advantages, their applicability in emerging areas of applications has been limited. One of the main reasons for this is the fact that clusters do not provide a single system image and thus are hard to program. In this work we address this problem by providing a single cluster image with respect to thread and memory management. We implement our system, CableS (**C**luster en**abled** thread**S**), on a 32-processor cluster interconnected with a low-latency, high-bandwidth system area network and conduct an early exploration of the costs involved in providing the extra functionality. We demonstrate the versatility of CableS with a wide range of applications and show that clusters can be used to support applications that have been written for more expensive tightly–coupled systems, with very little effort on the programmer side: (a) We run legacy pthreads applications without any major modifications. (b) We use a public domain OpenMP compiler (OdinMP [8]) to translate OpenMP programs to pthreads and execute them on our system, with no or few modifications to the translated pthreads source code. (c) We provide an implementation of the M4 macros for our pthreads system and run the SPLASH-2 applications. We also show that the overhead introduced by the extra functionality of CableS affects the parallel section of applications that have been tuned for the shared memory abstraction only in cases where the data placement is affected by operating system (WindowsNT) limitations in virtual memory mappings granularity.*

1. Introduction and Background

The shared memory abstraction is used in an increasing number of application areas. Most vendors are designing both small–scale symmetric multiprocessors (SMPs) and large–scale, hardware cache-coherent distributed shared memory (DSM) systems, targeting both scientific and commercial applications. However, there is still a large gap in the configuration space for affordable and scalable shared memory architectures, as shown in Figure 1. Shared memory clusters are an attractive approach for filling in the gap and providing affordable and scalable compute cycles and I/O.

Recently there has been progress in building high-performance clusters out of high–end workstations and low-latency, high-bandwidth system area networks (SANs). SANs, used as interconnection networks provide memory–to–memory latencies of under 10 s and bandwidth in the order of hundreds of MBytes/s, limited mainly by the PCI bus. For instance, the cluster we are developing at the University of Toronto uses Myrinet as the interconnection network and currently provides one–way, memory–to–memory latency of about 7.8 s and bandwidth of about 125MBytes/s. Similar clusters are being built at many other research institutions. Recent work has also targeted the design of efficient shared virtual memory (SVM) protocols for such clusters [29, 20, 32, 17]. These protocols take advantage of features provided by SANs, such as low–latencies for short messages and direct remote memory operations with no remote processor intervention [15, 11, 10], to improve system performance and scalability [20].

Despite the many advantages of clusters, their use is not widespread. One of the main reasons is that despite the progress on the performance side, it still is a very challenging task to port existing applications or to write new ones for the shared memory programming APIs provided by clus-

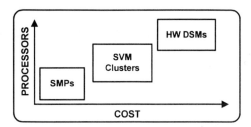

Figure 1. The architectural space for shared memory systems. Shared memory clusters may be able to fill in a gap in the cost-performance range and provide application portability across architectures that covers the full spectrum.

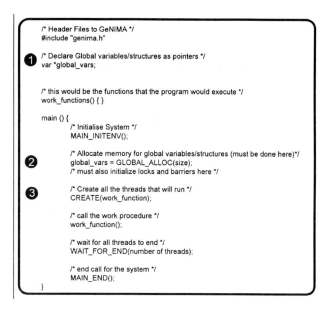

Figure 2. The programming template for many SVM systems. At Stage 1: all global variables are declared as pointers. Stage 2: global variables are allocated between the initialization sequence. Stage 3: threads are created.

ters. Many shared memory clusters are written according to M4–macros rules (Figure 2). Although these APIs provide sufficient primitives to write parallel programs, they also impose several restrictions: (i) Processes cannot always be created and destroyed on the fly during application execution. This is especially true on clusters that use modern SANs with support for direct remote memory operations. In these systems all nodes/processes need to be present at initialization to perform the initial mappings. (ii) Programmers allocate shared memory only during program initialization and should not free memory until the end of execution. For instance, these rules are followed by the SPLASH-2 applications that are usually used for evaluating shared memory systems. Also, placement of primary copies of shared pages is limited due to restrictions imposed by SANs on both the number of regions as well as the total amount of memory space that can be mapped. (iii) In most shared memory clusters the synchronization primitives supported are *lock/unlock* and *barrier* primitives. However, more modern APIs support conditional waits as well as other primitives. These, and other limitations are not very important for large classes of scientific applications that are well structured. However, they pose important obstacles for using clusters in areas of applications that exhibit a more dynamic behavior, such as commercially–oriented applications. In essence, current clusters that support shared memory provide a very limited single system image to the programmer with respect to process, memory management, and synchronization.

The goal of this work is to overcome the above limitations for existing and new applications written for the shared memory model. To achieve this we provide a more complete and functional single cluster image to the programmer by designing and implementing a *pthreads* interface on top of our cluster. We also perform a preliminary evaluation of the costs associated with the additional system functionality. Our system, *CableS* (**C**luster en**able**d

thread**S**), allows existing *pthreads* programs to run on our system with minor modifications. Programs can dynamically create and destroy threads, allocate global shared memory throughout execution, and use synchronization primitives specified by the *pthreads* API. More specifically, our system provides support for:

Dynamic memory management: *CableS* addresses a number of issues with respect to memory management. (a) It provides all necessary mechanisms to support different memory placement policies. Currently, *CableS* implements first touch placement, but can be extended to support others as well. (b) It provides the ability to allocate global, shared memory dynamically at any time during program execution. (c) It deals with static global variables in a transparent way.

Dynamic node and thread management: *CableS* allows the application to dynamically create threads at any point during execution. Currently, new threads are allocated to nodes with a simple, round–robin policy. When threads exceed a maximum number, a new node is attached to the application. On the fly, the system performs all the necessary initialization to support the *pthreads* API.

Modern synchronization primitives: *CableS* supports the conditional wait primitives.

The main limitation of *CableS* is that, although it provides a single system image with respect to thread management, memory management, and synchronization support, it does not yet include file system and networking support across cluster nodes. The general issue here is that operating system (OS) state is still not shared across nodes. However, this is beyond the scope of this work and we do not examine this further.

We demonstrate the viability of our approach and the versatility of our system by using a wide range of applications: (a) We run existing *pthreads* applications with minor modifications. (b) We use a public–domain OpenMP compiler, OdinMP [8], that translates OpenMP programs to *pthreads* programs for shared memory multiprocessors and run the translated OpenMP programs on our system. OdinMP [8] is designed for shared memory multiprocessors that support *pthreads*. Our system supports the OpenMP programs with no modifications to the OpenMP source and minor modifications to the *pthreads* sources. (c) We provide an implementation of the M4 macros for *pthreads* and we run some SPLASH-2 applications. We also show that the overhead introduced by the extra functionality affects the parallel section of applications that have been tuned for the shared memory abstraction *only* in cases where data is improperly placed due to OS limitations in virtual memory mappings granularity. In the SPLASH-2 applications most overhead is introduced during application initialization and termination.

The rest of the paper is organized as follows. Section 2 describes the design of *CableS*. Section 3 presents our experimental results. Section 4 presents related work and Section 5 discusses our high level conclusions.

2. System Design

CableS is a system built upon an existing state-of-the-art, tuned SVM system, *GeNIMA*, which provides the basic shared memory protocol. *CableS* supports a full *pthreads* (POSIX Threads IEEE POSIX 1003.1 [1]) API, which enables legacy shared memory applications written for traditional, tightly coupled, hardware shared memory systems to run on shared memory clusters. Within the *pthreads* API, *CableS* addresses the following issues: (i) Dynamic global memory management. (ii) Dynamic thread management. (iii) Support for modern synchronization primitives. Our main contribution is our memory extensions to support a transparent dynamic memory management.

2.1. Memory Subsystem

We deal with memory management issues at both the communication and SVM levels. First, we explain how the communication layer is coupled with the SVM layer. Secondly, we describe what limitations currently exist at the communication level, and how these limitations effect the system API. Finally, we describe how *CableS* addresses these limitations.

Nodes in modern clusters are usually interconnected with low–latency, high–bandwidth SANs that support user–level access to network resources [15, 10, 7]. By allowing users to directly access the network without OS intervention, these systems dramatically reduce latencies compared to traditional TCP/IP–based local area networks. Moreover, to further reduce latencies, SANs usually support direct remote memory operations: Reads and writes to remote memory are performed without remote processor intervention. This mechanism provides fast access to remote memory within a cluster. SVM systems on clusters interconnected with SANs take advantage of these features to reduce the overhead associated with propagation and updating of shared data [29, 20].

In these mechanisms, a node maps one or more regions of remote memory to the local network interface card (NIC) and then performs direct operations on these regions without requiring OS or processor intervention on the remote side. This mapping operation is called registration and usually requires work at both the sending as well as the receiving NIC.

2.1.1 Current SAN Limitations

Due to hardware resource limits (e.g., memory on the NIC) SANs [15, 6, 14, 11], incur a number of limitations:

One limitation is the number of memory regions that can be registered on the NIC (usually a few thousand). Usual solutions in SVM protocols to reducing the number of regions are: (a) To group shared pages in regions and map them in one operation. In this case, pages in the working set of a process may have their primary copies (homes) in remote nodes resulting in excessive network traffic and performance degradation. (b) To place the primary copies of pages in the working set on the node where the process runs. In this way the registration limitations may be violated since there will be a large number of non-contiguous memory regions that have to be registered. (c) To register the many, non-contiguous regions in one operation, including the gaps between regions. However, this results in registering essentially all the shared address space. This is not feasible due to the total amount of memory which can be registered. None of these solutions is satisfactory.

Another limitation is the total amount of memory that can be registered on the NIC (usually a few hundred MBytes). The only solution to this is dynamic management of registered memory [9, 4], which introduces additional costs but may allow for larger amounts of remote memory to be used for direct operations. Although we are exploring this alternative at the NIC level, this direction is beyond the scope of this work.

The amount of memory that can be pinned due to OS limitations, where a pinned page means that the page will never be swapped out of main memory. This is a fundamental limit in current OS design that cannot be overcome in SVM systems.

2.1.2 Current Limitations on SVM APIs

The above limitations inflict a number of constraints on SVM systems with respect to memory management:

Allocation and deallocation of global shared memory is limited. Many systems today allocate all global shared memory at initialization and deallocate it at program termination. Furthermore, static memory management requires all participating nodes to be present at application startup time. This simplifies significantly the task of providing a shared address space. Since all nodes are present at initialization, they can all perform at the same time all necessary steps of creating the shared portion of the virtual address space. Thus, resource requirements in memory and nodes need to be known up front, which is not always possible with applications that exhibit dynamic behavior, and in addition, resources may be overall, poorly utilized.

The amount of process virtual memory that can be allocated to global shared data is constrained. In many cases, although processes have available virtual address space, and the cluster has enough physical memory to efficiently support large problem sizes, the virtual memory cannot be used due to the above SAN limitations. This is going to be especially true as 64–bit processors are used in commodity clusters. Moreover, many shared memory applications exhibit access patterns to memory that result in a working set which consists of non-contiguous shared pages, further complicating registration issues.

There is no dynamic assignment of primary shared page copies to nodes (home placement and migration). The complex and expensive registration phase results usually in static management of the primary copies (homes) of shared pages. Thus, SVM systems, which take advantage of remote DMA (direct memory access) operations, do not usually provide dynamic and on–demand memory placement.

In the threads programming model, global shared variables are visible to all threads; however, this is not true in most SVM systems. Global static variables are not usually included in the shared address space. The compiler/linker automatically allocates these variables to a designated part of the virtual address space that is not part of the global address space. This imposes additional challenges in the process of porting existing shared memory applications to clusters.

So far, most of these issues have been dealt with by avoiding the problems. For instance, the SPLASH-2 applications have been written in a way that avoids all dynamic memory management issues. However, this is not (or should not be) true for most other shared memory applications, such as *pthreads* applications. The result is inflexible systems that are not easy to program. Tables 1 and 2 summarize the SAN limitations and constraints they impose on SVM systems.

SAN Limitations	Affects base SVM	Affects *CableS*
Number of registered regions	Yes	No
Total amount of registered memory	Yes	Yes
Total amount of pinned memory	Yes	Yes

Table 1. SAN limitations and constraints.

SVM Limitations	Addressed by base SVM	Addressed by *CableS*
Dynamic shared memory allocation and deallocation	No	Yes
Amount of virtual memory used for shared data	No	Partially (NIC)
Dynamic page placement	No	Yes
Global static shared variables	No	Yes

Table 2. SAN and SVM limitations and constraints.

2.1.3 Proposed Solution

Table 2 shows the issues that *CableS* deals with. *CableS* addresses the issues associated with the number of exported regions in SANs and with most SVM memory management limitations.

Reducing the number of registered regions: *CableS* uses double virtual mappings [19] for home pages. Initially, one contiguous part of the physical address space in each node is used to hold the primary copies of shared pages that will be allocated to this node. This part of the physical address space is always pinned, since it will be accessed remotely by other nodes (Fig. 3). The primary copies are mapped twice to the virtual address space of the process. One mapping is to a contiguous part of the virtual address space and is used only by the protocol to register the home pages with one operation, avoiding the registration limitations mentioned above. The second mapping is used by the application to access the shared data. For this mapping, the home pages are divided in groups of fixed size (in the current system 64 KBytes) and are mapped to arbitrary locations in the virtual address space of the process. It is important to note that these locations are not necessarily contiguous.

Dynamic allocation and deallocation: As the application requires more shared memory, it first allocates a region in the global virtual address space. Then, it determines which node will hold the primary copies of these pages according to some placement policy (currently first touch). When a home page is touched: (a) The home node extends the home pages section and registers the additional pages with the NIC. Then, it maps the virtual memory region to the newly allocated home pages (Fig. 3). As the pri-

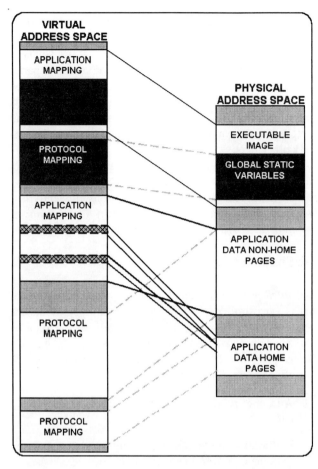

VIRTUAL ADDRESS SPACE

APPLICATION MAPPING

PROTOCOL MAPPING

APPLICATION MAPPING

PROTOCOL MAPPING

PROTOCOL MAPPING

PHYSICAL ADDRESS SPACE

EXECUTABLE IMAGE

GLOBAL STATIC VARIABLES

APPLICATION DATA NON-HOME PAGES

APPLICATION DATA HOME PAGES

Figure 3. The virtual memory map for the application and protocol regions.

mary copies of shared pages are placed in different nodes, the home pages portion of the physical address space is mapped to non-contiguous regions of the shared virtual address space in the home node. (b) Every other node in the system, registers the newly allocated virtual memory region with the NIC so that each node can fetch updates from the primary copies and rely on the OS to allocate arbitrary physical frames for these pages. The contiguous portion of the virtual address space that is exported is currently attached and exported as a single region. It is up to the communication layer to dynamically handle this region of registered virtual memory without statically reserving physical memory and NIC resources [9, 4]. **Dynamic placement and migration:** Implementing a dynamic placement policy requires that the system delays binding of virtual addresses until later in program execution. For instance, implementing a first touch policy, requires delaying binding until it is first read or written. *CableS* maintains information about each memory segment allocated in the global directory. During execution, when a node touches the segment, it uses the global directory to identify if the segment has

been touched by anyone else. If it has, then the segment is registered with the NIC and is mapped to the corresponding region on the home node (Fig. 3). If this is the first touch to the region, then the node becomes the home by updating the global information and by appropriately mapping the physical pages to its shared virtual address space so that the application can use it. Synchronization of the global information and ordering simultaneous accesses to a newly allocated region is facilitated through system locks. Table 2 mentions this feature as fully supported, but although we provide all necessary mechanisms for page migration, we do not yet provide a policy.

Amount of available virtual memory: The amount of virtual memory that can be used for shared data depends on the number of regions and on the total amount of memory the NIC can register and pin. *CableS* partially addresses this by taking advantage of the double mapping. Instead of exporting non-contiguous pages in the application map (Fig. 3), we export the single contiguous protocol mapping of the home pages (Fig. 3). Although, the total amount of memory that can be registered and pinned is still limited by the NIC, our approach allows certain applications, e.g OCEAN, to run larger problem sizes.

Global static variables: *CableS* deals with global static variables in a transparent way. It uses a type quantifier *GLOBAL* in WindowsNT:

```
#define GLOBAL _declspec(allocate("GLOBAL_DATA"))
```

to allocate these global variables in a special area within the executable image (Fig. 3) [1]. At application initialization, the first node in the system becomes the primary copy for this region. All necessary mappings are established to other nodes as they are attached to the application. Thus, static global variables of arbitrary types can be shared among system nodes. This approach can be used in other operating systems. For example, in Linux the *__attribute__ ((section ("GLOBAL_DATA")))* has similar functionality.

Finally, *CableS* does not attempt to deal with the restrictions on the amount of memory that can be registered and pinned because these are issues that are better dealt at the NIC level (Table 1). However, this work is beyond the scope of this paper, which focuses at SVM library level issues.

2.2. Thread Management

In a distributed environment, threads of execution need to be started and administered on remote systems. For this purpose, *CableS* needs to maintain and manage global state that stores location and resource information about each thread in an application. *CableS* uses per application global

---

[1] Making this region part of the shared address space in NT is not straight forward, since the system does not seem to allow remapping of this area in the process virtual address space. For this reason we extend the VMMC driver to provide the necessary supporting functionality.

state, called the application control block (ACB). This state is updated by all nodes in the system via direct remote operations as well as notification handlers. *CableS* maintains the most up to date system information on the first node where the application starts (master node). To ensure consistency of the ACBs, updates are performed either by the master node through remote handler invocations or by node update regions in which the system guarantees that the node is the exclusive writer.

The thread management component of the *pthreads* library is hinged around thread creation. Thread creation in *CableS* involves one of three possible cases: (i) Create a thread on the local node. Local thread creation is equivalent to a call to the local OS to create a thread. (ii) Create a thread on a remote node that is not used by this application. This operation is called attaching a remote node to the application. When *CableS* needs to attach a new node to the application, the master node M creates a remote process on the new node N. Node N, starts executing the initialization sequence and performs all necessary mappings for the global shared memory that is already allocated on M. N then retrieves global state information from M including shared memory mappings and sends an initialization acknowledgment back to M. M broadcasts to all other nodes in the system that N exists and that they can establish their mappings with N. At the end of this phase, node N has been introduced into the system and can be used for remote thread creations. (iii) Create a thread on an already attached remote node.

The remaining thread management operations involve mostly state management, mainly, through direct reads and writes to global state in the ACB. For example, in the case of *pthread_join()*, a thread waits until the ACB indicates that the particular thread being waited for has completed its execution.

Most traditional SVM systems create one thread per processor; *CableS* allows multiple threads per processor. These threads are scheduled by the local OS and compete for global system resources. Threads can be terminated at any time via a cancel mechanism, or can terminate by completing execution. *CableS* provides mechanisms to terminate threads, and to dynamically detach a node when there are no longer any threads remaining on the node.

2.3. Synchronization Support

The *pthreads* API provides two synchronization constructs: *mutexes* and *conditions*. Current SVM APIs that mostly target compute-bound parallel applications provide two other synchronization primitives, locks and barriers. Since mutexes and locks are very similar, we use the underlying SVM lock mechanism to provide mutexes in the *pthreads* API. The *pthreads* condition is a synchronization construct in which a thread waits until another thread sends a signal. Mutexes and conditions can be implemented either by spinning on a flag or by suspending the thread on an OS event. Although implementations that use spinning consume processor cycles, they are more common in parallel systems to reduce wake–up latency. Our implementation of *pthreads* mutexes and conditional waits uses spinning, when there is fewer threads per processor in a node, and switches to locks that spin for a specified time and then locally block [22].

Finally, global synchronization (barriers) can be implemented in *pthreads* with mutexes (or conditions). However, to support legacy parallel applications efficiently *CableS* extends the *pthreads* API to support a barrier operation *pthread_barrier(number_of_threads)*.

2.4. Summary

CableS provides a shared memory programming model that is very similar to a *pthreads* programming model for tightly–coupled shared memory multiprocessors, such as SMPs and hardware DSMs. Figure 4 shows an example of a *CableS* program. To run any *pthreads* program on *CableS*, the following modifications are required:

1. Add the *pthread_start()* and *pthread_end()* library calls.

2. Prefix all static variables that will be globally shared with the *GLOBAL* identifier.

3. Link with *CableS* library.

```
/* Header Files to CableS */
#include "CableS.h"

/* Declare Global variables/structures */
GLOBAL_DATA var *global_vars;
GLOBAL_DATA var other_global_vars;

/* this would be the functions that the program would execute */
work_functions() {
        /* pthread calls, pthread initializations and memory allocation calls */
}

main () {
        /* Initialise System */
        pthread_start();

        /* pthread calls, pthread initializations and memory allocation calls */

        /* end call for the system */
        pthread_end();
}
```

Figure 4. The current programming model for programs written for CableS

3. Results

In this section we present three types of results: (i) We provide microbenchmarks to measure the overhead of basic system operations. (ii) We demonstrate that legacy *pthreads* programs written for traditional hardware shared memory multiprocessors, such as SMPs, can run with minor modifications on *CableS*. We use a public domain OpenMP compiler, OdinMP [8], which is written for SMPs and hardware cache–coherent DSMs, to translate existing OpenMP programs to *pthreads* programs and run them directly on *CableS*. (iii) We study the impact of *CableS* on parallel programs that have been optimized for DSM systems by implementing the M4 macros on top of *pthreads* and running most of the SPLASH-2 applications.

3.1. Experimental Platform

The specific system we use is a 32–processor cluster consisting of sixteen, 2-way PentiumPro SMP nodes interconnected with a Myrinet network. Each SMP is running WindowsNT. The nodes in the system are connected with a low–latency, high–bandwidth Myrinet SAN [7]. The software infrastructure in the system includes a custom communication layer and a highly optimized SVM system. The communication layer we use on top of Myrinet is a user-level communication layer, Virtual Memory Mapped Communication (VMMC) [2, 10]. VMMC provides both explicit, direct remote memory operations (reads and writes) and notification–based send primitives. The SVM protocol used is GeNIMA [20], which is a home-based, page-level SVM protocol. The consistency model in the protocol is Release Consistency [13]. GeNIMA provides an API based on the M4 macros, which are extensively used for writing shared memory applications in the scientific computing community.

Table 3 shows the cost of basic VMMC operations on our cluster. Noticeable, VMMC provides a one way, end–to–end latency of around 7.8 s, which is to our knowledge, among the best performing systems using a Myrinet interconnect.

VMMC Operation	Overhead
1-word send (one-way lat)	7.8 s
1-word fetch (round-trip lat)	22 s
4 KByte send (one-way lat)	52 s
4 KByte fetch (round-trip lat)	81 s
Maximum ping-pong bandwidth	125 MBytes/s
Maximum fetch bandwidth	125 MBytes/s
Notification	18 s

Table 3. Basic VMMC costs. All send and fetch operations are assumed to be synchronous. These costs do not include contention in any part of the system.

3.2. Microbenchmarks

Table 4 shows the results from our microbenchmarking. We obtain these numbers on 2 and 4 node systems. For these tests there is no contention in system resources and there is no shared memory protocol activity (no application shared data is used). We run experiments multiple times and average costs over all executions.

Node attaching is the most expensive system operation since a new node needs to perform all initialization with other nodes in the system. This time will increase as more nodes are introduced since more import/export links need to be established. Some elements of node attaching are done in parallel, and the breakdowns will not exactly add up to the total. Additionally, the communication time includes the time for importing nodes, which potentially includes waiting time since a buffer can not be imported until the other node has exported it. The pthread_create() times show the cost of a remote create and the potential for pooling threads on nodes to save time.

Unlike the remote mutex cost, the local mutex cost refers to the case where the mutex was last locked/unlocked by a thread within the node and there is no communication involved. The first time cost refers to the case where the mutex is acquired for the first time. At that time the acquirer needs to perform additional bookkeeping.

Condition wait and signal involves mostly local processing and ACB direct read/write operations to update and retrieve condition information. These overheads are relatively low and depend only on direct remote operation costs, so they are not expected to vary much with the number of nodes. On the other hand, the current implementation of condition broadcast depends on the number of nodes waiting on the condition and involves processing for each node in the system and communication (one remote write) for each node waiting on the condition.

We also include execution values for two types of barriers. GeNIMA barriers are implemented in the original SVM system as native operations. The *pthreads* barrier is implemented using *pthreads* primitives: a mutex, a condition variable, and a shared variable. Since each synchronization variable is handled by a single node, this node becomes a centralization point. The difference in performance is due to the point–to–point nature of synchronization used in the *pthreads* version.

Segment migration involves determining if a segment has an owner and taking ownership of the page on the first touch. These two actions can be taken by any node, but the segment state is maintained on one node, so there is remote and local migration based on the need for this state information. Segment migration costs slightly more in the remote case since information needs to be read and written from and to the ACB owner node. Owner detection is the

CableS Mechanism	Total	Local CableS	Remote CableS	Local OS	Communication
attach node	3690 ms	1 ms	1978 ms	523 ms	1188 ms
local thread create	766 s	140 s	-	626 s	-
remote thread create	819 s	110 s	40 s	-	47 s
local mutex lock (first time)	33 s	10 s	-	-	23 s
local mutex lock	4 s	4 s	-	-	-
remote mutex lock (first time)	122 s	15 s	35 s	-	72 s
remote mutex lock	101 s	16 s	35 s	-	50 s
mutex unlock	6 s	6 s	-	-	-
conditional wait	30 s	5 s	-	-	15 s
conditional signal	100 s	14 s	-	2 s	85 s
conditional broadcast	110 s	7 s	-	2 s	101 s
GeNIMA barrier	70 s	-	-	-	65 s
pthreads barrier	13 ms	-	-	-	-
segment migration on ACB owner (first time)	159 s	92 s	-	67 s	-
segment owner detect on ACB owner	1 s	1 s	-	-	-
segment migration (first time)	252 s	95 s	-	65 s	92 s
segment owner detect (first time)	23 s	1 s	-	-	22 s
segment owner detect	1 s	1 s	-	-	-
administration request	20 s	2 s	-	-	18 s

Table 4. CableS execution times for the basic events. For node attach the remote OS time is 2031 ms and for remote create the remote OS time is 622 s.

page fault processing cost for a segment that does not need to migrate, but the page information needs to be examined. This processing is usually small but depends on whether the segment information is locally cached.

3.3. Supporting Legacy Pthreads Applications

To demonstrate the versatility of *CableS* we use OdinMP to compile three SPLASH-2 applications that have been written for OpenMP: FFT, LU, and OCEAN. OdinMP is written for translating OpenMP programs for SMP and hardware cache–coherent DSM systems. We also use three publicly available *pthreads* programs: (i) Prime numbers (PN), which computes all prime numbers in a user specified range. (ii) Producer–consumer (PC), a producer–consumer program which runs with two threads. (iii) Pipe (PIPE), which creates a threaded pipeline where each element stage consists of a calculation. Table 5 shows the *pthreads* programs which were run on *CableS* and the *pthreads* calls each of the programs makes, along with the average execution time of each function. We use this table to show the average cost of *CableS* operations during program execution (including any induced contention). PC only uses two threads and, therefore, runs on only one node. Performance-wise, PC shows the approximate cost of local API operations. PN, PIPE, and the OpenMP programs provide an indication of the average execution time of remote operations in *CableS*. We see that remote operations are about three orders of magnitude slower than local operations. With respect to synchronization operations, conditional waits and mutex lock operations include the cost of communication and the application wait time. Conditional signals and broadcasts are much faster than waits and mutexes since they involve sending only small messages to activate threads in remote nodes. Table 6 shows the speedups of the three OpenMP SPLASH-2 applications. These applications are written for SMP-type shared memory architectures and are not optimized for DSM (especially software) systems so the speedups are not indicative of the actual performance that can be obtained on DSM systems. The next section examines this aspect.

PROGRAM	4 procs.	8 procs.	16 procs.
FFT	1.61	2.05	2.44
LU	3.17	3.71	7.10
OCEAN	1.33	1.43	1.92

Table 6. Speedups for the three SPLASH-2 OpenMP programs on 4, 8, and 16 processors.

3.4. SPLASH-2 Applications

To investigate the overhead that *CableS* introduces in applications that have been tuned for the shared memory abstraction we provide an implementation of the M4 macros on *CableS* and run a subset of the SPLASH-2 applications

PROGRAM	C	J	L	Co	Ca	K	G	Cr	Lo	Un	Wa	Si	Br	Sp
PN								2254	23	2	6154	-	1	15677
PC								1.1	0.05	0.005	17	0.042	-	-
PIPE								1008	52	3	527	12	-	11249
OMP_FFT								1235	54	0.52	1382	0.146	1.1	12302
OMP_LU								1247	133	1	327	0.134	0.401	12412
OMP_OCEAN								1312	49	2	494	0.293	0.606	14222

Table 5. Shows pthread programs with their respective pthread function calls and execution times (in ms) for the basic API operations. Legend: C = pthread_create, J = pthread_join, L = mutexes, Co = conditions, Ca = thread cancel, K = thread specific information, G = program uses static global variables Cr = create, Lo = mutex locks, Un = mutex unlock, Wa = condition wait, Si = condition signal, Br = condition broadcast, Sp = spawn.

on two configurations: The original, optimized SVM system that we started from [20] and *CableS*. In *CableS* we use the *pthreads_barrier* call we introduced, as opposed to a mutex-based implementation of barriers. This choice is made for fairness reasons. Specific knowledge provided by the SPLASH-2 applications about global synchronization and exploited in the original SVM system should be exploited in *CableS* as well. Since *pthreads* was not designed for parallel applications that frequently use global synchronization we provide this new call for the purpose of this comparison.

The applications we use are: FFT, LU, OCEAN, RADIX, WATER-SPATIAL, WATER-SPAT-FL, RAYTRACE, and VOLREND. These applications have been used in a number of recent studies. We use the versions from [20]. Their characteristics and behavior have been studied in [31, 21]. FFT, LU, OCEAN share a common characteristic in that they are optimized to be single-writer applications; a given word of data is written only by the processor to which it is assigned. Given appropriate data structures they are single-writer at page granularity as well, and pages can be allocated among nodes such that writes to shared data are almost all local. The applications have different inherent and induced communication patterns [31], which affect their performance and the impact on SMP nodes. Water [31] and Radix [5, 16], exhibit more challenging data access patters for shared memory systems. These access patterns may result in false sharing depending on the level of sharing granularity. The problem sizes we use are: FFT-m22, LU-n4096, OCEAN-n514, RADIX-(n16777216, m33554432), WATER-32768 molecules, VOLREND-head, and RAYTRACE-car.512.env Figure 5 shows the execution times of each application in both system configurations for 1, 4, 8, 16, and 32 processors. We see that for five out of the eight applications, FFT, LU, RAYTRACE, WATER-SPATIAL, and WATER-SPAT-FL, the overhead of *CableS* is within 25% of the original system in the 32–processor configuration.

The other three applications, OCEAN, RADIX, and

VOLREND exhibit different behavior under the two systems. The large difference in OCEAN is due to a protocol optimization in the the original system which is not currently present in *CableS*. From the execution traces, the original system could not execute OCEAN with 32 processors, because of memory registration limits. However, *CableS*, with its memory extensions, was able to run OCEAN on 32 processors. RADIX and VOLREND are more interesting: Since *CableS* relies on remapping of virtual memory segments to dynamically allocate homes, home allocation is restricted due to WindowsNT limitations to a granularity of 64 KByte segments as opposed to the 4 KByte page size. In these applications, unlike the first set of applications, the large mapping granularity results in improper page placement for many pages and in high protocol and communication costs. Figure 6 shows the percent-

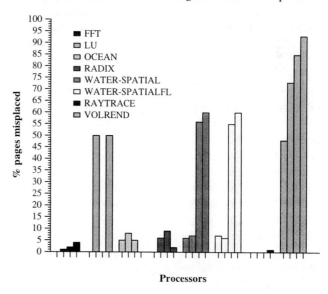

Figure 6. SPLASH-2 applications with their percentage of page misplacements for 4,8,16, and 32 processors

age of pages misplaced in *CableS* compared to the page–placement in the original system. FFT, OCEAN, RADIX, and RAYTRACE exhibit less than 10% of misplaced pages

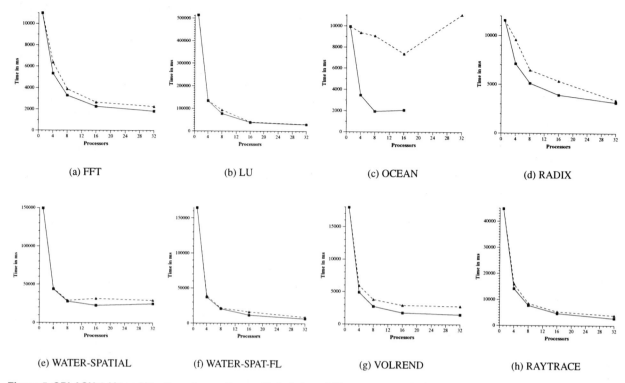

| (a) FFT | (b) LU | (c) OCEAN | (d) RADIX |

| (e) WATER-SPATIAL | (f) WATER-SPAT-FL | (g) VOLREND | (h) RAYTRACE |

Figure 5. SPLASH-2 M4 vs M4-pthread executions with 1, 4, 8, and 16 processors. Solid line is the M4 executions, and dashed line is M4-pthread executions

with small performance impact. We define a misplaced page as a page that *CableS* places on a different home node when compared against *GeNIMA*. For instance, in FFT misplaced pages cause approximately 2000 additional page faults per node. LU, WATER-SPATIAL, WATER-SPAT-FL, and VOLREND exhibit a large number of misplaced pages. This is not a problem in the two versions of WATER and LU due to the large computation to communication ratio (LU) and the infrequent synchronization (LU and WATER). LU exhibits a high percentage of misplaced pages at 8 and 32 processors. However, the application suffers only 200 additional read page faults which adds 50ms–100ms to the execution time. Thus the performance of the parallel section is almost identical between the two configurations. The execution time breakdowns are practically identical and are omitted for space reasons. Similarly, WATER-SPAT-FL is not affected by the misplaced pages. In VOLREND the misplaced pages result in high performance degradation. For example, with 32 processors the application shows a speedup of 12.09 on the original system, as opposed to only 6.49 on *CableS*.

Overall, we see that *CableS* introduces additional overhead in applications tuned for the shared memory abstraction only when it results in improper data placement due to the 64KByte–granularity mapping restrictions in WindowsNT.

4. Related Work

The *pthreads* standard is defined in [1]. *CableS* targets the implementation of a *pthreads* API on clusters of workstations. DSM-Threads [26] provides the same API on hardware cache–coherent DSM systems and discusses several implementation issues. *CableS*, instead, deals thoroughly with issues on modern SANs that support direct remote memory access. The authors in [12] examine how SVM protocols can be extended to reduce paging in cases where nodes have relatively small physical memories. Our focus is on dealing with limitations of SANs that support direct remote memory access and with providing dynamic thread and memory management. The Authors in [30] discuss home page migration issues in Cashmere. They examine protocol level extensions for migrating protocol pages among nodes. In our work, we investigate how SVM systems can be extended to support dynamic memory management. Shasta [27] is an instrumentation–based software shared memory system that was able to support challenging applications using the executable instrumentation mechanism. However, instrumentation–based, fine–grain software shared memory has its own limitations (e.g. depends on processor architecture) and the related issues and solutions can be very different from page–based shared virtual memory systems. There has also been some work on trying to eliminated registration limits at the NIC level. The authors in [9] address some of the limitations in the amount of memory that can be registered and pinned on modern SANs. However, they deal only with the send path and they do not address the related issues on the receive side. The authors in [4] try to reduce the overhead of dynamically managing registered memory on the NIC to avoid hardware and OS limits both on the send and receive sides. However, the issue of how the application working set size affects the required NIC resources and system performance is still not well understood.

Most other related work in the area has focused on the following four directions: (i) To improve the performance of SVM on clusters with SANs. There is a large body of work in this category [29, 23, 20, 32]. Our work relies on the experiences gained in this area and builds upon it to extending the functionality provided by today's clusters. (ii) To provide OpenMP implementations for clusters. Relatively little work has been done in this area. The authors in [24] provide an OpenMP implementation based on TreadMarks. They convert OpenMP directly into Tread-Mark system calls. In [28] the authors present a TreadMarks based system that deals with node attaching and detaching. They use the garbage collection mechanism of TreadMarks to move data among nodes, However, the communication layer used does not support direct remote memory operations, and this results in different mechanisms and tradeoffs. Our work attempts to synchronize all resources, including memory, with low level resource migration. (iii) To provide a *pthreads* interface on hardware shared memory multiprocessors, either shared–bus or distributed shared memory. Most hardware shared memory system and OS vendors provide a *pthreads* interface to applications [25]. In many systems, this is the preferred API for multithreaded applications due to the portability advantages. (iv) Finally, to provide a single system image on top of clusters. Projects in this area focus on providing a distributed OS that can manage all aspects of a cluster in multitasking environments and not as a platform for scalable computation. The authors in [3] provide a Java Virtual Machine on top of clusters. This work focuses on Java applications and uses the extra layer of the JVM to provide a single cluster image. Our work is at a lower layer. For instance, a JVM written for the *pthreads* API, such as Kaffe [18] could be ported to our system.

5. Conclusions

In this work we design and implement a system that provides a single system image for SVM clusters with modern SANs. Our system supports the *pthreads* API and within this API, provides dynamic thread and memory management as well as all synchronization primitives. Our memory management system deals with limitations of modern SANs that support direct remote memory operations. We show that this system is able to support *pthreads* applications written for more tightly–coupled, hardware shared memory multiprocessors. We use a wide suite of programs to demonstrate the viability of our approach to make clusters easier to use in new areas of applications, especially in areas that exhibit dynamic behavior. We also perform a preliminary evaluation of basic system costs.

Our results show that existing applications can run on top of *CableS* with few or no modifications and applications tuned for performance on shared memory systems incur additional overhead only when the 64-KByte granularity of mapping physical to virtual memory in WindowsNT results in improper data placement. The rest of the overhead introduced by *CableS* is limited to the initialization and termination sections of these applications.

CableS is a first step towards enabling a wider range of new applications to run unmodified on clusters. To facilitate further work with publicly–available, server–type applications we are porting *CableS* to Linux. We are also considering supporting a complete single system image on top of clusters that includes file system and networking support to allow a wider range of applications that have been developed for SMPs to run on clusters. In this direction, we are planning to examine commercial workloads, such as the Apache WWW server, and the Kaffe JVM that are usually run on small–scale SMPs.

6. Acknowledgments

We would like to thank the reviewers of this paper for their valuable comments and insights. Also, we thankfully acknowledge the support of Natural Sciences and Engineering Research Council of Canada, Canada Foundation for Innovation, Ontario Innovation Trust, the Nortel Institute of Technology, Communications and Information Technology Ontario, and Nortel Networks.

References

[1] International standard iso/iec 9945-1: 1996 (e) ieee std 1003.1, 1996 edition (incorporating ansi/ieee stds 1003.1-1990, 1003.1b-1993, 1003.1c-1995, and 1003.1i-1995) information technology – portable operating system interface (posix) – part 1: System application program interface (api) [c language].

[2] J. S. A.Bilas, C Liao. Using network interface support to avoid asynchronous protocol processing in shared virtual memory systems. In *Proceedings of the The 26th International Symposium on Computer Architecture*, Atlanta, Georgia, May 1999.

[3] Y. Aridor, M. Factor, A. Teperman, T. Eilam, and A. Schuster. A high performance cluster jvm presenting a pure single system image. In *ACM Java Grande 2000 Conference*, 2000.

[4] A. Basu, M. Welsh, and T. von Eicken. Incorporating memory management into user-level network interfaces. http://www2.cs.cornell.edu/U-Net/papers/unetmm.pdf, 1996.

[5] G. E. Blelloch, C. E. Leiserson, B. M. Maggs, C. G. Plaxton, S. J. Smith, and M. Zagha. A comparison of sorting algorithms for the connection machine CM-2. In *Proceedings of the 8th Annual ACM Symposium on Parallel Algorithms and Architectures*, pages 3–16, July 1991.

[6] M. Blumrich, K. Li, R. Alpert, C. Dubnicki, E. Felten, and J. Sandberg. A virtual memory mapped network interface for the shrimp multicomputer. In *Proceedings of the 21st International Symposium on Computer Architecture (ISCA)*, pages 142–153, Apr. 1994.

[7] N. J. Boden, D. Cohen, R. E. Felderman, A. E. Kulawik, C. L. Seitz, J. N. Seizovic, and W. Su. Myrinet: A gigabit-per-second local area network. *IEEE Micro*, 15(1):29–36, Feb. 1995.

[8] C. Brunschen and M. Brorsson. Odinmp/ccp - a portable implementation of openmp for c. *The 1st European Workshop on OpenMP*, 1999.

[9] Y. Chen, A. Bilas, S. N. Damianakis, C. Dubnicki, and K. Li. UTLB: A mechanism for address translation on network interfaces. In *Proceedings of the Eighth International Conference Architectural Support for Programming Languages and Operating Systems ASPLOS*, pages 193–203, San Jose, CA, Oct. 1998.

[10] C. Dubnicki, A. Bilas, Y. Chen, S. Damianakis, and K. Li. VMMC-2: efficient support for reliable, connection-oriented communication. In *Proceedings of Hot Interconnects*, Aug. 1997.

[11] D. Dunning and G. Regnier. The Virtual Interface Architecture. In *Proceedings of Hot Interconnects V Symposium*, Stanford, Aug. 1997.

[12] S. Dwarkadas, N. Hardavellas, L. Kontothanassis, R. Nikhil, and R. Stets. Cashmere-VLM: Remote memory paging for software distributed shared memory. In *Proc. of the Second Merged Symp. IPPS/SPDP 1999)*, 1999.

[13] K. Gharachorloo, D. Lenoski, and et al. Memory consistency and event ordering in scalable shared-memory multiprocessors. In *In 17th International Symposium on Computer Architecture*, pages 15–26, May 1990.

[14] Giganet. Giganet cLAN family of products. http://www.emulex.com/products.html, 2001.

[15] R. Gillett, M. Collins, and D. Pimm. Overview of network memory channel for PCI. In *Proceedings of the IEEE Spring COMPCON '96*, Feb. 1996.

[16] C. Holt, J. P. Singh, and J. Hennessy. Architectural and application bottlenecks in scalable DSM multiprocessors. In *Proceedings of the 23rd Annual International Symposium on Computer Architecture*, May 1996.

[17] L. Iftode, C. Dubnicki, E. W. Felten, and K. Li. Improving release-consistent shared virtual memory using automatic update. In *The 2nd IEEE Symposium on High-Performance Computer Architecture*, Feb. 1996.

[18] T. T. Inc. Wherever you want to run java, kaffe is there.

[19] A. Itzkovitz and A. Schuster. Multiview and millipage - fine-grain sharing in page-based DSMs. In *Operating Systems Design and Implementation*, pages 215–228, 1999.

[20] D. Jiang, B. O'kelley, X. Yu, A. Bilas, and J. P. Singh. Application scaling under shared virtual memory on a cluster of smps. In *The 13th ACM International Conference on Supercomputing (ICS'99)*, June 1999.

[21] D. Jiang, H. Shan, and J. P. Singh. Application restructuring and performance portability across shared virtual memory and hardware-coherent multiprocessors. In *Proceedings of the 6th ACM Symposium on Principles and Practice of Parallel Programming*, June 1997.

[22] A. Karlin, K. Li, M. Manasse, and S. Owicki. Empirical studies of competitive spinning for a shared-memory multiprocessor. In *Proceedings of the Thirteenth Symposium on Operating Systems Principles*, pages 41–55, Oct. 1991.

[23] P. Keleher, A. Cox, S. Dwarkadas, and W. Zwaenepoel. Treadmarks: Distributed shared memory on standard workstations and operating systems. In *Proceedings of the Winter USENIX Conference*, pages 115–132, Jan. 1994.

[24] H. Lu, Y. C. Hu, and W. Zwaenepoel. Openmp on networks of workstations. In *Proceedings Supercomputing*, 1998.

[25] F. Mueller. A library implementation of posix threads under unix. In *Proceedings of the USENIX Conference*, pages 29–41, Jan. 1993.

[26] F. Mueller. Distributed shared-memory threads: Dsm threads. *Workshop on Run-Time systems for Parallel Programming*, pages 31–40, April 1997.

[27] D. Scales and K. Gharachorloo. Towards transparent and efficient software distributed shared memory. In *Proceedings of the Sixteenth Symposium on Operating Systems Principles*, Oct. 1997.

[28] A. Scherer, H. Lu, T. Gross, and W. Zwaenepoel. Transparent adaptive parallelism on nows using openmp. In *Principles Practice of Parallel Programming*, pages 96–106, 1999.

[29] R. Stets, S. Dwarkadas, N. Hardavellas, G. Hunt, L. Kontothanassis, S. Parthasarathy, and M. Scott. Cashmere-2L: Software Coherent Shared Memory on a Clustered Remote-Write Network. In *Proc. of the 16th ACM Symp. on Operating Systems Principles (SOSP-16)*, Oct. 1997.

[30] R. Stets, S. Dwarkadas, L. Kontothanassis, , U. Rencuzogullari, and M. L. Scott. The effect of network total order, broadcast, and remote-write capability on network-based shared memory computing. In *The 6th IEEE Symposium on High-Performance Computer Architecture*, January 2000.

[31] S. Woo, M. Ohara, E. Torrie, J. P. Singh, and A. Gupta. Methodological considerations and characterization of the SPLASH-2 parallel application suite. In *Proceedings of the 23rd International Symposium on Computer Architecture (ISCA)*, May 1995.

[32] Y. Zhou, L. Iftode, and K. Li. Performance evaluation of two home-based lazy release consistency protocols for shared virtual memory systems. In *Proceedings of the Operating Systems Design and Implementation Symposium*, Oct. 1996.

User-Level Communication in Cluster-Based Servers *

Enrique V. Carrera, Srinath Rao, Liviu Iftode, and Ricardo Bianchini
Department of Computer Science
Rutgers University
Piscataway, NJ 08854-8019

{vinicio,rao,iftode,ricardob}@cs.rutgers.edu

Abstract

Clusters of commodity computers are currently being used to provide the scalability required by several popular Internet services. In this paper we evaluate an efficient cluster-based WWW server, as a function of the characteristics of the intra-cluster communication architecture. More specifically, we evaluate the impact of processor overhead, network bandwidth, remote memory writes, and zero-copy data transfers on the performance of our server. Our experimental results with an 8-node cluster and four real WWW traces show that network bandwidth affects the performance of our server by only 6%. In contrast, user-level communication can improve performance by as much as 29%. Low processor overhead, remote memory writes, and zero-copy all make small contributions towards this overall gain. To be able to extrapolate from our experimental results, we use an analytical model to assess the performance of our server under different workload characteristics, different numbers of cluster nodes, and higher performance systems. Our modeling results show that higher gains (of up to 55%) can be accrued for workloads with large working sets and next-generation servers running on large clusters.

1 Introduction

The number of Internet users has increased rapidly over the last few years. This large user base is placing significant stress on the computing resources of popular services available on the Internet. Clusters of commodity computers are currently being used to provide the scalability required by several of these services.

Several researchers and companies have concerned themselves with the cluster-based servers, e.g. [29, 31, 30, 24, 2, 3, 37, 11, 5, 12]. There are two main classes of servers in terms of how the clients' requests are distributed across the cluster: content-oblivious and content-aware servers. In a content-oblivious server the request distribution is based solely on a load metric, which is usually the number of open connections being handled by each node. Early servers were mostly of this type. However, content-aware servers are becoming ever more popular, as they can perform a more sophisticated request distribution. More specifically, in a content-aware server, request distribution decisions are affected by the actual content requested, so the cluster node that initially accepts a request (establishing a TCP connection with the client) and determines the content be-

ing requested may not be the node that should actually service the request. In that case, the request has to be forwarded to the most appropriate node, generating intra-cluster communication.

Content-aware distribution can be exploited to improve cache locality, as originally proposed in [24]. The idea is to aggregate the set of memories of the cluster into a large cache and distribute requests for files based on cache locality, as well as load balancing considerations. For their focus on cache locality, we refer to these servers as locality-conscious servers. We previously proposed and evaluated a portable locality-conscious WWW server, called PRESS, that relies heavily on efficient intra-cluster communication for good performance [12]. In fact, PRESS uses the Virtual Interface Architecture (VIA) [13] industry standard for user-level communication. User-level communication reduces the cost (or *processor overhead*) of message transfers by eliminating kernel traps and unnecessary data copying from the critical communication path. An interesting aspect of the standard is that it specifies remote memory accesses, i.e. operations that can read/write data from/to the correct memory addresses without intervention by the remote processor.

The evaluation in [12] showed that PRESS pays a small performance penalty for its portability, but did not consider the impact of the properties of the intra-cluster communication on the performance of our server. In particular, we did not consider the gains achievable by remote memory writes and zero-copy transfers. Furthermore, the effect of high overhead protocols and low bandwidth networks was only evaluated analytically for idealized workloads. Finally, the experimental evaluation was performed under favorable intra-cluster communication conditions, as the server nodes communicated over a gigabit-per-second network (Giganet) that implements VIA in hardware/firmware.

This paper extends our previous work by investigating the effect of the performance and features of the intra-cluster communication on the performance of PRESS. To set the study in context, we assessed the percentage of time each CPU running our server spends on intra-cluster communication, as opposed to external communication with clients and actually servicing requests. To determine this percentage we ran our server on an 8-node cluster using TCP and a Fast Ethernet switch for communication. Figure 1 presents the result of experiments with four WWW traces. The figure shows that more than 50% of the time is spent with intra-cluster communication for all traces, so there is great potential for user-level communication to improve performance. (The details about the infrastructure behind these experiments are presented later.)

*This research has been supported by NSF under grant # CCR-9986046.

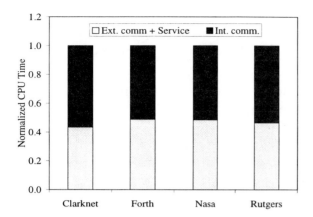

Figure 1: Time spent by PRESS (TCP/FE).

Thus, our three main goals are: (1) to assess the usefulness of remote memory writes and zero-copy in terms of performance; (2) to determine experimentally the intra-cluster communication parameters that have the greatest performance impact; and (3) to extrapolate our experimental results to investigate areas of the parameter space where user-level communication can be more useful. We accomplish these goals by evaluating versions of PRESS that utilize different protocol/network combinations and that exploit remote memory writes and zero-copy transfers to different extents. To be able to extrapolate from our experimental results, we use an analytical model of the performance of our server for varying communication characteristics, workload characteristics, and numbers of cluster nodes.

Our experimental results with an 8-node cluster and four real WWW traces show that network bandwidth affects the performance of PRESS by only 6%. In contrast, user-level communication can improve performance by as much as 29%. Low processor overhead, remote memory writes, and zero-copy all make small contributions towards this overall gain. (Network latency has no effect on throughput, so we did not consider it.) Our modeling results show that throughput gains of up to 49% can be accrued by user-level communication for large workload working sets and large numbers of nodes. These results also show that gains can reach 55% with next-generation servers, large working sets, and large numbers of nodes.

We believe that our findings have implications beyond our server. Communication in PRESS and other portable content-aware servers is so intensive that it is unlikely that other servers could accrue more significant improvements from user-level communication. Furthermore, even though we focus on servers with a content-aware request distribution and PRESS in particular, our observations should directly extend to other types (such as ftp, email, proxy, or file) and implementations of cluster-based servers, as long as files or file blocks are effectively transferred among the cluster nodes. A few examples of other servers in this class are the Swala WWW server [21], the Porcupine email server [30], and servers based on either the Federated File System [19] or Cooperative Caching Middleware [14].

The remainder of this paper is organized as follows. The next section section discusses user-level communication, VIA, PRESS, and the related work. Section 3 presents the methodology used in our experiments and discusses the performance results of our WWW server. Section 4 presents our model and its results. Finally, section 5 summarizes our findings and concludes the paper.

2 Background

2.1 User-Level Communication and VIA

The goal of user-level communication is to reduce the software overhead involved in sending and receiving messages, by removing the operating system from the critical communication path in a protected fashion. This goal is achieved by giving processes direct access to their network interfaces; the operating system in only involved in setting up the communication. In this way, the communicating parties can avoid intermediate copies of data, interrupts, and context switches in the critical path. The result of these optimizations is communication latency and bandwidth that approach the hardware limits.

There has been extensive research in user-level communication, e.g. [35, 17, 27, 34, 7, 6, 36, 1, 16]. This research led to the proposal of the VIA [15, 13] industry standard by a group of leading computer companies. In VIA, each communicating process can open directly accessible interfaces to the network hardware. Each interface, called *Virtual Interface* (VI), represents a communication end-point analogous to the socket end-point in a traditional TCP connection. In this way, pairs of VIs can be connected to create communication channels for bidirectional point-to-point data transfers. Each VI has a send and a receive queue. Processes post requests to these queues to send or receive data. The requests have the form of descriptors. Each descriptor contains all the information that the network interface controller needs to process the corresponding request, including pointers to data buffers. The network interface controller asynchronously processes the posted descriptors and marks them when completed. The processes then remove completed descriptors from the queues and reuse them for subsequent requests. In order to facilitate the removal of completed descriptors, VIA also specifies *Completion Queues* (CQs). A CQ can combine the notification of descriptor completions of multiple VIs into a single queue.

VIA provides two styles of communication. Besides the traditional send/receive data transfer model, it allows for direct access to the memory of remote machines. A remote memory access reads/writes data from/to the correct remote addresses without intervention by the remote processor. Regardless of the style of communication, the memory used for every data transfer in VIA needs to be "registered". The registration locks the appropriate pages in physical memory, allowing for direct DMA operations in the user memory buffers without the possibility of an intervening page replacement.

Finally, the VIA standard specifies three levels of reliability: unreliable delivery, reliable delivery, and reliable reception. In unreliable delivery, both regular and remote memory messages can be lost without being detected or retransmitted. In reliable delivery, all data submitted to transfer are guaranteed to arrive at the destination network interface exactly once and in order, in the absence of errors. If an error occurs, it is reported. Reliable reception is just like reliable delivery, except that a transfer is only successfully completed when the data have been delivered to the target memory location.

VIA has several successful implementations, e.g. Myrinet-VI [10], Giganet VIA [18], M-VIA [8], ServerNet VIA [32], FirmVIA [4]. Our experiments are made with Giganet VIA. This implementation supports VIA in hardware using its proprietary cLAN network interfaces connected through 2.5 Gbits/s full-duplex links. Giganet VIA does not support remote memory reads (only remote writes are supported) and reliable reception.

2.2 PRESS

Overview. PRESS is our portable cluster-based, locality-conscious WWW server [12]. Although WWW servers must service requests for both static and dynamic contents, in this paper we focus solely on PRESS as a server of static content (read-only files), since this type of content puts the most stress on the intra-cluster network.

Just like other locality-conscious servers [24, 3, 11, 5], PRESS is based on the observation that serving a request from any memory cache, even a remote cache, is substantially more efficient than serving it from disk, even a local disk. Essentially, the server distributes HTTP requests across the cluster nodes based on cache locality and load balancing considerations, so that the requested content is unlikely to be read from disk if there is a cached copy somewhere in the cluster.

PRESS assumes that HTTP requests are directed to the cluster using a standard method, such as Round-Robin DNS or a content-oblivious, load balancing front-end device. Thus, any node of the cluster can receive a client request and becomes the *initial node* for that request. When the request arrives at the initial node, the request is parsed and, based on its content, the node must decide whether to service the request itself or forward the request to another node. A request for a large file ($\geq$ 512 KBytes in our prototype) is always serviced locally by the initial node. In addition, the initial node is chosen as the service node, if this is the first time the file is requested or it already cached the requested file. If neither of these conditions holds, the least loaded node that is caching the requested content becomes a candidate for *service node*. This node is chosen as the service node either when it is not overloaded (i.e. its number of open connections is not larger than a user-defined threshold, $T = 80$ in our experiments) or when it is overloaded but so are the initial node and the least loaded node in the cluster. In this way, popular files end up replicated at multiple nodes for better load balancing.

A forwarded request is handled in a straightforward way by the service node. If the requested file is cached, the service node simply transfers it to the initial node. If the file is not cached, the service node reads the file from its local disk, caches it locally, and finally transfers it to the initial node. Upon receiving the file from the service node, the initial node sends it to the client. The initial node does not cache the file received from the service node to avoid excessive file replication across the cluster.

In order to be able to intelligently distribute the HTTP requests it receives, each node needs locality and load information about all the other nodes. Locality information takes the form of the names of the files that are brought into the caches, whereas load information is represented by the number of open connections handled by the nodes.

The dissemination of caching information is straightforward. Whenever a node either replaces or starts caching a file, it broadcasts that fact to the other nodes. Broadcasts of caching information are very infrequent in steady-state.

The dissemination of load information can be done in one of two ways: broadcasting and piggy-backing. When broadcasting, each node broadcasts its current load when the load is a certain number of connections (the load threshold) greater or smaller than the last broadcast value. When piggy-backing, the current load is appended to any message sent among the nodes. In this way, each message updates the load information of its sender on the receiver. Most of the experiments in this paper were performed with piggy-backing.

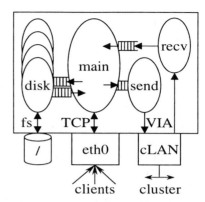

Figure 2: Basic PRESS architecture.

Communication architecture. PRESS is an event-driven server that was originally written to use VIA. Figure 2 shows a diagram with the basic architecture of our server. For highest performance, the main thread should not block. Thus, we use helper threads for disk access and communication. Disk threads are used to access files on disk to avoid stalling the main server thread, as suggested in [25].

In order to communicate inside the cluster, each cluster node sets up VI end-points with each other node. Two threads per node are responsible for sending and receiving messages; we refer to these threads as the send thread and the receive thread, respectively. These threads remain blocked until there is a message to be sent or received. The main server thread unblocks the send thread using a semaphore, after a *digest* of the message to be sent has been queued at a data structure that is shared by these two threads. When the send thread wakes up, it simply creates a message descriptor and places it at the corresponding send queue. The receive thread is unblocked by the arrival of a regular (as opposed to a remote memory write) message at one of the receive queues. When the receive thread wakes up, it simply determines which VI received the message and places a digest of the message at a data structure shared with the main thread. The main thread periodically polls this data structure. Remote memory writes have no effect on the receive thread. In fact, the receive thread is not even required, if all the communication is effected with remote memory writes.

Intra-cluster communication in PRESS occurs for five types of messages:

- Exchange of load information – very short messages carrying numbers of open connections;
- Exchange of caching information – short messages carrying file names;
- Request forwarding – short messages carrying file names;
- File transfer – long messages carrying file data; and
- Window-based flow control – very short messages carrying numbers of empty buffer slots.

As we explain above, load information exchanges may not require explicit messages because the local load values can be piggy-backed in other messages. In section 3 we analyze different load dissemination strategies and experiment with several possible implementations for each of these message types. The implementations differ in terms of the extent to which they use remote memory writes and copying.

Implementations that use remote memory writes can improve performance by not involving the receiver in the transfer. However, remote memory writes can also require more messages if copies are to be avoided. Furthermore, remote memory writes can involve significant polling overhead, especially for cluster configurations with a large number of nodes, when messages cannot be overwritten and must be handled quickly.

As an example of this tradeoff, a request forwarding message has to be handled quickly to reduce latency, so the main thread has to poll several queues (one queue for each node) fairly frequently to determine whether another node needs to receive a file. The regular message implementation of this message type reduces the amount of polling to the main thread polling of the single data structure it shares with the receive thread. However, this latter implementation requires data copying from the message descriptor to the shared data structure, so that the descriptor can be re-utilized by another message as quickly as possible, reducing flow control stalls.

In contrast, no overhead is associated with remote memory writes for messages implementing flow control or carrying load information. These messages do not require immediate attention and can be overwritten, which makes their implementation with remote memory writes much more efficient than with regular messages.

Besides the VIA implementation of PRESS, we also have a prototype of our server that uses TCP. The TCP version basically has the same structure of its VIA counterpart; the main differences are the replacement of the VI end-points by TCP sockets and the elimination of flow control messages, which is implemented transparently to the server by TCP itself.

Performance. PRESS compares favorably against other servers in terms of performance. Its single-node throughput is equivalent to that of the Flash server [25], as these two servers are based on similar optimizations. Flash has been shown superior to Apache in [25]. In [12], we experimentally show that the multi-node throughput of the original version of PRESS on 8 nodes is within 7% of that of scalable LARD [3], a highly efficient but non-portable locality-conscious server. Using analytical modeling, we showed that portability should cost no more than 15% in terms of performance, even for large (96-node) clusters.

2.3 Related Work

The main contribution of this paper is to quantify the performance impact of user-level communication and several messaging characteristics on cluster-based servers. Previous studies of user-level communication were performed either for microbenchmarks [6, 35, 27, 36, 15, 10, 8, 32] or in the context of scientific applications [28, 23, 33]. This paper extends those studies to real, non-scientific applications, in particular to the now very popular cluster-based servers.

As far as we are aware, in only one other paper [22] has the performance of a server been evaluated as a function of network parameters. The study considered a single-processor NFS server and the effect of the parameters of the network that connects the server to its clients. In contrast, our work concentrates on the impact of network parameters and characteristics on the inter-node communication of cluster-based servers.

The only previous communication sensitivity studies of cluster-based servers were done by ourselves in [5, 12]. However, our previ-

Logs	Num files	Avg file size	Num requests	Avg req size
Clarknet	28864	14.2 KB	2978121	9.7 KB
Forth	11931	19.3 KB	400335	8.8 KB
Nasa	9129	27.6 KB	3147684	21.8 KB
Rutgers	18370	27.3 KB	498646	19.0 KB

Table 1: Main characteristics of the WWW server traces.

ous evaluations did not consider the ability to perform remote memory writes and to avoid data copies. Moreover, the effect of protocol overhead and network bandwidth was not assessed experimentally. PRESS and the analytical model we use in this paper were introduced in [12]. The server and model used here are modified versions of those in that paper. PRESS has been modified to use piggybacking, to communicate with TCP as well as VIA, and to exploit remote memory writes and zero-copy to various degrees. The model has been modified to consider remote memory writes and zero-copy.

Previous studies of VIA have been performed in the context of parallel and/or distributed applications [8, 32, 28]. Thus, this paper extends the small body of work on this industry standard, while evaluating several of its main features (low overhead, remote memory write, copy avoidance) for cluster-based servers. In contrast with this paper, other studies of remote memory write have concentrated on microbenchmarks (e.g. [17, 1]) and do not consider the impact of different messaging characteristics on the usefulness of this primitive.

3 Experimentation

3.1 Methodology

Cluster hardware and workloads. Our cluster is comprised by 8 Linux-based PCs with 300 MHz Pentium II processors, 512 KBytes of second-level cache, 512 MBytes of memory, a SCSI disk, and interfaces to switched Fast Ethernet and Giganet (cLAN) networks.

Besides our main cluster, we use another 10 Pentium-based machines to generate load for the servers. These clients communicate with the server using TCP over a Fast Ethernet switch. For simplicity, we did not experiment with a content-oblivious front-end device; we used the equivalent strategy of having clients send requests to the nodes of the server in randomized fashion with equal probabilities. The clients reproduce four WWW server traces. All these traces have been used in previous studies. Clarknet is a trace from a commercial Internet provider, Forth is from the FORTH Institute in Greece, Nasa is from NASA's Kennedy Space Center, and Rutgers contains the accesses made to the main server for the Computer Science Department at Rutgers University in the first 25 days of March 2000.

We eliminated all incomplete (due to network failures or client commands) requests in the traces and ended up with the characteristics listed in table 1. The traces cover a relatively wide spectrum of behavior. The number of files ranges from about 9100 to 28900 with an average file size between roughly 14 and 28 KBytes. The average size of the files serviced ranges from about 9 to 22 KBytes.

Metrics. We focus solely on the throughput (and messaging behavior, of course) of the different versions of our server, since server latencies are almost always low compared to the overall latency a

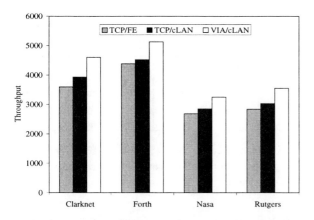

Figure 3: Throughput for protocol/network combinations.

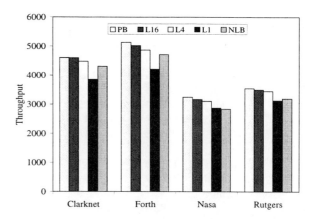

Figure 4: Throughput for different dissemination strategies.

client experiences establishing connections, issuing requests, and waiting for replies across a wide-area network. In order to determine the maximum throughput of each version of the server, we disregarded the timing information in the traces and made clients issue new requests as soon as possible. Before starting our measurements, we warm the node caches executing our traces for 5 minutes.

3.2 Effect of Overhead and Bandwidth

In this section we present the performance results of PRESS running on our cluster with three protocol/network combinations. For all these combinations the communication with the clients is through TCP over the Fast Ethernet network. The combinations are:

- TCP/FE. Intra-cluster communication uses TCP through additional Fast Ethernet interfaces. Under this protocol/network combination, sending a 4-byte message takes 82 microseconds, whereas the observed bandwidth achieved for 32-KByte messages is 11.5 MBytes/s.

- TCP/cLAN. The server still uses TCP for all the intra-cluster communication, but the cLAN is used for this communication. This implementation runs the complete TCP stack, just like TCP/FE; it does not take advantage of the reliability and message ordering properties of the cLAN. Under this combination, sending a 4-byte message takes 76 microseconds and the observed bandwidth is 32 MBytes/s with 32-KByte messages.

- VIA/cLAN. The server uses VIA over cLAN for all the intra-cluster communication. Under this combination, sending a 4-byte message takes 9 microseconds. The network peaks at 102 MBytes/s bandwidth for 32-KByte messages.

Figure 3 plots the throughput of PRESS for our four traces under the three different protocol/network combinations. By comparing TCP/FE and TCP/cLAN we can isolate the effect of network bandwidth on performance, since cLAN bandwidth is a factor of 3 higher than that of Fast Ethernet and overheads are virtually the same. This comparison shows that increased network bandwidth provides relatively small performance benefits, even for the traces that involve large requested files (Rutgers and Nasa). The average difference in performance between TCP/FE and TCP/cLAN over all traces is 6%.

The comparison between TCP/cLAN and VIA/cLAN isolates the effect of processor overhead on performance, since the VIA overhead

is a factor of 8 lower than that of TCP and network bandwidth is not a serious performance factor as we just saw. This comparison shows that the gains that can be accrued by exploiting a protocol with lower processor overhead are more significant, ranging from 14% for Forth to 17% for Rutgers.

3.3 Effect of Strategies for Load Information Dissemination

The results presented in the previous section correspond to the version of PRESS that piggy-backs load information in the messages exchanged among the nodes. As the load at a node can change frequently, this piggy-backing strategy may leave other nodes with an inconsistent view of the amount of load at the node. Such an inconsistent view may cause PRESS to make poor load balancing decisions.

Based on this observation, in this subsection we evaluate the cost of utilizing a more aggressive strategy for distributing load information in the VIA/cLAN implementation. More specifically, we consider a strategy that directs a node to broadcast its current load when the load value is a certain number of connections (load threshold) greater or smaller than the last broadcast value. In effect, we study the tradeoff between the level of consistency of the load information and the overhead of the extra messages. Given that we rely on user-level communication over a high-bandwidth network for these experiments, this tradeoff may be favorable to exchanging more messages. As we see next, this is *not* the case.

Figure 4 presents the throughput of PRESS for five different load information dissemination strategies. The rightmost bar for each trace represents the base line case: no load balancing at all (labeled "NLB"). The next three bars from right to left represent load thresholds of 1 ("L1"), 4 ("L4"), and 16 ("L16") connections. The leftmost bar represents the throughput of the default, piggy-backing implementation ("PB"). The number of messages, bytes, and the average size of messages involved in each of these implementations is presented in table 2.

We can make several observations from this figure. The first observation is that avoiding load information broadcasts is always the best approach, even under such favorable communication conditions. In fact, broadcasting with a load threshold of 1 connection can perform worse than not doing load balancing within the cluster at all,

Version	Msg type	Num msgs (K)	Num bytes (MB)	Avg msg size
NLB	Load	0.0	0.0	0.0
	Flow	1203.6	15.3	13.0
	Forward	2075.5	107.1	52.9
	Caching	39.0	2.2	58.9
	File	2699.8	19479.4	7388.4
	TOTAL	6017.8	19604.0	–
L1	Load	29902.2	458.8	15.7
	Flow	8279.0	105.1	13.0
	Forward	1605.9	82.9	52.9
	Caching	52.5	3.0	58.8
	File	2092.4	15052.3	7366.4
	TOTAL	41932.0	15702.2	–
L4	Load	6176.6	96.4	16.0
	Flow	2636.2	33.5	13.0
	Forward	1879.1	97.0	52.9
	Caching	48.6	2.8	58.8
	File	2445.1	17687.3	7407.4
	TOTAL	13185.6	17917.0	–
L16	Load	342.2	5.3	16.0
	Flow	1155.6	14.7	13.0
	Forward	1839.2	94.9	52.9
	Caching	51.5	3.0	58.8
	File	2389.4	17194.8	7369.1
	TOTAL	5777.8	17312.8	–
PB	Load	0.0	0.0	0.0
	Flow	1152.4	19.1	17.0
	Forward	1984.6	110.2	56.8
	Caching	48.1	3.0	62.8
	File	2576.8	18580.5	7383.7
	TOTAL	5761.9	18712.7	–

Table 2: Intra-cluster communication and dissemination strategies.

especially for the traces that exhibit higher throughput (i.e. faster load variations). Increasing the threshold reduces the number of messages tremendously (as shown in table 2) and increases overall performance. However, the best implementation is indeed the one that uses piggy-backing; it combines the minimum number of messages with good enough load balancing.

As one would expect, using remote memory writes for the load broadcasts improves the performance of L1 significantly, improves the performance of L4 slightly, and does not affect L16. Even when using remote memory writes for load broadcasts, the piggy-backing version is at least as efficient as any other version of PRESS.

3.4 Effect of Remote Writes and Zero-Copy

To evaluate the usefulness of remote memory writes and zero-copy transfers, we developed 5 other versions of PRESS, numbered from 1 to 5. The version we studied so far, labeled "VIA/cLAN" in figure 3 and "PB" in figure 4, is called version 0. The versions differ in the extent to which remote writes and zero-copy are utilized. In all versions, load information is piggy-backed in other messages and intra-cluster communication uses VIA over cLAN. A summary with the description of each version of PRESS appears in table 3.

Message				Versions		
	V0	V1	V2	V3	V4	V5
Flow	reg	rmw	rmw	rmw	rmw	rmw
Forward	reg	reg	rmw	rmw	rmw	rmw
Caching	reg	reg	rmw	rmw	rmw	rmw
File	reg	reg	reg	rmw	rmw + 0-cp RX	rmw + 0-cp TX and RX

Table 3: Communication characteristics of PRESS versions. Keys: reg = regular, rmw = remote memory writes, 0-cp = zero-copy, TX = send, RX = receive.

Version 0 only utilizes regular messages, i.e. a receiver is interrupted to handle an arriving message and data copies are made at the sender and at the receiver for all message types. Note that most of the data copies in version 0 are of no serious performance consequence (very little data are involved in each case), except for the copies made at the sender and receiver of a file transfer message. The copy at the receiver side is unavoidable when using regular messages, since files can be bigger than message descriptors and the corresponding descriptor must be freed as quickly as possible for use by another message. The copy at the sender side could be avoided, provided that we could either: make all cache pages unswappable and available to VIA, or manage a smaller cache of unswappable and available pages with low overhead.

Version 1 improves on version 0 by using remote memory writes for flow control messages. In this type of messages only a word of data is transferred per message. The messages do not require immediate attention and can be overwritten.

Version 2 improves on version 1 by using remote memory writes for forward and caching information messages, as well as flow-control messages. Forward and caching messages are very similar in that a file name is transferred in each message, the messages can not be overwritten, and polling fairly frequently for these messages can improve performance. At each node, two circular buffers are allocated for forward and caching messages for each other node. As each node knows the location of its private buffers at every other node, it keeps track of exactly where the next file name should be written in the memories of remote nodes. Polling is done by looking at message sequence numbers stored at the last position of each (fixed-size) buffer entry. A receiver determines that the next message has not yet been completely received if its sequence number is not equal to the last sequence number plus 1. Processors poll for these messages at the end of the main server loop.

Version 3 improves on version 2 by adding remote memory writes for file transfers. The data structures for these transfers are a small circular buffer that is similar to the forward and caching buffers just described and a large circular buffer for the actual file data. These two buffers are allocated by each node for each other node. Again, because each node knows the location of its private buffers at every other node, it keeps track of exactly where to write the memories of remote nodes. The sender of a file then writes the file data to the large buffer and the file information to the small buffer. The file information includes a pointer to the beginning of the file in the large buffer. Again, polling by the receiver is done on the sequence numbers at the end of the server loop. When the receiver detects the arrival of a file, it copies it to another buffer and sends it back to the requesting client.

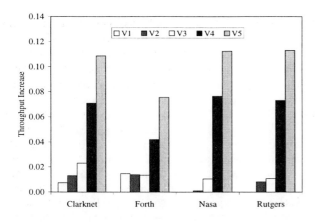

Figure 5: Throughput for the RMW and zero-copy versions.

This version does not require a receive thread, as all communication is performed with remote memory writes.

Version 4 improves on version 3 by having the receiver of file data send the data to the client right out of the large communication buffer. By doing this, version 4 eliminates the expensive data copy made at the receiver of a file transfer message.

Finally, version 5 improves on version 4 by eliminating the data copy at the transmitter of a file transfer message. For that, all the pages corresponding to cached files are registered in VIA.

Figure 5 depicts the throughput increase of the different versions of PRESS for each trace on our 8-node cluster server. The throughput increases are determined with respect to version 0. Table 4 lists the number of messages and bytes that each version transfers. Results for version 0 are labeled "PB" in table 2.

The figure shows that versions 1 and 2 produce minimal improvements in comparison to version 0. This is explained by the relatively small number of messages of these types. Version 3 does not significantly improve performance either, even though interrupts for message reception and the receive thread itself have been eliminated. The reason for this surprising result is that using remote memory writes requires two messages per file (one with the file data and one with metadata), rather than a single message. The effect of this increase can be observed by comparing the number of file messages and the total number of messages in versions 2 and 3 in table 4.

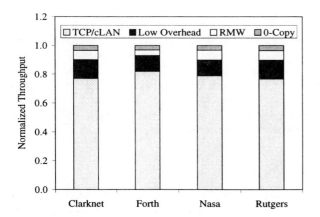

Figure 6: Summary of contributions.

Version	Msg type	Num msgs (K)	Num bytes (MB)	Avg msg size
V1	Flow	1161.6	4.5	4.0
	Forward	2001.5	111.1	56.8
	Caching	51.0	3.1	62.8
	File	2594.0	18610.7	7346.6
	TOTAL	5808.2	18729.4	–
V2	Flow	1856.7	7.3	4.0
	Forward	1980.1	102.2	52.8
	Caching	51.6	2.8	54.8
	File	2567.4	18452.2	7359.7
	TOTAL	6455.8	18564.5	–
V3	Flow	4194.2	65.5	16.0
	Forward	2026.2	120.4	60.8
	Caching	51.1	3.1	62.8
	File	4644.4	18818.3	4149.1
	TOTAL	10915.9	19007.3	–
V4	Flow	4603.4	70.5	15.7
	Forward	2122.3	126.1	60.9
	Caching	47.2	2.9	62.8
	File	4870.2	19827.9	4169.0
	TOTAL	11643.1	20027.5	–
V5	Flow	5176.5	75.2	14.9
	Forward	2230.7	132.5	60.8
	Caching	47.4	2.9	62.8
	File	5117.7	20754.5	4152.7
	TOTAL	12572.4	20965.1	–

Table 4: Intra-cluster communication, RMW, and zero-copy.

In contrast, versions 4 and 5 do exhibit non-trivial performance benefits. The benefits from version 4 range from 4% for Forth to 8% for Nasa, averaging 6.6%. Version 5 outperforms all other versions, reaching improvements that range from 8% for Forth to 11% for Rutgers. The gains achieved by these two versions stem from avoiding large data copies. *Note however that remote memory writes have commonly been studied in the literature in scenarios where they obviate the need for data copies at receivers (e.g. [28]), so we credit the gains achieved by version 4 to remote memory writes and the gains of version 5 to zero-copy transfers.*

Overall, by comparing version 5 against the TCP/cLAN implementation, we find that user-level communication improves throughput by as much as 29%, averaging 26%. No specific property of this type of communication is responsible for the vast majority of the gains. Low processor overhead is responsible for about 15%, remote memory writes for file transfers are responsible for about 7%, and zero-copy file transfers are responsible for about 4%. A summary of these results is presented in figure 6. The throughput gains provided by low overhead, remote memory writes, and zero-copy transfers are stacked above the base TCP/cLAN throughput.

4   Modeling

In this section we analytically extrapolate our experimental results to a broader range of parameters. Our goal is to determine the benefits that can be achieved by low processor overhead, remote memory

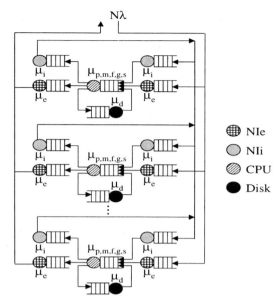

Nλ

⊕ NIe
◯ NIi
▨ CPU
● Disk

Figure 7: Model of a locality-conscious server.

writes, and zero-copy transfers under a variety of current and future scenarios. We now turn to a description of the model.

4.1 The Model

Figure 7 depicts our open queueing model of a portable locality-conscious server such as PRESS running on a cluster of N PCs with an intra-cluster or "internal" network and an "external" network that connects the cluster to the outside world. The model mimics our own cluster.

The model assumes that all queues are M/M/1. In the model, requests for files arrive at a rate $N \times \lambda$. Assuming that the traffic to the nodes is perfectly balanced, the probability that a request is assigned to a specific workstation is the same for all the workstations $(1/N)$. Thus, each external network interface receives requests with a rate λ and processes them at a rate μ_e. The initial processing of requests (reading and parsing) is done by the CPU at a rate μ_p. If the requested file is cached locally the node just replies to the request at a rate μ_m. If the file is cached only remotely, the request is forwarded by the CPU at a rate μ_f. Each internal interface processes forwarded requests and replies at a rate μ_i.

After a request is received by the service node, the server tests whether the requested file is cached and, if so, the file is sent back by the CPU to the initial node through the internal cluster network with a rate μ_s. Otherwise, the node must first read the file from disk, store it in its memory, and then transfer the file across the cluster (again with a rate μ_s). Each disk receives read requests with a rate $(1 - H) \times \lambda$ (where H is the probability that a requested file is cached in main memory) and processes them at a rate μ_d. The CPU of the initial node receives the reply of a forwarded request at a rate μ_g. Finally, when the requested file is ready to be sent out, it is sent at a rate μ_e.

Other important parameters to our model are the cache size per node (C), the average size of the requested files (S), and the file request distribution. This latter parameter deserves further comments. In this study, we concentrate on heavy-tailed distributions of access,

such as the ones exhibited by WWW servers [9]. Such distributions can be approximated by means of Zipf-like distributions [9], where the probability of a request for the i'th most popular file is proportional to $1/i^\alpha$ with α typically taking on some value less than unity.

With these parameters, we define the total cache space and the average cache hit rate for a locality-conscious server. The cache space is $C_{lc} = N \times C$ bytes if no file replication is allowed, or $C_{lc} = N \times (1 - R) \times C + R \times C$ bytes, if an R percentage of the main memory is used for file replication. The average cache hit rate can be defined as: $H = z(n, F)$, where $z(n, F)$ represents the accumulated probability of requesting the n most accessed files in a Zipf-like distribution of the requests to F files. The number of cached files (n) is equal to $\min(C_{lc} \div S, F)$. Furthermore, the percentage of requests forwarded to another workstation can be defined as: $Q = (N - 1) \times (1 - h) \div N$, where the hit rate for replicated files (h) is equal to $z(\min(R \times C \div S, F), F)$. Note that our use of $z(n, F)$ to describe hit rates effectively means that the most accessed files are always cached in the model.

To simplify the presentation, we define the locality-conscious hit rate (H_{lc}) as a function of a single-node server's hit rate (H_{sn}) as follows: $H_{lc} = z(\min(C_{lc} \div S, f), f)$, where f is such that $H_{sn} = z(C \div S, f)$. In the same way, we define the percentage of requests forwarded to another node as: $Q = (N - 1) \times (1 - h) \div N$, where $h = z(R \times C \div S, f)$.

Note that all the above definitions assume that the probability of an unreplicated file to be cached by a specific workstation is the same for all the workstations $(1/N)$. The first two columns of table 5 summarize the model parameters and their descriptions.

As our model assumes a cost-free distribution algorithm, cost-free caching information dissemination and message flow control, perfect load balancing, and does not consider cache replacements and contention for network wires and memory and I/O buses, it provides an *upper bound on the throughput* achievable by these servers.

Parameter Values. We carefully selected default values for our model parameters. The value of R was chosen to maximize the performance of the servers. To concentrate solely on processor overhead, remote memory writes, and zero-copy, we assume peak bandwidths for the internal and external networks. The service rate of the external network interface, μ_e, was selected assuming that the interface provides 100 Mbits/s full-duplex links with 4-microsecond overhead at the network interface per message. These parameters approximate the characteristics of our Fast Ethernet network interface cards. The service rate of the internal network interface, μ_i, was selected assuming that the interface provides 1 Gbit/s full-duplex links with 3-microsecond overhead at the network interface per message. These parameters approximate the characteristics of our Giganet interface cards. The fixed cost in the μ_m, μ_s, and μ_g rates are based on measurements we took by running a single request at a time through our own real server on two cluster nodes. The μ_d and μ_p rates are based on these same measurements.

4.2 Results

To collect predictions from the model, we instantiate its parameters and solve its traffic equations using standard linear algebra techniques. To validate the model, we compared the throughputs of version 5 and TCP/cLAN on 8 nodes against the corresponding model

Param	Description	Definition or Default Value
R	Percentage of replication	15%
α	Zipf constant	0.8
μ_i	NIi transfer rate	$(0.000003 + size/125000)^{-1}$ ops/s
μ_e	NIe transfer rate	$(0.000004 + size/125000)^{-1}$ ops/s
μ_p	Request read/parsing rate by CPU	5882 ops/s
μ_m	Client reply send rate (after stored locally) by CPU	$(0.00027 + S/12500)^{-1}$ ops/s
μ_d	Disk access rate	$(0.0188 + S/3000)^{-1}$ ops/s
μ_f	Intra-cluster request forwarding rate by CPU	31250 ops/s – VIA 3676 ops/s – TCP/cLAN
μ_s	Intra-cluster reply send rate by CPU	$(0.00003 + S/125000)^{-1}$ ops/s – VIA $(0.00027 + S/125000)^{-1}$ ops/s – TCP/cLAN
μ_g	Intra-cluster reply reception rate by CPU	$(0.00003 + S/125000)^{-1}$ ops/s – VIA $(0.00027 + S/125000)^{-1}$ ops/s – TCP/cLAN
C	Total cache space	C = 128 MBytes $C_{lc} = N \times (1 - R) \times C + R \times C$
H	Cache hit rate	$H_{sn} = z(\min(C \div S, F), F)$ $H_{lc} = z(\min(C_{lc} \div S, F), F)$
h	Cache hit rate for replicated files	$h = z(\min(R \times C \div S, F), F)$
Q	Percentage of requests forwarded	$Q = (N - 1) \times (1 - h) \div N$

Table 5: Model parameters and their default values. S = avg file size in KBytes; $size$ = avg transfer size in KBytes. F = number of files.

predictions. These comparisons show that the version 5 performance is within 2% of the model results for traces with large average file sizes (Nasa and Rutgers). For traces with small average file sizes (Clarknet and Forth), version 5 is within 20% of the model results. The TCP/cLAN performance is within 15% and 25% of the model results for large and small average file sizes, respectively. These validation results demonstrate that the model provides a looser upper bound for traces with small average file sizes than with large average file sizes. On average, modeling and experimental results are within 14% of each other.

Effect of processor overhead. We start by studying the benefits achievable by lowering processor overheads for a wide range of workload working set sizes and numbers of cluster nodes. To simplify the analysis, we model variations in working set size using the cache hit rate of a single-node server; as the working set size increases, the cache hit rate decreases.

Figure 8 plots the throughput improvements that can be accrued by running a portable locality-conscious server with VIA-based intra-cluster communication in comparison to a similar server that uses TCP for the same purpose. The internal network bandwidth we assume, 128 MBytes/s, is the same for both systems, as listed in table 5. We also assume an average file size of 16 KBytes. The figure shows that for small numbers of nodes and very low hit rates, the throughput does not improve as a result of the lower processor overhead. The reason is that the disks are the performance bottleneck in this area of the parameter space. As the hit rate or the number of nodes is increased, the amount of data that can be cached also increases, and we start to see throughput improvements. For a fixed hit rate, increasing the number of nodes leads to significant throughput improvements at first, but quickly improvements level off. The reason for this effect is that intra-cluster communication increases by a factor of $1/(N \times (N - 1))$ for each node that is added to the system, where N is the size of the current configuration. For small N, increases in intra-cluster traffic are significant; for large N, they approach 0. Overall, improvements are most significant, 37%, for 128 nodes and 36% hit rate.

We now study throughput improvements due to lowering processor overheads as a function of average file sizes and numbers of nodes. Our real traces exhibit average file sizes of 8.8 to 21.8 KBytes and we expect average file sizes to continue growing. In figure 9, we investigate average file sizes of up to 128 KBytes, assuming a 90% single-node hit rate. The figure shows that improvements are most significant, 48%, for 4-KByte files and large numbers of nodes. As we increase the average file sizes, throughput improvements decrease significantly to about 4%. The reason for this result is that the overhead quickly becomes a small fraction of the overall cost of transferring messages.

These results suggest that lowering processor overheads can provide higher benefits than we found experimentally, but only for large working set sizes compared to the size of a single memory. Increases in average file sizes actually reduce the achievable improvements. Real life file sizes tend to continuously increase, which points to decreasing benefits. Depending on whether real life working sets grow faster than memory sizes, we may see greater benefits from low processor overhead, but they will likely not exceed 48%.

Effect of remote memory writes and zero-copy transfers. We now turn to studying the benefits achievable by exploiting remote memory writes and zero-copy transfers, again as a function of a range of single-node hit rates and numbers of nodes. Figure 10 plots the throughput improvements that can be accrued by exploiting these mechanisms in VIA with respect to a server that only uses regular, 1-copy VIA messages. The performance parameters are those listed in table 5. Again, we assume a 16-KByte file size. The figure shows the same overall trends as in figure 8. The main difference is that the maximum gain here is only 12%.

Figure 11 plots the improvements due to remote memory writes and zero-copy transfers, as a function of average file sizes and numbers of nodes. We again assume a 90% hit rate on a single node.

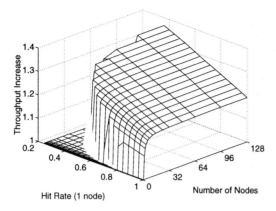

Figure 8: Gains achievable by lowering overheads, as a function of hit rate and number of nodes.

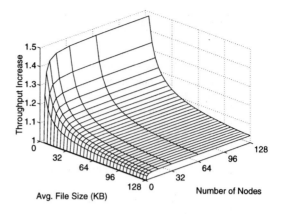

Figure 9: Gains achievable by lowering overheads, as a function of average file size and number of nodes.

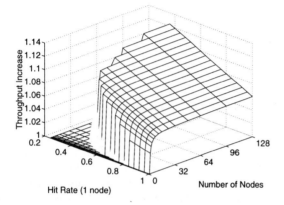

Figure 10: Gains achievable by using RMW and 0-copy, as a function of hit rate and number of nodes.

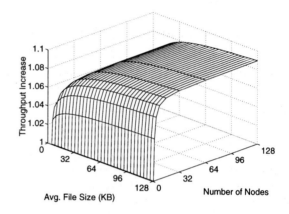

Figure 11: Gains achievable by using RMW and 0-copy, as a function of average file size and number of nodes.

For small file sizes, most of the benefit comes from avoiding interrupts with remote memory writes. As we increase the size of files, the throughput gains increase, now mostly as a result of zero-copy, and eventually reach 9%. It is somewhat surprising that the benefit of zero-copy does not grow almost linearly with the file size. This is because, as files become larger, the CPU spends longer to send them back to clients, continuously diminishing the fraction of time spent on intra-cluster communication. Varying the number of nodes has the same effect as we observed above.

These results suggest that exploiting remote memory writes and zero-copy transfers can provide slightly higher benefits than we found experimentally, but only for large working set sizes. Increases in average file sizes do not significantly increase the achievable improvements. Depending on whether real life working sets grow faster than memory sizes, we may see greater benefits from these mechanisms, but it is unlikely that they will exceed 12%.

Future systems. The above results show that in the best of circumstances user-level communication can increase throughputs by 49% (37% coming from low processor overhead as shown in figure 8 and 12% coming from remote memory writes and zero-copy transfers as shown in figure 10), assuming the characteristics of our cluster. It is important also to consider higher performance systems. In particular, we now consider the effect of faster processors and higher

performance TCP implementations.

Faster processors would not increase the throughput improvements we have found. The reason for this is simply that gains from user-level communication are most significant when the processor is the bottleneck. Thus, increasing the speed of the processor scales all the relevant parameters by the same factor, keeping throughput improvements the same. This effect has been recognized before in [20].

Higher performance TCP communication *can* have an impact on throughput improvements. In particular, higher performance communication can be achieved with a higher bandwidth network and a zero-copy TCP implementation along the lines of the IO-lite operating system [26]. The idea is to use the cached file data, which is constantly pinned to memory, as a large TCP buffer. File data can then be sent to clients or to other nodes without copying them out of the cache. We expect next-generation operating systems to include such zero-copy optimizations.

We modeled such a system by halving the μ_m parameter and halving the fixed cost of the TCP versions of the μ_f, μ_s, and μ_g parameters of table 5. The results are shown in figure 12, assuming 16-KByte files, and figure 13, assuming 90% hit rate. The figures show that, under the best of circumstances, the throughput improvement provided by user-level communication can reach 55%.

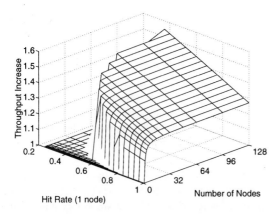

Figure 12: Gains achievable by user-level communication, as a function of hit rate and number of nodes.

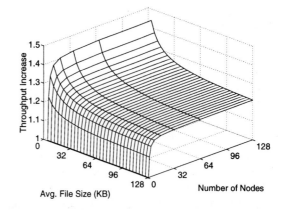

Figure 13: Gains achievable by user-level communication, as a function of average file size and number of nodes.

5 Conclusions

In this paper we have quantified the impact of user-level communication and network bandwidth on the performance of a content-aware server. Our results demonstrated that processor overhead, remote memory writes, and zero-copy can all provide performance gains, whereas network bandwidth is not as important.

Based on our results and experience, we conclude that low overhead, remote memory writes, and zero-copy transfers should continue to be provided and exploited in future user-level communication systems. In addition, we conclude that user-level communication can improve the performance of content-aware servers by as much as 49% for current operating systems and 55% for next-generation operating systems. Whether such high gains will ever be achieved depends on working sets growing faster than memories.

References

[1] S. Araki, A. Bilas, C. Dubnicki, J. Edler, K. Konishi, and J. Philbin. User-Space Communication: A Quantitative Study. In *Proceedings of Supercomputing '98*, November 1998.

[2] M. Aron, P. Druschel, and W. Zwaenepoel. Efficient Support for P-HTTP in Cluster-Based Web Servers. In *Proceedings of the USENIX 99 Annual Technical Conference*, Monterey, CA, June 1999.

[3] M. Aron, D. Sanders, P. Druschel, and W. Zwaenepoel. Scalable Content-Aware Request Distribution in Cluster-Based Network Servers. In *Proceedings of USENIX'2000 Technical Conference*, San Diego, CA, June 2000.

[4] M. Banikazemi, V. Moorthy, L. Herger, D. K. Panda, and B. Abali. Efficient Virtual Interface Architecture Support for the IBM SP Switch-Connected NT Clusters. In *Proceedings of the 14th International Parallel and Distributed Processing Symposium*, Cancun, Mexico, May 2000.

[5] R. Bianchini and E. V. Carrera. Analytical and Experimental Evaluation of Cluster-Based WWW Servers. *World Wide Web Journal*, 3(4):215–229, December 2000.

[6] M. Blumrich, K. Li, R. Alpert, C. Dubnicki, E. Felten, and J. Sandberg. Virtual Memory Mapped Network Interface for the SHRIMP Multicomputer. In *Proceedings of the 21st Annual International Symposium on Computer Architecture*, pages 142–153, Chicago, IL, April 1994.

[7] N. J. Boden, D. Cohen, R. E. Felderman, A. E. Kulawik, C. L. Seitz, J. N. Seizovic, and W.-K. Su. Myrinet: A Gigabit per Second Local Area Network. *IEEE Micro*, 15(1):29–36, February 1995.

[8] P. Bozeman and B. Saphir. A Modular High Performance Implementation of the Virtual Interface Architecture. In *Proceedings of the 2nd Extreme Linux Workshop*, Monterey, CA, June 1999.

[9] L. Breslau, P. Cao, L. Fan, G. Phillips, and S. Shenker. Web Caching and Zipf-like Distributions: Evidence and Implications. In *Proceedings of IEEE INFOCOM 99*, pages 126–134, New York, NY, March 1999.

[10] P. Buonadonna, A. Geweke, and D. Culler. An Implementation and Analysis of the Virtual Interface Architecture. In *Proceedings of Supercomputing '98*, Orlando, FL, November 1998.

[11] E. V. Carrera and R. Bianchini. Evaluating Cluster-Based Network Servers. In *Proceedings of the 9th IEEE International Symposium on High Performance Distributed Computing*, pages 63–70, Pittsburgh, PA, August 2000.

[12] E. V. Carrera and R. Bianchini. Efficiency vs. Portability in Cluster-Based Network Servers. In *Proceedings of the 8th Symposium on Principles and Practice of Parallel Programming*, Snowbird, UT, June 2001.

[13] Compaq Corp., Intel Corp., and Microsoft Corp. *Virtual Interface Architecture Specification, Version 1.0*, 1997.

[14] F. M. Cuenca-Acuna and T. D. Nguyen. Cooperative Caching Middleware for Cluster-Based Servers. In *Proceedings of the 10th International Symposium on High Performance Distributed Computing*, San Francisco, CA, August 2001.

[15] D. Dunning and G. Regnier and G. McAlpine and D. Cameron and B. Shubert and F. Berry and A. M. Merritt and E. Gronke and C. Dodd. The Virtual Interface Architecture. *IEEE Micro*, 18(2):66–76, March 1998.

[16] R. dos Santos, R. Bianchini, and C. L. Amorim. A Survey of Messaging Software Issues and Systems for Myrinet-Based

Clusters. *Parallel and Distributed Computing Practices, special issue on High-Performance Computing on Clusters*, June 1999.

[17] C. Dubnicki, L. Iftode, E. Felten, and K. Li. Software Support for Virtual Memory-Mapped Communication. In *Proceedings of the 10th International Parallel Processing Symposium*, April 1996.

[18] Giganet. *Giganet cLAN Cluster Switch*. http://www.giganet.com/.

[19] S Gopalakrishnan *et al.* The Federated File System. Technical report, Department of Computer Science, Rutgers University, 2000. In preparation.

[20] T. Heath, S. Kaur, R. Martin, and T. Nguyen. Quantifying the Impact of Architectural Scaling on Communication. In *Proceedings of the 7th IEEE Symposium on High-Performance Computer Architecture*, January 2001.

[21] V. Holmedahl, B. Smith, and T. Yang. Cooperative Caching of Dynamic Content on a Distributed Web Server. In *Proceedings of the 7th IEEE International Symposium on High Performance Distributed Computing*, pages 243–250, July 1998.

[22] R. Martin and D. Culler. NFS Sensitivity to High Performance Networks. In *Proceedings of the International Conference on Measurement and Modeling of Computer Systems*, April 1999.

[23] R. Martin, A. Vahdat, D. Culler, and T. Anderson. Effects of Communication Latency, Overhead, and Bandwidth in a Cluster Architecture. In *Proceedings of the 24th International Symposium on Computer Architecture*, June 1997.

[24] V. S. Pai, M. Aron, G. Banga, M. Svendsen, P. Druschel, W. Zwaenepoel, and E. Nahum. Locality-Aware Request Distribution in Cluster-based Network Servers. In *Proceedings of the 8th ACM Conference on Architectural Support for Programming Languages and Operating Systems*, pages 205–216, San Jose, CA, October 1998.

[25] V. S. Pai, P. Druschel, and W. Zwaenepoel. Flash: An Efficient and Portable Web Server. In *Proceedings of the USENIX 99 Annual Technical Conference*, June 1999.

[26] V. S. Pai, P. Druschel, and W. Zwaenepoel. IO-Lite: A Unified I/O Buffering and Caching System. *ACM Transactions on Computer Systems*, 18(1):37–66, 2000.

[27] S. Pakin, M. Karamcheti, and A. Chien. Fast Messages (FM): Efficient, Portable Communication for Workstation Clusters and Massively-Parallel Processors. *IEEE Parallel and Distributed Technology*, 5(2):60–73, April 1997.

[28] M. Rangarajan and L. Iftode. Software Distributed Shared Memory over Virtual Interface Architecture: Implementation and Performance. In *Proceedings of the 3rd Extreme Linux Workshop*, October 2000.

[29] Resonate. *Resonate Central Dispatch*. http://www.resonateinc.com/.

[30] Y. Saito, B. N. Bershad, and H. M. Levy. Manageability, Availability and Performance in Porcupine: A Highly Scalable, Cluster-Based Mail Service. In *Proceedings of 17th ACM Symposium on Operating Systems Principles*, December 1999.

[31] ServerIron. *ServerIron*. http://www.foundrynetworks.com/products/Webswitches.html.

[32] E. Speight, H. Abdel-Shafi, and J. K. Bennett. Realizing the Performance Potential of the Virtual Interface Architecture. In *Proceedings of the International Conference on Supercomputing*, pages 184–192, Rhodes, Greece, June 1999.

[33] R. Stets, S. Dwarkadas, L. Kontothanassis, U. Rencuzogullari, and M. Scott. The Effect of Network Total Order, Broadcast, and Remote-Write Capability on Network-Based Shared Memory Computing. In *Proceedings of the 6th International Symposium on High-Performance Computer Architecture*, January 2000.

[34] H. Tesuka, A. Hori, and Y. Ishikawa. PM: A High-Performance Communication Library for Multi-User Parallel Environments. Technical Report TR-96015, Real World Computing Parnership, November 1996.

[35] T. von Eicken, A. Basu, V. Buch, and W. Vogels. U-Net: A User-Level Network Interface for Parallel and Distributed Computing. In *Proceedings of the 15th ACM Symposium on Operating Systems Principles*, pages 40–53, Copper Mountain, Colorado, December 1995.

[36] K. G. Yocum, J. S. Chase, A. J. Gallatin, and A. R. Lebeck. Cut-Through Delivery in Trapeze: An Exercise in Low Latency Messaging. In *Proceedings of the IEEE Symposium on High-Performance Distributed Computing*, Portland, OR, August 1997.

[37] H. Zhu, B. Smith, and T. Yang. Scheduling Optimization for Resource-Intensive Web Requests on Server Clusters. In *Proceedings of the 11th Annual ACM Symposium on Parallel Algorithms and Architectures*, pages 13–22, June 1999.

Pipelining and Microarchitecture

Using Internal Redundant Representations and Limited Bypass to Support Pipelined Adders and Register Files

Mary D. Brown   Yale N. Patt

Electrical and Computer Engineering
The University of Texas at Austin
{mbrown,patt}@ece.utexas.edu

Abstract

This paper evaluates the use of redundant binary and pipelined 2's complement adders in out-of-order execution cores. Redundant binary adders reduce the ADD latency to less than half that of traditional 2's complement adders, allowing higher core clock frequencies and greater execution bandwidth (in instructions per second). Pipelined 2's complement adders allow a higher clock frequency, but do not reduce the ADD latency. Machines with redundant binary adders are compared to machines with 2's complement adders and the same execution bandwidth and bypass network complexity. Results show that on the SPECint95 benchmarks, the average IPC of an 8-wide machine with 1-cycle redundant binary adders is 9% higher than a machine using 2-cycle pipelined adders.

Pipelined functional units and multi-cycle register files may require multi-level bypass networks to guarantee that an instruction's result is available any cycle after it is produced. Multi-level bypass networks require large fan-in input muxes that increase cycle time. This paper shows that one level of bypass paths in a multi-level bypass network can be removed while still achieving within 3% to 1% of the IPC of a machine with a full bypass network.

1. Introduction

Future microprocessors require greater execution bandwidth for higher performance. The first step towards increasing the bandwidth is to reduce the ALU latency—along with the things that feed the ALUs, such as the scheduling logic and bypass networks—so that the execution core can be clocked at higher frequencies. Taking this first step increases execution bandwidth and reduces the latency for executing chains of dependent instructions. In the Intel Pentium 4, the core clock frequency was set by the ALU and bypass network latency [10]. Other parts of the chip, such as the fetch engine, could provide the required execution bandwidth at lower clock frequencies.

To further increase the execution bandwidth, it is necessary to pipeline the functional units or increase the number of functional units. The three execution core configurations shown in Figure 1 all provide an execution bandwidth of 2 instructions per cycle. Configuration A shows 2 ALUs, each with 1-cycle latency. Configuration B shows 2 ALUs, each pipelined over 2 cycles. Dependent instructions cannot execute in back-to-back cycles in this configuration. Configuration C also shows 2 ALUs pipelined over 2 cycles, but it allows intermediate results to be forwarded from the first stage of the ALU. This allows a dependent chain of instructions to execute in consecutive cycles.

In each configuration, the bypass mux for one input of one ALU is shown. The ALU inputs for Configurations A and B can receive data from the register file or the outputs of either ALU. The ALUs in Configuration C can receive the data from the register file or either stage of either ALU. The outputs of Stages 1 and 2 are used as inputs to Stage 1, but only the outputs of Stage 2 are written back to the register file. For one-cycle operations, forwarding from Stage 1 is necessary so that dependent operations can execute in consecutive cycles. For multi-cycle operations, the output from Stage 1 is an intermediate result. Because results are available from multiple stages but only written to the register file in Stage 2, a multi-level bypass network is used.

Programs with a large amount of exposed ILP can exploit high execution bandwidth. Programs with little exposed ILP benefit from low execution latency. Given a constant cycle time, all three configurations provide the same bandwidth. Configuration A is the best as it provides low latency. Configuration B has a long latency. Configuration C has long latency for final results, but also provides low-latency intermediate results.

Our results show that for machines with an execution bandwidth of 8 instructions per cycle, an ideal machine using 1-cycle adds will have an average IPC 8% higher than

289

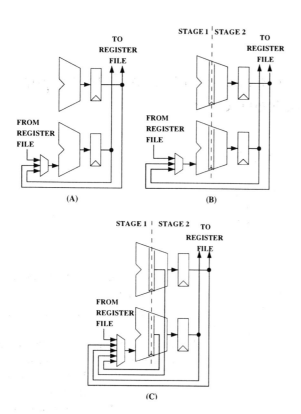

Figure 1. Three ALU configurations.

a machine with 2-cycle adds on the SPECint2000 benchmarks, and 11% higher on the SPECint95 benchmarks. A machine with redundant binary adders and the same bypass network complexity can be used to reach within 1% of the IPC of the ideal machine. Because the multi-level bypass networks for pipelined adders and register files may increase the cycle time, this paper also investigates limited bypass networks and the schedulers to support them. One level in a multi-level bypass network can be removed while still achieving within 3% to 1% of the IPC of a machine with a full bypass network.

Section 2 discusses some background and related work. Section 3 reviews redundant binary arithmetic and discusses which operations can be performed with redundant binary inputs. Section 4 discusses execution cores with redundant binary adders and limited bypass networks. Section 5 shows experimental results, and Section 6 concludes.

2. Background and Related Work

One technique for pipelining adders is to use pipelined digit-serial adders [6]. An example of this concept, called *staggered adds*, was implemented in the Intel Pentium 4 [10]. When staggering a 32-bit add over two cycles, the carry-out of the 16th bit and the lower half of the result are produced in the first cycle, and the upper half of the result is

produced in the second cycle. Back-to-back dependence execution is possible by forwarding the lower half of the result and its carry-out in the first stage, and then forwarding the second half of the result in the second stage. Conventional 2's complement carry-lookahead adders have a critical path that grows logarithmically with respect to the number of bits in the data. Using a 2-stage, staggered adder is unlikely to cut the effective add latency in half unless the latency is set by control signal propagation.

Redundant binary arithmetic can be used to further reduce the effective ALU latency. When integers are in a redundant binary representation, they can be added without a carry propagation through the entire length of the data operands. Hence redundant binary adders have a latency that is independent of the data size, and a much shorter critical path than 2's complement adders. Data can be forwarded between dependent ADDs in redundant binary representation. A redundant binary number must be converted back to 2's complement before it can be stored in memory or used by some types of instructions.

Redundant binary arithmetic has been a steady area of computer arithmetic research since the 1950's [3]. Although the ILLIAC III used a redundant binary adder-subtractor for fast multiplication and division [2], redundant binary arithmetic has mainly been used in adders that are internal to hardware multipliers and dividers [12]. The reason for its limited use is that results of redundant binary operations must be converted back to 2's complement using a conventional (slow) adder with a full carry-propagation. Hence redundant binary adders only show a performance improvement relative to 2's complement adders when these format conversions can be avoided or moved off the critical path of program execution. Conversions can be avoided when executing a chain of dependent redundant binary operations and forwarding the intermediate results in redundant binary representation [7].

Multi-cycle register files and pipelined functional units that produce intermediate results require extra levels of bypass buses for data to be available any cycle after it is computed [5, 17]. Larger, multi-level bypass networks will have longer forwarding delays. There are several techniques to reduce forwarding delays. One technique is to interleave the bit slices of several functional units within a cluster. The functional units, input multiplexors, and latches within a cluster are stacked and aligned such that for each bit slice, the data wires of all functional units are adjacent.

Another technique to reduce forwarding delays is to remove selected bypass paths altogether. Ahuja et. al. [1] demonstrated that certain bypass paths were rarely used. By removing these buses from an in-order pipeline and scheduling code to avoid pipeline stalls, performance was close to that of a pipeline with a complete bypass network. On the VIPER VLIW microprocessor [8], each functional unit had a bypass path to only itself and its closest functional unit in order to reduce the bypass network complexity. Nagarajan et. al. [13] use an array of ALUs with bypass paths only to nearby ALUs. Instructions are statically assigned to ALUs such that forwarding delays are reduced.

Cruz et. al. [5] examine removing the first level of a 2-level bypass network used with a 2-cycle register file. IPC was degraded because dependent instructions could no longer execute in back-to-back cycles. They point out that if the second (rather than the first) level of the bypass network were removed, there would be a 'hole' in data availability—that is, results are available the first cycle after they are produced, then are not available in the following cycle, and then are later available from the register file. This paper examines limited multi-level bypass networks that cause holes in data availability. Section 4.3 will explain how to schedule instructions around these holes.

3. Redundant Binary Arithmetic

This section presents an overview of the redundant binary number system that we utilize to make fast adders. Section 3.1 describes the redundant binary representation. Section 3.2 describes how to convert between redundant binary and 2's complement representation. Section 3.3 describes how addition works in the redundant binary number system and implementation of a redundant binary adder. Section 3.4 discusses the delays of redundant binary adders relative to carry-lookahead adders. Section 3.5 describes overflow in the redundant binary system and detection of 2's complement overflow. These sections are primarily a review of information presented in previous work [2, 3, 9, 11, 16]. Section 3.6 describes how other operations used in a modern instruction set, specifically the Alpha ISA, may be handled in a redundant binary system.

3.1. Overview

Most current ISAs use 2's complement representation for integers. Two's complement representation has several attractive properties: (1) addition and subtraction operations work the same way regardless of whether the numbers are positive or negative, (2) there are approximately the same number of positive and negative values represented with a given number of bits, and (3) N bits can be used to represent 2^N possible values—that is, each distinct pattern of 0s and 1s represents only one value, and each distinct value has only one representation.

Redundant number systems can have more than one representation for a given value, so they require more bits for representing the same range of integers as 2's complement representation. However, many redundant number systems do have an advantage over 2's complement, which is that

addition can be performed in constant time regardless of operand size. There are many redundant number representations; we will limit our discussion to one such representation called *signed digit* representation.

Signed-Digit number representations were first described by Avizienis [3]. Each digit of a number in signed-digit representation may be either positive or negative. In this paper, we will only discuss a specific signed-digit representation commonly called *redundant-binary* representation where each digit can take on any value from the set {-1, 0, 1}. Because there are three possible values of a digit, two bits are required to encode each digit.

In conventional unsigned binary format, the ith digit represents 2^i multiplied by 0 or 1. In redundant binary representation, the ith digit represents 2^i multiplied by -1, 0, or 1. An n-digit redundant binary number X $= x_{n-1}, x_{n-2}, ..., x_0$, where $x_i \in \{-1, 0, 1\}$ represents the value $\sum_{i=0}^{n-1} x_i 2^i$. For example, the 4-digit number $\langle 0, 1, 0, -1 \rangle$ represents $2^2 - 2^0 = 3$. Three could also be represented by $\langle 0, 0, 1, 1 \rangle$ in redundant binary.

3.2. Conversion To/From 2's Complement

A redundant binary number is converted back to 2's complement by means of a subtraction with carry propagation. Suppose the redundant binary number X is represented by two sets of bits, X^+ and X^-, representing the positive and negative powers of 2, respectively, that are added to compute the value. For example, if $X = \langle 0, 1, 0, -1 \rangle$, then $X^+ = \langle 0, 1, 0, 0 \rangle$ and $X^- = \langle 0, 0, 0, 1 \rangle$. The 2's complement representation of X can be computed by subtracting X^- from X^+ in the 2's complement number system.

The conversion from 2's complement to redundant binary is straightforward. All bits except the most significant bit of the 2's complement number are assigned to the positive component, X^+. The most significant bit of the 2's complement number is assigned to the most significant digit of X^- so that the number will retain the correct sign.

If the values 1, 0, and -1 are encoded as $\langle 0, 1 \rangle$, $\langle 0, 0 \rangle$, and $\langle 1, 0 \rangle$, respectively (i.e. one bit indicates the digit is negative, the other indicates it is positive), then converting from 2's complement to redundant binary requires no logic; the path can be hardwired. The conversion from redundant binary back to 2's complement requires a 2's complement subtraction circuit with full carry propagation.

3.3. Implementation

Redundant binary addition limits carry propagation to at most two digits. The computation of the ith digit of the sum is a function of digits i, $i-1$, and $i-2$ of both inputs.

Several possible logic diagrams for one digit-slice of a redundant binary adder were shown in previous works [12,

16]. One logic diagram is shown in Figure 2. The intermediate output h_i is a function of digit i. The output f_i is a function of digit i and h_{i-1}. The sum for digit i is a function of digit i, h_{i-1}, and f_{i-1}.

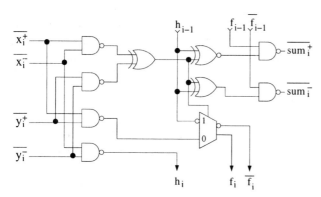

Figure 2. One Digit-Slice

3.4. Delays of Redundant Binary Adders

The critical path through one bit slice of a redundant binary adder, which is also the critical path through the whole adder, consists of seven transistors with fan-outs less than or equal to 4.

Several researchers have compared the delays of redundant binary adders to 2's complement carry-lookahead (CLA) and carry-select adders. Makino et. al. [12] fabricated a multiplier that used redundant binary adders. They simulated several redundant binary adders and CLAs using SPICE2 with a 0.5-μm CMOS process technology. They found that a redundant binary adder was 2.7 times faster than a redundant binary to 2's complement converter, and 3 times faster than a conventional 64-bit CLA.

Nagendra et. al. [15] compared the delays of 32-bit CLA and signed-digit adders optimized for performance. They found that their signed-digit adder, which used a radix-4 signed-digit representation, was 2.6 times as fast as the CLA. The same authors found a carry-save adder, which uses a redundant representation similar to the redundant binary representation described in this paper, to be twice as fast as their signed-digit adder [14].

3.5. Overflow

Integer overflow occurs when the result of a computation is too large to fit within a fixed number of bits. With 2's complement, this is easily detected by examining the signs of the sources and destination.

With a chain of redundant binary additions, carry-outs can quickly propagate towards the most significant digit of a number. For example, when the value 1 is repeatedly incremented in redundant binary using an adder built

from the circuit in Figure 2, the representations of the resulting values will be $\langle 0, 0, 0, 1\rangle$, $\langle 0, 0, 1, 0\rangle$, $\langle 0, 1, 0, -1\rangle$, $\langle 1, -1, 0, 0\rangle$, $\langle 1, -1, 1, -1\rangle$, and so on. Non-zero digits propagate left faster in redundant binary than in 2's complement. It is possible for there to be a carry-out of the most significant digit, while the value of the number may still be representable with fewer digits. When this scenario, called *bogus overflow*, occurs, either the carry-out is 1 and the most significant digit is -1, or vice-versa. This can be easily avoided by using one of several techniques [2]. One technique exploits the fact that the representations $\langle 1, -1\rangle$ and $\langle -1, 1\rangle$ can be converted to $\langle 0, 1\rangle$ and $\langle 0, -1\rangle$, respectively. When bogus overflow occurs, the sign of the most significant digit is complemented.

In addition to correcting for bogus overflow, 2's complement overflow must still be detected. Two's complement overflow will occur if any of the following events occur:

- The carry-out is still -1 or 1 *after* correcting for bogus overflow.

- The most significant digit is -1 and the rest of the result is negative. In order for the result to have the same value as if it were computed in 2's complement, the most significant digit should be set to 1.

- The most significant digit is 1 and the rest of the result is not negative. In order for the result to have the same value as if it were computed in 2's complement, the most significant digit should be set to -1.

3.6. Other Operations

Not all operations in modern instruction sets can be computed in the redundant binary system. This section discusses which integer instructions in the Alpha ISA can execute in redundant binary format.

Arithmetic Operations. Addition, subtraction, and multiplication using redundant number systems has been demonstrated in previous work [2]. The Alpha ISA also has three additional arithmetic instructions, CTLZ (count the leading zeros of an operand), CTTZ (count the trailing zeros of an operand), and CTPOP (count the number of set bits in an operand). CTLZ and CTPOP require the operand to be in a unique representation, which means they should be executed in 2's complement format. CTTZ may be executed in redundant binary by counting the trailing non-zero digits.

Byte Manipulation and Logical Operations. The byte manipulation instructions extract data from one or more bytes of their operands. If individual bytes are extracted from a redundant binary number, the result, when converted back to 2's complement, may be incorrect. Hence byte operations are performed in 2's complement. Bitwise logical operations (e.g. XOR) also require the inputs to be in 2's complement to produce the correct result. One exception is when the two source register operands of a logical operation are the same register. This is the standard way to implement the MOVE operation in the Alpha ISA.

Conditional Operations. Conditional moves and branches test for values greater than, equal to, or less than zero; or they check to see if the least significant bit of a value is set. Both number systems require an OR circuit to test for zero. Testing for positive or negative values in 2's complement is straightforward: the value is negative if the most significant bit is set. In redundant binary, the sign of a number is determined by the most significant digit with a value other than zero. If this digit is -1, the number is negative; otherwise it is positive. Testing the least significant bit of a number in redundant binary format requires a 2-input OR of the two bits comprising the least significant digit of the number. In summary, all conditional move and branch instructions may be executed in redundant binary format, although an additional circuit is needed to test for positive or negative values.

Shifts and Scaled Adds. The Scaled Add instruction of the Alpha ISA shifts one of the inputs to the left by two or three bits before adding it to an immediate value. Scaled Adds and Left shifts will work in the redundant binary system by shifting digits rather than bits. If the most significant bit of the result is 1, it should be changed to -1 because the number would be negative in 2's complement representation. For example, the number $\langle -1, 1, 0, 1 \rangle$ (-3 in decimal representation) would become $\langle -1, 0, 1, 0 \rangle$ (-6) when shifted left by one digit. A right shift may not produce the correct result in redundant binary. Right shifts are performed with 2's complement inputs.

Memory Access Instructions. Loads and Stores can compute memory addresses in redundant binary format. The cache index is formed from a subset of the bits of the 2's complement representation of the memory address, and is not easily formed from the redundant binary representation. Sum Addressed Memory [9] (SAM) can be used to avoid converting the address to 2's complement.

In conventional data caches, the cache index is an input to a decoder. The output of this decoder is a one-hot vector that asserts one word line for a row of the cache. SAM uses a different type of decoder from conventional caches. A SAM decoder accepts two numbers, a base and a displacement, as input, and produces a one-hot vector of word lines. The one-hot vector is produced using a separate equality test for each word line rather than a full carry-propagating addition. The Sun UltraSPARC III uses Sum Addressed Memory to avoid the base + displacement calculation normally needed for address computation [11]. SAM can be used to

index the data cache with a single redundant binary number by treating the positive and negative components of the number as the two SAM inputs.

It is also possible to use a modification of SAM to eliminate the base + displacement calculation when the base register is in redundant binary format. This modified SAM has three inputs: the positive and negative components of a redundant binary number and a 2's complement displacement. The modified SAM consists of a conventional SAM preceded by a circuit similar to a carry-save adder. The critical path through the modifed SAM is, at worst, the critical path through the conventional SAM preceded by a 3-input XOR gate. In our experiments, we assume that all machines utilize SAM to avoid the base plus displacement calculation.

Data loaded from memory is already in 2's complement format because data is stored in the caches and main memory in 2's complement representation.

Quadword to Longword Forwarding. Alpha supports both quadword (64-bit) and longword (32-bit) data types. A quadword instruction may forward its result to a longword instruction. The lower 32 bits of the quadword are extracted to form the longword input. In order to extract the lower half of a quadword in redundant binary format, the same mechanism used for correcting bogus overflow and conditions for testing 2's complement overflow must be used at the 32nd digit in addition to the 64th digit. When 2's complement numbers are converted to redundant binary, the 32nd bit should be hardwired to the negative portion of the 32nd digit of the redundant binary representation so that longwords will retain the correct sign.

Summary of Instruction Classifications. Table 1 classifies the fixed-point instructions of the Alpha ISA according to their input and output formats. If the format is listed as RB, operands can be in either redundant binary or 2's complement format. If the format is TC, operands must be in 2's complement format. The fourth column of the table indicates the fraction of dynamic instructions belonging to each class. On average, 33% of the instructions with register destinations produce results in redundant binary format, and about 25% of the instructions require at least one input in 2's complement format.

4. The Execution Core

This section describes how redundant binary adders and limited bypass networks can be incorporated in an execution core. Section 4.1 discusses two possible execution core configurations. Section 4.2 discusses limited bypass networks. Section 4.3 discusses solutions for two scheduling problems: scheduling in a machine with redundant binary adders (and hence multiple data formats) and scheduling in

Instruction	Input Formats(s)	Output Format	Fraction of Inst. Stream
ADD, SUB, MUL, LDA, LDAH, CMOVLBx, SxADD, SxSUB, SLL	RB	RB	18.0%
CMOVLT, CMOVGE, CMOVLE, CMOVGT †	RB	RB	0.4%
CMOVEQ, CMOVNE ‡	RB	RB	0.5%
Memory Access	RB	TC	36.6%
CMPEQ ‡	RB	TC	0.5%
CMPLT, CMPLE, CMPULT, CMPULE †	RB	TC	3.9%
conditional branches † ‡	RB	—	14.4%
Other	TC	TC	25.7%

†test for positive/negative values requires extra logic tree or wired-OR
‡test requires subtraction for comparison

Table 1. Instruction Classifications

a machine with limited bypass networks.

4.1. Core Configurations

This section discusses two possible execution core configurations. The first uses a physical register file that stores data in 2's complement representation. The second uses two or more copies of the physical register file: some using 2's complement representation and some using redundant binary representation. Although each entry in a redundant binary register file requires twice as many bits of state as an entry in a 2's complement register file, fewer bypass paths are needed when redundant binary register files are used.

Only TC Register Files. If register files only store data in 2's complement, the output of the ALUs producing redundant binary results (i.e. the *RB-output* ALUs) must be converted back to 2's complement before it can be stored. Figure 3 shows an example of an RB-output ALU, an ALU that accepts only 2's complement inputs (i.e. a *TC-input* ALU), and part of the bypass network.[1] Three bypass levels are required for any RB-output ALU. The paths in bold hold data in redundant binary format. The first two bypass levels (BYP-1 and BYP-2) of the RB-output ALU can be used by any RB-input functional unit, but they cannot be used by TC-input functional units.

Consider the dependency graph and pipeline diagram in Figures 4 and 5. The ADD gets the result of the SLL (Shift Left Logical) from the first bypass path (BYP-1). The AND gets the result of the SLL in 2's complement format from BYP-3. The SUB gets the ADD's result from BYP-1 and

---

[1]This example and all further examples in this section assume the redundant binary addition and logical operations take one cycle, the format conversion takes two cycles, and the register file access takes one cycle. Bypass paths needed to bypass values from the register file write stage to the register file read stage are not shown in the figures.

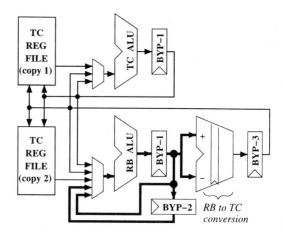

Figure 3. ALUs with TC Register Files

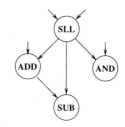

Figure 4. Dependency Graph

	Cycle:	1	2	3	4	5	6	7
(RB ALU)	SLL	RF	EXE	CV1	CV2	WB		
(TC ALU)	AND				RF	EXE	WB	
(RB ALU)	ADD		RF	EXE	CV1	CV2	WB	
(RB ALU)	SUB			RF	EXE	CV1	CV2	WB

Figure 5. Pipeline Diagram.

the SLL's result from BYP-2.

TC and RB Register Files. In the second configuration, the inputs to TC-input functional units come from 2's complement register files and 2's complement bypass paths. The inputs to other functional units come from redundant binary register files and bypass paths in either representation. Figure 6 shows an example with one TC-input ALU and one RB-output (and TC or RB-input) ALU. This configuration requires the same number of bypass paths as a machine with only TC ALUs. There is no second-level bypass, and BYP-3 is only used by the TC-input ALU and TC register file. The timing of operations is the same as when using all TC register files.

4.2. Limited Bypass Networks

The number of bypass levels, and hence the number of bypass paths, required in a full bypass network increases linearly with the number of cycles between execution and

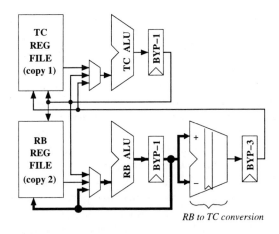

Figure 6. ALUs with TC and RB Register Files

the last stage of register file write-back. This section explains how bypass levels can be removed.

Most instructions execute as soon as their last (or only) source operand is available. When an instruction executes immediately when its last source operand becomes available, the input comes from a first-level bypass path (i.e. BYP-1). Hence the first-level bypass paths are used more often than any others. An instruction would only need a second-level bypass in the following cases:

- it had a second source that became available the cycle before the last available source

- it was stalled for one cycle because another instruction was granted execution

- it was just recently placed in the scheduling window and was scheduled at its earliest opportunity.

None of these situations occur very frequently.

The machine with only TC register files was modeled with a limited bypass network: the second bypass level (BYP-2) was removed, and the output of BYP-3 was not used as a bypass for the RB-input ALUs. For RB-input instructions, the result of an RB-output instruction is available in redundant binary format immediately after it is produced, and then there is a 2-cycle hole in data availability. After that, the result is available from the register file. For TC-input instructions, the result is available from BYP-3, and then from the register file.

For the dependency graph shown in Figure 4, this limited bypass network would result in the pipeline schedule shown in Figure 7. The AND gets the result of the SLL from BYP-3. The SUB is delayed by three cycles and retrieves both source operands from the register file (or a bypass path within the register file, depending on the register

file design). Performance results of this machine and a conventional 2's complement machine with a limited bypass network are discussed in Section 5.2.

Cycle:	1	2	3	4	5	6	7	8	9	10
(RB ALU) SLL	RF	EXE	CV1	CV2	WB					
(TC ALU) AND						RF	EXE	WB		
(RB ALU) ADD		RF	EXE	CV1	CV2	WB				
(RB ALU) SUB						RF	EXE	CV1	CV2	WB

Figure 7. Pipeline Diagram.

This paper only investigates the removal of entire levels of bypass paths. Further restrictions in bypass networks may be made with little loss in IPC with the help of instruction steering. This topic remains an area of future work.

4.3. Scheduling

The use of multiple data formats can present scheduling problems due to variable times for result availability. For example, a SUB dependent on an ADD may be scheduled one cycle after the ADD, but a logical instruction dependent on an ADD must wait 3 cycles (1 for the addition, 2 for the format conversion) before it can be scheduled.

There are many scheduling techniques to handle this problem. One technique is to use separate schedulers for the different classes of operations identified in Table 1. The result tag broadcasts, or wakeup signals, from a scheduler for RB-output instructions to a scheduler for TC-input instructions can be latched for 2 cycles to account for the format conversion. The use of separate schedulers is warranted since these two classes of instructions execute on different functional units. Another technique is to associate the result of a redundant binary operation with two resources (i.e. physical register numbers or tags): one resource indicates that the result is available in redundant binary format; the other indicates the result is available in 2's complement.

The limited bypass network described in Section 4.2 will create holes in data availability. Wakeup array-style scheduling logic [4] can be used to schedule around these holes. Figure 8 (a) shows a block diagram of this scheduling logic. The wakeup logic contains information about each instruction that specifies which resources (i.e. source operands or functional units) are needed. One input to the wakeup logic is a wire for each resource, called the RESOURCE AVAILABLE line, which is asserted if that resource is available. The wakeup logic for an instruction monitors the RESOURCE AVAILABLE lines for the required resources. When all required RESOURCE AVAILABLE lines are asserted, the instruction requests execution. When it is granted execution by the select logic, a shift register that acts as a countdown timer to count the instruction's latency is enabled. The output of the shift register is the RESOURCE AVAILABLE line for that instruction, and it indicates when dependent instructions may be scheduled. For example, the timer in Figure 8 (b) would be used for a 2-cycle instruction (assuming the scheduling operation takes 1 cycle). To handle holes in data availability, the initial value in the shift register would interleave 0s and 1s according to which levels of the bypass network were missing.

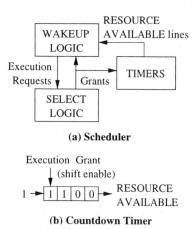

(a) Scheduler

(b) Countdown Timer

Figure 8. Scheduling logic

5. Experiments

5.1. Machine Model

The SPECint95 and SPECint2000 benchmarks were simulated using an execution-driven simulator for the Alpha ISA. All benchmarks were run to completion using modified input sets to reduce simulation time. Some characteristics of the machine model are shown in Table 2. The pipeline latency was a minimum of 13 cycles: 6 for fetch and decode, 2 for rename, 1 for schedule, 2 for register file read, a minimum of 1 for execution, and 1 for retirement.

Branch Predictor	48KB hybrid gshare/PaS, 4096-entry BTB 2 basic blocks per cycle fetched
Decode, Rename, and Issue Width	8 instructions
Instruction Cache	64KB 4-way set associative (pipelined) 2-cycle directory and data store access
Instruction Window	128 Reservation Station Entries
Execution Width	4 or 8 functional units
Data Cache	8KB 2-way set associative (pipelined)
Unified L2 Cache	1MB, 8-way, 8-cycle access contention for 2 banks is modeled
Memory	100-cycle access contention for 32 banks modeled

Table 2. Machine Configuration

Machines with 4 and 8 functional units were studied because the effects of execution latency depend on the exe-

cution bandwidth. As execution bandwidth increases, performance is more dependent on the latencies of instructions on the critical path. All other machine parameters remained constant so that the amount of exposed ILP changed as little as possible. All functional units were homogeneous. The use of special-purpose functional units would have made it difficult to make a fair comparison between redundant binary and conventional execution cores because the classes of operations that would execute on each type of functional unit depend on the data representation.

All machines had a 128-entry instruction window and select-2 schedulers (i.e. schedulers that pick 2 instructions per cycle for execution on 2 functional units). The 4-wide machine had two schedulers, each holding 64 instructions. The 8-wide machine had 4 schedulers, each with 32 instructions. Groups of two consecutive instructions were steered to each scheduler in a round robin manner. The 8-wide machine was partitioned into two clusters, each with 4 functional units. If a result produced on a functional unit in one cluster had to be forwarded to a functional unit in the other cluster, there was a 1-cycle propagation delay.

For both execution widths, four machines were modeled: a **Baseline** machine, the RB (redundant binary) machine with TC register files and a limited bypass network (**RB-limited**), the RB machine with both TC and RB register files (**RB-full**), and the **Ideal** machine. The **Baseline** machine used 2-cycle, pipelined 2's complement ALUs. The **RB** machines used 1-cycle redundant binary adders with 2-cycle format converters. The **Ideal** machine used 1-cycle 2's complement arithmetic units. The execution latencies for the machines are given in Table 3. The **RB-limited** machine used the bypass network described in Section 4.2. All machines had the same number of bypass paths.

Instruction Class	Base	RB (TC result)	Ideal
integer arithmetic	2	1 (3)	1
integer logical	1	1	1
integer shift left	3	3 (5)	3
integer shift right	3	3	3
integer compare	2	1 (3)	1
byte manipulation	2	1 (3)	1
integer multiply	10	10	10
fp arithmetic	8	8	8
fp divide	32	32	32
loads, stores (SAM decoder)	1	1 (3 for stores)	1
dcache latency	2	2	2

Table 3. Instruction Class Latencies

5.2. Results

Figure 9 shows the IPC of the 8-wide machines on the SPECint2000 benchmarks. For each benchmark, the first bar shows the IPC of the **Baseline** machine; the next two bars represent the **RB** machines, and the last bar represents the **Ideal** machine. The **RB-full** machine had an IPC 7% higher than the **Baseline** machine, and within 1.1% of the **Ideal** machine. Figure 10 shows the results on the SPECint95 benchmarks. The **RB** machine had an IPC 9% higher than the Baseline machine, and within 2% of the Ideal machine. Overall, the **RB-limited** machine performed within 2% of the **RB-full** machine.

The results for 4-wide machines are shown in Figures 11 and 12. Fast functional units have less of an advantage on the 4-wide machines because the execution bandwidth is a bottleneck for the amount of exposed ILP in these benchmarks. On the SPECint2000 benchmarks, the **RB-full** machine has an IPC 5% above the **Baseline** machine, and within 0.5% of the **Ideal** machine. On the SPECint95 benchmarks, the **RB-full** machine has an IPC 6% above the **Baseline** machine, and within 1.3% of the **Ideal** machine. Overall, the **RB-limited** machine performed within 2.3% of the **RB-full** machine.

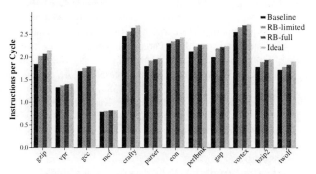

Figure 9. 8-wide machines, SPECint2000.

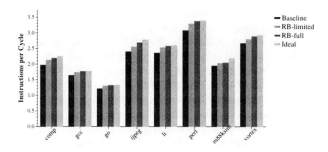

Figure 10. 8-wide machines, SPECint95.

Format Conversions. The IPC of the **RB** machines is lower than that of the **Ideal** machine because of the format conversions that were on the critical path of execution. There are four cases of data bypasses: (1) a 2's complement result is forwarded to a 2's complement operation, (2) a 2's complement result is forwarded to a redundant binary operation, (3) a redundant binary result is forwarded to a redundant binary operation, and (4) a redundant binary result

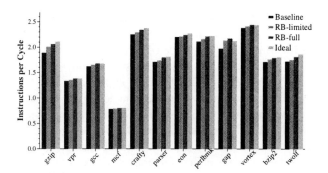

Figure 11. 4-wide machines, SPECint2000.

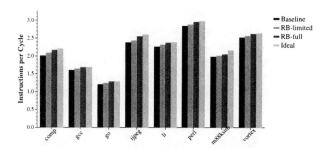

Figure 12. 4-wide machines, SPECint95.

is forwarded to a 2's complement operation. Only the fourth case requires a format conversion. Figure 13 shows a distribution of the four cases for the 8-wide **RB-full** machine on the SPECint2000 benchmarks. Only last-arriving bypassed source operands (i.e. source operands that delay an instruction's execution) are included in the distribution. The number at the top of each bar indicates the fraction of all dynamic instructions that had at least one bypassed source operand. The numbers at the bottom indicate the fraction of the data bypasses that required format conversion (RB to TC). For example, on the bzip2 benchmark, 2.4% of 69% of all dynamic instructions were delayed because of a format conversion. Because a majority of the last-arriving sources are from memory loads, which produce 2's complement results, few last-arriving sources required format conversions.

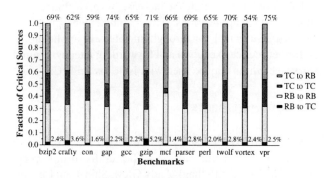

Figure 13. Potentially critical bypass cases.

Limited Bypass Networks. To evaluate the potential of using a scheduler that can support holes in data availability, the **Ideal** machine was modeled with limited bypass networks. Because it had a 2-cycle register file, three levels of bypass paths were required for a full bypass network. Five limited bypass configurations were modeled: **No-1** had no first-level bypass paths, **No-2** had no second-level bypass paths, **No-1,2** had no first or second-level bypass paths, and so on. The difference between the **Ideal** machine and the **No-1** machine is the effect of increasing all execution latencies by one cycle. In the **Ideal** machine, 21% to 38% of the instructions did not receive any sources off of the bypass network, 51% to 70% retrieved a source operand from the first-level bypass bus, and 5% to 14% of the instructions received a source operand from another bypass path. Because the first-level bypass paths are heavily utilized, those machines that do not remove the first-level bypass paths perform the best. The harmonic means of the IPC over all 20 benchmarks for each machine are shown in Figure 14. The 4-wide **No-1,2** machine outperformed the 8-wide **No-1,2** machine because the 8-wide machines are clustered, and both machines have ample execution bandwidth for the long execution latencies.

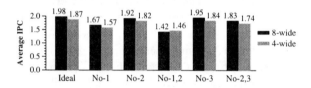

Figure 14. IPC with Limited Bypass Networks.

6. Conclusions

Redundant binary adders have about half the latency of 2's complement adders. As a result, an execution core built from redundant binary adders can be clocked at a higher frequency, resulting in greater execution bandwidth and lower execution latencies. Our results show that redundant binary adders provide a significant increase in performance for latency-critical applications. Two's complement, pipelined adders are sufficient for throughput-intensive applications. To further reduce execution and forwarding latency, limited bypass networks may be used with little loss in IPC.

Acknowledgements

We would like to thank Jared Stark and the anonymous referees for their comments on earlier drafts of this work. We would also like to thank Andy Glew, Shih-Lien Lu, and Chris Wilkerson for their valuable discussions. This work was supported in part by Intel and IBM. Mary Brown is supported by an IBM Cooperative Graduate Fellowship.

References

[1] P. S. Ahuja, D. W. Clark, and A. Rogers. The performance impact of incomplete bypassing in processor pipelines. In *Proc. of MICRO-28*, pages 36–45, 1995.

[2] D. E. Atkins. Design of the arithmetic units of ILLIAC III: Use of redundancy and higher radix methods. *IEEE Trans. on Computers*, C-19:720–732, Aug. 1970.

[3] A. Avizienis. Signed-digit number representations for fast parallel arithmetic. *IRE Transactions on Electronic Computers*, EC-10(9):389–400, Sept. 1961.

[4] M. D. Brown, J. Stark, and Y. N. Patt. Select-free scheduling logic. In *Proc. of MICRO-34*, 2001.

[5] J.-L. Cruz, A. González, M. Valero, and N. P. Topham. Multiple-banked register file architectures. In *Proc. of ISCA-27*, pages 316–324, 2000.

[6] M. D. Ercegovac. On-line arithmetic: An overview. *SPIE Real-Time Signal Processing VII*, 495:86–93, Aug. 1984.

[7] A. Glew. Processor with architecture for improved pipelining of arithmetic instructions by forwarding redundant intermediate data forms. U.S. Patent Number 5,619,664, 1997.

[8] J. Gray, A. Naylor, A. Abnous, and N. Bagherzadeh. VIPER: A VLIW integer microprocessor. *IEEE Journal of Solid-State Circuits*, 28(12):1377–1383, Dec. 1993.

[9] R. Heald, K. Shin, V. Reddy, I.-F. Kao, M. Khan, W. L. Lynch, G. Lauterbach, and J. Petolino. 64-KByte sum-addressed-memory cache with 1.6-ns cycle and 2.6-ns latency. *IEEE Journal of Solid-State Circuits*, 33(11):1682–1689, 1998.

[10] Intel Corporation. *IA-32 Intel Architecture Software Developer's Manual With Preliminary Willamette Architecture Information Volume 1: Basic Architecture*, 2000.

[11] W. L. Lynch, G. Lauterbach, and J. I. Chamdani. Low load latency through sum-addressed memory (SAM). In *Proc. of ISCA-25*, pages 369 – 379, 1998.

[12] H. Makino, Y. Nakase, H. Suzuki, H. Morinaka, H. Shinohara, and K. Mashiko. An 8.8-ns 54 x 54-bit multiplier with high speed redundant binary architecture. *IEEE Journal of Solid-State Circuits*, 31(4):773–783, Apr. 1996.

[13] R. Nagarajan, K. Sankaralingam, D. Burger, and S. W. Keckler. A design space evaluation of grid processor architectures. In *Proc. of MICRO-34*, 2001.

[14] C. Nagendra, M. J. Irwin, and R. M. Owens. Area-time-power tradeoffs in parallel adders. *IEEE Transactions on Circuits and Systems*, 43(10):689–702, Oct. 1996.

[15] C. Nagendra, R. M. Owens, and M. J. Irwin. Power-delay characteristics of CMOS adders. *IEEE Tran. on Very Large Scale Integration (VLSI) Systems*, 2(3):377–381, Sept. 1994.

[16] N. Takagi, H. Yasuura, and S. Yajima. High-speed vlsi multiplication algorithm with a redundant binary addition tree. *IEEE Trans. on Computers*, C-34(9):789–796, Sept. 1985.

[17] D. M. Tullsen, S. J. Eggers, J. S. Emer, and H. M. Levy. Exploiting choice: Instruction fetch and issue on an implementable simultaneous multithreading processor. In *Proc. of ISCA-23*, pages 191–202, 1996.

Loose Loops Sink Chips

Eric Borch
Intel Corporation, VSSAD
eric.borch@intel.com

Eric Tune*
University of California, San Diego
Department of Computer Science
etune@cs.ucsd.edu

Srilatha Manne   Joel Emer
Intel Corporation, VSSAD
[srilatha.manne, joel.emer]@intel.com

Abstract

This paper explores the concept of micro-architectural loops *and discusses their impact on processor pipelines. In particular, we establish the relationship between* loose loops *and pipeline length and configuration, and show their impact on performance. We then evaluate the* load resolution loop *in detail and propose the* **distributed register algorithm** *(DRA) as a way of reducing this loop. It decreases the performance loss due to load mis-speculations by reducing the issue-to-execute latency in the pipeline. A new loose loop is introduced into the pipeline by the DRA, but the frequency of mis-speculations is very low. The reduction in latency from issue to execute, along with a low mis-speculation rate in the DRA result in up to a 4% to 15% improvement in performance using a detailed architectural simulator.*

1   Introduction

Micro-architectural loops are fundamental to all processor designs. We define micro-architectural loops as communication loops which exist wherever a computation in one stage of the pipeline is needed in the same or an earlier stage of the pipeline. Loops are caused by control, data, or resource hazards.

Figure 1 illustrates the basic components of a loop. The *initiation stage* is the stage where data from a succeeding stage is fed back. The *resolution stage* is the stage that computes the result needed by a preceding stage. The *loop generating instruction* is the instruction which initiates the loop. For branches, the loop generating instruction is a branch, the loop initiation stage is the fetch stage, and the

---

[1]Eric Tune did this work while at VSSAD.

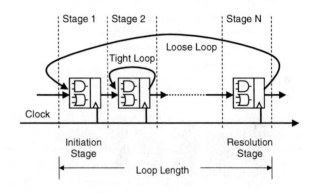

Figure 1. Micro-architectural loops

loop resolution stage is the execute stage. *Loop length* is defined to be the number of stages traversed by a loop, and the *feedback delay* is the time required to communicate from the resolution stage to the initiation stage. *Loop delay* is the sum of the loop length and feedback delay. Loops with a loop delay of one are referred to as *tight loops*; all other loops are referred to as *loose loops*.

With a loop delay of one, tight loops feed back to the same pipeline stage. Figure 2 shows examples of tight loops in the Alpha 21264 processor, such as the next line prediction loop and the integer ALU forwarding loop [3]. The next line prediction in the current cycle is needed by the line predictor to determine the instructions to fetch in the next cycle, while the ALU computation in the current cycle is required in the ALU in the next cycle to support back-to-back execution of dependent instructions. Tight loops directly impact the cycle time of the processor because the information being computed is required at the beginning of the next cycle.

Loose loops extend over multiple pipeline stages. Examples of loose loops in the Alpha 21264 (Figure 2) are the *branch resolution loop* and the *load resolution loop*. The

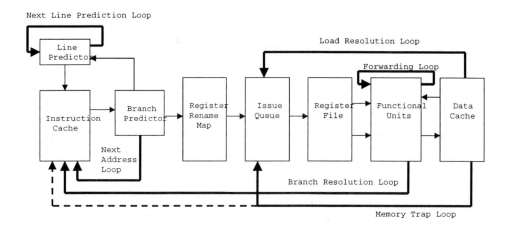

Figure 2. Examples of micro-architectural loops in the Alpha 21264 processor [3], represented by solid lines. If the recovery stage is different from the initiation stage, it is shown by a dotted line.

branch resolution loop is caused by a control hazard resulting from the existence of an unresolved branch in the pipeline. The fetch unit does not know with certainty which instruction to fetch until the branch resolves. The load resolution loop is caused by a data hazard resulting from an unresolved load operation, e.g., did the load hit in the cache or not. The loop occurs because instructions dependent on the load cannot issue until the issue queue knows the time at which the load data will be available.

Loose loops can impact performance by restricting the pipeline's ability to do useful work. The simplest way to manage a loose loop is to stall the pipeline while waiting for the loop to resolve. Since no progress is made while the pipeline stalls, performance will be negatively impacted. Thus, an alternative technique of speculating through the loop is often used. Speculating through a loop improves performance by attempting to make progress while the loop resolves instead of simply waiting. Stalling the processor means that no progress is made every time a loose loop is encountered, while speculating through the loop allows progress to be made, except when there is a mis-speculation.

Stalling the processor is often an acceptable solution when the loop length is small. With a simple, 5 stage pipeline, a single cycle branch bubble may not have a significant impact on performance. Stalling the processor is also a tenable solution when the loop occurs infrequently. The memory barrier loop in the Alpha 21264 is an example of an infrequent loop. When a memory barrier instruction is encountered in the pipeline, the mapping logic stalls the memory barrier instruction and all succeeding instructions. The instructions are released to issue when all preceding instructions have completed.

As pipelines get longer and/or loops occur more frequently, speculation is used to manage loose loops and maximize performance. There are many examples of speculation in the Alpha 21264, such as branch prediction, load hit prediction, and memory dependence prediction. As long as there are no mis-speculations, loose loops do not impact performance because the pipeline is always doing useful work.

When mis-speculations occur, however, the pipeline has done work which must be thrown away. The pipeline must then recover, and restart processing from the mis-speculated instruction. Mis-speculation recovery may occur at the loop initiation stage or, due to implementation reasons, at an earlier stage in the pipeline which we call the *recovery stage*. The presence of a recovery stage introduces a recovery time, that is, the time it takes the useful instructions to refill the pipeline from the recovery stage to the initiation stage. For example, the initiation stage for load/store reorder traps in the 21264 is the issue stage, while the recovery stage is the fetch stage. The dotted lines in Figure 2 illustrate where the recovery stage is earlier than the initiation stage.

The best performance is achieved when there are no mis-speculations. Every mis-speculation degrades performance. Clearly the frequency of loop occurrence (i.e., the number of loop generating instructions) and the mis-speculation rate are first order determinants of the performance lost. How much performance is lost per mis-speculated event is a complex function of a number of parameters. One measure of this is the amount of work discarded due to each mis-speculation. We term this *useless work*.

The product of the frequency of loop occurrence and the mis-speculation rate determines the number of times useless work is done. For example, the number of branch mis-speculation events is greater in programs with a high occurrence of branches and a high mis-prediction rate, such as integer programs. The amount of useless work due to each mis-speculation is a function of the time required to resolve the loop, and the time required to recover from the mis-speculation. The greater these latencies, the greater the impact of the mis-speculation.

The lower bound of this time is equal to the loop delay plus the recovery time. The actual latency is augmented by any queuing delays within the loop. For instance, the branch resolution loop length for the Alpha 21264 encompasses 6 stages, the feedback delay is 1 cycle [3], and there is no recovery time. Thus, the minimum impact of a mis-speculation is 7 cycles.

The long pipelines in current generation processors increase the loop delay for many loose loops. The Pentium4 design, for example, has a pipeline length greater than 20 stages and a branch resolution latency on the order of 20 cycles [12]. Pipeline lengths are increasing for two reasons: higher operating frequency and more architecturally complex designs. A high operating frequency shrinks the clock cycle, resulting in fewer stages of logic fitting within a cycle [1]. Operations that required only one cycle in the past now take multiple cycles. Architectural advances that increase overall processor throughput also increase pipeline lengths. Wide issue widths, out-of-order instruction issue, speculation, and multi-threading increase the amount of logic on the processor, and more logic often requires more pipeline stages to complete an operation.

This paper looks at the impact pipeline lengths, pipeline configurations, and loose loops have on processor performance. We show that performance is not just affected by the overall length of the pipeline, but by the length of critical portions of the pipeline that are traversed by key loose loops. In particular, we focus on the load resolution loop and the impact loop length and queuing delay have on this loop. Based on our analysis, we propose a design modification called the **distributed register algorithm (DRA)**. It moves the time consuming register file access out of the issue to execute path and adds a register caching mechanism. Using the detailed ASIM [4] architectural simulator, we show speedup improvements of up to 4% to 15% relative to the base model.

The rest of the paper is organized as follows. Section 2 describes the base architecture and details the load resolution loop. Section 3 shows the impact pipeline lengths and configurations have on performance. Sections 4 and 5 discuss the reasoning behind the proposed design modification and detail the DRA. Results are presented in section 6. Section 7 explains the relation of our work to prior work related to register files, and section 8 concludes the paper.

2 Processor Model

We modeled our base processor to be comparable to next generation super-scalar processors [5, 10]. It is an 8-wide issue machine with branch prediction, dynamic instruction scheduling, and multi-threaded execution. It contains a unified, 128 entry instruction queue (IQ), and has up to 256 instructions in flight at any time. The minimum pipeline delay for an integer operation with single cycle execution latency is similar to the Pentium4 [12], around 20 cycles, assuming no stalls or queuing delays in the pipeline. Other operations may take longer depending on their execution latency.

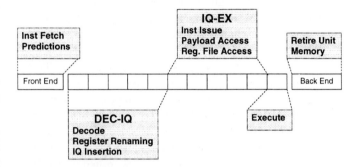

Figure 3. Pipeline of base architecture

Figure 3 shows the pipeline of the simulated machine. In this work we focus on the latency between instruction decode and execute. These are labeled in the figure as **DEC-IQ** (decode to insertion into the instruction queue) and **IQ-EX** (issue from instruction queue to execute). Many micro-architectural loops traverse this portion of the pipeline, such as the branch resolution loop and the memory dependence loop, and processor performance is highly sensitive to the length of this region.

Our simulated architecture uses a clustered design similar to the 21264 [14]. In particular, we cluster the instruction scheduling logic. As noted in [2], issuing M instructions out of an instruction queue of N entries is difficult to implement when M and N are large. In our case, $M = 8$ and $N = 128$. Therefore, we allocate or slot the instructions at decode to one of eight functional unit clusters. Now the problem of issuing M out of N instructions is reduced to issuing one out of approximately $N/8$ instructions, assuming that instructions are distributed uniformly to all clusters. The DRA uses the cluster allocation information to determine which functional units receive which source operands. This is described in detail in Section 5.

2.1 Pipeline Latency

The DEC-IQ latency is 5 cycles in the base model. The 5 cycles are required for instruction decoding, register renaming, wire delay, and insertion of the instruction into the IQ. The latency from IQ-EX is also 5 cycles, which is required for determining which instruction to issue, reading the pertinent information from the instruction payload, performing register file access, and delivering the instruction and the source operands to the functional units. The IQ only contains the dependency information required to determine when an instruction is ready to issue. The instruction payload contains the rest of the state for the instruction, such as physical register numbers, op codes, and offsets.

Register file access takes 3 cycles, with two of the cycles required purely to drive data to and from the register file. The wiring delay is due to the large register file required to support an 8 wide issue, out-of-order, SMT machine with both physical registers and architectural state for all threads. Furthermore, we require 16 read ports and 8 write ports to support 8-wide issue.

The register file design could have fewer ports. The full port capability is not needed in most cases because either the operands are forwarded from the execution units, or the number of instructions issued is less than 8, or not all instructions have 2 input operands and one output operand [15]. However, there are implementation problems with reducing the number of ports. First, which operands are being forwarded is not known at the time of issue, and the register file and forwarding structure are accessed simultaneously, not sequentially. Accessing them sequentially would add additional delay into the IQ-EX path. Therefore, we cannot suppress the reading of the register file on a hit in the forwarding logic. Second, if there are fewer read port pairs than functional unit clusters, a complex switching network is needed to move operands to the correct functional units. This also adds additional delay into the IQ-EX path. Third, if 16 operands are needed in a cycle, there must be some logic to stall or suppress instructions that will not be able to read their operands. For these reasons, a register file with full port capability can be easier to implement and manage, and reducing the number of ports adds unnecessary complexity.

2.2 Managing Issue Loops

The 5 cycle IQ-EX latency introduces some challenging architectural problems. The long latency produces two loose loops that are managed in different ways to optimize performance.

2.2.1 Forwarding Buffer

A loose loop exists between the execution stage and the register file read stage. A value computed in the execution stage needs to be written back to the register file before dependent instructions can read the value. Forwarding logic is added in the execution stage to shrink this loop from a loose loop to a tight loop. Without forwarding, dependent instructions must wait to issue until their operands are written to the register file. While these instructions stall, the pipeline has fewer instructions to execute, resulting in less available

work. Forwarding enables instructions to get their operands from the forwarding logic in the ALUs without having to wait for them to be written to the register file. It replaces this loose loop with a tight loop in the execution logic that makes the result computed in a previous cycle available in the current cycle.

The base model contains a *forwarding buffer* which retains results for instructions executed in the last 9 cycles. Five of these cycles are required to cover long latency operations and limit the number of write ports on the register file. The other four cycles cover the time it takes for the resulting data to be written to the register file. The forwarding buffer is required for the base architecture to work. As will be discussed in Section 5, it is also an integral part of our redesign for the register file.

2.2.2 Load Resolution Loop

The load resolution loop is caused by the non-deterministic latency of loads. Although the latency of a cache hit is known, whether the load will hit, miss, or have a bank conflict in the cache is unknown. This makes it difficult to know when to issue load dependent instructions so that they arrive at the functional units in the same cycle that the load data arrives. It is this unknown that necessitates a loose loop. As with all loose loops, the pipeline could either stall or speculate. The Alpha 21064 and 21164 processors stall the pipeline [7, 8] until the load resolves, while the Alpha 21264 can speculatively issue dependent instructions and recover on a load miss [3].

In our base processor, stalling load dependent instructions effectively adds 5 cycles to the load-to-use latency. Stalling may prevent useful work from getting done. To avoid this, the base processor speculatively issues load dependent instructions, i.e., it predicts that all loads hit in the data cache.

To help discuss the load resolution loop, we define two terms. The *load dependency tree* is defined to include the instructions directly or indirectly dependent upon the load. The set of cycles in which any instructions within the load dependency tree may issue speculatively is called the *load shadow*. In the 21264, the load shadow for integer loads starts 2 cycles after the load issues, and ends when the load signals a data cache hit or miss [3].

Load Mis-speculation Recovery As long as the load hits, there is no penalty for the speculation. A miss, however, requires a costly recovery action. For correct operation, all instructions within the load dependency tree that have already issued must be reissued after the load resolves. Implementation choices can further increase the mis-speculation penalty. In the Alpha 21264, the amount of useless work can be even higher on an integer load miss because all in-

302

structions issued in the load shadow, whether they are in the load dependency tree or not, are killed and reissued. Fortunately, most programs have a high load hit rate, and the overall cost of recovering from mis-speculations is significantly less that the cost of a non-speculative policy.

We also have a choice of recovery points for a load mis-speculation. We could make the recovery stage the issue stage, by reissuing load dependent instructions from the IQ. Alternatively, the fetch stage could be the recovery stage by flushing the pipeline and re-fetching instructions starting with the first instruction after the mis-speculated load. Re-fetching is easier to implement, but it dramatically increases the loop recovery time. Our results show that it performs significantly worse than reissue. Hence, it was not considered further.

IQ Pressure Our base architecture reissues instructions on a load miss. Unlike the 21264, we do not reissue all instructions issued within the load shadow; we only reissue instructions that are within the load dependency tree. The number of instructions reissued is equal to the useless work performed due to load mis-speculations. For each reissued instruction, there was a previous issue of the same instruction that was killed.

Although load speculation with reissue performs better than no speculation or speculation with re-fetch, it puts additional pressure on the IQ. The reissue mechanism requires the IQ to retain all issued instructions until it is notified by the execution stage that the instructions do not have to reissue. The occupancy time of instructions in the IQ is therefore a function of the IQ-EX latency. The longer the instructions reside in the IQ after issuing, the less space there is for new, unissued instructions. In our base model, the loop delay is 8 cycles (loop length of 5 cycles and feedback delay of 3 cycles). Thus, it takes 8 cycles from the time an instruction issues to the time the IQ is notified by the execution stage that the instruction does not have to reissue and can be removed. Once an instruction is tagged for eviction from the IQ, extra cycles are needed to clear the entry. If the machine is operating near full capacity of 8 IPC, more than half the entries in the IQ may be already issued instructions in the load dependency tree waiting for the load to resolve. The instruction window effectively shrinks, resulting in less exposed instruction level parallelism (ILP), and potentially, a reduction in useful work.

3 Impact of Loop Length

As pipeline lengths increase, so do the loop lengths for many loose loops, resulting in more useless work done per mis-speculation. In this section we quantitatively look at the impact longer pipelines have on performance. Furthermore, we also investigate various pipeline configurations

and show that performance is a function of not just the length of the pipeline, but the configuration of latencies across the pipeline.

3.1 Increasing Pipeline Lengths

Figure 4 shows the results from increasing the pipeline length of our base machine running a sampling of integer, floating point, and multi-threaded benchmarks. The decode to execute portion of the pipeline is varied from 6 to 18 cycles, in increments of 4 cycles (2 cycles each for DEC-IQ and IQ-EX). Speedup numbers are shown relative to the 6 cycle case.

We use the Spec95 benchmark suite in our analysis. For single threaded runs, we skip from 2 to 4 billion instructions, warm up the simulator for 1 to 2 million instructions, and simulate each benchmark from 90 to 200 million instructions. The multi-threaded benchmarks are simulated for 100 million instructions total for both threads. Each program in the multi-threaded run skips the same number of instructions as in the single-threaded run. All benchmarks are compiled with the official Compaq Alpha Spec95 flags.

The greater the pipeline length, the longer the loop delay for loops which traverse the pipeline between decode and execute. Figure 4 shows that increasing the pipeline length by 12 cycles results in a performance loss of up to 24% due to mis-speculation on loose loops. The two primary loops in this region are the branch resolution loop and the load resolution loop. All benchmarks show a reduction in performance as the pipeline lengthens.

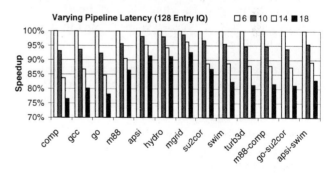

Figure 4. Performance for varying pipeline lengths. Pipeline length is varied between *decode* and *execute*. Performance is shown relative to the case with **6** cycles between decode and execute. Numbers less than 100% indicate a performance loss. Note that the Y-axis begins at 70%.

Integer programs are generally impacted by mis-speculations on the branch resolution loop. *compress*, *gcc* and *go* perform a significant amount of useless work due to branch mis-predictions. Furthermore, they are also burdened by load misses, resulting in additional performance degradation. *m88ksim*, however, does not have as many branches or branch mis-predictions as the other integer benchmarks, resulting in less sensitivity to the branch resolution loop delay.

We expected floating point programs to be sensitive to the load resolution loop primarily due to a large number of load operations and a high load miss rate. Some programs behave as expected, such as *turb3d* and *swim*. Both programs have a reasonable number of loads and load misses in the data cache, indicating many mis-speculation events. *turb3d* also suffers from a fair number of data TLB misses, where recovery from the beginning of the pipeline impacts performance, not just the latency of the IQ-EX portion.

Two programs, *hydro* and *mgrid*, also have a large number of loads and a high data cache miss rate, but are not particularly sensitive to pipeline length. Unlike *turb3d* and *swim*, both these programs also suffer from misses in the second level cache. Therefore, the performance of these programs is dominated by the long main memory access latency. The loop delay of the load loop, even with a long pipeline, is insignificant in comparison to the main memory access latency.

apsi has a reasonably high data cache miss rate; however, the amount of useless work performed due to load mis-speculations, as indicated by the number of instructions reissued, is small. The relatively low IPC of *apsi*, combined with the small amount of useless work performed per mis-speculation, suggests that *apsi* has long, narrow dependency chains restricting ILP. Therefore, the performance of *apsi* is determined more by program characteristics than by the load resolution loop delay.

su2cor does not suffer from many branch or load mis-speculations. However, analysis shows that there is a measurable amount of useless work resulting from branch mis-predictions, as noted by the number of instructions killed due to branch predictions. Therefore, although the number of branch mis-speculations is small, the resolution latency is large due to queuing delays in the pipeline. Increasing the pipeline length only exacerbates the situation since the loop length defines the lower bound for resolution latency.

Pipeline length impacts multi-threaded performance in the same manner as it impacts the component programs. However, the degree of impact is generally less than that of the worst performing component program. For example, *go-su2cor* has a smaller performance loss than *go* alone. In multi-threaded execution, the availability of multiple threads prevents the pipeline from issuing deeply down a speculative path [16]. Furthermore, when a mis-speculation occurs on one thread, the other thread(s) can continue doing useful work while the mis-speculated thread recovers.

3.2 Not All Pipelines are Created Equal

Figure 5 shows the results from varying the pipeline configuration while retaining the same overall pipeline length. The syntax **X_ Y** represents the latency from DEC-IQ (**X**), and IQ-EX (**Y**). Note that $X + Y$ is constant. The speedup shown is relative to the 3_ 9 configuration, with 3 cycles from DEC-IQ and 9 cycles from IQ-EX. The results indicate that not all pipelines are created equal, and reducing the latency from IQ-EX improves performance by up to 15%, even when the overall length of the pipeline remains the same.

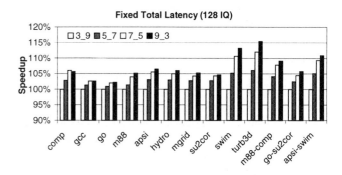

Figure 5. Performance for a fixed overall pipeline length. The first number in the legend represents the cycles from DEC-IQ, while the 2nd number represents the cycles from IQ-EX. All data is shown as speedup relative to to the 3_9 case. Note the y-axis begins at 90%.

Loose loops determine how sensitive the processor is to various pipeline configurations. Loose loops in our base processor either traverse the entire decode to execution portion of the pipeline (branch resolution loop), or traverse just the IQ-EX portion (load resolution loop). There are no loops which exist only within the DEC-IQ section. By moving pipeline stages from the IQ-EX portion to the DEC-IQ portion, we reduce the length of loops contained within the IQ-EX region without jeopardizing loops in other sections.

The benchmarks with the greatest performance improvement in Figure 5 (*swim, turb3d,* and *apsi-swim*) are a subset of the programs that showed the most sensitivity to increasing pipeline lengths in Figure 4. The rest of the benchmarks are either sensitive to the branch resolution loop length, which does not change in these simulations (*compress, gcc, go, m88ksim, su2cor, m88ksim-compress* and *go-su2cor*), or are impacted by other benchmark characteristics such as low ILP (*apsi*) or misses to main memory (*hydro* and *mgrid*).

Reducing the IQ-EX latency, even at the cost of increasing DEC-IQ latency, improves performance. The access to a large register file dictates much of this latency. Farkas, et.

al. [11] also note that large register files might limit the performance benefit of wide, super-scalar machines. In the rest of the paper, we present the **distributed register algorithm** (DRA). It reduces the IQ-EX latency and the latency of the overall pipeline by moving the time consuming register file access out of the IQ-EX path and placing it in the DEC-IQ path. This primarily reduces the loop delay of the load resolution loop, resulting in less capacity pressure on the IQ and less useless work done due to load mis-speculations.

4   Distributed Register Algorithm

Much of the IQ-EX latency is determined by the register file access time of 3 cycles. Therefore, the obvious method for reducing the IQ-EX latency is to move the register file access out of this path and replace it with a register cache. Register caches are small, generally on the order of 16 to 32 entries. Given their size, they can be placed close to the functional units. The size and placement reduce register access delays and transfer latencies, allowing a register access latency of one cycle in the general case. This effectively shrinks the IQ-EX latency from 5 cycles to 3 cycles, resulting in a shorter load resolution loop delay and less wasted work on a load miss.

A register cache contains a subset of all registers; hence a register cache, unlike a register file, can suffer from operand misses. The data hazard resulting from not knowing whether the operand will hit or miss in the register cache introduces a new loose loop to the pipeline, called the *operand resolution loop*. The operand resolution loop has a high frequency of loop occurrence — every instruction that has input operands is a loop generating instruction. Since the number of mis-speculation events is the product of the frequency of loop occurrence and the mis-speculation rate, even a small operand miss rate is detrimental to performance. If the number of register cache misses is high enough, then the amount of work wasted due to register cache misses can offset the savings from a reduced IQ-EX latency.

Register caches must be small to reduce access latency. Given that they are fully associative structures, they need to be on the order of 16 to 32 entries to achieve a single cycle access latency. A small register cache results in a high miss rate for our base architecture because determining which values to insert into the cache is a difficult task. Register values are frequently used just once [6], so many of the entries in the register cache may never be accessed if they are forwarded to the consumer through the forwarding buffer. Also, the number of cycles between the availability of operands for an instruction can be quite large in a wide issue, out-of-order machine.

Figure 6 shows the cumulative distribution function for the time (in cycles) between when an instruction's first operand is available, and when the second operand is available for *turb3d*. The time is zero for instructions with only one operand. 25% of all instructions have 25 cycles or more between the availability of operands. In fact, even the 9 cycle forwarding buffer in our base architecture only covers about 50% of all instructions. Other benchmarks show similar characteristics. A register cache may need to be of comparable size to a register file to hold all the relevant information for the instructions in flight.

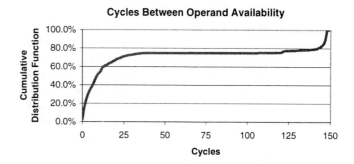

Figure 6. Cumulative distribution function of the time in cycles between when an instruction's first operand and second operand is available. Data is shown for *turb3d*.

To increase the capacity of the register cache without increasing the access latency, the DRA takes advantage of the clustered architecture of the base model and places a small register cache called a *clustered register cache* (CRC) within each functional unit cluster. There are eight CRCs, each with 16 entries. This effectively increases the size of the register cache to 128 entries.

To more effectively manage the entries in the CRC, the DRA does one of two things. First, each CRC only stores those operands required by instructions assigned to that functional unit cluster. An instruction is assigned a functional unit cluster when it is decoded. Therefore, the DRA may direct the operands for this instruction to a specific cluster. Note that the same operand may be stored in multiple CRCs if it is consumed by instructions assigned to different clusters.

Second, each CRC only stores operands for a consuming instruction that is unlikely to get the operand through other means. To achieve this, we note that one can classify operands by how a consuming instruction gets those operands. The three classes are: *completed operands*, *timely operands*, and *cached* operands.

Completed operands are already in the register file when a consuming instruction is decoded and can be read at any time. These operands tend to be associated with global registers such as the global pointer and stack pointer. However, if a register is alive long enough, it can be a completed operand for many instructions. The DRA reads completed operands from the register file in the DEC-IQ path — after the register is renamed and before the instruction is inserted into the IQ. When the instruction enters the IQ, the operand is inserted into the payload for retrieval when the instruction issues. Accessing the register file out of the issue path was proposed by Tomasulo and others [13].

Timely operands are those where the consumer of the operand is issued not long after the producer of the operand has issued. The forwarding buffer already inherent to our base model handles this category of operands by storing all values computed in the last 9 cycles.

Cached operands are those that are inserted into the CRCs. To reduce the capacity pressure on the register cache, only those operands who have consuming instructions that neither pre-read the operand from the register file nor read it from the forwarding buffer are placed in the register cache. This can happen when an instruction's operand is not in the register file for pre-read, nor does the instruction issue soon enough after its producer to get the value from the forwarding buffer.

Note that the classification of an operand is determined by where the consuming instruction got the operand. Thus, an operand with many consumers could be a completed, timely, and cached operand for each different instruction.

5 DRA Implementation

In our proposed architecture, operands are delivered to the functional units in one of 4 ways.

- Pre-read from the register file: If the operand(s) exists in the register file at decode time, (i.e. a completed operand), it is pre-read from the register file and sent to the IQ.

- Read from the forwarding logic: The base pipeline has 9 stages of forwarding logic to handle requests for timely operands that were produced in the previous 9 cycles.

- Read from the CRC: CRC lookup happens in parallel with the lookup in the forwarding buffer. There is a 16 entry CRC in each of the eight functional unit clusters that provides cached operands.

- Read from register file on an operand miss: If, during execution, the operand is not available through any of the means above, then the operand misses. A miss signal is sent to the register file. The operand is read and delivered to the IQ payload where it waits for the instruction to reissue. This is the recovery path resulting from a mis-speculation on the operand resolution loop.

The hardware for this scheme is shown in Figure 7, and consists of a *register pre-read filtering table* (RPFT) combined with one *cluster register cache* (CRC) and one *insertion table* for each functional-unit cluster. This is in addition to structures that already exist in our base model, specifically one forwarding buffer per cluster, and a monolithic register file.

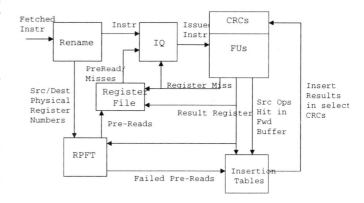

Figure 7. Distributed register algorithm (DRA) block diagram.

5.1 Cluster Register Cache (CRC)

There are 8 functional unit clusters in our base architecture, and there is a CRC associated with each cluster. Each CRC is placed close to it's functional unit cluster to reduce wire delays. Our studies show that a 16 entry CRC is more than adequate to meet our needs. Since only one instruction per cycle executes in a functional unit cluster, only 2 read ports are required per CRC. However, 8 write ports are needed to handle the maximum number of register values computed per cycle. The CRC, similar to the forwarding buffer, uses a fully associative lookup requiring the use of a CAM structure.

The CRCs use a simple FIFO mechanism to manage insertion and removal of entries. A more complex mechanism would be cumbersome and unnecessary because most register values are only read once before being overwritten [6]. We modeled a few mechanisms that had almost perfect knowledge of which values were needed, but the performance improvement over our simple FIFO scheme was negligible. Furthermore, register cache capacity pressure is reduced by filtering the operands that get inserted in the CRC.

Register cache insertions are filtered in one of two ways. First, only the CRC associated with the functional unit cluster an instruction will execute on receives the input register operands for that instruction. Our base model uses clustered issuing logic similar to the Alpha 21264, and instructions are slotted to a particular functional unit cluster (or arbiter according to the 21264 nomenclature) at the time of decode. Therefore, it's known at decode which source operands are required in each functional unit cluster. Second, only those operands that have consumers that have not read the operand when it leaves the forwarding buffer get inserted into the CRC's. This means that if all consumers of an operand either pre-read it from the register file or receive the value from the forwarding buffer, then the value is not stored in any CRCs.

The base architecture already contains the logic to determine the functional unit cluster an instruction will execute on. However, the second filtering mechanism, determining whether the operand is procured from the register file or the forwarding buffer, requires additional hardware. Two new structures, the *register pre-read filtering table (RPFT)* and the *insertion table*, address these issues.

5.2 Register Pre-read Filtering Table (RPFT)

The RPFT stores information about the validity of the registers. It has one bit associated with each physical register. When the bit is set, it indicates that the register is valid in the register file. The operand stored in that register is a completed operand and can be pre-read prior to issue. The bit is set when an operand is written back to the register file. If the bit is clear, the producer of that operand is in flight, and the operand is not in the register file. The bit is cleared when the renamer notifies the RPFT that it has allocated a physical register to be written by an instruction.

After the register renaming stage, the physical register numbers for an instruction's source operands are sent to the RPFT. If the bit for a register is set, then the value in the register file is pre-read and forwarded to the payload portion of the IQ. If the bit is clear, the source register number for the input operand is sent to the insertion table associated with the functional unit cluster the instruction is slotted to.

The number of 1-bit entries in the RPFT equals the number of physical registers in the machine. The structure requires 16 read ports, and 8 write ports to handle 8-wide issue. Weiss and Smith used a similar algorithm to work around stalling instructions when they saw a true dependency [13]. In their algorithm, a bit set in the scoreboard indicated a true dependency on an un-computed result, and the dependent instruction was placed in the reservation stations along with the register identifiers for the un-computed operands.

5.3 Insertion Table

There is an insertion table associated with each CRC and functional unit cluster. It keeps count of the number of outstanding consumers of an operand that will execute on the functional unit cluster and that have not yet read the operand. The number of entries in an insertion table is dictated by the number of physical registers. Each entry is 2 bits wide. A non-zero entry value indicates that the operand is needed by instructions assigned to the insertion table's functional unit cluster. An entry is incremented when the insertion table receives the source register number from the RPFT, and it is decremented every time the associated register is read from the forwarding buffer.

With 2 bits per entry, the insertion table entries can indicate a maximum of 3 consumers for each operand per cluster. However, most operands have few consumers, so 2 bits is more than adequate.

When an operand is written back (from the forwarding buffer) to the register file, a copy is also sent to each of the insertion tables. If the insertion table entry associated with the operand is zero, it is highly likely that there are not any consumers of this operand in-flight and the value is discarded. For all functional unit clusters where the insertion table entry for an operand is non-zero, there are consumers in flight. The operand is written into the CRCs for those functional units and the insertion table entries are cleared. Note that operands can reside in multiple functional unit clusters as long as there are outstanding consumers for that operand that will execute on each of those clusters.

5.4 Misses

Mis-speculations occur on the operand resolution loop because the DRA, as implemented, does not guarantee a successful pre-read or a hit in the forwarding buffer or CRCs. Misses happen for one of two reasons. Operands may get dropped from the CRCs before being read due to capacity pressure and the FIFO replacement policy. Operands may also not get inserted into the CRCs because we saturate at 3 consumers per operand. This occurs when an operand has more than 3 consumers slotted to the same functional unit. For each operand hit in the forwarding buffer, the count for that operand in the insertion tables gets decremented by one. If there are at least 3 hits in the forwarding buffer on a single operand, then the count in the functional unit's insertion table goes to zero and indicates no consumers are in-flight that need this operand. Thus, the operand does not get inserted in the CRC, and any subsequent consumers executing on the same functional unit take an operand miss.

If one (or both) of an instruction's operands miss in the CRC or forwarding buffer, an invalid input is returned in place of the real value, and the instruction produces an invalid operand. When this happens, signals are sent to both the register file and the IQ. The correct input operand value is read from the register file and sent to the IQ, and the IQ readies the instruction for reissue. The instruction is ready to reissue as soon as the operand reaches the IQ payload. In addition to reissuing the instruction with a missing operand, all instructions in the dependency tree that have already issued will also signal the need to reissue as soon as they read the invalid operand resulting from a miss in the CRC. The logic to manage mis-speculations on the operand resolution loop is similar to the logic that manages mis-speculations on the load resolution loop. The only additional hardware required is the wiring to stall the front end of the pipeline while the missing operands are read from the register file and forwarded to the instruction payload.

5.5 Stale Register Values

The CRC associated with each functional unit is implemented as a simple FIFO structure to avoid the problems associated with managing a complex insertion and replacement algorithm. As a result, stale data needs to be accounted for in the CRC in order to guarantee correctness. Although rare, a CRC could have stale operands if there is not much pressure on the structure. A physical register may be reallocated while the old register value resides in the CRC.

This case is handled when the register is reallocated. The destination register numbers are sent to the RPFT, and these are also forwarded to all CRCs. If the CRC contains an operand for a reallocated register, then that entry is invalidated. Note that there are many cycles between when the CRC receives the reallocated registers and when the register is written with a new value. Therefore, we have enough time to invalidate the entries in the CRC. An alternate method would time out the operands in each CRC after a certain period of time.

6 Results

The basic premise behind the DRA is that we remove the expensive register file access from the IQ-EX stage and overlap it with part of the DEC-IQ stage. By doing so, we remove latency from a critical portion of the pipeline and possibly increase the latency in other portions of the pipeline.

In our base processor model, moving the register file access reduces the IQ-EX latency from 5 to 3 cycles while the DEC-IQ latency remains the same. Register file lookup takes 3 of the 5 IQ-EX cycles. However, one of these cycles is still required for accessing the forwarding buffer and the CRCs, resulting in a 3 cycle IQ-EX latency. In the DEC-IQ portion, the physical register numbers are available at the end of the second cycle, providing 3 cycles for accessing the register file and sending the data to the IQ payload. Given

that accessing the register file and driving data to the functional units takes 3 cycles in the base machine, we should be able to drive data to the payload in the same time. Hence, the DEC-IQ portion remains 5 cycles.

We also ran experiments with longer register file access latencies of 5 and 7 cycles to determine the impact the DRA has on potential future designs. In the case of a 5 cycle access latency, the base architecture's IQ-EX latency is 7 cycles. The DRA implementation removes the 5 cycle register file access latency, but needs 1 of these cycles to access the forwarding buffer and CRCs. Thus, it shrinks the IQ-EX stage to 3 cycles. The DEC-IQ latency increases by 2 to a total of 7 cycles. This is because the register renaming is complete after the 2nd cycle of DEC-IQ, and it still takes 5 cycles to access the register file and deliver the operands to the IQ. For the 7 cycle register read latency, the IQ-EX stage remains at 3 cycles and the DEC-IQ stage increases to 9 cycles.

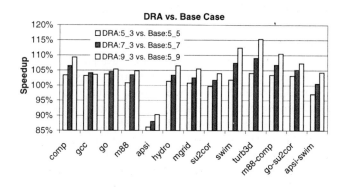

Figure 8. Performance improvements with the DRA relative to the base architecture. The **DRA:D1_D2 vs. Base:B1_B2** syntax shows the pipeline latencies for each configuration. D1 and D2 are the latencies from DEC-IQ and IQ-EX, respectively, for the DRA. B1 and B2 represent the same latencies for the base configuration. Both configurations have the same register file access latency. Note the graph starts at 85%.

We modeled the architecture described using the ASIM [4] simulation infrastructure with a very detailed, cycle level, execution driven processor model. ASIM forces consideration of logic delays by mimicking hardware restrictions within the processor model. This makes it very difficult to model instantaneous, global knowledge over the entire model. In hardware, for example, there is a non-unit delay between the IQ and the functional units. Therefore, there is a lag between the time events occur in the functional units and the time the IQ makes decisions based upon these events. ASIM enforces propagation delay restrictions in the simulated model, and does not allow us to make decisions based upon global knowledge that may lead to inaccuracies in our simulations.

Figure 8 shows the results using the DRA for the three different register access latencies. Performance is shown as speedup of the DRA implementation relative to a non-DRA implementation. For example, the first bar, **DRA:5_3 vs Base:5_5**, shows the relative speedup of a DRA implementation with a 5 cycle DEC-IQ latency and a 3 cycle IQ-EX latency relative to a base pipeline with no DRA and a 5 cycle latency for both DEC-IQ and IQ-EX. Both configurations have a 3 cycle register file access latency. The second and third bar in each cluster shows similar information for a 5 and 7 cycle register file access latency, respectively.

With the exception of *apsi* and *apsi-swim*, performance improves with a DRA for all configurations. We see an improvement of up to 4%, 9% and 15% for register file access latencies of 3, 5, and 7 cycles, respectively. Performance improves not only because we shift the cycles from IQ-EX to DEC-IQ, but because we also shorten the pipeline by 2 cycles in each case. Those programs that are the most sensitive to pipeline lengths (*compress, m88ksim-compress*) and/or IQ-EX latencies (*swim, turb3d*) benefit the most.

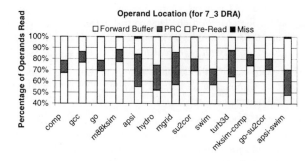

Figure 9. Hit and miss rates for operand values. Hits are further segmented into hits from register pre-read, hits from the forwarding buffer, and hits from the DRA. Numbers are shown for the 7_3 DRA case, i.e., 7 cycles from DEC_IQ, 3 cycles from IQ_EX, and a 5 cycle register file access latency. Note the graph starts at 40%.

The reason performance degrades is because of mis-speculations on the operand resolution loop. Not only will the instruction that suffered an operand miss reissue, but all of the instructions in the dependency tree that have issued will also reissue. Figure 9 shows that performance is very sensitive to operand miss rate. The figure shows the hit and miss rates for register operand values. Hits are further segmented into hits in the register file during pre-reading, hits in the forwarding buffer, and hits in the CRCs. On average, more than half the operands are read from the forwarding buffer. The remaining operand reads are distributed equally between being pre-read from the register file, and read from the CRCs. Most benchmarks have an operand miss rate well

under 1%, and do not suffer a performance impact from operand resolution loop mis-speculations. However, even a small miss rate of 1.5% can have a substantial impact on performance, as *apsi* shows. In this case, the work wasted due to mis-speculations on the operand resolution loop outweighs any benefit resulting from a shorter pipeline.

There are two reasons why *apsi* suffers a 10%-14% performance loss. First, there is the relatively high miss rate of 1.5%. This, combined with a high frequency of loop occurrence, results in a large number of reissued instructions and much wasted work. Second, *apsi* is not particularly sensitive to pipeline lengths as shown in Figure 4. A 12 cycle increase in pipeline length only degraded performance by 9%. Therefore we gain little by shortening the pipeline, and suffer the penalty of high operand miss rates and instruction reissue. The combination of the two situations contributes to the performance loss in *apsi*.

7 Related Work

Hierarchical register files are not a new idea. The Cray-1 had two sets of two-level register files. More recently, Zalamea et. al. explored two-level hierarchical register file designs[17]. However, in both cases, compiler support was required to explicitly move values between different levels of the register file.

Cruz et. al. proposed a hierarchical register file design that does not require compiler support [6]. They use a single register file with a highly ported upper-level portion that acts as a register cache, and a lightly ported lower-level that acts as a register file. The design proposed by Cruz has a number of shortcomings for our architecture. First of all, they use mechanisms to manage the entries in their register cache that require current information from the instruction scheduling unit. However, given the latencies in our pipeline, it is impossible to gather this knowledge and act on it in a timely manner. Another problem with the design is the non-deterministic delay for instruction execution that depends on whether the operands are attained from the register cache or register file. Due to the non-deterministic delay, the dependents of an instruction cannot be scheduled with certainty. If an instruction's dependents are issued with the assumption that the instruction will "hit" in the register cache, then the dependent instructions must stall if the instruction ends up accessing the slower register file. Stalling instructions which have been issued entails complex control which can add to the critical path of the processor [9]. Finally, the lower-level register file design has fewer ports than the number of functional units. Hence, there is no mechanism to handle the case where all instructions issued miss in the register cache. Even though this is an unlikely event, it must be accounted for.

8 Summary and Conclusions

In this paper, we explored micro-architectural loops resulting from hazards in the pipeline. In particular, we focused on a subset of micro-architectural loops, called loose loops, that impact processor performance by forcing the pipeline to stall or speculate until the loop resolves. We showed that the performance impact of loose loops is related to the pipeline length and configuration. In particular, performance is especially sensitive to the length of the issue to execute section of the pipeline due to the load resolution loop. Reducing the latency of issue to execute improves performance even as the overall length of the pipeline remains the same.

Based on our analysis, we proposed the the DRA as a way of reducing the issue to execute latency. The DRA moves the time consuming register file access out of the issue to execute path and replaces it with the clustered register cache (CRC). Using a very detailed architectural simulator, we showed performance improvements of up to 4% to 15%, depending on the pipeline configuration, with the DRA.

Much of our future work focuses on improving the design of the DRA. For example, retaining pre-read operands in the instruction payload requires a large amount of hardware. Therefore, a more efficient design might be to forward the pre-read values to each cluster to be held in another register cache close to the functional units. In addition, we'd like to investigate a more efficient method of invalidating stale entries in the CRCs. Also, further analysis of benchmarks like *apsi* needs to be done to determine how we can reduce or eliminate the performance loss.

Acknowledgments

The authors would like to acknowledge the following individuals for their contribution to this work: Matt Reilly for his insightful comments and corrections, Chaun-Hua Chang for clarifying the register file design, and Dean Tullsen for reviewing the paper. We would also like to thank the reviewers for their comments and suggestions.

References

[1] Vikas Agarwal, M. S. Hrishikesh, Stephen W. Keckler, and Doug Burger. Clock rate versus IPC: The end of the road for conventional microarchitectures. In *Proceedings of the 27th Annual International Symposium on Computer Architecture*, pages 248–259, Vancouver, British Columbia, June 12–14, 2000. IEEE Computer Society and ACM SIGARCH.

[2] R. I. Bahar and S. Manne. Power and energy savings via pipeline balancing. In *Proceedings of the 28th Annual International Symposium on Computer Architecture*, Gotenburg, Sweden, July 2001. IEEE Computer Society and ACM SIGARCH.

[3] Compaq Computer Corporation. *Alpha 21264 Microprocessor Hardware Reference Manual*, July 1999.

[4] Compaq Computer Corporation. *The ASIM Manual*, August 2000.

[5] Compaq Computer Corporation. *Alpha 21464 Internal Design Specification, Rev. 0*, 2001.

[6] José-Lorenzo Cruz, Antonio González, Mateo Valero, and Nigel P. Topham. Multiple-banked register file architectures. In *Proceedings of the 27th Annual International Symposium on Computer Architecture*, pages 316–325, Vancouver, British Columbia, June 12–14, 2000. IEEE Computer Society and ACM SIGARCH.

[7] Digital Equipment Corporation. *Alpha 21164 Microprocessor Hardware Reference Manual*, 1994.

[8] Digital Equipment Corporation. *DECchip 21064 and DECchip 21064A Alpha AXP Microprocessors Hardware Reference Manual*, 1994.

[9] John H. Edmondson, Paul I. Rubinfeld, Peter J. Bannon, Bradley J. Benschneider, Debra Bernstein, Ruben W. Castelino, Elizaabeth M. Cooper, Daniel E. Dever, Dale R. Donchin, Timothy C. Fischer, Anil K. Jain, Shekhar Mehta, Jeanne E. Meyer, Ronald P. Preston, Vidya Rajagopalan, Chandrasekhara Somanathan, Scott A. Taylor, and Gilbert M. Wolrich. The internal organization of the Alpha 21164, a 300-mhz 64-bit quad-issue CMOS RISC microprocessor. *Digital Technical Journal*, 7(1):119–135, 1995.

[10] Joel Emer. Ev8: the post-ultimate alpha. Keynote at International Conference on Parallel Architecture and Compilation Techniques, September 2001.

[11] Keith I. Farkas, Norman P. Jouppi, and Paul Chow. Register file design considerations in dynamically scheduled processors. In *Proceedings of the Second International Symposium on High Performance Computer Architecture*. IEEE, January 1996.

[12] G. Hinton, D. Sager, M. Upton, D. Boggs, D. Carmean, A. Kyker, and P. Roussel. *The Microarchitecture of the Pentium4 Processor*. Intel Corporation, February 2001.

[13] M. Johnson. In *Superscalar Microprocessor Design*, 1991.

[14] R. E. Kessler, E. J. McLellan, and D. A. Webb. The alpha 21264 microprocessor architecture. In *Proceedings of the International Conference on Computer Design*, October 1998.

[15] M. Reilly. Lost cycles due to register port contention. In *htttp://segsrv.shr.cpqcorp.net/arana/qbox/register_cache2.html*. Compaq Computer Corporation, February 1998.

[16] J. S. Seng, D. M. Tullsen, and G. Z. N. Cai. Power-sensitive multithreaded architecture. In *Proceedings of the International Conference on Computer Design*, October 2000.

[17] J. Zalamea, J. Llosa, E. Ayguade, and M. Valero. Two-level hierarchical register file organization for VLIW processors. In *Proceedings of the 33rd Annual IEEE/ACM International Symposium on Microarchitecture (Micro-33)*, pages 137–146, Los Alamitos, CA, December 10–13 2000. IEEE Computer Society.

Evaluation of a Multithreaded Architecture for Cellular Computing

Călin Caşcaval   José G. Castaños   Luis Ceze   Monty Denneau   Manish Gupta

Derek Lieber   José E. Moreira   Karin Strauss

Henry S. Warren, Jr.

IBM Thomas J. Watson Research Center

Yorktown Heights, NY 10598-0218

{cascaval,castanos,lceze,denneau,mgupta,lieber,jmoreira,kstrauss,hankw}@us.ibm.com

Abstract

Cyclops is a new architecture for high performance parallel computers being developed at the IBM T. J. Watson Research Center. The basic cell of this architecture is a single-chip SMP system with multiple threads of execution, embedded memory, and integrated communications hardware. Massive intra-chip parallelism is used to tolerate memory and functional unit latencies. Large systems with thousands of chips can be built by replicating this basic cell in a regular pattern. In this paper we describe the Cyclops architecture and evaluate two of its new hardware features: memory hierarchy with flexible cache organization and fast barrier hardware. Our experiments with the STREAM benchmark show that a particular design can achieve a sustainable memory bandwidth of 40 GB/s, equal to the peak hardware bandwidth and similar to the performance of a 128-processor SGI Origin 3800. For small vectors, we have observed in-cache bandwidth above 80 GB/s. We also show that the fast barrier hardware can improve the performance of the Splash-2 FFT kernel by up to 10%. Our results demonstrate that the Cyclops approach of integrating a large number of simple processing elements and multiple memory banks in the same chip is an effective alternative for designing high performance systems.

1. Introduction

With the continuing trends in processor and memory evolution, overall system performance is more and more limited by the performance of the memory subsystem. The traditional solution to this problem, usually referred to as the von Neumann bottleneck, is to design ever larger and deeper memory hierarchies. This results in complex designs where most of the real estate is devoted to storing and moving data, instead of actual data processing. Even within the processing units themselves, significant resources are used to reduce the impact of memory hierarchy and functional unit latencies. Approaches like out-of-order execution, multiple instruction issue, and deep pipelines have been successful in the past. However, the average number of machine cycles to execute an instruction has not improved significantly in the past few years. This indicates that we are reaching a point of diminishing returns as measured by the increase in performance obtained from additional transistors and power.

This paper describes the Cyclops architecture, a new approach to effectively use the transistor and power budget of a piece of silicon. The primary reasoning behind Cyclops is that computer architecture and organization has become too complicated and it is time to simplify. The Cyclops architecture is founded on three main principles: (i) the integration of processing logic and memory in the same piece of silicon; (ii) the use of massive intra-chip parallelism to tolerate latencies; and (iii) a cellular approach to building large systems.

The integration of memory and logic in the same chip results in a simpler memory hierarchy with higher bandwidth and lower latencies. Although this alleviates the memory latency problem, access to data still takes multiple machine cycles. The Cyclops solution is to populate the chip with a large number of thread units. Each thread unit behaves like a simple, single-issue, in-order processor. Expensive resources, like floating-point units and caches, are shared by groups of threads to ensure high utilization. The thread units are independent. If a thread stalls on a memory reference or on the result of an operation, other threads can continue to make progress. The performance of each individual thread is not particularly high, but the aggregate chip performance is much better than a conventional design with an equivalent number of transistors. Large, scalable systems can be built with a cellular approach using the Cyclops chip as a building block [2]. The chip is viewed as a cell that can be replicated as many times as necessary, with the cells interconnected in a regular pattern through communication links provided in each chip.

Cyclops is a research project and the architecture is still evolving. In this paper we describe one particular configuration that we have evaluated. We shall focus on two features that we have demonstrated to improve performance substantially: (i) the memory hierarchy, particularly the novel cache organization, and (ii) the mechanism for fast synchronization. The current design point for Cyclops calls for 128 thread execution units. These thread units are organized in groups of four, called *quads*. Each quad includes one floating-point unit, shared by the four thread units in the quad, and a 16 KB cache unit. Main memory is organized in 16 independent banks of 512 KB each, for a total of 8 MB, and it is shared by all threads in the chip. We want to emphasize that these numbers represent just one of many configurations possible. The total numbers of processing units and memory modules are mainly driven by silicon area, so as to maximize floating-point performance. The degrees of sharing for floating-point and cache units were selected based on instruction mixes observed in current systems [8]. We continue to study these trade-offs in parallel with the hardware design [3], to obtain the best performance.

Designing an effective cache organization for a large SMP like the Cyclops chip is always a challenge. Conventional approaches to cache coherence, such as snooping and directories, have scalability and cost problems (as measured in silicon area). Our approach consists of a software-controlled, non-uniform access, shared cache system. The threads of execution share the multiple cache units in the chip, but each thread is more tightly coupled to one particular unit. Software controls the placement of data in the cache, allowing high-affinity data (*e.g.*, thread stack) to be placed in the cache unit closer to a particular thread. We evaluate the efficacy and efficiency of the Cyclops memory hierarchy through measurements using the STREAM benchmark.

Likewise, designing effective synchronization mechanisms for large SMPs is a challenge. Our initial experiments with memory-based synchronization demonstrated that software barriers for a large number of threads could be very slow, with a degrading performance on important benchmarks [4]. These measurements motivated the development of dedicated hardware barriers in the chip. We evaluate the performance improvements resulting from these fast barriers through measurements using the FFT kernel from the Splash-2 benchmark suite.

The rest of this paper is organized as follows. Section 2 presents a detailed description of the Cyclops architecture. Section 3 describes our simulation environment and presents performance results for the STREAM [11] and Splash-2 FFT [22] benchmarks. Section 4 discusses related work. Finally, Section 5 presents our conclusions and discusses plans for future work.

2. The Cyclops architecture

The architecture of the Cyclops chip is a hierarchical design, shown in Figure 1, in which threads share resources at different levels of the hierarchy. The main idea behind the design is to integrate in one chip as many concurrent threads of execution as possible. Instead of hiding latencies, through out-of-order or speculative execution, Cyclops tolerates latencies through massive parallelism. With this design each thread unit is simpler and expensive resources, such as floating-point units and caches, are shared between different threads.

The architecture itself does not specify the number of components at each level of the hierarchy. In this section we describe a possible implementation of the Cyclops architecture with components determined by silicon area constraints and most common instruction type percentages. We expect these numbers to change as manufacturing technology improves. Also, the balance between different resources might change as a consequence of particular target applications and as our understanding of the different trade-offs improves.

In this paper we consider a 32-bit architecture for Cyclops. The proprietary instruction set architecture (ISA) consists of about 60 instruction types, and follows a 3-operand, load/store RISC design. The decision of using a new simplified ISA bears on the goal of a simpler design. For designing the Cyclops ISA we selected the most widely used instructions in the PowerPC architecture. Instructions were added to enable multithreaded functionality, such as atomic memory operations and synchronization instructions.

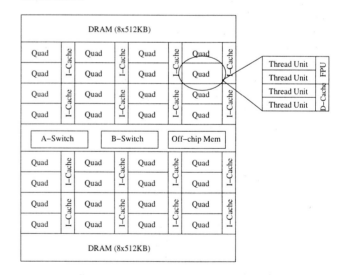

Figure 1. Cyclops chip block diagram.

We evaluate a design with the following characteristics: 128 thread units, each unit containing a register file (64 32-

bit single precision registers, that can be paired for double precision operations), a program counter, a fixed point ALU, and a sequencer. The thread units are very simple computing processors that execute instructions in program order (completion may be out-of-order). Most instructions execute in one cycle. Each thread can issue an instruction at every cycle, if resources are available and there are no dependences with previous instructions. If two threads try to issue instructions using the same shared resource, one thread is selected as winner in a round-robin scheme to prevent starvation. If an instruction cannot be issued, the thread unit stalls until all resources become available, either through the completion of previously issued instructions, or through the release of resources held by other threads.

Groups of four thread units form a *quad*. The threads in a quad share a floating-point unit (FPU) and a data cache. Only the threads within a quad can use that quad's FPU, while any thread can access data stored in any of the data caches. The memory hierarchy has non-uniform access latencies. Thus, threads have faster access to their local data cache than to a remote cache. The floating-point unit consists of three functional units: an adder, a multiplier, and a divide and square root unit. Threads can dispatch a floating point addition and a floating point multiplication at every cycle. The FPU can complete a floating point multiply-add (FMA) every cycle. With a clock cycle of 500 MHz, in .18μm CMOS technology, it achieves a peak performance of 1 GFlops per FPU, for a total chip performance of 32 GFlops.

2.1. Memory hierarchy

A large part of the silicon area in the Cyclops design is dedicated to memory. This memory is distributed on two hierarchical levels, main memory and caches for data and instructions, further described in this section.

Our design uses 16 banks of on-chip memory shared between all thread units. Each bank is 512 KB of embedded DRAM, for a total of 8 MB. The banks provide a contiguous address space to the threads. Accesses to the memory banks go through a memory switch, shown in Figure 2, thus the latency to any bank is uniform. Addresses are interleaved to provide higher memory bandwidth. The unit of access is a 32-byte block, and threads accessing two consecutive blocks in the same bank will see a lower latency in burst transfer mode. The physical memory address is 24 bits, giving a maximum addressable memory of 16 MB. The peak bandwidth of the embedded memory is 42 GB/s (64 bytes every 12 cycles, 16 memory banks).

Each of the 16 KB data cache (one per quad) has 64-byte lines and a variable associativity, up to 8-way. The data caches are shared among quads. That is, a thread in a quad can access data in other quads' caches, with lower

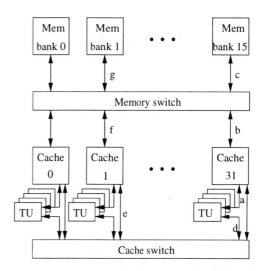

Figure 2. Cyclops memory hierarchy.

latency than going to memory. All remote caches have the same access latency, higher than the local cache access latency, since they are accessed through a common switch, as shown in Figure 2. The peak bandwidth out of the caches is 128 GB/s (8 bytes per cycle, 32 caches).

In the same figure we have marked the paths that a data item will traverse in different scenarios. For example, if a thread unit (TU) in quad 31 accesses data present in its local cache, the data will come through the path marked *a*. For a local cache miss, the request will go through path *a* to the local cache, will propagate to memory following the path *bg*, and come to the thread following *gba*. A remote cache request for cache 1 will go through the path *de*. A remote cache hit into cache 1 will come through *ed*, while a remote cache miss will follow the path *fcfed*.

The hardware does not implement any cache coherence mechanism to deal with multiple copies of a memory line in different caches. However, the architecture supports an entire spectrum of access schemes, from no coherence at all to coherent caches shared at different levels. The levels range from sharing across the entire chip down to sharing within each quad. Any memory location can be placed in any cache under software control. The same physical address can be mapped to different caches depending on the logical address. Since a physical address is limited to 24 bits, we use the upper 8 bits of the 32-bit effective address to encode cache placement information. The encoding, presented in Table 1, allows a thread to specify in which cache the data accessed is mapped. We call this *interest group* encoding, and it works as follows: the *q* bits in the first column in Table 1 specify a number that defines one set of caches, shown in the second column of the table. If the set contains more than one member, the hardware will select one of the caches in the set, utilizing a scrambling function

Table 1. Interest group encoding

Encoding	Selected Caches	Comments
0b000 0 0 0 0 0		thread's own
$0b00q_4q_3q_2q_1q_0 1$	$\{0\}, \{1\}, ... \{31\}$	exactly one
$0b00q_3q_2q_1q_0 1\ 0$	$\{0,1\}, \{2,3\}, ... \{30,31\}$	one of a pair
$0b00q_2q_1q_0 1\ 0\ 0$	$\{0,1,2,3\}, ... \{28,29,30,31\}$	one of four
$0b00q_1q_0 1\ 0\ 0\ 0$	$\{0, ... 8\}, ... \{24, ... 31\}$	one of eight
$0b00q_0 1\ 0\ 0\ 0\ 0$	$\{0,1, ... 15\}, \{16,17, ... 31\}$	one of sixteen
0b001 0 0 0 0 0	$\{0,1, ... 31\}$	one of all

so that all the caches are uniformly utilized. The function is completely deterministic and relies only on the address such that references to the same effective address get mapped to the same cache.

If all references use the interest group 0b00100000, the caches behave as a single 512 KB coherent unit shared across the chip. This is the default used by our system software. Each piece of data is mapped only to a single cache. A drawback of this scheme is that given a uniform distribution of accesses, only one out of 32 accesses will be in the local cache. The other non-zero interest groups partition the caches in different ways, from two units of 256 KB each to 32 units of 16 KB each. In each of those cases, one effective address identifies one, and only one, cache location. Hence, the cache coherence problem does not arise when using those interest groups. For example, an interest group of 0b00010001, indicates that the data should be cached in cache number 8, while an interest group of 0b00010010 indicates either cache 7 or cache 8. When using the interest group zero (0b00000000), each thread accessing that data will bring it into its own cache, resulting in a potentially non-coherent system. The cache selected depends on the accessing thread. This means that the same memory location can be mapped to multiple caches. Without coherence support in hardware, it is up to user level code to guarantee that this potential replication is done correctly.

An important use of this flexible cache organization is to exploit locality and shared read-only data. For example, data frequently accessed by a thread, such as stack data or constants, can be cached in the local cache by using the appropriate interest group. The same constant could be cached in different caches by threads in separate quads by using interest group zero and a physical address that points to the same memory location.

A data cache can also be partitioned with a granularity of 2 KB (one set) so that a portion of it can be used as an addressable fast memory, for streaming data or temporary work areas. The threads sharing a data cache have to agree on a certain organization for a particular application. This feature can potentially result in higher performance for applications that are coded to use this fast memory directly, instead of relying on the dynamic, and often hard to control, cache behavior.

Instruction caches are 32 KB, 8-way set-associative with 64-byte line size. One instruction cache is shared by 2 quads. Unlike the data caches, the instruction caches are private to the quad pair. In addition, to improve instruction fetching, each thread has a Prefetch Instruction Buffer (PIB) that can hold up to 16 instructions.

Some applications require more memory than is available on the Cyclops chip. To support these applications, the design includes optional off-chip memory ranging in size from 128 MB to 2 GB. In the current design the off-chip memory is not directly addressable. Blocks of data, 1 KB in size, are transferred between the external memory and the embedded memory much like disk operations.

2.2. Communication interface

The Cyclops chip provides six input and six output links. These links allow a chip to be directly connected in a three dimensional topology (mesh or torus). The links are 16-bit wide and operate at 500 MHz, giving a maximum I/O bandwidth of 12 GB/s. In addition, a seventh link can be used to connect to a host computer. These links can be used to build larger systems without additional hardware. However, this is not focus of this paper.

2.3. Synchronization primitives

An additional feature of the Cyclops chip is the fast interthread hardware barrier, provided through a special purpose register (SPR). It is actually implemented as a wired OR for all the threads on the chip. Each thread writes its SPR independently, and it reads the ORed value of all the threads' SPRs. The register has 8 bits and we use 2 bits per barrier, thus providing 4 distinct barriers. One of the bits holds the state of the *current* barrier cycle while the other holds the state of the *next* barrier cycle. In one cycle, all threads participating in the barrier initially set their *current* barrier cycle bit to 1. The threads not participating in the barrier leave both bits set to 0. When a thread is ready to enter a barrier, it atomically writes a 0 to the *current* bit, thereby removing its contribution to the current barrier cycle, and a 1 to the *next* bit, thereby initializing the next barrier cycle. Each thread then reads back its register and spins, waiting for the value of the *current* bit to become 0. This will happen when all threads have written a 0 to that bit position in their special purpose registers. Roles are interchanged after each use of the barrier. Because each thread spin-waits on its own register, there is no contention for other chip resources and all threads run at full speed. Performance data for the fast barrier operations are presented in Section 3.3.

3. Experimental results

In this section we describe our simulation environment for executing Cyclops code and evaluating the performance of the Cyclops chip. We also report experiments with two different benchmarks: the STREAM benchmark is used to assess the sustained memory bandwidth and overall performance of the Cyclops chip when executing vector kernels; the FFT kernel from the Splash-2 benchmark suite measures the performance impact of Cyclops' fast barrier mechanism.

3.1. The Cyclops simulation environment

Cyclops executables (kernel, libraries, applications) are currently being generated with a cross-compiler based on the GNU toolkit, re-targeted for the Cyclops instruction set architecture. This cross-compiler supports C, C++, and FORTRAN 77. An architecturally accurate simulator executes instructions from the Cyclops instruction set, modeling resource contention between instructions, and thus estimating the number of cycles each instruction executes. The simulator is parametrized such that different architectural features can be specified when the program runs.

The performance parameters for the simulated architecture are shown in Table 2. The upper section shows instruction latencies, in cycles. The execution column is the number of cycles the functional unit is busy executing the instruction. The additional cycles after which the result becomes available are shown in the latency column. The lower section summarizes the hardware parameters used in simulations.

Table 2. Simulation Parameters.

Instruction type	Execution	Latency
Branches	2	0
Integer multiplication	1	5
Integer divide	33	0
Floating point add, mult. and conv.	1	5
Floating point divide (double prec.)	30	0
Floating point square root (double prec.)	56	0
Floating point multiply-and-add	1	9
Memory operation (local cache hit)	1	6
Memory operation (local cache miss)	1	24
Memory operation (remote cache hit)	1	17
Memory operation (remote cache miss)	1	36
All other operations	1	0

Component	# of units	Params/unit
Threads	128	single issue, in-order, 500 MHz
FPUs	32	1 add, 1 multiply, 1 divide/square root
D-cache	32	16 KB, up to 8-way assoc., 64-byte lines
I-cache	16	32 KB, 8-way assoc., 32-byte lines
Memory	16	512 KB

Each chip runs a resident system kernel, which executes with supervisor privileges. The kernel supports single user, single program, multithreaded applications within each chip. These applications execute in user mode. The kernel exposes a single-address space shared by all threads. Due to the small address space and large number of hardware threads available, no resource virtualization is performed in software: virtual addresses map directly to physical addresses (no paging) and software threads map directly to hardware threads. The kernel does not support preemption (except in debugging mode), scheduling or prioritization. Every software thread is preallocated with a fixed size stack per thread (selected at boot time), resulting in fast thread creation and reuse.

Before going into the detailed analysis of the memory bandwidth and hardware barriers, we present parallel speedups obtained on a subset of the Splash-2 benchmarks (see Figure 3). While not optimized specifically for Cyclops, most of these benchmarks reach appropriate levels of scalability, comparable to those reported in [22].

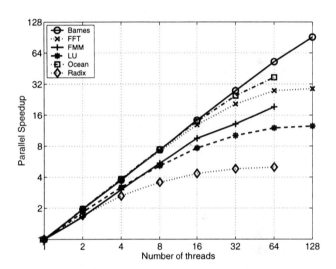

Figure 3. SPLASH2 parallel speedups.

3.2. Experiments with the STREAM Benchmark

The STREAM benchmark [11] is a simple synthetic benchmark program that measures sustainable memory bandwidth and the corresponding computation rate for simple vector kernels. It is intended to characterize the behavior of a system for applications that are limited in performance by the memory bandwidth of the system, rather than by the computational performance of the CPU. The STREAM benchmark consists of four vector kernels: Copy ($c_i = b_i$), Add ($c_i = a_i + b_i$), Scale ($b_i = s \times c_i$), and Triad ($a_i = b_i + s \times c_i$), which operate on vectors a, b, and c of double-precision floating point elements. To investigate the behavior of the memory subsystem, we run the benchmark for different values of n, the vector length. We report the measured bandwidth following the STREAM convention:

315

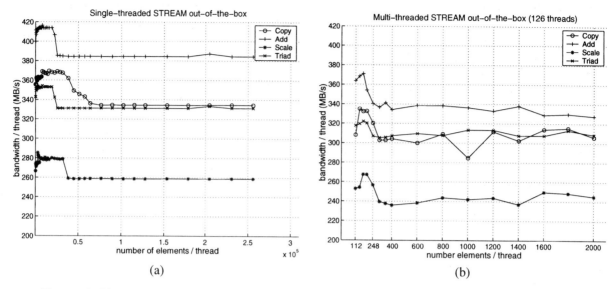

Figure 4. Single- and multi-threaded (126 threads) STREAM out-of-the-box performance

Copy and Scale move $2n$ 64-bit double words per run, whereas Add and Triad move $3n$ double words per run. We perform ten runs per experiment and report the highest performance result. STREAM specifies that each vector size should be at least four times the size of the last level cache or 1 million elements, whatever is larger. Unfortunately, since the main memory of a Cyclops chip is 8 MB we cannot satisfy the million-element requirement. The largest vector size we use is 252,000 elements, or approximately 2 MB. This is four times the size of the combined data caches.

3.2.1. STREAM out-of-the-box.
We started by running the STREAM benchmark directly out-of-the-box as a single-threaded computation. Results as a function of vector size are reported in Figure 4(a). This figure shows the transition between in-cache and out-of-cache modes of operation, as the vector size increases. The transition for Add and Triad happens for smaller vector sizes since those operations use three vectors. Copy and Scale use two vectors each. We also run 126 copies of the benchmark as a multithreaded computation, where each thread performing its own benchmark independently. Although the total number of threads in the chip is 128, only 126 could be used for the benchmark because two of them are reserved for the system. Results, in terms of average memory bandwidth sustained by each thread, as a function of vector size *per thread* are reported in Figure 4(b). Although the curves are not as smooth, we can still observe a transition between in-cache and out-of-cache modes at 200-300 elements per thread.

The thread in the single thread run achieves a higher performance compared to each individual thread from the multithreaded run, as can be seen in Figure 4. This happens because in the multithreaded run, the threads are contending for shared bandwidth. The aggregate bandwidth achieved by the multithreaded version corresponds to the sum of the bandwidths observed for all 126 threads. For large vectors, that bandwidth is from 112 (for Add) to 120 (for Triad) times larger than for the single-threaded case.

3.2.2. Multithreaded STREAM.
We then proceeded to evaluate the parallel execution of a single STREAM benchmark. The code was parallelized by hand using *pthreads*. We perform experiments to measure the impact of loop partitioning, use of local caches, thread allocation policies, and code optimization. We also compare multithreaded STREAM execution in Cyclops to execution on a commercial large-scale shared memory system.

Loop partitioning: Using the Cyclops cache system as a single 512 KB cache, we studied both block and cyclic partitioning of loop iterations among the threads. We note that block and cyclic partitioning of iterations correspond to block and cyclic access patterns for each thread. To avoid all threads hitting the same region of memory at the same time, in the cyclic mode threads were combined in groups of eight, and each group started execution from a different region of the iteration space. By combining threads in groups of eight we allow for reuse of cache lines, which contain eight double-precision elements.

Results for the blocked and cyclic partitioning are shown in Figure 5(a) and (b). For the same vector size, the performance achieved in blocked mode is better than that achieved in cyclic mode. In blocked mode, each thread loads one cache line from main memory to cache and uses the other seven elements later. In this case, each cache line is used by only one thread. In cyclic mode, each cache line is accessed

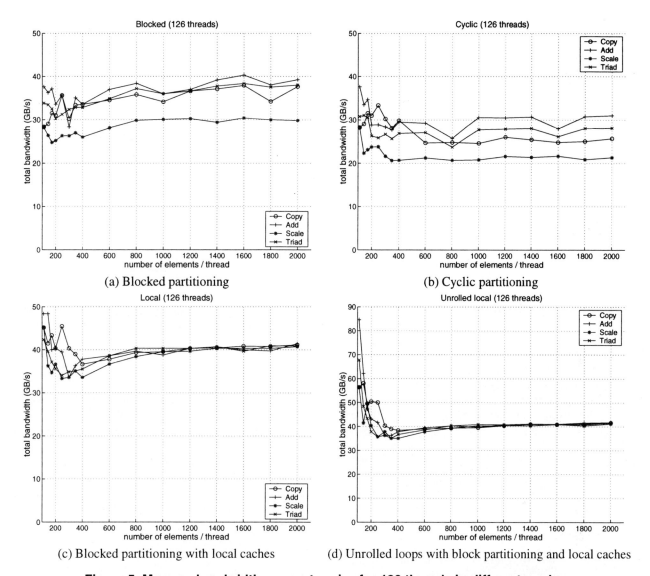

(a) Blocked partitioning

(b) Cyclic partitioning

(c) Blocked partitioning with local caches

(d) Unrolled loops with block partitioning and local caches

Figure 5. Memory bandwidth vs. vector size for 126 threads in different modes.

by the eight threads in a group. The threads access the same cache line at approximately the same time, while the cache line is still being retrieved from main memory. Because of that, each thread will have to wait longer to get the data it needs. Therefore, the average waiting period for the data is greater in cyclic mode.

Taking advantage of local caches: In the measurements reported above, data accessed by one thread is always spread over all quads. As a result, most of the accesses (on the order of $\frac{31}{32}$) are remote cache references. The access time to a local cache is three times faster than the access time to a remote cache (6 cycles *vs.* 17 cycles). To improve performance, we use the interest group feature of Cyclops to force all vector elements accessed by a thread to map into its local cache. False sharing was avoided by mak-

ing the block sizes multiples of cache lines and aligning the blocks to cache line boundaries. For the same vector size, performance with vector blocks mapped to the local cache are better than with distributed caches (Figure 5(c)). For small vectors we observe improvements of up to 60% in total bandwidth. Although the improvements are smaller for large vectors, as performance is limited by the main memory bandwidth, we still see a 30% improvement for Scale.

Thread allocation policies: By default threads are sequentially allocated. That is, threads 0 through 3 are allocated in quad 0, threads 4 through 7 are allocated in quad 1 and so on. We can also use a balanced thread allocation policy. With that policy, threads are allocated cyclically on the quads: threads 0, 32, 64, and 96 in quad 0, threads 1, 33, 65, and 97 in quad 1, and so on. We measured the im-

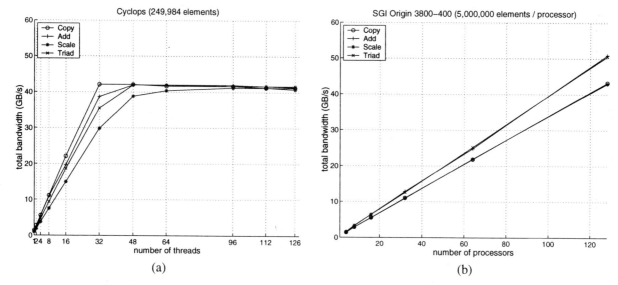

Figure 6. Comparing performance of (a) Cyclops with unrolled loops, local caches, balanced thread allocation policy and block partitioning (vector size is 249,984 elements) *vs.* **that of (b) SGI Origin 3800-400 (vector size is 5,000,000 elements/processor).**

pact of the balanced policy when used with the local cache mode. The balanced policy improves results for local access mode when less than all threads are used. In general, with the balanced policy there is less pressure from the threads to each cache. In the case of Copy, the bandwidth with the balanced policy can be up to 20% higher than with the unbalanced policy. When all threads are being used, the allocation makes no difference because all quads have four threads active.

Code optimization (unrolling): When the original STREAM benchmark code is compiled, the resulting instruction sequence inside the loops is: load the operands, execute the operation and store the result. Since there are dependences between the instructions, a thread has to stall until its load/store operations are completed. Issuing other independent instructions while the load or store instructions execute is desirable. That can be achieved by unrolling the code. We perform a four-way unrolling of the code by hand, because the GNU compiler does not handle it satisfactorily.

Figure 5(d) shows that loop unrolling, combined with blocked partitioning and the use of local caches, improves the overall performance for small vectors, since other useful instructions are being issued while the load/store operations complete. In the case of long vectors, overall performance is constrained by main memory bandwidth, and unrolling does not make a difference.

Comparing with a commercial machine: The best STREAM results for Cyclops, for different numbers of

threads, are compared with the published results for the SGI Origin 3800/400 in Figure 6. We used a large fixed vector length for Cyclops, which forces out-of-cache operation. The published results for the SGI Origin used vector lengths that were a function of the number of processors. We note that the vector sizes for the Origin are much larger, and that Cyclops does not have enough memory to run that size. Nevertheless, it is remarkable that a single Cyclops chip can achieve sustainable memory bandwidth similar to that of a top-of-the-line commercial machine.

3.2.3. Conclusions from the STREAM benchmark tests. It is clear from the measurements that the best performance in STREAM for Cyclops is achieved with a combination of block partitioning of the data, use of local caches, and code optimization. The balanced thread allocation policy also improves performance, but only in combination with a local cache policy and only when not all threads are being used. Unrolling the code helps to improve performance because it increases the number of useful instructions between load/store dependences and thus reduces the number of stalls by a thread. However, for large problem sizes the memory bandwidth becomes the real limiting factor and unrolling loses its impact.

3.3. Hardware barriers validation

We compared the performance of the hardware barrier feature of Cyclops against a software implementation, using the FFT kernel from the Splash-2 [22] benchmark suite. The

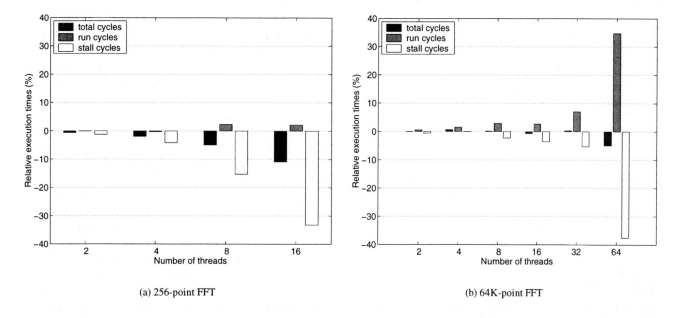

| (a) 256-point FFT | (b) 64K-point FFT |

Figure 7. Hardware *vs.* software barriers in SPLASH2 FFT.

software barriers are a tree based scheme: on entering a barrier a thread first notifies its parent and then spins on a memory location that is written by the thread's parent when all threads have completed the barrier.

Figure 7 shows the performance improvement of the hardware barriers over the software implemented barriers for two input data sizes: a 256-point and a 64K-point FFT. The benchmark requires the number of points per processor to be greater than or equal to the square root of the total number of points, and the number of processors to be a power of two. Because of the first constraint, in the 256-point version the maximum number of threads is 16. Due to the second constraint and the fact that some threads in the Cyclops chip are reserved by the system, the maximum number of threads in the 64K-point version is 64. In the figure, we show the relative improvement in performance as percentage bars. For each benchmark we present three bars: total number of cycles, run cycles – in which the threads were busy computing, and stall cycles – in which threads were stalled for resources. Negative bars represent a reduction in the number of cycles, and therefore an improvement in performance. We note that in general the number of run cycles increases for the hardware barrier implementation, while the number of stalls decreases significantly. This is in line with the expectations. The hardware barrier implementation executes more, cheaper instructions, that do not contend for shared memory. The performance gain is about 10% for the 256-point FFT with 16 threads, and about 5% for the 64K-point FFT with 64 threads.

4. Related work

Our design for Cyclops is ambitious, but within the realm of current or near-future silicon technology. Combined logic-memory microelectronics processes will soon deliver chips with hundreds of millions of transistors. Several research groups have advanced processor-in-memory designs that rely on that technology. We discuss some of the projects that are related to Cyclops.

The MIT RAW architecture [1, 21] consists of a highly parallel VLSI design that fully exposes all hardware details to the compiler. The chip consists of a set of interconnected tiles, each tile implementing a block of memory, functional units, and switch for interconnect. The interconnect network has dynamic message routing and a programmable switch. The RAW architecture does not implement a fixed instruction set architecture (ISA). Instead, it relies on compiler technology to map applications to hardware in a manner that optimizes the allocation of resources.

Architectures that integrate processors and memories on the same chip are called Processor-In-Memory (PIM) or Intelligent Memory architectures. They have been spurred by technological advances that enable the integration of compute logic and memory on a single chip. These architectures deliver higher performance by reducing the latency and increasing the bandwidth of processor-memory communication. Examples of such architectures are IRAM [14], Shamrock [10], Imagine [15], FlexRAM [9, 18], DIVA [7], Active Pages [13], Gilgamesh [23], MAJC [19], and Piranha [5]. In some cases, the PIM chip is used as a co-processor (Imagine, FlexRAM), while in other cases it is used as the main engine in the machine (IRAM, Shamrock, MAJC, Piranha). Cyclops uses the second approach. Another difference is that some architectures include many (32-64), relatively-simple processors on the chip (Imagine, FlexRAM) and others include only a handful (4-8) of processors (IRAM, Shamrock, MAJC, Piranha). Cyclops belongs to the first class.

Simultaneous multithreading [6, 20] exploits both instruction-level and thread-level parallelism by issuing instructions from different threads in the same cycle. It was shown to be a more effective approach to improve resource utilization than superscalar execution. Their results support our work by showing that there is not enough instruction-level parallelism in a single thread of execution, therefore it is more efficient to execute multiple threads concurrently.

The Tera MTA [16, 17] is another example of a modern architecture that tolerates latencies through massive parallelism. In the case of Tera, 128 thread contexts share the execution hardware. This contrasts with Cyclops, in which each thread has its own execution hardware. The Tera approach, however, can tolerate longer latencies to memory and supports the design of a machine without caches.

5. Conclusions

In this paper we have described the Cyclops architecture, a highly parallel processor-and-memory system on a chip. The Cyclops chip is intended to be used as a building block for scalable machines. Cyclops minimizes the impact of memory and functional unit latencies not through complicated architectural features, but through the use of massive parallelism. We have measured the performance attained from two of Cyclops' distinguishing features: its memory subsystem organization and its hardware support for fast interthread barriers. We have demonstrated that a single Cyclops chip can achieve sustainable memory bandwidth on the order of 40 GB/s, similar to a top-of-the-line commercial machine. We have also shown that the fast barrier hardware can improve the performance of an FFT kernel by up to 10%.

As future work, we plan to investigate the performance of Cyclops in more detail [3]. In particular, we want to study the impact of its fault tolerance features. Although we did not discuss this aspect of the Cyclops architecture here, the chip is expected to function even with broken components. For example, if a memory bank fails, the hardware will set a special register to specify the maximum amount of memory available on the chip and will re-map all the addresses so that the address space is contiguous. If thread units fail, there is enough parallelism in the chip so that useful work can still be accomplished. If an FPU breaks, an entire quad will be disabled, but there are 31 other quads

available for computation. From a system perspective, in which multiple chips are connected together, an application with knowledge of the machine status can adapt its communication patterns based on chip availability. We have only started to explore the system software components necessary to take advantage of these architectural features. It will be important to characterize the impact of faults on overall chip and system performance.

Finally, we need to discuss two important limitations of the Cyclops architecture. First, combined logic and memory processes have a negative impact: the logic is not as fast as in a pure logic process and the memory is not as dense as in a pure memory process. For Cyclops to be successful we need to demonstrate that the benefits of this single-chip integration, such as improved memory bandwidth, outweigh the disadvantages. Second, due to its single-chip nature, Cyclops is a small-memory system. The external DRAM is not directly addressable and the bandwidth to it is much lower. We can expect future generations of Cyclops to include larger memory, but the current ratio of 250 bytes of storage to MFlop of compute power (compared to approximately 1MB/1MFlop in conventional machines) will tend to decrease.

The result is that Cyclops systems are not single purpose machines such as MD-Grape [12] but are not truly general purpose computers either. Our architecture targets problems that exhibit two important characteristics. First, they should be able to exploit massive amounts of parallelism, on the order of a million processors in very large systems. Second, they should be compute intensive. Examples of applications that match these requirements are molecular dynamics [4], raytracing, and linear algebra.

Finally, we should stress that the results presented in this paper were obtained through simulation. Although we are confident of the general trends demonstrated, the results need to be validated through real measurements in hardware. As we proceed to complete the design of Cyclops and build prototypes, we will have the capability to perform those measurements.

References

[1] A. Agarwal. Raw computation. *Scientific American*, August 1999.

[2] F. Allen et al. Blue Gene: A vision for protein science using a petaflop supercomputer. *IBM Systems Journal*, 40(2):310–328, 2001.

[3] G. Almasi, C. Caşcaval, J. G. Castaños, M. Denneau, D. Lieber, J. E. Moreira, and H. S. Warren, Jr. Performance evaluation of the Cyclops architecture family. Technical Report RC22243, IBM T. J. Watson Research Center, November 2001.

[4] G. S. Almasi, C. Caşcaval, J. G. Castaños, M. Denneau, W. Donath, M. Eleftheriou, M. Giampapa, H. Ho, D. Lieber,

J. E. Moreira, D. Newns, M. Snir, and H. S. Warren, Jr. Demonstrating the scalability of a molecular dynamics application on a Petaflop computer. In *Proceedings of the 2001 International Conference on Supercomputing*, pages 393–406, June 2001.

[5] L. Barroso, K. Gharachorloo, R. McNamara, A. Nowatzyk, S. Qadeer, B. Sano, S. Smith, R. Stets, and B. Verghese. Piranha: A scalable architecture based on single-chip multiprocessing. In *27th Annual International Symposium on Computer Architecture*, pages 282–293, June 2000.

[6] S. Eggers, J. Emer, H. Levy, J. Lo, R. Stamm, and D. Tullsen. Simultaneous multithreading: A platform for next-generation processors. *IEEE Micro*, pages 12–18, September/October 1997.

[7] M. W. Hall, P. Kogge, J. Koller, P. Diniz, J. Chame, J. Draper, J. LaCross, J. Brockman, W. Athas, A. Srivasava, V. Freech, J. Shin, , and J. Park. Mapping irregular applications to DIVA, a PIM-based data-intensive architecture. In *Proceedings of SC99*, November 1999.

[8] J. L. Hennessy and D. A. Patterson. *Computer Architecture A Quantitative Apporach*. Morgan Kaufmann, second edition edition, 1996.

[9] Y. Kang, M. Huang, S.-M. Yoo, Z. Ge, D. Keen, V. Lam, P. Pattnaik, and J. Torrellas. FlexRAM: Toward an advanced intelligent memory system. In *International Conference on Computer Design (ICCD)*, October 1999.

[10] P. Kogge, S. Bass, J. Brockman, D. Chen, and E. Sha. Pursuing a petaflop: Point designs for 100 TF computers using PIM technologies. In *Frontiers of Massively Parallel Computation Symposium*, 1996.

[11] J. D. McCalpin. Sustainable memory bandwidth in current high performance computers, 1995. http://home.austin.rr.com/mccalpin/papers/bandwidth/.

[12] MD Grape project. http://www.research.ibm.com/grape.

[13] M. Oskin, F. T. Chong, and T. Sherwood. Active pages: A computation model for intelligent memory. In *International Symposium on Computer Architecture*, pages 192–203, 1998.

[14] D. Patterson, T. Anderson, N. Cardwell, R. Fromm, K. Keeton, C. Kozyrakis, R. Thomas, and K. Yelick. A case for intelligent RAM: IRAM. In *Proceedings of IEEE Micro*, April 1997.

[15] S. Rixner, W. Dally, U. Kapasi, B. Khailany, A. Lopez-Lagunas, P. Mattson, and J. Owens. A bandwidth-efficient architecture for media processing. In *31st International Symposium on Microarchitecture*, November 1998.

[16] A. Snavely, L. Carter, J. Boisseau, A. Majumdar, K. S. Gatlin, N. Mitchel, J. Feo, and B. Koblenz. Multiprocessor performance on the Tera MTA. In *Proceedings Supercomputing '98*, Orlando, Florida, Nov. 7-13 1998.

[17] A. Snavely, G. Johnson, and J. Genetti. Data intensive volume visualization on the Tera MTA and Cray T3E. In *Proceedings of the High Performance Computing Symposium - HPC '99*, pages 59–64, 1999.

[18] J. Torrellas, L. Yang, and A.-T. Nguyen. Toward a cost-effective DSM organization that exploits processor-memory integration. In *Sixth International Symposium on High-Performance Computer Architecture*, January 2000.

[19] M. Tremblay. MAJC: Microprocessor architecture for Java computing. Presentation at Hot Chips, August 1999.

[20] D. M. Tullsen, S. J. Eggers, and H. M. Levy. Simultaneous multithreading: Maximizing on-chip parallelism. In *Proceedings of the 22nd Annual International Symposium on Computer Architecture*, pages 392–403, June 1995.

[21] E. Waingold, M. Taylor, D. Srikrishna, V. Sarkar, W. Lee, V. Lee, J. Kim, M. Frank, P. Finch, R. Barua, J. Babb, S. Amarasinghe, and A. Agarwal. Baring it all to software: Raw machines. *IEEE Computer*, pages 86–93, September 1997.

[22] S. C. Woo, M. Ohara, E. Torrie, J. P. Singh, and A. Gupta. The SPLASH-2 programs: Characterization and methodological considerations. In *International Symposium on Computer Architecture (ISCA)*, June 1995.

[23] H. P. Zima and T. Sterling. The Gilgamesh processor-in-memory architecture and its execution model. In *Workshop on Compilers for Parallel Computers*, Edinburgh, Scotland, UK, June 2001.

Author Index

Revised November 7, 2001